THE COLLEGEVILLE BIBLE COMMENTARY

THE
COLLEGEVILLE BIBLE COMMENTARY

BASED ON THE NEW AMERICAN BIBLE

New Testament

General Editor

ROBERT J. KARRIS, O.F.M.

THE LITURGICAL PRESS

COLLEGEVILLE, MINNESOTA

NIHIL OBSTAT: Robert C. Harren, J.C.L.
Censor Deputatus

IMPRIMATUR: ✝ Jerome Hanus, O.S.B.
Bishop of St. Cloud
October 19, 1988

Cover photos: Mosaic under main altar of the Church of the Multiplication of Loaves at Tabgha, *Placid Stuckenschneider, O.S.B.* Harbor town of Skala on the island of Patmos from the chapel over the Cave of the Apocalypse, *Roger Kasprick, O.S.B.* Jewish woman, view of Jerusalem, and Chapel of the Beatitudes (on spine), *Richard T. Nowitz.*

Printed in the United States of America.

95 96   8 7 6 5 4 3 2

Library of Congress Cataloging-in-Publication Data

The Collegeville Bible commentary : based on the New American Bible.
     p.   cm.
   Contents: [1] Old Testament / general editor, Dianne Bergant —
[2] New Testament / general editor, Robert J. Karris.
   ISBN 0-8146-2210-0 (Old Testament). — ISBN 0-8146-2211-9 (New
Testament)
   1. Bible—Commentaries. I. Bergant, Dianne. II. Karris, Robert
J.
[BS491.2.C66 1992]
220.7'7—dc20   92-23578
                                                                              CIP

CONTENTS

PREFACE

Today we are witnessing an increased interest in the Bible. Women and men from all walks of life are enrolling in classes, attending workshops, and organizing study groups. Guided reflection on the biblical tradition is a fundamental component of evangelization programs such as the Rite of Christian Initiation of Adults (RCIA) and RENEW. Prayer groups look for leaders who can guide them beyond private interpretation into the spiritual depths of the tradition. People are searching for new insights and are turning to biblical scholars to provide them. Non-specialists are no longer satisfied with a merely devotional understanding of the Bible. They are asking literary, historical, and theological questions that require learned answers.

In an effort to address this need, The Liturgical Press commissioned thirty-four respected scholars to provide individual booklets that together would interpret the entire Roman Catholic canon. Utilizing the most recent critical methods and incorporating the fruits of contemporary scholarship, they brought to completion in 1986 the *Collegeville Bible Commentary*, a series of thirty-six booklets, each including questions for review and discussion. The wide selection of authors resulted in a variety of theological positions and methodological approaches, which contributed to the richness of the enterprise. There was a consistent attempt throughout to be sensitive to contemporary concerns. This project was completed in a little over five years, thus ensuring the up-to-date character of the interpretation. In 1988 the authors of the New Testament commentaries redid their works in the light of the revised edition of the New Testament of the New American Bible.

These two volumes bring together the commentaries of all thirty-six booklets. Their comprehensiveness make them invaluable resources, enabling the reader to refer easily to the interpretation of any or all of the biblical books. Besides being used for Bible study, they can also serve as references for liturgy planning, homily preparation, and biblical prayer services. These volumes are an admirable response to the injunction of the Second Vatican Council: "Access to sacred Scripture ought to be wide open to the Christian faithful" (*Dei Verbum*, no. 22).

DIANNE BERGANT, C.S.A.
General Editor, Old Testament Commentary

ROBERT J. KARRIS, O.F.M.
General Editor, New Testament Commentary

ABBREVIATIONS

OLD TESTAMENT

Gen	Genesis	Prov	Proverbs
Exod	Exodus	Eccl	Ecclesiastes
Lev	Leviticus	Song	Song of Songs
Num	Numbers	Wis	Wisdom
Deut	Deuteronomy	Sir	Sirach
Josh	Joshua	Isa	Isaiah
Judg	Judges	Jer	Jeremiah
Ruth	Ruth	Lam	Lamentations
1 Sam	1 Samuel	Bar	Baruch
2 Sam	2 Samuel	Ezek	Ezekiel
1 Kgs	1 Kings	Dan	Daniel
2 Kgs	2 Kings	Hos	Hosea
1 Chr	1 Chronicles	Joel	Joel
2 Chr	2 Chronicles	Amos	Amos
Ezra	Ezra	Obad	Obadiah
Neh	Nehemiah	Jonah	Jonah
Tob	Tobit	Mic	Micah
Jdt	Judith	Nah	Nahum
Esth	Esther	Hab	Habakkuk
1 Macc	1 Maccabees	Zeph	Zephaniah
2 Macc	2 Maccabees	Hag	Haggai
Job	Job	Zech	Zechariah
Ps(s)	Psalm(s)	Mal	Malachi

NEW TESTAMENT

Matt	Matthew	1 Tim	1 Timothy
Mark	Mark	2 Tim	2 Timothy
Luke	Luke	Titus	Titus
John	John	Phlm	Philemon
Acts	Acts	Heb	Hebrews
Rom	Romans	Jas	James
1 Cor	1 Corinthians	1 Pet	1 Peter
2 Cor	2 Corinthians	2 Pet	2 Peter
Gal	Galatians	1 John	1 John
Eph	Ephesians	2 John	2 John
Phil	Philippians	3 John	3 John
Col	Colossians	Jude	Jude
1 Thess	1 Thessalonians	Rev	Revelation
2 Thess	2 Thessalonians		

OTHER ABBREVIATIONS

NAB	New American Bible	RSV	Revised Standard Version
NEB	New English Bible		

PALESTINE IN THE
TIME OF JESUS

Miles
0   40

Kms
0   40

MEDITERRANEAN

SEA

PHOENICIA

LEBANON MTS.

SYRIA

Sidon

Abila•
ABILENE

Damascus•

Zarephath

▲ MT. HERMON

Tyre•

•Caesarea Philippi

Ptolemais•

GALILEE

Chorazin
Capernaum• •Bethsaida

Magadan• Lake

Cana• Tiberias• Galilee

MT. CARMEL▲

•Nazareth

Nain• ▲ MT.
TABOR

•Gadara

Caesarea•

TEN TOWNS

Salim•

SAMARIA Aenon•

Samaria•

•Gerasa

▲ MT. EBAL

MT. GERIZIM ▲• Sychar

Jordan River

P
E
R
E
A

Joppa•

•Arimathea?

Ephraim•

Jericho• •Bethany

Emmaus• •Bethany

Azotus• Jerusalem••

Qumran•

Ascalon

JUDEA •Bethlehem

Gaza•

•Hebron

Dead

Sea

IDUMEA

N
A
B
A
T
E
A

© United Bible Societies, 1978

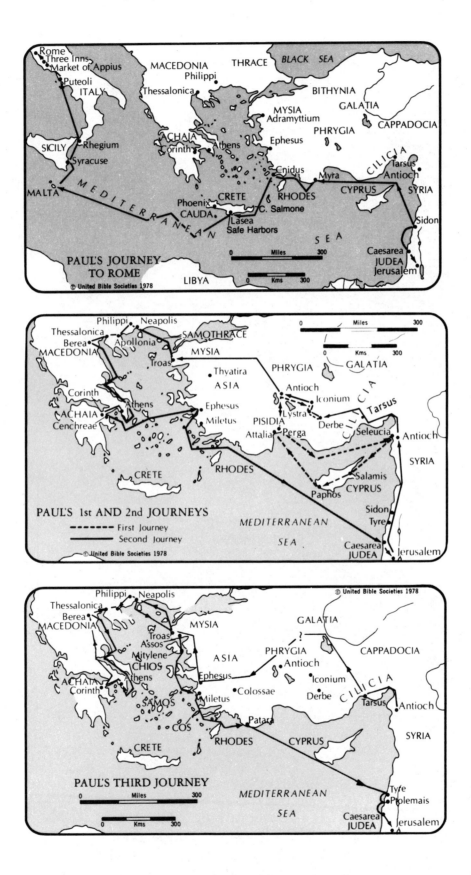

PAUL'S JOURNEY TO ROME

Rome
Three Inns
Market of Appius
Puteoli
ITALY
SICILY
Rhegium
Syracuse
MALTA
MEDITERRANEAN
MACEDONIA
Philippi
Thessalonica
ACHAIA
Corinth
Athens
PHOENIX
CAUDA
Lasea
Safe Harbors
CRETE
RHODES
C. Salmone
Cnidus
Myra
CILICIA
Tarsus
Antioch
CYPRUS
SYRIA
Sidon
Caesarea
JUDEA
Jerusalem
SEA
LIBYA
THRACE
BLACK SEA
BITHYNIA
GALATIA
CAPPADOCIA
MYSIA
Adramyttium
PHRYGIA
Ephesus
© United Bible Societies 1978

Miles 0 300
Kms 0 300

PAUL'S 1st AND 2nd JOURNEYS

Philippi Neapolis
SAMOTHRACE
Thessalonica
Berea
Apollonia
MACEDONIA
Troas
MYSIA
Thyatira
ASIA
PHRYGIA
GALATIA
Antioch
Iconium
Tarsus
CILICIA
Lystra
Derbe
Corinth
Athens
Ephesus
Miletus
PISIDIA
ACHAIA
Cenchreae
Attalia
Perga
Seleucia
Antioch
SYRIA
CRETE
RHODES
Salamis
CYPRUS
Paphos
Sidon
Tyre
MEDITERRANEAN
SEA
Caesarea
JUDEA
Jerusalem

Miles 0 300
Kms 0 300

- - - - First Journey
———— Second Journey

© United Bible Societies 1978

PAUL'S THIRD JOURNEY

Philippi Neapolis
Thessalonica
Berea
MACEDONIA
Troas
Assos
Mitylene
CHIOS
MYSIA
ASIA
GALATIA
PHRYGIA
Antioch
CAPPADOCIA
Ephesus
Colossae
Iconium
Derbe
CILICIA
Tarsus
Antioch
ACHAIA
Corinth
Athens
SAMOS
Miletus
COS
Patara
SYRIA
CRETE
RHODES
CYPRUS
Tyre
Ptolemais
Caesarea
JUDEA
Jerusalem
MEDITERRANEAN
SEA

© United Bible Societies 1978

Miles 0 300
Kms 0 300

xi

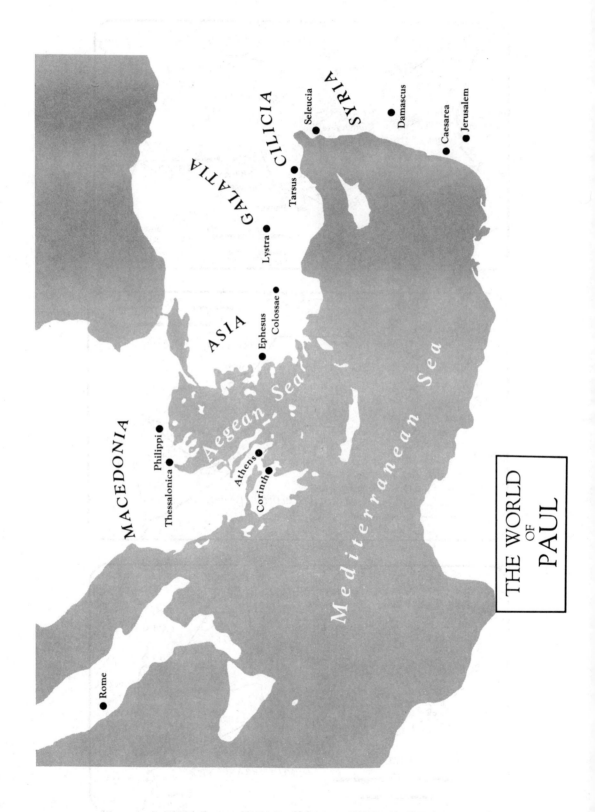

THE WORLD
OF
PAUL

THE
NEW TESTAMENT

MATTHEW

Daniel J. Harrington, S.J.

INTRODUCTION

Tradition and newness in tension

Matthew's Gospel has a strongly Jewish flavor. Its special concerns are to place Jesus of Nazareth within the traditions of God's chosen people and to show how this same Jesus burst the bonds of those traditions and brought them to fulfillment. From beginning to end, there is a tension between tradition and newness. Neither pole of the tension is rejected. The interplay between the two generates life and fresh insights.

Matthew takes pains to point out how this or that event in Jesus' life fulfills the prophecies of the Old Testament. All through the account of the passion and death, he assures us that those terrible events conform to God's will as expressed in the Old Testament. Nevertheless, at certain points (see 5:21-48) Jesus seems to contradict or abolish some precepts of the law. He can do so because, as the Son of God, he is the authoritative interpreter of the Jewish tradition.

The identity of Jesus is expressed in terms that have rich Old Testament backgrounds. Jesus is the Son of David, the Messiah or Christ, Wisdom, and so forth. All these titles express aspects of Jesus' identity, but no one of them alone is an adequate description of him. The two most prominent terms are Son of Man and Son of God. The former title reflects Jesus' way of referring to himself and probably has some connection with the heavenly figure of Dan 7. The latter title could be used in the Old Testament with reference

to the king (see Pss 2 and 110). When applied to Jesus, however, these titles take on new meaning and go far beyond whatever content may be attributed to them in the Old Testament.

The identity of God's people is also worked out in the tension between tradition and newness. Matthew has no doubt that Israel is God's people, and so a major thrust of his Gospel is to show the continuity between Israel of old and the new thing that God has done in Christ. But after the coming of Jesus, who are God's people and who inherits the kingdom of God? Matthew's answer is simple and straightforward: Those who follow Jesus are God's people. Attachment to Jesus the Jew makes membership in God's people possible even for those who are not Jewish by birth (see 21:41, 43). Those Jews who do not accept this new definition of God's people are said to belong to "their synagogues" (see 4:23; 9:35; 10:17; 12:9; 13:54), which are also called the synagogues of the hypocrites (6:2; 23:6, 34).

Sources and structure

When the person whom we call Matthew determined to write about Jesus, he decided to write a Gospel—a literary form something like a biography. Though surely not a biography in the nineteenth- or twentieth-century use of the term, Matthew's Gospel does follow the story of Jesus of Nazareth from his birth, through his public activity as a preacher and a healer, up to his death and resurrection. Matthew could have written a long letter or a poem or a chronological report of the events in Jesus' life; instead, he chose to write a narrative about Jesus. His Gospel is a collection of stories that portray Jesus as a powerful and living person. By means of these vivid stories we are invited to become part of the story of Jesus, the Son of Man and the Son of God.

Matthew did not compose the Gospel entirely out of his own imagination and experience. He appears to have had at his disposal several written sources. In chapters 3–4 and 12–28 he drew heavily on Mark's Gospel. Mark wrote before Matthew did, and so it is fair to call Matthew's Gospel a revised and greatly expanded version of Mark's Gospel. Furthermore, in about two hundred verses Matthew and Luke are so much alike that it is reasonable to assume that both evangelists made independent use of a common source. This source was a collection of Jesus' sayings that circulated in Greek in the fifties of the first century A.D. This source used by Matthew and Luke is usually designated by the letter Q (from the German word for "source," *Quelle*). Finally, Matthew had access to sayings and stories that no other evangelist had. This material peculiar to Matthew's Gospel is often designated by the letter M.

The fact that Matthew depended very much on existing material indicates that his story of Jesus is deliberately traditional. But in addition to handing on the traditions about Jesus, Matthew also interpreted these traditions in order to bring out certain aspects and to speak to certain problems that the Christian community of his time faced. Perhaps his most original literary contribution was the general structure that he imposed on the story of Jesus. Since Matthew was telling the story of Jesus, he was clearly obligated to follow the pattern provided by the life of Jesus. Since he had access to Mark's Gospel, he could not disregard entirely the outline of Jesus' life provided by it. Q was simply a collection of sayings, and so the evangelist had more freedom in using it.

What structure does Matthew's story of Jesus take? The most obvious features are the beginning and end of the Gospel. Mark's story of Jesus began with Jesus' adult years, but Matthew in chapters 1–2 goes back to his birth and infancy. Mark's story ends with the death

of Jesus and the discovery of the empty tomb in Jerusalem. Matthew in chapters 26–28 follows Mark very closely, but he adds the story of Jesus' appearance to the eleven disciples in Galilee (28:16-20). Between chapters 1–2 and 26–28, Matthew presents five major speeches by Jesus: the Sermon on the Mount (chs. 5–7), the missionary discourse (ch. 10), the parables discourse (ch. 13), the advice to a divided community (ch. 18), and the eschatological discourse (chs. 24–25). We must not assume that these five speeches are exact transcriptions of sermons given by Jesus on five occasions; rather, everything about them indicates that Matthew has constructed the speeches out of traditional materials and imposed upon them their present literary structures. Matthew was obviously very interested in Jesus' teaching and went to great lengths to highlight it.

The five speeches of Jesus are an important structural principle in the Gospel, and they are separated from one another by large blocks of narrative material. When we look at the Gospel as a whole, the following general outline emerges:

1:1–2:23	The genealogy and itinerary of Jesus
3:1–4:25	The beginning of Jesus' ministry
5:1–7:29	The Sermon on the Mount
8:1–9:38	The powerful deeds of Jesus
10:1-42	The missionary discourse
11:1–12:50	The importance of Jesus and the rejection of him
13:1-53	The parables concerning the kingdom of God
13:54–16:4	Miracles and controversies
16:5–17:27	The way to the cross
18:1-35	Advice to a divided community
19:1–23:39	Growing opposition to Jesus
24:1–25:46	The coming of the kingdom
26:1–28:20	The death and resurrection of Jesus

Authorship and historical setting

Originality of authorship was not an important value in the culture in which the Gospel of Matthew was written. The title "According to Matthew" was most likely not part of the first edition of the text, and no explicit claim is made in the Gospel that its author was an eyewitness to the events described in it. The Gospel is basically an anonymous composition. But calling the Gospel "anonymous" does not mean that we know nothing about the author. The evangelist was a Christian who was well versed in Jewish methods of teaching, living in Syria or some other area in which Jewish influence was strong, around A.D. 85. He sought to show that those who acknowledge Jesus as the Messiah will inherit the kingdom of God.

The traditional ascription of the Gospel to Matthew the tax collector (see 9:9) who became an apostle (see 10:3) generates more problems than it solves. Why is the same tax collector named Levi, the son of Alphaeus, in Mark 2:14? How did a tax collector, living on the fringes of Jewish religious life, produce such a religiously sophisticated Gospel? Why did an eyewitness depend on written sources like Mark and Q, and never put forward the claim that he saw this or that take place? Perhaps the church for which the Gospel was written took the apostle Matthew as its "patron saint." Or perhaps the apostle Matthew was responsible for some of the special material (M) in the Gospel.

The tradition of the existence of an Aramaic or Hebrew version of Matthew also generates more problems than it solves. The church historian Eusebius quotes the early Christian writer Papias to the effect that Matthew collected the "oracles" in the Hebrew languages and then others translated or interpreted them. Does this statement refer to the completed Gospel, or to the Old Testament quotations used in it, or to the sayings of Jesus? Why does Papias say Hebrew, when Jesus spoke Aramaic? Did Papias have any special reasons for placing Matthew's Gospel before Mark's? All these questions indicate that the ascription to Matthew the apostle and the tradition of an Aramaic or Hebrew version of Matthew involve too many problems for us to place much reliance on them in interpreting the Gospel.

Matthew's Gospel was put into final form around A.D. 85, perhaps in Antioch of Syria. That means that the Christian community had existed for about fifty years since Jesus' death, and about fifteen years since the Jerusalem temple had been destroyed in A.D. 70. This dating is based to a large extent on what appears to be a partial description of the events of A.D. 70 in 22:7: "The king was enraged and sent his troops, destroyed those murderers, and burned their city." Other possible allusions to the destruction of Jerusalem occur in 21:41 and 27:25.

The Matthean community was a mixed group, but the majority apparently were Jewish Christians. By A.D. 85 it had become clear that not all Israel was going to accept Jesus as the Messiah of Jewish expectations and that non-Jews represented a very promising missionary field (see 28:19). Matthew was encouraging a largely Jewish-Christian community to recognize itself as the legitimate heir of God's promises to Israel. He also wished them to broaden their missionary horizons to include the Gentiles. Antioch in Syria would have been an appropriate location, but there is no absolute certainty on this matter.

This commentary

The following commentary on the Gospel of Matthew aims to explain clearly and simply what the evangelist whom we call Matthew was trying to say to his first readers. It pays particular attention to the literary structures and the theological concerns of the passages. Since the readers of this commentary live in a world that differs greatly from that of the original readers of the Gospel, historical information and explanations about cultural presuppositions are also supplied. The goal of the expositions is to allow twentieth-century readers to share more deeply in the excitement that the Gospel of Matthew must have inspired among its first readers.

COMMENTARY

I. THE GENEALOGY AND ITINERARY OF JESUS

Matt 1:1-2:23

1:1-17 The genealogy of Jesus the Messiah (see Luke 3:23-38). The genealogy at the beginning of the Gospel establishes Jesus' place within the Jewish tradition. Jesus is the son of Abraham and of David as well as the continuation of David's line after the exile of 587 B.C.E. The names in the genealogy up to Abiud in verse 13 are found in the Old Testament, and here they are arranged in three sets of fourteen names each (v. 17). Israel's history is traced from its beginning with Abraham (v. 2), through its high point with King David (v. 6) and its low point in the Babylonian Exile (v. 11), to its fulfillment in Jesus the Messiah (v. 16). Luke emphasizes Jesus' universal significance by tracing his lineage back from Joseph to Adam (see Luke 3:23-38), but Matthew is concerned with rooting Jesus of Nazareth in the heritage of God's chosen people, Israel.

The literary flow of the genealogy is disturbed by the inclusion of the names of four women. Not only is the occurrence of women's names in a Jewish genealogy unusual, but what is known about them from the Old Testament makes their appearance all the more surprising. Tamar (v. 3) disguised herself as a prostitute and conceived her sons by Judah, her father-in-law (see Gen 38). Rahab (v. 5) was a prostitute of Jericho whose life was spared on account of her collaboration with Joshua's spies (see Josh 2; 6). The tradition that she was the mother of Boaz is found only in Matthew's Gospel. Ruth (v. 5) was a Moabite who joined herself to Israel through her husband's family (see Ruth). The "wife of Uriah" (v. 6) was Bathsheba; King David shamefully arranged her husband's death in battle and took her as a wife (2 Sam 11).

The appearance of these four unusual women in the genealogy of the Messiah prepares for the surprising birth of Jesus in verses 18-25. Just as their inclusion breaks the genealogical pattern of "A became the father of B" and just as what is known about them from the Scriptures indicates some kind of irregularity, so the birth of Jesus breaks the tradi-tional pattern (v. 16) and is highly irregular. Thus, the genealogy of Jesus in Matt 1:1-17 goes in two directions: It stresses the continuity of Jesus with the great figures of God's people ("son of Abraham . . . son of David"), and it also prepares for the very irregular and indeed unique birth narrated in the following passage.

1:18-25 The birth of Jesus (see Luke 2:1-7). The story of Jesus' birth is really an extension of the genealogy. Its primary concern is Jesus' right to a place in the messianic genealogy through Joseph, and its climax comes in Joseph's resolve to make Jesus a Davidic child by assuming the legal obligations of paternity. The tension between continuity with the Jewish tradition (legal paternity through Joseph) and the sharp break with tradition (the miraculous conception of Jesus) develops the basic theme already raised in the genealogy.

Engagement or betrothal in Jewish society of Jesus' time involved a much stronger commitment than it does in modern Western society. The description of Joseph's embarrassment and his plans in verses 18-19 may presume his suspicion that Mary had been raped or seduced. As a devout observer of the Old Testament law, Joseph could not take Mary as his wife (see Deut 22:23-27). Not wishing to subject Mary to the shameful trial of the woman suspected of adultery (Num 5:11-31), he decided to forgo the public procedure and took upon himself the responsibility for the divorce. Divorce proceedings were carried out, not in a law court, but rather on the initiative of the male (see Deut 24:1).

Joseph's plans are interrupted in verses 20-23 by the appearance of a messenger from God in a dream—a device familiar from the Old Testament account of the birth of Samson (Judg 13). The angel's message assumes the virginal conception of Jesus by the Holy Spirit and concentrates on the names of the Messiah. As the legal son of Joseph, Jesus will be named the "Son of David" (v. 20). His given name is Jesus, which is related to the Hebrew verb for "save." This name is entirely appropriate because, in Matthew's perspective and in the faith of all the early Christians, Jesus saved the people of God from their sins. The third name applied to Jesus appears in the citation from Isa 7:14: "and they shall name him Emmanuel." As a sign to King Ahaz and his royal court, the prophet Isaiah had announced that a certain woman would bear a son. The early Christians took the Greek translation of "young woman" as "virgin" to confirm their belief in the virginal conception of Jesus. But Matthew may have been more interested in the child's name "Emmanuel." In Hebrew, "Emmanuel" means "God with us," and this expresses the significance of Jesus for Matthew and the early church. A similar note is struck in the final verse of the Gospel: "And behold, I am with you always, until the end of the age" (28:20).

The dream allayed Joseph's fears. Not only had Mary not been raped or seduced, but this child has been conceived by the Holy Spirit and deserves the names Son of David, Jesus, and Emmanuel. Joseph acts in accordance with the divine communication and takes Mary to be his wife (v. 24). The statement in verse 25 that he did not have sexual relations with her before the birth of Jesus neither affirms nor denies the perpetual virginity of Mary.

The whole of Matt 1:1-25 serves both to situate Jesus firmly within God's people and to call attention to his extraordinary status. On the one hand, he is the descendant of Abraham and David and the fulfillment of the promises and hopes attached to those great Old Testament figures. On the other hand, the mode of his birth is highly unusual, and the names given to him—Jesus and Emmanuel— suggest that he far surpasses any of his ancestors.

2:1-12 Wise men worship Jesus at Bethlehem. Each of the four episodes in chapter 2 revolves around a place name: Bethlehem, Egypt, Ramah, and Nazareth. Jesus was known as a Galilean (see John 7:41-42) from the town of Nazareth. The four scenes in the chapter explain how Jesus the Son of David was born in Bethlehem, how he was taken to Egypt in order to avoid the threat of death, why he did not return to Bethlehem, and how Nazareth came to be his home. Each episode includes an Old Testament quotation that contains the name of a place. This appeal to the Old Testament indicates that the Messiah's itinerary was guided by the will of God.

After situating the place of Jesus' birth in Bethlehem and its date late in the reign of King Herod the Great (37–4 B.C.E.), the first episode

introduces wise men from the East who possess astronomical and astrological knowledge. The "star" that they observed may have been the conjunction of the planets Jupiter and Saturn. There may also be a reference to speculations based on Num 24:17 ("A star shall advance from Jacob") that connected the Messiah's birth with the appearance of a star.

Efforts at identifying the star should not divert attention from the more central concerns of the passage. The threefold occurrence of "do him homage" in verses 2, 8, 11 expresses the basic theme, and the contrast between the Magi and Herod (and those on his side) is developed in the course of the story.

In response to the imperfect revelation given in the star, the Gentile wise men come to worship Jesus. But they need to learn from the Jewish Scriptures that the Messiah is to be born in Bethlehem (vv. 5-6). They proceed to Bethlehem and worship the infant Messiah. From the three kinds of gifts listed in verse 11, the tradition of *three* wise men developed in the fifth century; in the eighth century the three were given names.

The faith of the Gentile wise men stands in contrast to the cynical cunning of Herod. As an Idumean whose Judaism was suspect, Herod would naturally fear all Jewish messianic movements as threats to his political power. Even though he had access to the Scriptures and could see plainly what the prophet Micah (see Mic 5:1; 2 Sam 5:2) had said about the place of the Messiah's birth, Herod was not willing to worship the newborn king. The episode of the wise men reflects the early church's experience of the Gentiles' readiness to accept the gospel and the disappointing slowness of all Israel to receive it. It also prepares for the recognition of Jesus as King of the Jews (Matt 27:11, 29, 37) and for the universal mission of the disciples (Matt 8:11-12; 28:18-20).

2:13-15 The flight into Egypt. The structure of the story of the flight into Egypt is similar to that of the birth story in 1:18-25. It consists of the angel's appearance to Joseph in a dream, a command and the reason for the command, Joseph's determination to carry out the command, and a quotation from the Old Testament.

Egypt was a common place of refuge for Jews of this time, and only after the death of Herod in 4 B.C.E. was it safe for Jesus to return to Palestine. The quotation from Hos 11:1 ("Out of Egypt I called my son") places this part of the Messiah's itinerary within the framework of God's will. It not only identifies Jesus as the Son of God, but it also suggests that he is the personification of the people of God. Just as God called Israel of old out of Egypt in order to create a special people for himself, so he calls Jesus out of Egypt into the land of Israel in order to create a new people (see Matt 21:41, 43). The principle of continuity between the old people and the new people is Jesus the Jew.

2:16-18 The slaughter of children in Judea. Although the slaughter of innocent male children two years and under is consistent with Herod's ruthlessness in defending his throne during the last years of his reign, there is no record of this event in any ancient source outside of Matthew's Gospel. The quotation from Jer 31:15 focuses on Ramah, a place about five miles north of Jerusalem. Ramah was the place where Rachel, the wife of Jacob, died; it was also the place where the Jews in the sixth century B.C.E. gathered for their march into the Babylonian exile.

Herod's savage action is a repetition of Pharaoh's slaughter of the Israelite children in Egypt (Exod 1:15-22). Indeed, this episode and the preceding ones seem to suppose a reversal of the Exodus story: Jesus is taken to Egypt for his own safety, and the king of Jerusalem represents unbelief and hardness of heart. Herod acts as the enemy of God's people represented by the newborn Messiah. The Old Testament passage explains Herod's action as consistent with God's will but does not condone or justify it.

2:19-23 Jesus' arrival in Nazareth. After Herod's death in 4 B.C.E., his kingdom was divided among his sons. Archelaus ruled Judea, Samaria, and Idumea from 4 B.C.E. to A.D. 6. The story of how Jesus got to Nazareth follows a now familiar pattern: the angel's appearance to Joseph in a dream, a command and the reason for it (see Exod 4:19), Joseph's determination to carry out the command, and a quotation from the Old Testament. The precise source of the quotation is not certain; the texts most often cited as possible sources are Judg 13:5, 7 and Isa 11:1. At any rate, the episode explains why Jesus was connected with Nazareth and why he began his public ministry in Galilee.

The tension between the continuity with the Jewish tradition and the new act of God in Jesus that was so prominent in Matt 1:1-25 also emerges in chapter 2. Each point in the Messiah's itinerary is grounded in a quotation from the Old Testament, and the individual episodes contain phrases and characters reminiscent of certain biblical passages. On the other hand, the Gentile wise men come to worship the newborn king of the Jews while Herod does everything in his power to destroy him. The future of the people of God seems to rest with Jesus of Nazareth—the Son of God who has been called from Egypt to live and work and die in the land of God's own people.

II. THE BEGINNING OF JESUS' MINISTRY

Matt 3:1–4:25

3:1-12 John's preparation for Jesus (see Mark 1:2-8; Luke 3:1-18; John 1:19-28). In the summary of the preaching of John the Baptist, material from the Markan and the Q sources has been used. Matthew's most important contribution comes at the very beginning (v. 2), where John's preaching is summarized in exactly the same words as Jesus' preaching is summarized in 4:17: "Repent, for the kingdom of heaven is at hand." Both preachers demand a radical conversion of the whole person to God, and both urge it as preparation for the new age when the God of Israel will be acknowledged as the Lord by all creation. That time is very close at hand.

The first part of the material about John the Baptist (vv. 1-6) makes John's activity a part of the momentous and eventful time of Jesus ("in those days") and locates him in the wilderness of Judea—the area in which the community that has given us the Dead Sea scrolls had its center. The relation of John to Jesus is explained by the quotation from Isa 40:3: John's preaching in the wilderness prepares the way for Jesus. The description of John's haircloth and belt in verse 4 reminds the reader of the prophet Elijah's clothing as described in 2 Kgs 1:8. John cultivates the prophet's lifestyle and can be aptly described as the new Elijah (see Matt 11:14; 17:11-13). The Jewish historian Josephus (*Antiquities* 18:116-119) confirms that John drew large crowds for his exhortations to justice and piety. He describes John's ritual of baptism as a symbolic action signifying that conversion of heart had taken place.

In verses 7-10 John's preaching is directed to members of two Jewish groups ("the Pharisees and Sadducees") that will furnish unbelieving opposition to Jesus throughout the Gospel. They are warned to reform their lives as a preparation for the decisive intervention of God ("the coming wrath"). They are warned not to rely on their Jewish descent ("Abraham as our father") to protect them. The references to "children" and "stones" probably reflect a play on two very similar Aramaic (or Hebrew) words. Finally, they are warned that the time is short ("the ax lies at the root"). In the coming time of judgment prior to the fullness of God's kingdom, it is the fruit of good deeds that will count. John's stress on repentance, action now, and "bearing fruit" in good deeds foreshadows Jesus' instructions to his own disciples.

The second sample of John's preaching (vv. 11-12) subordinates John to Jesus. In this context "the one who is coming after me" must be Jesus. In verse 11 John protests that he is not even worthy to act as the slave of Jesus by carrying his sandals, and he contrasts his own symbolic water-baptism with the immersion in the Holy Spirit and the refining fire of judgment that will complete Jesus' proclamation of God's kingdom. The traditional image of the last judgment as a harvest is used in verse 12. The judgment will separate the good ("wheat") from the bad ("chaff"); it is very near.

Whatever the historical relationship may have been between John the Baptist and Jesus (and their followers), Matthew and the other New Testament writers took care to draw John into the circle of Jesus' influence and to subordinate him to Jesus. Far from contradicting Jesus, John preaches precisely the same things: conversion of heart, the coming of God's kingdom, and bearing fruit in good deeds. Far from engaging in a rivalry with Jesus, John makes it clear from the start how much the person and baptism of Jesus surpassed him and his baptism. John the Baptist emerges as a faithful "Christian" preacher! His warnings have relevance not only to the Pharisees and Sadducees but also to Christians.

3:13-17 The baptism of Jesus (see Mark 1:9-11; Luke 3:21-22). That Jesus was baptized by John is undoubtedly a historical fact. According to the Gospel accounts, Jesus received from John a baptism connected with the forgiveness of sins. It is inconceivable that the early Christians, who held Jesus in such high esteem, would have invented a story in which Jesus received something from John and that this reception would involve the baptism of repentance (see Matt 3:2, 6, 8, 11).

Indeed, the early church's embarrassment at Jesus' having been baptized by John is reflected in the dialogue found only in Matt 3:14-15. John demonstrates his humility and reveals his prophetic insight that Jesus is the "one to come." Jesus' first words in the Gospel are a request that he be baptized by John because this is in accord with God's will; it must be done in order to fulfill the divine plan. Thus Matthew explains how Jesus the sinless one could have received a baptism of repentance.

Jesus' emergence from the waters of the Jordan (vv. 16-17) is accompanied by several extraordinary, supernatural phenomena with long and rich Old Testament backgrounds. With the opening of the sky, the separation between heaven and earth is broken through (see Ezek 1:1; Isa 64:1). The descent of the Holy Spirit "like a dove" recalls the activity of the Spirit of God in the creation (see Gen 1:2). The voice from heaven describes Jesus in phrases taken from various Old Testament passages (Gen 22:2; Ps 2:7; Isa 42:1). The story reaches its climax in the identification of Jesus as the Son of God.

The theories that the events following the baptism occurred as a private vision granted to Jesus and that only then did Jesus become conscious of his divine sonship have no foundation in Matthew's account. The public character of the signs in verses 16-17 and the message referring to Jesus in the third person ("This is . . .") leave no doubt that, for Matthew, these events could have been experienced by onlookers. Matthew's primary concern is to show that at the very beginning of Jesus' public ministry he is publicly acknowledged as the Son of God. This in turn makes clear the significance of everything that Jesus will do in the course of that ministry. His is the ministry of God's own Son. A new age under the power of God has begun, and in it all the plans of God will be fulfilled.

4:1-11 The testing of God's Son (see Mark 1:12-13; Luke 4:1-13). The theme of Jesus as the Son of God that is so prominent in the baptism account is developed in the story of the temptation. The passage is best entitled the "testing of God's Son," because the first two tests are introduced by the phrase "if you are the Son of God." The tests and Jesus' responses to them show what kind of Messiah and Son of God he really is. The setting in the desert (v. 1) and the use of the number "forty" (v. 2) suggest a contrast between ancient Israel and Jesus. During its wandering in the wilderness after the escape from Egypt, ancient Israel was tested and found wanting. Where ancient Israel failed, Jesus now triumphs.

Mark's narrative of the testing of Jesus (Mark 1:12-13) contains only two verses, but Matt 4:1-11 and Luke 4:1-13 provide a lengthy debate in which the devil presents three tests and Jesus answers with three quotations from the Book of Deuteronomy. After forty days and nights of fasting, Jesus would be very hungry. So the first test (vv. 3-4) is the temptation to change stones into bread in order to feed himself. Jesus takes his reply from Deut 8:3: The Son of God is fed by the word of God, not by bread alone.

The second test (vv. 5-7) involves Jesus' being taken up to the highest point on the wall surrounding the Jerusalem temple. There he is tempted to throw himself down and call on God for aid, thus fulfilling Ps 91:11-12. Jesus takes his reply this time from Deut 6:16: The Son of God does not put his Father to such foolish and magical tests.

The third test (vv. 7-10) promises all the kingdoms of the world to Jesus if he will offer worship to the devil. Jesus' reply is taken from Deut 6:13: The Son of God offers worship only to his heavenly Father.

What kind of a Son of God is Jesus? His conduct during the three tests makes it clear that he does not seek to satisfy his own material needs, to make a miraculous display of his status and power, or to enter into partnership with the devil for the sake of political authority. Jesus emerges as totally obedient to the will of his Father, especially as that will is expressed in the words of the Old Testament Scriptures. His attitude provides a model for Christians who may be tempted to pay too much attention to material goods, to provoke God, or to seek influence and wealth without regard for justice and morality. Having personally withstood the assaults of Satan on these matters, Jesus is able to free others from their tyranny.

4:12-17 Preaching God's kingdom (see Mark 1:14-15; Luke 4:14-15). After being identified publicly as the Son of God in the baptism account (3:13-17) and after proving what kind of Son of God he is (4:1-11), Jesus journeys from Judea to Galilee in order to begin his public ministry (4:12-17). Unlike Mark (see Mark 1:14-15), Matthew feels obligated to explain in some detail why the Messiah should exercise his ministry in Galilee rather than in Jerusalem and Judea. John's arrest by Herod Antipas (a son of Herod the Great) and the danger that spelled for Jesus were not sufficient reasons for this move. As was the case in Matt 2:1-23, geography is explained in light of the Scriptures: Jesus' Galilean ministry is in accord with the words of Isa 9:1-2, and thus in accord with God's will.

The substance of Jesus' preaching is summarized in Matt 4:17: "Repent, for the kingdom of heaven is at hand." The same message was attributed to John the Baptist in 3:2. The first part of the message contains the command calling for a complete conversion and reorientation of life. The second part supplies the reason for the command: The definitive display of God's power and judgment and the establishment of his rule over all creation are near. In fact, as we will see, the ultimate victory of God is being inaugurated in the ministry of his Son.

4:18-22 The call of four fishermen (see Mark 1:16-20; Luke 5:1-11). Matthew's story of the call of the first disciples is very similar to Mark 1:16-20. In the overall plan of Matthew's Gospel, it introduces three of the disciples who will form Jesus' inner circle among the Twelve: Peter, James, and John. It also prepares for the presence of the disciples at the Sermon on the Mount (5:1) and for the promise to Peter (16:17-19). Jewish teachers did not usually call their own disciples; rather, prospective disciples sought out a teacher with a good reputation for learning and holiness. This account emphasizes the extraordinary attractiveness and magnetism of Jesus.

The first disciples encountered Jesus in their everyday occupation of fishing in the Sea of Galilee—then as now, an important and profitable business in Israel's economy. Without any preparation and with little or no deliberation, they leave behind their business and their families in order to follow Jesus. Discipleship is first and foremost being with Jesus, and the quick response of the first disciples ("at once" according to verses 20, 22) suggests how appealing the invitation to be with Jesus must have been. But discipleship also involves sharing in the mission of Jesus ("fishers of men" according to verse 19), and that dimension too is stressed from the very beginning.

4:23-25 A summary of Jesus' activities (see Mark 1:39; Luke 4:44). Almost every word in the summary of Jesus' preaching, teaching, and healing activities is found in some passage in Mark (see Mark 1:39; 1:28; 3:10; 3:7-8). Although Jesus' activity is confined to the region of Galilee, word of it spreads to the whole province of Syria. The outward movement of Jesus' reputation as a teacher and healer results in the movement of many people toward him. People suffering from all kinds of diseases are brought to him, and they are cured (v. 24). People from every region of Israel except Samaria join the crowds that follow him (v. 25). Such people, along with the disciples, form the audience for the Sermon on the Mount (see 5:1; 7:28).

By way of preparation for the Sermon on the Mount, Matthew has established Jesus' superiority to John the Baptist (3:1-12), recounted the divine acknowledgement of Jesus as the Son of God (3:13-17), and shown what kind of Son of God Jesus is (4:1-11). He has also explained why Jesus taught and healed in Galilee (4:12-17) and how he attracted an inner circle of disciples (4:18-22) and a larger circle of interested followers (4:23-25). The Sermon on the Mount (5:1–7:29) will reveal what a powerful teacher Jesus is.

III. THE SERMON ON THE MOUNT

Matt 5:1–7:29

The Sermon on the Mount is the first of Jesus' five major speeches in the Gospel. It is obviously related to the Sermon on the Plain in Luke 6:20-49 but is more than three times as long. Matthew has gathered together traditional sayings and shaped them into an epitome of Jesus' teaching. The basic thesis of the Sermon is stated in 5:20: "Unless your righteousness surpasses that of the scribes and Pharisees, you will not enter into the kingdom of God."

The introductory section (5:1-20) describes those who are blessed (5:3-12), the role of the disciples (5:13-16), and the role of Jesus (5:17-19). The second major section (5:21-48) contrasts the holiness or righteousness of the experts in the interpretation of the Old Testament law ("the scribes") and the better holiness or righteousness taught by Jesus. The third section (6:1-18) warns against the purely external holiness cultivated by groups like the Pharisees, and the fourth section (6:19–7:29) furnishes more advice for Christians in their pursuit of holiness.

The teachings contained in the Sermon on the Mount have been interpreted in many different ways: principles of Christian ethics, counsels of perfection, ideals that are impossible to practice, and so forth. For Matthew, these teachings are the directives of Jesus the Messiah and Son of God, whose authority far surpasses that of every other teacher (see 7:29). They are presented as a sample of Jesus' basic demands made on his disciples and as an expression of Christian values. They presuppose the personal experience of Jesus and the good news of God's coming kingdom, and thus they offer practical advice on how to respond to Jesus and his preaching.

5:1-2 The setting. The site for the Sermon is a mountainside, presumably in Galilee. In the Bible and in other religious literatures, the mountain is frequently a privileged place for revelations of or from God. The fact that Jesus' first extensive block of teaching is set on a mountainside gives it special importance. The audience for the Sermon has already been introduced. It certainly contains the disciples chosen by Jesus (4:18-22). It also includes some of the crowd (4:23-25), as both the beginning (5:1) and the end (7:28) of the Sermon indicate. The Sermon is intended for a wider audience than the inner circle of Jesus' followers.

5:3-12 The beatitudes (see Luke 6:20-23). The beatitudes declare "blessed" or "happy" some surprising people. The beatitude is a literary form common in the Old Testament book of Psalms. There persons or groups are declared to be blessed or happy (see Pss 1:1; 32:1-2; 41:1; 65:4; 84:4-5; 106:3; 112:1;

128:1), and sometimes the reason for the declaration is supplied. The Matthean beatitudes differ from the Old Testament models in their references to the coming kingdom of God and to the reversal of human values that accompanies it. The four beatitudes in Luke 6:20-23 are commonly thought to reflect the form ("Blessed are you . . .") and the content (blessings on the poor, the hungry, the weeping, and the persecuted) of Jesus' preaching more closely than the Matthean beatitudes do. Matthew's version tends to spiritualize ("poor in spirit" . . . "hunger and thirst for righteousness") and contains further beatitudes that do not add appreciably to the content of Luke's version.

The first set of beatitudes (vv. 3-6) proclaims as happy the poor in spirit (those whose condition demands total trust in God), the sorrowing (see Isa 61:2-3), the meek (see Ps 37:11), and those who hunger and thirst for righteousness (those whose central task in life is the fulfillment of God's will). Their happiness is largely future, but it also extends into the present time. By living out the values of the kingdom of heaven here and now, they anticipate and share the happiness that a fuller form of life with God will bring. God is the source of all their happiness.

The second set of beatitudes (vv. 7-10) also climaxes with a reference to righteousness, just as the first set did (see v. 6). Here a blessing is pronounced upon the merciful, the honest (see Ps 24:3-4), the agents of peace, and those who suffer on account of their search for righteousness. They too are promised future happiness from God. The final beatitude in verses 11-12 (see Luke 6:22-23) develops the theme of persecution for the sake of Jesus and relates this to the persecution suffered by certain Old Testament prophets.

5:13-16 The role of the disciples (see Mark 9:50; Luke 14:34-35). The role of the followers of Jesus is expressed by the images of salt and light. In Jesus' time, salt was used not only to improve the taste of food but also to preserve meat and fish. When Jesus compares his followers to salt (v. 13), he says that they improve the quality of human existence and preserve it from destruction. In Jesus' time, the only lamps available were small dish-like devices in which oil was burned. By our standards these lamps did not give off much light, but in the time before electricity their light must have seemed very bright. When Jesus calls his disciples the light of the world (vv. 14-15), he says that their actions serve as a beacon of light in a dark world. The disciples are challenged to let their light shine (v. 16) as a witness to their fidelity to Jesus and his heavenly Father.

5:17-20 The role of Jesus. The role of Jesus is treated with reference to the Old Testament, or rather, the Old Testament is treated with reference to Jesus. Jesus came to reveal the true meaning of the Old Testament, to express what the law and the prophets wished to say, and thus to bring it to fulfillment (v. 17). The saying in verse 18 appeals to the Jewish idea that the law is eternal, or at least that it remains in force "until all things have taken place" (the fullness of God's kingdom, or perhaps the death and resurrection of Jesus). In its context in the Sermon on the Mount, "these commandments" in the third saying (v. 19) may refer to Jesus' own instructions rather than to the precepts of the Old Testament. Jesus appears as the authoritative interpreter of the Jewish tradition, the one who is able to bring to light its most profound aspects. The final saying (v. 20) demands that Jesus' disciples surpass the scribes and Pharisees in seeking righteousness; otherwise they cannot enter God's kingdom. This saying states the basic thesis of the entire Sermon and gives structure to the various sayings contained in the three remaining sections.

5:21-26 Murder and anger. The second part of the Sermon (5:21-48) contrasts the scribes' ideal of holiness based on the literal reading of Scripture and Jesus' more radical and demanding teaching. This contrast is carried out by means of six antitheses in which the words of the Old Testament ("You have heard") are placed beside the sayings of Jesus ("But I say to you"). The antitheses illustrate how Jesus came to "fulfill" the law and the prophets by explaining the meaning of the Old Testament commandments at their deepest levels. In some cases, the biblical precept is extended in order to get at the root disposition beneath the forbidden action. In other cases, the precept itself is pushed so far as to be effectively repealed or superseded. Sayings on topics having some connection with the subject matter of the six antitheses are also included.

The first antithesis (vv. 21-26) concerns the prohibition against murder (Exod 20:13; Deut 5:17). Jesus' followers cannot be satisfied with merely avoiding the act of murder but must also curb the anger and the insults that lead to murder. The three courts or places of judgment mentioned in verse 22 (judgment or the local court, the Sanhedrin, the fiery Gehenna) would normally be connected with trying a case of murder, but here they are related to anger. The point is that anger should be taken as seriously as murder is. Two illustrations of putting away anger and being reconciled to others are provided in verses 23-26. The first instance (vv. 23-24) suggests that reconciliation may even take precedence over participating in worship at the temple, and the second instance (vv. 25-26) warns against letting a dispute go so far as to end up in court, where the judgment could go against one.

5:27-30 Adultery and lust. The second antithesis demands that lust as the root cause of adultery (Exod 20:14; Deut 5:18) be avoided. The mention of the lustful look in verse 28 is developed by means of the sayings about the right eye (v. 29) and the right hand (v. 30) being occasions of sin (see Matt 18:8-9). The salvation of the whole person is of more value than the preservation of any one part that may lead to sin.

5:31-32 Divorce. The antithesis concerning divorce seems to repeal or reject the permission and procedure found in Deut 24:1. According to Jesus, divorce is not allowed (see Luke 16:18; 1 Cor 7:10-11; Mark 10:2-12; Matt 19:3-12). The Matthean versions of Jesus' teachings on divorce include some kind of exception: "unless the marriage is unlawful" (5:32; 19:9). The Greek word is *porneia*, which refers to some sort of sexual misconduct or irregularity. In Acts 15:20, 29 *porneia* has to do with marriages contracted within the degrees of kinship forbidden by Lev 18:6-18, and thus technically incestuous unions. These exceptive clauses were probably intended to deal with members of the Matthean community who were already in such irregular marriages before they became Christians.

5:33-37 Oaths. The antithesis regarding oaths also seems to go so far beyond the Old Testament prohibition against swearing falsely (Lev 19:12; Num 30:2; Deut 23:21) as to do away with it entirely. At a time when oaths and vows were proliferating in Judaism,

Jesus recommends that his disciples simply be honest and straightforward in their speech. No human being has control or ownership of the heavens, the earth, or Jerusalem. Only God does. We cannot even control our own bodies completely. Therefore, no one has the right to make an oath based on such things as witnesses.

5:38-42 Retaliation (see Luke 6:29-30). In the fifth antithesis the Old Testament law of retaliation (Exod 21:23-24; Lev 24:19-20; Deut 19:21) is also pushed to the point of abrogation. The law of retaliation ("an eye for an eye and a tooth for a tooth") was intended to restrict vengeance and to keep violence within limits. Jesus urges his followers to forgo even the limited retaliation allowed by the Old Testament and thus to interrupt the whole cycle of revenge. The disciples must not adopt the attitudes and actions of their enemies, and four practical examples of non-retaliation in the face of evil are provided in verses 39-42 (see Luke 6:29-30). Each example challenges accepted, instinctive human behavior patterns.

5:43-48 Love of enemies (see Luke 6:27-28, 32-36). The final antithesis demands that Jesus' followers love not only the members of their own national or religious group (Lev 19:18) but even their enemies. This new demand is based, not on human nature, but on the example of God. It is human nature (represented by the tax collectors and pagans) to love those who love you and to greet only members of one's own family. But God makes the sun rise on good and bad alike, and rain falls on both the just and the unjust. When God's love and care for all people are taken as the standard, the disciples of Jesus cannot limit their love to their own group or their own nation. The disciples' perfection reflects and is measured by God's perfection.

6:1-4 Almsgiving. Three religious practices that would have been especially important for the Pharisees are treated in the third major part of the Sermon (6:1-18). After stating the general principle that religious acts should be done to honor God and not simply to better one's own reputation (v. 1), the passage considers almsgiving (vv. 2-4), prayer (vv. 5-15), and fasting (vv. 16-18). Each section contains a description of behavior that should be avoided, an instruction on the proper attitude, and the promise of a reward from God. Pious self-display is criticized, not the pious actions in themselves.

In a society without a highly organized welfare system, the obligation to offer charity (vv. 2-4) to the poor, the defenseless, and the sick was taken very seriously by religious people. In verse 2 Jesus criticizes those who make a great display of their charity by means of the image of blowing a horn. He calls such people "hypocrites," a term that originally referred to actors on a stage but here carries the sense of "phonies." The charge of hypocrisy is also leveled against the scribes and Pharisees in chapter 23. Jesus' disciples are instructed to be so free from religious showiness that they do not even seek the self-satisfaction of knowing what they are giving (6:3). Both verses 2 and 3 rely on obvious exaggerations in order to contrast self-seeking and selflessness in religion. The God who sees acts hidden from human sight will surely reward charity given without fanfare (v. 4).

6:5-15 Prayer (see Luke 11:2-4). The section on prayer begins the same way as the preceding section did. Here the behavior to be avoided is making a public spectacle of oneself in prayer (v. 5). The only fitting reward for such prayer is the public notoriety that it attracts. Indeed, prayer offered to win human praise is not prayer at all. Jesus' disciples are instructed to avoid making a public display of themselves in prayer (v. 6). That public prayer should be condemned outright was unthinkable for Jews like Jesus and Matthew, and it is not condemned here. Rather, another exaggerated statement is used in order to underline the warning against religious showiness. God will reward only genuine prayer offered in sincerity to him.

Attached to this teaching are sayings on prayer (vv. 7-8), a sample prayer (vv. 9-13), and sayings on forgiveness (vv. 14-15). In Jewish piety the prayer of petition was very important, and Jesus' disciples are warned not to confuse quantity with quality (v. 7). God as a loving Father knows the needs of his children even before they make their requests, but he wants them to ask in confidence and trust (v. 8). In petition, we do not so much inform God of some situation as express our dependence and faith.

The so-called Lord's Prayer or Our Father (vv. 9-13) is offered as a sample. Most of its phrases have close parallels in Jewish prayers of the time. The shorter and perhaps more primitive version in Luke 11:2-4 addresses God simply as "Father" and lacks petitions found in Matt 6:10, 13. The Matthean version begins with a typically Jewish form of invocation in prayer: "Our Father in heaven." The three "you-petitions" are addressed directly to God (vv. 9b-10) and pray for the coming of God's kingdom. They ask that God let the time come when he will be recognized as the Holy One by all creation, that the fullness of his kingship be revealed to all creation, and that the perfection with which his will is done in heaven should extend to earth also. The three "we-petitions" (vv. 11-13) ask for physical and spiritual well-being in the difficult period before the fullness of God's kingdom. They ask that God provide the bread we need today, that the forgiveness we receive from God may lead us to forgive those who have wronged us ("debts" is a metaphor for sins), and that in the time of testing accompanying the coming of God's kingdom we may not fall prey to the Evil One.

The saying on forgiveness (vv. 14-15) is joined to the Lord's Prayer because it concerns the same issue that the second of the "we-petitions" (6:12) treats. It makes our willingness to forgive one another the necessary condition for God's willingness to forgive us our sins.

6:16-18 Fasting. The section on fasting follows the pattern set in the sections on almsgiving and prayer. There were special days designated for fasting in the Jewish calendar, and pious Pharisees fasted two days a week. Not the act of fasting itself, but rather making a public display of one's fast, is criticized in verse 16. Jesus' disciples are instructed to disguise their fasting by looking as if they are preparing for a holiday (v. 17). God will know that they are fasting and will reward them accordingly (v. 18).

6:19-34 Trust in God (see Luke 12:33-34; 11:34-36; 16:13; 12:22-34). The final section of the Sermon (6:19-7:29) gives advice regarding the Christian pursuit of holiness. The basic theme is the decision for or against God. The major topics bear some relation to the "we-petitions" in the Lord's Prayer: trust in God to provide food and clothing ("Give us today our daily bread"), avoiding the condemnation of others ("as we forgive our debtors"), approaching God as Father with our requests

("Our Father in heaven"), and traveling the narrow and hard way ("deliver us").

The material in the first part (vv. 19-34) concerns various aspects of the choice between God and earthly wealth. The sayings on true riches in verses 19-21 (see Luke 12:33-34) contrast the fragile nature of earthly treasures and eternal treasure with God, who rewards those who give alms, pray, and fast in secret (vv. 1-18). The following saying (vv. 22-23) assumes that the eyes are the conduits for the entire body. In this context (see Luke 11:34-36), it refers to the need for sound spiritual vision if the person is to act properly. Those whose vision is not focused on obedience to God will plunge their whole selves into darkness. The decision for or against God carries over into all dimensions of the person's life. The choice between God and earthly wealth is made explicit in verse 24 (see Luke 16:13), where the latter is personified as Mammon ("that in which one puts trust or faith").

The sayings on care and anxiety in verses 25-34 (see Luke 12:22-34) seek to free the followers of Jesus from excessive concern about food and clothing (see v. 31) by means of several considerations. They are urged to reflect on God's care as shown in nature (the birds and the wild flowers) and to realize that human beings are even more important in God's sight. They are asked to admit that worrying does not really solve anything (v. 27) and to recognize that if their heart is set on serving God alone, these matters will take care of themselves (v. 33). The God whom they address in prayer as Father knows all that they need.

7:1-6 Avoiding condemnation (see Luke 6:37-38, 41-42). The followers of Jesus are warned to avoid condemning other people ("stop judging"). This is the prerogative of God on the day of judgment. The way in which they deal with others in this matter will determine in large part the way that others and God himself will deal with them (vv. 1-2). This does not rule out the practice of correction within the community (see 18:15-18), but such correction must be carried out with an awareness of one's own failings and prejudices (vv. 3-5). It also does not rule out discernment and discretion in dealing with hostile outsiders or even with apostate and unrepentant Christians (v. 6).

7:7-11 Approaching God in prayer (see Luke 11:9-13). In prayer, God is to be approached with boldness and confidence. The importance of the prayer of petition is underlined ("ask . . . seek . . . knock"), and the efficacy of such prayers is assumed (vv. 7-8). The way that a human father cares for his children and gives them good gifts when they ask him is used in verses 9-11 to illustrate the way that the heavenly Father answers petitions in prayer.

7:12 The golden rule (see Luke 6:31). The so-called golden rule of verse 12 about treating others as you would wish them to treat you is not original or unique to Jesus. Matthew's primary interest was the use of it as a summary of the Old Testament tradition. The Jewish teacher Hillel offered a similar teaching ("What you do not like, do not do to your neighbor") and asserted that the rest of the law and the prophets is a commentary on this (see Tob 4:15).

7:13-27 Decision for or against God (see Luke 13:24; 6:43-44; 13:25-27; 6:47-49). The Sermon concludes with a series of contrasts regarding the decision for or against God. The image of the two ways in verses 13-14 (see Luke 13:24) is common in the Old Testament and was developed in the Dead Sea scrolls and in the early Christian writing called the *Didache*. The idea that the gate is narrow and the way is constricted is noteworthy in Matthew. The false prophets of verses 15-20 (see Luke 6:43-44) are to be judged in accordance with Deut 13:1-5 and 18:20-22. Does the prophet's word come true? Does the prophet lead the people astray? The results (or fruits) show the prophet's character (the tree).

The sayings in verses 21-23 (see Luke 13:25-27) also focus on the relationship between word and action: It is not enough merely to say "Lord, Lord," for only doing God's will gives entry to his kingdom. The firm foundation mentioned in verses 24-27 (see Luke 6:47-49) includes both word and deed.

7:28-29 Conclusion. The Sermon on the Mount ends as the four other major speeches of Jesus in the Gospel do (see 11:1; 13:53; 19:1; 26:1): "Jesus finished these words." The contrast between the authority displayed by Jesus and the lack of authority on the part of the scribes (see Mark 1:22) was important to Matthew and his community as they experienced the split between the church and the synagogue ("their scribes").

IV. THE POWERFUL DEEDS OF JESUS

Matt 8:1–9:38

Having illustrated the power of Jesus as a teacher by the Sermon on the Mount, Matthew now gives examples of his power as a healer and a wonder-worker in chapters 8–9. Jesus is powerful in both word and deed. Nine acts of power are arranged in three groups of three (8:1-17; 8:23–9:8; 9:18-34). The groups are divided from one another by non-miraculous materials (8:18-22; 9:9-17; 9:35-38) in which the theme of discipleship is prominent. Both the Sermon and the mighty acts of Jesus are set in the framework of his ministry in Galilee (see 4:23; 9:35).

8:1-4 Power over leprosy (see Mark 1:40-45; Luke 5:12-16). The first cycle of Jesus' mighty deeds (8:1-17) presents demonstrations of his power over leprosy, paralysis, fever, and demonic possession. He shows mercy to the marginal people of Jewish society: lepers, Gentiles, servants, women, and the possessed.

Matthew's version of the healing of the leper (vv. 1-4) contains a transitional sentence (v. 1), the leper's request for healing (v. 2), Jesus' response and the miraculous healing (v. 3), and the final instruction that the healed man show himself to the priest in the temple (v. 4). The key words are "make clean" or "cure," which appear in the request for healing (v. 2), in Jesus' response (v. 3a), and in the narrator's description of what took place (v. 3b).

The Matthean account is simpler than Mark 1:40-45. The references to Jesus' emotions in Mark 1:41, 43, as well as the report about the public impact of the healing in Mark 1:45, are absent. In Matt 8:2, Jesus is addressed as "Lord," which not only heightens his dignity but also places the miracle in the framework of praying faith. The simpler structure also helps to highlight Jesus' concern that the Old Testament law regarding lepers who had been cleansed (Lev 14:2-9) be fulfilled exactly. The authority of Jesus as Messiah and Son of God, how he should be approached in prayer, and his fulfillment of

the Old Testament emerge as the central themes in Matthew's account.

8:5-13 Power over paralysis (see Luke 7:1-10; John 4:43-54). The themes of Jesus' authority and power are carried on in the healing of the centurion's servant. But here special attention is given to a non-Jew's act of faith in Jesus' power. The centurion was a Gentile soldier (probably a Syrian) who was stationed at the military garrison in Capernaum. Whereas Luke's account portrays him as communicating with Jesus through intermediaries (the elders of the Jews and friends), Matthew pictures him in a dialogue of faith directly with Jesus. His request in verse 6 is prefaced with the title "Lord," and his response to Jesus' willingness to cure his paralyzed servant highlights the power of Jesus' word (v. 8). As a military man, he knows the force of a verbal command in a well-run army, and so he believes that the word of Jesus is powerful enough to cure his servant (vv. 8-9).

The Gentile centurion's faith is praised as surpassing anything that Jesus has encountered among God's chosen people (v. 10). It is seen as anticipating the situation after Jesus' death and resurrection when the Gentiles will find a place among God's people at the heavenly banquet (and in the church) and many Jews by birth will be excluded for their unbelief in Jesus (vv. 11-12). As a response to the centurion's display of faith, Jesus carries out the act of healing (v. 13).

8:14-17 Power over fever and demons (see Mark 1:29-34; Luke 4:38-41). In 8:14-17, Matthew compresses Mark's accounts of the healings of Peter's mother-in-law and of the many sick at Capernaum. Besides omitting the Markan context, Matthew also omits the mention of Simon (Peter), Andrew, James, and John. Jesus miraculously heals the woman, and as proof of the healing she serves him (not them, as in Mark 1:31). In the account of the general healing (vv. 16-17), Matthew leaves out what he regards as extraneous details as well as Jesus' refusal to let the demons speak. On the other hand, in verse 17 he adds the notice that in this healing activity Jesus brings to fulfillment the prophecy of Isa 53:4. This quotation not only carries on the theme of Jesus as fulfilling the Old Testament but also serves to identify Jesus as the Suffering Servant of God.

8:18-22 The demands of discipleship (see Luke 9:57-60). The first and second triads of Jesus' acts of power (8:1-17; 8:23–9:8) are separated by sayings on the radical demands of discipleship. In the first instance a scribe addresses Jesus as "Teacher" and offers to follow him anywhere, only to be warned that Jesus the Son of Man gives no guarantee of security. In the second instance a "disciple" requests permission to attend to the burial of his father (see 1 Kgs 19:20), but the Lord demands that he choose between discipleship and family obligation. This is an extreme way of making the point that the call to follow Jesus supersedes all other obligations and that it may even involve cutting family ties. Such sayings are designed to force us to reflect on the seriousness and significance of discipleship. Their extreme character creates a tension that can only be resolved by accepting the call.

8:23-27 Power over the sea (see Mark 4:35-41; Luke 8:22-25). The second cycle of Jesus' mighty acts (8:23–9:8) reveals his power over the sea, the demons, and sin. Matthew's account of the stilling of the storm (vv. 23-27) drops some details found in Mark 4:35-41 and makes more explicit the themes of discipleship and faith. In verse 23, Jesus takes the initiative, and the disciples "follow" him (a technical term for discipleship). Thus the material on discipleship in verses 18-22 is connected with Jesus' power over the sea.

It is possible that Matthew's readers were sensitive to one or more of the following symbolic equivalencies: the sea as the forces of chaos allied against God, the storm as the eschatological earthquake, and the boat as the church. Their request in verse 25 takes the form of a prayer: "Lord, save us! We are perishing!" Jesus' response to their prayer takes over Mark's theme of the disciples' obtuseness and describes it under the term "little faith." Although they have some faith, the disciples still have a long way to go before they reach perfect faith. Under Matthew's careful editorship, the theme of Jesus' power is complemented by the themes of discipleship and faith made concrete in prayer to Jesus as Lord.

8:28-34 Power over demons (see Mark 5:1-20; Luke 8:26-39). The second act of power in this series is located by Matthew at Gadara, which was much closer to the shore of the Sea of Galilee than Gerasa is (see Mark 5:1). It concerns two men possessed by demons rather than one man as in Mark 5:2, perhaps because Matthew has combined Mark 1:21-28 and 5:1-20 into a single, short account. The demoniacs fade from the scene and give way to the demons, who address Jesus as the Son of God and complain that they should not be disturbed until the coming of the kingdom (v. 29). Then the demons request that Jesus send them into a herd of swine (unclean animals for Jews), and their "prayer" is granted by Jesus (vv. 31-32). The focus of the Matthean account is the dialogue between Jesus and the demons and his display of power over them.

9:1-8 Power over sin (see Mark 2:1-12; Luke 5:17-26). Matthew's story of the healing of the paralytic and the forgiveness of his sins omits Mark's descriptions of the crowd and the difficulty that the friends encounter in bringing the sick man to Jesus. The effect of this compression is to keep the theme of the forgiveness of sins in the spotlight. The faith of the friends is noted (v. 2), and the conversation between the scribes and Jesus serves to establish his authority both to forgive sins and to bring about physical healing. The healing itself (vv. 6-7) is offered as a visible proof of the Son of Man's power to work wonders even in the realm of the invisible or the spiritual (the forgiveness of sins). The statement in verse 8 that the crowd praised God for giving such authority to human beings suggests that in Matthew's community Jesus' authority to forgive sins was viewed as having been transmitted to members of the church (see 18:15-20).

9:9-17 The defense of the disciples (see Mark 2:13-22; Luke 5:27-39). The section that separates the second and third triads of Jesus' acts of power (8:23–9:8; 9:18-34) begins with the call of the tax collector Matthew in 9:9. In Mark 2:14 and Luke 5:27 he is named "Levi." His name may have been changed in our Gospel to make him one of the Twelve (see 10:3) and/or because the community in which the Gospel was written retained a traditional attachment to the apostle Matthew. There is no reason to suppose that the tax collector-turned-disciple had two names. Tax collectors were suspect to pious Jews on the grounds of their collaboration with the Roman officials and their practice of extorting more than was owed to the government. Jesus' willingness to accept such a person as a disciple prepared the way for the acceptance of all kinds of people into the church.

Jesus' practice of dining with tax collectors (v. 9) and sinners (vv. 10-11) scandalized the Pharisees, for whom ritual purity and table fellowship were important religious practices. They ask Jesus' disciples why he does this. In verses 12-13, Jesus himself supplies three explanations: (1) the spiritually sick need him most; (2) Hosea 6:6 bears witness to the greatness of God's mercy; (3) Jesus came to call sinners to conversion of heart. Then in verse 14 disciples of John the Baptist, for whom ascetic practices like fasting would have been important, ask why Jesus' disciples do not fast. They are told that the time of Jesus the bridegroom is not a fitting one for fasting (v. 15); when he is taken away from them, there will be ample time for fasting. The radical newness of Jesus and the incompatibility between his message and the old forms of piety are brought out in verses 16-17 by means of the images of the new cloth and the new wine.

9:18-26 Power over death (see Mark 5:21-43; Luke 8:40-56). The third cycle of Jesus' mighty acts (9:18-34) reveals his power over death and chronic illness, blindness, and speechlessness. The stories of the revival of the synagogue leader's daughter and the healing of the woman with the hemorrhage had already been intertwined in Mark 5:21-43. In verses 18-26, Matthew has greatly simplified the Markan narrative in order to make the theme of faith stand out even more sharply. According to verse 18, the ruler knew that the girl was already dead but still believed that Jesus could restore her to life. The way in which the girl's restoration to life is described in verse 25 ("arose") connects this miracle to Jesus' own resurrection. In verses 20-22 every detail not relevant to the theme of faith in Jesus' power is omitted. The words that are translated as "cured" and "saved" are part of the New Testament vocabulary of salvation.

9:27-31 Power over blindness. The second incident in the third cycle was probably designed to combine the two stories found in Mark 8:22-26 and 10:46-52 (see also Matt 20:29-34). The Matthean account revolves around Jesus' question in verse 28 ("Do you believe that I can do this?") and the affirmative response by the two blind men. The heal-

ing is worked because of their faith (v. 29).

9:32-34 Power over speechlessness. The third section recounts in the briefest possible way the healing of a man who could not speak, and then contrasts two possible reactions: the amazement of the crowds at the unprecedented acts performed by Jesus, and the Pharisees' ascription of Jesus' power to Satan. The third cycle as a whole concerns the necessity of faith in Jesus' power and ends by noting that some people could witness the miracles and still refuse to believe that Jesus was sent from God.

9:35-38 The mission of the disciples. The final block of material on discipleship begins by repeating the description of Jesus' ministry that appeared in 4:23. Then the idea that discipleship involves mission is brought out by means of two images: the people are like sheep without a shepherd and like a harvest that needs workers to bring in the crops. God is the ultimate shepherd and harvest master, but he needs the cooperation of those who accept Jesus' invitation to discipleship. The three sections on discipleship in chapters 8-9 emphasize the radical demands that it can involve (8:18-22), the fact that all kinds of people can be called to it and the radical newness that it represents (9:9-17), and its missionary dimension (9:35-38).

V. THE MISSIONARY DISCOURSE

Matt 10:1-42

The idea that discipleship involves mission sets the stage for the second major speech by Jesus—the so-called missionary discourse in chapter 10. The sayings that make up this discourse have been gathered from various traditional sources and woven by the evangelist into a lengthy instruction on how the disciples of Jesus are to act (10:5-15) and what they can expect (10:16-42). The basic theme is stated in 10:24-25: "No disciple is above his teacher, no slave above his master. It is enough for the disciple that he become like his teacher, for the slave that he become like his master." Just as the disciples share in Jesus' power, so they must share his lifestyle and his sufferings.

10:1-5a Introduction (see Mark 3:13-19; Luke 6:12-16). After demonstrating his great powers as a healer in chapters 8-9, Jesus in 10:1 passes on to his twelve disciples the authority over demons and diseases that he had received from the Father. In his list of the Twelve (see Mark 3:16-19; Luke 6:13-16; Acts 1:13), Matthew stresses the primacy of Simon Peter ("first, Simon") and identifies Matthew as the tax collector of 9:9. The only significant disagreement among the various lists of apostles involves Thaddaeus, who in Luke 6:16 and Acts 1:13 is called Judas the son of James and in some manuscripts of Matthew and Mark is named Lebbaeus.

10:5b-15 What the disciples are to do (see Mark 6:7-13; Luke 9:1-6). The disciples' mission is limited to the people of Israel (vv. 5b-6), and they are to avoid entering the cities of non-Jews and Samaritans (whose Judaism was suspect in the eyes of Judeans and Galileans). Only after the death and resurrection of Jesus does the mission to the latter groups begin (see 28:19). The disciples' mission (vv. 7-8) replicates and extends the mission of Jesus in preaching the coming of God's kingdom and in healing the sick (see 4:23). As discipleship has been offered to them as a gift, so they are to offer it to others.

Wandering preachers representing various philosophies and religions were a common sight in the world of Jesus' time. Jesus' disciples are instructed not to be anxious about money or baggage or lodging, but rather to depend on the charity of their hearers (vv. 9-13). Their lack of concern for money, clothing, and lodging allows them to carry out the mission in a more single-minded way. It also bears witness to their trust in God's care for them and to their conviction that what has been freely received should be freely given. When the preachers are rejected in a place (vv. 14-15), they are to react without violence and only symbolically ("shake the dust from your feet"). They are to remain faithful to their task and trust that God will settle these matters in the final judgment. According to Gen 19, Sodom and Gomorrah were examples of extreme wickedness, especially with regard to hospitality.

10:16-25 Hostility (see Mark 13:9-13; Luke 21:12-17). The remainder of the missionary discourse tells the disciples what they are to expect. They can expect the same treatment that Jesus himself receives. Far from promising a mission free from conflict or opposition, Jesus prepares his disciples for hostility. They are sent as defenseless creatures ("sheep") among predators ("wolves"), and so they are urged to be shrewd while retaining their guilelessness (v. 16). In being tried and punished (vv. 17-18) by Jewish religious leaders ("their synagogues") and by Roman governmental officials ("governors and kings"), they share in Jesus' own passion (see 26:57-68; 27:11-26). Among the terrors awaiting the disciples are the anxiety connected with speaking at a public trial (v. 19), divisions within families and subsequent acts of betrayal (v. 21), hatred (v. 22), and persecution (v. 23). These terrors are outweighed by confidence in the Spirit (v. 20) and in their ultimate vindication when God's kingdom comes (v. 22).

In verse 23b the "towns of Israel" refers to the Jewish regions of Palestine, and "before the Son of Man comes" represents the coming of God's kingdom. According to Matthew's perspective, the coming of the Son of Man began with the death and resurrection and will terminate only at the end of time. The mission to Israel (10:5b-6) occupies the disciples until they receive the broader commission (28:19) that lasts until the end of this world. The sayings in verses 24-25 summarize the themes of the entire discourse and establish a link between the treatment accorded to Jesus by unbelievers and what the disciples of Jesus can expect.

10:26-33 Do not fear! (see Luke 12:2-9). Whatever the original contexts of the sayings in verses 26-33 may have been, here they serve to encourage the disciples to fearless confession in the face of opposition. Each saying is introduced by "Do not be afraid" (vv. 26, 28, 31) and attacks the fears that could cause the disciples to abandon their mission. The first saying (vv. 26-27) appeals to the inevitability of the coming of God's kingdom and Jesus' witness to it. Then the hypocrisy of the disciples' opponents will be revealed. The second saying (vv. 28-30) appeals to God's care for Jesus' disciples. Their opponents can destroy the body but not the soul. The third saying (vv. 31-33) appeals to the final judgment before God, which will be based on the disciples' faithfulness to Jesus during the conflicts that are part of their mission.

10:34-39 Family conflicts (see Luke 12:51-53; 14:26-27). Jesus does not guarantee the absence of conflict. In Jewish society of his time, family ties were far stronger than they are in the modern societies of the West.

But faithfulness to Jesus may involve the rupture even of these bonds. The passage is not an attack on family life as such, but it does insist that the disciples have a greater loyalty to Jesus than to the members of their families. In the extreme cases of having to choose between Jesus and one's family, Jesus demands absolute loyalty to himself. The sayings about the cross (v. 38) and losing one's life (v. 39) foreshadow Jesus' own fate and continue the theme of the disciples' identification with Jesus.

10:40-42 Receiving disciples of Jesus (see Mark 9:41). The concluding section of the missionary discourse reiterates the basic point of the discourse. The disciples are the representatives of Jesus. To receive them is to receive not only Jesus but also his heavenly Father (v. 40). Fitting rewards will be given to those who receive Christian prophets and holy men or even simpler Christians, because they all represent Christ and his heavenly Father.

VI. THE IMPORTANCE OF JESUS AND THE REJECTION OF HIM

Matt 11:1–12:50

The missionary discourse ends in 11:1, but nothing is said about the disciples' actual mission or their return. The spotlight remains on Jesus as he continues his work. The themes of unbelief and rejection that were so prominent in the missionary discourse are developed further in chapters 11–12, and we are given more information about Jesus' identity as the Messiah (11:1-6), the Wisdom of God (11:25-30), and the Servant of God (12:15-21).

11:1-6 Jesus as "the one who is to come" (see Luke 7:18-23). John's imprisonment had been mentioned in 4:12. The question in 11:3 regarding Jesus concerns his identity as "the one who is to come," which appears to have been a messianic title (see 3:11; 21:9; 23:39) derived from Ps 118:26 and Mal 3:1. Jesus' answer to John proves his messianic identity by listing the Messiah's deeds in terms of Isa 35:5-6 and 61:1. These deeds were described in chapters 8–9, and the list climaxes with the mention of the gospel having been preached to the poor (v. 5). The final saying (v. 6) declares "blessed" (see 5:3-12) those who do not find Jesus to be a scandal or a stumbling block. Though this beatitude may imply some misgivings on John's part concerning Jesus, it more likely prepares for the following incidents in which many people do find Jesus to be a stumbling block.

11:7-15 John the Baptist as Elijah (see Luke 7:24-30). The departure of John's messengers furnishes the occasion for Jesus' words about John's identity and the meaning of his rejection. John preached and baptized in the wilderness of Judah and lived very differently from the courtiers of Herod Antipas. Herod had John put in prison for questioning the propriety of his marriage to Herodias (see 14:1-12). In verses 9-10, 13, Jesus identifies John as a prophet but goes further by proclaiming him to be the fulfillment of Mal 3:1 (see Exod 23:20)—the prophet who will precede the coming of God's kingdom. This identification is made even more explicit in verse 14, when John is called Elijah. According to Mal 4:5, God would send Elijah the prophet from heaven before the great and terrible day of the Lord comes. But for all John's greatness, he has not yet inaugurated the decisive new age that the coming of God's kingdom will represent (v. 11). Nevertheless, John's imprisonment constitutes a violent attack against the coming kingdom (v. 12), an attack that will be repeated in the case of Jesus. Those who oppose the preaching of John and Jesus about the kingdom oppose the kingdom itself.

11:16-19 John and Jesus are rejected (see Luke 7:31-35). The austere and ascetic John was dismissed as having a demon (v. 18), and the joyful and expansive Jesus is rejected for keeping bad company (v. 19). Despite rejection by those who consider themselves wise, divine Wisdom will win out and confirm the actions of both John and Jesus. The beginning of the passage (vv. 16-17) compares the unbelievers to sullen children who refuse to play either the happy game of Jesus or the sad game of John.

11:20-24 Warnings to Galilean cities (see Luke 10:12-15). The Galilean cities in which Jesus had done his mighty deeds are given stern warnings. There are two pronouncements. Each contains a judgment ("woe"), an explanation and a comparison, and a prediction concerning the final judgment. First Chorazin and Bethsaida are threatened with "woe," because they have not repented in response to the deeds of Jesus. Their final judgment will be worse than that of the pagan cities of Tyre and Sidon (vv. 21-22). Then Capernaum (vv. 23-24) is threatened with woe, and its delusions of grandeur are compared to those of the king of Babylon as described in Isa 14:13-15. Capernaum too had refused to respond adequately to Jesus' deeds, and its final fate will be even worse than that of the wicked city of Sodom (see Gen 19:24-28). Both sayings of judgment assume the decisive importance of Jesus in human history.

11:25-30 Jesus as the Wisdom of God (see Luke 10:21-22). The themes of the decisive importance of Jesus and the rejection of him are linked in verses 25-30. Matthew has put together traditional sayings according to the following outline: the praise of the Father (vv. 25-26), the identity of Jesus (v. 27), and the invitation to come (vv. 28-30). Beginning with typically Jewish formulas of prayer, Jesus praises God for revealing to the simple and uneducated people, who were most receptive to Jesus, what has been hidden from the scholars and religious experts. Then in verse 27 Jesus asserts that God has granted him the revelation of himself as completely as a father discloses himself to a son. The relation between God and Jesus is so close that the only adequate terms for it are Father and Son. Therefore, only Jesus can pass on to others real knowledge of God. The language of verse 27 is very similar to many passages in John's Gospel (see John 3:35; 7:29; 10:14-15; 17:1-3).

In verses 28-30, Jesus expresses his invitation to discipleship in terms employed by Jesus ben Sira in Sir 51:23-27. Using the traditional image of the law as a "yoke," Jesus, the authoritative interpreter of the law (see 5:21-48), promises refreshment and rest in his wisdom school. All genuine searchers for wisdom are invited to come to Jesus. In Jesus, God's own wisdom dwells and can be learned.

12:1-8 Work on the sabbath (see Mark 2:23-28; Luke 6:1-5). Jesus' status as the authoritative interpreter of the law is exemplified in the incident of the disciples' plucking and eating grain on the sabbath. The disciples' actions would be considered the equivalent of reaping on the sabbath and therefore forbidden labor (see Exod 20:8-11; Deut 5:12-15). The Pharisees, who appear as the leaders of the opposition to Jesus and to his followers during most of the Gospel, protest against this unlawful act.

Jesus gives them four answers: (1) The disciples' act is compared to that of David and his followers in 1 Sam 21:1-6. In both cases a commandment was broken out of the need to satisfy physical hunger. Matthew has omitted the name of Abiathar the high priest from Mark 2:26, because in fact the high priest of the Old Testament story was Ahimelech. Thus the disciples of the Son of David had a good precedent in David himself. (2) In verses 5-6, Matthew cites an argument that is not present in Mark's account. The priests are allowed to perform acts of work in the Jerusalem temple on the sabbath on the principle that laws pertaining to the temple take precedence over laws pertaining to the sabbath. Perhaps the claim that Jesus is greater than the temple is implied here. (3) The quotation from Hos 6:6 ("I desire mercy, not sacrifice") is used to criticize the Pharisees' faulty scale of values. (4) Jesus as the Son of Man has the ultimate authority over the sabbath and even more right than David or the priests in the temple to overrule the Old Testament legislation regarding the sabbath.

In Matthew's community this passage would serve as a source of defenses against Jewish criticisms about early Christian laxity in observing the sabbath. The early Christians based their practice on the example and the authority of Jesus the Son of Man.

12:9-14 Healing on the sabbath (see Mark 3:1-6; Luke 6:6-11). The question of sabbath observance arises with respect to Jesus himself and takes the form of a debate. The place of the debate is "their synagogue"—an expression that suggests a sharp division between the Pharisees and the followers of Jesus. The question concerns the propriety of healing on the sabbath (v. 10), and Jesus' response involves a counter-question (v. 11) regarding the case of rescuing an animal on the sabbath (see Deut 22:4). If it is right to save an animal, how much the more is it right to save a human being (v. 12)!

As an illustration of good deeds done on the sabbath, Jesus restores to health the withered hand of a man in the synagogue. Why the good deed could not wait until after the sabbath or to what extent the man was in danger of death is not considered. Just as God desires mercy more than sacrifice, so good deeds override the sabbath regulations. Rather than convincing the Pharisees, Jesus' teaching and action only increase their opposition, to the point that they begin the plot to kill him (v. 14).

12:15-21 Jesus as the Servant of the Lord. In the midst of the rising opposition to Jesus from the Pharisees, Matthew pauses and places Jesus' response in the context of the Old Testament Servant of the Lord. Jesus was fully aware of the rising opposition (v. 15) but continued his healing activity and avoided publicity (vv. 15-16). His modesty and gentleness in the face of hostility are viewed as the fulfillment of Isa 42:1-4. By refusing to use violence against the Pharisees or to reveal himself openly, Jesus did not "contend or cry out." But other features in the Old Testament passage are also significant: Jesus' identity as the Servant of the Lord (see 3:17; 17:5), Jesus as especially endowed with the Holy Spirit, and his role in God's plan of salvation for the Gentiles. Matthew's identification of Jesus as the Servant of the Lord sets the stage for the debate with the Pharisees regarding the source of Jesus' powers. The thrust of their attack is that Jesus is in league with Satan. But Matthew's readers know that he is really the Servant of the Lord.

12:22-37 The source of Jesus' power (see Mark 3:19-30; Luke 11:14-23; 12:10; 6:43-45). The healing of a possessed man who was blind and mute provides the occasion for exploring the source of Jesus' power. The healing (v. 22) produces two reactions: wonder on the part of the crowds whether Jesus is the Son of David or Messiah (v. 23), and hostility from the Pharisees, who are convinced that he is the instrument of Satan (v. 24).

In response to the Pharisees, Jesus offers three arguments: (1) If Jesus' power over the demons were from Satan, Satan would be setting his own agents against themselves and thus destroying Satan's kingdom (vv. 25-26). (2) Jesus' exorcisms should be interpreted as good actions inspired by the Holy Spirit, just as the exorcisms performed by other Jewish exorcists are (vv. 27-28). (3) Jesus could not cast out demons unless he had some power over the chief demon (v. 29). The saying in verse 28, linking Jesus' exorcisms to the coming of God's kingdom, is very important for understanding all of Jesus' miracles: They are signs that, in Jesus, God's kingdom is break-

ing into the world and will reach its fullness in due time.

Having met the objections of the Pharisees, Jesus takes the offensive with three warnings: (1) Closeness to Jesus is absolutely essential, and the Pharisees must recognize it or run the risk of being on the wrong side when God's kingdom comes (v. 30). (2) The only unforgivable sin is attributing the work of the Holy Spirit to an evil spirit, as the Pharisees were doing in the case of Jesus. Failure to recognize the Son of Man for what he is may be understandable and even pardonable, but failure to recognize the source of his power is inexcusable (vv. 31-32). (3) The Pharisees' opposition to Jesus stems from their wickedness, and in the final judgment they will be judged with regard to their willingness or unwillingness to confess that Jesus is empowered by the Holy Spirit (vv. 33-37).

12:38-42 The sign of Jonah (see Luke 11:29-32). Despite all the miracles that Jesus had already worked, the scribes and Pharisees ask for more signs. The exasperated Jesus promises them only the sign of Jonah. The basic meaning of the sign of Jonah seems to involve the preaching of repentance to non-Jews and its acceptance by them. When the Old Testament prophet Jonah preached conversion of heart to the people of Nineveh, they acted on Jonah's preaching and repented (v. 41). The queen of Sheba came to Jerusalem to hear the wisdom of Solomon (see 1 Kgs 10:1-6), and she was duly impressed by him (v. 42). Jesus surpasses Jonah and Solomon, and so the scribes and Pharisees have good reason to repent. In verse 40, Matthew has given a second interpretation of the sign of Jonah: The three days spent by the prophet inside the fish (see Jonah 2) were a type or a foreshadowing of the three days between Jesus' death and his resurrection.

12:43-45 The evil spirit's return (see Luke 11:24-26). The passage about the evil spirit's return is joined to the sign of Jonah by its reference to "this evil generation" (vv. 39, 45), and to the entire section beginning at 12:22 by its concern with evil spirits. The activity of Jesus has made an impact on the evil spirits, but their power is far from broken. Matthew and his community probably viewed the Romans' destruction of Jerusalem in A.D. 70 as the fulfillment of Jesus' warnings.

12:46-50 The true family of Jesus (see

Mark 3:31-35; Luke 8:19-21). The long treatment of unbelief and rejection that began in the missionary discourse of chapter 10 and continued in the incidents of chapters 11–12 concludes with the definition of the true family of Jesus as those who do God's will. Matthew's account contains no explicit criticism of Jesus' relatives; they serve merely as a foil to emphasize the point that those who obey God constitute the real family of Jesus. In a society that placed a very high value on blood relationship, Jesus' teaching about his disciples forming a spiritual family would be quite challenging.

VII. PARABLES CONCERNING THE KINGDOM OF GOD

Matt 13:1-53

Jesus' parables about the kingdom form the third major discourse in the Gospel. A parable is a simile or metaphor drawn from everyday life or from nature. Its vividness or strangeness gains the hearer's attention but demands further reflection regarding the precise meaning. The kingdom of God refers to God's future display of power and judgment in which he establishes his rule over all creation. Its coming is basically God's work, though the cooperation of people in the present time is demanded. In Jesus' teaching, the kingdom has both present and future dimensions.

13:1-9 The seeds (see Mark 4:1-9; Luke 8:4-8). The first part of the parables discourse (13:1-35) envisions Jesus as sitting in a boat, with the crowds standing along the shore (vv. 1-3). The crowds are the mass of people. They are the object of Jesus' mission and are not yet totally incorrigible in their unbelief, like the scribes and Pharisees. The parable of the seeds (vv. 4-9) contrasts three kinds of wasted seeds with one kind of fruitful seed. The seeds were wasted because they landed on bad soils: a footpath (v. 4), rocky ground (v. 5), and among thorns (v. 7). But the seed that fell on good soil (v. 8) yielded great results. The parable uses repetition in order to build up a pattern of expectations and at the end changes the pattern in order to emphasize the real point of the story. It explains why Jesus' preaching of the kingdom of God has not been universally accepted and encourages those who have accepted it to keep on bearing fruit

in good works. The seed growing in the good soil will achieve enormous results.

13:10-17 Why Jesus used parables (see Mark 4:10-12; Luke 8:9-10). The contrast between the fruitful seed and the wasted seeds continues in the explanation of why Jesus used parables as a teaching device. The disciples want to know why he teaches in parables when he could use simple and direct speech (v. 10). In response to their question, Jesus asserts that the gift of understanding is given to the disciples but not to others (vv. 11-12) and that the disciples are blessed with special sight and hearing (vv. 16-17). Because the others fail to see and hear Jesus' plain teachings about the kingdom, he is forced to use the mysterious speech of the parables (v. 13). The general lack of understanding of Jesus' teaching is explained in verses 14-15 as the fulfillment of Isa 6:9-10. The spiritual dispositions of the disciples (the fruitful soil) render them capable of seeing and understanding, while the others remain incapable of seeing and understanding at all because their spiritual dispositions are not capable of allowing the seed to bear fruit.

13:18-23 The explanation of the seeds (see Mark 4:13-20; Luke 8:11-15). The hearers of the parable of the seeds were clearly expected to draw some equivalencies: the seed is Jesus' preaching of the kingdom; the good soil is proper dispositions; the bad soils are improper dispositions; the fruitful seeds are the disciples; the wasted seeds are the unbelievers. But the explanation of the parable given in verses 18-23 goes beyond these obvious correspondences and focuses on the reasons why the seeds failed or prospered. Whether this explanation goes back to Jesus or was worked out in the early church is a point of debate.

According to the explanation, the bad soils are lack of understanding (v. 19), superficiality (v. 21), and division within oneself (v. 22). The corresponding obstacles to belief are the "evil one" (v. 19), tribulation or persecution (v. 21), and worldly cares and the desire for wealth (v. 22). In the good soil, however, the message of Jesus is taken in and yields remarkable results (v. 23).

13:24-30 The grain and the weeds. The parable of the grain and the weeds uses another agricultural comparison to explain the lack of universal acceptance of Jesus' preaching. Jesus sowed good seed, but the evil one has sown a kind of weed that is difficult to distinguish from the grain in the early stages of growth. The parable concerns the proper attitude toward the mixed reception accorded to Jesus. The harvest (v. 30) was a common Old Testament and Jewish symbol for the final judgment, and so the advice is tolerance and patience until God renders his definitive decision. In verses 28-29 the disciples are restrained from any attempt at forcibly rooting out the unbelievers among their fellow Jews. This separation will accompany the final appearance of the kingdom.

13:31-35 The mustard seed and the leaven (see Mark 4:30-32; Luke 13:18-21). The parables of the mustard seed and the leaven use everyday things to illustrate the dynamic of the kingdom of God. The activity of God in the ministry of Jesus seems as small as a mustard seed or as a little yeast, but its result in the fullness of God's rule will be very great. These comparisons suggest that in Jesus' preaching, the kingdom already has a present dimension and that the process moving toward its fullness has in some way been inaugurated. The part of Jesus' discourse that was addressed to the crowds ends (vv. 34-35) by explaining that he used parables in order to fulfill Ps 78:2. The quotation also calls attention to Jesus' exalted status as the one who can reveal the mysteries of the universe.

13:36-43 The explanation of the grain and the weeds. At this point Jesus turns away from the crowds and concentrates on his disciples. To their request for an explanation of the parable of the grain and the weeds, he first responds in verses 37-39 with a catalogue of equivalencies that serves to decode the parable, though according to verses 10-17 the disciples should not need such aids. Then in verses 40-43 he provides a scenario for the events surrounding the last judgment. The latter feature has the effect of shifting the focus from patient tolerance in the present (as in verses 24-30) to the spectacular events that will constitute the end of the world. Again there is a debate regarding the origin of this explanation of the parable. Did it come from Jesus, the early church, or the evangelist?

13:44-50 The treasure, the pearl, and the net. The parables of the treasure and the pearl in verses 44-46 illustrate the zeal with which the kingdom should be pursued. They express the great value of the kingdom, the joy that it brings, and the total commitment that it deserves. The parable of the fish net in verses 47-50 reminds us that the coming of the kingdom will include a final judgment in which good and bad will be separated and receive their fitting rewards and punishments.

13:51-53 Conclusion. The parables discourse ends with a saying that expresses well the ideal to which the evangelist aspired: the ability to see the radically new act of God in Christ in the light of the Old Testament tradition. Such a person understands the relation between the new (Christ) and the old (Jewish tradition). The discourse closes in the customary way (see 7:28; 11:1; 19:1; 26:1).

VIII. MIRACLES AND CONTROVERSIES

Matt 13:54–16:4

13:54-58 Rejection at Nazareth (see Mark 6:1-6; Luke 4:16-30). The themes of unbelief and rejection continue in the incidents about Jesus at Nazareth (vv. 54-58) and the death of John the Baptist (14:1-12). The reference to Jesus as teaching in "their synagogue" (v. 54) suggests a separation between Jesus' followers and other Jews, and probably reflects the situation that existed when Matthew's Gospel was written. The description of Jesus as the "carpenter's son" (v. 55) shows that the people of Nazareth do not know what the readers of the Gospel know from 1:18-25. Their admiration quickly turns to disbelief—a fact explained in verse 57 by what seems to have been a proverb about the prophet's lack of acceptance in his home territory. Lack of faith on the people's part is presented in verse 58 as the explanation for Jesus' refusal to perform miracles there (see Mark 6:5-6).

14:1-12 John's death (see Mark 6:14-29; Luke 9:7-9). The tradition about the reaction of Herod Antipas (the son of Herod the Great) to Jesus is tied to the account of Jesus' activity in and around Nazareth. As the official in charge of governing Galilee from 4 B.C.E. to A.D. 39, Herod showed curiosity toward Jesus and wondered whether he might be John the Baptist restored to life (vv. 1-2). This provides the occasion for Matthew to tell the grisly story of John's execution and to connect the rejection of Jesus to the rejection of John (see

11:2-19). The description of Herod's marriage in verse 3 (see Mark 6:17) is not exactly correct, since Herodias had been married to another Herod, who was Herod Antipas' half-brother. In any case, the account in verses 3-12 develops the parallel between the tragic fate of John and what awaits Jesus. Both were regarded by the people as prophets, arrested on very flimsy grounds, executed on account of the weakness of a government official, buried by their disciples, and thought to have been raised from the dead.

14:13-21 The feeding of five thousand (see Mark 6:30-44; Luke 9:10-17; John 6:1-14). Matthew's concentration on the rejection of Jesus is interrupted by three miracle stories of varying length and content. Jesus' suspicion about Herod's interest in him leads him to depart to a deserted place, but the crowds continue to follow him. After curing some of the sick, Jesus provides enough food for five thousand men, plus women and children (vv. 15-21). Matthew's account is similar to Mark's, except that it is more concise and places the disciples in a better light. Matthew 14:16-18, when compared with Mark 6:37-38, softens the disciples' lack of understanding. The disciples appear as partners in the discussion and share in feeding the crowds. The language of Matt 14:19, when compared with that of Matt 26:26, suggests that the feeding was viewed as an anticipation or preview of the Last Supper and thus of the church's celebration of the Eucharist. The fish (v. 19) and the twelve baskets of leftovers may point beyond the Last Supper to the banquet of the Messiah at the final coming of the kingdom.

14:22-33 Walking on the water (see Mark 6:45-52; John 6:15-21). The transitional passage in verses 22-23 situates the disciples at sea and Jesus alone in prayer on the mountain. The disciples are on their own, and they are faring badly. The boat may well be a symbol of the church (see 8:23). In the disciples' time of need, Jesus comes to rescue them and appears as the lord over the powers of nature (vv. 24-27). Into this episode Matthew has inserted the story of Peter's attempt to walk on the water and his subsequent failure on account of his little faith (vv. 28-31). Peter represents the disciples (and all Christians) in his enthusiastic love and insufficient faith. In his fright he addresses Jesus with a prayer ("Lord, save me"), and he receives a criticism about the smallness of his faith. The story climaxes with the adoring confession from the disciples that Jesus truly is the Son of God (vv. 32-33).

14:34-36 Healings at Gennesaret (see Mark 6:53-56). The healings at Gennesaret constitute the third member in this series of miracle stories and repeat the theme of the great impression made by Jesus on the general public. The very favorable reaction to Jesus stands in contrast to the rejection at Nazareth in 13:54-58 and the hostility shown to him by the scribes and Pharisees in 15:1-20.

15:1-20 The controversy about ritual purity (see Mark 7:1-23). Jesus' three acts of power are followed by a controversy with the Pharisees and scribes. The specific issue for debate is the disciples' failure to observe the rules of ritual purity as exactly as the Pharisees did (v. 2). The Pharisees had built up a body of tradition designed to ensure the observance of the written law. They also wished to extend to all Israelites the rules that originally applied only to members of priestly families on the grounds that Israel is a priestly people. Thus they expected Jesus and his followers to observe the rules of priestly purity spelled out in Lev 22:1-16.

The first part of Jesus' response (vv. 3-9) attacks the Pharisees' idea of tradition. Jesus argues that sometimes their tradition leads to breaking the clear commands of the law (vv. 3-6). The commandment about honoring one's parents is stated in the law both positively (Exod 20:12; Deut 5:16) and negatively (Exod 21:17). But the Pharisees' tradition, according to Jesus, allows a person to place property under sacred vow as a means of preventing the parents from having access to it. Thus a pious fiction provides the excuse for disregarding and getting around a sacred obligation encouraged by the law. The words of Isa 29:13 are used to brand such behavior as hypocrisy. The tradition that claims to protect the law actually violates it.

The second part of Jesus' response (vv. 10-20) concentrates on the specific issue of ritual purity. The statement in verse 11 to the effect that there is only moral uncleanness is very radical, since large parts of the Old Testament law concern ritual uncleanness contracted by touching and by eating certain foods. Only a firm faith in Jesus as the authoritative interpreter of the law could allow Matthew and his community to accept such a revolutionary teaching.

To the basic statement in verse 11 are joined a very harsh judgment on the Pharisees (vv. 12-14) and an explanation for the disciples of Jesus (vv. 15-20). When informed about the Pharisees' offense at his teaching, Jesus denies their spiritual roots (v. 13) and condemns them as blind guides leading others to destruction (v. 14). Peter's request for an explanation of Jesus' teaching in verse 15 assumes that "parable" means "mystery" or "riddle." Jesus' explanation in verses 17-20 merely expands and makes concrete the radical statement in verse 11. Moral purity alone is important, and the evil designs of the mind make a person morally impure and issue in the kinds of action forbidden by the Old Testament. The complaint raised against Jesus' disciples in verse 2 has no validity, because the whole tradition of ritual impurity and purity has no validity.

15:21-28 The healing of the non-Jewish woman's daughter (see Mark 7:24-30). The pattern of three miracles and a controversy story found in 14:13–15:20 is repeated in 15:21–16:4. The first healing takes place in the area surrounding the southern Phoenician cities of Tyre and Sidon, and involves the possessed daughter of a non-Jewish woman. In fact, the healing is simply the occasion for a dialogue of faith between the Gentile woman and Jesus. In verse 22 she tries to initiate the dialogue with a prayer and addresses Jesus as Lord and Son of David, but is rebuffed by Jesus on the ground that his mission during his ministry prior to his death is confined to the Jews (v. 24). When the woman persists in her prayer ("Lord, help me"), Jesus again rebuffs her with a sharp saying that equates non-Jews with dogs, and Jews with sons and daughters of God (v. 26). The woman has the presence of mind and the cleverness to point out that even dogs are given crumbs and scraps from their masters' tables (v. 27). This display of faith so impresses Jesus that he grants her request that her daughter be healed. This story of salvation being offered to Gentiles through faith in Jesus would have encouraged the church's mission to the Gentiles after Jesus' death and resurrection. In God's plan of salvation, pride of place belongs to the Jews ("the children"). But Jesus himself praised

and respected the remarkable faith of non-Jews (see also 8:5-13).

15:29-31 The healing of many people. The second miracle story in this series summarizes Jesus' many acts of healing (see 12:15-21; 14:34-36). After the geographical introduction in verse 29, words and phrases from Isa 35:5-6 and 29:18-19 are used to describe the kinds of physical maladies (v. 30) and the remarkable changes brought about by Jesus the healer. At the center of the account is the person of Jesus (v. 30). The sick are brought to him and he cures them.

15:32-39 The feeding of four thousand (see Mark 8:1-10). The third miracle story involves the feeding of another large crowd of people. It has many features in common with the feeding of the five thousand in 14:13-21. The two accounts differ chiefly in the numbers: loaves (five versus seven), baskets of leftovers (twelve versus seven), and the number of men (five thousand versus four thousand). Jesus' compassion for the crowds (v. 32) leads him to supply their physical needs, and the language in which the multiplication is described (v. 36) again suggests Eucharistic overtones (see 14:19; 26:26). There is no good reason to view this miracle as the "Gentile feeding" as opposed to the "Jewish feeding" of 14:13-21. The two passages may represent independent accounts of a single event.

16:1-4 The controversy about signs (see Mark 8:11-13; Luke 12:54-56). Just as the preceding series of miracle stories in 14:13-36 ended with a controversy story in 15:1-20, so the second series of miracle stories in 15:21-39 ends with a controversy in 16:1-4. Despite all the miracles that Jesus has worked, the Pharisees and Sadducees want some further sign that he is from God. Although the Pharisees and Sadducees opposed each other on many points, here they appear to be united in opposing Jesus.

The reply in verses 2-3 does not occur in some important manuscripts of the Greek text. Whether it belonged in the original Gospel text or not, its basic point is that Jesus' miracles are signs of God's coming kingdom. The opponents know enough to predict the weather from the color of the sky, but they are blind to the real nature of Jesus' miracles. The sign of Jonah could be the offer of salvation to the Gentiles (see 8:5-13; 15:21-28), but in light of 12:40 the evangelist probably understood it to be the death and resurrection of Jesus.

IX. THE WAY TO THE CROSS

Matt 16:5–17:27

16:5-12 The leaven of the Pharisees and Sadducees (see Mark 8:14-21). With the so-called discourse on the leaven, Jesus turns to his disciples and instructs them throughout the rest of the chapter. His instructions concern the teaching of the Pharisees and Sadducees (16:5-12), the identity of Jesus and Peter (16:13-20), the cross and resurrection (16:21-23), and the discipleship of the cross (16:24-28).

In the discourse on the leaven (vv. 5-12), the disciples' failure to bring bread along for their journey is joined to Jesus' puzzling warning against the leaven of the Pharisees and Sadducees (v. 6). The leaven apparently refers to a corrupting influence. By substituting "Sadducees" for Mark's "Herod" or "Herodians" (see Mark 8:15), Matthew prepares for the concluding explanation (v. 12) that the leaven describes the corrupting teaching of the Pharisees and Sadducees.

Jesus' response to the disciples' misunderstanding takes the form of five questions in verses 8-11. Allusion is made to the feedings of the five thousand (14:13-21) and the four thousand (15:32-39), with the implication that the disciples should know by now that Jesus is capable of caring for their physical needs. The disciples again show weakness of faith—a characteristic way of describing the imperfect condition of Jesus' closest followers in Matthew (see 6:30; 8:26; 14:31). Though Jesus' rebuke of the disciples seems quite sharp, it is not nearly as cutting as the series of questions in Mark 8:17-21. At any rate, the disciples' slowness to understand shows how much they need to be instructed about Jesus and about what it means to follow him.

16:13-20 The identity of Jesus and Peter (see Mark 8:27-30; Luke 9:18-21). Peter's confession of faith begins as a dialogue between Jesus and the disciples. It takes place near Caesarea Philippi in northern Palestine and marks the initial step of the journey that will issue in Jesus' passion and death in Jerusalem.

When Jesus asks concerning popular speculations regarding his identity, the disciples list some current opinions (v. 14). According to 14:2, Herod Antipas thought that Jesus was John the Baptist restored to life. The return of Elijah was expected to accompany the coming of God's kingdom (see Mal 4:5-6). The reference to Jeremiah is found only in Matt 16:14 (see Mark 8:28; Luke 9:19), and it may indicate that the similarities between the prophet Jeremiah and Jesus were recognized (see Matt 2:17; 27:9).

In the second stage of the dialogue (vv. 15-16), Jesus asks not for popular speculations but rather for the disciples' own assessment. As is often the case in this section of Matthew (see 15:15; 16:22; 17:24; 18:21), Peter appears as the spokesman for the group and proclaims Jesus to be the Messiah. (*Messiah* is a Hebrew word that means "anointed one"; its Greek translation is *Christos*.) Peter's confession of Jesus as the Messiah reflects the disciples' hope that Jesus would deliver Israel from its enemies and establish God's kingdom on earth.

Up to verse 16b, the account closely parallels Mark 8:27-29. But to Mark's narrative Matthew adds in verse 16b a further specification of Jesus' identity ("the Son of the living God") and Jesus' promise to Peter in verses 17-19. This addition changes the flow of the story in Peter's favor. Whereas in Mark 8:27-33 the confession of faith is passed over and gives way to a misunderstanding on Peter's part, in Matthew the confession brings a solemn blessing on Peter.

The phrase "Son of the living God" in verse 16b corrects and transcends any false implications present in the title "Messiah." The blessing in verse 17 declares that Peter's confession was a revelation from God, and verse 18 promises that Peter is the rock on which the Christian community will be built after Jesus' death and resurrection. No power opposed to God will be able to destroy that community. Finally, in verse 19 Peter is portrayed as the "major-domo" or prime minister in the kingdom proclaimed by Jesus (see Isa 22:15-25). His exercise of the power to bind and loose (see 18:18) will be confirmed by God. The content of that power is not completely clear. It may involve laying down rules and giving exemptions, imposing or lifting excommunications, forgiving or not forgiving sins, or even performing exorcisms.

The language of the passage is very Semitic, and clearly verses 16b-19 transmit an early tradition. There is a debate about whether this blessing was uttered by Jesus during his earthly ministry or after his resurrection (see 1 Cor 15:5; Luke 24:34). Other scholars trace its origins to the church at Antioch in Syria. Whatever its origin, the passage praises Peter as the recipient of a divine revelation (v. 17), declares him to be the foundation of the community (v. 18), and gives him special authority (v. 19). With the command to silence in verse 20, Matthew rejoins Mark's account.

16:21-23 The first prediction of the passion (see Mark 8:31-33; Luke 9:22). The first prediction of the passion removes any doubts about what kind of Messiah Jesus is. In verse 21 Jesus proclaims unambiguously that his earthly future will involve suffering and death in accord with his Father's plan ("he must go to Jerusalem"). The content of the passion prediction closely parallels the events of Matt 26–28. Despite his confession of faith and the blessing in response to it, Peter in verse 22 rejects the possibility that Jesus' messiahship could involve suffering. In verse 23 Peter's attitude is rebuked sharply as coming from Satan, as a stumbling block in Jesus' way, and as purely human thinking.

16:24-28 The discipleship of the cross (see Mark 8:34–9:1; Luke 9:23-27). Sayings on the cost and reward of discipleship follow the first prediction of the passion. The saying about taking up the cross in verse 24 (see 10:38) connects the fate of the disciples with Jesus' own fate. Whereas in 10:1 the disciples were given a share in Jesus' power displayed in chapters 8–9, here they are warned that discipleship also involves a share in the cross. The sayings in verses 25-26 revolve around the theme of life and suggest that only in letting go of self and letting God do the guiding can we ever find freedom and happiness. In verse 27 the typically Jewish belief in rewards and punishments as being determined at the coming of God's kingdom in the judgment is given a Christian interpretation: Jesus the Son of Man will be in charge. Whatever verse 28 may have originally referred to (the imminent coming of the kingdom, the death and resurrection, Pentecost), here it serves as an introduction to the transfiguration in 17:1-8. In that event the disciples receive a preview of the Son of Man's glorious coming in the kingdom.

17:1-8 The transfiguration (see Mark 9:2-8; Luke 9:28-36). The story of the transfiguration of Jesus is a preview of the Son of Man's coming in his kingship (see 16:28). Some interpreters have argued that the account originally told of an appearance of the risen Lord and has been put back into the earthly ministry of Jesus. But the narrative has very little in common with the resurrection appearances in the Gospels. The transfiguration seems to have been a historical experience of a visionary character. The reference to "six days later" in verse 1 is puzzling, though the traditional significance of the mountain as a privileged place of divine revelation suggests an allusion to God's appearance to Moses on Sinai (see Exod 24:16). Here as elsewhere in the Gospels there is an inner circle of disciples constituted by Peter, James, and John. The word "transfigured" used in verse 2 to describe what happened to Jesus indicates a change of form or shape. The disciples experience a glimpse of Jesus' lordship as it will be fully manifest at the coming of the kingdom. The order of the names of Moses and Elijah in verse 3 makes it clear that they represent the law and the prophets of the Old Testament.

Matthew's primary interest in the account of the transfiguration is the disciples' reactions to the event. In verse 4 Peter addresses Jesus as "Lord" and asks his permission to erect the three booths. Apparently he hoped that all of them would remain in this glorious atmosphere until the kingdom came. The disciples' hopes are raised still higher in verse 5 with the voice from the cloud (a Jewish image of God's presence) that affirms Jesus' special status in exactly the same terms as at the baptism (see 3:17). The awesome character of the experience frightens the disciples (v. 6), but Jesus acts as a comforter and encourages them not to be afraid (v. 7).

17:9-13 The sequel to the transfiguration (see Mark 9:9-13). The sequel to the transfiguration connects the preview of Jesus' glory with his suffering, death, and resurrection. In verse 9 the transfiguration is characterized as a vision, and the disciples are warned not to talk about it until after the resurrection. In contrast to the disciples in Mark 9:10, they apparently understand what rising from the dead means. Their question about Elijah in verse 10 refers to the tradition based on Mal 4:5-6 that the prophet Elijah would return from heaven before God's kingdom would come. Jesus' reply in verses 11-12 accepts this tradition as valid but asserts that Elijah had already come in the person of John the Baptist (see 11:14). Just as John was not recognized but rather underwent suffering and death, so Jesus as the Son of Man will be misunderstood and put to death (see 14:1-12). In case there were any doubts about the identification of John the Baptist as Elijah, Matthew adds that the disciples then realized that Jesus had been speaking about John the Baptist (v. 13).

17:14-20 The healing of the possessed boy (see Mark 9:14-29; Luke 9:37-43). Matthew's account of the healing of the possessed boy is much shorter than Mark's. Indeed, the issue is not so much Jesus' power to heal, as it is in Mark, but rather the disciple's failure to heal as due to their "little faith" (v. 20). The lengthy description of the boy's condition in Mark 9:17-18, 20-22, 25-26 is condensed considerably, and he is simply described as being affected by the phases of the moon ("a lunatic"). The boy's father in verses 14-15 approaches Jesus in a prayerful way ("knelt down before him . . . 'Lord, have pity'"). Given the way that Matthew tells this story, the stern rebuke in verse 17 seems to be directed at the disciples; this is confirmed in verse 20, where they are criticized for their "little faith."

The mention of little faith is the occasion for using the saying on faith the size of the mustard seed. The mustard seed is tiny (see 13:31), and the point of the saying is that even a small amount of faith can have dramatic effects. The connection between the story in verses 14-19, whose point is the ineffectiveness of the disciples' faith, and the saying in verse 20, whose point is the great power of even a little faith, is purely formal. In other words, the two units have been joined only because they deal with "little faith" and despite the fact that the meaning in each unit is quite different. Some manuscripts include as verse 21 the saying found in Mark 9:29. Yet, if the passage were originally part of Matthew, there would be no good reason why it should be omitted in the other ancient manuscripts. It most likely was added to Matthew's text in the process of copying.

17:22-23 The second prediction of the passion (see Mark 9:30-32; Luke 9:43-45). The second prediction of the passion reminds us that the fate of suffering and death awaits Jesus in Jerusalem. The term "handed over" in verse 22 suggests that these events will take place with God's permission and in accord with his plan. Unlike the disciples in Mark 9:32, who do not understand the prophecy and are afraid to ask about it, the disciples in Matt 17:23 understand it very clearly.

17:24-27 The temple tax. When questioned about whether Jesus paid the tax for the upkeep of the Jerusalem temple and the sacrifices offered there (see Exod 30:11-16; Neh 10:32-33), Peter, as the spokesman for Jesus, answers affirmatively (vv. 24-25a). But the story goes on to make it clear that Jesus had no real obligation to do so. The illustration used in verses 25b-26 is based on Jesus' identity as the Son of God. Just as kings gather taxes from foreigners but not from their own sons, so God (whose house the Jerusalem temple is) demands taxes from people in general but not from his Son Jesus. The story ends in verse 27 with the miraculous provision of the money for paying the tax.

Although Jesus was under no obligation to pay the temple tax, he did pay it in order to avoid giving scandal to anyone. After A.D. 70, when the Jerusalem temple had been destroyed and the Jewish temple tax was diverted to provide for the upkeep of the pagan temple of Jupiter Capitolinus in Rome, this story would have furnished advice for the Jewish members of Matthew's community. As free children of God through Jesus, they are not obliged to pay the tax but should do so in order to avoid further problems (see Rom 13:1-7; 1 Pet 2:13-17).

X. ADVICE TO A DIVIDED COMMUNITY

Matt 18:1-35

The fourth of the five major discourses of Jesus (see chs. 5–7; 10; 13; 24–25) has been aptly described as Matthew's advice to a divided community. The evangelist has taken sayings from various sources and arranged them to supply guidance for Christian communities as they try to deal with status-seeking, scandal, lapses, reconciliation, and forgiveness. The two major parts of this discourse concern the care of the "little ones" (18:1-14) and the proper attitude toward community members who have sinned (18:15-35).

18:1-4 Greatness in God's kingdom (see Mark 9:33-37; Luke 9:46-48). The occasion for the discourse is provided by the disciples' question about who is the greatest in God's kingdom (v. 1). Their question had a context in Jewish society of the time, since there was a good deal of speculation about position and status in the coming kingdom. The community that gave us the Dead Sea scrolls even arranged the communal meals according to rank within the group. The meals were supposed to mirror what would happen when God's kingdom comes.

As an answer to the disciples' question, Jesus points to a child (v. 2) and urges the disciples to become like children (v. 3). In ancient society the child had no legal rights or standing and was entirely dependent on the parents. The child necessarily received everything as a gift. Likewise, no one through rank or status has a real claim on God's kingdom; only those who recognize this fact and receive the kingdom as a gift will enter it (v. 4). The child is presented as a symbol of those without legal right or claim to the kingdom, not as a model of innocence or humility. All speculations about rank in the coming kingdom and about the present as a mirror of the future are dismissed as a tragic misunderstanding of God and his kingdom.

18:5-10 Scandalizing little ones (see Mark 9:42-48; Luke 17:1-2). In this section the word "child" takes on a different meaning. In the preceding passage it referred to one without legal status, but here it describes a simple and good-hearted member of the community who can be led astray. The saying about receiving a child in Jesus' name in verse 5 expresses an identity between the little ones and Jesus. He dwells in them in a special way. Those who would lead them astray are given three sharp warnings: (1) It is better to be dead than to cause one of these little ones to stumble on the path of discipleship (v. 6). (2) Personal responsibility for scandal cannot be dismissed on the ground that scandal is inevitable (v. 7). (3) Anything—even going without a foot or a hand or an eye—is better than giving scandal within the community (vv. 8-9). This third warning may presuppose the image of the community as the body of Christ, from

which offending members are to be cut off or excommunicated. The passage closes in verse 10, as it began in verse 5, with a reference to God's special care and concern for the "little ones."

18:12-14 Little ones who stray (see Luke 15:3-7). What happens if one of the little ones does go astray? This passage compares God to a shepherd who searches out those sheep that stray. The search is not automatically successful ("And if he finds it," v. 13), but the return of the "strays" gives great pleasure to God. God wishes that none of the little ones should ever perish or be damned (v. 14). Note that a distinction is drawn between those who stray and those who perish.

18:15-17 Reconciling a sinner. The second major part of Jesus' fourth discourse (18:15-35) concerns attitudes toward community members who have sinned. The first section (18:15-17) outlines the various steps to be taken when one Christian sins against another. At each stage (personal discussion, discussion before witnesses, discussion before the whole community), the aim is to win the erring Christian back to the community. Even the drastic step of excommunication probably was intended to shock the offender into reconciliation. Similar procedures were employed by the Dead Sea community, on the basis of Deut 19:15. The designation of the excommunicated member as a Gentile or a tax collector in verse 17 is odd in view of Jesus' openness to both groups. Here the terms simply describe people who were excluded from the mainstream of Jewish religious life.

18:18-20 Binding and loosing. In their present context within Jesus' advice to a divided community, the sayings about binding and loosing (v. 18) and the two or three gathered in Jesus' name (vv. 19-20) probably refer to the community's power to exclude erring members as a last resort. In verse 18 the disciples (see 16:19, where Peter alone receives the power) are promised that God will stand behind their decisions on earth. In verses 19-20 the agreement of the community joined in prayer will be accepted by God as binding, because he is present in the community's prayer in a special way. The momentous and painful character of cutting off one who has ignored the community is balanced to some extent by the community's confidence that God approves its decisions.

18:21-35 Forgiveness. Having dealt with the extreme case of the totally incorrigible member and the extreme punishment of excommunication, the discourse turns to the more ordinary experience of forgiveness and reconciliation within the community. The situation is the same as that of 18:15: "If your brother sins against you . . . ." In this case, however, the erring person listens to the offended party or to the several witnesses or to the community as a whole. How many times should such a person be forgiven? Once again Peter serves as the spokesman for the group and gives what he imagines to be a very generous answer to his own question. Seven times (v. 21). Jesus corrects Peter and answers: Seventy-seven times. The new number is not to be taken literally. The point is that Christians have no right to place any limit on forgiveness.

Why Christians may not set limits to forgiveness is illustrated by the parable of the merciless steward (vv. 23-25). This parable puts in story form the second "we-petition" of the Lord's Prayer: "And forgive us our debts, as we forgive our debtors" (6:12). In other words, God's willingness to forgive us depends on our willingness to forgive others (see 6:14-15). The actions of the king in the parable indicate that he is to be identified with God. He demands a reckoning (v. 23), is approached as lord (v. 26), and shows great mercy in writing off the huge debt (v. 27). Yet the merciless servant failed to learn from the example of the king, and his cruelty toward the other servant results in the revocation of his own forgiveness (vv. 28-34). The story warns us that the forgiveness granted to us by God will be revoked unless we are willing to forgive others (v. 35). The unforgiving are excluded from God's mercy. Those who wish to receive God's mercy must show mercy toward others.

XI. GROWING OPPOSITION TO JESUS

Matt 19:1–23:39

19:1-12 Marriage and divorce (see Mark 10:1-12). The fourth discourse ends in the usual manner ("When Jesus finished"), and Jesus enters Judean territory (19:1). For Matthew (as for Mark), Galilee is the place of revelation (see 4:12-17) and Judea is the place of rejection and death. Jesus continues to attract great crowds and to heal the sick (v. 2).

As a way of testing Jesus, the Pharisees question him about marriage and divorce. The phrasing of their inquiry in verse 3 ("for any cause") places Jesus' teaching in the context of the Jewish debate about the grounds for divorce. According to Deut 24:1, the husband wrote out the terms of the divorce, presented it to the wife, and thus ended the marriage. The grounds for divorce in Deut 24:1 ("because he finds in her something indecent") are vague. In Jesus' time, one school restricted divorce to the case of adultery on the woman's part, and another school was far more free in its interpretation, to the extent that a woman could be divorced if she was a bad cook or not beautiful. It was assumed that divorced men and women could marry again, though the Temple Scroll from Qumran casts doubt on this for members of some Jewish circles at least.

Matthew's presentation of Jesus' teaching on marriage and divorce in verses 4-9 first cites Gen 1:27 (v. 4) and Gen 2:24 (v. 5) to the effect that in God's original plan of creation marriage was indissoluble and no human agent could end such a union (v. 6). In the Old Testament (see Deut 24:1-4) divorce was allowed only as a concession to human weakness. This was not God's original intention (vv. 7-8). Once again Jesus assumes the role of the authoritative interpreter of the law, and in verse 9 he forbids divorce and remarriage absolutely, except for the case of *porneia*—most likely a marriage contracted within the degrees of kinship forbidden by Lev 18:6-18 (see the commentary on Matt 5:32). There is little doubt that Jesus regarded marriage as indissoluble (see Mark 10:11-12; Luke 16:18; 1 Cor 7:10-11). But it is not easy to know whether in this case Jesus was stating an ideal or laying down a command.

The radical nature of Jesus' teaching on this topic (it does away with Deut 24:1-4) leads the disciples in verse 10 to question whether it is advisable to marry at all. In 19:11 Jesus clearly states that celibacy is a gift from God and is not for all (v. 11). According to verse 12, Christian celibacy is a response to the experience of God's kingdom as made present in the teaching and example of Jesus. It is not based on male suspicion of women, cultic purity, or the demands of community life. The Dead Sea community also seems to have had both married and celibate members.

19:13-15 Children and the kingdom (see Mark 10:13-16; Luke 18:15-17). As someone with a reputation for holiness, Jesus' blessing was much sought for children (v. 13). The assumption was that the power of holiness somehow went forth from him and communicated itself to others. The occasion is used to teach about receiving God's kingdom. As was the case in 18:1-4, the child represents those without legal claims or rights, those who must necessarily receive everything as a gift. The kingdom is for those without pretensions to status and superiority, for those who recognize that it is a gift.

19:16-30 Wealth and the kingdom (see Mark 10:17-31; Luke 18:18-30). The theme of wealth as a possible obstacle to perfect discipleship is raised in the story of Jesus' encounter with the rich young man. When asked what is necessary to have eternal life, Jesus invites the young man ("If you wish") to enter eternal life by observing the Ten Commandments and the command to love one's neighbor as oneself (vv. 16-20). When he replies that he has already been observing these commandments, Jesus invites him to a new stage ("If you wish to be perfect") in verse 21. For this person, perfection as a disciple of Jesus involves distributing his wealth to the poor and sharing in the insecurity and the trust that were characteristic of the earthly Jesus and his first followers. The young man was unable to accept Jesus' invitation to the new stage of perfection beyond the observance of the law (v. 22).

The rich young man's inability to accept Jesus' challenge sets the scene for general teachings on wealth as an obstacle to discipleship in verses 23-26. Not only is it difficult for the rich to enter God's kingdom (v. 23); it is practically impossible, as the saying about the "eye of a needle" in verse 24 makes clear. The disciples' amazement in verse 25 stems from their assumption that wealth is a sign of divine favor. In verse 26 Jesus teaches that no one can enter the kingdom because of his or her own possessions or achievements; the kingdom is God's gift.

As the spokesman once again, Peter asks about the rewards for accepting Jesus' challenge to radical poverty (vv. 27-30). Peter had left his fishing business in Galilee (see 4:18-22) and his family (see 8:14-15). The risks and sacrifices of Jesus' first followers should not be minimized. In the "new age" of the kingdom, they will share in the glory of the Son of Man (v. 28) and will be rewarded with an even better social and religious community (v. 29). The odd saying about the reversal of positions between the first and the last in verse 30 is illustrated in the following parable.

20:1-16 The parable of the good employer. By bracketing the parable in 20:1-15 with the sayings about the first and the last in 19:30 and 20:16 and by placing it in the context of the rewards for the disciples (19:27), the evangelist makes it illustrate Jesus' promise that the disciples, now considered the last, will be the first in receiving rewards (see 20:8). In the context of Jesus' ministry, the parable was probably addressed to his opponents who criticized him for preaching the good news of the kingdom to tax collectors and sinners. In that setting, the parable is best entitled "the good employer." The employer is God as revealed in Jesus as his representative.

The good employer hires workmen at dawn for the usual daily wage of one denarius and sends them off to work in his vineyard (vv. 1-2). Other workmen in verses 3-7 are hired at various times during the day (midmorning, noon, midafternoon, late afternoon), but their wages are not specified ("whatever is just"). In verse 8 the employer commands that the workers be paid in the reverse order of their hiring and that all receive the same wage (v.11). To the complaints of those who had worked all day (vv. 11-12), the employer answers that he has been just in paying the agreed wage to them (vv. 13-14); they have no right to complain if he wants to be generous to others (v. 15). God's own justice and generosity are used to explain why Jesus preached the kingdom to both the already pious and the lost sheep of Israel (see 10:6). If they accept his preaching, both groups will be granted an equal share in God's kingdom.

20:17-19 The third prediction of the passion (see Mark 10:32-34; Luke 18:31-34). The third prediction of the passion occurs on the road leading up to Jerusalem, which is located in a mountainous region. This prediction is more detailed than the two previous ones (16:21; 17:22-23) and mentions explicitly the Jewish and Gentile tormentors of Jesus. Matthew's version specifies crucifixion as the mode of Jesus' death.

20:20-28 Places of prominence in the kingdom (see Mark 10:35-45). The question of status in the coming kingdom (see 18:1-4) appears again with the request by the mother of James and John that her sons should have places of special prominence in the kingdom. In Mark 10:35-37 the two disciples make the request on their own. Jesus replies in verses 22-23 that (1) in order to share in his kingdom, the disciples must share his cup of suffering, and (2) it is not his prerogative to assign positions of prominence in the kingdom. The indignation of the other disciples in verse 24 furnishes the occasion for Jesus to teach about service to others as the way of leadership in his community. Then leadership as power according to Gentile patterns ("lord it over them") is contrasted with leadership after the pattern of Jesus, the servant and slave of all (vv. 25-27). This style of leadership as service to others is grounded in the example of Christ's sacrificial death as a "ransom for many" (v. 28).

20:29-34 The healing of two blind men (see Mark 10:46-52; Luke 18:35-43). The story of the healing of the two blind men at Jericho parallels the healing of Bartimaeus in Mark 10:46-52, but there are many differences. In Matthew's account there are two blind men (for a similar phenomenon, see 8:28), and more attention is paid to their faith in Jesus' power than to the process of the healing. They address Jesus in verses 30, 31, and 33 in the language of prayer. They call him "Lord" and "Son of David." The irony is that those who are blind physically have the spiritual insight to recognize Jesus for who he really is. Jesus the merciful healer then gives them physical sight (v. 34), and they join the band of his disciples.

21:1-11 The Messiah's entrance (see Mark 11:1-11; Luke 19:28-38; John 12:12-19). Jesus' entry into Jerusalem is made from the east, from the Mount of Olives, which was connected with the "day of the Lord" in Zech 14:4. Matthew understood the event as the fulfillment of Isa 62:11 and Zech 9:9 (Matt 21:5). Isa 62:11 ("Say to daughter Zion") is fulfilled by the enthusiastic reception given to Jesus by the crowds (v. 8) and the greeting given to him as the Son of David in the words of Ps 118:25-26 (v. 9). The whole city is in-

terested in Jesus, and he is identified as the prophet from Galilee (vv. 10-11). Zech 9:9 is fulfilled in the humble manner in which Jesus enters the city. The two beasts of burden ("the ass and the colt") in verses 2, 7 fulfill in an overly literal way the double mention of the animal in the Old Testament passage. Jesus' entrance into Jerusalem was the entrance of the Messiah and so conformed fully to Old Testament prophecy and Jewish expectations. However, it was also the entrance of a humble person, not that of a military conqueror.

21:12-17 The Messiah's temple (see Mark 11:15-19; Luke 19:45-48; John 2:13-22). The Messiah's first actions in the holy city involve the temple of Jerusalem. His action in overturning the commercial enterprises in the outer court of the temple (v. 12) is also presented as fulfilling Old Testament prophecies. According to Isa 56:7, the temple should be a house of prayer; according to Jer 7:11, those businessmen have turned it into a den of thieves.

Besides this symbolic protest against the commercialization of the temple, Jesus also cures the blind and the lame. The presence of the blind and the lame in the temple area was probably not welcomed by the temple officials (see 2 Sam 5:8). Up to this point, the Pharisees had been the chief opponents of Jesus, but now and throughout the rest of the Gospel the chief priests and elders emerge as the major enemies. Angered by Jesus' demonstration, the healings in the temple area, and the popular enthusiasm for Jesus, the opponents ask for an explanation in verse 16. The explanation that Jesus offers is that the children's enthusiasm is simply the fulfillment of Ps 8:3. With that, Jesus departs for Bethany, a village east of Jerusalem, and spends the night there.

21:18-22 The cursing of the fig tree (see Mark 11:12-14, 20-24). The cursing of the fig tree is the only miraculous action of Jesus that does any harm or works destruction. In fact, it is best seen as a symbolic or prophetic action: When the Messiah came to search for the fruits of righteousness in the holy city, he found nothing there. The action prefigures the fall of Jerusalem and the destruction of the temple in A.D. 70. Matthew's emphasis on the miraculous character of the action ("immediately the fig tree withered") in verses 19, 20 sets the stage for the sayings in verses 21-22 on the extraordinary power of prayer offered in faith. The disciples can share in the power of Jesus if they have faith like his. As is customary in Matthew's Gospel (see especially chs. 8–9), the display of Jesus' miraculous power dissolves into a teaching on the dynamics of prayer and faith.

21:23-27 Jesus' authority (see Mark 11:27-33; Luke 20:1-8). The debate about Jesus' authority in verses 23-27 is the first in a series of controversies between Jesus and his opponents. The series is interrupted by three parables in 21:28–22:14 and rejoined in 22:15-46. In the first controversy the opponents are the chief priests and elders of the people. This group will be instrumental in getting Jesus put to death. The point of controversy is the authority (v. 23) on which Jesus had entered the city, cleansed the temple, healed the lame and the blind, and taught.

Jesus' response takes the form of a question to his questioners (vv. 24-25). He promises to answer their question if they will first state publicly whether John's baptism was from God or purely human. Jesus' question puts his opponents on the defensive: If they say "from God," they admit their stupidity and lack of spiritual insight in not taking up John's cause. If they say "purely human," they risk the anger of the many people who regarded John as a prophet sent from God. Jesus' counter-question reduces his opponents to silence ("We do not know"). They have been put to shame, and Jesus has come away from the debate with honor (v. 27). The controversy also continues the parallel between John the Baptist and Jesus. Matthew's readers know that God was the source of the authority for both John and Jesus.

21:28-32 The two sons. The controversies are interrupted by three parables dealing with the culpability of Jesus' opponents (vv. 28-32), the punishment allotted to them (vv. 33-43), and the carrying out of that punishment (22:1-14). The parable of the two sons (vv. 28-32) assumes that Jesus' preaching of God's kingdom is a pivotal moment in Israel's religious history. Just as the second son initially refused the father's command but later repented and obeyed (v. 30), so the tax collectors and prostitutes (v. 31) are now reforming their lives in response to Jesus and are entering the kingdom. Just as the first son promised to obey but did nothing (v. 29), so the profess-

edly and publicly religious opponents of Jesus fail to act upon Jesus' message of the kingdom. The opponents' culpability consists in their refusal of Jesus' preaching and stands in sharp contrast to the openness and resolve of those whom they despise. In verse 32 the parallel between John and Jesus continues: The dynamic of the parable of the two sons was present in John's ministry also. The conversion of the tax collectors and sinners to the way of righteousness should inspire Jesus' opponents to accept his preaching, and not to regard him with suspicion and hostility.

21:33-46 The tenants (see Mark 12:1-12; Luke 20:9-19). The parable of the tenants concerns the punishment allotted to the religious and political leaders of Israel. The parable obviously alludes to the description of Israel as God's vineyard in Isa 5:1-7, and many of the phrases in verse 33 are taken directly from that Old Testament passage.

God is the owner of the vineyard; he has leased out his property to the religious and political leaders. Many servants (prophets) were sent to the vineyard, but they all met the same bad fate (vv. 34-36). The owner expects that at least his son (Jesus) will be received with respect. In fact, he receives even worse treatment, to the point of being killed outside the vineyard (vv. 37-39). When the owner himself comes, he will punish the tenants by destroying them (v. 41) and taking away their claim to preeminence in God's kingdom (v. 43). The vineyard will be leased to others (the church), and the people of God in Christ will yield an abundant harvest. The opponents' rejection of Jesus ("the stone") is the reason for their punishment. This brings to fulfillment Ps 118:22 (v. 42). Matthew's community would find in this parable an explanation for the destruction of Jerusalem by the Romans in A.D. 70 and a justification for its claim to be the true people of God.

The saying about the stone in verse 44 is absent from many early manuscripts and may have been added in other manuscripts from Luke 20:18 because of the thematic connection with Matt 21:42. The major enemies of Jesus—the chief priests and the Pharisees—recognize that these parables concern them (v. 45) but fear to arrest Jesus because the crowds consider him to be a prophet (see 21:11, 26).

22:1-14 The royal marriage feast (see

Luke 14:15-24). The parable of the royal marriage feast concerns the punishment of Jesus' opponents (especially vv. 5-7) and has many features in common with the parable of the tenants in 21:33-46. The marriage feast or banquet was a popular way of imagining what life in the coming kingdom would be like. The king and his son clearly represent God the Father and Jesus respectively. The invitation offered by the first group of servants (prophets) is refused (v. 3), but the invitation given by the second group of servants (perhaps John the Baptist and Jesus) encounters not only indifference (v. 5) but also hostility, to the point that those servants are executed (v. 6). The vivid description in verse 7 of how the king's army destroyed those murderers and their city surely brought to the minds of Matthew's first readers the Roman conquest of Jerusalem in A.D. 70. Because the professedly and publicly religious people of Israel refused the invitation to the kingdom of God, a general invitation has been made (vv. 8-10) to all kinds of people, including tax collectors and prostitutes (and perhaps even non-Jews).

Mere acceptance of the invitation, however, does not guarantee participation in the banquet, as the incident in verses 11-13 makes clear. Guests at a wedding banquet would be expected to appear in clean and neat clothing. When the king (God the Father) sees a man who is not dressed properly, he questions him in a cool manner ("My friend") and has him ejected from the banquet hall. Being a tax collector or prostitute is no more a guarantee of salvation than being a Pharisee or chief priest is; rather, one must receive Jesus' invitation to the kingdom and act upon it so that when the banquet actually begins, one will be properly prepared to participate. In this context the saying in verse 14 suggests that the invitation to the kingdom has been offered to all kinds of people, but only a few of them act upon it in such a way as to be allowed to participate in the banquet of the kingdom.

22:15-22 Taxes to Caesar (see Mark 12:13-17; Luke 20:20-26). After the three parables directed at Jesus' opponents, the series of controversies is rejoined. The second controversy concerns paying taxes to the emperor. The opponents are the Pharisees, who as religious people resented paying taxes to a foreign government, and the Herodians, who

may have administered the system of taxation in Palestine. The two groups join forces to trap Jesus. If he affirms that taxes should be paid, he loses the esteem of the religious nationalists. If he denies that taxes should be paid, he is subject to arrest as a political revolutionary.

The Pharisees and Herodians approach Jesus in a flattering but hypocritical manner (v. 16), and then spring their question about whether it is lawful to pay taxes to the emperor (v. 17). Recognizing their hypocrisy (v. 18), Jesus eludes their trap by asking them to show him a coin bearing the image and the name of the emperor. The very fact that both the Pharisees and the Herodians use the emperor's coin implies that they should pay taxes to the emperor (v. 21). Jesus, however, moves the debate to another level by challenging his opponents to be as observant in paying their debts to God as they are in paying their debts to the emperor. The opponents are revealed as hypocritical and not really religious, and Jesus gains honor for having recognized their character and having eluded their trap.

22:23-33 Resurrection (see Mark 12:18-27; Luke 20:27-40). The third controversy in the series focuses on belief in the resurrection of the dead. The conservative, priestly party of Sadducees denied the resurrection of the dead on the grounds that it appears in Old Testament books other than the Pentateuch. The Sadducees accepted as authoritative only the first five books of the Bible. The references to belief in resurrection appear in Isa 25:8; 26:19; Ps 73:24-25; and Dan 12:2.

The objection of the Sadducees in verses 24-28 uses the practice of levirate marriage described in Deut 25:5-10 (the obligation of a man to marry the wife of his dead brother) in order to reduce belief in the resurrection to absurdity. Instead of unraveling their argument, Jesus charges that they understand neither the Scriptures nor the power of God (v. 29). They fail to understand God's power (v. 30), because the resurrected life will be entirely different from the present life. Since there will be no marriage then, the Sadducees' argument on the basis of levirate marriage is groundless. They also fail to understand the Scriptures (vv. 31-32), because Exod 3:6 ("I am the God of Abraham, the God of Isaac, and the God of Jacob") presupposes that the patriarchs of Israel were still alive in Moses' time. Therefore, the resurrection of the dead is taught in the Pentateuch.

22:34-40 The greatest commandment (see Mark 12:28-34; Luke 10:25-28). The fourth controversy revolves around the greatest commandment in the Old Testament. The questioners are the Pharisees in the person of a lawyer (vv. 34-35). Jewish teachers of Jesus' time were frequently asked to summarize the law in a brief statement. For example, Hillel summarized the law in a way that is much like the so-called golden rule of Jesus (see 7:12): "What you hate for yourself, do not do to your neighbor. This is the whole law; the rest is commentary. Go and learn." Jesus' summary of the law consists of two commandments that encourage love of God (Deut 6:5) and love of neighbor (Lev 19:18). These two commandments are the threads on which the entire law hangs. With this answer, Jesus proves his fidelity to the Jewish tradition and his commitment to a spirituality that emphasizes the essentials.

22:41-46 The Messiah (see Mark 12:35-37; Luke 20:41-44). In the fifth controversy in the series, Jesus asks the Pharisees about the Messiah. They respond correctly that the Messiah is David's Son (v. 42). Jesus' further question in verses 43-44 assumes (as Jews of his time did) that David was the principal author of the Book of Psalms and that the Scriptures, under the Spirit's inspiration, contained prophetic statements about the future. In Ps 110:1, David refers to the Messiah as "my lord." Therefore, the Messiah must be superior to David, and "Son of David" is not an adequate title for the Messiah. A more sufficient title is "Lord." This controversy and the two preceding ones illustrate the superior ability of Jesus in interpreting the Scriptures. Those opponents who claimed great knowledge of the Scriptures are reduced to silence (v. 46).

23:1-12 Warnings against the scribes and Pharisees (see Mark 12:38-40; Luke 20:45-47). The controversies with, and the parables against, Jesus' opponents culminate in a stinging attack in 23:1-39. The passage contains a severe warning to avoid the religious style of the scribes and Pharisees (vv. 1-12), seven woes against the scribes and Pharisees (vv. 13-36), and a final lament over Jerusalem (vv. 37-39). The seven woes have

led some interpreters to view chapter 23 as the introduction to the fifth major speech, with the woes corresponding to the beatitudes of chapter 5. But the abrupt changes of audience and the subject matter of chapter 24 indicate that chapter 23 is best taken with the preceding material about Jesus' opponents.

The audience for Jesus' attack on the scribes and Pharisees consists of his disciples and the crowds (v. 1). The scribes were religious intellectuals, skilled in interpreting the Old Testament and in applying it to everyday life. The Pharisees belonged to a religious fraternity that expressed its fellowship in communal meals and prided itself on the exact observance of the law. Not every scribe was a Pharisee, nor was every Pharisee a scribe. A modern Christian equivalent to the phrase "scribes and Pharisees" would be something like "theologians and Jesuits." The scribes and Pharisees in verses 2-3 are said to occupy the chair of Moses, which was the way of describing the seat of honor in the synagogue from which the teacher delivered his teaching. The audience is urged to follow their teachings but to avoid their hypocrisy. It is difficult to square verse 3 with the many other statements in chapter 23 and elsewhere in the Gospel that criticize the teachings, and not merely the practices, of the scribes and Pharisees. Their imposition of the priestly regulations on lay people contrasts with the easy yoke and light burden of Jesus (see 11:28-30).

The opponents' love of self-display and desire for honorific titles are criticized in verses 5-10. Among their showy practices are enlarging the small scroll boxes (phylacteries) worn during prayer (see Exod 13:9; Deut 6:8; 11:18); lengthening the tassels worn at the four corners of the cloak (see Num 15:38-39; Deut 22:12); competing for the places of honor at social and religious gatherings; and seeking after prestigious titles like "rabbi," "father," and "master." These titles are rejected in verses 8-10 on the grounds that only God deserves the title "father" and only Jesus merits the title "master." Religious showiness is rejected in verses 11-12 in light of the Christian ideal of leadership as service to the community (see 20:25-28) and the dynamic of humility and exaltation.

23:13-36 Woes against the scribes and Pharisees (see Luke 11:37-52). Pronouncing a "woe" on someone or some group expresses grief at their sorry state and warning of the very bad consequences to follow. The first of the seven woes against the scribes and Pharisees (v. 13) accuses them of hindering people from entering God's kingdom, perhaps by their opposition to Jesus and his disciples. The second woe (v. 15) accuses them of making great missionary efforts in gaining converts but actually doing harm to the converts' spiritual lives. The third woe (vv. 16-22) refers to the Pharisees' attempts at discouraging oaths sworn by the most sacred things (the temple, the altar, God) and shifting the oaths to less important things (the gold of the temple, the gift on the altar, heaven). Jesus rejects this campaign as ridiculous casuistry.

The fourth woe (vv. 23-24) criticizes the opponents for neglecting the most important concerns of the law (justice, mercy, and fidelity) on account of their obsession with calculating the religious taxes to be paid on vegetables and spices. This overwhelming interest in trivia (the gnat) leads them to overlook the big things (the camel). The fifth woe (vv. 25-26) and the sixth woe (vv. 27-28) both contrast a pure exterior with a rotten interior. The opponents' concern with the ritual purity of cups and dishes used at meals is not matched by their efforts at moral purity. So wide is the gap between external appearance and internal reality that the opponents may be described as "whitewashed tombs" (v. 27).

The seventh woe (vv. 29-36) reflects the widespread building of tombs and shrines for martyred prophets around Jerusalem. Jesus accuses the scribes and Pharisees of being the physical and spiritual descendants of the people who were originally responsible for these martyrdoms. Proof of this charge is the hostility shown to Jesus and his followers in the present and in the future (v. 34). The retribution promised against "this generation" (vv. 35-36) would have been interpreted in Matthew's community as the destruction of Jerusalem by the Romans in A.D. 70. Abel (see Gen 4:1-16) was the first righteous person to be killed, and Zechariah (see 2 Chr 24:20-22) is presented as the last canonical prophet to have been martyred.

23:37-39 Concluding lament (see Luke 13:34-35). Jesus' final lamentation over Jerusalem characterizes the city as murderer of the prophets and opponent of the Messiah (v. 37). Therefore God will cease to dwell in the temple (v. 38), and Jesus the Messiah will not be seen there until he returns as judge with the coming of the kingdom of God. Jesus speaks as God's prophet decrying Israel's apostasy and as the Messiah who is to come again in glory.

XII. THE COMING OF THE KINGDOM

Matt 24:1-25:46

The fifth and final discourse concerns the events surrounding the future coming of God's kingdom. Since the kingdom will mark the end of history as we know it, the discourse is often called the "eschatological discourse" (from *eschaton*, the Greek word for "end"). The first part (24:1-36) relies heavily on Mark 13:1-37 and describes the events that must happen before the end will come. The second part (24:37-25:30) contains parables and other traditional materials that encourage an attitude of watchfulness. A picture of the last judgment (25:31-46) concludes the discourse.

24:1-3 The setting (see Mark 13:1-4; Luke 21:5-7). The scene of the discourse is set in verses 1-3. Jesus had entered the temple area in 21:23 and foretold that God would desert the temple in 23:38. His prediction of the temple's destruction in 24:2 would represent an accomplished fact for Matthew's community after A.D. 70. Seated on a place with traditional connections to the coming of the kingdom (see Zech 14:4; Matt 21:1), Jesus talks with the full circle of disciples. They ask him when (1) the temple will be destroyed, and (2) he will come as the Son of Man, and the world as we know it will end. In his reply Jesus is careful to make a distinction between these two happenings.

24:4-14 The early stages (see Mark 13:5-13; Luke 21:8-19). Jews of Jesus' time believed that great sufferings would accompany the coming of God's kingdom. The first section of Jesus' answer to the disciples' questions warns against mistaking the early stages of those sufferings (v. 8) for the final stage. Among the events in the first stage are the appearance of false messiahs (see Acts 5:33-39) or even persons claiming to be Jesus returned from heaven (v. 5); wars between nations (vv. 6-7a); and various natural disasters (v. 7b).

The Christian community will not be immune from the "labor pangs" of the kingdom.

It will experience persecution and hatred from outside (vv. 9-10a) as well as apostasy, false prophets, and widespread tepidity within the community (vv. 10b-12). The only appropriate attitude for loyal Christians is patience (v. 13). They are assured that the end will not come until the gospel has been preached throughout the world. Matthew's community had already seen some of the religious, political, and natural disasters mentioned in verses 5-8. It had probably also experienced firsthand the problems proper to the church (vv. 9-13). An important motive for writing the Gospel was to encourage the community to preach the good news of Jesus the Messiah to all the people of the world (see 28:19).

24:15-22 The great tribulation (see Mark 13:14-20; Luke 21:20-24). The time of the great tribulation will begin with the so-called abomination of desolation (v. 15). That phrase originally referred to the attempt of the Syrian king Antiochus IV Epiphanes to set up an altar to Baal Shamen in the Jerusalem temple in 167 B.C.E. (see Dan 9:27; 11:31; 12:11). It was probably used again with reference to the emperor Caligula's plan to have a statue of himself erected in the temple in A.D. 40. Perhaps Matthew identified it with the Roman profanation and destruction of the temple in A.D. 70 or with some still future event.

In either case, Jesus presents instructions in verses 16-18 on how to avoid the great tribulation by fleeing to safe refuges in the mountains, by coming down from the roof by the outside staircase and not bothering to try to rescue anything inside the house, and by not bothering to pick up one's coat left by the side of the field. The point is clear: Get out of the way, and be quick about it! In verses 19-20, he takes pity on pregnant women and nursing mothers (who could not move quickly) and hopes that the great tribulation will not occur during the cold, rainy season or on the sabbath (when travel would be either very difficult or contrary to the Jewish law).

This tribulation will be the greatest that the world has ever seen or ever will see (v. 21). But on account of the patient members of the Christian community (see v. 13), God has shortened this period of tribulation. If he had not done so, no human being could survive at all. Whatever connections may

have been made between the advance of the Roman army in A.D. 70 and the great tribulation, the language used to describe the tribulation far outdistances those historical happenings. The tribulation signals the end of the world as we know it.

24:23-36 The coming of the Son of Man (see Mark 13:21-32; Luke 21:25-33). The graphic description of the coming of the Son of Man (vv. 29-31) is sandwiched between two warnings not to be deceived about when he is to come (vv. 23-28, 32-36). The disciples (and Matthew's readers) should not be misled by false messiahs and false prophets even if they can work miracles, or by rumors about the Messiah being in the desert or in hiding (vv. 23-26). The actual coming of the Son of Man will be sudden and public, like a lightning bolt (v. 27). Its signs will be unmistakable and unambiguous, just as the vultures signify the presence of a carcass (v. 28).

Nearly every phrase in the description of the Son of Man's coming (vv. 29-31) can be found in the Old Testament passages concerning the coming of God's kingdom. After great cosmic disturbances (see Isa 13:10; Ezek 32:7; Amos 8:9; Joel 2:10, 31; 3:15; Isa 34:4; Hag 2:6, 21), the Son of Man will come on the clouds of heaven (see Dan 7:13-14). The tribes of the earth will beat their breasts (see Zech 12:10), and the trumpet blast will begin the last judgment (see Isa 27:13). The judgment will vindicate the chosen ones of the Son of Man, who is pictured here as a superhuman figure with divine authority. Early Christian tradition identified him with Jesus, the humble and suffering Son of Man.

The fig tree (vv. 32-33) is one of the few trees in Palestine that sheds its leaves annually. Thus it allows the intelligent observer to tell the time of year from its stages of growth. Likewise, when all the signs listed in verses 3-22 have come to pass, then people will know that the Son of Man is near (v. 33). The prophecy that all these events will take place in the present generation (v. 34) is balanced by the insistence that only the Father knows exactly when the Son of Man will come (v. 36). It is not possible to identify "all these things" (v. 34) with the death and resurrection of Jesus. A second, glorious arrival of Jesus is clearly intended. The passage makes clear that not even the Son himself knew the precise moment.

24:37-44 Pictures of the Son of Man's coming (see Mark 13:32-37; Luke 17:26-30, 34-36). The second part of the eschatological discourse (24:37–25:30) consists of parables about the coming of the Son of Man and related traditions. In the parables there is frequently a division of people into two groups. The coming of some figure (the Son of Man) is uncertain or delayed, but suddenly it happens. Rewards and punishments (the last judgment) are handed out. The lesson is watchfulness in the present. Watchfulness is responsible service of God shown in the careful fulfillment of one's duties until the Son of Man comes.

The first section (vv. 37-44) combines several pictures in order to describe the arrival of the Son of Man (v. 37). The Noah parable (vv. 37-39) contrasts Noah and the other people of his generation. The flood came upon them suddenly and had dire consequences for many. The pictures of the two men in the field (v. 40) and the two women grinding meal (v. 41) emphasize the suddenness of the coming and the separation that it will bring. Since the exact hour of the coming is unknown, the only appropriate attitude is constant watchfulness (v. 42). This attitude is encouraged further by the story of the homeowner (v. 43). If a homeowner knows when a thief is coming, he exercises watchfulness at that time. But since the time of the Son of Man's coming remains unknown, the watchfulness must be constant (v. 44).

24:45-51 The two servants (see Luke 12:41-48). The parable of the two servants contrasts watchfulness and lack of vigilance. The faithful and wise servant (vv. 45-47) does his duty. When the master returns and discovers him at work, he is abundantly rewarded. The wicked servant (vv. 48-51) takes advantage of the master's prolonged absence by mistreating the other servants and wasting time in foolish pleasures. The master will certainly return sometime. When he does, the wicked servant will be punished. The lesson is that constant watchfulness will be rewarded and lack of vigilance will be punished when the Son of Man comes.

25:1-13 The ten bridesmaids. The parable of the ten bridesmaids contains many features already familiar from the preceding parables. The ten bridesmaids are divided into two groups: the foolish and the wise. The foolish ones have made no provisions for lighting their torches, while the wise ones have. The story assumes the Palestinian custom of the bridegroom's going to the bride's house in order to make the marital agreement with his father-in-law. When the bridegroom returns with the bride to his own home, the wedding feast can begin. The bridesmaids are expected to meet the bridegroom and the bride as they approach the house. The foolish bridesmaids are sure that the bridegroom will not arrive at night, but the wise ones recognize that he can arrive at any time (vv. 2-4). The bridegroom is delayed (v. 5), but he finally arrives at a most unexpected time (v. 6). The foolish bridesmaids are caught by surprise and are unable to obtain oil in time for the beginning of the wedding feast (vv. 7-10). The door is locked, and they are refused entrance (vv. 11-12). Once more, the lesson is constant watchfulness (v. 13).

25:14-30 The talents (see Luke 19:11-27). The parable of the talents has many elements found in the preceding passage, but it concentrates on the judgment scene (vv. 19-30). The master (the Son of Man) goes away and distributes various sums of money to three servants. The Greek word that describes these sums is "talents." The parable is the source of the English term "talent" as the description of a natural ability that can be improved by diligent practice. Though there are three servants in the parable, they really constitute two groups: the two who invest and double the amount, and the one who buries the money. The master is away for a long time, and suddenly he returns and demands an accounting (v. 19). The accounting is clearly the last judgment. It involves rewards for the two servants who doubled the sums given to them (vv. 20-23) and punishment for the servant who did nothing (vv. 24-30). Constant watchfulness demands fruitful action and even boldness.

25:31-46 The judgment of the nations. The eschatological discourse reaches its climax and conclusion with the scene of the last judgment. Even though the story compares the Son of Man to a shepherd, it probably should not be classed as a parable, since the judgment is presented in a direct and straightforward way. When the Son of Man comes in his glory (see 24:29-31), he will divide "all the nations" into two groups (vv. 31-33). Those who have done good deeds for one of "these least brothers of mine" (v. 40) will be blessed (vv. 34-40), but those who have failed to do these deeds for one of "these least ones" (v. 45) will be condemned (vv. 41-46). The good deeds are feeding the hungry, offering hospitality to the homeless, clothing the naked, comforting the sick, and visiting the imprisoned. These deeds deserve a reward at the last judgment because of the relationship of identity between the Son of Man and "the least" (vv. 40, 45).

Who are "all the nations" (v. 32), and who are "the least" (vv. 40, 45)? The usual interpretation understands "all the nations" as including all humanity, and "the least" as including people in distress of some kind. Therefore, at the final judgment all humanity is to be judged according to acts of kindness done to poor and suffering people. But is this what Matthew and his community understood by the story? In Matthew's Gospel, "nations" and "all the nations" usually refer to people other than Israel (see 4:15; 6:32; 10:5, 18; 12:18, 21; 20:19, 25; 21:43; 24:7, 9, 14; 28:19). In several passages (see 10:40-42; 18:6, 14), the "least brothers" seem to be Christians. If these terms have the same meaning in 25:31-46 that they have elsewhere in the Gospel, "all the nations" are the Gentiles who have not explicitly accepted either Judaism or Christianity, and "the least" are Christians with whom the Gentiles have had some contact. According to this interpretation, the Gentiles will be judged according to acts of kindness done to Christians (see 10:40-42).

XIII. THE DEATH AND RESURRECTION OF JESUS

Matt 26:1–28:20

Almost eighty percent of Matthew's passion account is identical in vocabulary and content with Mark's account. Matthew adds some materials that tend to develop themes already present in Mark 14-16. Jesus is even more obviously in command of the events, and everything proceeds according to God's will as revealed in the Old Testament.

26:1-5 The plot (see Mark 14:1-2; Luke 22:1-2; John 11:45-53). The introductory scene sets the major figures on stage. Jesus tells his disciples plainly that at Passover time he will be arrested and crucified (vv. 1-2). Passover is the spring festival commemorating ancient Israel's release from slavery in the land of Egypt. The major opponents of Jesus are not the scribes and Pharisees, but rather the chief priests and elders gathered around the high priest Caiaphas (vv. 3-5). Passover was a pilgrimage feast that attracted large crowds to Jerusalem, and so the opponents wish to avoid setting off a revolution by arresting a popular religious teacher from Galilee during that time.

26:6-16 The anointing (see Mark 14:3-11; Luke 22:3-6; John 12:1-8). At a house not far from Jerusalem, a woman shows Jesus the signs of respect and hospitality by anointing his head with some expensive ointment. The disciples' complaint that the ointment could have been sold and the proceeds given to the poor (vv. 8-9) furnishes the occasion for Jesus to interpret the woman's action. The first interpretation (vv. 10-11) concerns the extraordinary status of Jesus and the special privilege connected with the time of his earthly presence. The second interpretation (vv. 12-13) suggests that the anointing is a preparation for Jesus' burial. The Hebrew word Messiah means "anointed," and from the very start the passion of Jesus is the story of the Messiah's suffering and death. The woman's beautiful deed stands in sharp contrast to Judas' plans to betray Jesus (vv. 14-16). Matthew suggests that Judas' motive was greed (v. 15) and that the thirty pieces of silver promised to him fulfilled Zech 11:12.

26:17-25 The meal at Passover time (see Mark 14:12-21; Luke 22:7-14, 21-23; John 13:21-30). Matthew's account of the preparations for the Passover meal (vv. 17-19) focuses on Jesus' command in directing the course of events. Jesus is very much in charge. Although Matthew follows Mark in interpreting the meal as marking the actual beginning of the Passover festival, the reference in John 18:28 and the supposed activities of the chief priests and elders during these days indicate that it more likely took place on the evening before the first day of Passover. At the meal, Jesus predicts that one of the Twelve will betray him (vv. 20-25). In verse 25, Matthew makes it clear that Jesus knew that his betrayer was Judas. The other disciples' addressing Jesus as "Lord" (v. 22) contrasts with Judas' "Rabbi" (v. 25). The enormity of the betrayal is brought out by the fact that the one sharing the meal with Jesus would hand him over. The fact that God's plan is being fulfilled (v. 24) does not absolve Judas of responsibility for Jesus' death.

26:26-29 The Eucharist (see Mark 14:22-26; Luke 22:15-20). Jesus' actions and words with the bread and the wine anticipate and interpret his impending death. What happens to the bread in verse 26 will happen to Jesus' body, and what happens to the cup of wine in verse 27 will happen to his blood. Sharing in the bread and wine means sharing in Jesus' death. The "blood of the covenant" (v. 28) alludes to Exod 24:8, where Moses seals the old covenant by sprinkling the people with blood, and "on behalf of many" suggests some connection with the atoning suffering of the Servant of the Lord in Isa 53:12. The expiatory or atoning value of Jesus' death is underlined by "for the forgiveness of sins." According to verse 29, Jesus' meal with the disciples anticipates the heavenly banquet that will be part of God's kingdom. This account of the Last Supper brings together many aspects of the church's Eucharistic celebration: Passover meal, memorial of Jesus' death, covenant, sacrifice, and preview of the kingdom.

26:30-35 Peter's denial foretold (see Mark 14:27-31; Luke 22:31-34; John 13:36-38). The discussion between the disciples and Jesus on the Mount of Olives is further evidence that Jesus knew what awaited him and that all these events were proceeding according to God's will as expressed in the Old Testament. He tells them that their faith in him will be shaken this very night, and that his arrest and their scattering will fulfill Zech 13:7 (v. 31). He also commands them to go to Galilee, which is the place of revelation (see 4:13-17) and the site of the climactic resurrection appearance (see 28:16-20). Jesus even knows that Peter will deny him three times before dawn (v. 34). Peter's self-confident boast (vv. 33, 35) sets the scene for the dramatic story of his denial in 26:69-75.

26:36-46 Prayer in Gethsemane (see Mark 14:32-42; Luke 22:39-46). The account of Jesus' prayer in Gethsemane presents him as the obedient Son of God who accepts God's will that he suffer and die (vv. 39, 42, 45-46) and the disciples as needing instruction on how to remain on guard in times of trial (vv. 40-41, 43, 45-46). Gethsemane (v. 36) was a small olive garden on the Mount of Olives, and once again the inner circle of disciples consists of Peter, James, and John (v. 37). The wording of Jesus' statement to the disciples in verse 38 reflects phrases found in Pss 42:5, 11; 43:5. Jesus prays three times, and returns three times to find the disciples asleep. The content of the prayers (vv. 39, 42) indicates that Jesus had to school himself to accept the suffering that awaited him. His final summons to the disciples (vv. 45-46) shows perfect submission to the Father's plan and confidence that the power of his evil opponents is only temporary.

26:47-56 The arrest (see Mark 14:43-50; Luke 22:47-53; John 18:3-12). The story of Jesus' arrest first describes how Judas arranged to betray Jesus to the chief priests and elders (vv. 47-50). In the crowded and excitable conditions of Jerusalem during the Passover pilgrimage, careful planning was needed if a riot was to be avoided. Judas determined on the typical signs by which a disciple would greet his teacher—the embrace (vv. 48-49) and the greeting "Rabbi" (v. 49). Jesus' response is the cool greeting "Friend" (see 20:13; 22:12), and with that he is arrested.

The incident of the cutting off of the ear of the high priest's servant (v. 51) provides the occasion for Jesus to repeat that these events are taking place in accord with God's will and the Old Testament Scriptures (vv. 52-54). Jesus' parting words to the crowds (vv. 55-56) emphasize his political innocence and harmlessness as well as his recognition that the disciples' desertion was the fulfillment of Zech 13:7 (see 26:31).

26:57-68 The trial before the Sanhedrin (see Mark 14:53-65; Luke 22:54-55, 63-71; John 18:13-14, 19-24). The trial of Jesus before the Sanhedrin is located at the high priest's house (v. 58) and involves the chief priests, scribes, and elders. After fruitless efforts at developing a case against Jesus (vv. 59-60), two charges are made: He threatened to destroy the temple (v. 61), and he claimed to be the Messiah (v. 63). The charge about threatening to destroy the temple probably reflects Jesus' preaching that the coming of the kingdom would demand a new kind of worship (see Mark 14:58; John 2:19-21; Acts 6:14) or may have a connection with his prophetic cleansing of the temple (see 21:12-17). The charge about his messiahship suggests that the

Jewish and Roman authorities viewed Jesus as one more in the series of political-religious agitators so common in Palestine during this period.

Instead of meeting these charges directly, Jesus in verse 64 speaks about the coming Son of Man (see Dan 7:13-14). The reaction is swift and furious. The high priest calls it blasphemy (v. 65). The council sentences him to death (v. 66). Others mock him and challenge him to play the prophet (vv. 67-68). Even though both Mark and Matthew understood this proceeding at the high priest's house to have been a legal trial, the Fourth Gospel's understanding of it as an investigation something like our grand-jury proceeding (see John 18:13-14, 19-24) is more likely on historical grounds.

26:69-75 Peter's denial (see Mark 14:66-72; Luke 22:56-62; John 18:15-18, 25-27). Peter's denial of Jesus is highly dramatic. His partner in conversation progresses from simply a maid (26:69), to a maid plus the bystanders (v. 71), to the crowd of bystanders (v. 73). His denials advance from a plea of ignorance (v. 70), to a denial accompanied by an oath (v. 72), to cursing and swearing followed by an outright denial that he knew Jesus (v. 74). The crowing of the cock at dawn (vv. 74-75) brings the shock of recognition that Jesus' prediction in verse 34 has come to pass. Peter's cowardice under pressure stands in sharp contrast to Jesus' faithfulness unto death.

27:1-2 The delivery of Jesus to Pilate (see Mark 15:1; Luke 23:1-2; John 18:28-32). The story of the handing over of Jesus to Pilate assumes that the Jewish leaders held a second legal proceeding at daybreak and passed the death sentence on Jesus. Pilate was the military governor of Judea from A.D. 26 to 36. His headquarters were at Caesarea on the Mediterranean shore, and he came to Jerusalem during the Passover pilgrimage to keep order.

27:3-10 The death of Judas. Matthew's story of Judas' death continues the theme of Old Testament fulfillment, since the goal and climax of the passage is the quotation presented in verses 9-10. That quotation, though attributed to Jeremiah (v. 9), actually joins phrases from Zech 11:12-13 and Jer 18:2-3; 19:1-2; 32:6-15. The story also proves that Jesus, who knew beforehand what Judas was plotting, was correct in his judgment about

the terrible fate of his betrayer (see 26:24). Matthew describes Judas' death as a suicide by hanging (v. 5). A somewhat different account appears in Acts 1:16-20. A third concern of the passage is the responsibility of the Jewish leaders for Jesus' death. They have condemned Jesus to death (v. 3). They do not deny his innocence (v. 4). Their scruple about adding blood money to the temple treasury leads them unwittingly to fulfill the Old Testament text (vv. 6-8).

27:11-26 The trial and sentencing of Jesus (see Mark 15:2-15; Luke 23:3-5, 13-25; John 18:33–19:16). The account of Jesus' questioning and sentencing by Pilate places the responsibility for Jesus' death on the Jewish leaders. The chief priests and elders manipulate the Roman governor (v. 12). The portrayal of Pilate as weak and indecisive contrasts with other ancient characterizations of him as inflexible, merciless, and obstinate. His question to Jesus in verse 11 probably carried a political nuance. Although Jesus was in fact the Messiah and thus the genuine King of the Jews, his only response to Pilate is silence (v. 14), perhaps in accord with Isa 53:7 and Ps 38:12-14. Pilate could not have understood the spiritual nature of his messiahship.

The practice of giving amnesty to a prisoner at Passover time is known only from the Gospels. Given the choice of Jesus or Barabbas, the chief priests and elders manipulate the crowd to have Pilate free Barabbas and crucify Jesus (vv. 15-18, 20-23). Jesus' innocence is confirmed by the report of a dream experienced by Pilate's wife (v. 19), and the Jewish leaders are charged with acting out of jealousy at Jesus' popularity (v. 18). When asked what crime Jesus had committed, the crowd gives no answer (v. 23).

By offering the crowd a choice between Jesus and Barabbas, Pilate had apparently hoped to release Jesus. The plan backfired. Seeing that a riot was developing (and he had come to Jerusalem to prevent a riot), Pilate declares Jesus to be innocent and places the responsibility on the crowd for the death of Jesus (vv. 24-25). The crowd accepts the responsibility. The scourging was intended to weaken Jesus so as to shorten the time of crucifixion (v. 26). The episode as a whole (vv. 11-26) stresses that the Roman governor allowed Jesus to be crucified, not because he was guilty of a crime, but rather because the crowd, incited by the chief priests, forced him into it.

27:27-31 The mockery (see Mark 15:16-20; John 19:2-3). The account of the mockery of Jesus contains two features that run through the entire account of Jesus' death in verses 27-50: (1) The way in which the soldiers are described in verse 27 is reminiscent of Ps 22:16: "A company of evildoers encircles me." Psalm 22 is the psalm of the righteous sufferer, and Matthew, following Mark and other early Christians, saw in that psalm an explanation of Jesus' death. The crucifixion was part of God's plan for the Messiah. (2) "Messiah" is preeminently a royal title in the Jewish tradition, and Jesus is mocked as a king. He is given a mock robe, crown, and sceptre. The soldiers kneel before him and address him as "King of the Jews." Right from the start and with exquisite irony, Matthew emphasizes that Jesus suffered as the King of the Jews in accordance with Psalm 22.

27:32-44 The crucifixion (see Mark 15:21-32; Luke 23:26-43; John 19:17-27). The crucifixion story begins when Simon of Cyrene, a Jew from North Africa, is forced to carry Jesus' cross (v. 32). Golgotha (v. 33) was a small hill just outside the wall of Jerusalem at that time; criminals could not be executed within the walls of the holy city. The offer of wine mixed with gall (v. 34; see also v. 48) fulfills Ps 69:21. The two major themes of the crucifixion account appear in verses 35-37: The division of Jesus' garments fulfills Ps 22:18, and the charge on which Jesus was crucified involves his identity as King of the Jews.

Three groups insult the crucified Jesus in verses 38-44: the passers-by (vv. 39-40); the chief priests, elders, and scribes (vv. 41-43); and the robbers crucified along with Jesus (v. 44). They unwittingly fulfill Ps 22:7-8. The content of their mockery reflects the two charges raised against Jesus at his trial before the council in 26:57-68: the threat to destroy the temple and the claim to be the Son of God or Messiah. The opponents are correct in calling Jesus the King of the Jews (v. 37), even though they do not realize the truth of their statement.

27:45-54 The death of Jesus (see Mark 15:33-39; Luke 23:44-48; John 19:28-30). Even in death, Jesus remains the righteous sufferer of Psalm 22. His last words (v. 46) are a direct quotation from Ps 22:1. The darkness over the land of Judea (v. 45) may have been an eclipse or a sandstorm that fulfilled Amos 8:9 or Exod 10:22. Jesus' use of Psalm 22 on the cross (v. 46) does not preclude an experience of intense suffering. In fact, the words of the psalm express most appropriately his feelings of abandonment and his subsequent reaffirmation of his total trust in the Father. The confusion about Elijah (vv. 47-49) probably reflects Jewish traditions about the prophet's roles as forerunner of the Messiah and helper of people in distress. The description of Jesus' death in verse 50 is simple and even understated.

Jesus' death is accompanied by several signs (vv. 51-54) that help Matthew's readers to understand its significance. First, the curtain in the Jerusalem temple is torn (v. 51a). This signifies either the end of the barrier between God and humanity or the end of the old covenant. Then in verses 51b-53 (and only in Matthew) the signs that were expected to accompany the coming of God's kingdom occur. Those signs are described in terms found in Ezek 37 and indicate that Jesus' death inaugurates a new stage in history that will culminate in the resurrection of the dead. Finally, in verse 54 the centurion and his men, who were surely non-Jews, confess that Jesus was truly the Son of God. Their confession provides a model for all non-Jews who accept Jesus as the Son of God.

27:55-61 The burial of Jesus (see Mark 15:40-47; Luke 23:49-56; John 19:38-42). The account of Jesus' burial establishes that he was really dead and that on Easter Sunday morning the women did not go to the wrong place. Matthew describes Joseph of Arimathea as a rich disciple of Jesus and thus avoids the possible inference from Mark 15:43 that Joseph had shared in the Sanhedrin's condemnation of Jesus. Unless Jesus had really died, Pilate would not have allowed the release of the corpse (v. 58) and Joseph would not have placed the corpse in the burial cave (vv. 59-60). The women, who had known Jesus for a long time (v. 55), saw him die and also saw the tomb in which the corpse of Jesus had been placed (v. 61).

27:62-66 The guard at the tomb. The same points made in the preceding account are emphasized in the story of the guarding of Jesus' tomb, a passage found only in Matthew's Gospel. For the first time in the passion narrative, the Pharisees appear along with the chief priests (v. 62) and demand that Pilate establish a guard around Jesus' tomb. Their suspicion that Jesus' disciples might steal his corpse probably reflects the Pharisees' response to the early Christian preaching about the resurrection of Jesus. According to Matthew, Pilate refused their request. So the opponents established their own guard at the tomb, thus affirming that Jesus really died and that they too knew where he was buried.

28:1-10 The empty tomb (see Mark 16:1-8; Luke 24:1-12; John 20:1-10). No one witnessed the resurrection of Jesus, nor does Matthew suggest that anyone did. He and the other evangelists tell only about the empty tomb and the appearances of the risen Lord. The explanation for the emptiness of the tomb is that Jesus had been raised from the dead (v. 6). The women, who had seen Jesus die and knew exactly where he had been buried on Friday afternoon, return to the tomb early on Easter Sunday morning (v. 1). They encounter an angel who had rolled back the large round, flat rock fitted into the groove at the entrance of the tomb and who had terrified the guards dispatched by the chief priests and Pharisees (vv. 2-4). The angel explains the emptiness of the tomb in verses 6-7 with reference to Jesus' three passion predictions (see 16:21; 17:23; 20:19). The women, inspired by both joy and fear, hasten to tell the disciples (v. 8). On the way they encounter the risen Lord and do him homage (v. 9). He instructs them in verse 10 to tell the disciples to leave Jerusalem (the place where Jesus was rejected) and to go to Galilee (the place of revelation). After his resurrection, he too goes to Galilee (see 26:32).

28:11-15 The report of the guards. The story of the guards and the chief priests explains why the guards assigned by the chief priests and Pharisees (see 27:65-66) and present at the angel's appearance (see 28:4) did not come forward and make public what they had experienced. According to this account (only in Matthew's Gospel), the guards were bribed by the chief priests and elders to say that the disciples stole Jesus' body from the tomb. The opponents do not deny that Jesus died and was buried, but they do reject the resurrection of Jesus as the explanation of the empty tomb. Instead, they circulate the false story that Jesus' body was stolen.

28:16-20 The great commission. The appearance of the risen Jesus on the mountain in Galilee is a very important scene in the overall plan of Matthew's Gospel. The mountain (see 5:1; 17:1) and Galilee (see 4:12-16) are preeminent places of revelation. The eleven disciples are the Twelve minus Judas. Their doubts (v. 17) may involve the possibility of having such an experience at all or the propriety of worshiping Jesus. In either case, their doubts vanish quickly. They, like the women in verse 9, worship Jesus (see 2:1-12).

The so-called great commission of verses 18b-20 consists in the statement about Jesus' authority (v. 18b), the command to make disciples (vv. 19-20a), and the promise of Christ's abiding presence until the fullness of God's kingdom comes (v. 20b). Thus it summarizes the three major themes of Matthew's Gospel: (1) Supreme and universal authority has been given to Jesus by his heavenly Father. Therefore he far surpasses every other human being and deserves all the exalted titles given to him. (2) The disciples are to share their discipleship with all people (not simply their fellow Jews) and to hand on Jesus' teaching to them. The largely Jewish community for which Matthew wrote his Gospel probably needed some encouragement to share their faith with non-Jews, and the statement in verse 19a was most likely understood as a reference to the Gentile mission. The wording of the command to baptize (v. 19b) undoubtedly reflects a baptismal formula used in the Matthean community. (3) The promise of Jesus' continuing presence with the disciples and their successors brings to fulfillment the name "Emmanuel" ("God is with us") given to Jesus at conception (see 1:23), in accordance with Isa 7:14. The promise assumes a "time of the church" between the inauguration of God's kingdom through Jesus and its fullness at the end of the world. The spirit of the risen Jesus will guide and protect the church during this time.

MARK

Philip Van Linden, C.M.

INTRODUCTION

Mark's Gospel: one of four portraits of Jesus

It is commonly accepted by the majority of contemporary New Testament scholars that Mark's Gospel was the first to be written and that it was a source used by Matthew and Luke in the composition of their Gospels. (The Gospel of John, it seems, developed out of a tradition that did not know of the other three Gospels.) God's purpose in inspiring *four* evangelists was not primarily to "preserve the facts" about Jesus' life on earth but to meet the many different needs of the people in the newly formed first-century Christian community. God chose several believers to communicate the "good news" about Jesus in such a way that the various spiritual needs of the early church community could be met.

The Christian community today is also made up of people with a great variety of spiritual needs, and its faith can be nourished by the four inspired "Jesus portraits" of Mark, Matthew, Luke, and John. When Christians choose to encounter Mark's Jesus, they meet with that side of Jesus that is the simplest of the four, and very demanding! They discover that Mark's version of Jesus' life centers on his death and on the meaning of suffering. When they open themselves to involvement with Jesus as Mark presents him, they realize that they too are invited to discover the meaning of life and death as he did, namely, by radical trust in God and by loving service to others' needs.

A glimpse at the whole of Mark's Gospel

The overall plan and framework of Mark's Gospel is simple and involving. As his drama unfolds, his readers will be involved in the mystery of who Jesus is and what it means to be his follower. The Gospel develops gradually in three stages. In the *first stage* (chs. 1–8), Mark's readers are drawn into a relationship with the powerful healer and preacher, Jesus of Nazareth. During this first stage no one seems to understand Jesus' true identity, not even his disciples. Suddenly, in the encounter at Caesarea Philippi, what had been hinted at earlier (e.g., 3:6: "they took counsel . . . against him . . . to put him to death") becomes clear: "The Son of Man must suffer greatly . . . be killed, and rise after three days" (8:31). In this first climax of his Gospel, Mark's readers also learn that the way of Christ is the way of the Christian (8:34: "Whoever wishes to come after me . . ."). Theirs too is the way of the cross!

The *second stage* of Mark's Gospel (chs. 9–15) gradually reveals to its readers the concrete means of true Christian discipleship. This is summed up best in 10:45, where Jesus says: "The Son of Man did not come to be served but to serve and to give his life as a ransom for many." And that is precisely what happens in the second climax of the Gospel, as Jesus dies for his people (chs. 14–15).

Jesus' death, however, is not the end. For the *third stage* of the Gospel of Mark begins

903

with the proclamation of Jesus' resurrection and with his going to Galilee ahead of his disciples (16:6-7). It is at the empty tomb that Mark's readers take the place of Jesus' first followers and become the major characters in his Gospel drama (16:8). It is as his Gospel ends that Mark challenges his readers most dramatically to respond to Jesus in their lives with trust, and not with the trembling and bewilderment of the women at the tomb! The third stage of Mark's Gospel continues in the life of the church, until the risen Lord comes again.

The characters and themes in Mark's Gospel

Mark's narrative account of Jesus' ministry, death, and resurrection emphasizes certain themes that were of great importance in the early church. It is also important for the Christian community of the twentieth century to meditate upon them: (1) the *humanity* of Jesus; (2) *trust* as the heart of discipleship; and (3) *service to others* as the daily way of taking up Jesus' cup and cross.

1) Of the four Gospel portraits of Jesus, Mark's is by far the one that best reveals *the human side of Jesus*. While Mark's Jesus spends most of his time performing incredible acts of mercy, which reveal that he is God's Son, he is also depicted as a most human Lord. Only Mark preserves those details that bring out how sharp (1:25), deeply grieved and angry (3:5), or indignant (10:14) Jesus could be with those around him. Mark alone adds the touching detail to the story of Jesus' raising of the little girl from her deathbed: "she should be given something to eat" (5:43). Only Mark's Jesus looks at the rich man and *loves him* (10:21) before he challenges him to give up all to follow him. Mark's Jesus is often discouraged by his inability to get his own disciples to understand him and his mission (e.g., 4:13; 8:14-21). Mark reveals a Jesus who is at once the powerful Son of God and a most human person. Mark's readers will sense that the Jesus of this Gospel is very approachable, because he has experienced life as they have, with all its disappointments and its loves, with all its joy and sadness.

2) Mark believes that the truest sign of being Jesus' disciple is *trust*. He challenges his readers to a radical trust in the risen Lord in a most provocative way by portraying Jesus'

first disciples as slow-witted, even blind. Mark's Jesus looks for *trust in who he is*, but the disciples respond with *amazement and fear to what he does*! They see who Jesus is on one level (their Messiah-Savior, who gives them bread, in 6:34-44 and 8:1-10). But they are blind to him on another level (their Messiah-Suffering Servant, who gives them life through his death, in 10:35-45). The Jesus who could give sight to the physically blind (8:22-26; 10:46-52) could not give insight and understanding to his most intimate followers!

The blindness of Jesus' disciples is one of the tragic threads of Mark's narrative. In presenting them in this way, however, Mark hopes that his Christian readers will *see* better than Jesus' first disciples did. He hopes that they will trust in Jesus, not as the "instant cure-all Messiah," but as the one whose death gives meaning to the life and suffering they experience.

3) A final cluster of Markan images is closely related to Mark's presentation of the human Jesus and the blind disciples. Jesus' challenge to trust in him leads to *the cup and the cross*. And in concrete daily life, Jesus' cup and cross take the form of being "the slave of all" and serving others rather than being served by them (10:44f.). Although Mark's Gospel does not give long lists of "how to" serve God and others, its readers cannot avoid the model of Mark's Jesus as the suffering servant of all. They know that they must seize every opportunity to serve others in charity if they want to be his followers.

It is in the garden of Gethsemane that the major themes of Mark's Gospel seem to come together. In his agony there, the human heart of Jesus is "troubled and distressed" (14:33). The one who has challenged his disciples to trust in God alone comes close to giving up himself: "Father . . . take this cup away from me." However, as his disciples sleep, Jesus continues his prayer in faith: "but not what I will but what you will" (14:36). Anyone searching for the meaning of Christian life and discipleship in Mark's Gospel can turn to the Gethsemane passage (14:32-42) and hear it all summed up: "Give yourself to the suffering Messiah. Trust as he did, even though he would rather not have trusted. Join him in serving the needs of your brothers and sisters, even unto death."

The Gospel of Mark in the liturgy

For centuries most of the readings at Sunday Eucharists were chosen from the Gospel according to Matthew. With the renewal of the liturgy after the Second Vatican Council, there came a major restructuring of the Gospels to be proclaimed on Sundays. Mark's Gospel became the "Cycle B Gospel," read on most Sundays from January to November every third year (1988, 1991, 1994, etc.). Weekday Eucharists feature Mark's Gospel even more regularly, daily during the eight weeks that precede the Lenten season. Consequently, by being open to the Liturgy of the Word, Christians can now experience the person and message of Mark's Gospel on a regular basis, in union with all those who share in the church's liturgy. With all of God's people, they are invited to follow Mark's Jesus from his baptism and first preaching (1:7-11 and 1:14-20: Third Sunday in Ordinary Time) to his last days before entering upon his passion (13:24-32: Thirty-third Sunday in Ordinary Time). The liturgical experience of Mark's Gospel can thus be very formative of the church's relationship with Jesus. It can also serve as a weekly, even daily, rallying call to deeper involvement in service to others, which is the hallmark of the Markan Christian.

The author and his times: A matter of urgency

According to some fathers of the early church (e.g., Papias, A.D. 135; Irenaeus, A.D. 200; and Origen, A.D. 250), the "Gospel according to Mark" was the work of an associate and interpreter of Peter. The Acts of the Apostles links a certain "John Mark" with Peter (Acts 12:12), and the First Letter of Peter concludes with encouragement from Peter and greetings from "Mark my son" (1 Pet 5:13). Most scholars today feel that the tradition of Peter's influence on Mark's Gospel was more practical than historical, that is, such a tradition assured this Gospel of apostolic authority ("It came to the church through Mark from Peter!"), which was so important in the formative years of the church. From the Gospel itself, it is possible only to identify its author as a zealous member (pastor?) of the second-generation church, who seems to be writing around the time of the destruction of Jerusalem by the Roman army in A.D. 70 (see especially 13:1-23 for indications of this time-frame).

It also becomes evident as one reads Mark's Gospel that his message is a most urgent one. It seems that Mark and his community belonged to that part of the early Christian community which believed that Jesus was going to return very soon, *as he said* (9:1; 13:30-31). In order to be on guard and ready for his glorious return as "Son of Man coming in the clouds . . . to gather his elect" (13:26-27), Mark urges his Christians to learn from his Jesus the meaning of radical, here-and-now discipleship, as if there is no tomorrow.

And so it begins, "the gospel of Jesus Christ, the Son of God," according to Mark.

COMMENTARY

"AND SO IT BEGINS"

Mark 1:1-45

The Gospel of Mark begins with a powerful title sentence. In his theme verse, Mark announces his belief that *Jesus of Nazareth*, who had lived among the people of Palestine for some thirty years, healing their sick and teaching them the goodness of God, and who had been put to death among thieves, *is indeed alive as the risen Christ, the Son of God.*

Mark, unlike Matthew and Luke, does not relate anything about the infancy of Jesus; instead, he immediately introduces his readers to the adult Jesus through his forerunner, John the Baptist. Mark's readers are quickly drawn into the drama of Jesus' active ministry. They witness Jesus' miraculous power and the ensuing conflicts with those who fail to understand his life's mission. The drama that begins here in chapter 1 will eventually unfold in the final mystery of conflict and power, the death and resurrection of Jesus. It is in the crucified and risen Jesus that Mark and his Christian readers find their source of hope and strength for living as Jesus did.

1:1 The Son of God. Mark's first verse is more power-packed than a casual reading would suggest. It is more than a title verse, announcing the Gospel's central character: Jesus Christ, the Son of God. It also provides the key to understanding the succeeding sixteen chapters. That is because in only one other place in the Gospel does a human being proclaim that Jesus is Son of God (the centurion who put Jesus to death, in 15:39). This prepares Mark's readers to question their own faith-convictions about Jesus of Nazareth. According to Mark, no one else would recognize Jesus' true identity while living with him and witnessing his powerful teaching and healing. In his first verse, Mark gives his readers the clue to the end and purpose of his whole Gospel: to know Jesus as the Son of God is to believe that he is their suffering Messiah, who died on the cross and who now lives as their risen Lord. Mark's Jesus asks his disciples to follow him to life on his way—the way of loving service, even unto death.

1:2-8 John points to Jesus. John the Baptist has only one function in the Gospel of Mark: he is the one who points to Jesus as the Messiah. His call for conversion to God through baptism and the forgiveness of sins, as well as his clothes and food, makes him the new Elijah (see 2 Kgs 1:8) sent by God "to prepare the way of the Lord." John recognizes that one more powerful is soon to come after him. Although Jesus will be baptized by John, it is clear that even John knows his subordinate role in the Jesus drama. As Mark's narrative unfolds, he will present John the Baptist again, in 6:14-29. There, by his death at the hands of King Herod, John will fulfill the role of pointing to Jesus' death, just as here his baptism with water points to Jesus' baptism "with the Holy Spirit." John's whole courageous life and death point to Jesus of Nazareth. He is a model of total witness to Christ for Mark's readers.

1:9-11 God confirms John's preaching. What John's preaching points to, God himself confirms. Although Jesus comes from Nazareth to be baptized by John in the Jordan River (Matthew, Luke, and John diminish John's role in Jesus' baptism), Mark makes it very clear that it is God himself who blesses Jesus. It is God who rends the heavens, sends his Spirit upon Jesus in the form of a dove, and says: "You are my beloved Son. With you I am well pleased." God likewise has descended upon Christians in their baptism, making them favored sons and daughters of God. As Mark's readers follow *the* Son, they learn how to be like him. They see how he let the Spirit of his baptism lead him to drink the cup of suffering at the end of his life of service and interpret his impending death as a second "baptism" which his disciples would share (10:35-45).

1:12-15 Jesus' journey begins. Mark's version of the temptation in the desert is much shorter than Matthew's or Luke's. Its brevity, however, makes its significance more direct. The Spirit leads Jesus into the desert. Tempted and tested there by Satan for forty days, as the people of Israel were tested before him, Jesus is protected by God through his angels. Mark's two verses state simply that Jesus has withstood the test and is ready for his brief but saving life of service to God and humanity. Experiences of temptation and weakness were not unknown to the Son of God. Mark thus tells his readers that the protecting spirit of Jesus is with them in their weakness just as God was with him in his desert experience.

With John's arrest (v. 14), Jesus' work begins. Mark's "gospel of Jesus Christ, the Son of God" began at verse 1. Now the "good news of God" begins, as Jesus' first words are heard: "This is the time of fulfillment" (v. 15). Yes, says Mark, God's reign of power has begun in Jesus, who is God's good news in person. Jesus' announcement would have exhilarated the faithful Israelites of his day. However, he immediately links the good news with an equally important call for radical response: "Therefore, repent and put all your trust in the gospel of God that I bear!" In these brief inaugural words of Jesus' ministry, Mark summarizes the gospel message that Jesus preached: the very power of God is available to those who open themselves to Jesus and to his gospel way of loving service.

1:16-20 The call of the first four followers. Jesus, who has just begun preaching about the kingdom of God and conversion, effects what he preaches. Immediately after Jesus says "Come after me" to the brothers Simon and Andrew, James and John, they turn from family and lifework as fishermen to follow him. In this brief but very striking scene, Mark shows how powerful and direct Jesus' call to share in his mission can be. He also holds up as a model for his readers the immediate and total response of the four. But if Mark's readers are to gain the full impact of this passage, it is vital that they be aware of how Simon (named Peter by Jesus in 3:16), James, and John will respond elsewhere in the Gospel. (Andrew is mentioned only three other times: when Simon's mother-in-law is cured, 1:29; when Jesus names him among the Twelve, 3:18; and when he is with Peter, James, and John again, talking with Jesus about the end of the temple, 13:3.)

This first involvement of Peter, James, and John with Jesus is only the beginning of an exciting yet tension-filled journey. These three will be the only ones whom Jesus permits to share in four experiences in which he most clearly reveals the power and purpose of his life (healing and giving life, in 1:29-31 and 5:37-43; the glory-filled transfiguration, in 9:2-13; the message about the future times, in 13:1-37). At the same time, they will be the ones who will most seriously misunderstand their Lord and fail him at crucial points of

their intimacy with him (Peter at Caesarea Philippi, in 8:27-33; James and John seeking "to be first," in 10:35-45; all three of them in the garden of Gethsemane, 14:32-42; Peter's denial, in 15:66-72).

The eager and total response of the disciples here, once seen in Mark's overall drama, draws the readers of the Gospel into a tension that will be experienced over and over as the journey with Jesus unfolds. For Mark, to "come after" Jesus and to join in his mission means to walk a journey of life-giving exhilaration and draining confusion, of overwhelming power and powerlessness. It is an invitation to respond, "Yes, I leave all and follow you," not only in one radical conversion experience but continuously until the end.

1:21-28 Spellbound and amazed by his teaching and power. Mark's readers do not learn *what* Jesus teaches in the Capernaum synagogue, but they do learn *how* he teaches ("with authority," vv. 22 and 27), and *what effect* his powerful teaching has (people are "astonished" and "amazed," vv. 22 and 27; the unclean spirit is overwhelmed, v. 26). The repetition of the phrase "with authority" (found twice, at v. 22 and v. 27) indicates that Mark wants the events of Jesus' first teaching and first powerful action to be seen as intimately related. He not only speaks with authority—he also acts with power!

It is important to know that for Mark and his first-century Christians the "unclean spirit" (v. 23) and other "demons" (see 1:32; 3:11, 15, 22; 5:2, etc.) represented evil, mysterious powers who were hostile to God, health, and goodness. These demons were thought to be so perceptive that they could know who was a representative of God's power. Here, the "unclean spirit" reveals Jesus as "the holy One of God" (v. 24) and cunningly tries to thwart his mission for goodness. Jesus' two commands are sharper and more forceful than the challenges of the unclean spirit. For *Jesus' word effects what it says:* the unclean spirit leaves the man, shrieking one last time as he goes down in defeat (v. 26). The "amazed" bystanders acknowledge the teacher's authority, yet they still have to ask: "What is this?" (v. 27).

Mark's intention here is to make his readers confident in their Lord as teacher and healer. However, the allusion to the people's amazement (v. 27), which caused Jesus' reputation to spread throughout Galilee (v. 28), also has another purpose. It is precisely the people's response of being *amazed* (1:27 and 5:20), or *astounded* (2:12 and 5:42) that will eventually bring other hostile forces to seek to destroy Jesus (see 6:14-29, where Herod is threatened by Jesus' reputation and ends up beheading John the Baptist). Mark wants more from his readers than amazement; he wants them to be alert when Jesus reveals himself in less appealing ways. "Will you also be amazed when Jesus begins to teach that the Son of Man has to suffer much, be rejected by the chief priests, be put to death, and rise three days later (8:31)? Will you recognize him for who he is when he hangs on the cross, abandoned by most of his followers who were amazed by his first signs of power?"

The followers of Mark's Jesus can have much confidence in Jesus as wonderworker. However, those who want to follow the "amazing one" must also go the way he goes. They must deny themselves, take up their cross, and follow after him (8:34).

1:29-31 Simon's mother-in-law. In verse 29, Mark has Jesus move immediately from his first powerful miracle to another. The visit to Simon's mother-in-law turns into a second sign that God's kingdom of wholeness is present in him. In 1:25 Jesus cured with a word; here he cures sickness by a touch (1:31). His touch saves as surely as his word. The fact that the woman's cure is immediate and total is made clear by Mark's emphasis on how she resumes her duties of hospitality, waiting on her guests in verse 31.

1:32-34 The Messiah and his secret. Jesus' first day of ministry does not end with sundown. That evening "the whole town" gathers around him with their sick and possessed. His first day of preaching and healing has given them hope that God is at work among them. After Jesus has cured many, Mark's readers first hear the curious phrase "not permitting them (the demons) to speak, because they knew him" (v. 34). This reminds Mark's readers of the "Quiet!" of 1:25 and prepares them for what they will hear repeatedly in Mark's Gospel (1:44; 3:12; 5:43; 7:36; 8:26; 8:30; 9:9). Mark presents Jesus as being very reserved about letting his reputation as miracle-worker spread. This reticence is called the "messianic

secret." By emphasizing such secrecy regarding Jesus' identity as Messiah, Mark hopes that his Christian readers will accept Jesus' true identity, on his terms, in the context of his entire life and mission. Mark's Jesus will reveal himself as Messiah by being powerless on the cross. Christians are free to proclaim Jesus as their Messiah and Lord only when they accept his way of suffering messiahship along with his miraculous works.

1:35-39 The good news spreads. Jesus rises early and withdraws to a desert place to pray alone (v. 35), because he knows that the people are seeking him out *only* because of his miraculous powers. They have misunderstood him, and so he must move on to neighboring villages and continue his ministry of preaching and healing throughout all of Galilee (v. 39). Not even Simon can hold him back, for not even Simon understands where Jesus' way leads. Perhaps Mark's readers, who already know the end of the journey, will profit much from their own desert experiences of prayer with "the misunderstood Messiah."

1:40-45 The leper is healed and misunderstands. The healing of the leper is a remarkable scene, full of marked contrasts. It is a fitting conclusion to Mark's first chapter. The powerful but misunderstood Messiah is approached directly by a person who is normally denied any contact with healthy people. This outcast's trust in Jesus is met by the pity and power of his touch and word. However, the leper's exhilaration at his cure is dampened by a stern repetition of Jesus' prohibitive messianic secret: "Tell no one anything!" (v. 44). (Only the priest is to know, because only his word can allow the outcast to re-enter the society from which his sickness has kept him.)

Instead of following Jesus' word, the cured man tells everyone! And Jesus' mission is thwarted as soon as it begins: "It was impossible for Jesus to enter a town openly" (v. 45). Through this concluding story of chapter 1, Mark asks all Christian followers to take Jesus at his word. He asks them to take Jesus seriously, as he is, at his pace on the journey, and in his time. To be a Christian is to respond to Jesus' word with fidelity, whether that word is "Be made clean" or "Tell no one anything!"

JESUS IN CONFLICT

Mark 2:1–3:6

In Mark's first chapter, Jesus' appearance as teacher and healer had drawn the sick, possessed, and needy to him "from everywhere" (1:45). Now, in this section of five closely related scenes (2:1–3:6), Jesus' activity on behalf of those in need will draw the scrutinizing attention and threatening ire of the scribes and Pharisees, who make their first appearance in the Gospel.

The Markan drama continues to portray a powerful Jesus, whose "teaching with authority" (1:27) still issues forth in miraculous cures of the sick. But now there is more. Now it becomes evident that Jesus' claims to forgive sins (2:5) and to be "lord of the sabbath" (2:28) are the cause of open conflict with the religious leaders of his day.

As Mark's readers journey with Jesus from the cure of the paralytic (2:1-12) to the cure of the man with the withered hand (3:1-6), they will sense an increasing tension. They will be lifted up with joy by Jesus' powerful but gentle love of the needy and outcast. They will swell with pride at their Lord's wise teaching, which will eventually bring his wise antagonists to silence (3:4). At the same time, they will sense the dark place where all these "successful encounters" lead. They will sense that the Son of Man already stands in the shadow of the cross, even before Mark makes it clear at 3:6, when he concludes this section: "The Pharisees went out and immediately took counsel with the Herodians against him to put him to death." How well Mark prepares his Christian followers for the ultimate conflict of Jesus' life!

2:1-12 "My son, you are forgiven/healed." Back in Capernaum, Jesus is surrounded by great numbers of people again (v. 2; see 1:33). As he preaches to the crowd, four friends of a paralyzed man lower him on his mat through the roof so that he can be close enough for Jesus to see him and cure him (vv. 3-4). (Such extraordinary means to get close to Jesus emphasized the faith of these friends as well as the overwhelming size of the crowd Jesus attracted.) Jesus responds to this act of faith, not by healing the man immediately, but by touching off the first of a series of controversial dialogues with the onlooking scribes and Pharisees. When Jesus says, "Child, your sins are forgiven" (v. 5), he is as much as saying, "It is God whom you approach." (In the Old Testament, only God is capable of forgiving sins; and it was expected that he would do so only at the end of time.) It thus becomes clear why the scribes murmur "he is blaspheming" (v. 7) and why Jesus brings it all out in the open. His claim to be able to forgive sins better reveals his identity as Son of God than do the miracles he performs.

Aware of the silent censure his forgiving word has caused in the crowd, Jesus proceeds to prove that "the Son of Man has authority to forgive sins on earth" by commanding the man to rise and walk in the sight of everyone (vv. 8-11). In concluding this miracle, Mark asks his readers to praise God for his presence in their midst as the forgiver-healer, just as the crowd did (v. 12), even in the face of those who do not believe.

It is significant that Mark has chosen to present this miracle and teaching about Jesus' power to forgive sins so early in his Gospel drama. It shows that the need for the experience of God's forgiveness was as important to first-century Christians as it is today. Mark's readers praise God for saying clearly, even today, "My sons, my daughters, I absolve you from your sins."

2:13-22 Jesus and Levi; eating and fasting. After the conflict with the Pharisees over his dealing with the paralytic, Jesus continues to teach the crowds and to gather his first band of disciples (v. 13). He calls a tax collector, Levi, who immediately leaves his work to follow him (v. 14). It is significant that Jesus chooses his followers from among those with simple or even despicable occupations (e.g., Levi would be held in contempt by his fellow Jews because he cooperated with the Romans in exacting taxes for the emperor. His profession would place him among the recognized sinners of the Jewish people).

Even more significant is the fact that Jesus goes to Levi's house to associate with other "sinners" (v. 15). This provokes the scribes, who object, "Why does he eat with tax collectors and sinners?" (v. 16). This Jewish teacher, in contrast to the Pharisees, seeks out sinners to follow him. He even eats with them! The entire scene ends with a general statement from Jesus: "Those who are well do not need a physician, but the sick do" (v. 17).

By relating this second conflict situation, Mark encourages his readers to understand that to follow Jesus means that their meals, especially their Eucharistic meals, must include people who are aware of their weakness and of their need of healing. This stands in contrast to anyone who might think that only those who are "righteous" may participate in the meal. Indeed, the meal at which Jesus is present as *the* righteous one is the meal at which the sick and the sinner are most welcome. Paradoxically, then, the Christian Eucharist is for those who seem "not to belong," but really do!

If Jesus' eating habits challenged the life style of the Jewish leaders, so also did his disciples' style of fasting (vv. 18-22). When confronted by the question why his disciples do not fast (v. 18), Jesus responds with his own question: "Why fast while the groom is at the wedding?" Drawing on Old Testament imagery (wedding imagery often referred to God's presence with his people, and fasting was seen as preparation for God's coming), Mark's Jesus is as much as saying that God's kingdom is now present in his person. Indeed, he goes on, once the groom is "taken away" (a reference to his death), the guests will fast until he returns in his glory (v. 20). As Mark's readers await that final coming of Jesus, they fast with a certain hope and joy in him.

Mark's readers today can live with the same joyful hope that Mark held out for his first readers. They too can understand the meaning of the two parables (the unshrunken cloth sewn on an old cloak, v. 21; and the new wine in old wineskins, v. 22), which are meant to teach that a true follower of Jesus does not fast for the wrong reasons. The kingdom of God has already been established. When Christians choose to fast, Mark implies, it is to heighten their anticipation of the full joy of the heavenly banquet they will share in. At the Eucharist, Christians already celebrate the groom's presence with them in sacrament. When they fast, they proclaim their hope in the fullness of union with him to come.

2:23-28 The lord of the sabbath. Mark next relates a peculiar incident about Jesus' disciples picking grain as they walk along with him on a sabbath. Again, the actions of Jesus and his followers cause a furor among the Pharisees. In response to their protest, Jesus argues from Scripture that even David took exception to the law for the sake of his hungry followers (1 Sam 21:2-7). Mark's Jesus goes on to proclaim that God created the sabbath for human beings, and not vice versa. Those who follow Jesus are to interpret the whole Jewish law by living according to God's spirit of the law, namely, loving kindness. Later in his Gospel, Mark will make it clear that all laws are summed up in the one law of Christ, his dual commandment of love. When a Christian chooses "to love God and one's neighbor as oneself," that one will be approved by the Lord (12:28-34).

The importance of this sabbath incident in Mark's Gospel lies in the summary character of its last verse. When Jesus says that the "Son of Man is lord even of the sabbath," he is summing up his own authority. Mark's readers will remember that this entire section began with Jesus' telling the crowd at Capernaum that "the Son of Man has authority to forgive sins on earth" (2:10). What happens next, on the same sabbath (3:1-6), will show how this claim of Mark's Jesus channels the flow of the whole Gospel. The Pharisees will stop arguing and begin plotting against the Son of Man. The die is cast!

(A note on the title "Son of Man": Jesus never refers to himself as the Son of God in Mark's Gospel. He often calls himself the Son of Man. This title, from Dan 7:13, came to be understood as referring to the future redeemer of the Israelite nation. Mark's use of the "Son of Man" title points rather to *the means* that the Redeemer would use to save his people, namely, his suffering and death on the cross. Mark's intention becomes even clearer when the reader notes that the next time the "Son of Man" title is used is in 8:31, in the first explicit prediction of Jesus' suffering and death.)

3:1-6 The withered hand and the plot. Jesus' mercy toward the man with the withered hand is the climax of the section that began with Jesus' cure of the paralyzed man (2:1-12). Its climactic nature becomes evident when one notices three things. First, Mark places this synagogue cure on the sabbath, immediately after the statement that Jesus is lord of the sabbath. The cure is concrete proof of his claim to lordship. Secondly, a dramatic change of rhythm in the narrative becomes evident when one reads the withered-hand passage in connection with the four preceding ones. Here it is Jesus who asks the provocative question ("Is it lawful to do good on the sabbath . . . ?," v. 4), not the Pharisees, as they do in 2:7, 16, 18, 24. Here Jesus is angry with them (v. 5), instead of them being upset with him. In fact, now the complainers have nothing to say (v. 5)! Thirdly, after Jesus shows his merciful power by perfectly restoring the man's hand, the Pharisees withdraw to plot how they might destroy Jesus (v. 6).

Mark concludes this series of five "conflict stories" on a sobering note. His readers cannot help but see that Jesus' way of life is leading to his death (v. 6). They also realize that Mark will suggest that the same is true for those who follow the "Son of Man" (8:31-38). Nevertheless, no matter what tension Mark's readers will experience while trying to live the Christian life, Jesus will be there on their behalf. Mark has assured his readers that Jesus will respond generously to their faith in him (2:5), because he has come for the needy (2:17) as a merciful Lord of the sabbath (2:27 and 3:4-5).

REFLECTING ON THE MEANING OF DISCIPLESHIP

Mark 3:7-35

Good storytellers involve their listeners in their stories by the use of various techniques, such as character development, comparison and contrast, vivid detail, pacing, etc. In his first two chapters Mark has already shown that he is a good storyteller. He has begun to reveal the human side of Jesus' character by certain details that Matthew and Luke leave out of their accounts (for example, only Mark describes Jesus' grief and anger during the cure of the man with the withered hand, 3:5). He has already established a mounting tension in his drama by placing the five conflict stories of 2:1–3:6 (they "took counsel against him to put him to death," 3:6) after the "success story" of chapter 1 ("people kept coming to him from everywhere!" 1:45).

Mark the storyteller also has a message he wants to convey by his Jesus story, and so he wants to give his readers time for reflection. That is why he presents a brief summary pas-

sage here (3:7-12). It not only sums up Jesus' overwhelming appeal to the crowds (vv. 7-10), but it also reminds his readers that Jesus did not want his identity as God's Son to be proclaimed for the wrong reasons (vv. 11-12; see the comment on "secret" in 1:32-34). Mark hopes that this pause for reflection will prepare his readers for the rest of their journey with Jesus. Their walk with him will often be confused by "great crowds and multitudes" in search of only a part of what Jesus and Christians come to give (vv. 7-8). It will be complicated by forces bent on obstructing the path that leads to the fulfillment of the Lord's mission (vv. 11-12). Therefore, Mark rounds off this part of his Jesus story with two passages (the choice of the Twelve, vv. 13-19, and the conflict about Beelzebul, vv. 20-35) which help his readers to understand the true meaning of Christian discipleship.

3:13-19 Called by name to be with Jesus. By the time Mark wrote his Gospel in A.D. 70, most of those who had been Jesus' first disciples were no longer present to lead the Christian community. In this passage, in which Jesus' choice of the first twelve disciples is described, Mark emphasizes for the Christians of his day two important elements of discipleship: "being with Jesus" and "being named" by him.

The first ingredient of Christian discipleship emphasized here is being a "companion" of the Lord (v. 14). To be Jesus' "disciple" is to be a "learner," and to learn from him it is necessary to be with him. From this point on in the Gospel narrative, Jesus will keep his Twelve close to him. They will learn from him the mysteries of the kingdom (in parables, 4:1-34). They will also discover the difficulties of his way (chs. 8–16, in which Jesus details his way of the cross and the cost of following him). The fact that Mark has Jesus choose his Twelve on the mountain (v. 13) not only indicates the solemnity of the moment but also points to other scenes of the Gospel when the disciples will be with Jesus on other mountaintops, for example, to witness the transfiguration in 9:2-10 and to see him in agony on the Mount of Olives in 14:26-42. Mark's readers are asked to be with Jesus and to learn from him in experiences of mysterious glory and painful agony.

A second element of Christian discipleship is located in the meaning of "being named" by Jesus. In Genesis, because God had "named" the heavens and the earth and all creatures, they became God's own possession (Gen 1:3-10). When God gave Adam the command to name the animals, Adam shared God's own power over them (Gen 2:20). To be "named" by Jesus means to be possessed by him, to be under his control. It also means that those named by him will share in his power (vv. 14-15). In this brief passage, Mark's readers, baptized "in the name of Jesus," hear the invitation to be companions with the risen Lord and to learn from him how to share in his mission and power.

3:20-35 Possessed by God and doing God's will. Once Jesus has come down from the mountain with his twelve companions, many people crowd around him, so much so that he and his disciples cannot even manage to eat (v. 20). Mark's readers will notice various reactions to Jesus and to his ministry among the people. His family is "standing outside." They have come to protect him from doing too much. They think he is "out of his mind" (v. 21). Important scribes have come from Jerusalem to see why Jesus is so popular. They claim that he is "possessed by Beelzebul" and that he expels demons with Satan's help (v. 22). After Jesus has cleverly and forcefully responded to these accusations (vv. 23-30), Mark's readers learn what the proper reaction to Jesus is. They learn that, of all those who crowd around Jesus, the only ones who can really be considered his brothers and sisters are those "who do the will of God" (vv. 32-34). Jesus expects his followers to have the same single-minded dedication to God's will as he does. Such dedication may lead to conflicts with people like the Jerusalem scribes. It may seem "crazy" or "overdone" to others, even to members of one's own family! But this is what it means to be "family" with Jesus.

Jesus' response to the accusation that he is possessed by the devil is brief and pointed. In two parables about divided kingdoms and divided houses (vv. 24-27), he shows how self-defeating it would be if he, who drives evil spirits out of people (3:11), were an agent of Satan! Jesus also points out that the only unforgivable sin belongs to his accusers, who refuse to accept the power of God's Holy Spirit at work in him (vv. 28-30). Jesus is possessed by *God's* spirit, and so are all those who choose to do God's will.

THE MYSTERY OF THE KINGDOM; THE POWER OF JESUS

Mark 4:1-35

Chapter 4 begins and ends with Jesus in a boat. Mark's readers will hear him teaching the crowds "in parables" about the kingdom of God. This preaching will be followed by Jesus' revelation of his power over the raging sea. Jesus not only preaches about the power of the kingdom, but he also practices what he preaches!

4:1-20 Teaching in parables. C. H. Dodd, a renowned British Scripture scholar, describes what a parable is and how it was meant to function in the time of Jesus. "At its simplest, the parable is a metaphor or simile drawn from nature or common life, arresting the hearer by its vividness or strangeness, and leaving the mind in sufficient doubt about its precise application to tease it into active thought." Here in chapter 4, Mark puts his readers in touch with the first-century world of parables. They will hear how Jesus used the familiar in a new way, inviting his listeners to new thought about God and God's kingdom. In effect, Jesus' parables say that God's ways may not be our ways. They call for conversion.

In Jesus' first parable (vv. 3-8), Mark's readers hear that something small, like a seed (or like the small Christian community of A.D. 70), could grow (or not grow) and yield (or not yield) much grain, depending on whether the soil was good (or thorny or rocky or hardened like the footpath). A good parable, by its nature, is open-ended and gives the hearer the choice to respond on various levels. Mark's hope in relating this parable is that his Christians would respond: "Let *us* be good soil! Let *us* be full of hope, even in the fragile times of our beginnings as a small community! *We* want God's seed to produce one hundredfold *in us*, as Jesus promised it would!"

The private discussion between Jesus and his disciples (vv. 10-12) sounds as though Jesus is giving the crowd ("those outside," v. 11) no chance to understand him or become his followers. This is very strange, considering that parables were meant to stimulate their hearers to conversion. What is going on in the harsh verse 12 (taken from Isa 6:9-10) is this: The early church knew that certain people had heard Jesus' word and had rejected him; they also knew that others ("you" disciples, in v. 11) had believed in him. Mark therefore shows that Jesus, like Isaiah before him, brought a message that truly caused people to take a stance, either for him or against him. Jesus' parables, says Mark, were intended to bring all people to God's kingdom, but some chose to remain "outside." Mark's readers are asked to be open to God's word in their day. They are challenged to let his word draw them "inside," into a deeper faith-relationship with their risen Lord.

Although Jesus' first parable was originally an open-ended invitation to radical involvement with him, the explanation that follows it (in vv. 13-20) becomes a practical, point-by-point application of the parable's details to the life of Mark's Christians. Listening carefully to this explanation, they could respond: "Yes, we understand the parable for our time (v. 13). We know that the seed is God's word (v. 14). But we also can see how the various types of seed stand for those people who respond to the word differently (vv. 13-20). Some of us have let Satan lead us away from the faith (v. 15). Some of our number let pressure and persecution wear us down (vv. 16-17). Others of us are struggling with cravings for money and other things of this world that draw us away (vv. 18-19). Nevertheless, we want to hear the word, take it to heart, and be true followers of Jesus' way" (v. 20).

4:21-34 Hearing the word in parables. After the parable of the seed and its explanation, Mark records five other parables that are meant to enable his audience to take Jesus' word to heart more personally and more profoundly. By the parable of the lamp (v. 21), Mark suggests that his readers will have to ponder the meaning of Jesus' life and message much more thoroughly for themselves before they can share it fully with others (vv. 22-23). The parable-like saying about getting back "in the measure you give" (v. 24) is much like the preceding parable about the lamp. Mark's readers must continuously grow in their understanding of Jesus for themselves, or they will lose what they think they possess. The parable of the sleeping farmer (vv. 26-29) shatters the illusions of those who think that they can control the coming of God's kingdom. Indeed, says Mark, "God's ways are not our ways! We must be patient and let God be

God!" The last parable of chapter 4 is also about a seed, the smallest of all seeds, the mustard seed (vv. 30-32). Even though the early Christian community was small in number, this parable assures Mark's readers that all their efforts will be fruitful in the growing kingdom of God—if they will just understand (see vv. 33-34).

Mark summarizes how the people "heard" Jesus' parables: some attentive ones "were able to understand" them (v. 33), while the disciples understood them perfectly because "he explained everything in private" to them (v. 34). With such special tutoring, Jesus' disciples would seem ready to prove their enlightened discipleship. The following scene on the sea is proof that they were *not* ready!

4:35-41 Jesus stills the storm and calls for faith. In this first storm scene (see 6:45-52 for a similar account), Mark's Jesus gives his disciples an opportunity to show that they have come to know him for who he really is. They have shared in the secrets of the kingdom (4:1-34), and they have been with him as he healed all sickness and drove out demons (chs. 1-3). Now they are with him on the raging sea, and he sleeps! (v. 38). They think that he does not care for them (v. 38), after all they have seen him do on behalf of those in need. After quieting the violent storm with a word, "Quiet! Be still!" (v. 39), Jesus turns to his disciples (and Mark's readers) and asks: "Why are you so terrified? Do you not yet have faith?" (v. 40). The first disciples' only response is: "Who then is this?" (v. 41). Mark wants his Christians, with their knowledge of Jesus' entire life, death, and resurrection, to be assured of his protection in their times of stress and confusion. He asks for more than "great awe" (v. 41) at Jesus' stilling of the storm. He asks for deep here-and-now faith from all who struggle to understand the meaning of Jesus' life, death, and resurrection in their own daily experience of Christian living.

THE MIRACLES GO ON

Mark 5:1-43

The disciples, the Jewish leaders, and the Jewish crowds have all seen Jesus calm devils and the sea. They have heard him preach about conversion and the kingdom of God.

After all this, the disciples still ask, "Who then is this?" (4:41). With the first miracle of chapter 5, Mark has Jesus reach out beyond Jewish boundaries to see if non-Jews will recognize him for who he really is (in 5:1-20, the cure of the demon-crazed man takes place in Gerasene-Gentile territory, east of the Jordan River). When Jesus returns home from this amazing encounter with non-Jews, he meets with increasingly more profound faith in him (from a Jewish synagogue official, Jairus, in 5:21-24 and 35-43, and from a simple, suffering woman in the crowd, in 5:25-34). It would seem that after these three miraculous events Jesus' disciples would understand his purpose and mission better. However, because the chapter ends with yet another reference to "the secret" ("He gave strict orders that no one should know this," 5:43), Mark's readers realize that Jesus still wants his followers to see more in him than a powerful worker of miracles.

5:1-20 Jesus reaches out to non-Jews: The Gerasene demoniac. Mark's vivid description of the possessed man, who violently roars around the tombs and hillsides of Gerasene territory (vv. 1-5), sets the stage for Jesus' encounter with him (vv. 6-10). Even before Jesus drives the devils from the man (strangely, the devils within the man *ask* Jesus to send them into a herd of swine, which he does, vv. 11-13), the possessed man comes to Jesus, pays him the homage due to God alone, and recognizes him as God's Son (vv. 6-7). Like other possessed persons before him (see 1:24; 1:34; and 3:11), this man sees and proclaims what the disciples and the Jewish crowds do not: Jesus is God's Son!

When the people of the village come out to see if the swineherds' incredible story is true, they find their well-known wild man "sitting there clothed and in his right mind" (vv. 14-15). They also presumably see two thousand pigs afloat in the sea. Naturally, they are filled with fear. They cannot fathom the power of Jesus and ask him to leave their land before he shocks them any more. It was obviously easier for them to cope with a violent possessed man than it was to deal with the one who had the power to cure him (vv. 16-17). The healed man, so long tormented and isolated from society, asks if he can stay with Jesus (v. 18). Although Jesus does not let him come along with him, he does not tell him

to keep quiet about the cure, as he has so often done after his miracles. The consequence is that the non-Jews throughout the region of the Ten Cities hear what God's mercy has done for him through Jesus (vv. 19-20). By this remarkable miracle, Mark not only displays Jesus' loving concern for one outcast but also sets the stage for Jesus' mission to all non-Jews.

Mark's community of Jewish *and* Gentile Christians would be very alert as Jesus enters the foreign land of Gerasa (v. 1). They would be anxious to see how the keepers of swine (obviously Gentiles, since this was an occupation prohibited to Jews) might react to Jesus (vv. 11-17). They would recognize in this event Mark's way of describing the initial step in Christianity's spread to the Gentiles. Indeed, the Christian faith of Mark's day, which was adhered to by Jew and non-Jew alike, was rooted in Jesus' own loving outreach. Christianity had no limiting boundaries of race or nationality. Jesus' saving word and power were intended for all of God's people.

5:21-43 Jesus and women: life and trust. In Mark's Gospel Jesus is closely involved with women nine times. Here in verses 21-43, Mark's readers enter into two of Jesus' more moving encounters with women (Jairus' daughter and the woman with the hemorrhage). Both stories begin with someone seeking out Jesus, the healer. Both stories end in the cure of a person who had been hopelessly sick. Even the way Mark intertwines the two stories (the story of Jairus' daughter begins, the account of the hemorrhaging woman is related in full, and the Jairus story is then completed) shows that Mark wants his readers to hear one important message common to both: "Do not be afraid; just have faith" (v. 36)! The father of the little girl trusts Jesus even after hearing the report that she is dead (vv. 35-40). He is invited to witness Jesus' healing touch and word, and then sees his little girl walking around alive (vv. 41-42). The woman shows her trust by touching Jesus (v. 27) and by coming forward in spite of her fear (v. 33). She learns that her faith is rewarded by peace and lasting health (v. 34). Like Jairus and the woman, Christians of every age are urged by Mark to approach Jesus confidently with earnest appeals on behalf of the sick and dying.

Even as he reports Jesus' miraculous power, Mark preserves the human side of Jesus. For example, the one who has more healing power than the physicians of his day (he cured the woman who had spent all her money and twelve years of time in going to doctors, who failed to help her, v. 26) did not know who touched him (v. 30). Likewise, the one who raises the little girl from her deathbed (v. 41) is also sensitive to her need for something to eat (v. 43). Such details make Mark's Jesus very approachable. He was not a perfect human (for example, he did not know everything), but he was perfectly human (he was full of compassion). Mark's readers can trust him now as those in need did when he walked on this earth. He is sensitive to the needs of those who seek him out.

It is important that Mark's readers notice the details in this passage that point to the climax of the Gospel. Such hints reveal Mark's desire to keep his readers moving with Jesus to the place where his journey leads. For example, Peter, James, and John, who witness the raising of the dead girl here, will soon question what "to rise from the dead" means (9:10). Likewise, the fearful, trembling woman with a hemorrhage points to the three women who will leave the empty tomb "seized with trembling and bewilderment," so afraid that they say nothing to anyone (16:8). There is almost no section of Mark's Gospel that does not draw his readers to its conclusion. Mark asks his readers, women and men, to stay with Jesus to the end. Even when life's confusion and tragedies get them down, Mark's readers are reminded: "Fear is useless. What is needed is trust in God, who brings life, even from death."

OF BREAD AND BLINDNESS

Mark 6:1–8:26

In chapters 1 to 5 Mark has highlighted Jesus' miracles and power over cosmic forces: over demons, over raging seas and winds, over sickness and death. He has also let his readers know that the proper Christian response to Jesus' power is faith in him, not terror or fear (4:40 and 5:36). In chapters 6 to 8 Mark will continue his picture of the powerful Jesus. However, he will emphasize even more how blind Jesus' disciples are to the meaning of Jesus' power (6:52 and 8:14-21).

Mark's readers will also notice a new emphasis in these chapters, namely, the breads. In chapters 6 to 8 Mark will repeatedly connect bread with the disciples' lack of understanding of Jesus. It gradually becomes clear that Mark is suggesting to his Christians that they will recognize the true meaning of Jesus for themselves only when they realize what their Eucharistic sharing of the bread really means. (The Eucharist commemorates their union with the risen Lord, who came to his glory through his suffering and death.) It is by "bread and blindness" that Mark's Jesus leads his followers to the halfway point and first climax of the Gospel, that is, to the revelation by Jesus to Peter and the disciples that the road to his final glory (and theirs) is by way of much suffering and death (8:27-38).

6:1-6 He was too much for them in Nazareth . . . and they for him! Jesus' disciples are with him as he teaches a large synagogue crowd in his hometown, Nazareth. While many of Mark's readers are interested in this passage because of its reference to Jesus' "brothers and sisters" (v. 3), Mark's own interest lay elsewhere. (Because of the Catholic church's teaching on the virginity of Mary, this mention of Jesus' brothers and sisters causes questions to be asked. However, neither this section nor 3:31-35, where his brothers and sisters are mentioned again, says anything definitive about Mary's virginity or Jesus' blood family, because in Mark's day "brothers and sisters" could refer to cousins, stepbrothers or stepsisters, or members of the extended family, as well as to blood sisters or brothers.) Mark passes on the account of the hometown folks' rejection of Jesus for a special reason: to provide an important transition and surprising contrasts at this point of his drama. The passage is transitional, for it bridges the greatest of Jesus' miracles (raising the girl from death) with the sharing of his healing power with the disciples (6:7-13). The surprising contrasts lie not so much in his town's rejection of him ("A prophet is not without honor . . .," v. 4) as in his discouragement and ineffectiveness in their midst: "So he was not able to perform any mighty deed there, apart from curing a few. . . . He was amazed at their lack of faith" (v. 5). Up to this point people have always been amazed and fearful in Jesus' presence. Here Jesus is amazed at them and at the lack of faith he finds in Nazareth. Mark's readers, no matter how familiar they are with Jesus, might well evaluate the depth of their faith in him in order to allow him to be as effective as he wants to be in their midst.

6:7-13 The apostles are sent to preach and to expel demons. Rejected by his own, Jesus preaches elsewhere and sends his twelve disciples out with special instructions and powers. The reader will remember that Mark has carefully prepared for this important moment when Jesus sends the apostles out. First, he had Jesus call them personally (1:16-20). Then he selected twelve special ones to accompany him (3:13-19). The Twelve, tutored by Jesus and present with him as he healed many from sickness and evil (chs. 3–5), are now ready to become "ones sent out" (the Greek word for "apostle" means "one sent out"). The specific order to expel unclean spirits (v. 7) is accompanied by further details regarding clothing, what to bring, where to stay, and what to do when they are rejected (vv. 8-11). These detailed directions were indications for the early church of the need to move quickly and to be dependent on God's care. Were Mark's Christians in A.D. 70 as trusting in God as Jesus called his Twelve to be? What are the specific apostolic mission orders for today's apostles who read Mark's Gospel? One thing seems clear: Mark is asking all his readers to consider prayerfully how to balance their eager action in building up God's kingdom with their trust in God's own loving involvement in their lives.

6:14-29 King Herod, John the Baptizer, and Jesus. This rather long account of the death of John seemingly interrupts the flow of Mark's story about Jesus. However, it is likely that Mark presents this account here in order to prepare his readers for Jesus' death, much in the same way that John's first appearance in the Gospel prepared for Jesus' coming on the scene (1:2-11). A careful reading will indicate how John's death was truly a foretelling of Jesus' own death. Consider the clues. Although Herod was wrong about John being "raised up" (v. 16), Jesus will indeed be raised up (16:6-8). Like Herodias (v. 19), the chief priests want to kill Jesus but have to go about it by devious means because of what the people might do (11:18 and 14:1-2). Like Herod (v. 20), Pilate will have Jesus put to death even though he does not know what

crime Jesus has committed (15:14). Finally, like John's disciples (v. 29), a follower of Jesus will get his dead body and "lay it in a tomb" (15:46). Such clues show that Mark wants his readers to see the fate of their Lord in the fate of his forerunner John. Mark also wants his readers to be so much like John, preparing others for the experience of Jesus in their lives and in death, that people will confuse them with Jesus too. Herod thought that Jesus was John come back to life. Will others think that Jesus has come back to life when they witness the life of Mark's Christian community, then and now?

6:30-52 Crowds, breads, and the walk on the water. The short passage in 6:30-33 serves to "round off" the missioning of the Twelve (in 6:7-13). It also prepares Mark's readers for the rest of chapter 6, which features two closely related and marvelous manifestations of Jesus' identity as their Lord: first, as the one who feeds his people abundantly (with bread, 6:34-44); secondly, as the one who is with them in the most serious conflicts of their lives (on the raging sea, 6:45-52).

Although the apostles need time alone with Jesus (v. 31), he responds first to the greater need of the crowd that has found his place of refuge (v. 33). The first miracle of the breads (6:34-44) reveals for Mark and the early church that Jesus is as powerful and as loving as the God of Exodus 16, who provided manna for his wandering people in the desert. When Jesus pities them, "for they were like sheep without a shepherd" (v. 34), he becomes for Mark's readers the Good Shepherd of Ezekiel 34, tending his needy flock and teaching them at great length (v. 34). These allusions to the Old Testament remind Mark's readers of God's providence in the past. When, however, Mark has Jesus take the loaves, raise his eyes to heaven, pronounce a blessing, break the loaves, and give them to the disciples to distribute (v. 41), Mark's Christians become conscious of their present experience of the Lord in the Eucharist. The details of Jesus' *past* care for his hungry people are experienced in the *present* when his needy followers come to him for nourishment. Mark's readers share in the abundance of leftovers (v. 43)! God cares for God's people in Eucharist!

Immediately after the multiplication of the loaves, Mark presents a second scene in which

Jesus calms a wind-swept sea on behalf of his fearful disciples (6:45-52; recall 4:35-41). As the wind begins to toss the boat around, Jesus comes walking toward them on the water (v. 48; in 4:38 Jesus was in the boat with them, but he slept). Jesus' calming of the sea *and* the disciples (vv. 50-51) would be further signs for Mark and his readers that Jesus was their Lord of creation. Only God had such mastery over the sea (e.g., Gen 1:1-10). Only "I AM" had the power to divide the Red Sea for the Hebrew people (Exod 3:14 and 14:21). Even the strange phrase "He meant to pass by them" (v. 48) would point to Jesus' identity as Lord. (In Exod 33:22, God set Moses in the hollow of the rock and covered him with his hand until *he had passed by*. This was to protect Moses from seeing God's face, which meant death in Old Testament times.) Although Jesus intended to "pass by them," he reveals a new way of God's protecting the chosen people: he comes to be with those who are afraid. He assures them with his word: "IT IS I!"

The back-to-back miracles of the breads and the walk on the water would seem to be enough to convince anyone that God was once more among the people in the person of Jesus. However, when Mark says that the hearts of Jesus' disciples were hardened (v. 52), it seems that he is looking for something more from his readers. He hopes that they will question their own degree of intimacy with their risen Lord. In their own wind-tossed times, some forty years after Jesus' death and resurrection, would the reassuring words of Jesus ("Do not be afraid!") be enough for them? Or was the fear of the first disciples still present in the Christian community? Mark hopes that his readers will come to understand the meaning of *all* the events, including Jesus' humiliating death, as they understand more about the loaves. He hopes that their fears will be resolved when, at the Eucharist, they come to understand their own suffering in the light of Jesus' sacrifice for them and for all his people.

6:53-56 The touch that heals. Chapter 6 ends with the summary statement that "as many as touched the tassel on his cloak were healed" (v. 56). What a contrast! The crowds (of vv. 53-56) ran to Jesus wherever he put in an appearance. His disciples, however, the ones closest to him, "were completely as-

tounded . . . their hearts were hardened" (vv. 51-52). The enthusiastic crowds also stand in sharp contrast to the antagonistic Pharisees who gather around and against Jesus in chapter 7. This brief passage helps Mark's readers, who wish to be intimate disciples of Jesus, to focus their faith on the only one whose touch can heal them of the brokenness and lack of meaning in their lives.

7:1-23 Conflict over eating bread and serving God. After Mark has shown how successful Jesus' mission of healing among the crowds has been (6:53-56), he reminds his readers of the heavy cloud that hangs over his entire Gospel drama. He now reports the detailed and sharp conflict between Jesus and the Pharisees over the issue of what and how to eat properly. It was conflicts like this one (and those already recorded in 2:1-3:6) that would bring to completion the Pharisees' plot, how they might "put him to death" (3:6).

What Jesus teaches in this passage is as important for Mark's readers today as it was in A.D. 70. Jesus, presented here by Mark as the clever Jewish rabbi, turns the Pharisees' challenge about the manner in which his disciples prepared to eat bread (it is unlike their traditional rites of purification, vv. 2-5) into a wide-sweeping exposure of their "lip service" interpretation of God's law (quoting Isa 29:13 in vv. 6-7). He continues with a second example of their false piety, the *qorban* tradition, which would deny parents the care due them by their children (vv. 9-13). (Scholars are hard pressed to find such a lack of filial piety in Jewish rabbinic tradition, which indicates that this *qorban* tradition was probably some extreme and isolated circumstance of Jesus' or Mark's day.)

Finally, Mark's Jesus expresses the timeless principle that it is not what or how one eats that makes a person clean or unclean. It is what comes from inside the depths of the person that makes one pure or impure (v. 15). Then, as if Jesus' stance were not clear enough, Mark has Jesus explain his powerful one-liner to his disciples. External things, like the food one eats, do not make a person evil. It is one's actions, inspired from within, that show when a person is not living according to God's commands (see the list in vv. 17-23). Mark hopes that his readers will look to the various ways they are living in relationship with others to see if they are responding to

God "from within" (with their whole being) or merely with "lip service" (with superficial nods to tradition).

Why Mark presents this heavy conflict passage here is just as important as the message it contains. This conflict section interrupts a chain of six miracle stories (it comes after the feeding of the multitude, the walk on the water, and the healing of the crowds; it is followed by the healing of the Canaanite child, the cure of the deaf-mute, and the second feeding of the multitude). Mark seems to have at least two reasons for doing this. First, this heightens the tension of his drama, suggesting that anyone who chooses to follow Jesus as healer will be involved in many conflicts for the sake of the gospel, perhaps even with religious leaders and structures. Secondly, the conflict passage builds on his theme of the slow-witted disciples, because they need special tutoring again (here in v. 17), as they did earlier (in 4:10, 34). Thus Mark challenges Christian leaders within his audience to reevaluate the way they understand and pass on the Christian tradition entrusted to them.

7:24-37 Non-Jewish women and men are healed and spread the news. The two miracle stories that conclude chapter 7 are linked by the now familiar Markan theme of Jesus' desire for secrecy (see the comment on 1:32-34). Before healing the Syro-Phoenician's daughter, "he entered a house and wanted no one to know about it" (v. 24). After curing the deaf-mute, "he ordered them not to tell anyone" (v. 36). Of course, people *did* recognize him. They *did* spread the news of his healing power (vv. 24, 36-37). But even as Mark faithfully and readily records the marvels that Jesus performed, his secrecy theme does not allow his readers to forget that the true glory and identity of their Lord were only fully revealed in the death he underwent on their behalf.

The Syro-Phoenician woman who asked Jesus to heal her possessed daughter would seem to have had two counts against her from the start. Being a woman and a non-Jew, it is no wonder that she crouched at the feet of this male Jewish preacher, begging him for help (vv. 25-26)! The first-century readers of Mark's Gospel would not be overly surprised at Jesus' harsh-sounding refusal to give to Gentiles (the dogs) what rightfully belonged to the Jews (the children of the household).

They would be surprised, though, that Jesus would allow a Gentile woman to persist in her pleading and even play off his own words to get what she wanted: "Lord, even the dogs under the table eat the children's scraps!" (vv. 27-28). Her persistence forces Jesus to make an exception to the rule (i.e., take care of your own people first, then go to others, v. 27). He cures her possessed daughter by a word as a reward for her mother's staying power and faith in him (v. 29).

Mark's readers would hear in this passage several invitations to action: first, to imitate the persistence of the woman, even when things seem hopeless; second, to imitate Jesus' "breaking the rules" on behalf of an "outsider"; and third, to examine their openness to those of other faiths, especially the Jews, the first "sons and daughters of the household."

The story of the deaf-mute is like a gate swinging back and forth. It swings back to the story of the Syro-Phoenician woman, because the deaf-mute also comes from a non-Jewish part of Palestine (v. 31). It swings forward to the next chapter, to the story of the blind man (8:22-26), which closely parallels this cure. Both the deaf-mute and the blind man are brought to Jesus by others (v. 32; 8:22). Both times Jesus takes the men away from the crowd (v. 33; 8:23) and touches them, using spittle to heal them (vv. 33-35 and 8:23, 25).

These obvious parallels make it clear that Mark wants the two cures to be read side by side. In this way, Mark's readers will hardly be able to miss that Jesus is the Messiah promised by Isaiah long before when he said: "Then will the eyes of the blind be opened, the ears of the deaf be cleared" (Isa 35:5-6; see Mark 7:37). However, with the final parallel element in the two stories (Jesus' request for secrecy in 7:37 and 8:26), Mark asks his readers to remember another Isaian passage that Jesus has fulfilled by his life and life-giving death: "Who would believe what we have heard? . . . He was spurned and avoided by all, a man of suffering, accustomed to infirmity . . . . pierced for our offenses, crushed for our sins. Upon him was the chastisement that makes us whole, by his stripes we were healed" (Isa 53:1-5).

Jesus, for Mark, was the perfect fulfillment of all Isaiah's prophecies. He was the promised Messiah who healed the deaf, the mute, and the blind. He was also the innocent one who suffered on behalf of his people. For Mark and his readers, Jesus is the one who says: "Follow me on my way. Care for my people, until there are no longer any sick or hurting people on this earth. But know that in your healing service of others you will experience the same pain that I experienced in making you whole. Stay with me. I will provide the nourishment you need" (see 8:1-10, which follows).

8:1-10 Jesus feeds the crowd again. The second time that Mark's compassionate Jesus feeds the hungry crowds (8:1-9; recall 6:34-44) is another foreshadowing of the Eucharist (14:22-26), so important to Mark and to his community. Some readers think that this is the report of an actual second feeding incident (noting that there are many *differences* from the first feeding, e.g., the numbers of people and loaves, the different geographical locale, etc.). Others wonder if this might be a second written version of one and the same feeding event, pointing out the *similarities* in the two accounts, e.g., the pity Jesus feels, the similar words and gestures he uses, the same basic marvelous deed performed, etc. They also point to the disciples' question in 8:4 and believe that it makes no sense if the disciples have just seen Jesus feed five thousand people with five loaves in chapter 6.

Whatever the solution to this debate, it is fairly clear that Mark has included this second feeding account to make sure that the Gentile members of his community know they are welcomed to the Eucharist from the very beginning. (Notice that Jesus is still in Gentile territory at this point, 7:24, 31, and 8:10. Notice also the phrase in verse 3, "Some of them have come a great distance," i.e., "from afar," which is a well-known early Christian way of referring to Gentile converts.) Mark thus claims that Jesus is the giver of bread, ready to satisfy hungry followers of whatever background. He also suggests that the Christian Eucharist is the place for true Christian community to form, where people of diverse backgrounds become one in the Lord who gives bread to all in great abundance.

Was Mark's first audience in need of hearing that the Eucharist was meant to gather various segments of that community together? Are the readers of Mark's Gospel today in need of the same message, as people of the various Christian churches struggle to become

one again in worship as well as in mission? Perhaps Mark wants all his readers to hear Jesus say: "Today my heart is moved with pity *for you*. You hunger for unity. I want you to 'become one body, one spirit' in me" (Eucharistic Prayer III).

8:11-13 This age seeks a sign. This brief encounter with the Pharisees is little more than a transition passage. It links the second feeding (8:1-10) with the scene of Jesus in the boat with his disciples, asking them *eight* times to try to understand who he really is (8:14-21). Yet, this small transitional passage serves the purpose of heightening even more the severely strained relationship between Jesus and the Pharisees. It is wrought with emotion and tension. In Matthew's version (Matt 12:38-42), Jesus gives a clear, self-possessed answer to the Pharisees' demand for a sign: they shall be given the sign of "the prophet Jonah," signifying Jesus' three days in the tomb before his resurrection. Here in Mark's version, Jesus only "sighs from the depths of his spirit" (v. 12). He leaves them, without satisfying their desire for any words or actions concerning a "heavenly sign."

In this way, Mark portrays a Jesus who is so human, so much like his readers, that they could identify with him in his frustration with the religious leaders of his day, just as they have identified with him in his pity for the hungry crowd in the preceding passage. Mark's Jesus is one like them in all things. They will be like him in all things, even in frustrating conflicts with the unbelieving religious leaders of their day.

8:14-21 Jesus seeks recognition and understanding. In two previous episodes on the sea (4:35-41 and 6:45-52), Jesus has revealed himself as Lord over the sea, and in both cases his disciples' "hearts were hardened" (6:52). Once again on the lake with them, Jesus wants them to see who he is. This time he instructs them to keep their eyes open and not to be like the bad "leaven of the Pharisees and the leaven of Herod" (v. 15). (The latter saw Jesus as a popular wonder-worker who threatened their authority as religious and political leaders of the people.) Since the disciples "had forgotten to bring bread along," they missed Jesus' point about the leaven of the Pharisees (vv. 14 and 16). Consequently, with a barrage of eight questions, Jesus makes his followers realize that they misunderstand him as much as the Pharisees do (v. 17). They who were with him as he healed the deaf-mute (7:31-37) have ears but are not hearing (v. 18). They who were witnesses of his feeding the multitudes with bread (chs. 6 and 8) "still do not understand" that he alone is enough nourishment for them (v. 21).

When Jesus asks how much bread is left over (v. 20), it marks the seventeenth time that the breads have been mentioned in chapters 6 to 8 and the last time bread occurs until the Last Supper scene at 14:22. As the end of the "Bread and Blindness" section of his Gospel draws near, Mark hopes that his readers will examine their appreciation of the Christian community's celebration of the Eucharist. He also invites them to see, to hear, and to understand the many ways that their Lord (the "one loaf" of v. 14?) wants to be involved in their lives.

8:22-26 A blind man sees perfectly, gradually. By now, the fact that Jesus heals yet another person is nothing special to the readers of Mark's Gospel. However, to anyone following the developing threads of the Gospel drama to this point, this is a very special cure. That is because this is the first blind person to be healed. He is also healed "in stages," just before the passage in which Peter and the disciples begin to get a glimpse of the way Jesus must go (vv. 27-38). These special details lead Mark's readers to the realization that the blind man of chapter 8 is much more than an individual whom Jesus cured in A.D. 30. He is the symbol of the first disciples and of all disciples of Jesus, ever in need of his enlightening touch. Mark's readers have begun to see more clearly. Are they ready to go forward with Jesus on his way?

THE WAY OF JESUS BECOMES CLEARER

Mark 8:27-10:52

In the first eight chapters of his Gospel, Mark has portrayed the people around Jesus, both friend and foe, as people blind to the true meaning of his miraculous works (nineteen miraculous events conclude with 8:21: "Do you still not understand?"). What follows are two and a half tightly knit chapters, bound together by the blind-man story just concluded (8:22-26) and a second blind-man story that will end with the cured man following

Jesus "on the way" to Jerusalem, the goal of his journey and the end of his way (10:52 and 11:1). Between these two "book-end" blind-man passages, Mark has placed three clear predictions of Jesus' passion, each followed by his disciples' continued lack of comprehension.

As these chapters unfold, so unfolds Jesus' revelation of himself as the one who will rise from the dead (in each of the predictions and in 9:2-9). But of course the disciples do not understand this either (9:10)! Perhaps the most important thing to happen in these chapters is the way in which Mark turns the various miracle stories and dialogues into opportunities for explicit "teaching moments" about the meaning of the Christian life and its radical demands. Thus, the miracles in the first half of the Gospel are replaced by hard teachings in the second half.

If there is any general call that the readers of these chapters will hear, it will be the call to be as trusting as little children in the service of others. (The word-fields of "little child" and "servant" dominate these chapters as "the breads" and "blindness" dominated chapters 6-8). Perhaps by the account of the second blind man's cure (end of ch. 10), those who *hear* Jesus' message and teachings will finally *see* that the person they follow and the mission they share is radical but simple, tiring but transforming, impossible for them alone but not for God. His is a way of service and self-giving that gives life to others and preserves one's own.

8:27-9:1 Revelation of the way of the Messiah and his followers. As Mark's readers approach Caesarea Philippi with Jesus and his disciples (v. 27), they arrive at the first major climax of Mark's Gospel drama. (The second climax is the passion account, chs. 15-16). Until now, Mark has been revealing who Jesus is in the mighty deeds he has done. Along with this revelation, Mark has also reported Jesus' reluctance to have people believe in him only because of those wondrous deeds. (Recall the "secret" of 8:26; 7:36; 5:43, etc.) This Caesarea Philippi passage is the heart of the matter. Jesus now says explicitly that his way is a way of suffering. The way of the Messiah is the way of the cross.

Mark, Matthew, and Luke all record this important passage. However, whereas Peter's confession of faith gets rewarded with "the keys to the kingdom of heaven" in Matthew's Gospel (Matt 16:19), Mark only reports that Peter is told not to tell anyone that Jesus is the Messiah (v. 30). Mark knew what Peter meant by "Messiah," namely, "the powerful deliverer of God." Mark also knew that Jesus understood that title differently, i.e., that it signified that he was "the Son of Man, [who] must suffer greatly and be rejected . . . be killed, and rise after three days" (v. 31).

The account goes on to show that Peter and the disciples were not ready for this. They wanted a leader who would deliver them from pain, not one who would experience pain and death himself! Consequently, Peter rebukes Jesus (v. 32), angering Jesus to the point of sending Peter away as if he were the devil himself (v. 33). Indeed, when Mark shifts the focus of the scene from Peter to the crowd and the disciples (v. 34), his readers find out that they also must share the disciples' struggle with the hard, cold reality that Jesus is not the "instant cure-all" person they would like him to be. They can hear him speak directly to them, saying: "Whoever wishes to come after me, must deny himself, take up the cross, and follow in my steps!" (v. 34).

Even today's reader finds it hard to swallow the absolute and radical statements that follow: "For whoever wishes to save her/his life will lose it . . . ." (v. 35); "What could one give in exchange for one's life!" (v. 37). Yes, says Mark, all who call themselves followers of Jesus must lose their lives for Jesus' sake and the sake of the gospel (v. 35). Mark thus pushes his readers to the edge. Either they give themselves in total trust to the suffering Messiah they follow, or they open themselves up to the awful prospect of hearing an unfavorable judgment: "The Son of Man will be ashamed of them when he comes in his Father's glory with the holy angels" (v.38).

Although Mark's readers in A.D. 70 were not among those standing there in A.D. 30 (9:1), his urgent challenge was still theirs, because "the kingdom of God coming in power" could be upon them at any time. Likewise, although twentieth-century readers of Mark's Gospel might not share his expectations of an imminent return of Jesus in glory and judgment, the urgency of this whole section of his Gospel does provoke profound questions for individual Christians and for the whole church. If Mark's readers are to take his Jesus

seriously, how can they begin today to live the Christian life more radically? What are the times and circumstances in which they can be people of gospel values in the midst of their world today? Mark's Jesus will respond to these questions with some concrete means in chapters 9 and 10. For now, Mark allows his readers to sit back and respond to these questions before he takes them up a high mountain with Peter, James, and John (9:2-8).

9:2-13 Revelation of glory (and suffering). It almost seems that Mark knows his readers will be exhausted after the encounter at Caesarea Philippi, because he follows it six days later with one of the most refreshing and consoling events of his Gospel—the transfiguration. Jesus takes Peter, James, and John up the mountain with him, the same three whom he had brought with him when he restored the little girl to life (v. 2; recall 5:37-40). The three have a glimpse of Jesus in his dazzling glory (v. 3). When they see him conversing with Elijah and Moses, they are awe-struck at the realization that Jesus is the fulfillment of the prophets (Elijah) and of all the law (Moses).

Peter wants to capture the consoling moment and keep Jesus, Moses, and Elijah there with them (v. 5). However, Mark does not allow his readers to linger on the mountaintop any longer than Peter, James, and John do. Instead, God's voice from the cloud repeats what it had said earlier at Jesus' baptism: "This is my beloved Son" (1:11). Then the voice adds: "Listen to him!" (v. 7). Mark's readers do not have to think hard to remember what Jesus has spoken for them to hear (8:34-9:1). Their refreshing pause on the mountain is over. Glimpses of glory that Christians receive from God are real, but according to Mark, they are given so that Christians can move on with him, and with him alone (v. 8).

Any enlightenment that Peter, James, and John received on the mountain seems dulled as Mark reports the conversation they have with Jesus on the way down (vv. 9-13). Jesus knew, says Mark, that they would have difficulty accepting the fact that he would have to suffer and die before rising from the dead. Consequently, he tells them not to get themselves or others excited about the glory of the transfiguration event until after he has risen from the dead (v. 9). They ask about the role Elijah is to play in the restoration of God's people, to which Jesus responds with a question of his own about the suffering role of the Son of Man (v. 12). Then he answers their question, saying that Elijah has already come and fulfilled his role (1 Kgs 19:2-10; likewise, Mark's Jesus is referring to John the Baptizer as "Elijah, his forerunner"). Thus, as this section ends, Peter, James, and John, as well as Mark's readers, are left to respond to Jesus' unanswered question (v. 12): "Why does Scripture say of the Son of Man that he must suffer greatly and be treated with contempt?"

9:14-29 "I do believe! Help my unbelief!" The healing of the possessed boy is one of the longest miracle stories in Mark's Gospel (only the expulsion of the demons in 5:1-20 is longer). It is also one of the more detailed stories, becoming a bit complicated in the repetition of some of those details (e.g., in v. 22 the father of the boy tells Jesus what he has *already* told him in v. 18; the crowd gathers twice within the same story in vv. 15 and 25). Despite its length and detail, there is a very clear and simple message that Mark wishes to convey: Anything is possible to one who trusts (v. 23), and trust is deepened by prayer (v. 29)!

Although Jesus is the one who heals the boy (vv. 25-27), it is the father's profession of faith that Mark holds up for his readers to imitate. Even in the most desperate moments, when prayer and trust seem useless, Jesus invites his followers to go one step further and pray like the boy's father: "I do believe! Help my unbelief!" (v. 24). Perhaps the alert reader of the Gospel will hear the echoes of Jesus' message all along (e.g., "Do not be afraid; just have faith" in 5:36; "Please, Lord, even the dogs under the table eat the children's scraps" in 7:28), calling for a persistent and ever more radical trust in him. The same theme will carry over into the following passages, in which the total trust of little children becomes the model of what is needed to take part in the kingdom of God (9:35-37 and 10:13-16).

9:30-32 The second (of three) predictions of death and resurrection. Jesus' disciples were not able to expel the demon from the young boy (9:18) because of the lack of belief among the people (9:19) and because of their own lack of prayerfulness (9:29). Is it surprising, then, that the disciples will fail to understand the meaning of Jesus' second prediction of his death and resurrection (vv. 31-32)? Mark's note that "they were afraid to question him" about this prediction (v. 32) might help his readers to deal with the fact that the Twelve abandoned Jesus in his passion and death. It might also encourage his readers to pause, take stock of their own fears, and confidently express them in prayer with their Lord.

9:33-50 Some radical demands of discipleship. Each evangelist records those teachings of Jesus that meet the needs of his readers. Here we notice some concerns that Mark hopes his community will face: (1) ambition among themselves (vv. 33-37); (2) envy and intolerance of others (vv. 38-41); and (3) scandalizing others (vv. 42-48).

The first concern, the evil of ambition, is a major one for Mark as pastor of his community. (This becomes even clearer in chapter 10 when the third passion prediction is followed by another warning against ambition, 10:35-45). How ambitious Jesus' disciples are! They argue about who is the most important among them (9:33-34) instead of trying to understand the meaning of their leader's passion prediction (9:32)! The response of Jesus (and Mark) is direct and simple: to be "important" among Jesus' followers means to be a humble servant, not a proud "first" (v. 35). In verses 36-37 Mark's Jesus presents himself and the child as models of openness to others: "Whoever receives one child such as this in my name receives me." What a contrast this is to the disciples' interests (in v. 34)! How different from their closed attitudes toward others (in vv. 38-42)!

Mark's second concern, the pettiness of arrogance and envy, is exposed when John and other disciples try to exclude a "non-member" from doing ministry in the name of Jesus (v. 38). Jesus (and Mark) challenge the disciples to be tolerant and open to others of good will: Working in Jesus' name brings its reward to anyone who "is not against us!" (vv. 40-41).

A third concern, the danger of causing scandal to others (v. 42), is met by Jesus' (and Mark's) harsh, traditional imagery of the unquenchable fires of Gehenna (vv. 43-48). In order to avoid those fires, Jesus' followers must be extremely cautious of giving bad example to anyone. Indeed, it would be better to cut off an arm or leg and enter heaven maimed than to give scandal to others and be thrown into hell!

Mark concludes this demanding section of his Gospel with a confusing but powerful mixed metaphor. Jesus claims that his followers will be cleansed ("salted" by the fire of v. 49) so that they can be at peace within and with others (the useful, tasty salt of v. 50). He thus presents a highly seasoned mixture of challenges to his own disciples and readers in A.D. 70 and today. His readers must reflect upon the liveliness of their gospel spirit. They must also root out the evils of ambition, envy, and scandal wherever they exist in their midst.

10:1-12 The Pharisees ask about divorce; Jesus responds. Journeying south from Capernaum (see 9:33), Jesus finally comes to Judea (10:1), on his way up to Jerusalem (10:32). In Judea, Jesus continues to preach his demanding message (begun in 8:34-38 and 9:33-50). However, in chapter 10 there seems to be an intentional attempt on Mark's part to establish a certain pattern and rhythm that gradually build up to the climax of his Gospel. The Markan arrangement consists of three passages in which Jesus meets with individual characters (the Pharisees of v. 2; the young man of v. 17; and James and John in v. 35). Then Mark's Jesus uses the encounters to teach his Twelve privately (v. 10, v. 23, and v. 41). These three similar passages are rhythmically balanced by three interspersed "models" for the Christian disciple to imitate (the child of vv. 13-16; Jesus himself in vv. 32-34; and the blind man in vv. 46-52).

The first encounter of chapter 10 has to do with the ever important issue of the fidelity of spouses in the marriage relationship (vv. 1-12). The early church was careful to preserve Jesus' attitudes concerning significant matters of daily living. Here Mark passes on the earliest tradition of Jesus' attitude toward marriage and divorce (vv. 6-9). While other teachers allowed men to divorce their wives in certain circumstances, Jesus taught that it was not permissible "to separate what God has joined together," using Gen 1:27 and 2:24 as authority for his interpretation. In other words, the Jesus tradition made it clear that it was not permissible for a man to divorce his wife. After Jesus talks privately with the Twelve (v. 10), Mark passes on what had come to be the earliest adaptation of Jesus' words for the Christian community, namely, if a man or a woman should have to divorce his or her spouse, he or she could not remarry without being considered an adulterer (vv. 11-12).

In these few verses, today's readers of Mark's Gospel can see the early church's struggle with one of the most painful areas of concern in the contemporary church and society—the meaning of fidelity in marriage relationships. At the core of Mark's Gospel message is Jesus' challenge to spouses to live in faithful and perpetual union until death. At the same time, recognizing the hard reality of life, even this early Gospel seems to allow for the separation (without remarriage, however) of spouses who can no longer love one another as husband or wife. (Matthew's Gospel, at 19:9, adds another "exception clause," which shows how this vital issue was dealt with in Matthew's community.) Thus, there are some whom Mark's Jesus will challenge to continue to be faithful forever. There are others whom he will challenge to adapt, as the early church did, to the needs and feelings of those who no longer can live with their spouses.

10:13-16 The model of the child: total trust. Perhaps Jesus' teaching concerning fidelity in marriage inspired Mark to follow that passage (10:1-12) with the image of the child (vv. 13-16). Mark claims in these verses that only a childlike trust will enable his Christians to live up to Jesus' demands in the concrete day-to-day relationships they have, in the family and elsewhere. Once more the disciples seem to want to avoid hearing the truth. They scold the people for bringing children to Jesus (v. 13). In turn, Jesus' human compassion is aroused to passionate indignation with them. Only Mark records Jesus' anger with the disciples and his tender touching of the children (vv. 14 and 16).

When Jesus says that it is only to those who are as needy and receptive as children that the kingdom of God belongs (vv. 14-15), he invites his readers to delve more deeply into the realization of their own human helplessness. Only thus can the power of their God and Father live in them. The positive acceptance of one's own powerlessness and God's power draws Mark's readers very close to the experience of having the kingdom of God established in their hearts. As Jesus will say in the next section of the Gospel, "For human beings it is impossible but not for God. All things are possible for God" (10:27).

10:17-31 The rich man asks about everlasting life; Jesus looks at him with love. In Matthew's version of this encounter, Jesus tells the rich man: "If you wish to be perfect, go, sell what you have, and give to the poor" (Matt 19:21). In Mark's account there is no "if" clause. The one who wants to follow Mark's Jesus must give up all he or she has, give the proceeds to the poor, and then follow him (v. 21). What a demanding person Mark's Jesus is! Here is an eager, prospective disciple, who has kept all the commandments since his childhood (v. 20). He wants everlasting life (v. 17). Jesus looks on him with love, but then challenges him beyond his capacities (see v. 22: "He went away sad . . .").

Mark's Jesus turns to his disciples and makes it clear to them that having many possessions is an almost insurmountable deterrent to possession of the kingdom of God (vv. 23-25). This overwhelmed Jesus' disciples (v. 26) and probably overwhelmed Mark's first readers as thoroughly as it challenges his readers today. Mark calls for the trust of the child in its parents: "All things are possible for God" (v. 27; recall the model of the child in 10:13-16). However, that challenging response did not satisfy Peter, just as it probably did not satisfy Mark's Christians, who had already left so much to follow Jesus (v. 28). In verses 29-31, Mark assures his readers that anyone who is detached from everything and everyone, so that he or she can follow after Jesus, will receive a hundredfold of family members and possessions in this life, while inheriting everlasting life in the age to come. (Mark's readers will note that those who leave all for Jesus will also receive "persecutions," v. 30. Even when he assures his Christians of their reward, Mark's Jesus reminds them that they stand in the shadow of the cross.)

In the world of today, just as in the time of Jesus and Mark, security in possessions and in money can pull people away from depending on God as the true source of their life, here and hereafter. Like the man in the Gospel story, all of Mark's Christians are called to radical discipleship. To follow Jesus still means to go and sell what one has. To be for Jesus still means to be for the poor. The man in the Gospel story wanted everlasting life. The Christian way to everlasting life is to be poor. Jesus' way is to rely solely on God, for whom all things are possible!

10:32-34 The "Suffering Servant" predicts his fate for the third time. Mark records Jesus' third and final prediction of his death and resurrection, with some details that were missing in the previous two predictions: it would happen in Jerusalem; and the Gentiles would mock him, spit at him, and flog him before killing him (vv. 33-34). As the end of Jesus' way draws closer, the more explicitly he identifies himself with the suffering servant of Isaiah, who would heal his people by the very stripes, chastisement, and harsh treatment he would endure for their sakes (Isa 53:1-7).

The manner in which Mark sets the scene for this third prediction is significant: "They were on the way, going up to Jerusalem, and Jesus went ahead of them" (v. 32). Jesus knows where they are headed and what awaits him in Jerusalem. But the disciples follow, "amazed," and the crowd trails along in fear. By this time the reader must wonder what effect such predictions had on the first disciples, especially when two of the Twelve (James and John) show that they have completely misunderstood what he has said (see next passage, 10:35-45). Mark hopes that his unfolding Gospel drama will have a more lasting effect on his Christian readers. He hopes that they will consciously choose to model their lives on Jesus, the Suffering Servant, who walks ahead of them.

10:35-45 James and John ask about glory; Jesus gives them the cross. The request of James and John to sit at Jesus' right and left in glory makes up the next to last scene before Jesus arrives in Jerusalem, the place of his death. It seems almost impossible that these two disciples could ask such an ambitious and inappropriate question after Mark's Jesus has been describing his way of suffering so clearly, since 8:31! (Matthew casts James and John in a better light, having their mother pose the request, Matt 20:20.)

Jesus responds to their request with a challenging question of his own: "Can you drink the cup I shall drink or be baptized with the baptism with which I am baptized?" (v. 38). Since "the cup" and "baptism" language is symbolic for Mark of Jesus' agony and death to come, it is obvious that Jesus is challenging James and John to take very seriously what it means to follow him to glory. Then, in response to their eager "We can" of

v. 39, Jesus divides the issue: You shall share in my cup, in my baptism, in my death. But it is up to someone else, my Father, to give out the seats of glory! (v. 40).

Jesus thus concludes the dialogue in such a way that James and John get a profound (and unwanted?) answer to their ambitious request. The answer is not a simple "yes" or "no," but a challenge: "Perhaps the Father will reserve the seats for you, *if* you willingly take on my cross, my cup, my baptism." Who among Mark's readers in A.D. 70 or today is eager to go "all the way" with Jesus?

Verse 41 is the transition verse by which Mark draws his own Christian readers more explicitly into the dialogue. Today's reader of the incident might become indignant with James and John, as the other ten disciples did, and say, "How selfish they are!" However, Mark's Jesus calls *all* of his followers together and says: "It is not only in this one incident that Christians manifest selfish, unchristian attitudes. Whoever wants to follow the Son of Man must take an uncompromising stance against such non-gospel values as 'lording it over others'" (v. 42). To be a Christian is to be a servant, as Jesus was (v. 45). To be first and greatest is to serve the needs of all, as Jesus did (v. 44). That is the way to glory for a disciple of Mark's Jesus!

Because this scene features James and John, two of Jesus' most intimate disciples (remember that they were with him at the transfiguration, 9:2-9, and that they will be with him in the garden of his agony, 14:32-42), Mark's message here is especially relevant to anyone in a leadership position in the church. It is a "servant leadership" that Mark calls for. The church's leaders are meant to be the first to "drink the cup," daily serving the needs of their brothers and sisters, whatever those needs are, whenever they are perceived. If this call seems too radical and even impossible to fulfill, Mark next offers his readers the example of someone else—the blind beggar Bartimaeus of verses 46-52—who probably thought his situation was hopeless.

10:46-52 The model of the blind man: "I want to see!" The cure of blind Bartimaeus concludes this demanding section of Mark's Gospel drama, just as the cure of the other blind man (8:22-26) concluded the "Bread and Blindness" chapters (6–8). In contrast to the first blind man, who was brought to Jesus by others (8:22), Bartimaeus cries out on his own initiative: "Jesus, Son of David, have pity on me!" (v. 47). The title he gives Jesus, "Son of David," indicates that he, a *blind* beggar, actually *sees who Jesus is* more clearly than the disciples and crowd who have been with him all along! Although some people try to quiet the man (v. 48), his persistence wins out. Jesus has his disciples call him closer (v. 49). Bartimaeus responds with great enthusiasm and comes to Jesus. He becomes the one and only person in Mark's Gospel who calls Jesus "Master." (This particular way of addressing Jesus appears in the New Testament only here and at John 20:16, when Mary Magdalene meets the risen Jesus near the empty tomb.)

In the Gospel of Matthew, the parallel story has two blind men call for Jesus' help; and Jesus, moved with compassion, *touched their eyes* (Matt 20:33-34). Here in Mark's version of the incident, Jesus need not touch Bartimaeus. He does not even have to say "Your faith has saved you" (as Luke has it, in 18:42), because Bartimaeus' cry and actions reveal his deep faith. Jesus is his master! It is just such profound trust in Jesus that Mark wants to elicit from the Christian recipients of his Gospel.

When the blind man immediately received his sight and started to follow Jesus "on the way" (v. 52), Mark offers a smooth transition to the next section of the Gospel (i.e., the *end* of the road, Jerusalem and Calvary, chs. 11–15). More important, however, he offers his community the hope and encouraging example of this early disciple of Jesus (the phrase "to follow him on the way," was a familiar designation for discipleship in the early church). Consequently, after Mark presents the very difficult teachings of Jesus about the Christian attitude toward divorce, riches, and ambition (earlier in ch. 10), this miracle-discipleship story becomes Mark's rallying call to his Christian readers in their own situation, on their own way of the cross: "You have nothing to fear from him! Get up! He is calling you!"

ON TO JERUSALEM

Mark 11:1–13:37

This major section of Mark's Gospel begins with Jesus' entry into Jerusalem

(11:1-11) and ends with his long discourse about the Jerusalem temple and the "days of tribulation" (13:1-37). Throughout these three chapters, Mark's readers will find themselves involved with Jesus in a series of foreboding incidents that build up to his betrayal, passion, and death in Jerusalem (chs. 14–15). Almost all of the scenes in chapters 11 to 13 are conflict-ridden, showing Jesus in confrontation with the religious leaders of Jerusalem over the issues of prayer and piety (11:12-25 and 12:28-44); life after death (12:18-27); tribute due to Caesar (12:13-17); and Jesus' authority in all such matters (11:27-33). This series of conflict stories will remind Mark's readers of earlier conflicts (2:1–3:6), which ended with the Pharisees' plotting with the Herodians how they might destroy Jesus (3:6). This time the plotting leads to his arrest and death (14:43-52 and 15:21-26).

By his choice of the various scenes for these three critical chapters, Mark leaves no doubt in his readers' minds about what the basis of their Christian discipleship is: they are to put their trust in God (11:22), and they must put that trust into action by loving their neighbor as themselves (12:31). Their models will be two: (1) the sincere scribe of 12:28-34 and (2) the poor widow, whose generous trust in God urged her to give "from her poverty, all she had, her whole livelihood" (12:44).

11:1-11 Jesus' entry into Jerusalem. Mark's account of Jesus' triumphal entry into Jerusalem functions much as the transfiguration event did earlier (9:2-8). It is another exhilarating moment on the otherwise long and arduous "way" of Jesus to his saving passion and death. Because Jerusalem was the holy city of God, and because the details of Jesus' arrival there (vv. 7-10) point to the coming of Israel's Prophet-Savior (e.g., "See, your king shall come . . . riding on an ass, on a colt, the foal of an ass," Zech 9:9), Mark's first readers would not be able to miss the obvious connection: *Jesus was the longed-for Savior of Israel!* They could join the crowds and shout: "Hosanna! The reign of God and of our father David has begun with Jesus' coming!"

However, because Jerusalem was also the city of Jesus' death, Mark is quick to play down the enthusiasm surrounding Jesus' entry. (This nuance in Mark's Gospel becomes evident when his account is compared with Matthew's version, which has "the very large crowd spread their cloaks on the road," Matt 21:8, and "the whole city was shaken" at his entry, Matt 21:10.) Consequently, the way Mark presents this episode allows his readers to rejoice in the risen Lord's kingship over them while not allowing them to forget the cost of being his disciples, namely, that they must deny their very selves, take up their cross, and follow in his steps (8:34).

The exhilarating moment of the entry into Jerusalem has come and gone. After a night's rest at Bethany with the Twelve, Jesus returns to the city for the final days and the final act of the Gospel drama (11:11-12).

11:12-25 The cursed fig tree and the cleansing of the temple. At first reading, the story of Jesus and the fig tree (vv. 12-14 and 20-21) is one of the strangest in the Gospels. It is uncharacteristic enough of Jesus to curse a fig tree for not having fruit on it. But when Mark includes the detail that "it was not the time for figs" (v. 13), Jesus appears even more unreasonable, and the incident becomes more difficult to understand.

Two keys are needed to unlock the meaning of this strange passage. First, Mark's readers may recall that the fig tree was a common Old Testament image for Israel (e.g., Hos 9:10). Therefore, Jesus' cursing of the tree would symbolically stand for his anger with the Jewish people. But why does Mark's Jesus curse Israel at this point of the Gospel drama? (Remember that the people have just welcomed him triumphantly into Jerusalem!) A second key to understanding this passage is its immediate context, which reveals an angry Jesus driving the buyers and sellers from the sacred temple area. They have turned what was meant to be "a house of prayer for all peoples" into a "den of thieves" (v. 17, quoting Isa 56:7). Consequently, Mark's readers can see why he wove the fig-tree passage together with the cleansing of the temple. The withered fig tree (v. 21) is meant to symbolize the fruitless side of Jewish temple piety in Jesus' time.

This passage might well challenge Mark's Christian readers to evaluate the depth of their own faith. In contrast to the superficial ceremony of the old temple, Mark hopes that they will have the type of profound trust in God that can move mountains (vv. 22-23). In verses 23-24, Mark's Jesus uses very bold, even exaggerated, language to say that by faith and prayer his people will be able to do what seems impossible, as well as receive *whatever* they ask for in prayer. (Remember the similarly strong "image with a point" in 10:25: "It is easier for a camel to pass through the eye of a needle than for one who is rich to enter the kingdom of God.")

Jesus and the early church believed in the infinite power of prayer. It seems that the only thing Mark's readers cannot hope to receive in prayer is an escape from their share in the suffering way of the Lord. For example: "Amen, I say to you, there is no one who has given up house or brothers or sisters or mother or father or children or lands for my sake and for the sake of the gospel who will not receive a hundred times more now in this present age: houses and brothers and sisters and mothers and children and lands, *with persecutions*, and eternal life in the age to come (10:29ff.).

Mark concludes his description of Jesus' type of true piety by saying that anyone who prays with forgiveness for those who have offended them shall be forgiven in turn by the Father in heaven (v. 25). Although Mark does not relate the Our Father in his Gospel, as Matthew and Luke do, this little section brings out the attitudes of radical trust and forgiveness that are expected of children in their lives and in their prayer.

11:27-33 The lines of authority are drawn: conflict! The chief priests and scribes, who were looking for a way to destroy Jesus after he had cleansed the temple (11:18), question him "by what authority" he teaches and acts as he does (v. 28). This is not a simple question put by one teacher to another. It is a most serious challenge, the first in the final series of challenges that Jesus will face from the religious leaders of his day (11:27–12:44).

Mark's readers will notice how each conflict ends with a victorious Jesus silencing his opponents, the experts in Jewish law and scriptures. Here, for example, in verses 29-33, Jesus takes their question about his authority and turns it into his own clever question about the authority of John the Baptizer (v. 30). Since the scribes feared what others, friends or foes of John, might think of their response (vv. 31-32), they are forced to admit: "We do not know" (v. 33). What began as a threat to Jesus' authority ends as an example of how little authority (and courage) his antagonists

had! Mark wants his readers to take pride in the confounding wisdom of their teacher, Jesus. He also might be cleverly questioning his readers as to how they use the authority they possess in the church or how courageously they challenge the way others use the authority vested in them.

12:1-12 The parable of the vineyard: the rejected stone (son) is the cornerstone. For the first time since chapter 4, Mark has Jesus "speak to them in parables" (v. 1), namely, in the parable of the vineyard and the evil tenants (vv. 3-8). This is the last parable Mark records, and what a perfect last parable it is! By it, Mark anticipates the final act of his whole Gospel drama, since the rejection of the owner's son (v. 8) looks to the crucifixion of Jesus, and the reaction of the owner (vv. 9-11) points to the resurrection, when God vindicates Jesus' death.

Mark's Christian readers would understand the various elements and the deeper message of this parable as clearly as the scribes and chief priests to whom it was addressed ("They realized that he had addressed the parable to them," v. 12). The care of the vineyard (the people of Israel) had been entrusted by God to the leaders of the Jewish people (the "tenant farmers"). They treated the son (Jesus) as ruthlessly (vv. 6-8) as they had treated the Old Testament prophets before him (vv. 2-5). Because they did so, they no longer have any authority with God's new people. Rather, that authority now rests with the leaders of the early church (v. 9).

Mark conveys the same message when he has Jesus quote Psalm 118. Only the key image changes, namely, the "son" becomes the cornerstone (vv. 10-11). As Mark prepares his readers for their encounter with Jesus' death, he makes it clear where the blame for the Son's death lay—with the Jewish leaders. He also challenges Christian leaders to examine the relationship they have with Christ, "the cornerstone." For them, this parable is food for serious thought about how they are caring for the church entrusted into their hands by the risen Lord.

12:13-27 Of tribute due to Caesar and to the living God. Mark moves from his last parable to two more of Jesus' conflict encounters with Jewish leadership. The first concerns the tax due to the emperor (vv. 13-17), and the second has to do with belief in resurrection and life after death (vv. 18-27). Mark's readers will discern a similar pattern in both encounters. First, the leaders approach Jesus with trick questions, obviously trying to "ensnare him in his speech" (v. 13). The Pharisees and Herodians ask if a good Jew should pay taxes to the Roman emperor or if that is against the law of Moses (v. 14). Then the Sadducees, who were known for not believing in the resurrection, ask a legalistic and cynical question about marriage relationships in the risen life (v. 23).

In response to their questions, Jesus shows a cunning wisdom that unveils their intent to trip him up. He exposes their hypocrisy in one case (v. 15) and shows their shallow understanding of their own Scriptures in the other (v. 24). Good Jews (and good Christians in Mark's audience) are expected to pay "tax tribute" to lawful civil leaders and "praise and true allegiance tribute" to God (vv. 15-17). Jews (and Christians) who really understand their sacred Scriptures should also know that "the God of Abraham, the God of Isaac, the God of Jacob" (and of the risen Jesus) is "not God of the dead but of the living" (vv. 24-27).

The cumulative result of these two encounters is that Mark's readers, like those first involved with Jesus, might be "amazed" at Jesus' wisdom (v. 17) and at his dedication to his Father, the God of life. But Mark wants more than amazement—he wants his Christians to imitate their Lord by being courageous apostles of truth and life themselves. How they are to be such apostles is up to them in their own circumstances. However, the following passage will give them a concrete model to follow.

12:28-34 The scribe who was close to the reign of God. After all the scheming and malicious questioning from the elders and scribes, for Jesus to claim that a scribe is "not far from the kingdom of God" (v. 34) is quite remarkable. Yet, upon examining this dialogue over which is the "first of all the commandments" (v. 28), Mark's readers can readily approve of the scribe's sincerity and honest attempt to understand the underlying basis of Jesus' way. Jesus responds to his question with the traditional *Shema* prayer, which every Israelite prays twice daily: "Hear, O Israel! The Lord our God is Lord alone!" (v. 29). Since the Lord is one, Jesus and the *Shema* continue, one's whole being (heart, soul, mind, and strength)

should love God (v. 30). Jesus then adds a second command: "You shall love your neighbor as yourself." In effect, he makes the first of all the commandments into one dual commandment ("There is no greater commandment than *these*," v. 31).

The scribe appreciates Jesus' response. He sees how Jesus has combined two commands given to Israel by Moses (Deut 6:2 and Lev 19:18). He also hears in Jesus' response more than Jesus has said! He hears in it the echo of the prophet who declared that love, not sacrifice, is what God desires of all people (v. 33, quoting Hos 6:6).

Mark's readers know how correct the scribe was, because they knew that Jesus practiced what he taught. He had loved God and his neighbor unto death. His sacrifice was love! As they leave the crowds, who no longer "dared to ask him any more questions" (v. 34), Mark's readers might well ask themselves how their love of God is verified by their love of neighbor. They might ask how their sacrifice and liturgical worship of God are made manifest in their sacrifices for others. Mark's report of this encounter thus challenges his Christians to be like Jesus and also like this singular scribe, who had such insight into the ways of the kingdom. It also prepares them for the last two episodes of chapter 12, which will contrast the generous piety of the widow with the empty prayer of certain scribes (12:38-44).

12:35-37 Jesus is David's Lord and God's Son. Up to this point in chapter 12, the scribes have been asking Jesus challenging questions. He now asks them one: "How do [you] claim that the Messiah is the son of David" (v. 35), when David himself (in Ps 110:1) refers to the Messiah as "my Lord" (v. 36)? Mark's readers know that Jesus is their Messiah. They also know that he was of Davidic descent. However, Mark wants his readers to acknowledge even more, namely, that Jesus is the Son of God. Some people put Jesus to death because he claimed to be "the Son of the Blessed One" (14:61-64). How will Mark's readers renew their commitment to their Lord, who is also David's Lord and God's Son?

12:38-44 The poor widow shows the scribes the meaning of religion. The last time Mark presents Jesus in the temple is one of the most dramatic moments of his whole Gospel. Jesus first warns people to beware of the scribes, who pray long and loud in order to be seen and respected as "the holy ones" (vv. 38-39). At the same time, because they "devour the houses of widows" (v. 40), they show how empty their prayer is. (They also disobey a special commandment given to their ancestors by Moses: "You shall not wrong any widow or orphan or stranger," Exod 22:21.)

To this story of hypocrisy Mark has added the touching picture-example of the poor widow (vv. 41-44). Look at her, says Mark's Jesus. She puts much less money in the box than the wealthy ones (v. 41), but she, from her poverty, has contributed all she had, her whole livelihood" (v. 44). Her offering is a sign of what total dependence on God really means. The widow thus becomes a model of faith for Mark's readers. If they imitate her generous and trusting faith, they will also be imitating Jesus, who likewise gave up his very life for the many (chs. 14-15)!

13:1-4 The end of the temple and the end of "all these things." As Jesus and the disciples leave the temple area, Mark has Jesus predict that "there will not be one stone [of these great buildings] left upon another" (v. 2). They respond to Jesus' remarkable statement with an important related question: "Tell us, when will this happen? And what sign will there be when all these things [i.e., the world as we know it] are about to come to an end?" Mark's readers today might not see how the disciples' question about the end of the world follows logically from Jesus' prediction about the end of the temple. They will understand the connection, however, if two significant facts are made clear: (1) the early church saw the destruction of Jerusalem as a pre-eminent sign of the soon-to-come end of the world; and (2) the early Christians for whom Mark was writing had *already* witnessed that destruction of Jerusalem (in A.D. 70 by the Roman army). Such historical background will help today's readers of Mark's Gospel understand this important chapter.

It is also helpful for Mark's readers to realize the special type of literature they will be involved with for the rest of chapter 13. All of Jesus' talk about "the end" and the signs that will accompany it belongs to the type of first-century writing known as "apocalyptic." In the early church, apocalyptic writing was used to communicate hope to fearful people by revealing how God would definitively save

his faithful ones from any and all evil forces at the end of time. Apocalyptic literature made up a small (in content) but very significant (in meaning) part of Christianity's first gospel message. (Such writing was rather common in certain Old Testament communities, which were longing for the coming of their Messiah to deliver them from foreign, pagan rulers. See, for example, the Book of Daniel, chapters 7–12, written about 150 B.C., which describes the coming of the Son of Man in terms very similar to those found here in Mark's Gospel. See also New Testament writings like Matt 24–25, Luke 21, 1 Thess 4–5, and the Book of Revelation, which reflect the early church's keen consciousness of the Lord's absence and its expectations of his imminent return in glory.) It is in chapter 13 that Mark passes on to his community the early church's hopeful preoccupation with Jesus' return. It is here that Mark describes the attitudes to be adopted by his readers in the time between Jesus' resurrection and that return.

13:5-23 Christian alertness and endurance in "the end times." Mark begins Jesus' apocalyptic speech with a section (vv. 5-23) that exemplifies very well two ways in which apocalyptic language is meant to move its readers to response and action. First, the catch phrase that begins and ends this section ("See that no one deceives you" at v. 5, and "Be watchful" at v. 23) signals his readers to be very alert to their response to certain misleading preachers in their midst ("who come in my name," v. 6, and "false messiahs and prophets," v. 22) who say the end is already here because of certain signs (for example, wars, v. 7; earthquakes, v. 8; persecution, vv. 9-13). The proper Christian response, says Mark, is not to panic (v. 7) but to persevere. Mark encourages his readers to view their perseverance in times of tension as a positive sign of God's protecting Holy Spirit with them until the end (vv. 9 and 11). Even more important, Mark demands that his readers be alert to means of spreading the good news about Jesus "to all nations" (v. 10), because only when that missionary effort is concluded can the end really come.

A second characteristic of apocalyptic speech is that some events that have already begun to happen (in the past and present) are cast as a part of the future scheme of things. This mode of writing was meant to assure the readers of the reliability of those parts of the message that really do pertain to the future. For example, Mark's readers can say, "Yes, some families already have broken up and have been divided because some of their members chose to follow Jesus" (vv. 12-13). They can also say, "Yes, 'the desolating abomination' of Roman idols already stands in Jerusalem, where the holy temple once stood" (v. 14). At the same time, what is most important is that they realize that the Lord *will* protect his faithful ones when the end really comes, even shortening the days of distress for the sake of those he has chosen (v. 20). In fact, reports Mark, the most reliable sign of the end of time is yet to come, namely, the glorious return of the Son of Man (to be described in vv. 24-27).

By being in touch with the nature of apocalyptic writing, the readers of chapter 13 can experience the urgency of the early church's waiting and watching for the return of their absent Lord (vv. 15-19). They can also hear Mark's invitation to put aside useless and fearful calculation of deadlines regarding the end of the world, in order to live courageously in the present as discerning and alert missionaries of Jesus' gospel.

13:24-27 The consoling coming of the Son of Man. While apocalyptic writing is recognized by its scary and dark imagery of trials, tribulations, and turmoil in the heavens (vv. 24-25), there is also the consoling light at the heart of it all, which overcomes the darkness. Here that consolation takes the form of the glorious Son of Man, Jesus, coming on the clouds to gather his chosen and faithful ones from all over the earth (vv. 26-27). Mark borrows this encouraging picture of God's deliverance from the promises of the Old Testament prophet Daniel (Dan 7:13-14). Mark's readers today, as well as his first readers, might well be lifted up by this promise of God's final victory over whatever difficulties or darkness envelop them and their world. Encouraged by this hopeful vision, they can accept more readily their responsibilities to be a consoling light for those who may not yet have experienced the hopeful side of the gospel promises.

13:28-37 "We do not know when, but it is near, so persevere!" Just as surely as Jesus' other predictions have come to pass (his death and resurrection, the fall of Jerusalem,

the trials his followers would endure), so also will he come again in glory to save his chosen ones. This encouraging message of 13:3-27 concludes with the final call of Jesus to his faithful followers: "The end is near and will happen soon. You will see the signs of the end (vv. 29-31) just as clearly as you see the coming of summer by the new leaves on the fig tree (vv. 28-29)." *"But,"* underlines Mark's Jesus, "since no one knows the day or the hour when the end will come, be watchful and be alert (vv. 32-33). Look around you like the gatekeeper (v. 35). Do not be found sleeping (v. 36), but 'watch!'" (v. 37).

The apocalyptic chapter 13 ends with Mark's sharp challenge for all his readers (not only for Peter, James, John, and Andrew of v. 3). He asks them to persevere in their faith, even in dark days of suffering on behalf of the gospel. It should be clear to Mark's readers that it is their duty to be alert missionaries of that gospel in the present, since the Son of Man entrusted it into their hands until his return in glory.

THE SON OF MAN WILL BE PUT TO DEATH AND WILL RISE THREE DAYS LATER

Mark 14:1-16:8

The very familiar account of the death and resurrection of Jesus is the climax of Mark's involving drama. Everything has been leading to these three chapters, and Mark tells the passion story in such a way that many of the key themes of his Gospel are now drawn together. For example, *the disciples* still fail to have any clear sight or faithful confidence in the Lord they follow. Indeed, they all scatter in the garden when one of them betrays Jesus to his killers with a kiss (14:43-52). Likewise, the alert reader will see how the important images of *bread* and *cup* (developed through chs. 6-8 and 10) come together in the Eucharistic passage that precedes Jesus' agony in the garden (14:22-26). A third developing theme of the earlier chapters, namely, Jesus' identification of himself as the *suffering Son of Man*, finds its climax at the foot of the cross, when the Roman centurion declares at Jesus' death: "Truly this man was the Son of God!" (15:39).

By now, Mark's readers expect some of the developments that occur in these closing chapters. Yet, Mark's passion account also surprises his readers with a very abrupt ending (16:8). When the women leave the tomb and say nothing to anyone because they were afraid (16:8), Mark's readers are left to complete the story with their own careful reflection and response. Why did Mark end the Gospel in this strange way? When did the women overcome their trembling and bewilderment and carry out the mission given to them by the young man at the tomb (16:7)? What about the readers' own hesitation to be courageous proclaimers of Jesus' message? While Mark's readers know that most of Jesus' predictions have come true, two are left unfulfilled. First, did Jesus ever appear to the disciples in Galilee, as he had promised (14:28)? (The reader knows that he did, but *not* from Mark's account.) Second, will Jesus keep his promise to return "in the clouds with great power and glory . . . and gather his elect . . . from the end of the earth to the end of the sky," as he had promised (13:26-27)? This certainly has not happened yet!

The ending of Mark's Gospel is, therefore, more like the beginning of something else. It is as if Mark is saying that the Gospel is not over yet. In fact, Mark's ending leaves his readers with the startling realization that they have to conclude the Gospel by living out its values. What seemingly began as Mark's account of the *past* life of "Jesus Christ, the Son of God" (1:1) ends with the dramatic invitation that all his readers be faithful imitators of Jesus, the servant Son of Man (10:45), *in the present*, until he comes again to establish the reign of God in power (8:38 and 9:1)!

14:1-11 The preparations for Jesus' death and burial. The first verses of the passion narrative set the scene and the emotional tone for all that is to follow. While the chief priests are afraid to arrest Jesus because "there may be a riot among the people" (v. 2), one of the Twelve makes it easy for them by arranging to hand him over, thereby changing their fear into jubilant anticipation (vv. 10-11). In the midst of the plotting and planning for Jesus' death, Mark places the story of the woman at Bethany (vv. 3-9), whose bold act of reverence for Jesus "will be told in her memory wherever the good news is proclaimed throughout the world."

Typically, those with Jesus do not understand what is going on around them. They fail to see that the woman's act of anointing is the anticipation of Jesus' burial (v. 8). Their intentions are good (the money could be given to the poor, v. 5), but their infuriation with the woman (vv. 4-5) shows that they missed the point of her symbolic action. It should have reminded them of the reality of Jesus' suffering way! Mark does not want *his* readers to miss the point. To care for the poor is a key part of following Jesus (recall the challenge to the rich man in 10:21). But Jesus' followers must also choose *all* that is involved in being his disciples, even to the extent of giving their lives in service of the needs of all, in imitation of the suffering Son of Man (10:44-45).

14:12-26 Jesus makes his own preparations: the Passover Eucharist. Jesus' triumphal entry into Jerusalem (11:8-11) had been preceded by his remarkable prediction that the disciples would find a "colt on which no one has ever sat" (11:2-7). A similarly remarkable prediction precedes the Passover supper that Jesus will celebrate with his disciples (see 14:12-16). Such amazing circumstances prepare Mark's readers for a very special part of the Jesus story.

The Passover meal of the Hebrews celebrated their deliverance from Egypt. ("The Lord will go by, striking down the Egyptians. Seeing the *blood* . . . on the doorposts, the Lord will *pass over* that door and not let the destroyer come into your houses to strike you down," Exod 12:23). As Jesus' Passover meal with his disciples begins, an unnamed (for now) and pitiable disciple is symbolically singled out as the one who will bring about Jesus' betrayal and, ironically, the new deliverance of God's people (vv. 17-21).

Such dramatic preparation leads to Mark's account of the first Eucharistic meal (vv. 22-25), which was as central to his Christian community's life then as it is today. Certainly Mark was faithful in passing on the early church's tradition that the Christian Eucharist is the *new Passover*. Jesus' saving death and resurrection was God's new and perfect way of delivering all people. Mark's Christians shared in the new covenant of Christ's body and blood when they shared the Eucharistic bread and cup! At the same time, Mark uses the occasion of the first Eucharist to round off a special theme he has been developing in regard to the disciples' blindness. (*Bread* has not been mentioned since chapters 6–8, where the disciples did not see the deeper meaning of Jesus' miracles, especially with "the breads"; *the cup* has not been mentioned since 10:35-45, when Jesus made clear its intimate connection with his death.) Consequently, Mark is telling his readers that those who wish to share in Jesus' Eucharistic cup (now and at the heavenly banquet, v. 25) must first choose to share fully in Jesus' way of suffering service (10:45a: "The Son of Man did not come to be served but to serve"). They must participate actively in Jesus' mission on earth, which involves pouring out their lives "for *many*" (v. 24), always in imitation of him (10:45b: "The Son of Man has come . . . to give his life as ransom *for many*").

14:27-31 "The sheep will be dispersed." After Jesus and his disciples arrive at the Mount of Olives (vv. 26-27), he makes three more predictions: (1) the sheep (his disciples) will be scattered at his death (v. 27); (2) once risen, Jesus will go to Galilee before them (v. 28); and (3) Peter will deny him three times "before the cock crows twice" (v. 30). Despite the protests of Peter and the others, Mark's readers know that two of these predictions will shortly (and sadly) be fulfilled. The disciples will all desert Jesus and flee (v. 50), and Peter will deny him (vv. 66-72). However, the prediction about seeing him in Galilee will be left unfulfilled, even when Mark's Gospel ends (16:8). Mark challenges his readers to ponder the meaning of this unfulfilled prediction as they enter the garden with Jesus, Peter, James, and John (v. 32).

14:32-42 The garden experience: model of radical trust. Mark's account of Jesus' agony in the garden is actually two moving scenes in one. In the first (vv. 33-36), Mark's readers are privileged to witness Jesus' profound humanity, as he is overwhelmed by fear and sadness at the prospect of his imminent death (i.e., the cup of v. 36). They also recognize in his final acceptance of his Father's will the ultimate act of his loving humanity, i.e., his choice to give up his life for the Father and for all people.

The second scene (vv. 37-42) focuses the readers' attention on the disciples who fall asleep as Jesus struggles in prayer. Mark hopes that his readers will face life and choose to be human like Jesus, not like the disciples. The profundity of Jesus' choice to take the cup can

be grasped, ironically, only by certain readers of Mark's Gospel—that is, only those who have come as close to despair as Jesus did in the garden can really identify with him. Mark hopes that Jesus will be for them a realistic (truly human) model of trust and love in their painful "hour" (v. 41) of Christian and human life!

14:43-52 It all starts to fall into place: the betrayal and arrest. Once Jesus has made the decision to give himself up to his Father's will (v. 36), the other pieces of the passion account quickly fall into place. Immediately after Jesus is betrayed by the kiss of Judas (vv. 44-45), he is arrested and led off as if he were a common robber (v. 48). Mark makes it clear, in verse 49, that the arrest of the innocent Jesus, like the rest of his passion experience, is in accord with Old Testament prophecies about the way the Messiah of Israel would be treated by his own people.

Three other details in the passage bring out how oblivious Jesus' companions are to what is really happening. One of them thinks he can stop violence with violence (v. 47). All the rest leave him alone (v. 50). And even the young man who does follow, "wearing nothing but a linen cloth," runs away as soon as Jesus' enemies try to seize him (vv. 51-52). These details of Mark's passion account serve not only to recall for his readers "the way it all happened" but also to stimulate them to ask themselves how far they would go in staying with Jesus and his gospel values in their own difficult life situations.

14:53-65 The trial and the verdict and the sentence: Death! The so-called trial of Jesus is full of false and trumped-up charges against him. In response to such testimony, Jesus "was silent and answered nothing" (v. 61). The high priest's verdict of guilty (v. 64) comes only when the "silent one" does acknowledge that he is "the Messiah, the Son of the Blessed One," who will sit with God ("the Power") in the heavens, and who will "come with the clouds of heaven" as judge in the last days (v. 62). It is ironic that none of the *false* testimony can disprove Jesus' innocence (v. 55). It is only when he speaks *the truth* about himself that he is condemned to death (v. 62)! Certainly Mark's readers would be proud of their Lord's perseverance in the face of this humiliating trial and the mocking taunts and spittle that accompany it (v. 65). But will they be any more faithful to him than Peter was (see the next passage) when their faith is severely tested?

14:66-72 Peter denies Jesus three times. As Jesus had predicted (14:27), all his disciples deserted him in the garden and fled (14:50). As he had predicted (14:30), even Peter denies him, not once but three times (vv. 66-72). Peter's tears (v. 72) indicate his remorse, however, and his sorrow could be encouraging to any of Mark's readers who may at times have been unfaithful followers of Jesus. For they know that the one who denied his Lord three times would go on to experience the mercy of a forgiving God and become the early church's greatest apostle among the Jews (Gal 2:8) after the resurrection. Through the tears of Peter, Mark offers a great deal of hope to any of his Christian readers who lack courage and trust. It is never too late for them to say with contrite hearts: "Yes, *I am with* the Nazarene, Jesus!"

15:1-15 The chief priests and Pilate hand over "the king of the Jews." It is clear from the start of this passage (15:1: "As soon as morning came") how anxious the Jewish priests are to get the cooperation of the Roman official, Pilate, in putting Jesus away. Earlier the high priest had asked Jesus, in Jewish terms, if he was "the Messiah, the Son of the Blessed One." The Roman now asks, in terms that have political meaning for him, if Jesus is "the king of the Jews" (15:2). Jesus accepts the title given him by Pilate (15:3), which is the equivalent of saying "guilty" to the charge of high treason. (There is no king in Roman territory but Caesar!) Even so, Pilate sees through the charges made against Jesus (15:10: "He knew, of course, that it was out of envy that the chief priests had handed him over"). He tries to release Jesus instead of Barabbas, but the priests influence the crowd to ask for Barabbas (v. 11). Pilate ends up "wishing to satisfy the crowd," which calls for Jesus' death: "Crucify him!" (vv. 11-15). In so doing, Pilate plays out his cowardly role in the Gospel drama. Though convinced of Jesus' innocence, he still yields to pressure and hands him over to be scourged and crucified. And Jesus begins to drink deeply from "the cup."

15:20-32 The climax: they mocked and crucified him. Once again, after the intrigue of "the trials" that shows how innocent Jesus

really is, the horrible events of the passion quickly unfold. After Jesus is scourged (v. 15), he is dressed "in purple" and "crowned" with thorns by the Roman soldiers, who mockingly call him "King of the Jews" (vv. 16-20). Through all the spitting and the beating he receives, Jesus remains silent. Mark's readers would certainly recognize in this the fulfillment of the Isaian prophecy concerning the Messiah: "I gave my back to those who beat me. . . . My face I did not shield from buffets and spitting" (Isa 50:6).

The climax of the Markan drama comes in Jesus' crucifixion. The readers of Mark's Gospel will notice that some familiar details are missing as they read Mark's account of the way of the cross. For example, the lamenting women of Jerusalem (Luke 23:27-31) do not meet him on the way. Likewise, *both* of the men who are crucified with Jesus join the passers-by in taunting Jesus (vv. 27-32), unlike what is recorded by Luke in the memorable exchange between Jesus and the "good thief" (Luke 23:40-43). Consequently, Mark's readers are left with the starkest of pictures. Their Lord hangs alone on the cross, exposed to the mockery of the people he came to save.

One of the last cries of mockery (v. 32: "Let the Messiah, 'the King of Israel,' come down now from the cross that we may see and believe") becomes for Mark a profound challenge to his readers' faith. Will they believe in Jesus precisely because he did *not* come down from the cross? Will they be able to see meaning in their own inexplicable suffering in the light of the absurd suffering of their Messiah and King? Will they be able to see the positive, saving value of their suffering as St. Paul did: "In my flesh I am filling up what is lacking in the afflictions of Christ on behalf of his body, the church" (Col 1:24)?

15:33-41 In his death Jesus is seen as the Son of God. Mark's readers have now come with Jesus to *the* moment that all his life has prepared for. Along with Jesus' "blind" disciples, they have walked with Jesus as he has shared life and healing power with others (chs. 1-8). They have learned what is necessary to be enlightened and true Christian disciples (chs. 9-13). All that is needed now is for them to stay with him to the end!

It is in the dark hour of Jesus' death (v. 33) that Mark's readers see the light. It is there, at the foot of the cross, that they hear their

Lord's cry, "My God, my God, why have you forsaken me?" (v. 34). Mark does not want his Christians to mistake Jesus' cry for what it is not (as did the bystanders, who thought it was simply a desperate appeal for Elijah's help, vv. 35-36). Rather, he wants them to recognize in Jesus' last words and death the ultimate act of self-giving and trust. Like the Psalmist who first uttered this cry (Ps 22:2), Mark's Jesus believes that God will hear him (Ps 22:25) and will give him life, precisely because he suffered and died out of love and obedience! Who would ever believe that life could come from death? Yet Mark wants his readers to believe that this *is* true, not only for Jesus but also for anyone who will follow in his steps. Who would expect a Gentile centurion to be the first to declare that Jesus is "the Son of God"? Yet Mark asks his readers to see the *living* Son of God most clearly in his humble and loving *death*, just as the pagan centurion did.

15:42-47 Jesus is buried by Joseph of Arimathea. Near the end of Jesus' ministry in Jerusalem, he had met with a scribe who was "not far from the kingdom of God" (12:28-34). For Mark's readers, that scribe's sincere response to Jesus was more authentic than the response of Jesus' own disciples. Once again, in the burial scene, it is not Jesus' disciples who respond properly, but Joseph of Arimathea, "a distinguished member of the council" (15:43). He was bold enough to take reverent care of Jesus' burial (vv. 43-46). Thus, even as he relates the account of Jesus' burial, Mark prods his readers to have more faith than Jesus' first disciples. Pilate's inquiry as to whether Jesus was already dead (v. 44) also becomes an important detail for Mark. Such insistence on finality prepares Mark's readers for the most striking reversal of the entire Gospel, namely, the proclamation of the young man at the tomb: "Do not be amazed! You seek Jesus of Nazareth, the crucified. He *has been raised;* he is not here. Behold the place where they laid him" (16:6).

16:1-8 The end is the beginning! Go now and tell that he is risen! "They said nothing to anyone, for they were afraid" (16:8). This is how the women respond to the wonderful news of Jesus' resurrection. This is also how Mark ends his Gospel. (It is generally agreed that verses 9-20 were added to Mark's Gospel later by those who could not believe that

Mark would end it as he did!) By ending it this way, Mark actually invites his readers to step in and take the place of the women at the empty tomb. The women failed to carry out the mission orders they received from God's messenger (the young man "clothed in a white robe," v. 5). Mark wants his disciples, men and women, to spread the good news that God has brought life from death by raising Jesus from the dead (vv. 6-7). He wants them to do so without the fear, bewilderment, or trembling of the three women at the tomb (v. 8).

Mark's readers might well ask how they could be any better as disciples than the women and men who were with Jesus during his life, at his death, and at the empty tomb. Mark would probably answer this way: "It is for you that this Gospel has been written! Persevere as faithful followers of the Jesus I have presented to you. His resurrection is not the end! He has gone ahead of you as the servant Messiah. Now you must care for the needs of those most in need, until he comes again. He has given meaning to suffering and has brought life from death. Trust in him and give his life to those who have no hope. Whatever you do, let others know by your courageous words and your lives of service that you have heard the Lord's call and that you have chosen to follow his lead until you see him, as he has promised."

THE THREE "OTHER ENDINGS" OF THE GOSPEL

16:9-20 +

Although virtually all of today's scholars of the Bible believe that Mark had a purpose in ending his Gospel abruptly at 16:8, this was not always the case. Some first- or second-century Christians tried to "complete" his Gospel drama by adding scenes that they thought Mark should have added himself.

The first extra ending, the so-called *Longer Ending* (vv. 9-20), includes appearances of the risen Jesus to Mary Magdalene and to the disciples. These visions were meant to inspire the early missionary church to "go into the whole world and proclaim the gospel to every creature" (v. 15). The church's missionaries had nothing to fear, because the ascended Lord

(v. 19) was with them in their preaching (v. 20) and would confirm their message with special signs of his protection and power (vv. 17-18). Alert readers will notice some themes in these verses that are unlike anything they have seen before in Mark's Gospel. They may also recognize in them echoes of familiar scenes from the other Gospels, gathered together to round off Mark's abrupt ending (for example, Mary Magdalene meets with Jesus alone in John's Gospel, 20:11-18; the appearance to the two disciples is reminiscent of Luke's Emmaus appearance, 24:13-35; and the commission to "go into the whole world to preach" sounds like the ending of Matthew's Gospel, 28:16-20).

The so-called *Shorter Ending*, when read immediately after 16:8, was another attempt of the early church to end Mark's Gospel more smoothly. It reverses the fear and silence of the women at the tomb and shows how the message of the resurrection came to be proclaimed through "Peter's companions."

The *Freer Ending*, preserved in the Freer Gallery in Washington, D.C., is a fifth-century addition to the Longer Ending. Appearing between verses 14 and 15, it excuses the disbelief and stubbornness of the disciples found at 16:14.

Although the church has recognized these "added endings" as worthy of inclusion in the inspired text, none of them is as inspiring and involving as Mark's own. Mark's abrupt ending leaves it up to his readers to "complete" his Gospel in their lives.

LUKE

Jerome Kodell, O.S.B.

INTRODUCTION

The Gospel of Luke is the first half of a two-part work that tells the story of the origins of Christianity from the infancy of Jesus until the arrival of Paul, the foremost preacher, in Rome around A.D. 60. Just the length of the Gospel and of its companion volume, the Acts of the Apostles (more extensive than the contribution of any other individual New Testament writer), would have made its author a prominent influence on Christian theology and spirituality. But he is in addition a gifted writer, organizing his materials creatively and telling his story with clarity and artistic coloring. Dante called Luke the "scribe of Christ's gentleness" because of his emphasis on Jesus' mercy to sinners and outcasts. Some of the most memorable Gospel stories of divine mercy are found only in Luke (the widow of Naim, the prodigal son, Zacchaeus).

The author and his audience

At the beginning of his Gospel, Luke recognizes the work of those who have gone before. He is not trying to replace the earlier Gospel of Mark, but he sees the need for a new account for a new generation in different circumstances. Luke is a Greek-speaking Christian, possibly a convert of Paul, writing in Antioch (Syria) or Asia Minor (modern Turkey) late in the first century—probably in the eighties. The Christian church is quickly becoming more Gentile than Jewish in composition; it is no longer confined to Palestine but is a configuration of communities scattered throughout the Roman Empire. Its language is not Aramaic but Greek. Luke wants to show the continuity of this modern Greek church with Jesus and the early Hebrew community. He finds that he can trace these roots best by adding a sequel to the story of Jesus, connecting the two parts thematically while preserving the historical distinctions. He uses the Gospel of Mark, editing it according to his own needs, and other written and oral sources besides, some from traditions used also by the evangelist Matthew.

To Luke's readership, the geography, language, and religious and political conditions of Palestine were foreign and remote. Most were unfamiliar with the Jewish writings that the preachers often referred to in explaining the story of Jesus. The Christians of Asia Minor and Europe were concerned to be good citizens of the Roman Empire, a government that had been treated as an intruder by many of Jesus' contemporaries in Palestine. Many of the new generation of Christians were not poor but well-to-do, more urban than rural. The question arose, either spontaneously or with help from their pagan neighbors: Why are we Greeks following a religion with so much of a Hebrew core? How did the news about Jesus get here? Were our missionaries reliable? Are we by now independent of happenings in Jerusalem?

These Christian citizens of the Roman Empire would have heard, of course, of the destruction of Jerusalem by the Roman army, a catastrophe foretold by Jesus and interpreted as punishment for sin. Did this indicate that they should cut their Jewish roots? How could Jesus' words to a Hebrew audience a half century earlier be appropriate to a modern Greek audience? All this would have been heightened by their neighbors' pervasive hostility to Christianity and by subtle persecution in many forms, particularly social and economic.

Issues like these swirled about Luke as he conceived his two-part work. He addressed these and more, directly and indirectly. He wanted his readers to know that they had been included in God's plan of salvation from the beginning, even though historically the Jews were the first to hear the message as the channel for all others. The story of salvation unraveled according to the exact plan of God, just as was promised in the Old Testament. It is a journey to the kingdom under the guidance of the Holy Spirit. The Gospel portrays the beginnings of the Christian story, from the first announcement of the fulfillment of salvation until its achievement in the death and resurrection of Jesus. The Acts of the Apostles tells of the rise and development of the church, pointing out the major decisions and turning points as the leaders were guided by God into the Gentile mission. Once the church's decision to evangelize all people, not only Jews, is made definitively (Acts 15), the story follows the apostle Paul as he carries the gospel across the Empire, into Europe and eventually to the center of the contemporary world, Rome.

Themes

Every preacher of the gospel delivers the fundamental proclamation of salvation in Jesus Christ. But each one develops the insights into the mystery that come from personal reflection and experience and that are needed by a particular audience. There are four written Gospels; there might have been many more. They tell us the same basic story about Jesus and interpret its meaning. Their approach to the subject is like that of four painters assigned to produce portraits of the same person. Each evangelist brings to the task a personal relationship to Jesus, individual talents, a particular experience of Christian life in a certain place or places, a wealth of material learned in the community or researched in other ways. Some of Luke's prominent themes are the following.

1. Salvation for all. The realization that God wants to save all people goes back to the earliest times in Israel's life as a people (Gen 13:2). All the communities of the earth would find blessing through the Hebrews. The early Jewish Christians knew this well, but they had to struggle with the question: Does God mean to open up salvation in Jesus to everyone directly, or should we bring converts in through Judaism? The decision had already been made in favor of universal salvation by the time any of the Gospels were written, so this theme is present beginning with the earliest, the Gospel of Mark. But reflection on this truth proceeded in various directions. Luke seems to have the most thoroughgoing message of universal salvation. Matthew's Gospel, for example, has the mandate to preach to all nations (Matt 28:19), but Jewish rejection of Jesus still smolders (Matt 27:25). Luke is not affected by this kind of anguish, and he stresses that Jesus is still available for Jews who turn to him (Acts 3:17-20).

2. Mercy and forgiveness. This theme has already been pointed out as distinctive of Luke's portrait of Jesus. In this Gospel, Jesus is constantly concerned to help the poor, the sinner, the outcast. Shepherds instead of Magi come to his crib (2:8-18); he welcomes the sinful but penitent woman at a Pharisee's meal (7:36-50); he speaks well of Samaritans (10:30-37); he seeks hospitality from a tax collector (19:1-10). The place of women in Luke's Gospel is also noteworthy in this regard. Women were second-class, often mistreated citizens of the world at that time. Jesus befriended women (10:38-42) and accepted their help (8:1-3); they did not weaken in faithfulness at the time of his passion and death (23:49; 24:1; Acts 1:14).

3. Joy. Luke's Gospel radiates the joy of salvation. The joy flows from a confidence in God's love and mercy as demonstrated in the teaching and action of Jesus described in the previous section. The births of John the Baptist and Jesus are announced as causes of great joy (1:14; 2:10). The repentance of a sinner is a source of great joy in heaven (15:7-10). The Gospel ends with the disciples returning to Jerusalem full of joy after Jesus' ascension (24:52).

4. The journey. All three synoptic Gospels (Matthew, Mark, Luke) begin the account of Jesus' public ministry with John's preaching from Isaiah: "Make ready the way of the Lord, clear him a straight path" (Isa 40:3). The mission of Jesus is presented as the continuation and culmination of the "way of the Lord" that began when Abraham left his homeland, and continued with the Exodus from Egypt led by Moses and, later, the return from the Babylonian captivity. Luke capitalizes on the journey theme to organize the central section of his Gospel (9:51–19:44) around the final journey of Jesus from Galilee to Jerusalem.

The Father's guidance of Jesus and the church brings to the fore emphases on the role of the Holy Spirit and the place of prayer. Luke is occasionally referred to as the "Evangelist of the Holy Spirit" or the "Evangelist of Prayer." The role of the Spirit begins before Jesus' birth (1:35, 67). Jesus is led by the Spirit into the desert (4:1) and on returning announces that he is the one foretold on whom the Spirit rests (4:18). This theme continues even more strongly in the Acts of the Apostles as the Spirit empowers the disciples to preach the gospel (Acts 2:1-17). The Spirit guides the emerging church in deciding how to expand the mission (15:28) and leads the missionaries on their journeys (16:6-7). Prayer is the context for the opening announcement of salvation (Luke 1:10). Jesus prays before choosing the Twelve (6:12); he is praying as he is about to be transfigured (9:29) and when the disciples ask him to teach them to pray (11:1). Prayer characterizes the community in Acts (Acts 1:24; 2:42; 3:1).

5. Modern Christian living. Luke is determined to make the teaching of Jesus applicable to his readers living a middle-class life in a cosmopolitan society. He indicates that good citizenship is compatible (and expected) with Christianity. This is more evident in Acts than in Luke's Gospel. Paul's Roman citizenship is carefully noted (Acts 16:37-40; 22:26), and his honorable civic conduct is insisted on (18:14-16). But already in the Gospel, Jesus is presented as an observant citizen maligned by false charges (Luke 20:25; 23:2). His death was at the hands of the Roman magistrate, true, but one who was too weak to free Jesus as he was convinced he should (23:1-25). If these good citizens were persecuted—the implication might further be—don't be alarmed at your own mistreatment in the cause of Christ.

The question of possessions is treated often. In Luke, Jesus' beatitudes are harsh and stark: "Blest are you poor . . . . Woe to you rich" (6:20, 24), but overall there is no simplistic message of personal despoilment. The point is rather that one must not be enslaved by attachment to possessions (12:13-43; 14:25-33); they must be expended on others (18:22). Renunciation extends even to one's personal relationships. Not even one's own family must come between the disciple and Jesus (14:26).

6. Fulfillment of prophecy. Jesus' mission of salvation had been prepared from ages past. Luke incorporates a surprising amount of Old Testament teaching for his Greek readers, though not as much as Matthew does. One of Luke's favorite usages is "it must happen"—"it had to happen" (2:49; 4:43; 9:22). The cross, the way of suffering, was a puzzle to his Greek readers—how revolting that the Savior, Son of God and King, should be treated so shamefully. Luke repeats again and again that the suffering had to be: it is the way to glory (18:31-33; 24:26).

7. Ascension. Luke sees the goal of Jesus' mission as "to be taken (up) from this world" (9:51; 24:51). The ascension comes in the event of the resurrection; it is the act of glorification whereby Jesus takes his place at the right hand of the Father. The ascension is crucial to Jesus' saving work, because it is through this glorification that the Spirit is released on the church (Acts 2:33) and salvation is made available for all people.

OUTLINE OF THE GOSPEL

COMMENTARY

PREFACE

Luke 1:1-4

Luke's preface is like a memo clipped to a book manuscript, describing the book's contents and explaining why it has been written. The book in this case is not only his Gospel but also the companion volume, the Acts of the Apostles. Acts has its own preface as well, also addressed to Theophilus (presumably a prominent Christian convert), describing its connection with the Gospel (Acts 1:1-3).

While introducing his book and giving his reasons for writing, Luke also tells us a fair amount about himself and the readers he is trying to reach. He admits that he is not one of the original eyewitnesses of the deeds and words of Jesus; he is a "second-generation" Christian like his readers. The classical Greek style of his preface indicates that he is an educated convert writing for others like himself scattered throughout the Roman Empire. The gospel story has already had wide circulation through traveling preachers and through the teaching of established Christian communities; it has even been circulated in written form by this time. Only one product from these "many" earlier gospel-writers, however, has come down to us in complete form—the Gospel of Mark, which Luke uses as a source.

Since the story of Jesus is already familiar to Luke's audience, what is to be gained in going over the same territory? Does this writer have a better interpretation, more information, new stories? Luke does not try to lure his readers with flashy promises; his whole emphasis is on establishing the reliability of the information they have already received. He has made his own painstaking investigation into the gospel and intends to set it out in an orderly fashion so that any doubts may be laid to rest. Skepticism had naturally arisen concerning the authenticity of a Jewish religion in a Greek world, and as the years went on, the far-flung Christian communities had tended to become disconnected from their Palestinian origins. Luke wants to help his non-Jewish brothers and sisters in the Lord to trace their roots back to the historical Jesus (Gospel) and to follow the growth of Christianity as the early church spread from Jerusalem to Asia Minor to Rome (Acts).

PART I: BEGINNINGS

Luke 1:5–2:52

Luke's account of the conception, birth, and infancy of Jesus is one of his finest creations. There was nothing in Mark's Gospel to guide him. Matthew has an infancy narrative, but there is every indication that Luke and Matthew had no knowledge of each other's work. Rather, they composed their accounts separately at a time when the church was reflecting back beyond Jesus' public ministry to his earthly beginnings.

The traditional preaching outline began with Jesus' baptism (as is evident in the sermons of Peter and Paul in Acts, and in the structure of Mark's Gospel). The infancy stories were added to the front of that outline to serve as a prologue to the main narrative. A prologue announces the themes to be pursued in the body of the work. Both Luke and Matthew proclaim the good news in advance in a kind of mini-gospel based on the birth and infancy of Jesus. If Luke's infancy narrative had been lost before his Gospel began to circulate, we wouldn't know it had existed, because there are no clear references back to these chapters in the later account of the public ministry. But the reverse is not true—there are many references forward to the later developments. What we know about the infant Jesus comes from the teaching of the adult Jesus and the early church's reflection on his life, death, and resurrection. Who is this child? He is Messiah and Lord (Acts 2:36). What does his coming mean? He will save his people from their sins (Luke 24:47). A reader's understanding of the prologue depends on his or her understanding of the rest of the book. It means much more when read a second or third time after the entire book has been read. The infancy narrative grows in meaning the more the life, death, and resurrection of Jesus resound in the faith of the reader.

Both Luke and Matthew stress the fulfillment of Old Testament promises in the story of Jesus' beginnings. Matthew does this by explicit "formula quotation" (Matt 1:22-23; 2:15, 17-18), but Luke prefers to indicate the fulfillment through hints and allusions. Luke also puts his stamp on the material by subtle structural organization, especially by paralleling the origins of John and Jesus. Both births are announced by the angel Gabriel and come as a resounding surprise to all, including their parents. They are circumcised on the eighth day according to Jewish law, but their names are assigned by the angel. A parent interprets each child's coming in a canticle. In comparing the two boys, however, Luke carefully demonstrates Jesus' superiority. Luke's craftsmanship is also noticeable in the construction of the annunciation scenes, which are based on a standard birth-announcement pattern from the Old Testament (Isaac: Gen 17; Samson: Judg 13):

1. An angel appears (or the Lord himself).
2. There is apprehension and fear.
3. The angel reassures the recipient, then announces the birth.
4. An objection is raised.
5. The angel gives a sign.

1:5-25 Announcement of John's birth. Luke begins his story of Jesus and the Christian church with the introduction of the parents of John the Baptist. We should notice the very Jewish beginning of this Gospel for the Greeks. Zechariah and Elizabeth come out of the heart of Judaism. They are both of a priestly tribe, blameless in their observance of the Mosaic law. Further, Luke subtly relates them to the ancient Hebrew parents Abraham and Sarah, who were also advanced in years and childless, but able to believe in a divine surprise (Gen 17:1-20).

The scene is set in the temple in Jerusalem, where the hopes of the people of God were always centered. Luke's Gospel will likewise end in the temple (24:53). The angel allays Zechariah's fear and announces the promise: "Your wife Elizabeth will bear you a son." He is described as an ascetic Nazirite (Num 6:1-21) and compared to Elijah the prophet. Zechariah's objection is answered with his loss of speech. Perhaps the harshness of this sign is due to the fact that he asked for proof and not simply for information, as Mary did (1:34).

By the time Zechariah returns home, there is an aura of expectancy among the people. Dramatic events of salvation are underway. The conception of John takes place as foretold, unknown to the world at large. At this point, it is still only an elderly Jewish couple who know that God has begun another important intervention, the most important of all, in the history of their people.

1:26-38 Announcement of Jesus' birth. If continuity with Hebrew history and hopes was stressed in the announcement of John's birth, the radical newness of God's saving action is the focus of the announcement of the birth of Jesus. The scene shifts from Judea, center of Jewish life and worship, to Galilee, a province scorned as a secondary outpost in Judaism. This location for the momentous proclamation is only a minor surprise compared with the announcement itself. This child will not only be "great in the sight of [the] Lord" like John (1:15); he will be called "Son of the Most High." John's birth was made possible by natural means through the healing of sterility; Jesus will be born of a virgin. John will be filled with the Holy Spirit while in the womb; Jesus is conceived by the power of the Spirit. John will be a prophet; Jesus will be the final and eternal King of Israel.

Mary is mystified by the angel's greeting. How is she the highly favored one, blessed among women? It is not because of something she has done, but because of God's choice of her for a special role in his salvation. She responds with the classic words: "I am the handmaid of the Lord." Mary is the model Christian disciple from the beginning. Her physical motherhood was a unique grace, but her motherhood on the spiritual plane is one shared by all who make the same faithful response she did (8:21). The larger implications of Mary's response to the angel were summarized succinctly at Vatican Council II: "At the message of the angel, the Virgin Mary received the word of God in her heart and in her body, and gave life to the world" (*Constitution on the Church*, 53).

1:39-56 Visit to Elizabeth. Zechariah had been promised that his son would be filled with the Holy Spirit (1:15). Once Jesus is conceived by the power of the Holy Spirit, the Spirit can become active in others. John receives the Spirit in the presence of Jesus; the Spirit fills Elizabeth, and later Zechariah and Simeon. This foreshadows the future glorification of Jesus, which will release the Spirit on all (Acts 2:33). Elizabeth's question, "And how does this happen to me, that the mother of my Lord should come to me?" recalls the words of King David when the ark of the covenant was being brought back to Jerusalem after having been captured by the Philistines: "How can the ark of the Lord come to me?" (2 Sam 6:9). The ark symbolized the presence of Yahweh, the God of Israel. Mary's visit to Elizabeth sanctifies her home with the presence of the Lord.

Mary's canticle, traditionally called the *Magnificat* because of its first word in Latin translation, is a mosaic of Old Testament quotations and allusions interpreting the coming of Jesus. The hymn is strongly influenced by the canticle sung by Hannah, the mother of Samuel the prophet, after the birth of her son through divine intervention (1 Sam 2:1-10). Both canticles see these actions of God as part of a longstanding process of overthrowing proud human expectations and exalting the lowly. Mary's word for it is "mercy."

1:57-80 The birth of John. John's father, mute till now, regains his power of speech as soon as the name designated by the angel is confirmed. The people are filled with fear— not terror, but awesome reverence in the face of God's wonderful deeds. They are not simply shocked but show their awareness of deeper meaning in the events.

Zechariah's canticle (the *Benedictus*), like that of Mary, weaves traditional Hebrew quotations and themes into a hymn of praise. His hymn is described as a "prophecy" under the inspiration of the Holy Spirit. Prophecy in this fundamental biblical sense does not mean primarily a foretelling of the future, as in modern parlance, but a divinely enlightened proclamation of the meaning of events. Zechariah sees in the birth of his son God's remembrance of his covenant promises to David (2 Sam 7:8-16) and the definitive salvation for all the people. In the first part of the canticle, the salvation hoped for sounds roughly like the overthrow of national enemies (a concept of Messiah that would plague Jesus during his ministry), but in later verses salvation is understood more profoundly as freedom from sin (see Acts 2:38).

Luke's way of ending this story of John's birth is a good indication of his technique in keeping the reader's attention on one episode at a time, even though several events are interlocked. Verse 80 has John growing up from infancy to manhood and taking his place in the desert even before Jesus' birth is described. He is stationed there for his next appearance in the story thirty years later (3:1-3).

2:1-7 The birth of Jesus. The scene shifts again, now from the lonely Judean wilderness and from small villages in the hills of Galilee and Judea to the vast arena of the Roman Empire. The mysterious events recounted in chapter 1, still hidden and local, will have significance for the whole world. Emperor Augustus orders that a census be taken. Joseph and Mary, law-abiding citizens, make the journey to Joseph's ancestral city.

The census under Quirinius has caused much debate. Quirinius did not become governor in Syria until A.D. 6; shortly afterward he conducted the census in Judea that provoked the rebellion of Judas the Galilean (Acts 5:37). If Jesus' birth is situated during the reign of Herod the Great (Luke 1:5), it cannot have taken place during this census several years later. Among the various solutions proposed, the most satisfactory views Luke as associating a number of loosely related historical events around the time of Jesus' birth in order to fix its context in the minds of his readers, without intending ironclad accuracy. The precise dating of these remote Judean events cannot have been too important to Greeks of the Empire seventy or eighty years later. But the realization that Palestine was part of the Syrian province at the time of Jesus' birth might bring those events closer to Luke's readers in Antioch, the center of the church's missionary thrust in his time.

Mary gives birth to her "first-born son." This does not mean, as the Fathers of the church commented from earliest times, that she had other children later. "First-born son" is a legal designation for the one who has special privileges and position under the Mosaic law (Deut 21:15-17). Christian faith understands Jesus to be the "first-born of many brothers" in a spiritual sense (Rom 8:29). The swaddling clothes and the manger illustrate the poverty and humility of Jesus' birth, but the wrappings are also a subtle reminder of his royalty. Hidden here is a parallel with the birth of King Solomon: "In swaddling clothes and with constant care I was nurtured. For no king has any different origin or birth" (Wis 7:4-5).

2:8-20 The shepherds hear the good news. The humble King's birth is proclaimed first to the lowly. The shepherds were generally poor and to some extent outcasts, considered by the "respectable" to be ignorant, dirty, and lawless. Like the hated tax collectors, these outcasts are ready for the gospel. The appearance of God's messenger lights up the sky (Deut 33:2); there is fear and reassurance as at the annunciation to Mary. It is through these lowly ones that the message of salvation comes to the whole people of Israel. The titles "Messiah" and "Lord" will be the theme of the early preaching (Acts 2:36); though mentioned here in the prologue, these titles cannot be fully understood until the resurrection and the outpouring of the Spirit.

The angels announce peace as a gift of God's favor. Augustus was revered for having established peace in the Empire in 29 B.C.E. after a century of civil strife. But the Pax Romana is an exterior calm enforced by military power. True peace will come through Jesus (John 14:27). The shepherds go "in haste" to Bethlehem, eager (as Mary was: Luke 1:39) to respond to the news of salvation. Their telling of the events provokes the astonishment that will later accompany the work of Jesus and the early gospel preachers (5:26; 8:56; Acts 8:13). Sometimes this surprise and wonder lead nowhere, but those who listen to the shepherds respond by glorifying and praising God, while Mary, the ideal recipient of God's word and the model (after Jesus) of Christian prayer (8:21; 11:27-28), reflects on God's words and deeds in her heart.

2:21-40 Jesus comes to the temple. Jesus' parents obeyed imperial law at the time of his birth; now they are portrayed as observant Jews, fulfilling the prescriptions of the religious law concerning circumcision and the presentation of the first-born to the Lord. The scene at the temple is slightly confused because Luke has entwined two separate ceremonies. The Book of Exodus required the presentation and redemption of the first-born son because the first-born sons "belong" to the Lord who saved them when the Egyptian first-born were destroyed at the Passover (Exod 13:15). Leviticus described the ceremony for the ritual purification of the mother forty days after giving birth (Lev 12:1-8). On this occasion she was to offer a lamb and a pigeon or a turtledove, but a poor couple was permitted to bring only two pigeons or doves.

The emphasis is less on the purification of Mary than on the presentation of Jesus in the temple, where he will receive a more official recognition as the promised Savior of Israel. The temple symbolizes for Luke the continuity between Judaism and Christianity. The first announcement of the definitive act of salvation takes place in the temple (1:11), Jesus teaches in the temple (19:47), and the disciples continue to worship in the temple well into the new age (24:53; Acts 3:1).

Simeon and Anna are faithful, humble Israelites waiting in the temple for the revelation of God's salvation. Just and pious (see 1:6), they are open to the Holy Spirit's inspiration. Simeon recognizes Jesus as the Anointed of the Lord and in his *Nunc Dimittis* (2:29-32) further prophesies that Jesus will be a "light for revelation to the Gentiles." In blessing the parents, he warns that this child will be a sign opposed and that Mary will be pierced with a sword. With these two utterances of Simeon, we are given a foreshadowing of the universal salvation that will be proclaimed in Jesus and of the necessity of suffering in the mission of this Messiah. The shadow of the cross falls across the Holy Family. The later followers of Jesus are not to be surprised that suffering is encountered in their pursuit of a gospel life. Even families and friendships will be broken up as "the thoughts of many hearts" are laid bare, because the peace Jesus brings will not be a counterfeit covering secret divisions (12:51-53).

2:41-52 Jesus in his Father's house. Verse 40 sounds like a conclusion setting the stage for Jesus' adult career. The story of Jesus' origins seems to be complete with the family's return to their hometown after his birth and the fulfillment of the law's prescriptions. But a unique story has been added. It serves to illustrate the wisdom and grace with which this boy is said to be endowed and makes even more evident his special mission and destiny. Like many childhood stories of famous people, this one is recalled because it shows glimmers in Jesus' boyhood of the qualities that will emerge in a superior way in his manhood.

Jesus and his parents journey to Jerusalem for the feast of Passover. The next time Luke portrays Jesus on his way to Jerusalem it will be for the Passover again; it will be his final trip to Jerusalem, and the Jewish feast will coincide with his own Passover. Jesus is also "lost" then for three days before he reappears as the victorious risen Lord.

At his presentation, Jesus was unable to speak for himself; others interpreted his identity and mission for him. Now he proclaims the meaning of his life. He states the priority of God's claim in his mission. His life has a meaning that transcends the relationships of his human family. Thus he confirms the sword prophecy of Simeon. The astonishment of Jesus' parents is difficult to reconcile with the revelations surrounding their child's birth. This is a sign that some of the infancy stories were originally passed along independently of one another. It also underlines the fact that the full understanding of Jesus' identity and mission awaits the resurrection.

PART II: THE MESSIAH IS PREPARED

Luke 3:1–4:13

3:1-6 John the forerunner. Luke took pains to describe the historical context of the birth of Jesus. He is even more thorough in setting the scene for the beginning of John's ministry. The majestic first sentence reflects the ancient tradition that began the gospel story with John's Jordan ministry (Mark 1:1-4; Acts 10:37). There is also a change in Greek style at this point. Luke has already shown his mastery of classical Greek (1:1-4) and given an example of Hebrew-flavored Greek in the infancy stories; now for the rest of the Gospel he writes in the Greek style of the Septuagint, the Old Testament translation familiar to his readers.

After the death of Herod the Great, his kingdom had been divided among his children as a tetrarchy (four provinces). By the time of the events recorded here, a Roman procurator had been placed in charge of Judea, because Herod's son Archelaus had made such a mess of his rule there. The Herod mentioned here is another son, Antipas, about whom Luke has information not found elsewhere (23:7-12; Acts 13:1). There was only one ruling high priest at any particular time; in this case it was Caiaphas, but Annas is mentioned because he retained the title and exercised important influence in retirement (see Acts 4:6).

The call of John is patterned on that of Old Testament prophets (see Jer 1:2). He is the last of the old dispensation, serving as a bridge to the new. He prepares the way of the Lord that led from Egypt to Israel and now,

through Jesus, leads into the messianic kingdom. John's baptism was a ritual act expressing the willingness of individual Hebrews to join the movement of renewal. It counted on an interior disposition of repentance without which there could be no forgiveness.

Luke extends the Isaiah quotation further than Mark or Matthew (vv. 5-6) in order to incorporate the promise of universal salvation that is so important to him and his Gentile readers. The confirmation of this promise given here at the beginning of Luke's writing (see also 2:32) comes at the end of his two-part work in Paul's announcement that salvation has indeed come to the Gentiles (Acts 28:28).

3:7-20 John the prophet. Through a series of questions (as in Acts 2:37), this new prophet is given the opportunity to explain what repentance means. Words or titles are not enough. A child of Abraham must demonstrate his or her heritage in deeds. This is done especially in sharing with the poor and in social justice. John's message is consistent in this with the doctrine of his prophet-predecessors.

John is approached by two groups whose professions were considered questionable by the Pharisees: the tax collectors, who customarily made handsome profits by overcharging their compatriots; and the Jewish soldiers who belonged to the Roman peacekeeping force. John does not require that they give up their jobs, but that they perform them fairly and honestly.

John's activity gave rise to speculation about the Messiah. Expectation had been high for decades; several pseudo-prophets and pseudo-messiahs had already appeared (Acts 5:36-37), leaving disappointment but only adding to the expectancy. John gives an official answer to "all" in Israel: "One mightier than I is coming." In comparison with the Messiah, John considers himself lower than the lowest slave: only a non-Jewish slave could be required to loosen his master's sandal strap, and John will not even venture that.

John contrasts his baptism with that of Jesus. The point is not that one baptism is with water, the other in the Holy Spirit and fire (the early church also baptized in water from the beginning), but that John's baptism is *only* in water, that is, a ritual sign expressing outwardly what the person must express inwardly. The baptism of Jesus will be definitive: it will be an act of God bringing salvation (Holy Spirit) and judgment (fire). The image of fire is expanded by reference to the process of separating wheat from chaff. A "winnowing fan" or shovel tosses the mixture into the air; the heavier kernels of wheat fall to the floor, while the chaff blows away for later burning (Isa 21:10).

John the prophet challenges Herod to repentance for his marriage to Herodias, the wife of Philip. Luke does not repeat the details of Herod's marriage nor of his crime against John. Here he simply mentions the imprisonment. Later there will be a reference to the martyrdom of John, but obliquely after the fact (9:9). The vivid details had obviously had wide circulation by this time, thanks to Mark's account; Luke did not think it necessary to repeat the story.

3:21-38 Son of God, Son of Man. Jesus joins the pilgrimage to the Jordan to be baptized by John. In his case, however, the baptism is the occasion for his special anointing as the Messiah (Acts 10:38). Luke presents him as the last one to be baptized by John, the climax of John's baptismal ministry. Immediately after this, a new era begins. The heavens are opened, signaling a visitation of God with a new revelation for the people (Isa 63:19). The Holy Spirit comes on Jesus to reside with him "bodily" (Greek text). The voice from heaven identifies Jesus as the long-awaited Anointed One with the words of messianic Psalm 2: "You are my son" (v. 7) in combination with an allusion to Isa 42:1, where God's servant is described as "my chosen one with whom I am pleased." Jesus is announced as the expected messianic king, but his kingship will not be exercised in pomp and power; it will be a mission of humble self-sacrifice.

Luke waits till this point in his narrative to insert Jesus' family tree (unlike Matthew, who uses the genealogy to start his book). Perhaps he does this to emphasize the dramatic importance of the anointing by the Spirit at the Jordan as the inauguration of Jesus' public ministry.

There are many differences between the lists of Luke and Matthew. Some of the differences have received plausible explanation; others remain a source of debate. Matthew traces Jesus' ancestry beginning with Abraham; Luke takes it all the way back to Adam.

These decisions fit well with the purposes of the evangelists: Matthew is interested in Jesus' Jewish credentials for the sake of his Hebrew Christian readers; Luke, writing for Gentiles, wants to show from the beginning that Jesus brings salvation for all the children of Adam. Mary is not mentioned, though the fact of her virginal motherhood is recalled (v. 23). Both genealogies trace the descent through Joseph, the legal father of Jesus. The vague reference in verse 23—"about thirty"—is one of the New Testament's rare clues to Jesus' age during his ministry (see John 2:20). Much of the kind of biographical detail that catches our eye, in fact, was irrelevant to the gospel preachers and writers, who were presenting the meaning of Jesus rather than a collection of facts about him.

4:1-13 Testing in the wilderness. Before he launches out into his preaching and healing ministry, Jesus is led by the Spirit to the wilderness of Judea for a forty-day period of preparation. The Palestinian desert is not the sandy waste of the Sahara. The parts around the Dead Sea are utterly barren, but most of the Palestinian desert is semi-arid, with some vegetation, particularly in the winter. It was a dangerous place, uncharted, inhabited by wild animals and bandits. The wilderness was believed to be the haunt of demons (Isa 13:21; 34:14); it is no surprise that Jesus met the devil there. But Jesus' forty days in the desert is meant to trigger an association with Israel's forty years of wandering in the desert after the Exodus. Stephen's speech in Acts describes these as years of testing and failure for the people of God (Acts 7:39-43). Jesus is also tested in the desert but remains faithful.

The account in Mark says only that Jesus was tested, but Matthew and Luke describe three temptations. These are typical of the temptations Jesus faced throughout his life and typical as well of the testing his followers will undergo. In the first and third temptations, the devil addresses Jesus as Son of God but tries to make him deviate from the path of filial obedience to the Father. Jesus is tempted to turn stones into bread, that is, to use his power for his own ends rather than to be the Messiah planned by his Father; and he is taunted to test the Father's word rather than go forward on his mission in faith. The second temptation is an attempt to make Jesus give to someone else the allegiance that belongs to God. The devil claims that the power and glory are at his disposal; he is a liar and not to be trusted, but many before and after Jesus have fallen for this temptation.

Jesus answers all three temptations with the scriptural word of God, quoting from the Book of Deuteronomy, which described Israel's apostasy in the desert (Deut 8:3; 6:13-16). The devil even tries to use Scripture himself (vv. 10-11), but Jesus is quick to turn aside the challenge to his Father's fidelity. Scripture is no more authoritative than any other word if it is wrongly interpreted. The second and third temptations are transposed in Luke and Matthew, though it is apparent they are both working from the same written source. It was probably Luke who changed the order of the scenes in order to place the climax of the series in Jerusalem, which he highlights as the focus and pivot of Jesus' saving work and the life of the early church (Luke 9:51; Acts 1:4). The story breaks off with the devil departing "for a time." The reader will be alerted to the devil's heightened activity at the beginning of the passion account (22:3).

PART III: THE MINISTRY IN GALILEE

Luke 4:14–9:50

Jesus returns to Galilee fresh from his victory over the devil. This section shows Jesus in the early days of his mission, preaching and healing in his native area before he makes the decisive turn toward Jerusalem (9:51) and his passion, death, and resurrection.

4:14-30 Acclaim and rejection. The account of Jesus' return to his hometown embodies the gospel story in miniature. Jesus is met initially with praise and acclaim, but this response sours through jealousy and suspicion until his own people are seeking his life. As an observant Jew, Jesus customarily worshiped in the synagogue. In the sabbath service there were two readings, one from the Pentateuch (the first five books of the Bible) and a second from the prophets. Jesus took this second lesson, probably by prearrangement, opening the scroll to Isaiah (61:1-2) and reading a promise of the restoration of Israel. The original context is the anointing of a prophet, but the figure of the promised Messiah, the kingly Anointed One, is also implied in Jesus' usage of the text. He is the spirit-

bearer foretold by Isaiah (Isa 11:2), the Prophet and Messiah who will usher in a new age of freedom and divine favor.

There is an air of expectancy (as before the baptism in 3:15) as Jesus sits to interpret the reading (a synagogue teacher might either sit or stand). He announces that the day of fulfillment has come. The "today" he speaks of is the inaugural day of the "year acceptable to the Lord." That day continued to unfold until the goal of Jesus' glorification (ascension), when it became the eternal day of salvation. The listeners were impressed by his preaching, but just at this point a jarring note is heard: "Isn't this the son of Joseph?" In Mark's account of this Nazareth visit, the cloud of suspicion is described more thoroughly (Mark 6:2-3). Luke has modified Mark's chronology by moving this story earlier in the Galilean ministry. As a result, the mention of deeds done in Capernaum (actually deeds still to be done) is awkward.

Jesus compares himself to two great prophets of ancient Israel, noting that they served non-Israelites because their own people were not open to their ministries. The implication is that he, too, a prophet not accepted by his own people, will take his message to outsiders. This prospect threatens his listeners, arousing murderous thoughts. The same judgment on Israel will be made by Paul with similar results (Acts 22:21). The hostility does not overcome Jesus for the time being; he still has a mission to accomplish in fulfillment of God's plan. In the decisive act of rejection that results in his death, Jesus will seem to be destroyed but will emerge victorious (Luke 24:26).

4:31-44 A day at Capernaum. Jesus moves on to Capernaum, a city on the north shore of the Lake of Galilee, which becomes his headquarters during the period of the Galilean ministry. Following the Gospel of Mark, Luke presents a typical day in the life of Jesus, a sabbath in Capernaum. Jesus appears in the local synagogue as God's authoritative preacher and representative, bringing an official attack on the power of Satan. The unclean spirit recognizes the kind of challenge that has been issued: "Have you come to destroy us?" Jesus does not permit the demon to speak, probably to demonstrate his authority over the spirit world, but possibly also Luke has in mind here the "messianic secret," a theme developed by Mark (Mark 5:43). Jesus does not want his identity known before he is able to invest the title Messiah with its true meaning. Again the people are struck with awe at his words and deeds redolent of divine authority. But amazement does not necessarily lead to faith (Luke 4:22; 5:26).

From the synagogue Jesus goes to Simon's house for the main sabbath meal. Simon Peter is so well known in the Christian tradition by this time that Luke does not introduce him to the readers. Jesus finds Simon's mother-in-law with a fever, which he "rebukes" as he had the demon. Jesus has come to free the people from whatever binds them, whether demons or diseases or other handicaps that keep them in bondage. Verses 40-41 indicate that Jesus' merciful ministry to the demoniac and to Simon's mother-in-law were simply dramatic examples taken from his general practice. The evidence piles up until the demons no longer have to guess at Jesus' identity; he still requires their silence.

Jesus' reception at Capernaum is the opposite of that at Nazareth. The people try to keep him in their midst. But even this is a way of holding him bound, and Jesus escapes from these friends just as he had from his enemies. He is not tied down to one group or one place—he has been sent to all the people. In mentioning the "synagogues of *Judea*," Luke is using Judea in the broader sense of all Palestine without specifying which part of the country, even though at this period Jesus' mission has been limited to Galilee in the north. He is implicitly offering salvation to the whole nation.

5:1-11 Jesus calls the fishermen. Jesus continues his ministry in the territory around the Lake, here called Gennesaret after the fertile plain on its northwest shore. Jesus' preaching is called "the word of God" for the first time. He will describe the word as a life-giving source for those who receive it in faith (8:21; 11:28); the ministry of this word will continue in the church (Acts 4:31; 6:2). The introduction of this term at the beginning of the episode signals that the calling of the fishermen and their response is an occasion of the effective proclamation of the word of God.

In Mark's version of the call of the first disciples (Mark 1:16-20), the scene is shared by two sets of brothers. Here the spotlight is on Simon, with his partners in the background

(Andrew is not even mentioned by name). Jesus seems familiar with this group and they know him (see 4:38; John 1:35-42). While the fishermen are doing their morning cleaning of the nets and hanging them to dry, Jesus uses Simon's boat to distance himself from the crowd a little in order to preach. The water would have helped his voice carry. With verse 4, the crowd is suddenly gone, and the rest of the scene is interaction and dialogue between Jesus and Simon.

Simon is called to obedience based on faith. It was certainly not reason that provoked this fisherman to cast his nets back into the water at the instigation of this carpenter from the inland hills. Fishing was best at night; if nothing had been caught then, daytime fishing was useless. But Simon placed his trust in Jesus: "But at your command, I will lower the nets." The result is a marvelous catch of fish.

Now Simon is called Peter for the first time, "the Rock," the name he will later have as the leader of the church. His eyes are opened through his act of faith, and he falls before Jesus. Peter is the first person in the public ministry to call Jesus "Lord" (no longer only "Master": v. 5). Suddenly we realize that the story has been more than the initial calling of the fishermen disciples. From earliest times the church has seen herself as the "bark of Peter" in which faith in Jesus is tested (Mark 4:35-41; Matt 8:23-27). Jesus chooses Simon's boat, sending him into deep water and calling for a decision based solely on personal faith. The faith of Simon's response is what makes him the rock on which the church is built (Matt 16:18).

Simon Peter is aware of the distance between himself, a sinner, and the Lord. His natural reaction is to plead unworthiness. The divine holiness is too much for a human to bear (Exod 20:19). But Jesus has not come to drive sinners from his presence. He rather associates sinful people with himself in his ministry, if they will put their trust in him. They must leave *everything* (a Lukan stress: 5:28) and follow him. The three stories following this one show Jesus "catching men" (5:11), involving himself with the outcasts and sinners.

5:12-16 A leper comes to Jesus. Lepers were thoroughly ostracized at the time of Jesus. They were considered a menace to society. Jesus shows his ability to break through the social prohibitions to help these outcasts. "Leprosy" was a term used to cover any number of skin diseases, not only Hansen's disease. It was considered particularly difficult to cure; therefore, the man's request indicates the strength of his faith in Jesus. Whenever a skin disease of this sort seemed cured, the afflicted person reported to the priests, who were the examiners appointed to protect society's interests. This disease was also connected with ability to participate in public worship. Rules for examination and purification rituals ("what Moses prescribed") are given in the Book of Leviticus (chs. 13 and 14).

Jesus does not stand at a distance like one fearing contamination. He touches the afflicted man. The use of touch in healing was shown earlier to be characteristic of his healing ministry (4:40). Despite his instruction to keep his work secret, his reputation continues to spread. Crowds come, as people always must, to hear the word of God and to be healed. Jesus does not let his busy mission interfere with his communion with his Father. He takes time to get away from the crowds to pray. Perhaps his notoriety kept before him the temptation to personal goals (4:1-12), and he felt the need of prayer to keep his ministry in proper focus.

5:17-26 The healing of a paralyzed man. The question of the nature and source of Jesus' authority has arisen before (4:22, 32, 36). Here Jesus displays his authority before leaders of Judaism from all over the country. This is the first of four conflict stories leading up to the laying of a desperate plot (6:11). Some men (four, according to Mark 2:3) have heard about Jesus' healing power and want to bring their paralyzed friend to take advantage of the opportunity. The strength of their concern for their friend and of their faith in Jesus is evident from the lengths they are willing to go. They make the awkward ascent to the roof (probably by an outside stairs), carrying the man on his mat. The roofs of Palestinian houses were made of tiles or of mud and thatch. The man is lowered into the presence of Jesus, surely amid much complaining by the crowd. Both Mark and Luke mention that it was the faith of the man's friends that evoked Jesus' statement of forgiveness. The action of faith has been decisive in the two preceding stories. Here, for the only time in the Gospels,

an adult is healed because of the faith of someone else—a strong testimony to the bonds that faith forms among Jesus' followers.

The paralyzed man and his bearers were probably surprised by Jesus' statement of forgiveness rather than physical healing. This also stuns the scribes and Pharisees, who complain, correctly, that forgiveness of sins is in the hands of God. Jesus has come with an offer of thoroughgoing salvation, not one that stops at the surface. He has performed the more difficult inner healing and now will cure the limbs of the man. But he uses the occasion to demonstrate his power to forgive sins as well as to heal bodily ailments, and to identify the source of his authority. He is the "Son of Man": this title has its primary reference in the Book of Daniel, where the Son of Man receives dominion and kingship. Jesus uses this title to describe his authority now and at the time of judgment (6:5; 9:26; 12:8). The reaction to this event is astonishment, but this time also praise of God, both by the healed man and by the onlookers.

5:27-32 A tax collector is called. Jesus' attitude toward sinners was glimpsed in the exchange with Simon Peter (vv. 8-11). Now, after the healing of a sinner, Jesus' attitude toward sinners is given more explicitly. Tax collectors were classed as sinners because of the dishonesty and injustice associated with their profession. Jesus does not talk to Levi privately but calls him in the midst of his business, and goes to a public banquet where a "large crowd" of tax collectors and other friends of Levi are present. The Pharisees emphasize the impropriety of sharing a meal with these people, who, besides being sinners, would have had contact with Gentiles and thus been ritually unclean. Jesus uses a proverb to explain his stance: he has come to help those in need and will go out to them. Those who will not recognize their own need are not ready for the doctor.

This story may have been recalled to give a norm for relations in the early church. The question of preaching to Gentiles and eating with them looms large in the Acts of the Apostles (10:28; 11:3). Jesus' example gave warrant for transcending the traditional boundaries of ministry. The story showed that even an unclean public sinner could respond to the preaching with the same total self-gift as the first disciples did (5:11, 28).

5:33-39 The old and the new. These verses deal with questions arising from Christian differences from Judaism, beginning with practices during Jesus' own lifetime. The Pharisees fasted on Monday and Thursday (see 18:12) as well as for the regular Jewish observances, and John the Baptist encouraged fasting as well. The challenge to Jesus here is more an introduction to the statement about the bridegroom than an emphasis on a Christian posture against fasting (and prayers). Jesus was apparently much freer on such questions (see 7:34) but did not undervalue fasting (Matt 6:16-18). Acts shows the early Christians regularly praying and fasting (Acts 2:42; 13:3; 14:23).

Jesus compares the present time of his ministry to a wedding, implying that this is a foretaste of the messianic banquet. Fasting as a sign of mourning is inappropriate. There is a veiled reference to the passion in the mention of the removal of the groom. The followers of Jesus did mourn at that time (24:17-38) before they became aware of the resurrection and Jesus' continuous presence in their midst (24:52). In Acts, fasting is part of praying for the Holy Spirit's guidance rather than an expression of mourning.

A different kind of answer to the question about fasting is given in the two sayings about the coats and the wineskins. The gospel life proclaimed by Jesus is something entirely new. It was born in the matrix of Judaism, but it must be allowed to develop on its own, adapting in ritual, in religious observances, in social practices, in doctrine, according to its own principles. If Christianity is fettered to Judaism, it will be ruined. The sayings have wider application in terms of any kind of clinging to past ways for their own sake.

6:1-11 Jesus and the sabbath. The final two conflict stories in this series deal with Jesus' attitude toward the sabbath. Judging from the number of such stories in the Gospels (see 13:10-17; 14:1-6), confrontations about the sabbath must have been frequent during his ministry. In the first incident, Jesus' disciples are doing what would have been allowable by the Mosaic law (Deut 23:26), but on the sabbath this could technically be described as a forbidden work of "harvesting" in the Pharisaic interpretation.

In Mark, the Pharisees question Jesus about his disciples, but Luke has them address the disciples directly so that Jesus can intervene on their behalf as their master and defender. He uses an incident from the Old Testament to defend their actions. When David was hiding from Saul with a band of followers, he went to a local shrine to ask for food. The only food available was the holy showbread, which no one but priests consumed. The priest in charge allowed the bread to be eaten, because the disciplinary restrictions of the law gave way before human need (1 Sam 21:2-7). In the application here, if David's authority to interpret the law is accepted, how much more ought one accept the authority of the Son of Man as "Lord of the sabbath."

Immediately Jesus demonstrates his lordship by an act of healing. The sequence is the same as in the healing of the paralyzed man (5:21-25). In the case of the man with the withered hand, the scribes and Pharisees are no longer just responding to problematic actions of his ministry, but are actively scrutinizing him to find difficulties. Jesus knows by now that it is useless to try to keep his acts of power secret. He does not avoid the confrontation with his enemies on this occasion, but provokes it in order to make another statement about the sabbath and to expose to the scribes and Pharisees their own false motives.

The Pharisaic interpretation of the law allowed medical intervention on the sabbath for birth, circumcision, and mortal illness. Jesus doesn't ask merely whether it is lawful to heal on the sabbath, but asks about the purpose of the sabbath: If the sabbath was given by God to his people for their good, shouldn't an observant Jew do good instead of evil on the sabbath? In posing the question this way, Jesus implies that in this case, not to do the good that can be done is an act of evil—letting a person suffer needlessly. His enemies cannot hear what he is saying; their minds are already made up.

6:12-16 The Twelve Apostles. Luke places the choice of the Twelve just before the "Great Discourse" so that it can take on the character of an official instruction for the whole church assembled under its leaders. The importance of Jesus' decision in selecting the Twelve is underscored by mention of his all-night vigil. He calls all the disciples together, choosing the core group from among them.

Three of these we have met before and will meet again (Peter, James, and John), one other will have a large role later (Judas Iscariot); but the rest are mentioned only here by Luke's Gospel (see also Acts 1:13). The fact that there are Twelve is itself important, because these Christian leaders are to rule over the renewed Israel in place of the patriarchs of old (Luke 22:29-30).

The Twelve are called "apostles," from the Greek word *apostello*, meaning "to send out." Andrew is now mentioned along with Simon Peter, his brother, then the Zebedee brothers. Philip and Thomas are known from John's Gospel (John 1:43-48; 20:24-29). Of Bartholomew and James son of Alphaeus we know nothing more from the New Testament. Matthew is called a "tax collector" in Matt 10:3. The second Simon is called the "Zealot," a title that aligns him with the Jewish nationalists plotting the expulsion of Rome. Judas son of James is mentioned also in John's Gospel (John 14:22), but otherwise only in Luke's writings (Acts 1:13), where he takes the place of Thaddaeus in the traditional list (Mark 3:18; Matt 10:3). Probably these are two names for the same person. The meaning of "Iscariot" is a matter of speculation; it may mean "man of Kerioth" (a village in Judea).

6:17-49 The sermon on the plain. At this point in his narrative, Luke incorporates part of the material Matthew had included in the Sermon on the Mount (Matt 5-7). But instead of staying on the mountain to deliver his discourse, Jesus comes down from the mountain like Moses descending to deliver the law to the people (Exod 34:15). As before, people crowd around him to hear the word of God and to be healed (5:1, 15).

6:20-26 The blessings and the woes. The differences between this passage and the eight beatitudes in Matthew are striking. The best explanation is that the two evangelists received a common core of material from the preaching tradition, some of which had already been adapted by various Christian communities, and further edited it for the needs of their own readers. Luke's beatitudes correspond to the first, fourth, second, and eighth in Matthew's list, but with significant variations.

The point has been made that Matthew's beatitudes suggest what Jesus' disciples ought to be, whereas Luke's describe what they actually are. This should not be carried too far. Luke's own readership included wealthy and middle-class citizens of the Empire. To be "poor" involves a state of dependence, which is what both sets of beatitudes are aiming for. The fourth Lukan beatitude holds the key. It is not good simply to be poor or hungry or persecuted, but one is fortunate to be dispossessed or mistreated for the sake of the Son of Man. The prophets of old were treated shamefully though they were God's spokesmen (Jer 15:15; Amos 7:10-12). More pertinently, so was Jesus (Luke 13:33).

The reason for the woes to the rich and well-fed is not given here but may be sought in other parts of the Gospel. The rich did not use their wealth to help the needy (16:19-31), hoarding it rather for themselves (12:21). They did not recognize the source of their gifts (21:3-4) or were trapped by them (18:24-25). Riches kept such persons from trusting God (12:22-34). They are compared to the false prophets who always found friends because of their falsely optimistic statements (Jer 5:31; Mic 2:11).

6:27-35 Love of enemies. The radical love of Jesus and his heavenly Father, the love that must be the mark of the Christian, is presented clearly and emphatically in these verses. The test of discipleship is the love of enemies, which makes sense by no earthly standard and must be based on faith. Three times the sequence "love, do good, give" is repeated (vv. 27-30, 32-34, 35) to bind the admonition into mnemonic phrases. If you love, do good and lend to your friends—that is merely good politics or good business. To be a child of the Most High more is required. Even the Golden Rule in the middle of these verses (v. 31) seems tinny against such a dazzling standard.

6:36-42 Relationships. It is in the call for compassion that Jesus calls God "Father" for the first time in his public ministry (see 2:49), though he has implied this relationship in verse 35. To be like the Father is to be compassionate, which means, as the subsequent sentences unfold, not to judge or condemn, but to forgive offenses and to give without counting the cost, as God himself has done. He will not be outdone in repaying the generosity.

Luke uses the saying about the blind leading the blind in a different context than Matthew does. There it is a stricture against the Pharisees; here it is a warning against false teachers in the Christian community. The true Christian teacher will always remain a disciple of the Master, not changing or "surpassing" his instruction. The famous image of the splinter and the beam drives home the point about judging others (v. 37). The passage says nothing about fraternal correction that is an action generated by love; the hypocrite, blinded by his own sin, is interested only in exposing another's weakness.

6:43-49 A tree and its fruit. Jesus uses two different fruit-tree images to make the point about the source of a person's actions: in verse 43, the fruit tells whether or not the tree is healthy; in verse 44, the fruit verifies the variety of tree. Those who call upon Jesus as Lord must demonstrate the reality and the quality of the relationship. They will be able to do this if they hear his words and put them into practice (8:15, 21).

Both Luke and Matthew end the discourse with the comparison of the two builders. The example has been adapted to different audiences. Matthew's story seems to reflect the Palestinian situation, where a house could easily be built on exposed rock without digging; Luke's good builder has to dig to reach rock (more likely in Asia Minor). Matthew's foolish builder builds on sand, which Luke does not mention; his vulnerable house is one that is built on top of the ground. Matthew's house is destroyed as much by wind as by water on the exposed Palestinian plain; Luke's house seems to be in a city, protected from wind but vulnerable to a flood that would wash away a house built on the surface.

7:1-10 The centurion and his servant. Stories like this one from Jesus' ministry were crucial during the debate of the early church concerning the mission to the Gentiles. The nationality of the centurion is not given, but he was not a Jew (v. 5). He would have been a member of Herod's peacekeeping force (see 3:14) rather than a member of the imperial army, which had no forces in Galilee at this date. In Luke, this incident foreshadows the various statements in Acts that God knows no partiality; rather, "The man of any nation who fears God and acts uprightly is acceptable to him" (Acts 10:34-35; see 15:9). If even the observant Jews of Jesus' own time brought a non-Jew to Jesus, and if Jesus went to him

without quibble—the church's argument must have run—why shouldn't Jewish Christians accept Gentiles?

The centurion is introduced as a compassionate man seeking the compassion of Jesus. His Jewish friends argue in his favor that he has been generous to their people. In the light of what Jesus has just said about selfless generosity, this would not have been the compelling motive of his action. The centurion surprises him with his humility and his faith. Possibly the officer's thoughtfulness is implied here, too: he would have known that entering the house of a Gentile rendered a Jew ritually unfit for worship. But it is the centurion's faith, not the good works that captivated the man's Jewish friends, that Jesus wants to impress on his listeners. The healing is mentioned almost as an afterthought.

7:11-17 The widow and her son. Another demonstration of Jesus' compassion follows in the Galilean village of Naim. The comparison of Jesus to the prophetic figures of Israel's past underlies the narrative. His action of revivifying the son of a widow along with the expression "he gave him to his mother" alludes to the earlier act of power by Elijah (1 Kgs 17:23). When the people see what has happened, their reaction is to recognize a "great prophet." Jesus' compassion for the woman draws him to the scene. As in the previous story, there is a possibility of ritual uncleanness (by touching a corpse: Num 19:11). The response of the people is first fear, but ultimately the praise of God, as in the healing of the paralyzed man (Luke 5:26). Faith is not mentioned preliminary to the deed as in the healing of the centurion's servant; but the action elicits faith in the form of divine praise.

7:18-35 Jesus and John. John has been confined in prison (3:20), but his disciples have kept him abreast of Jesus' ministry. Now he sends two of them to ask Jesus point-blank whether he is "the one who is to come," using an expression for the expected Messiah originating in the prophecy of Malachi (Mal 3:1). There might also be an overtone of expectancy for the awaited prophet-like-Moses (Deut 18:15) with whom both John and Jesus are connected in popular estimation (John 1:21; 6:14). Why did John doubt that Jesus was the one expected? Probably in the stories of Jesus' compassion and in his message of love of enemies and forgiveness John did not see the exercise of eschatological judgment he had predicted for the one to come who is "mightier than I" (Luke 3:16-17). Luke's own faith is unmistakable in the statement that John "sent them to the *Lord* to ask . . . ."

The disciples arrive at a time when they can observe Jesus' healing ministry. Jesus responds to John's question by interpreting his action through texts from Isaiah that envision the days of messianic deliverance: the blind seeing, cripples walking (Isa 29:18-19; 35:5-6). The two disciples are told to relate to their teacher "what you have seen and heard." This will be the mission of the early church; the apostles will carry it out even at the risk of persecution and death (Acts 4:20). Jesus understands his work as the unraveling of the program he had proclaimed in his inaugural sermon at Nazareth, "glad tidings to the poor . . . a year acceptable to the Lord" (Luke 4:18-19). John is warned that even he may block God's plan if he is not ready to adapt himself to divine surprise. The statement of verse 23 is, of course, addressed not only to John but to people of any age: Jesus as he was and is has frequently been found a stumbling block; his true image has suffered many distortions.

This encounter is followed by Jesus' glowing description of John. He is not a reed wavering in the wind, but a staunch prophet of the Lord whose unyielding fidelity lands him in prison. He is even more than a prophet—he is the one selected to be the forerunner of the Messiah, the messenger who comes in the spirit of Elijah (Mal 3:23; Luke 1:17). No one born of woman is greater than he, but even the least born into the kingdom is greater. This is a paradoxical way of stating the importance of being in the kingdom, no matter what one's human credentials. There is no notion here that John was excluded from the kingdom (see 13:28).

Those who had benefited by John's ministry praise God when they hear Jesus' testimony about him. Luke sees in the Jewish leaders' refusal to receive John's baptism a sign that they are closed to God's plan for them. The evangelist contrasts this attitude with Jesus' commitment to fulfill God's designs (18:31). The "people of this generation" are not willing to open themselves to God's action in Jesus and will not cooperate any more than obstinate children do. They find excuses to reject John, and then opposite excuses to reject Jesus. God's plan (his "wisdom"), however, will prove its validity in the lives of those who embrace it.

7:36-50 The loving woman. Though Jesus is willing to dine with outcasts (5:29), he does not reject invitations from the well-to-do (11:37; 14:1). A "sinful woman" approaches him in Simon the Pharisee's house in the presence of the other invited guests. It is a moment of embarrassment for Simon and for the woman as well, whose courage is shown by her action; but shown more importantly is her faith in Jesus and her trust that he will receive her with compassion. The guests were reclining, so Jesus' feet were exposed behind him.

Simon judges that Jesus cannot be a prophet because he allows a sinner to touch him. Simon overlooks his own sinfulness and misunderstands Jesus' prophetic ministry. At an earlier meal with "sinners," Jesus had compared himself to a doctor (5:31). Jesus does know who the woman is, but Simon does not even "see" her until challenged by Jesus (v. 44). To open his eyes, Jesus tells the parable of the money-lender. Simon is forced to admit that the one forgiven the larger debt is more grateful. But he does so hesitantly, perhaps even sneeringly—"I suppose"—wary of being caught in a trap by the clever carpenter.

But with the admission the Pharisee is already caught. Jesus draws out the comparison of gratitudes point by point: you provided no water, she washed with her tears; you gave me no kiss, she kissed my feet; you did not anoint my head, she anointed my feet. The climax of Jesus' pronouncement and of the story comes in verse 47, which may be translated two different ways with vastly different meanings. The New American Bible's original version of the Greek is defensible—"her many sins are forgiven because of her great love"—but the revised translation of 1986 is more consistent with the parable in verses 41-42: "her many sins have been forgiven; hence, she has shown great love."

Jesus says that the woman has already been forgiven her sins; that is evident because of her love. She would not be able to show such love unless she had first accepted love (forgiveness, acceptance). The forgiveness has set her free to love. When Jesus says "Your sins are forgiven," he is confirming what is already true in her; in the different context of the healing of the paralyzed man, Jesus forgave the sins at the moment of declaration (5:20). It is not that her love has earned forgiveness. By faith she accepted Jesus' (God's) loving forgiveness that saved her (see 1:77) and is now able to love.

Jesus' pronouncement in verse 47 interprets the parable of the money-lender. The woman has received "five hundred days' wages" worth of forgiveness, or a great amount. We do not know about Simon, but the implication is that he has been forgiven a lesser amount and is less able to show gratitude and love. This does not mean that one has to be a great sinner to love greatly. We all need "five hundred days' wages worth" of forgiveness, but we may be blind to our sinfulness or too fearful or proud to ask that our debt be written off. And then we are chained to our guilt, which keeps us from the freedom of love.

8:1-3 Jesus' women companions. Jesus now undertakes a systematic preaching tour of the local towns and villages, accompanied by the Twelve and by several women and others who helped provide for their needs. These women had been healed by Jesus and were expressing their gratitude in this way. It would have been exceptional for a traveling preacher to associate women with himself, so this is another sign of Jesus' openness and concern for all and his ability to transcend prejudice and custom. Two of these women, Mary Magdalene and Joanna, will be named among the first witnesses of the resurrection (24:10); perhaps they and others of this group are implied among those waiting with the Twelve for the outpouring of the Spirit after the ascension (Acts 1:14).

8:4-21 Listening to the word of God. This section on response to the gospel message contains two parables with commentaries; it climaxes with a pronouncement of Jesus on the basis of the proper relationship of his disciples to him. The parable of the sower (or more properly, of the *sowing*) appears in all three Synoptics (Mark 4:3-8; Matt 13:4-8). The parable itself (vv.5-8) is open to more than one interpretation, but the commentary (vv. 11-15) describes what must have been the most common interpretation in the early church. The seed is the word of God, which will bear fruit in a receptive heart (fertile ground), but which may be ineffective in other

soils for any number of reasons: the birds = the devil; no moisture = buckling under to persecution; thorns = cares, riches, and pleasures. In verses 13-15, the listener is compared to the seed rather than to the soil. Characteristic of Luke is the emphasis on perseverance (v. 15; see 21:19; Acts 11:23).

After telling the parable, Jesus calls for attention to the deeper meaning of his preaching (v. 8), something he must have done often to shake his hearers into listening more carefully (see 14:35). When the disciples ask him to explain the meaning of the parable privately, he assures them that the "mysteries" (hidden designs) of God's reign are revealed to them, and then utters the puzzling statement that parables are meant to keep others from understanding. Jesus obviously does not want his listeners, whoever they are, to be prevented from understanding (the reverse of the admonitions in verses 8 and 18 and of the parable of the lamp in verse 16). He uses the quotation from Isa 6:9 to describe the case that, in fact, some will see but not perceive, hear but not understand, because of hardness of heart. The phrasing is a form of Hebrew overstatement that translates awkwardly. It is even harsher in Mark's version (Mark 4:12), which both Luke and Matthew (Matt 13:13-15) have softened.

The parable of the lamp is applied here to the revelation of the "mysteries of the kingdom of God" mentioned in verse 10. God means for the proclamation of Jesus, now somewhat limited in its scope and even necessarily secret, to go out into the world. This will be the mission of the apostles (Acts 1:18). Jesus urges his listeners again to "take care how you hear," for those who are open to the word of God will become richer and richer in the life it engenders and nourishes (see v. 8), but those who do not listen will find that the spiritual life that seems to have germinated will wither away (see v. 6). The section concludes with the visit of Jesus' family, which gives him the opportunity to assert for his followers that the fundamental relationship to him is not through blood ties or other earthly connections but through hearing and acting on the word of God.

8:22-25 The storm on the lake. The identity of Jesus has been a recurring issue during the Galilean ministry (4:22, 34, 41; 7:16). Now for the third time the question is asked point-blank: "Who is this?" (v. 25; see 5:21; 7:49). Still once more will it arise (9:9) before Peter makes his profession of faith in Jesus as the Messiah (9:20). This time it is the disciples themselves who raise the question as they experience his power while they are alone with him on the lake. The early Christian community saw this story as a call to faith in Jesus who is present in the church during stormy times.

8:26-39 The Gerasene disciple. After exhibiting his power over the storm, Jesus demonstrates his authority over the demons in Gentile territory. Further, he works a dramatic transformation in a human life. The man is said to be "possessed" by demons. This English term is too strong. The Greek in verse 27 says he "had" demons, in verse 36 that he was "demonized" (see Mark 1:32), but the modern notion of possession, leading even to replacing the ego, is foreign to the New Testament. The unclean spirit turns out to be a regiment ("legion" was an imperial army term), which recognizes Jesus as did other demons.

The man's condition is dangerous to himself and to others, and has persisted over a long time. This is no ordinary exorcism. Its lasting effects could be doubted, which is probably why Jesus agrees to send the demons into the swine—for visible proof that the demons have left the man. They ask not to be sent to "the abyss." The word used could mean Sheol, the underworld of the dead (see Rom 10:7), but here it means the prison of evil spirits (2 Pet 2:4; Rev 9:1-11). Jews, for whom pork was unclean, would have thought it appropriate that the demons were sent into the swine.

The local people are terrified by what has taken place. Their fear does not lead to praise of God (5:26) but to the rejection of Jesus. Luke's favorable treatment of Gentiles does not blind him to the possibility of their failure. The loss of the swine impresses them more than the transformation of the man, who, when the people arrive, is sitting at Jesus' feet in the attitude of a disciple listening to his word (see 10:39). The man wants to follow Jesus (like the women who had been healed: 8:1-3), but his vocation is to share what has happened to him with his own people.

8:40-56 Jesus and the two daughters. The demonstration of Jesus' power over disease and death completes a cycle of four miracle stories. Luke links the raising of the girl with the earlier incident at Naim by adding to the account in Mark that she was an only daughter. Several touches in the synoptic narrative tradition link the stories of the little girl and the woman. Both are called daughter; the father and the woman fall at Jesus' feet; the girl's age and the duration of the woman's condition coincide; they are both affected "immediately" by contact with Jesus; and the centrality of faith is highlighted in both events. Luke adds that the girl is "saved" (v. 50: rather than "spared"), the same word used to describe the healing of the woman (v. 48).

The woman with the hemorrhage touches the tassel of Jesus' cloak and is healed in a way that is almost magical. To remove this overtone of superstition (which Luke himself detests: Acts 8:9-11; 19:19), the tradition emphasizes that Jesus' power has gone out in response to faith, and that the healing has been more than physical. The trust in Jesus that prompted her to come forward is like that of the woman known to be a sinner (7:37-38), and Jesus' final word to both of them is exactly the same: "Your faith has saved you; go in peace" (7:50; 8:48). Peter does not call Jesus "Lord" but "Master" in verse 45, as he did on an earlier occasion when he was uncertain about the extent of Jesus' power and knowledge (5:5).

Jesus' care for the woman seems to have delayed him just long enough to prevent his saving the girl's life. Jesus reassures Jairus, "Do not be afraid; just have faith." Fear had ruined his visit to the Gerasenes (8:37). Jesus takes his three closest disciples with him. Luke changes the traditional order of the names of James and John (see 5:10) to prepare for the teamwork of Peter and John in Acts (Acts 3:1, 11; 4:1; 8:14). The mourners at Jairus' house are not ready for the surprise Jesus brings (see 7:23); they laugh at him, remaining closed to God's action.

9:1-9 The apostolic mission. The ministry in Galilee is coming to an end. The material in the first part of this chapter shows Jesus preparing his closest disciples for accompanying him on the journey to Jerusalem and continuing his work later. He shares with them his own power and authority, gives them a vision of his glory, and makes it clear that his mission and theirs will involve humiliation and suffering. The Twelve are "sent" (*apostello*) with instructions to imitate the Master in taking nothing along. Christ's disciples must concentrate on the mission, not on their own needs, depending on the good will of the people to whom they bring the gospel. Thus there must be no special concern for accommodations, and certainly no idea of making a profit from the task. The Jews would shake pagan dirt from their sandals when leaving Gentile territory. Here the practice is a warning that people closed to the gospel proclamation are cutting themselves off from salvation (see Acts 13:51).

This expansion of Jesus' mission draws the attention of more people, including Herod Antipas, the tetrarch of Galilee, who will be curious (v. 9) and even alarmed about Jesus until his death (13:31-33; 23:6-12). We are informed of John's death through the allusions in verses 7 and 9. Jesus' preaching and mighty works remind people of prophetic figures of the past, especially Elijah. But his identity remains a matter of debate.

9:10-17 The feeding of the people. Jesus takes the apostles away for a time, probably to rest and to discuss their experiences. Luke specifies the place as Bethsaida, the hometown of some of the Twelve (John 1:44). When interrupted by the needs of the crowds, Jesus again preaches and heals. The implication may be that though the disciples have been given a share in his ministry, they cannot take Jesus' place; this will be even more evident in their inability to take care of the hungry crowd without his help. The feeding of the five thousand had a meaning for the early church in the responsibility of the leaders to feed the flock, particularly with preaching and the Eucharist. The wording of verse 16 draws our attention to the Last Supper and to the Eucharist, a source of superabundant nourishment to those who receive Jesus' word and his healing.

9:18-27 The Messiah of God. Jesus' absorption in prayer signals the approach of a decisive moment (see 3:21; 6:12). He is ready to confront his followers with the question that has been tantalizing audiences since the beginning of his ministry: "Who is this?" (8:25). They give the standard response about public opinion: John, Elijah, a prophet (vv. 7-8). When he asks for their own conclusion, Peter speaks up for the rest: "The Messiah of

God." This answer is correct, as we know from the preview during Jesus' infancy, but it may be misunderstood (23:35), so Jesus imposes silence until he has a chance to instruct them in the true meaning of his Messiahship. Peter's leadership role is highlighted as he answers this crucial question in the name of the other disciples (see Acts 2:14).

Immediately Jesus gives the first of three predictions of his passion (see Luke 9:44; 18:31-33), using the title "Son of Man," which he preferred and which in this context seems interchangeable with "Messiah." There should be no mistaken identity: Jesus will not be the Messiah of popular expectation, capitalizing on national patriotism to remove the yoke of Rome and restore Davidic rule. He will suffer, be rejected by the leaders God's people, and be killed. Only then will he be vindicated. His followers must follow in his steps, taking up the cross (the Lukan version adds "daily"). To deny one's very self and to lose one's life does not mean an ego-suppression that would be psychologically harmful; it means giving up control over one's destiny and opening oneself to true self-knowledge by laying aside the image constructed from worldly illusions about the meaning of life. The stakes are high: one's response now will determine the outcome of the great judgment (v. 26). Jesus' remark that some of his companions will not die till they have seen the reign of God refers, in its Marcan setting, primarily to the experience of the transfiguration; Luke's usage expands this to the experience of the resurrection and the gift of the Holy Spirit (Acts 2:32-36).

9:28-36 The glory of God's Son. The transfiguration is a dazzling contrast to the message of suffering and humiliation. The two extremes need to be held together, as always in the gospel tradition, in order to accept Jesus as he is—Son of Man and Son of God. Several details recall the Sinai experience of God: Moses, the mountaintop, the cloud (Exod 24:9-18). Jesus is seen as God's Son in his heavenly glory. He is "changed in appearance" (v. 29), as he will be in his glorified resurrection body (Mark 16:12). Appearing with him are two key Old Testament figures, Moses the Lawgiver and Elijah the Prophet. They are a sign that Jesus will fulfill the expectations of the Hebrew people. In fact, they speak with him about his own *exodus*—his death, resurrection, and, in Luke's theology, especially his ascension—which he will "accomplish" in Jerusalem.

The three intimate disciples behave disappointingly. They fall asleep, as they will later at a crucial moment (22:45). Peter, confronted with divine glory, fails to call Jesus by the title "Lord," which adequately identifies him as the Savior, and babbles incoherently about building earthly tents for the heavenly beings. The revelation climaxes with the voice from the clouds as at Jesus' baptism. He is God's Son, his Chosen One (Ps 2:7; Isa 42:1). The admonition "listen to him" underscores the importance of what Jesus has been saying about his own mission and the nature of discipleship.

9:37-50 Jesus returns from the mountain. Jesus mission is not an aloof solitude on the mountain but a ministry to the children of God. On his return, he immediately becomes involved with human need, a beloved and chosen Son (2:22; 9:35) serving another beloved son, an only child (a Lukan detail). The disciples had begun their mission with the power to overcome "all demons" (9:1), but they are unable to cast this spirit out. This experience, added to that of the loaves (9:13) and the transfiguration, puts their power in perspective as a participation in the messianic authority of Jesus. They still need his help; further, their ministry is not magical, but dependent on faith. Jesus shakes them out of their awe by repeating the prediction of his passion. They do not understand. Luke's phraseology stresses that their inability to penetrate this mystery was according to the divine plan. Full understanding must await the resurrection with the gift of the Spirit. But the disciples may have refrained from inquiring further because of uneasiness about the harsh conclusions for their own lives that had followed from the first prediction (9:23-24).

Elsewhere Jesus says that the disciples must become like little children (18:17; Matt 18:3-4). This point emerges from his saying here, but in an oblique way. He emphasizes the seeming unimportance or insignificance of the little child in a world with selfish interests. The child and others who are helpless and "least" in the world's eyes are the greatest in the kingdom. A true disciple recognizes Jesus in them. Whoever serves these least ones shares in their worldly insignificance and is great in the kingdom. The incident of the strange exorcist, originally independent of the foregoing, is added here as an example of the kind of openness to others just commented on. The disciple of Jesus does not sit in judgment (6:37) but waits for the fruit to emerge (6:43-44) and is ready to accept the action of God in unexpected people and places.

PART IV: THE JOURNEY TO JERUSALEM

Luke 9:51–19:44

Jesus now makes the decisive turn toward Jerusalem and the accomplishment of his *exodus* (v. 31). The theme of the final journey is already in Mark (Mark 10:1, 32), but Luke has developed it to show Jesus' commitment to the Father's plan (9:62; 13:33). He keeps the reader alert to the journey theme (13:22; 17:11) and lengthens this section by inserting a sizable addition to Mark's narrative (Luke 9:51-18:14), containing several stories and sayings he received from independent sources. Besides knitting the separate episodes together under the journey motif, Luke binds the section together thematically by inserting it between two children episodes in Mark (Mark 9:36-37; 10:13-16). The journey of Christian discipleship is characterized by the lowliness of a child, characterized by availability for God's action and dependence on God.

9:51-62 The beginning of the journey. Jesus' journey to Jerusalem is a march toward exaltation ("to be taken up") in fulfillment of God's plan. The earthly journey of Jesus serves also as the framework for the progress of the church in the time after the ascension. We find ourselves on the way toward Jerusalem with the Lord. But the march to glory, as Jesus has already warned, is a path through suffering. The disciples must expect to be treated no better than the Master. The cost of Christian discipleship is clearly stated as the journey gets underway.

The hostility of the Samaritans is not the personal hatred Jesus will meet in Jerusalem. It is evidence of the national or racial prejudice between Samaritans and Jews. Jesus' disciples cannot expect to be free from this treatment, but the answer is not retaliation. James and John must learn to avoid useless clashes and to look for new places to spread the kingdom.

Illusions are dispelled for would-be disciples. The person who offered himself with absolute availability (v. 57) is told the cost: you will be less secure than the foxes and the birds. Another responds to Jesus' call with the request that he be allowed to take care of one of the most sacred duties under the law, the burial of a parent. The urgency of the gospel supersedes this claim. Jesus' saying means that those who do not respond to the gospel call will be spiritually dead; they will have time to bury the physically dead. Elijah gave permission to his disciple Elisha to bid good-bye to his family (1 Kgs 19:19-21), but the call of the reign of God is more urgent than that.

10:1-20 The mission of the seventy-two. Only Luke among the evangelists tells of this second mission of disciples. He probably means it to have special significance for the missionary activity of the church after the departure of Jesus. According to rabbinic teaching, there were seventy-two nations in the world (based on the reading of Gen 10 in the Greek Septuagint). The disciples are to go "ahead of him," therefore not announcing themselves or their own message, but preparing the way for Jesus. This is the continuing charge of Christian preachers. The missionaries are sent in twos in order to give a witness that can be considered formal testimony about Jesus and the reign of God (see Matt 18:16). Jesus urges prayer for more harvest workers. The Lord of the harvest is concerned about its progress, of course, but he has made his own response to the need somehow dependent on the active concern of those sent into the mission.

Again, there is no room for illusion. The disciples will be lambs among wolves, defenseless, completely dependent on the Lord of the harvest for whatever is needed. Several of the admonitions to these disciples repeat the instructions to the Twelve (9:1-5). The admonition to greet no one is another emphasis on the urgency of the gospel task. The peace they offer seems like a tangible gift or even a living reality with a mind of its own. This notion of peace rests on the biblical concept of the word of God as being not only a message but somehow an embodiment of God's own personality and power (Isa 55:10-11; Jer 20:8-9). The peace-wish of the Christian missionary is more than an expression of good will—it is the offer of a gift from God of which

they are privileged to be the ministers and heralds (see 1:2; Acts 6:4). Those who bring spiritual gifts can expect their physical needs to be taken care of by the beneficiaries (v. 7; see Gal 6:6).

Because the proclamation of the gospel is the word of God, it is not to be treated as a merely human message—"take it or leave it." There are harsh consequences for closing ears and hearts to the news of God's reign. Jesus makes drastic comparisons for the obstinate cities of Galilee where he centered much of his ministry. Chorazin and Bethsaida will be no better off than Sodom. And proud Capernaum, Jesus' "headquarters" in Galilee, has learned nothing from the Jewish heritage that was preparing for the coming of the Messiah. Tyre and Sidon, Gentile cities, would have been able to read the signs that Capernaum overlooked. The conclusion of the instruction is a reminder of the deeper dimension of the mission: the disciples are bringing Jesus and the Father to their listeners.

On their return, the seventy-two are amazed at the power that has been given them through the name of Jesus. They have driven out demons, furthering Jesus' attack on Satan's dominion in this world. Jesus envisions Satan falling from the sky through their ministry, another way of saying that the eschatological or final battle between good and evil is taking place now; the victory is being won in Jesus' name (John 12:31; Rom 16:20). But the disciples must not lose their perspective. The prize is not human glory through feats of power but heavenly glory through following Jesus to Jerusalem, to Calvary. The divine registry is a theme in Jewish literature (Exod 32:32; Dan 12:1).

10:21-24 Jesus the revealer. This passage gives a rare glimpse into the personal prayer of Jesus. In Luke's arrangement (differing from Matthew's by the insertion of the return of the missionaries: see Matt 11:20-27), the prayer is an exuberant outcry provoked by the disciples' happy report on the success of their mission. Jesus speaks intimately to God as "Father," praising him for letting these "little ones" understand what is really going on in the world: not an endless round of superficial activity, but a decisive battle between good and evil. The humble disciple is able to see and hear what prophets and kings looked forward to, a truth which, because of its simplicity, is often hidden from the worldly great and worldly wise. The revelation of the meaning of existence is under God's full control; it cannot be bought, nor can it be deduced by human cleverness.

Jesus is the revealer of the Father. The phraseology here is very similar to that of John's Gospel (John 1:18; 6:46). The Son mediates knowledge of the Father as he wishes: he can share with others his special relationship to the Father. Very shortly Jesus will give the disciples a share in his intimate prayer (11:1-4).

10:25-37 The Good Samaritan. This story and the following one together give a complete picture of Christian discipleship in terms of love of neighbor (active service) and love of Jesus (prayer). They combine to illustrate the way to everlasting life given in the lawyer's answer (v. 27). When he responds with the statement about love of God and love of neighbor, the lawyer is quoting from the ancient Hebrew prayer, the *Shema* (Deut 6:4-5), linking it to a saying from Lev 19:18. This combination was evidently original with Jesus (Mark 12:29-31) and known to the lawyer, who used it when Jesus turned the question back to him. To "justify himself" (because Jesus has made the lawyer's question seem easy), he raises the disputed question about the identity of the neighbor. In the Leviticus text, the neighbor is one's fellow Israelite.

As a parable, the story of the Good Samaritan is intended to challenge a wrong but accepted pattern of thought so that values of the kingdom can break into a sealed system. This it does by showing a Samaritan, a member of the people despised and ridiculed by Jews, performing a loving service avoided by Jewish religious leaders. This would have been shocking and, for many Jews, unbelievable and unacceptable. The impact in Luke's Gospel is heightened in view of the Samaritan inhospitality of 9:52-53.

This story, once accepted, also gives a vivid example of the fulfillment of the love commandment. The lawyer's question implies that someone is not my neighbor. Jesus' story replies that there is no one who is not my neighbor. "Neighbor" is not a matter of blood bonds or nationality or religious communion; it is determined by the attitude a person has toward others. The priest and the Levite were well-versed in the demands of God's law and,

like the lawyer, would surely have been able to interpret it for others. But they missed its deepest purpose, while the Samaritan, by practicing love, showed that he understood the law.

10:38-42 Martha and Mary. To judge from the story of the Samaritan, Martha should have been praised for her practical service to Jesus. Her action, in fact, is neither praised nor condemned, but she is challenged to consider her priorities. The whole gospel is not contained in loving service to others, no matter how important that is. Christian discipleship is first and foremost personal adherence to Jesus. There must be time to listen to his "word" (v. 39: singular in Greek); devotion to Jesus is the "one thing required." This relationship shows itself in loving service, but without prayer, care for others' needs may not be love.

The Good Samaritan parable and the story of Martha and Mary, then, serve to illustrate the double commandment (10:27) in reverse order: the action of the Samaritan emphasizes love of neighbor; the action of Mary emphasizes love of God.

11:1-13 Jesus teaches his disciples to pray. The disciples realize that the right relationship to the Father (and to Jesus) is sought in prayer. Jesus, like John the Baptist, must have a distinctive insight into prayer flowing from his mission. In response to the disciples' question, he reveals the Lord's Prayer. Here the setting is a time of prayer; in Matthew's Gospel, the Lord's Prayer is part of the Sermon on the Mount (Matt 6:9-13).

Comparison of the two forms of the Lord's Prayer reveals that the structure and content are basically the same, reflecting the original instruction of Jesus. They were shaped by different community traditions at a very early stage. Matthew's text, an adaptation for liturgical use, has been used in worship down to our day; the briefer text of Luke, though less familiar, is probably closer to the original phrasing of Jesus. Both begin with Jesus' distinctive address for God, "Father" (Hebrew: *Abba*), and pray first for the glorification of God's name on earth and the full establishment of his kingdom. Then they turn to the disciples' needs: God's continual protection day by day and his sustaining support in the face of the "final test" at the end of time. In slightly different wording, both formulas relate God's forgiveness of us to our forgiveness of others.

The story of the midnight visitor and the sayings following it are a strong admonition to perseverance in prayer. God always responds to our prayer in ways that are best for us, though not perhaps in ways that we would expect or like. The extravagant examples of the sleeping friend and the father who would give snakes and scorpions to his children drive home the absurdity of thinking of the heavenly Father as harsh or cruel. God wants the best for us—which ultimately is the Holy Spirit, the gift of the age to come (see Acts 2:17). "Ask. . . seek . . . knock" are three different descriptions of petitionary prayer; but "seek" also implies the search for the kingdom of God and union with the Father.

11:14-28 Jesus and Beelzebul. The words and deeds of Jesus often provoke amazement in the witnesses, with varying reactions: praise of God (5:26), questions (4:36), wonder (9:43). The crowd viewing the casting out of the mute demon is closed to the meaning of the event. Some put the worst possible interpretation on Jesus' act of power, others demand even further signs before they will believe. This is the kind of hardness of heart that even ten plagues would not penetrate (Exod 7–11).

"Beelzebul" was a popular name for the master of demons. Jesus points out the absurdity of the accusation. If he is working for Beelzebul, Beelzebul is destroying his own kingdom. Other Jewish exorcists fall under the same suspicion. No, Jesus' routing of the demons is a sign that a stronger power is manifesting itself, a power that can only be from God and a sign of the inbreaking of the kingdom. Jesus compares himself to a victorious warrior carrying away the very arms Satan has been relying on. He warns his critics that there is no middle ground: if you do not side with Jesus, you are in the army of Satan. The point is pressed with the example of the wandering unclean spirit. If the place vacated by the demon is not incorporated into God's reign, it still virtually belongs to the kingdom of Beelzebul; and false security will make it even more susceptible to Satan's domination.

A woman in the crowd cries out in admiration for Jesus' deed and his wisdom in answering the critics. Her comment takes the form of praise of the mother who had brought him into the world, with the implication that this achievement and the physical relationship with such a son must make her completely happy. Jesus responds that true happiness consists in hearing the word of God and keeping it. Earlier he had said that physical motherhood is subordinate to this spiritual relationship open to all (8:21; see 6:47-48), not excluding Mary, of course, but intimating where her real excellence lies (see 2:19, 51).

11:29-36 The sign of Jonah. Jesus takes up the remarks of those asking him for a further sign of his spiritual authority (v. 16). He himself is sign enough for the present generation. He compares himself to Jonah, at whose coming the Ninevites reformed their lives (Jonah 3:5). Jesus, too, has a message of salvation, if the people will only heed it. The queen of Sheba had come to investigate the rumors of Solomon's wisdom and wealth (1 Kgs 10:1-13). At the judgment, all these Gentiles, like the inhabitants of Tyre and Sidon (Luke 10:13-14), will be recognized as more open to God's will than these chosen people of his.

The saying about the lamp, used earlier in the context of listening to the word of God (8:16), is repeated here in a similar context. Jesus and the gospel proclaimed by him are the light (lamp) God offers to his people. To refuse this light (for example, by seeking signs) is to prefer darkness in one's life. The lamp of the gospel is always burning, but it is not necessarily burning for you (v. 36). A secondary application of the lamp image is to one's eyes, understood as the window that can be fogged or shaded and thus keep the light from entering the person.

11:37-54 Woes to the Pharisees and the lawyers. The host is surprised that Jesus does not perform the ritual ablutions, though this custom was only a Pharisaic practice not required by the law. His puzzlement provokes a reply that was more than he bargained for, not an answer to the specific question of ritual washing but a full-scale condemnation of a general religious attitude associated with the Pharisees. The speech is preserved in a considerably different order in Matt 23.

Jesus accuses the Pharisees of emphasizing externals in religion while overlooking in their own conduct the breach of essentials. He mentions the absurdity of religiously cleaning the outside of a cup while one's own inside is full of evil. The antidote to greed, he says, is to give away one's money in alms. Luke records several sayings of Jesus about the need to be poor (6:20; 14:33; 12:21), but he also shows that riches are not condemned as long as they serve the needs of others and do not make one a slave (12:15; 19:8; 16:13). The tithes that the Pharisees were paying should have led in this direction, but instead had become a decoy covering the neglect of justice and charity (v. 42; see 17:12). Their blindness had made them a danger to those they were supposed to lead.

This speech offends one of the lawyers at table. These lawyers or experts in the teaching of Moses are otherwise called "scribes" (v. 53), but Luke has adopted here a term that would be more understandable to his Greek readers (see 10:25). The scribes did not necessarily belong to any particular Jewish group, but most of them were in fact Pharisees. Jesus accuses them of using the law as a rod to punish the people instead of interpreting it for them as a gift from God. They have taken away the "key of knowledge," the means for true understanding of God and salvation, and by misusing the law have been themselves misled.

The criticism of the scribes and Pharisees leads to a condemnation of the practices of their ancestors, an especially stinging rebuke. Stephen would be stoned for accusing Israel of murdering its prophets (Acts 7:52-54). Jesus calls the present generation to account for the blood of God's messengers, from Abel, the son of Adam and Eve (Gen 4), to Zechariah, the son of Jehoida, the chief priest during the reign of King Joash of Judah (837–800 B.C.E.), who was killed in the temple when he tried to call the nation back to true worship (2 Chr 24:17-22). As a result of this outburst, the animosity of the Jewish leaders is no longer subtle. They manifest their hostility and set traps for Jesus.

12:1-12 Fearless discipleship. The size of the swelling crowd is in contrast to the attitude of the religious leaders. Jesus continues to use the way to Jerusalem as a school for his disciples. Note, he says, the hypocrisy of the Pharisees. They think that their surface respectability will keep what is underneath from being discovered. A saying used earlier about the revelation of God's word is now used to teach that all personal secrets will be revealed on the day of judgment. The point is enforced with the images of exposure to daylight and an announcement from the rooftops.

All this leads to an admonition to the disciples (called "friends" here for the only time in the Synoptic Gospels; see John 15:13-15) to be open and aboveboard in their adherence to Jesus and his gospel. They should not let human fear keep them from openly living their faith. Humans can only kill the body. The only one to fear (in the sense of realistic reverence because of his authority over our destiny) is God, who decides life and death, reward and punishment. But this fear is not the cowering of a slave before a cruel master; God is Father. He cares even for the dime-a-dozen sparrows. Therefore one of his own children should know nothing of enslaving fear. "You are worth more than many sparrows." This could not have been said with a straight face. Jesus dispels fear with a smile in the midst of harsh language (see v. 24).

In the Acts of the Apostles, the fearlessness of gospel proclamation is a sign of the presence of the Holy Spirit (Acts 4:29-31). Jesus will treat his disciples as they have treated him. Their fidelity or their inconstancy will not remain hidden. The saying in verse 10 promises, though, that there is always the possibility of repentance for denying the Son of Man. "Blaspheming against the Holy Spirit" means the denial of God's desire or ability to save. This attitude, as long as it exists, makes forgiveness impossible.

12:13-21 The poor rich man. Jesus is interrupted in his instruction of the disciples by a man who wants help in acquiring his rightful share of the family inheritance. Besides being rude, the interruption betrays an insensitivity to what Jesus has just said about matters of essential importance. Rabbis were often asked to arbitrate in family disputes. Jesus certainly has the authority to do this (even more as the Son of Man), but he sees behind the question the very greed he warned the Pharisees about (11:39-42). He uses the opportunity to tell a parable about the trap of possessions.

The rich man would be the envy of most people—so wealthy that he does not have room to store his goods. But he is a fool because in the midst of his good fortune he has lost the sense of what is really important. He imagines that he can control his life. Possessions create this kind of illusion. The rich man is really poor in the sight of God. He does not even think about the possibility of sharing what he has with others. The implications of this story will be carried further in the tale of another rich man (16:19-31).

12:22-34 The care of a loving Father. The discussion of possessions leads to one of Jesus' most radical statements about the life of faith. What he says here about the conduct of life goes directly against the normal human approach: striving to get life under control by arranging for all immediate needs and wants and by covering all contingencies. Jesus says that worry about such things is a sign of lack of faith (v. 28) and a misunderstanding of our God. What is condemned here is not foresight and industry but an anxious approach to life that subconsciously denies that God is a loving Father who has everything carefully under his control.

In the desert, Jesus had won his own battle with this temptation by declaring that there is more to life than food (4:4). And no matter how protective and solicitous one is for health and safety, the length of life is completely under God's control. God takes care of the birds. He adorns the flowers and gives sunshine and moisture to the grass, which will soon perish. You are meant to live in his kingdom forever: will he not take care of you? Freedom from frantic anxiety is a sign of faith. The primary concern is the establishment of God's kingdom (Lord's Prayer: 11:2), not one's own. It is absurd to let life be consumed in the building of a vanishing kingdom when the Father wants to give you his own eternal kingdom.

Finally Jesus comes back to the admonition to give alms (11:41). Parting with what one depends on is the best way to learn the freedom of the kingdom. The attitude toward earthly goods is not an indifferent or innocent question; it is the barometer of what is really important in a person's life.

12:35-48 Waiting for the Master's return. The mention of the kingdom, the thief, and the treasure prompts Luke to add here some sayings of Jesus about the coming of the Son of Man at the end of the world (*parousia*) and the judgment. Central to the test of faith is the challenge of constant readiness for the Master's return. In several ways Jesus empha-

sizes that the time of the return will be a surprise (17:20; Mark 13:33). Comparisons are made to the return of a master from a wedding, when the coming is certain but the timing is not, and to the coming of a thief, when not even the coming is certain. These sayings have been adapted to the situation of the early church as it experienced the delay of the coming, especially the instructions about the leaders of the community (vv. 41-48). But authentic sayings from Jesus are at the root of the discourse; for example, no disciple would have originated the comparison of the Son of Man to a thief (vv. 39-40).

The fastening of the belt recalls the preparations for the Exodus (Exod 12:11). The Hebrew people were to be ready to move immediately when the call of the Lord came. The disciples of Jesus are to be ready to open to the Master "immediately when he comes." The answer to Peter's question (v. 41) directs the discourse toward the Christian leaders especially. The care of what has been entrusted foreshadows the parable of the sums of money (19:11-27). The sayings on the distribution of responsibilities or gifts in the concluding verse of the section are clearly pertinent for those in authority, but they have a wider application for all on whom spiritual and temporal gifts have been bestowed.

12:49-59 The urgency of the kingdom. Jesus has given his disciples a glimpse of the culmination of his mission in the return of the Son of Man at the time of judgment. He is already engaged in the task of lighting a fire on the earth. Judgment is taking place as people decide for or against him. Fire is a symbol for the Holy Spirit as well (Acts 2:3-4); the fire of the Holy Spirit will be cast on the earth through the fulfillment of the events for which Jesus is heading toward Jerusalem. Jesus means by his "baptism" the plunge into this saving mission, a prospect that produces mixed emotions because of the suffering connected with it (see Mark 10:38-39). Some of his teaching on forgiveness and peace may have given the impression that he was spreading a soft gospel; John the Baptist seems to have worried about that (7:18-23). Jesus assures his listeners that Christian discipleship is costly, even causing division in the family (see Mic 7:6). The Gospels give us glimpses of differences of opinion about Jesus among his own kin (Mark 3:21; John 7:5).

The gospel challenge is clear. Anyone who can see the clouds or feel the wind can certainly see the signs of the times. It is hypocrisy to blind oneself to the evident signs of the coming of the kingdom. In trying to fool others, a hypocrite fools himself. There is still time for decision, warns Jesus, but do not put it off. When judgment comes, you will wish you had settled out of court.

13:1-9 Reform while there is time. Jesus continues his call for decision and reform by referring to contemporary disasters and telling a parable. Pilate was notorious for his harsh rule and his insensitivity to Jewish religious feelings. The first of these otherwise unknown incidents refers to the killing of some Galileans while they were offering sacrifice (probably in the Jerusalem temple at Passover). The second example involves what was probably a construction accident at the Siloam reservoir at Jerusalem. Popular wisdom associated disaster with punishment for sin (Job 4:7-9; John 9:2). Jesus says that in the present age good fortune and disaster are no indication of a person's spiritual state (see Matt 5:45). But in the judgment to come, those who have been evil will certainly experience disaster. Now is the time to produce evidence of a life dedicated to the kingdom (see 6:43-44). The time may even be extended for us as for the fig tree. But ultimately the judgment will come.

13:10-17 Healing and hypocrisy. Two sabbath incidents have already been presented (6:1-11). This sabbath cure is inserted here as an example of the hypocritical blindness Jesus has been describing (12:54-57). The synagogue official cannot see what is happening right before his eyes—the inbreaking of the kingdom in the freeing of this crippled woman from eighteen years of suffering. He has become too hobbled by the letter of the law to recognize its spirit. The Pharisees allowed animals to be taken care of on the sabbath (see 14:5); why begrudge this woman an extraordinary gift of God? The official's reaction is predictable: rather than confront the miracle-worker, he vents his ire on the people. The action produces division; the judgment is already taking place.

13:18-21 Two parables of the reign of God. These two parables stress the great results that can grow out of tiny beginnings. The small mustard seed becomes a shrub that may reach nine feet in height. A small lump of yeast helps the dough expand to several times its original size. Jesus uses these daily examples to give insight into the kingdom. The reign of God cannot be thoroughly described or explained in human language, but the world is full of signs of this reign. Parables give us flashes of understanding. From these two parables we learn primarily that we must expect the beginnings of the kingdom in the smallest happenings and (in the world's eyes) the most insignificant people. A crippled woman, for example, is a sign of the reign of God in the preceding narrative.

Though a parable usually has one principal focus, often an insight into the meaning of existence that upsets comfortable prejudices, it can be used for further applications. The early church saw a further meaning in the large mustard shrub and the birds as the gospel preaching spread and Gentiles found a home in the Christian community (v. 29). And the idea of yeast would lead naturally to the comparison with Christian influence in the world.

13:22-30 The narrow door. This section contains several references to the seriousness of the proclamation of God's reign and to the need for a sober decision to undertake the journey to Jerusalem with Jesus, a journey that will end in suffering and death (9:22-23). Luke reminds us that Jesus is still on the journey to Jerusalem according to God's plan. The question along the way offers him the opportunity to mention once again the difficulties involved in following him. He does not answer the question whether few will be saved, but he does say that many will not be. There is specific mention of the sad case of those who had been under the illusion that they were following Jesus but had maintained only a loose relationship with him. They ate and drank with him, indeed, but with no intimate fellowship; they heard his teaching but did not accept it as the word of God to be put into practice (8:21). Jesus' harsh words to "you evildoers" are meant as a challenge to the readers of Luke's Gospel to redirect their steps toward Jerusalem with Jesus while there is still time.

The patriarchs and prophets of Israel are waiting to share the banquet of the kingdom with those who are now on the way. Many of those who ate and drank with Jesus will not be there, but there will be others who never knew him while he was ministering in Israel. The gospel will be offered to the Gentiles; they will come into the kingdom from all over the world. Luke's Gentile audience would listen eagerly to these words, but they would also be challenged not to take for granted themselves their eating and drinking with Jesus at the Eucharist. The pronouncement closing this speech guards against both presumption and despair; as long as the journey is underway, some may fall away and others may still join.

13:31-35 The way of the prophet. The attitude of the Pharisees who bring the warning about Herod is not described, but their intervention is probably meant to be understood as hostility rather than helpfulness (see 11:53-54). Herod could have expressed a desire to get the troublemaker out of Galilee. Jesus' reference to "that fox" may be a way of recognizing the cunning in the threat that urges him on to the place where prophets traditionally met their fate. Twice Jesus describes his mission in terms of three days, surely meant here by Luke as a foreshadowing of the resurrection: ". . . on the third day I accomplish my purpose." The theme of the divinely appointed task is very strong. No matter what human rulers may want, Jesus has to follow the established pattern. Implied too is a warning that God will permit no interference in this plan, though kings will be permitted to cooperate in the execution of it (Acts 4:27). The confrontation between the prophets and their enemies often took place at Jerusalem or even in the temple (11:51; see Jer 26:20-24). Though historically the murders did not take place in Jerusalem exclusively (1 Kgs 18:4), Jerusalem stands for the heart of the land and its people, and symbolizes the stubbornness that counteracted the prophets (Acts 7:51-52).

Reminded of this tragic hostility of Jerusalem to the messengers of God, Jesus laments over the city, seeing himself as the last in the line of the prophets to meet destruction there. He foretells the abandonment of the "house," which should probably be interpreted as the whole city. Jesus will not be seen in Jerusalem before the allotted time. He still has to make the stages of the journey as it unfolds according to plan. But eventually he will come in the midst of cries of praise (19:38), which will only deepen the irony of his rejection.

14:1-6 Another sabbath cure. For the third time Luke presents a scene with Jesus in the house of a Pharisee (7:36; 11:37). The man with dropsy, a disease in which the body swells up with excess fluid, was presumably one of the guests. The possibility of a friend's cure might have provoked the host and his guests at least to discuss the propriety of this healing on the sabbath, but all are silent. Jesus then heals the man. He tries to open the minds of his hearers by showing the absurdity of denying healing on the basis of a law of the sabbath, the day given as a gift by God to refresh his people; the argument is similar to the one used in the synagogue (13:15).

14:7-14 Worldly honor and praise. Jesus addresses a parable to the guests and gives advice to his host. In both speeches he appeals to what would seem to be base motives. Guests are urged not to seek the first places at table, not because this sort of self-promotion and pride is wrong, but in order that they may later be honored. Honored guests, of course, were notorious for the ploy of coming late precisely to be noticed by the assembly as they went to their prominent seats. The point could be interpreted as a suggestion not to seek worldly honor openly but to employ false humility as a subterfuge. Dickens's Uriah Heep comes to mind. Jesus is using the worldly image, though, only because it is so familiar. His point is made in the pronouncement: "Everyone who exalts himself shall be humbled and he who humbles himself shall be exalted." Self-exaltation must not be sought either openly or secretly. Earlier Jesus had reprimanded his disciples for vying for rank (9:46-48).

A similar unworthy motive appears superficially in Jesus' words to the host. The impression is that an invitation to dinner is given for the sake of some reciprocal reward, whether only a return invitation or, in the case of serving the poor, the prize of resurrection with all the just. The point, though, is that in doing good we should serve freely, without regard for our own prospects, leaving the recompense to God. This is the way Jesus went about doing good, emptying himself for others without counting the cost. There is Semitic exaggeration in the statement that one should not invite friends, relatives, and neighbors. The kingdom is for everyone, and our hospitality is to embrace all, especially those who are overlooked by people with only selfish motives.

14:15-24 The great banquet. The mention of the resurrection prompts one of those at table to repeat a favorite maxim or beatitude: Happy are those who share the great banquet in the kingdom of God. This would not ordinarily evoke a response, but Jesus discerns a complacent attitude among the Pharisees and the lawyers toward their share in salvation. They feel protected by observing religious rules, even allowing observances to shut out new possibilities of good (vv. 1-6). He tells a parable about those who take a banquet invitation too lightly and because of their casual attitude lose their own right to a share at the table and are replaced by others. The original meaning concerned observant Jews complacent in their religion who might be surpassed by those they considered outcasts; the early church made the obvious comparison with Israel's rejection and the Gentiles' acceptance of the gospel.

The host in this story has typically invited his friends and relatives first (see v. 12), before turning to the poor and handicapped. It was customary in the social circles of the time to send a personal summons at the time of the dinner, even though an invitation had been sent earlier. It was also typical of Semites to refuse the summons politely so that the host's messengers could urge the invitation more strongly. This is the sense of "make them come in" in verse 23. By the time the summons comes, these invitees have had a change of plans. Perhaps the excuses were legitimate. A man could be released from military service to care for a new house or vineyard, or if recently betrothed or married (Deut 20:5-7; 24:5). But the guests have been too inconsiderate or careless to inform the host of their change of plans. They have not taken his hospitality seriously, and this makes him furious.

An invitation to the salvation banquet is not something to be taken lightly. Jesus implies that some at table with him do not appreciate the urgency of the situation. The host sent his servant out "quickly" to fill up the places. God's desire to fill his house is urgent; he wants as many as possible to partake of the messianic banquet. The final statement (v. 24) is directed to the gathering in the Pharisee's house ("you" is plural): If you take the happiness of sharing God's table in the kingdom too much for granted (v. 15), you may miss the urgent opportunities to respond to his summons by doing the good that he presents.

14:25-35 The cost of discipleship. Jesus moves on toward Jerusalem. The story of the carelessness of those invited to the banquet has been linked by the evangelist to other sayings spelling out the seriousness of discipleship. The call to follow Christ cannot be taken up half-heartedly (v. 35); such an attitude is a tragic miscalculation. These verses reestablish the tone set at the beginning of the journey toward Jerusalem (9:57-62).

Jesus returns to the theme of family division that might come because of the gospel (see 12:51-53). Jesus says his disciples must *hate* father and mother and family. This is another Semitic exaggeration to stress that anyone who stands in the way of thorough commitment to Jesus, even one's closest relations, must be renounced. "Hate" in this sense means "prefer less." This is the radical message of the cross (see 9:23).

Discipleship is thus an all-consuming vocation. It must be accepted with mature deliberation. Jesus uses two examples: a wise builder would not begin a project without assessing his ability to complete it; only a madman would go into a battle without considering the odds. The punch line for the Christian disciple is that renunciation is the salt of discipleship. When a follower of Jesus begins to hold anything back, discipleship becomes a charade. The salt parable has various applications. In Matthew's Gospel it is connected with the light image and used in terms of good example (Matt 5:13); in Mark, salt is the source of peace in the community (Mark 9:50).

15:1-10 Lost and found. This chapter is bound together by the theme of joy over the recovery of what was lost. All three parables apply to the return of the repentant sinner; the story of the prodigal son develops the theme of God's love and adds the contrast of the older brother's hostility. Jesus is surrounded by "tax collectors and sinners," causing murmuring among the scribes and Pharisees (see 7:39).

Jesus addresses his listeners directly: "What man among you . . . ?" What he suggests all will do in going after the one lost sheep is actually *not* what many of us would do, but the attractiveness of this extravagant individual concern makes the listener want to agree. In a split second we are drawn into God's world, seeing and acting as he would. The shepherd's joy is like God's joy; his dedication to the individual sheep, carrying it back to the flock, is a reflection of God's love. Francis Thompson's *Hound of Heaven* might be a commentary on this parable. The joy in heaven is over the change of heart (*metanoia:* see 3:3; 5:32) of the sinner. "No need of repentance" is ironic and tragic (see 5:32; 7:47).

A different image is used in a second parable to the same effect. The woman has lost one of her ten *drachmas,* Greek silver coins. She turns her house upside down in search of this one coin in ten. Perhaps it was part of her dowry and thus had added sentimental value. Her joy is like the joy in heaven over one repentant sinner. It needs to be shared. It is too great for one person. She and the shepherd invite their friends and neighbors for the thanksgiving party. What about the other nine silver pieces and the ninety-nine sheep—are they not important, too? Surely, but the joy of the kingdom breaks out of the ordinary categories of reason and good business. What was given up as lost has been found. It is like a new life, a resurrection, and must be celebrated.

15:11-32 The prodigal son. This story is probably the most famous of Jesus' parables. Besides being a classic of spiritual insight, it is a literary jewel. Through this story Jesus illustrates the earth-shattering acceptance available in the kingdom of God. The traditional title is too well entrenched to be changed, but it is a misnomer. The story is about a father and two sons, and its pivot is the father's prodigality in love to both of his sons rather than the younger son's wastefulness of worldly goods.

Under Jewish law, the first-born son received a double share of the inheritance (Deut 21:17). The younger son in this case was entitled to a third of the estate. The division of property ordinarily awaited the death of the father, and there were provisions in traditional law for penalties when the share was withdrawn ahead of time. This is not important here. By demanding his share and leaving, the younger son is cutting his ties with his family, with no regrets. He takes everything with him; there is no reasonable hope

that he will be back. His departure with a substantial share of the family estate also means a loss to his father and brother, adding to the latter's animosity.

Imagination can fill in the familiar story line that is compressed with great economy: the extravagant spending, the attraction of freeloading friends, the crash. For the Hebrew, caring for pigs evoked the idea of apostasy and the loss of everything that once identified the younger son as a member of his family and of God's people. He is even lower than the swine—they have access to the husks, but he does not.

Calamity finally brings him to his senses. He will return to his home as a hired servant. He carefully rehearses his speech, expecting to be treated with cold reserve and suspicion. But his father still loves him. He has been keeping vigil and sees his son coming "a long way off." Anything but coolly reserved, he runs to meet his son, hugging and kissing him. The son cannot get through his rehearsed speech. This reunion is almost identical to Esau's meeting with Jacob (Gen 33:4). Jacob remembers his crime against his brother and fears for his life. But Esau, like the father in this story, is interested only in reconciliation. The father cannot act quickly enough. He arranges for the finest robe, a ring and shoes, all of which classify the young man as a son of the household rather than a servant. There is no thought of recrimination, no policy of making the young man prove himself worthy. The only important thing is that he is alive. The son himself is more important than anything he has done.

The story would be complete as it stands with the return of the prodigal son and the father's open-armed acceptance. But another story interlocks with this one. The elder son's anger and self-righteousness make him resentful; not even the return of his brother will make him share the family celebration. Again the pivot is the father's love. He goes out to the elder son as he went out to the younger. He wants both of them to be happy. The elder son cannot see beyond propriety and is trapped in his own righteousness. The father does not deny the faithfulness of his elder son. He implies that all that is beside the point at this special moment. Something far more important is going on: a son and brother has returned from the dead. Everything else fades before that fact: "We had to celebrate and re-joice!" The Jacob story comes to mind again. At a later stage he has discovered, like Esau, the importance of reunion. When he discovers that his son Joseph is alive, he forgets recriminations and simply rejoices: "It is enough. My son Joseph is still alive!" (Gen 45:28).

A parable is not an allegory (in other words, there does not have to be an application for each part of the story), but besides experiencing the heavenly joy and the thorough acceptance of the younger son, we can see the father as God and put ourselves into the story. Am I like the father? Or like the elder or younger son? Do I have parts of all three in me? A parable this rich blossoms out with new meaning for each reader, and at each reading.

16:1-13 The right use of money. Jesus returns to the theme of use of wealth (see 12:13-34). The chapter begins and ends with parables. The story of the wily steward has been a problem for interpreters. Does Jesus encourage dishonesty? As verse 8 shows, he is rather contrasting the clever industry of the this-worldly with the lethargy of children of the kingdom. Whether the steward is moral or immoral in his actions is not the point of the comparison.

The steward has been careless in managing his employer's estate. Faced with expulsion, he knows that he will get no recommendation for a similar job. He is not physically capable of day labor, and begging would be too humiliating. While there is time, he uses his position to make friends for the bleak future. He reduces the debt of each of his master's debtors (only the first two instances are described), hoping they will remember. It appears that the steward has played fast and loose with his master's property. The charge against him was not dishonesty, however, but wastefulness and mismanagement; and in his preparations for the future he may not have been dishonest either. Stewards were often paid from the interest charged on loans. In the present case, the amounts he deducted from the individual debts may have been the (exorbitant) interest originally coming to him. Usury was against the law (Exod 22:24). By erasing this extra charge, the steward might have been seen as reforming his life and performing an act of justice!

Jesus' teaching, however, is an appeal for the "children of light" to be as enterprising in their pursuit of the kingdom as this steward was in trying to make a place for himself in this world. He follows this with a corollary on the use of worldly wealth in preparing for eternity. The crafty steward used his money to prepare an earthly dwelling, but earthly wealth, though it may be associated with evil (it is called literally "mammon of wickedness" in v. 9), can be put to good use for God's kingdom. It can be given as alms to the poor and lowly so that their benefactor may share with them a place in the kingdom (see 11:41; 12:21). This admonition looks ahead to the story at the end of the chapter.

A conclusion about stewardship is drawn for the followers of Jesus. As in this world, so in the kingdom: trustworthiness in small things leads to a greater trust. This refers to spiritual realities but is also concerned with physical stewardship (v. 13). The community of Jesus will have to deal with problems of spiritual and material stewardship (12:41-47; Matt 18:1-18). There is always the danger of subordinating the spiritual to the material without realizing that a new master has taken over.

16:14-18 The law, the prophets, and the kingdom. Jesus' statement that a person cannot serve both God and money triggers dispute and derision from Pharisees in the audience. They are described as "loving money" and obviously felt that they could combine worship of God and pursuit of riches. Jesus accused them of trying to prove their justice in the eyes of men, perhaps by almsgiving (see 21:1-4). They hold Jesus in contempt because his teaching on this matter is too rigorous and "unrealistic"; Jesus counters that their scale of values is contemptible to God.

The following three verses seem to break the flow of the chapter. They are sayings on the law collected from various places in Luke's sources (Mark 10:11-12; Matt 11:12-13; 5:18-32; 19:9). Why did the evangelist insert these sayings here before returning to the topic of wealth? The connection is to be found in the challenge to Jesus' whole moral teaching implied in the sneering reaction of the Pharisees. The law of Moses is the norm; Jesus has no business introducing his own law. Jesus replies that the law and the prophets have indeed been the norm, and even now that he is proclaiming the kingdom of God their validity does not cease. But the teaching of the kingdom brings into the open implications of the traditional teaching that were unrecognized.

John the Baptist is the turning point. He is the last of the Old Testament prophets, but, as the herald of Jesus, he belongs also to the preachers of the gospel. He is the bridge between old and new. From his time on, "everyone who enters does so with violence." The kingdom of God is open to every kind of person (3:10-14; 13:29), many of whom will still have to take aggressive action to find their way in. Luke will illustrate this later with the story of Cornelius, the first Gentile convert (Acts 10).

The way into the kingdom is open for the Pharisees, too, but it will not be the escape from observance implied by their derision. The law has abiding validity, but Jesus has the authority to interpret it correctly. His statement on divorce is an example of his interpretation (the most original form of the saying is found here and in Mark 10:11). In case the Pharisees think that Jesus' teaching waters down the law, they should note that his teaching on this point is stricter than that preached by their rabbis. They permitted a husband to divorce his wife on the basis of Deut 24:1. Jesus says divorce and remarriage is adultery.

16:19-31 The rich man and Lazarus. Jesus' teaching on the proper use of wealth is now illustrated by the story of two reversals of fortune. The rich man was oblivious to the needs of the beggar at his gate. He did not realize the seriousness of the present opportunity in preparing for the eternal future (vv. 8-9). It was not his wealth that kept him from Abraham's bosom, but his untrustworthy stewardship. The lives of the two men were quite different, and so were their deaths. Lazarus is carried away by angels, but the rich man is simply buried; it is the end for him, but the beginning for Lazarus.

The rich man is in the "netherworld," or Sheol, or Hades (as the Greek has it). It is a place hopelessly separated from the place of happiness with Abraham, though not synonymous with our "hell." The rich man can see Lazarus there (which probably increases his own torment). The rich man still thinks of Lazarus as his errand boy, first asking that he bring a drop of water to cool his tongue, then that he go to warn his brothers. Lazarus is probably surprised that the rich man knows his name. Abraham explains to the rich man why things have turned out this way. Though the man addresses Abraham as his father, he is Abraham's son only by blood relationship, not by the true spiritual relationship that effects salvation.

That the rich man wants Lazarus to go to his father's house is the first sign we have that he is concerned about others. But it is too late, and the action would be useless and inappropriate. They have Moses and the prophets. The word of God proclaimed through centuries in Israel should be enough. This statement harks back to Jesus' words about the law and the prophets in the center of the chapter (vv. 16-17). Jesus is still speaking to the Pharisees and still warning them that lip service to the law and superficial correctness in observance do not really mean listening to the word of God. Abraham closes with a statement that was probably embellished by the church in its transmission of the parable. Even resurrection will not convince those who are not disposed to listen attentively to the law and the prophets. This sentence adds an ironic twist and broadens the intended audience to all who read the story.

17:1-10 Four sayings on discipleship. As he makes his way to Jerusalem, Jesus continues to teach his disciples by sayings, stories, and his own example. It is inevitable, he says, that there will be stumbling blocks to faith and to the living of Christian discipleship because of Satan's interference and because of human misuse of freedom. The one who blocks another's way has a heavy responsibility to answer for. With the graphic image of the millstone, Jesus says it would be better to die than to become the source of another's failure.

Then, looking at the other side of the relationship (vv. 3-4), Jesus describes the proper attitude of the disciple who has been offended or "scandalized." It is an act of love to correct the brother who is a stumbling block for others. There is a false tolerance that permits a fellow disciple to continue down the wayward path. Jesus encourages correction and forgiveness. "Seven times" (v. 4) is a symbolic way of saying "every time."

The apostles ask for an increase of faith.

Jesus casts doubt on their possession of any faith. Maybe they are too self-assured because they are accompanying him to Jerusalem. He describes the power that comes through faith, using an exaggerated image for a memorable effect. The example of the treatment of a servant probably goes with Jesus' demurral about the apostles' faith. Servants of the Lord must beware of thinking that they deserve or can earn a special reward because of their service. Jesus may be alluding also to an attitude among Jewish religious leaders that correct observance deserves God's reward (see 18:9-12). The listeners would easily understand the example of master and servant relations. If good work is expected of the servant as an ordinary part of his duties, why should the disciple of Jesus think faithful service is not a basic requirement of following the master?

17:11-19 The grateful leper. The condition of lepers in the time of Jesus has been described (see 5:12-16). The group that meets him is composed of both Jews (Galileans) and Samaritans. The companionship of these usually bitter enemies indicates the desperation of their condition, which led them to depend on one another. Because they were required to avoid contact with non-lepers (Lev 13:45-46) but had to depend on their charity for survival, lepers haunted the outskirts of towns. This group shouted at Jesus from the proper distance; they had heard about his compassion and his healing power. Jesus simply gives a command, as Elisha did to the leper Naaman (2 Kgs 5:10-12), which could also be a test of their faith and obedience. They are to show themselves to the priests, whose responsibility it was to judge whether a leper was permitted to return to society (Lev 14:2). They obey his instruction, going to report their healing while they are as yet unhealed.

Only one of the group returns to express gratitude. He attributes the healing to God, openly singing his praises. The ingratitude of the others is a jarring note, but possibly the fact that the one grateful returnee was a Samaritan was more shocking at the time (vv. 16, 18). Jesus' final words to him are the message he gave to the woman in the Pharisee's house (7:50) and the woman cured of the hemorrhage (8:48). The faith of all the lepers led to their physical healing; perhaps it was

more than this for the others as well, but for the Samaritan at least, this healing brought "salvation," thorough wholeness and a proper relationship to God.

17:20-37 The coming of the reign of God. When Jesus sent the seventy-two disciples on their preaching mission at the beginning of his journey toward Jerusalem, he told them to proclaim the nearness of the reign of God (10:11). Earlier he had sent the Twelve to announce his reign (9:2). As he proceeds toward Jerusalem, the question arises, when will the reign of God come? Jesus answers first that the reign is already present (vv. 20-21) and then speaks of the definitive establishment of the kingdom at the end of the world (vv. 22-37).

The establishment of God's reign was expected with the coming of the Messiah (see 3:15). This would be the day of the Lord, a time of judgment and reward (Joel 2:1-2; 3:4-5). Jesus tells the Pharisees that knowledge of the time of the day of the Lord is not important. What is crucial is to recognize the presence of God's reign already in their midst. Jesus' ministry is the clear sign that God's reign has begun. No matter how clearly Jesus stated that the end cannot be calculated (v. 20; Mark 13:32-33) and that its timing is not a question to be concerned with (Acts 1:6-8), the question continued to arise as he went toward Jerusalem (19:11) and afterward in the church. Today it is still a major concern for many Christians, and the concern is still misplaced. Jesus' teaching on the question could not be clearer. Don't waste your time looking for signs and listening to clever calculations. Be aware that the reign of God is already in your midst; unless you give his present reign your full attention now, you will not be ready for the return of the Son of Man when it does occur. And no one can know when that will happen.

After calling attention to the present reality of God's reign, Jesus turns to his disciples to explain what is still to come. The presence of God's reign does not mean that the trials are over; there is still much suffering in store for Jesus (v. 25) and for his followers (v. 22). The disciples will be desperate for the coming of the Son of Man, and this will lead them to follow false prophets and misleading theories about his appearance. But when it happens, the appearance of the Son of Man will not be subtle or mysterious. Everyone will know. It will be as vivid as lightning across the sky. The contrast of the Son of Man's glory with the suffering that must precede will make his coming even more evident.

No matter when it happens, people will be unprepared. Worldly pursuits will captivate them, as they captivated those who lived in the days of Noah before the flood and the inhabitants of Sodom right up to the day of its destruction. That is why Jesus emphasizes the importance of recognizing the presence now of God's reign. It must govern our lives now, not just at the end; otherwise we will not be prepared to leave when the sudden call comes. One who is concerned about his possessions (14:33) will try to save them and be lost himself. Lot's wife is remembered as a person who was too attached to refrain from looking back (Gen 19:17, 26; see Luke 9:62).

The examples of the two men and the two women illustrate the suddenness of the coming of Christ and the readiness or unreadiness he will find. This has nothing to do with the "Rapture," a modern perversion of the scriptural teaching, which interprets these and the corresponding texts elsewhere (see Matt 24:37-41) as a description of the separation of good and evil people before the final coming. Verse 36 is omitted in most versions because it is a scribal insertion taken from Matt 24:40, adding the example of two men in the field to Luke's text. The proverb about the carcass and the vultures corresponds to the image of the lightning (v. 24). Jesus closes the instruction with a final stress on the dominant theme: the coming of the day of the Son of Man will be unmistakable. Meanwhile, do not devote your time and energy to signs and calculations but to living in readiness.

18:1-8 The corrupt judge and the widow. This parable on persistence in prayer shares many similarities with the parable of the man waking his neighbor at midnight (11:5-8). The context here is comfort and encouragement for the disciples as they await the coming of the Son of Man. Keep praying, don't lose heart.

The judge is completely unscrupulous, guided by neither divine nor human law. The widow is asking only for her rights; by Jewish law she was one of the special helpless ones who should be given priority (Deut 24:17-22). The judge's refusal to act may have been due to laziness, fear of her adversary, or her lack of importance in his eyes. He is finally moved to do her justice by fear of the consequences to himself if she persists in her request. Jesus contrasts the judge's insensitivity with God's care for his elect. If the unjust judge will act after persistent requests, will not God? But delay of an answer to prayer, and especially here the delay of the coming of the Son of Man, may cause followers of Jesus to give up. When the Master does come, some will have lost faith.

18:9-14 The Pharisee and the tax collector. Jesus was constantly combating the self-righteousness that he found such a sinister enemy of spiritual progress (5:32; 15:7). This parable is addressed directly to the self-righteous. The Pharisee and the tax collector are stereotypes of the good and the sinful person. The Pharisee prays with straightforward gratitude for his healthy spiritual state. There is no sign that he is trying to deceive. Pharisees did fast severely twice a week, on Mondays and Thursdays, for the good of the whole nation. And there is no reason to doubt that he tithed. The tragedy is that he does not understand the flawed nature of this prayer. He is deceiving himself. He does not look upon himself as God's servant but as one who deserves good of God for a job well done. Besides this pride, he is guilty of contempt for the tax collector.

The tax collector is conscious of his sinfulness. He knows that he does not deserve consideration because of anything he has done. The prayer he utters is one of the sources of the ancient Jesus Prayer: "Lord Jesus Christ, Son of God, have mercy on me, a sinner." It is this helplessness and dependence that opens one to God's grace; it is the spirit of the child. Earlier Jesus commended one who would say, after doing good work that was a duty, "We are unprofitable servants" (17:10). The debate over faith and works is already engaged here (see Rom 3:27-4:5). Jesus himself draws the shocking conclusion from the parable: the observant Pharisee goes home unjustified, the sinful tax collector is justified. The reversal maxim concludes the story (see 14:11).

18:15-17 Jesus and the children. At the beginning of his narrative of the journey to Jerusalem (9:51), Luke departed from the outline of Mark and began introducing material from sources either personal or common to Matthew and himself. At this point Luke begins to follow Mark again. In Mark, the episode of the children (Mark 10:13-16) is preceded by Jesus' statement on divorce and remarriage. But Luke uses it along with the story of the rich man, to which it is connected in Mark, as an illustrative sequel to the parable of the Pharisee and the tax collector. The tax collector has the attitude of a child, defenseless and expectant, while the Pharisee is like the rich man (vv. 18-25), not yet ready to give up control over himself.

The disciples are infected with the attitudes of the Pharisee and the rich man. They have no tolerance for children and what they stand for. In their view, Jesus is wasting his time on these children who are unable to comprehend the great work he is about. He startles them by saying that the reign of God belongs precisely to such as these children. This narrative later supported those in the developing church who argued for infant baptism.

18:18-25 Jesus and the rich man. Whether the official is a Pharisee or not, his self-righteous attitude (v. 21) is the same as that criticized by Jesus earlier (v. 11). Jesus contests the use of "good" in the address, not because he doubts his own goodness, but because this was an unusual way of addressing a rabbi and was probably meant in flattery. Jesus' perception was proved accurate when the man did not obey the instruction of the "good" teacher. Maybe this insight into his character explains the mention only of the "social" commandments of the Decalogue. The commandments dealing with love and service of God are much more subject to illusion.

Jesus does not draw the man into closer relationship immediately. But when he hears a wish to go further, Jesus offers him his own way of life (see 9:57-58). The ruler cannot take the step because of his wealth, so often a threat to life in the kingdom (14:33; 16:13). He seems to know deep down that Jesus has spoken the word he needs to hear, but he is too enslaved by his possessions to follow it through. This provokes Jesus' memorable remark about the camel and the needle's eye. Semitic exaggeration is used, not to deny the possibility of salvation for the rich (see v. 27), but to imprint indelibly in his hearers' minds the sinister influence that riches can be even on those sincerely desiring the reign of God.

18:26-34 The demands of discipleship. Jesus' listeners are shocked by his warning to the wealthy. They would have thought that prosperity was a sign of God's blessing because of a person's goodness (Prov 10:3, 22). Jesus does not retract the harshness (see 6:24) but enunciates the important principle that God is willing and able to save all who call out to him. Peter notes that the disciples have done what the rich ruler could not do, and asks rather crassly about the reward. Jesus promises an "overabundant return," without specifying his meaning (in Mark's version he adds "with persecutions": Mark 10:30), and speaks again of the priority of kingdom over family (see 14:26). Then to the Twelve Jesus makes the third prediction of his passion and resurrection, adding this time that these things will happen in fulfillment of prophecy. The meaning of his words is lost on them.

18:35-43 The blind man at Jericho. The approach to Jericho signals the final stage of Jesus' journey to Jerusalem. Here, as in the incident of the children, the disciples try to keep an "insignificant" person from bothering the Master. The evangelist continues on another level to present the life of the church as a journey with Jesus on the way of the Lord. The note that it is "the people walking in front" who reprimand the beggar is a subtle warning to church leaders who might overlook the needs of the powerless (see Acts 6:1). But it is for these lowly who express their need for salvation that Jesus has come. The present chapter is a gallery of such people: the widow, the tax collector, the children, now the blind beggar.

The beggar's name is given in Mark as Bartimaeus (Mark 10:46). Blind as he is, he cries out with inspired insight, calling Jesus by the messianic title "Son of David." When questioned, he goes further to identify Jesus as "Lord." In response to this faith, he receives the message of deliverance that by now is a stereotyped phrase: "Your faith has saved you" (7:50; 8:48; 17:19). Both the beggar and the witnesses see the ultimate meaning of this act of power and glorify God.

19:1-10 Jesus and Zacchaeus. The story of Zacchaeus is unique to Luke's Gospel. It serves to synthesize dramatically some key themes of discipleship as Jesus nears Jerusalem. First of all, Zacchaeus is a wealthy man—probably very wealthy as the "district supervisor" of the tax collectors. As a result, he would be seen by Jewish leaders as the "chief of sinners," bearing the responsibility for the dishonesty connected with the activity of all his field workers. The question of the proper use of wealth is thus addressed again, and also the issue of eating with sinners. There is the usual murmuring (see 5:30; 15:2). But the breach of decorum is even worse this time, because Jesus does not wait to be invited to the tax collector's house. He invites himself; the shepherd seeking the one lost sheep (v. 10; 15:4-7).

Zacchaeus, in spite of his reputation, is an attractive person. In our brief meeting, qualities akin to those of Peter emerge. Zacchaeus is spontaneous and impetuous, given to extravagant statements. But there is a deep genuineness. Though he is a person of some importance, his position does not prevent him from climbing the sycamore tree nor from publicly admitting his guilt and professing his repentance. Jesus takes the initiative in this conversion story (contrast the blind beggar: 18:38-43), but Zacchaeus had to be ready for the saving word or it would not have been effective (see 8:11-15). Jesus says this is a son of Abraham, even if he is a tax collector. He should not be ostracized because of his failings but helped to find his way back to the flock. Zacchaeus's gratitude is an illustration of the parable of the money-lender and the debtors (7:41-43). Jesus' love of him has awakened new possibilities of love and service.

19:11-27 The parable of the investments. Matthew has another version of this parable (Matt 25:14-30), involving only three servants and different sums of money (his "talents" are also much larger than Luke's *mnas*, translated here as "gold coins"). Luke has added the kingly coronation theme because of the popular anticipation of God's reign (19:11). In its present form the parable answers questions from the time of the early church about the return of Jesus and what to do in his absence. The additions have allegorized the parable, that is, made the individual elements more easily applicable to the story of Jesus.

After the resurrection Luke's readers saw in the reference to a faraway country Jesus' ascension to heaven, where he received the Father's glory and awaited the time when he would return as judge. The servants are not to sit around idle meanwhile nor simply preserve the *status quo*, but are to continue his work while he is away (Acts 1:8-11). The mention of the deputation hostile to his kingship is an allusion to the accession of Archelaus on the death of his father, King Herod the Great, about thirty years earlier. Archelaus had gone to Rome to seek imperial appointment as his father's successor, but a Jewish deputation to Caesar Augustus had managed to restrict Archelaus's rule to only part of the original kingdom. Subsequent cruelty and mismanagement led to Archelaus's early banishment by Rome.

Only three of the ten servants are mentioned in the king's review of accounts. The result of the review is the same as in Matthew's version. The enterprising servants are rewarded with more trust. The servant who played it safe out of fear is condemned for his conduct and loses his sum of money to the one with ten. This provokes criticism from those who dislike the king's largesse. They prefer wages gauged to work, like the vineyard workers in another parable (Matt 20:1-16). The saying in verse 26 appeared in a variant form in 8:18. Openness to God's action in Jesus continues to intensify one's share in the kingdom, but a closed or fearful heart is incapable of sharing these riches.

19:28-44 Arrival at Jerusalem. Jesus' long journey to Jerusalem reaches its goal as he enters from the east through the small villages of Bethphage and Bethany. Luke follows Mark closely here but adds material in verses 39-40 with faint similarities to Matthew's additions (Mark 11:1-10; Matt 21:1-9). Verses 41-44 are unique. In all three accounts this event marks the public acclamation of Jesus as the Davidic Messiah. Earlier he had silenced such acclaim (4:41; 5:14); now he defends the disciples (vv. 39-40) and the children (Matt 21:16) against the criticism of the leaders.

Behind this event and the narratives is the prophetic oracle of Zechariah:

"Rejoice heartily, O daughter Zion,
  shout for joy, O daughter Jerusalem!
See, your king shall come to you;
  a just savior is he,
Meek, and riding on an ass" (Zech 9:9).

Only Matthew makes specific reference to it (Matt 21:5). This background explains the mention of peace in Luke's account (vv. 38, 42). Riding on an ass was not so much an emphasis on humility as on peacefulness. Kings rode horses when they came in war (Jer 8:6); entering Jerusalem on an ass indicates the kind of kingship Jesus is exercising. The two disciples are sent to find an animal that has never been ridden before. Animals for certain types of ritual use had to be previously unused, like the cows chosen to pull the ark of the covenant (1 Sam 6:7; see Num 19:2). The Greek Septuagint version of Zech 9:9 speaks of a "new" colt.

To judge from the space devoted to it, the disciples' errand is considered very special. Perhaps Jesus' foreknowledge or messianic authority is implied in the mysterious instructions about getting the ass. When the disciples return they take an active part in the procedure, laying their cloaks on the colt and on the roadway, and helping Jesus to mount. Their cry of praise in Luke's account emphasizes that Jesus comes as king. Their words are similar to the words of the angelic chorus at Jesus' birth (2:14) to signal the fulfillment of the prophecy made then. The Pharisees think that Jesus' disciples have gone too far, making claims for him that he would not dare make. But Jesus replies that the time for proclamation of his full identity and mission has come. God's plan must be revealed now, even if the stones must be called into service.

Like Jeremiah at an earlier time (Jer 8:18-23), Jesus laments the blindness of Jerusalem to the evidence of God's plan for her. She will not accept the true peace he offers by his entry. Jesus foresees the days of Jerusalem's destruction by Rome in A.D. 70. Destruction came once when the city would not listen to Jeremiah and the other prophets; this time it will be because of failure to accept the Messiah.

PART V: SUFFERING AND VICTORY

Luke 19:45–24:53

Now that Jesus has arrived at Jerusalem, the drama will move quickly toward its divinely planned climax. Jesus goes to "take possession" of the temple as its legitimate teacher. In this setting the conflict with the Jewish leaders will heighten (chapter 20). He will speak of the last days of Jerusalem and of the world (chapter 21). Then will come the days of his Passover (chapters 22–23) and the victory of God in his new exodus (chapter 24).

19:45-48 Jesus comes to the temple. Luke's account of the cleansing of the temple is the shortest among the Gospels. It is one of the few episodes recounted by the Synoptics that also appears in John, where it occurs at the beginning of Jesus' ministry rather than at the end (John 2:13-17). Luke has played down the violence and gives no description of the activities Jesus objects to, letting the quotations from Isa 56:7 and Jer 7:11 be reason enough for expelling "those who were selling things."

Luke is more interested in showing the reason for the cleansing as the preparation for the true teacher to take his seat in the place designed for him. From now on Jesus makes the temple the center of his Jerusalem ministry. In the verses that conclude this section of temple teaching (21:37-38), Jesus is described as teaching daily in the temple, while spending his nights on the Mount of Olives, by implication in communion with his Father as the days of fulfillment draw near.

20:1-8 Teaching in the temple. Jesus has taken his place as the authoritative teacher in the temple. Chapter 20 begins with a general challenge to his authority by the religious leaders; then the remainder of this chapter and all the following give examples of Jesus' teaching activity amid the continuing attacks of his adversaries.

The group that comes to question Jesus first is an official delegation of the Sanhedrin, the supreme council, representing the three classes that comprised it: the high priests (former high priests and leaders of the four high priestly families), Pharisees (scribes of the Pharisee sect), and elders (leaders of the chief Jewish families). They ask for an explanation of "these things": Jesus' cleansing of the temple and assuming an official teaching role. Jesus counters with his own question about John the Baptist, whose baptism some or all of them had refused to accept (7:30). This throws them into the dilemma described in the text. They cannot answer, which is proof to Jesus (as it should be to them) that they have no right to be standing in judgment over Jesus' authority.

20:9-19 The parable of the tenant farmers. In their hearing, Jesus tells the people a parable in which the leaders recognize themselves (v. 19). The parable of the tenant farmers is clearly a description of the response of the Jewish leaders to Jesus, God's beloved Son. It is variously allegorized in the versions of Luke, Mark (Mark 11:27-33), and Matthew (Matt 21:23-27) to draw out the comparisons to the history of Israel and the sending of the prophets. Israel as a vineyard is a traditional theme (Isa 5:1-7; Ps 80). The sending of the beloved son is something new. The details of what happened to Jesus have affected the telling of the story; for example, the fact that the son is killed outside the vineyard in Luke and Matthew might reflect Jesus' crucifixion outside the city (see Heb 13:12).

When the audience hears that the tenants will be destroyed and that the vineyard will be given to others (the Gentiles), they cry out in disbelief. Can it be possible that the land of the promise, the kingdom given to David as a permanent inheritance, will pass to others? Jesus quotes Ps 118:22 on the irony of the rejected stone that becomes the keystone and then adds a saying of his own: the stone will crush its opponents. Jesus is the keystone of the spiritual building in which all his followers are "living stones" (1 Pet 2:4-8). The episode ends with the recurring theme of the hostility of the leaders and the openness of the people. Because of the readiness of the people to hear the gospel in spite of their leaders, the vineyard of the renewed Israel will contain sturdy Jewish roots in addition to the new Gentile growth (see Rom 11:17-18).

20:20-26 Caesar's taxes. In two successive episodes Jesus' teaching and authority are challenged by groups who are themselves at odds: first by the scribes and high priests (still smarting from the parable of the tenant farmers) and then by the Sadducees. The first group is described as waiting in the wings for an opportune moment to trap him through spies who would not be as immediately recognizable as the leaders themselves. The leaders expect Jesus to speak unfavorably of the Empire, which will give them grounds for handing him over to Pontius Pilate. When the time comes, they will accuse Jesus of opposing the payment of taxes in spite of his response here (23:2).

The spokesmen try to cajole Jesus into giving an answer defiant of the Empire. They describe him flatteringly as "showing no partiality," therefore able to utter the truth even if it should be critical of the emperor.

He teaches the "way of God" and is courageous and truthful enough to answer in God's favor even when it means that he must counteract worldly powers. They ask if it is right to pay taxes to the emperor. This is not a question about the justice of taxation, but whether a theocracy, a state under God's leadership, should pay taxes to an intruding pagan overlord.

The coin Jesus asked for was a denarius, the Roman coin that would have been used in paying taxes. Practically all of the imperial coins by this time would have carried the image of Tiberius Caesar, who had been ruling for at least fifteen years (see 3:1). Jesus avoids later quibbles by having his questioners identify the coin as Caesar's. His pronouncement on what is Caesar's and what is God's does not separate the world into two realms—one of the emperor and the other of God. God is Lord of all; when there is a conflict of interests, God's demand must be honored over any others. But the coin is proof of Caesar's political domain; like it or not, the citizens of Israel must give him what is his due (without, of course, denying the Lordship that belongs to God).

20:27-40 The Sadducees and resurrection. Jesus is challenged from another side by the Sadducees, who appear here in Luke for the only time (though they will be frequently on the scene in Acts [4:1-2; 5:17; 23:7-8]). The Sadducees were the aristocratic leaders who scorned the Pharisees and their "modern" beliefs and interpretations of the law. They were the conservatives, accepting only the first five books of the Bible (the Pentateuch) and not allowing the Pharisaic beliefs in the bodily resurrection of the just and the existence of spirits. Like the spies in the preceding incident, the Sadducees try to dispose Jesus for the answer favorable to their cause, in this instance by showing the absurdity of the doctrine of the resurrection.

By the law of levirate marriage (Deut 25:5-6; Ruth 3:9-4:12), a brother was supposed to raise up an heir for his childless dead brother so that the property would not leave the family and that his brother's name would continue in his posterity. The Sadducees pose a case that they think will force Jesus either to renounce the resurrection or to allow polyandry, which was considered immoral. Jesus replies that the succession of husbands is a problem for the Sadducees only because they have not thoroughly comprehended the meaning of the resurrection: resurrection life and current existence are two completely different things. In heaven the marriage relationship will be transcended by a new kind of relationship that will not involve procreation.

All three Synoptics record words of Jesus about the age to come (that is, after the final resurrection: Mark 12:25; Matt 22:30), but Jesus' phraseology in Luke (vv. 34-36) implies also that the age of the resurrection has already begun and that marriage has already lost its role as an absolute in human life (see Gen 1:28). Here is a hint that the state of celibacy (the state adopted by Jesus) has validity as a sign of the kingdom present and to come (see Matt 19:12). Those "judged worthy of a place in the age to come" are already children of the resurrection and no longer liable to death. They can imitate the angels in their complete absorption in God. Celibacy sacramentalizes this attitude of all Christians.

After saying this, Jesus takes up again the issue of the teaching of Moses with which the questioning began (v. 28). He shows that even Moses believed in a resurrection life when he spoke of God as the God of Abraham, Isaac and Jacob, who are still alive before him. Jesus' rebuttal of the Sadducees arouses the admiration of some of the scribes (probably Pharisees), but this was surely more of a political applause than a real adherence to the teaching of Jesus. As before (v. 26), Jesus' answer to their question has reduced his opponents to silence.

20:41-47 The Lordship of the Messiah. Jesus raises a question without giving the answer at the present time: if David (in Ps 110:1) calls the Messiah "lord," how can the Messiah be his son? Jesus was introduced as the son of David when his genealogy was given (3:33), and he has been correctly identified as the Messiah (9:20). The answer will come in the resurrection whereby Jesus, son of David and Messiah, will be exalted to God's right hand as the Lord (Acts 2:33-36). The criticism of the Pharisees made on the way to Jerusalem (11:41-43) is now made of the scribes (generally the same group) in the Jerusalem temple.

21:1-4 The widow's mite. Pursuing the theme of wealth and stewardship, Jesus draws the contrast between the temple contributions of the rich and a humble widow. He makes it clear that it is not what a person gives that expresses his or her generosity, but what one keeps. The beatitudes and the woes for the poor and rich are recalled (6:20, 24), as is the teaching on trust in providence (12:13-34). The scribes have just been condemned for going through the savings of people like the poor widow (20:47); earlier there was the charge of rapaciousness and laying impossible burdens on such people (11:39, 46). This reference to the evil conduct of the religious leaders forms a backdrop for the prediction of the destruction of the temple.

21:5-19 Prediction of the end. In Mark's version of this episode, Jesus comes out of the temple, allowing the disciples to get the impressive view that prompts their statement about the temple's beauty. Luke presents Jesus as teaching within the temple; this will be his last appearance in the temple, his final statement announcing its destruction. The destruction of the temple was connected in the popular mind with the end of the world. This had been true when Solomon's temple still stood: the Israelites felt that they were secure because of God's promise of an eternal heritage to David, and the temple was a symbol of divine protection. Jeremiah pointed out the illusion of relying on the earthly temple (Jer 7:4). Herod's temple was a glorious sight, too. Its adherents tended to base all their hopes on its sturdy security. Only the cataclysm of the end could shake it.

This connection of the fall of the temple with the end of the world leads Jesus to involve both ideas in answering their question "When will this happen?" First he speaks of the end of the world. This sermon on the end (*eschaton* in Greek) is commonly called the eschatological discourse. Fear and expectation will make people vulnerable to false messages and fake messiahs. They will point to apocalyptic signs (wars, earthquakes, plagues, signs in the heavens) to show that the end is near. Jesus has already said that the attempt to calculate the end is a waste of time (17:20-21). The signs he mentions can be observed in every age. They indicate that the end is indeed coming, but they are no help in determining the day or the hour.

The core of the discourse goes back to Jesus himself, but it has been affected by the experience of the early church in witnessing the fall of Jerusalem and the persecution of the first martyrs. Readers of the Gospel would be able to think of concrete examples of the persecution foretold by Jesus. In the mention of "kings and governors" they would see the faces of Herod and Pilate, and probably Agrippa I and Agrippa II, Felix and Festus (Acts 12; 24–26). Jesus' disciples are not to become frantic and anxious about the coming persecution. It will give them the opportunity to bear witness (Acts 3:15; 4:20). They must not worry about what to say in the time of trial; they will speak with a divine wisdom that no one can contradict (Acts 4:13). Family ties will not protect the disciple (Luke 12:51-53). Jesus' followers are to carry the cross all the way to Calvary, as he did. The promise that no harm will come to even one hair seems strange in the prediction of persecution. It is simply a graphic statement of the ultimate spiritual protection of all those who endure the persecution for the sake of Jesus.

21:20-24 The fall of Jerusalem. Jesus shortens the range of his vision from the end of the world to the destruction of Jerusalem. Luke modifies Mark's account, leaving no mention of the mysterious "abomination of desolation" or of the tempering of the disaster. He adds a description of the siege from postfactum information. The people in the Judean hills and countryside are warned not to flee into the city, where destruction is sure to descend. The mention of retribution and fulfillment brings prophetic judgment into the description of Jerusalem's fate. Writing for Gentiles, Luke highlights their role in Jerusalem's downfall. The enigmatic "times of the Gentiles" refers to the era of the Gentile mission, the beginning of which is recorded in the Acts of the Apostles.

21:25-38 The coming of the Son of Man. The "times of the Gentiles" will last until the end; their fulfillment (v. 24) brings Jesus back to the topic of the end of the world. The shaking of the cosmic forces will herald the coming of the end. Then the Son of Man, the risen Lord to whom judgment and authority have been given, will come in God's glory. It will be reason for panic for God's enemies, but the disciples should stand erect, expectant and ready like the people of the Exodus for God's deliverance (Exod 12:11).

The image of the fig tree is expanded by the addition of other trees for environments where figs might not be known. Spring budding is always a sign that summer is coming. The statement about the present generation (v. 32) seems difficult. It does not mean that the end of the world will come before the generation of Jesus passes (that generation had already passed at the time this was written). The emphasis of the statement is on the certainty of the events foretold by Jesus, and probably this means that the first of the events leading to the end of the world (the fall of Jerusalem) will happen within the experience of the present generation. The word of God, brought in the words of Jesus, bears witness to this prophecy (v. 33).

After describing the days of the coming of the Son of Man, Jesus urges on his listeners the proper conduct for awaiting his return. His warning is especially against the pleasures and cares represented by the "thorns" in the parable of the sower (8:14). These pressures of daily life lull people into false security. The exhortation to watch and pray foreshadows the same appeal during Jesus' agony in the garden (22:46). The section closes with a summary of Jesus' typical activity during these final days in Jerusalem (see 19:47). He taught in the temple during the day and spent the night in prayer on the Mount of Olives. Though the leaders were trying to put an end to him, the common people continued to be eager to listen to him.

22:1-6 The plotters and the betrayer. With the setting of the trap by the plotters and the betrayer, the story of the passion begins. Luke presents Jesus as the righteous man suffering martyrdom. He proceeds step by step according to the Father's plan. Jesus' pain is not diminished, but he endures it with an inner peace and is able to go out to others from the midst of his own agony (23:28, 34, 43).

The feasts of the Unleavened Bread and the Passover were originally two separate celebrations—the one an agricultural festival at the beginning of the barley harvest, the other a nomadic feast in which the first-born of the flock was sacrificed. Early in Israelite history the feasts were joined to commemorate the deliverance of Israel from Egypt. The Passover was observed on the first of the seven days of Unleavened Bread (v. 7). Jesus' enemies in the Sanhedrin hope for an opportunity to put him to death under the cover of the crowds thronging Jerusalem. The assistance of the temple guards would be needed should Jesus be arrested in the temple area.

After the temptations in the desert, Luke had remarked that the devil left Jesus to await another time. The opportune time has come (in John's Gospel, "the hour": John 13:1), and Satan enters Judas (see John 13:2, 27). The church realized that the enormity of the passion was beyond mere human agency. The evangelists note the tragic irony that the betrayer was one of the Twelve.

22:7-20 The Passover meal. Luke, like Mark and Matthew, presents the Last Supper as a Passover meal. In John's Gospel, the supper takes place the night before, and the death of Jesus occurs at the time of the sacrifice of the Passover lamb. Peter and John are sent to make the arrangements: the place, the food and its preparation, and needed attendants. Possibly Jesus did not specify the place clearly to avoid premature arrest in case Judas should overhear. Their signal is to be a man carrying a water jar: women usually carried jars and pitchers, men leather bottles.

Jesus realizes that the climax of his mission is approaching. His action dramatizes his own self-offering as the new Paschal Lamb. He will not eat the Passover supper again until it is fulfilled in the kingdom. The church understands this of the Eucharist, which he institutes in the following words, and of the eternal banquet of heaven (v. 30). Some modern translations omit verses 19b and 20 because they are missing in certain ancient sources, but the most recent critical texts (both Catholic and Protestant) contain them as authentic. At the Passover meal, the various dishes and cups were shared ritually with accompanying prayers and narratives. Jesus interrupts the customary flow of the ritual to offer himself to his disciples in the form of bread and wine. This signifies the making of a new covenant. In the old covenant the union of God and the people was symbolized by the sprinkling of the blood of an animal (Exod 24:5-8); now the union is perfect in the blood of one who is God and man. Jesus' followers are told to do what he has done in his remembrance. This refers both to the ritual action and to the self-gift it sacramentalizes.

The Eucharistic institution accounts come to us in two traditions, that of Mark and Matthew and that of Luke and Paul (1 Cor 11:23-25). Luke does not seem to be directly dependent on Paul, however, and is the only writer to mention two cups (the Passover meal called for four cups of wine).

22:21-38 Division at table. Luke's arrangement of the material makes the harshest contrast between the covenant action of Jesus and the action of the betrayer at the same table. Even presence at the Lord's table, Luke is saying to his readers, is no guarantee of fidelity to Jesus. The betrayal goes according to God's plan, but the one who carries it out still bears personal responsibility. The callousness of the whole group of the Twelve is revealed as their argument about which of them could be guilty of betrayal evolves into a dispute about their greatness. This dispute occurs at a different place in the other Synoptics (Mark 10:42-45; Matt 20:25-28). Jesus tells them that the kingdom has completely different categories of greatness than the world has. He notes ironically that those who tyrannize over their subjects are called "Benefactors": this was the case in Rome, Egypt, and other Gentile territories. The one who is great in the kingdom of God will be the one who serves in imitation of the Master himself. The Twelve will be given authority, however; they have shared the journey with Jesus (which is not yet finished), suffering the onslaughts of his enemies. They will become the new patriarchs of the renewed Israel of God.

Jesus addresses the leader of the new patriarchs by his Hebrew name. He says that Satan has asked to test the Twelve; the implication is that God's special permission is needed to interfere with the Twelve. Jesus' powerful intercession will help the leader. Jesus refers to the coming apostasy of Peter, from which he will return to strengthen his brothers. Peter does not accept the hint of his weakness and protests his allegiance and fidelity. Jesus then utters the prediction of his betrayal with unequivocal clarity. Peter must get over thinking that his special role among the Twelve was earned by his own strength. Jesus' promise of intercession is not idle.

In a parting message to all, Jesus asks them to recall the instructions they were given for the preaching mission (9:3). They had been told to rely on God's providence for the things they would need. Now, because of the impending crisis of Jesus' passion and death, and in view of the persecution sure to come on the early church, Jesus tells them to prepare themselves well for the struggle, even to taking up arms. He is speaking figuratively to alert them to the seriousness of the struggle, but they take him literally, producing two swords. "It is enough!" puts an end to a conversation that has been over their heads.

22:39-53 The agony and the arrest. Luke has streamlined and simplified Mark's account of the agony in the garden. Jesus does not select three disciples out of the group to accompany him; as a result, his admonition to pray so as not to be overcome by temptation is addressed to all the Twelve (and the readers) as a main theme (vv. 40, 46). Jesus himself is tested by his desire to avoid the cup, but he accepts the will of the Father. This is the climax of the struggle with Satan (see 4:1-13); an angel comes to his aid, so that he is able to pray with greater intensity. His sweat is not bloody but falls from him like drops of blood. Meanwhile the disciples, still unaware of the significance of what is going on in their midst, have fallen asleep. In the warning to them, we hear Jesus admonishing us to strengthen ourselves by fervent prayer for the persecution that will surely come to his followers.

The betrayer is again identified with tragic irony as one of the Twelve (v. 47). Still misinterpreting Jesus' words and their role as his disciples, his followers strike with the sword. Only in Luke's version does Jesus heal the servant's ear. He upbraids the arresting party for seeking him in an out-of-the-way place under cover of darkness, indicating that their deed cannot bear the light of day. What they are doing is indeed a sign of the "power of darkness" (v. 53). Jesus refers to the time of his passion as the "hour"; but the tone is not positive as in John's Gospel, where the hour is the time fulfilling the Father's plan (John 13:1; 17:1). Here it is "your hour" of darkness.

22:54-65 Peter denies Jesus. Unlike Mark and Matthew, Luke has no arraignment before the Jewish authorities before the morning session. At this point he focuses on Peter's denials, forgetting Jesus for the moment. Peter does not move about as in the other Synoptics, remaining rather in the courtyard, where he will be visible to Jesus after the cock crows. A woman and two men accuse Peter over a period of an hour or more. Luke probably means to show the endurance of Peter, who remains in the same place where he is in con-

stant danger of identification, as a sign of his willingness, though half-hearted, to stand by Jesus. When Jesus looks at him, he is not hopelessly crushed by remorse but is able to return as Jesus prayed he would (v. 32). The taunting punishment of Jesus is envisioned as taking place in the courtyard at the hands of the temple guard. His role as God's true prophet is mocked, which Luke regards as blasphemy against God (Greek text of v. 65). Luke does not mention the treatment of the Roman soldiers (Mark 14:65; Matt 26:67-68).

22:66-71 The Sanhedrin's decision. Luke's description of a single meeting of the Sanhedrin, taking place at daybreak, is more likely than that of Mark and Matthew, who describe a night meeting followed by a morning session to carry out the decision. A night meeting of the Sanhedrin is otherwise unknown. Jesus is unwilling to identify himself as the kind of Messiah popularly expected; rather, he speaks of himself as authoritative judge in his role as the Son of Man (Dan 7:13-14). They interpret this answer (correctly) as an affirmation of a special divine status; they can only view this as blasphemy, sufficient reason to condemn him to death (see Mark 14:62-64). The Sanhedrin is not empowered to impose the death sentence; they must submit their accusation to the judgment of the Roman authority.

23:1-12 Pilate and Herod. Pontius Pilate had been procurator, or Roman governor, of Judea for about five years (see 3:1). His seat of government was at the seacoast town of Caesarea, but he was in Jerusalem because of the large gathering of Jews for the feast of Passover. Luke follows Mark's outline but makes several additions to throw into relief Jesus' innocence. The Herod episode is also proper to Luke.

One of the charges is clearly false—the opposition to Roman taxes (see 20:20-25). Jesus has not spoken clearly to the Sanhedrin about being the Messiah (22:66), but he has not denied it; his entry into Jerusalem implied it (19:28-40). Luke has added the explanatory "a king" for the sake of his Greek readers. After Jesus' noncommittal reply, Pilate pronounces him innocent. No reason is given, because in abbreviating the account Luke has taken the arguments for granted. The charges are repeated, this time in terms that encompass Jesus' whole ministry as traditionally described, beginning in Galilee and eventually affecting the whole land (Acts 10:37).

The mention of Galilee gives Pilate the opportunity to divert the case to the tetrarch of Galilee, Herod Antipas, who was also in Jerusalem for the feast. Herod's curiosity about Jesus was mentioned earlier (9:9). Jesus does not respond to the request for a sign nor to the ill-motivated questions, as he never does in the Gospels. Herod's mocking treatment of Jesus ironically heals an enmity with Pilate (whose conduct cited in 13:1 may have been one of the causes). The cooperation of the two is later seen as the fulfillment of prophecy (Ps 2:1-2; Acts 4:25-28).

23:13-25 The death sentence. The second scene before Pilate is a threefold crescendo of Jesus' innocence, the crowd's hostility, and Pilate's weakness. Pilate tries various routes to convince the people of Jesus' innocence. But he is not strong or free enough to do what he knows is right. The people call for the release of the prisoner Barabbas under terms of what must have been a local custom authorized by the Judean procurators. Barabbas was a revolutionary and murderer who really would have constituted a danger to the stability of Roman rule. Verse 17 is omitted because it was an insertion from Mark 15:6.

Crucifixion is suddenly mentioned for the first time in verse 21. Luke does not explain why the crowds have become so violent (see Mark 15:11). Crucifixion was a cruel and humiliating punishment that the Romans inflicted only on slaves and non-Romans guilty of the worst crimes. Jews saw in this treatment the sign of a curse (Deut 21:23; Gal 3:13). Pilate tries to appease the crowd with a promise to have Jesus scourged—an absurdity if Jesus is innocent. Finally he cannot withstand the pressure. Jesus is delivered to the will of the crowd; their will is allowed to prevail, perverse as it is, because it coincides with the will of the Father (22:42).

23:26-31 The way of the cross. That the man pressed into service to Jesus was a Cyrenian would have been significant to the early Cyrenian converts (Acts 6:9; 11:20; 13:1). Simon is given the crossbeam, which had become too heavy for Jesus in his weakened condition. This would later be fastened to the upright that remained fixed in the ground at the site of execution. Luke adds to Mark's account the detail that Simon walked "behind

Jesus" to make him a symbol of the ideal disciple (14:27).

Jesus is being led to his death according to the Father's will, powerless now in the hands of his executioners. But he is the Lord, and on his way he makes another prophetic statement about Jerusalem (see 19:42-44). The women of Jerusalem who customarily solaced condemned prisoners are recipients of the divine pronouncement for the city as well as for themselves. They will wish to be hidden from the catastrophe soon coming upon Jerusalem (see Hos 10:8). Unlike the woman who rejoiced that Mary had borne and nursed Jesus (11:27), these women will rejoice if they have no children to suffer through the time of siege. Jesus leaves them with a proverb: Dry wood burns better than green. If the innocent Jesus has to suffer so much, what will be the fate of guilty Jerusalem?

23:32-49 Crucifixion and death. Luke does not use the Aramaic name "Golgotha" as the other evangelists do, but simply refers to the place of execution as "The Skull," a name that described the rock formation at Calvary. Jesus is crucified between two criminals (see 22:37; Isa 53:12). He utters the words of forgiveness that will become the hallmark of the innocent Christian sufferer, words echoed by Stephen, the first martyr (Acts 7:60). The dividing of the garments reflects the words of Ps 22:19. Though Luke does not exonerate the Jewish people completely from complicity in the death of Jesus, he continues to show that it was caused mainly by the hostility and jealousy of their leaders (v. 35). Luke has the scoffers refer to Jesus as the "chosen one" (as at the transfiguration: 9:35) rather than as the "king of Israel" (Mark 15:32; Matt 27:42), a title less striking to non-Jewish readers. The soldiers offer him their own cheap drink, which might be considered an act of kindness, but it is mockery to offer such a drink to a king.

The incident of the good thief is unique to Luke. The criminal who mocks Jesus is said to be blaspheming, a conclusion of Christian faith regarding Jesus' true identity. The other criminal asks Jesus to remember him when he begins his reign. He means the definitive messianic kingdom that Jews expected at the end of the present age, but in Luke's theology it also refers to the time of Jesus' exaltation through resurrection and ascension. Jesus promises him a place in "Paradise" *today*, because the death of Jesus is beginning the exodus (9:31) that will open a new way to salvation. "Paradise" goes back to the Persian term for an enclosed park and was used in the Greek Old Testament for the Garden of Eden in Genesis. Late Hebrew writings considered paradise an intermediate state of happiness of the righteous before the final judgment (4 Ezra 4:7; 2 Enoch 42:3). This intermediate state seems to have been the meaning of paradise here.

The triumph of darkness (22:53) now seems complete as Jesus nears death. Luke does not speak technically of an eclipse of the sun but of the failure of its light. The tearing of the curtain between the Holy Place and the Holy of Holies in the temple symbolizes that in Jesus a new access has been gained to God's presence and that a new dispensation has replaced the old. Jesus dies with a prayer of acceptance of the Father's will taken from Ps 31:6. The pagan centurion gives the verdict of innocent in climaxing a long build-up (rather than "Son of God" as in Mark 15:39; Matt 27:54). The crowd now beat their breasts—probably a combination of grief for the death of a man now recognized as innocent and of repentance for the wrongdoing in which they have participated. Luke did not report the desertion of the disciples in the Garden (see Mark 14:50; Matt 26:56). He implies that they have been helplessly and fearfully watching the events of the passion from a distance.

23:50-56 The burial of Jesus. Joseph of Arimathea (a town north of Jerusalem) is described in the same terms as Zechariah and Elizabeth (1:6) and Simeon (2:25). Like Simeon and Anna (2:38), he is awaiting the reign of God. The details of Jesus' burial in a new tomb bring Luke and the other Synoptics into rare coincidence with John's description (John 19:40-42). They do not, however, record an anointing of the body at this time.

The women from Galilee are still faithfully near to Jesus (see 8:1-3; Acts 1:14). The remark that they saw the tomb and the body (v. 55) is probably meant to counteract later rumors that the resurrection story was concocted when the women went back to the wrong (empty) tomb on Easter morning. Luke does not say when the spices were prepared—before or after the sabbath. Such preparations

for burial were not contrary to the sabbath observance, but Luke is taking extra pains to avoid the impression that anything was done without regard for the law of Moses.

24:1-12 Discovery of the resurrection. Luke's account of the discovery of the empty tomb follows Mark but adds the story of Peter's visit to the tomb (known in a different form by John: John 20:3-8). The Gospel stories of the resurrection surprise us by their disagreements: Was there one man or angel, or two? Did Peter go alone to the tomb or was John with him? Did Jesus appear to the disciples in Galilee or only in Jerusalem? These discrepancies have arisen because of word-of-mouth transmission. The fact that they have not been ironed out into a smooth story testifies to the authenticity of the experience behind them. The witnesses were convinced of what they had seen and heard and felt, and had no concern for editing the proclamation.

Jesus is referred to by the official title "Lord Jesus" (v. 3), which belongs to him because of the resurrection. The question to the women contains an implicit proclamation of faith and is addressed with many-layered meaning to the readers of the story as well: "Why do you seek the living one among the dead?" Jesus' resurrection has come about as foretold by himself and in fulfillment of the Father's will. What has happened to him is described in both passive and active forms: "he has been raised" (v. 6); he will "rise" (v. 7). Both of these usages are correct and are found elsewhere in the New Testament. The passive form is more frequent, expressing the truth that the whole work of salvation, including the resurrection of the Son of God, originates in God the Father.

The names of the women vary in the lists, but the name of Mary Magdalene is in all of them. Joanna was one of those mentioned as accompanying Jesus during his ministry (8:3). The third woman is called simply "Mary of James" in the Greek text; comparison with Mark 15:40 identifies her as James's mother rather than his wife.

24:13-35 An Easter walk to Emmaus. Two of the disciples who had been with the Eleven on Sunday morning (v. 9) leave for Emmaus after having heard the report of the women and of Peter. This story, another unique offering of Luke, has pattern similarities with the story of the baptism of the Ethiopian eunuch by Philip later on: a journey, the interpretation of Scripture, a significant action, and a mysterious disappearance (Acts 8:26-40). In the Greek text, the village of Emmaus is said to be "sixty stadia" from Jerusalem. A *stadion* was about six hundred feet, making the distance around seven miles.

Jesus is taken for another pilgrim returning home from the Jerusalem festival. The two disciples do not recognize him. Their eyes are "held back," an expression for spiritual blindness. Various appearance stories say that Jesus looked "different" (Mark 16:12; John 20:14; 21:4). His body has definitely been transformed by the resurrection, but the point in these descriptions seems to be that it takes faith, a gift of new eyes, to recognize the risen Lord. Readers are helped by knowing that some of Jesus' friends did eventually recognize him and testified to the reality of his resurrection, but even more by realizing that recognition of the Lord does not depend on his natural visibility.

The disciples are distressed by the death of Jesus and cannot believe that the event that has shaken their world is not known by another pilgrim. Cleopas is named, but not the other; perhaps Cleopas later exercised an important role in the Christian community. They describe Jesus as a mighty prophet, the long-awaited prophet-like-Moses (Deut 18:15; Acts 7:22). They had hoped he would be not only a prophet but the messianic deliverer of Israel (see 1:68). Again there is emphasis on the role of the leaders in Jesus' crucifixion (v. 20). The "third day" is probably remembered as part of a mysterious promise of Jesus (18:33). Even the accounts of the empty tomb did not lead them necessarily to conclude that he had risen, because the resurrection expected by the Jews was the general victory of all the just at the end. It was obvious to them that the end and the establishment of a new order had not come. They did not expect an individual resurrection in the midst of history.

Jesus upbraids them for their blindness. They have read the prophets all their lives but not recognized the fulfillment in the *necessary* suffering and death of Jesus (according to God's plan). The cross preceded the glory. This will be the pattern for his disciples (Acts 14:22). The disciples are struck by what Jesus has said and ask him to *stay* with them. The word "stay" or "abide" here may have richer

overtones, as in John's Gospel (John 14:17; 15:4-10). Jesus shares a meal with them, which is described so as to recall the multiplication of the loaves (9:16) and the Last Supper (22:19). In this "breaking of the bread" (an early name for the Eucharist: Acts 2:42, 46) they recognize him; immediately he disappears from their physical sight. They remember that their hearts were "burning" without their knowing why when he was explaining the Scriptures to them. Now they know that it was his risen presence they were experiencing. Luke's readers know that the same experience is available in the church in the Eucharist and in the reading of the Scriptures.

The experience of the risen Lord cannot be held in. It must be shared, proclaimed (Acts 4:20). By the time they return to Jerusalem, the good news is already known. Jesus has appeared meanwhile to Simon Peter, the leader of the Twelve; this appearance is not described in the Gospels. Luke closes his narration of the story with a reminder for his readers of its special significance for them: recognition came in "the breaking of bread."

24:36-49 Jesus appears to the community. If the reality of Jesus' spiritual presence in the church was emphasized in the preceding narrative, the physical reality of his resurrection body is emphasized here. From the earliest times in the church, there was a danger of docetism, the heretical belief that Jesus was God behind a thin veneer of humanity: thus his suffering was only playacting, and his resurrection was simply a return to a completely spiritual existence with no bodily effect. The Letters of John combated this error (1 John 4:2-3; 2 John 7). The present narrative stresses that Jesus' resurrection body is real. The disciples touch him; the marks of the passion are visible in his hands and feet; he eats with the disciples.

Their panic is not surprising, even though they have already heard about the earlier appearance. They are still excited and tense with the unfamiliarity of it all, and Jesus suddenly appears in their midst. His question to them is rhetorical, a way of introducing the Scriptural instruction that will help them to assimilate the truth of this marvelous event. The Old Testament is referred to in a traditional way by naming its three collections: law, prophets, and psalms (usually "writings"). His words commissioning them as witnesses of his resur-

JOHN

Neal M. Flanagan, O.S.M.

INTRODUCTION

This introduction is not intended to be an initial, preparatory summation of John's theology nor a presentation—with solutions—of the various problems regarding the author of the Gospel and the nature of his community. I prefer that the readers first have the opportunity to study through the Fourth Gospel as a journey of discovery. Only at the end, after they have assimilated much of what John himself has to say, will I attempt to pull elements together into a résumé.

The commentary is not a verse-by-verse study, though of course numerous individual verses will be considered. Insistence will be placed, rather, on the illumination of the successive Johannine themes as our author offers them to us.

Scholars are by no means in agreement as to the literary divisions intended by the author. My own strong preference is for those of C. H. Dodd, who divides the material into two main sections: the Book of Signs (chs. 2–12) and the Book of Glory (chs. 13–20). The Book of Signs is subsequently divided into seven thematic episodes. It is this division that I will follow here.

With sincere thanks I admit my debt to a long list of previous and contemporary scholars, but especially to C. H. Dodd, B. Lindars, R. E. Brown, J. L. Martyn, and O. Cullmann.

COMMENTARY

A. THE INTRODUCTION

John 1:1-51

The first chapter of John serves as an introduction to the whole Gospel, introducing the reader both to John's theology—what he believes about God and Jesus—and to Jesus' ministry. It contains a prologue and a series of testimonies.

a) 1:1-18 Prologue. The prologue serves somewhat like an overture to a formal musical composition. It may well have been written after the main body of the Gospel. (This is true of most prologues.) In its short span of eighteen verses, it states briefly what the whole of the Gospel will spell out over twenty-one chapters. It has both structure and content. The *structure* has been partially determined by the presentation of "wisdom personified" in the Old Testament books. There, as in Wis 9:9-12 or Prov 8:22-36, wisdom is first with God, then shares in creation, will come to earth, and there gift humankind. This same progression is found in our prologue. The other factor that has determined the structure is the Hebrew fondness for parallelism—notions being repeated in order—and for inverse parallelism, that is, repeated in inverse order. Visually, John's poetic prologue unfolds as follows.

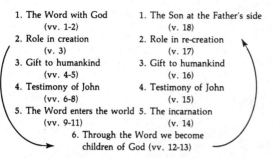

1. The Word with God (vv. 1-2)
2. Role in creation (v. 3)
3. Gift to humankind (vv. 4-5)
4. Testimony of John (vv. 6-8)
5. The Word enters the world (vv. 9-11)

1. The Son at the Father's side (v. 18)
2. Role in re-creation (v. 17)
3. Gift to humankind (v. 16)
4. Testimony of John (v. 15)
5. The incarnation (v. 14)
6. Through the Word we become children of God (vv. 12-13)

The movement of the prologue swings like the arm of a mighty pendulum, each point of which on the left side will be matched by an equivalent on the right.

In *content*, these eighteen verses speak of God's revelation, of how he has explained himself to us. It is this that accounts for the extraordinary title that our author uses—"the Word." Its best equivalent is "revelation." As we humans reveal ourselves through what we say and, even more, by what we do (our body language), so God through the centuries has offered his own self-revelation through act and speech. The prologue details this. God revealed himself through creation (vv. 2-5), but also through his Old Testament word (vv. 10-13), that is, through his covenants, the Mosaic writings, the prophets, and the wisdom literature. Those who opened their eyes and believed in this ancient revelation became "children of God . . . born . . . of God" (vv. 12-13). Finally God has revealed himself to the utmost through the incarnation of the Word, in whom God's glory, his presence, stands revealed as a sign of his enduring love (v. 14). (The Greek text tells us that the Word "pitched his tent" among us, a striking reference to God's Old Testament presence in the tent-tabernacle during Moses' wanderings with Israel in the desert.) To this incarnate Word John the Baptist has given testimony, a testimony that initiated the historical manifestation of Jesus, in whom the Father stands completely revealed and in whose fullness we, the Christian community, have all shared. The prologue ends with the upstroke of the pendulum arm to the right, in parallel to the very beginning of the poem. The Word, whose name is Jesus Christ (v. 17), is the Son, the only Son, who is "at the Father's side" (v. 18) and reveals him to those open to light and truth.

As you may have noticed, this explanation of the content of the prologue has ignored verses 6-8, the initial statement about John the Baptist, and in so doing has been able to interpret verses 9-13 as pre-incarnational, that is, as referring to the Old Testament revelation rather than to the historical presence of Jesus in the world. In our opinion, verses 6-8 occur where they do simply to balance the statement about the Baptist on the right side of the pendulum swing (v. 15). They are where they are, not for theological sequence, but for purely artistic reasons.

Consequently, verses 1-18 are an artistically fashioned poem summarizing the main point of John's theology: Jesus of Nazareth is God's supreme revelation, God's interpreter, his exegete. Being God himself (vv. 1, 18), he not only mediates God to us, he *immediates* him. He is God's wisdom speaking God's ultimate word about himself.

b) 1:19-51 Testimonies. This second section of chapter 1 contains a whole list of witnesses to Jesus who, one by one, identify Jesus for John's audience. Like the audience at a play, who by means of the printed program receive advance information about the actors, so these verses in John put the readers/hearers in a position of special knowledge as the drama of Jesus' life-story is played out. From the very beginning they are told who and what Jesus is. The testimonies flow as follows:

First day (vv. 19-28).
Witness: John the Baptist to priests and Levites.
Testimony: John is not Christ, nor the expected Elijah of Mal 3:23 (4:5 in some versions), nor the prophet of Deut 18:15, 18, but "the voice of one crying out in the desert," himself unworthy to untie the sandal strap of the one coming after him.

Second day ("next day" of vv. 29-34).
Witness: John the Baptist at sight of Jesus.
Testimony: Jesus is "the Lamb of God who takes away the sin of the world"; he who ranks before John; he on whom the Spirit descended and who baptizes with the Spirit; God's chosen One.

Third day ("next day" of vv. 35-39).
Witness: John the Baptist to two of his disciples, who go to Jesus about 4 p.m. and stay.
Testimony: "Behold, the Lamb of God." (This would be a reference to the paschal lamb and/or to the suffering servant of Isa 53:7, silent before its shearers.)

Fourth day(?) (vv. 40-42).
Witness: Andrew to Simon.
Testimony: "We have found the Messiah."

Fifth day ("next day" of vv. 43-51).
Witness: Philip to Nathaniel.
Testimony: "the one about whom Moses wrote in the law, and also the prophets."

Witness: Nathaniel.
Testimony: "You are the Son of God; you are the King of Israel."

Seventh day ("On the third day" of 2:1-11).
Witness: Jesus' Cana miracle.
Testimony: ". . . and so revealed his glory, and his disciples began to believe in him" (2:11).

Our author seems to be laying out an artistic first week in the good news of Christian re-creation to recall the first week of the creation story in the Book of Genesis. Both Genesis and John's Gospel begin with the identical phrase, "In the beginning." This is probably intentional. The succession of days in John are clearly marked except for the fourth, where the otherwise unnecessary reference to the two disciples going to Jesus about 4 p.m. and staying with him (v. 39) intends to say that they stayed overnight. Why else would John mention 4 p.m.? This first week of re-creation will conclude with the Cana miracle and the first manifestation that in Jesus is God's residing glory, his divine presence. "On the third day" of 2:1 should also remind us of *the* future supreme manifestation of God's glory, the resurrection.

This series of testimonies can be a source of confusion and difficulty for anyone who has read Mark's Gospel, in which the disciples come to their faith-knowledge of Jesus only hesitantly, timidly, and imperfectly—and that over a lengthy period of time. John seems to contradict Mark's picture. By the end of chapter 1 the Johannine disciples seem to know everything there is to know about Jesus, even his divinity. I think we must say that John is not attempting here to give a historical presentation of the first disciples' advance in faith. He has a different purpose in mind. He wishes to impress these christological statements on the minds of his audience at the very start of his dramatic presentation; therefore his actors appear in a succession of brief scenes to pass along the required information. The testimonies indicate that the Gospel's main interest is Christology. John may also wish to indicate through this procedure the way in which his own community advanced to its knowledge of Jesus: by moving from the circle of John the Baptist to the greater personage of Jesus, who was gradually recognized as the Lamb of God, God's chosen One, the Messiah, Son of God, and King of Israel. Jesus was the fulfillment of all the Old Testament hopes.

There is another purpose that John, a man of rich creative genius, may have intended. His list of characters in this first act/period of seven days seems to typify the basic personal elements of the Christian community. In order there appear: (1) John the Baptist, precursor to the new creation, whose sole function is to witness; (2) the Savior; (3) disciples who hear, follow, look for, and stay; (4) Peter, the rock; (5) missionaries like Andrew and Philip who spread the good news; (6) Nathaniel, the true Israelite in whom there is no guile, who, as some Jewish traditions expressed it, studied law under a fig tree and was rewarded. With this, the founding elements of the community are assembled. Let the drama begin!

The unexpected and ambiguous reference in verse 51 to a future vision of angels "ascending and descending on the Son of Man" insinuates the unifying function of Jesus. Like the angels on Jacob's ladder (Gen 28:12), he will join through himself the above and the below, the heavenly and the earthly.

B. THE BOOK OF SIGNS

John 2:1–12:50

Our author begins at this point what is aptly called "The Book of Signs." It moves by way of narrative and discourse through seven distinguishable episodes, or themes, and through seven sign-miracles. John's terminology regarding these sign-miracles is very distinct: they are "signs" pointing to some deeper theological truth. What the deeper truth is will frequently, but not always, be identified in the discourse. The material in these eleven chapters appears to be organized into theme clusters, which we will call "episodes."

2:1–4:42 Episode I: New Beginnings

In this section John will provide four different accounts—Cana, the temple, Nicodemus, the Samaritan woman—each of which will emphasize the newness that Jesus has brought into the world. The basic message throughout will be the same as that of Paul in 2 Cor 5:17: "The old things have passed away; behold, new things have come." John's Gospel is in many ways a Christian Genesis, a story of re-creation.

1. The Cana sign (2:1-12). With this account, located in the small town of Cana, north in Galilee, John begins his sign theology: "Jesus did this as the beginning of his signs" (v. 11). The question, as always in John, is: What does the sign mean? In this instance the meaning is multiple, but it is centered on one basic point: the arrival through Jesus of the new messianic age. What is changed in this incident is not simply water, but water for Old Testament ceremonial washings. It is changed not simply into wine, but into wine of highest quality and of surprising quantity (six jars, each holding fifteen to twenty-five gallons). Such a superabundance of wine was a frequent prophetic figure of speech for the dawning of the messianic age (Amos 9:13-14; Joel 3:18). The symbol was current also at the time of Jesus, as we read in the almost contemporary 2 Baruch 29: ". . . on each vine there shall be a thousand branches, and each branch shall bear a thousand clusters, and each cluster produce a thousand grapes, and each grape produce a cor [about 120 gallons] of wine . . . because these are they who have come to the consummation of time."

Changing Old Testament water into messianic wine, consequently, signifies, or signs, for John the passing of the old into the new. The messianic era has arrived. The feast symbolizes the messianic banquet. And the messianic bridegroom, he who supplies the wine, is Jesus himself (3:29). The allusion to the hour of Jesus' death in verse 4 may even mean that John wants his audience to think also of *the* messianic wine that will be the result and Eucharistic sacrament of Jesus' death.

Verse 4, "Woman, how does your concern affect me? My hour has not yet come," is extremely difficult to explain. Cancel the verse out and the story flows with ease. Leave it in, as the text itself demands, and we have the mother asking, Jesus responding negatively, yet the sign-miracle taking place. Leave it in, and we must ask: Why does Jesus call his mother "Woman"? Why is his verbal response negative but his action positive? Of what "hour" does Jesus speak? Explanations of all this are multiple and extremely divergent. One of the most probable is that verse 4 was not in the original pre-Gospel account, which presented a straightforward story of the incident in which the mother's request was answered by the son's positive response. The evangelist, however, who wished to use the story for his theme of new beginnings, inserted verse 4 to affirm, as do the other Gospels, that during Jesus' public life, until his hour came, his work was determined solely by the Father's will. It is this which is stated by the negative tone of the response and by the use of the impersonal "Woman."

John has also used this story to initiate his theology of glory. ". . . and so revealed his glory" (v. 11). This is the beginning of a magnificent Johannine conception of glory as being *God's manifested presence.* God glorifies us when he manifests himself in us; we glorify him when we manifest him to the world. In this instance at Cana, God's presence is manifested in his Son, his Revealer.

2. The temple purification (2:13-25). This is another newness or transformation story. The temple itself will be replaced. Destroyed in A.D. 70 by the soldiers of Titus' Roman army, its place as the center of worship and sacrifice, the site of God's presence and the visible symbol of his fidelity, will be taken by the risen body of Christ. The physical destruction of the temple was a spirit-crushing disaster for Israel. The loss was softened for Jewish Christians by this Johannine theology of the Christ-temple, which, indeed, Paul had already expanded into a doctrine of the Christian-temple (1 Cor 6:19).

This physical purification of the temple might remind us of the type of symbolic deeds acted out by the prophets; and, indeed, Jesus' approach to the temple on this occasion resembles that of Jeremiah (Jer 7). The action, though not a miracle, is a sign, a double sign. The temple, soon to be destroyed, stood in need of purification. And its function would be replaced by the risen body of Christ.

Jesus goes up to Jerusalem at Passover time

(v. 13) at the beginning of his ministry. This stands in contrast to the other Gospels, in which Jesus goes to Jerusalem but once, and then at the very end of his ministry. With regard to multiple visits, John is probably more correct historically. Our author has considerably more interest in Jerusalem than the other evangelists, an indication that his roots are more oriented in Jerusalem than in Galilee. The temple purification, however, probably occurred toward the end of Jesus' life, as the Synoptists (Matthew, Mark, Luke) indicate, serving as a final straw leading to Jesus' condemnation. John may well have transferred the story to this initial phase in Jesus' life because it fits so well into his "newness" theme and because he intends that Lazarus' resurrection (ch. 11) be the incident leading to the crucifixion (11:53; 12:10).

The mention of "forty-six years" in verse 20 is one of the clearest chronological indications given in the Gospels (see Luke 3:1 for another). This temple, which was finished in the early sixties, was begun by Herod in 20–19 B.C.E. The addition of John's forty-six years would date this scene to about A.D. 28.

Finally, there are four Johannine peculiarities that make their first appearance in this incident:

a) "The Jews" appear (v. 18) as the primary antagonists of Jesus. Certainly Jesus the Jew and his Jewish disciples had their share of difficulties with their Jewish contemporaries; but the marked distinction between Jesus and Jews must echo the later and sharper antagonism between Jews and Christians during the period of John's own community.

b) We find in verses 19-21 the first appearance of a dramatic technique by which the author makes his point through a progression from ambiguity to misunderstanding to comprehension. The ambiguity of verse 19 leads to the misunderstanding of verse 20 and to the final clarification of verse 21. This technique will occur frequently in the Gospel.

c) Verse 22 tells us that many of Jesus' words and acts were not understood during his lifetime but became intelligible only through the light of his resurrection. It is from this perspective that our evangelist writes.

d) Finally, in verse 23, John speaks of the many who believed because they could see the signs Jesus performed. We must be cautious here. John is not speaking of a deep and viable faith in this and the following verses; he is speaking of the initial faith of those who simply see the signs. It is not those who see that become the true disciples but those who understand. In the incident that follows we shall see a man attracted by signs (3:2) but with little understanding of what they mean.

3. Nicodemus (3:1-36). As a further development of the theme of "newness," John brings Nicodemus onto the scene, but in the night darkness that symbolizes lack of faith-light. Nicodemus has been attracted by Jesus' signs, an attraction not to be despised, yet at a distance from true faith. He has a role to play in the drama, for he is both a Jewish leader (v. 1) and a teacher of Israel (v. 10), a representative of so many interested Jews over the decades after Christ who have shown initial interest in Jesus. A dialogue ensues, animated once more by ambiguity and misunderstanding. Entrance into the "kingdom" (this expression is limited to vv. 3-5 in John, who prefers rather to speak of "life" or "eternal life") depends on being reborn through water and Spirit. Verse 3 speaks of birth "from above." The original Greek at this point can mean either "from above" or "again." John is quite capable of meaning both, though his future statement in verse 31 should incline us to put the greater emphasis on "from above." The "wind" of verse 8 might seem to introduce a jarring notion, but the Greek for "wind" and "spirit" is the same, *pneuma*; and our text is saying that the origin and movement of both wind and spirit is a divine mystery.

What begins as a dialogue in verses 1-10 turns into a monologue in verses 11-12 as Nicodemus disappears momentarily into the darkness from which he came. (He will reappear in better light in 7:50-52 and for a courageous action of discipleship in 19:39-42.) This pattern of dialogue turning to monologue is frequent in the Fourth Gospel, where minor characters are at times introduced simply to help develop an important theme. The Greek original is interesting at this juncture as singulars change to plurals, and Jesus addresses not simply Nicodemus but a world of Nicodemuses as well as John's readers and hearers. Thus verses 11-12 read in Greek: "Amen, amen, I say to you (singular) . . . but you (plural) do not accept our testimony. If I tell you (plural) about earthly things and you (plural) do not believe, how will you (plural) believe if I tell you (plural) about heavenly things?"

Verse 14 contains both an allusion to an Old Testament incident and the introduction of important Johannine theology. The elevated serpent in the desert refers to a fairly confusing incident in Num 21:9 in which a bronze serpent raised on a pole by Moses was a source of salvation (Wis 16:6). To this reference John adds that the Son of Man, too, "must be lifted up." This phrasing will be repeated three more times (8:28; 12:32, 34), and its theology of crucifixion-exaltation will be clarified as the Gospel proceeds.

Extremely important for Johannine and Christian theology is the conviction that God's love (v. 16) is the dynamic principle for world salvation. Jesus' God, John's God, our God is a God motivated by love so great that he has gifted the world with his own Son, not to condemn but to save.

John uses the word "world" (v. 17) in different senses. Here its use is neutral. The whole of creation, and in particular its human inhabitants, is the object of God's saving love. More frequently, as we shall see, "the world" will become symbolic for those who refuse to believe. It is mainly of these that verses 18-21 speak. Though Jesus has come to save and not to condemn, human actions play their own part in determining salvation and condemnation. Salvation is belief in Jesus (v. 18) accompanied by deeds done in God (v. 21). Condemnation is a from-within process, consisting in non-belief in the light that is Jesus, accompanied by the evil works done in the darkness. The light-darkness opposition should remind us of the same theme in the prologue (1:4-5).

Verses 22-30 present the Baptist's final witness to Jesus. They constitute such an obvious break between the preceding verses and those that follow (vv. 31-36) that many scholars believe they are out of place here. This need not be. John may have wanted to reintroduce the Baptist here to clarify through baptismal references what was meant by "born of water and Spirit" in verse 5. This reintroduction is admittedly awkward, but it might well serve this purpose. John's baptism (the site of Aenon near Salim in verse 23 is uncertain) leads into Jesus' form of baptism, the type suggested by verse 5. John's last testimony is given in verses 27-30. Here, as in 1:19-36, the Baptist stresses

Jesus' superiority. (This stressing may flow from the fact that John's own community had opposition from descendants of the Baptist's original followers who claimed that the Baptist, not Jesus, was the real Messiah.) "He must increase, while I must decrease," says the Baptist (v. 30). And with these apt words he disappears personally from the Gospel.

What follows in verses 31-36 seems to be a continuation of verse 21, interrupted by the paragraph concerning the Baptist. There is a sharp distinction in this Gospel between above and below, light and darkness, belief and unbelief—and all of this centers upon the person of Jesus who comes from above (v. 31) and testifies to what he has seen (v. 32) as the One whom God has sent (v. 34). To believe in Jesus is to accept the Father and the Father's love, to have and live eternal life. The content of the final verse, "Whoever believes in the Son has eternal life," both summarizes the whole of the chapter and ties the chapter's ending to identical statements in its centrally located verses 15-16. The "wrath of God" (v. 36) is the loss of life, the death and darkness that are willful unbelief.

4. The Samaritan woman (4:1-42). The evangelist has already presented us with various aspects of the "newness" that Jesus brings. It is the messianic wine of Cana, abundant and exquisite; the renovated temple of God; a rebirth in water and Spirit. In this next attempt to describe God's gift in Christ, John pictures it as *a spring of water*, life-giving, welling up into eternal life; as a *worship suitable to God who is Spirit*, a worship therefore in the Spirit of truth. He insists, moreover, that Jesus' food is the accomplishment of his Father's will. Part of that will is the missionary work in fields ripe for harvest.

This chapter is surely one of the most dramatically constructed in the Gospel. Divide it into its various speaking parts—(1) a narrator; (2) Jesus; (3) the Samaritan woman; (4) the disciples; (5) the townsfolk—and you have instant theater. Another element in the account that lends itself to dramatic presentation is the way the stage is cleared for dialogue with the woman by the disciples' departure (v. 8), and for dialogue with the disciples by the woman's exit (v. 28). Her jar, left behind in verse 28, acts like a stage prop to advise the audience that she will return. There is even dramatic progression in the faith-knowledge of the woman and her townsfolk. From simple knowledge that Jesus is a Jew (v. 9), the characters move to belief in him as prophet (v. 19), Christ (vv. 25-26, 29) and, finally, Savior of the world (v. 42).

The chapter, additionally, is excellently structured, focusing on the two central dialogues—the first with the woman, the second with the disciples. The structure is built like this:

Introduction (vv. 1-6), in which Jesus leaves Judea for Galilee to the north. Enroute he passes through Samaria, where, at Shechem, he rests at noon next to Jacob's well (still in useful existence today).

FIRST DIALOGUE (vv. 7-26), between Jesus and the Samaritan woman concerning:

a) *living water* (vv. 7-15). The water of Jacob's well is surpassed by the water that Jesus will give, "a spring of water welling up to eternal life" (v. 14).

Transition: Jesus' knowledge of the woman's past moves her toward faith: "Sir, I can see that you are a prophet" (v. 19).

b) *worship in Spirit and truth* (vv. 20-26). "Yet the hour is coming, and is now here, when true worshipers will worship the Father in Spirit and truth" (v. 23).

The woman begins to think in terms of the Messiah. Jesus states that it is he.

SECOND DIALOGUE (vv. 31-38), between Jesus and the disciples concerning:

a) *Jesus' food* (vv. 31-34). "To do the will of the one who sent me and to finish his work" (v. 34).

b) *the harvest* (vv. 35-38). "Look up and see the fields ripe for the harvest" (v. 35).

Conclusion (vv. 39-42). Belief of the Samaritans: ". . . we know that this is truly the savior of the world" (v. 42).

A few additional comments seem necessary to clarify even further the content of this moving chapter.

1. Jewish relationship with the Samaritans lodged between Galilee to the north and Judea to the south was bad, deep, and historically conditioned. About the year 722 B.C.E. the Assyrian army descended upon northern Israel with force, took its populace into an exile from which it never returned, and colonized its land with foreigners who partially adopted Israel's religion over the centuries but were always viewed by the Jews as hated, semi-pagan invaders. (2 Kgs 17:23-41 gives a brief summary of the story.) The woman, therefore, was justly surprised when the Jew Jesus spoke to her and indicated that he was even willing to drink from her water jar.

2. Jesus is described in very human terms in verse 6, sitting at the well, exhausted from his journey. John usually paints his portrait of Jesus in colors more definitely divine. The woman, too, is very human. Her appearance at the well about noon (v. 6), long after the village women would have replenished their water supply for the day, may indicate her isolated position in the town's society. Sexually immoral, she was left to herself and her merry-go-round retinue of men friends. Yet it is she who, rebounding from Jesus' healing words, becomes a missionary to her people. The Lord's word moves her from isolation to faith to mission.

3. The account, as happens frequently in John, may be telescoping different periods of time. It seems to reflect strongly the Church's post-resurrection mission to Samaria, such as is described in the work of Philip, Peter, and John in Acts 8:4-25. It may even be indicative of the life-story of John's community, which would then have included, and been influenced by, Samaritan converts. What I am proposing here is that John's literary technique has rather amazing depths and turns. He specializes in bi-level presentations. There are *theological bi-levels* when, as one out of many examples, the water changed into wine (ch. 2) really speaks of the old covenant giving way to the new. Both levels are present in the Cana story; both are intended by the author. And, in a way unexpected by us twentieth-century readers, there are also *historical bi-levels*. Events in Jesus' lifetime are interpenetrated by later events happening in the life of John's community. In this chapter, water symbolizes the eternal life given by the Spirit of truth, the theological bi-level. On the other hand, the encounter with the Samaritan woman is influenced by the later, post-resurrection outreach to the Samaritans, the historical bi-level.

4. Finally, it is important to note that the conversion of the Samaritans is effected, not

by any miraculous sign, but by *the force of Jesus' word*: "Many more began to believe in him because of his word. . .We have *heard* for ourselves, and we know that this is truly the savior of the world" (vv. 41-42). It is to this theme of the life-giving word of Jesus that John will turn in the following episode.

4:43–5:47 Episode II: Jesus' Life-Giving Word

This second thematic episode consists of three sections:

1. narrative healing of the official's son;
2. narrative healing of the infirm man at the pool;
3. discourse.

All three will emphasize the life-giving quality of Jesus' word.

1. Healing of the official's son (4:43-54). This account is prefaced by verses 43-45, which tie this incident to the preceding. Verse 44, ". . . a prophet has no honor in his native place" is a bit strange. It is probably the author's way of saying that the people of Jesus' own Galilee were overenchanted by miracles, and that the only proper response to Jesus at this point will be offered by a pagan official.

The story itself is strikingly similar to the Capernaum cure reported in both Matt 8:5-13 and Luke 7:1-10, but with the kinds of differences expected as the story was passed along in oral form. The sign-meaning of this "long-distance cure" is very clear. It is uniquely Jesus' word—he does nothing but speak—that gives life to this child "near death" (v. 47). *That* Jesus spoke is noted three times (vv. 50, 53); *what* he spoke is also mentioned three times (vv. 50, 51, 53). That is the insistence. Jesus' word gives life—to those who believe (vv. 50, 53).

The evangelist has couched Jesus' words in verse 48 in the plural: "Unless you (plural) people see signs and wonders, you (plural) will not believe." In so doing, he makes Jesus speak, not mainly to the quite admirable official, but to men and women of John's own day and ours. Thus, though the evangelist is willing to mention the signs (and this is now the second of them, says verse 54) and, perhaps, even to use an existing collection of them in his Gospel (2:11; 4:54; 20:30), he does not

overestimate their efficacy. They are important if their deeper meaning is understood. What is more important is to stand open and receptive to the life-giving power of Jesus' word.

2. Healing of the infirm man at the pool (5:1-18). This incident takes place in Jerusalem at a Jewish feast that John does not identify. What is important for him, and for us, is that it occurs on a sabbath (vv. 9-10, 16, 18). The pool has been located by modern archaeologists next to the Crusader Church of St. Anne. The excavations have shown that the pool was enclosed rectangularly by four porticoes, with a fifth running across the pool and dividing it into two sections. (John's knowledge of Jerusalem is good.)

Our text lacks a fourth verse, which speaks of an angel descending to move the water. This verse is missing in our oldest and best Greek manuscripts dating back to the second and fourth centuries, and was probably added by someone who wished to attribute the moving of the water in verse 7 to a direct heavenly intervention. The original text says simply that the water bubbled up on occasion and that healing power was attributed to it.

This sign-miracle follows the preceding one in rapid succession because it has the same theological bi-level, and John wants the two together to reinforce his teaching at this point. Again, it is Jesus' word—and only that—which gives life to a man whose body has been devitalized for thirty-eight years. And again, *what* Jesus spoke, "Take up your mat, and walk," is mentioned in almost identical terms three times (vv. 8, 11, 12).

One instructive yet sad part of the story is that the cured man, though he has directly seen and benefited from the sign, has not understood it. To him the sign has not revealed its meaning. He heads off to inform the adversaries that it was Jesus who had healed him and for whom they were looking (v. 15).

Verses 16-18 lead us from the narrative into the discourse, in which the theological meaning of the two cures will be spelled out in full. The early mention of the sabbath (v. 9) becomes important. To carry around a sleeping mat on the sabbath was contrary to the law. Yet Jesus authorized the action. In initial response to his critics (v. 17), Jesus compares himself to his Father. Since the Father works on the sabbath, as on all days, so can Jesus. This response is dangerous, since it places Jesus and the Father on a similar (equal?) plane. And so the dramatic plot thickens. Who is this Jesus who treats both God and the sabbath as his own family possessions?

Here again we are caught up, I believe, in a historical bi-level. The questions arising in verses 16-18 (sabbath rest and Jesus' divinity) are precisely those that John's own community faced in its dialogue with the Jews of its own neighborhood. Was Jesus really divine? What did the sabbath mean and enjoin for Christian Jews? The following discourse will treat the specific question of Jesus' relationship to his Father at greater depth.

3. The discourse (5:19-47). The main reason for considering units 1–3, the two cures and this discourse, as one literary unit is that all sections sound the one theme: the life-giving power of Jesus' word. He has just healed the official's son by saying, "You may go; your son will live" (4:50), and the infirm man with the words, "Take up your mat, and walk" (5:8). And now the discourse will underscore the theological depth of this same truth. Note how the words of Jesus keep coming back to this teaching:

> "For just as the Father raises the dead and gives life, so also does *the Son give life* to whomever he wishes" (v. 21).

> "Amen, amen, I say to you, whoever *hears my word* and believes in the one who sent me *has eternal life. . . . and has passed from death to life*" (v. 24).

> "Amen, amen, I say to you, the hour is coming, and is now here, when the dead will *hear the voice of the Son of God*, and those who hear *will live*. For just as the Father has life in himself, so also he gave to his Son the possession of life in himself" (vv. 25-26).

> ". . . because the hour is coming in which all who are in the tombs [like Lazarus in chapter 11] *will hear his voice and will come out*" (vv. 28-29a).

What has happened in John's construction is that Jesus' right to work on the sabbath because his Father works has developed into a consideration of the relationship between Father and Son on a more elevated and more general level. Notwithstanding the Jewish commandment of sabbath rest, it was always recognized that God's two primary activities did not, and could not, cease on the sabbath:

these were the divine acts of life-giving and of judgment. Both formed a constant part of God's life: babies were born and people did die on the sabbath. Our present discourse insists that what God does, the Son also does. The Father gives life, and so too does the Son, by his word. And a new point enters into consideration. As the Father judges, so too does the Son (vv. 22, 27, 30). In the Fourth Gospel, however, this judgment is not projected for the future. It occurs right now, depending on one's attitude toward Jesus. Whoever hears and accepts him receives eternal life and does not come under judgment (v. 24), since he or she thus hears and accepts the Father. Whoever responds negatively judges himself or herself by that very fact.

Now all of this—and one can justly imagine our author arguing the various points with his neighboring non-Christian Jews—leads to the impossible, incredible question: If this is all true, is not Jesus God, which, since the Father is certainly God, makes for two Gods? The language of the discourse becomes very circumspect at this point. Our author is certain of two facts—the divinity of Jesus and the oneness of God—which neither he nor the whole of Christian tradition has been able to reconcile completely, though believing in them ardently. The best John can do is to insist on the divinity of Jesus, while insisting equally on his dependence and obedience. And so here, as elsewhere when Jesus' divinity is stated, the discourse is also intent upon noting that "a son cannot do anything on his own" (v. 19); that the Father shows the Son "everything that he himself does" (v. 20); that the Father "has given all judgment to his Son" (v. 22); that the Father "gave to his Son the possession of life in himself" and "gave him power to exercise judgment" (vv. 26-27). In a word, and a strong word it is, "I cannot do anything on my own" (v. 30). Our author's predicament is clear, and we too are involved in it. Jesus, divine as he is, is not the Father; and the Father is God. Little wonder that Jewish Christians of the first century had difficulty explaining Jesus to their fellow Jews.

The final section of the discourse details the various witnesses that testify to Jesus. Above all, there is the Father himself who renders testimony (vv. 31-32). And there is John the Baptist for those who have been impressed by him (vv. 33-36). Then there are the works that Jesus has done through his Father's power, works that are visible words revealing both Father and Son (vv. 36-37). Finally—and this argument is aimed peculiarly at the Jewish community—there are the words of Scripture and Moses himself that testify to Jesus (vv. 39-47). "If you had believed Moses, you would have believed me, because he wrote about me" (v. 46). In the episode that follows, we shall see an example of how this Old Testament scripture could be utilized to evolve and describe a further theological characteristic of Jesus: his power to nourish as the bread of life.

6:1-71 Episode III: Jesus as the Bread of Life

This chapter will center on the one theme of Jesus as the bread of life. It has four clear divisions: (1) the multiplication of the loaves; (2) walking on the water; (3) the discourse; and (4) an epilogue of reactions.

Before speaking at all of the loaves miracle, it might be well to notice what has often been presented as a real difficulty in the order of John's Gospel and a possible proof that somehow, in its earliest history, its pages got mixed up. At the end of chapter 4, Jesus is found in Galilee. In 5:1 he goes up to Jerusalem. But in 6:1 he is again in Galilee. Geographically this is strange, to say the least, so that some commentators have suggested that chapter 6 be placed before chapter 5. None of the Greek manuscripts has this suggested reordering, and there are many good reasons for keeping the present disposition, while realizing that John need not be nearly so much interested in historical-geographical order as in organizing themes. Chapter 6, I believe, belongs where it is as a demonstration of the statement in 5:46-47 that Moses and Scripture refer to Jesus. This, as we shall see, is precisely what the discourse in chapter 6 will expound. I believe, too, that the reference to the sick in 6:2 points *back* to the identical Greek phrasing in 5:3. Finally, leaving chapters 5 and 6 in their present order gives us a combination of word and bread, the essential elements and order of Christian Eucharist, a combination that need not have escaped John's attention.

1. The multiplication of the loaves (6:1-15). The Jewish Passover (v. 4) was an unleavened bread feast, so the reference prepares us for the bread miracle that is about to take place. *This miracle is the only one narrated by all four evangelists:* by Mark twice, in 6:31-44 and 8:1-10; by Matthew twice, in 14:13-21 and 15:32-38; by Luke in 9:10-17. It must be that the primitive Christian Eucharist made the prefiguring loaves miracle common property in all the Christian communities. And, indeed, what Jesus does with the bread sounds like the rubrics for what the Christian minister continually did in the celebration of the Eucharist. In the accounts of Mark, Matthew, and Luke, Jesus *took* the bread and *blessed* and *broke* and *gave*. So would the Christian minister. John's description is equally ceremonial, but with one even more Christian peculiarity. In 6:11, Jesus took, *gave thanks*, and distributed. The Greek for "give thanks" is *eucharisteō*, which gives us our word for Christian Eucharist. It occurs again in 6:23. This same Eucharistic overtone is heard again in verses 12-13, where the fish have disappeared from the discussion, which speaks exclusively of the bread and the care to be taken of the remaining fragments. The ultimate *sign* (v. 14) of this miracle points to Jesus as the bread of life, particularly in the Eucharist.

The reaction in verse 14, "This is truly the Prophet, the one who is to come into the world," refers again (as in 1:21, 24) to the prophet like Moses (Deut 18:15, 18) who was expected in the final days. Jesus has just fed the people with bread; Moses did the same with the desert manna.

One final note of interest is that the two disciples who function in this manifestation of Jesus to the crowd are Philip and Andrew, the same two who in 1:41, 45 acted as apostles to Nathaniel and Simon Peter, and who will later be apostles to the Greeks (12:20-22). Their role in the Fourth Gospel is to reach out.

2. Walking on the water (6:16-24). It is striking that John's sequence—the loaves miracle followed by that on the Sea of Galilee—is identical to that of Mark 6:34-51 and Matthew 14:13-33. The tradition of this ordering must be very old. In all three accounts Jesus calms his disciples with the identical majestic phrase: "It is I. Do not be afraid" (John 6:20; Mark 6:50; Matt 14:27). As we shall see later, this phrasing, which in the Greek has no predicate and simply reads *egō* *eimi* = *I am*, has strong overtones of divinity, echoing the name for Yahweh found in Isa 43:10, 13, 25. Jesus is the divine presence; the disciples need have no fear.

There is a question as to why the water miracle should be situated at this point in a chapter that otherwise speaks exclusively of bread. What is it a sign of? No answer is completely satisfactory, but the following have been offered. (a) The Old Testament Passover miracles were manna bread plus the crossing of the Reed Sea, and water springing from the rock. Exod 14–16 ties together in tight sequence the account of the Reed Sea crossing and the gift of the desert manna. This traditional Exodus coupling of water and bread, found also in Ps 78:13-25, may have encouraged the first Jewish Christians to attach the Christian water-sign to that of the bread. They are so found in Mark 6, Matt 14, and now in John 6. (b) John is simply extending his theme of life-giving word by presenting Jesus as life-giver in time of famine and of storm. (c) The storm scene is intended as a sign of Jesus' divine status (the "It is I" of verse 19 masks the profound I AM of the original Greek) and his ever-helping presence, "do not be afraid" (v. 20).

The account closes (vv. 21-24) with the boat suddenly coming to land (this is seemingly miraculous too) and the crowd, or part of it, transferring itself to Capernaum to find Jesus. This will provide the audience for the discourse that now follows.

3. The discourse (6:26-59). The best way to understand this discourse is to recognize that it is a homily based on Jesus' teaching but elaborated extensively by a Christian preacher aided by Jesus' Spirit. In this sense, the whole discourse comes from the Lord. It centers on one biblical text, "He gave them bread from heaven to eat" (v. 31), and is therefore a conscious demonstration of the truth of 5:39, 46-47 that the Scriptures elucidate the person of Jesus. The pivotal text is a loose, by-memory combination of several possible Old Testament quotations:

Exod 16:4: "I will now rain down *bread from heaven* for you";

Neh 9:15: "*Food from heaven you gave them in their hunger*";

Ps 78:24: "He rained manna upon them for food and *gave* them *heavenly bread*";

Ps 105:40: ". . . and with *bread from heaven* he satisfied them."

All or some of these associated texts have been combined by the preacher into the one amalgam of verse 31. The homily is broken by the short interruptions of verses 30-31, 34, 41-43, 52, which, by introducing live dialogue, help to keep the audience's interest while at the same time pointing out the precise difficulties felt by both the Jews of Jesus' time and of John's own later period.

This homily on a biblical text—what the Jews would call a *midrash*—follows a phrase-by-phrase order. It will treat in order: *He gave; bread from heaven; to eat.* Let's observe this happen.

a) *He gave* (vv. 26-34). In this first section, the emphasis lies on the giving. Jesus will give (vv. 27, 34), not as Moses gave (v. 32) a perishable manna food of mortality, but as the Father, source of eternal life, gives (v. 32). Thus far, Jesus appears as the giver of bread and therefore as the new and superior Moses.

b) *Bread from heaven* (vv. 35-47). The insistence now shifts to the bread from heaven that Jesus not only gives but actually is (vv. 35, 38, 41, 42). It is important to note here that the operative verb is "believe." Jesus as bread from heaven is accepted and consumed through the belief required in verses 35, 36, 40, 47. What this means is that this is a faith nourishment. Jesus is bread from heaven, feeding all believers, in the same sense that Old Testament wisdom nourished all who accepted it (Prov 9:1-5). We might call this type of feeding "sapiential."

c) *To eat* (vv. 48-59). In this final section, the vocabulary changes radically. The significant words are "flesh," "blood," "eat," "drink." Note the constant repetition of "eat" in verses 49, 50, 51, 52, 53, 54, 58. "Feed on" (an even more physical verb in the Greek than "eat") occurs in verse 57 of the NAB. These verbs become overwhelmingly insistent, as does the constant reference to flesh and blood, food and drink. The meaning of the discourse has changed. Where in the preceding section Jesus nourished through wisdom-revelation those who believed, the verb "believe" has now completely disappeared and is replaced by "eat," "feed on." Our homilist is clearly speaking now of *sacramental* nourishment, of the food and drink that one eats and feeds upon, of the Eucharistic nourishment provided by the flesh and blood of the Son of Man (v. 53). The "Son of Man" phraseology tells us that this is not the physical flesh and blood of the earthly Jesus and that we are asked to eat and drink but the spiritual, Spirit-filled flesh and blood of the heavenly Son of Man. Verse 58 ties the homily together by referring back to the central phrase of verse 31.

What this homily has done, therefore, is to deliver a rich and multi-faceted exposition of the Jesus-as-Bread-of-Life theme. Jesus is first of all the *giver* of the bread, a new Moses. He is also the *bread of wisdom and revelation* who nourishes all who come to him in faith. He is, finally, the *Eucharistic* source of eternal life for all who eat and drink the flesh and blood of the heavenly and glorified Son of Man. Because John uses this Eucharistic material in this Bread of Life homily, it will not be too surprising—yet surprising enough—that the Eucharist will not be mentioned at the Last Supper. Its material has been transferred to this incident. John has also succeeded, with this transfer, to unite in this one chapter the essentials of Christian Eucharist, the word and the bread—the revealing word of verses 35-47 and the sacramental bread of verses 48-59.

4. Epilogue of various reactions (6:60-71). These final verses resume the murmuring criticisms of verses 41-43, 52 to describe a mounting crisis of faith for Jesus' disciples. "This saying is hard; who can accept it?" (v. 60). At this point in the text, our historical bi-levels (Jesus' time and John's later period) reappear. If these verses refer to Jesus' Galilean ministry, in which he hardly would have spoken of the Last Supper Eucharist, the critical reactions refer solely to the material of verses 26-47, and are a negative response to his presentation of himself as object of faith, as bread-wisdom giving life to those who believe in him. But the passage as a whole certainly reflects also the crisis (present for all Christian centuries) of John's own community, the difficulty involved in accepting Jesus as the sacramental bread of life. To this difficulty will be added the scandal of the ascent of the Son of Man "to where he was before" (v. 62). The first step of that ascent will be Jesus' elevation onto a cross on top of a hill.

The chapter concludes (vv. 66-71) with a presentation of two models. Peter is one. He takes the risk, opening himself to the Word whose revealing words give eternal life. "Master, to whom shall we go? You have the words of eternal life. We have come to believe and are convinced that you are the Holy One of God" (vv. 68-69). The other model is Judas. He will remain in the group, living a divided existence, but already moving into darkness and into the demonic power which that darkness symbolizes (13:26-30). His appearance here as future betrayer (v. 71) lends further proof to the belief that John is using Last Supper material in this latter part of the discourse to complete his total presentation of Jesus as the bread of life for the Christian community.

One final observation before leaving this rich chapter: verses 67, 70-71 speak of "the Twelve." Only here and in 20:24 (Thomas) does John use this terminology. He speaks, rather, and so very often, of "the disciples," his favorite description of Jesus' followers. John leans much more toward the equality of discipleship than the grading of hierarchy.

7:1–8:59 Episode IV: Identity Crisis

These two chapters, in which Jesus is both manifested and rejected as the prophet, Christ, the unique Son of the Father, and the divine I AM (*egō eimi*) are among the most difficult to synthesize in the Gospel. There is such an overwhelming richness of movement and content that the chapters are strongly resistant to external ordering by a commentator. Yet, elements of structural and theological order can be found.

1. Introduction (7:1-14). (a) The background of these chapters is the Jewish feast of Booths (or Tents or Tabernacles)—*Sukkoth* in Hebrew—an annual autumn feast of thanksgiving for the yearly harvest and for the historic Exodus miracles of the water and pillar of fire. The feast, similar to our Thanksgiving, was the most joyous and popular of the Jewish calendar; and during it the celebrants lived in branched huts reminiscent of those used during the harvest time and the desert wandering.

Two distinctive features of this week-long ceremony in September–October have made an impression on the text. Water was brought daily from the pool of Siloam to the temple, where it was poured over the altar as prayers were recited for the all-important winter rain. And the lights in the women's court flamed so brightly that the city was lit up by them. Water and light play a fairly important part in these two chapters.

b) The brothers (7:3-10) fare poorly in this episode. They see and cannot deny the works that Jesus is doing; yet their suggestion that Jesus should go public in Jerusalem, the heart and capital of the country, is banal and incorrect. Verse 5 reads literally: "neither did his brothers believe in him." This agrees with the picture of Jesus' family given in Mark 3:21, 31-35; 6:4. Happily, the brothers do form part of the post-resurrection church in Acts 1:14. They, too, had to struggle through failure into the Christian faith.

c) In general, chapters 7 and 8 report a hectic clash of dialogues and controversies as the Gospel turns toward the passion. Deep within the rapid disagreements lie the theological disputes that brought Jesus to the cross and, years later, forced John's community out of the synagogue.

d) The two chapters are linked together by their content, which repeats again and again the issues under discussion, and also by what is commonly called "literary inclusion," a statement toward the beginning that will be balanced, like two bookends, by a similar expression at the end. In this instance, the "in secret" (vv. 4, 10)—en kryptō in the original Greek text—is counterbalanced by the use of the same Greek root ekrybē, "hid," in 8:59. These bookends show that the author intends that these two chapters form a unit.

2. Parallel structure of 7:14-53. It is clear that this long section has been arranged into direct parallels, with the initial division of 7:14-36 neatly balanced by its equivalent in 7:37-52. At issue are the initial questions as to whether Jesus is the Christ and the prophet of Deut 18:15, 18.

a) *Jesus' teaching* (7:14-24). His doctrine is not his own but comes from God who sent him. Jesus speaks this doctrine faithfully. They, on the contrary, do not keep the law of Moses, which they profess. Why is it that they can circumcise on the sabbath but become so irate when Jesus cures a man on the sabbath? (5:1-10).

a') *Jesus' teaching* (7:37-39). On the last day of the week-long feast, Jesus invites all who thirst to come to him. Either from Jesus himself (the Greek text here is uncertain) or from those who believe in him will flow the rivers of living water, the Spirit. But the Spirit has not yet been given, nor will be given, until Jesus is glorified through the cross and resurrection.

b) *Discussion about Jesus* (7:25-31). The question here is whether or not Jesus is the Messiah (vv. 26-27, 31).

b') *Discussion about Jesus* (7:40-44). The discussion continues as to whether Jesus is the Messiah (vv. 41-42) and expands to ask whether he is the Prophet of Deut 18:15, 18. (John's admittance that the Messiah should be born in Bethlehem [v. 42] is strong proof that he himself believed that Jesus was born there.)

c) *Temple officers* (7:32-36) are sent by the chief priests and Pharisees to arrest Jesus. He responds that he will be with them for just a little while. Will he go to the Diaspora (v. 35), to the lands outside of Palestine to which, in fact, Christianity spread after Jesus' death?

c') *Temple officers* (7:45-52) report back to the priests and Pharisees that Jesus speaks as did no one previously, but their report is treated with authoritarian scorn. Nicodemus, passing from the night of 3:2 into considerably more light, defends Jesus, but to no avail.

3. Intense disputes (8:12-59). The clear and simple paralleling in the previous chapter disappears with our present material, in which there is a steady alternating of statements and responses on the part of Jesus and his opponents—the chief priests and Pharisees from verses 13-19, and the Jews from verses 22-57. The ball passes from one side to the other, with only occasional editorial comments (vv. 20, 27, 30, 59) to slow up the game. Whereas chapter 7 disputed the titles of "Messiah" and "the Prophet" as applicable to Jesus, chapter 8 discusses with passion two different issues. What is Jesus' relationship to the Father? Is it something so completely different, so unique, that God is his Father in a way that God is Father to no other human being? This controversy ranges through the whole of the chapter. Read for a moment 8:16, 18, 19, 26-27, 28-29, 38, 42, 49, 54. The issue refuses to stay down or go away. The negative side to it is that if Jesus is the unique Son of God, what do they become who refuse to believe in him? They themselves plead that Abraham is their father (vv. 33, 39) and that through him they are related to God. Jesus' answer is that, though they are from Abraham's stock (v. 37), they actually deny their family origin by refusing to do what Abraham did—*believe*. They turn thereby from the truth to be believed over to its opposite, a lie engendered by the devil (v. 44). If actions indicate parentage, theirs show the devil as their source, their father.

As if this issue were not powerful enough, another raises its head, and this an even more dangerous and troublesome one. Into the chapter comes the majestic designation of the divinity—the awesome, powerful I AM, the *egō eimi*. Used all alone, with neither noun nor adjective to accompany it, as it would be in "I am the good *shepherd*"; "I am *meek* and *humble*," it echoes the divine name found in Isa 41:4; 43:10, 13, 25; 48:12.

In this chapter the form I AM appears three times, in ever increasing clarity:

> 8:24: "For if you do not believe that I AM, you will die in your sins."

> 8:28: "When you lift up the Son of Man, you will realize that I AM . . . ."

If these two texts leave some slight doubt about the divine content of the phrase, the final incidence does not:

> 8:58: "Amen, amen, I say to you, before Abraham came to be, I AM."

Little wonder that "they picked up stones to throw at him; but Jesus hid and went out of the temple area" (8:59).

4. Theological questions and their historical bi-levels. This brief study of chapters 7 and 8 brings to the surface four questions regarding Jesus that were the object of intense and emotional controversy, first during Jesus' lifetime and later during the life of John's Christian community. During the time of Jesus—and later as well, but beginning with Jesus himself—there began the discussion as to whether he was indeed the awaited (a) *Messiah, the Christ*, as also (b) the *prophet like Moses* of whom Deut 18:15, 18 had written. It is this Jesus-level dispute that is apparent in chapter 7—but not in chapter 8. In this latter chapter the questions change, a sign probably that its contents are chronologically later than those of chapter 7. Now the controversy

heats up as the issues become even more important. Was, and is, Jesus the (c) *completely unique Son of the Father*, with a relationship so close that he and the Father become identical in will and work and word? Pushing this a step further, can and should Jesus be referred to as (d) *the divine I AM*? Is he God? These two—unique Son and I AM—are the awesome issues of chapter 8 (not of chapter 7). These are also questions, I believe, that originated only after the resurrection of Jesus—questions, then, of John's later community, whose affirmative answers put it in direct and powerful opposition to the Jewish synagogue, within which it had originated.

5. Further comments. This treatment of chapters 7 and 8 is already lengthy, but a few more comments seem required.

a) The reader may have noticed how often Jesus calls himself the one "sent"—sent by the Father, from above, from heaven. Just checking through chapters 7 and 8 brings to evidence ten occurrences: 7:16, 18, 28, 29, 33; 8:16, 18, 26, 29, 42. This word, while implying Jesus' divine origin, also indicates his obedience and subservience to the Father. It will assume a subtle importance in the following chapter.

b) ". . . no one laid a hand upon him, because *his hour* had not yet come" (7:30). Jesus' "hour" in John is a very specific period of time. At Cana (2:4), as here in 7:30, Jesus' hour is still in the future. We find in 7:39 that the Spirit had not yet been given, "because Jesus had not yet been glorified." The notions all coalesce. The Spirit will be given when Jesus' hour arrives, which is the hour of his glorification, of his elevation. In an instance of Johannine punning, this hour of glorification-elevation begins with the elevation onto a cross. At that precise moment, as the Son of Man is lifted up, will the divine I AM be manifested (8:27).

c) We have noted that the special adversaries of Jesus in 8:22-59 are "the Jews." It is very important for Christians reading, teaching, or especially preaching from the Fourth Gospel to realize that it can be used to promote anti-Semitism—and we all have had far too much of that over the centuries and particularly in our own. There are two points to be made here. One is that "the Jews" can be contrasted in our Gospel to a whole other segment of the population that is equally Jewish.

Take, for example, 7:13: "Still, no one spoke openly about him because they were afraid of *the Jews.*" In this context, all the "no ones" are Jewish people. Who, then, are "the Jews"? As adversaries of Jesus and as contrasted to the people of Jerusalem (7:25-26), they seem to be clearly identified with the Pharisees of 7:32, 47; with the chief priests and Pharisees of 7:45; and with the Sanhedrin and Pharisees of 7:48. Yet even here there are exceptions, as we see in the person of Nicodemus (7:50-51). In John, consequently, the unfortunate title "the Jews" represents the authorities, yet not all of them, who by choice and office opposed Jesus and his teaching. This would be but a small fraction of Jews in Jerusalem, to say nothing at all of the far greater majority of Jews living away from the capital city.

The second point is that by the time John is writing this Gospel, a change has occurred. Christians have come into existence. The majority would now be Gentile, but even Jewish Christians will have assumed their own Christian identity and been separated from their previous Jewish society. Contact between Jewish Christians and non-Christians has moved from tolerance to discussion to controversy to angry separation and excommunication. In this sorry evolution, the term "the Jews," which in Jesus' day represented just a small body of in-family adversaries, can be used to represent the Jews as a whole, resistant to Christian belief. This was a pitiable development, perhaps inevitable; but the ill feelings of John's time will be thoroughly immoral if perpetuated in our own century. The long and heavy legacy of hate and murder that has piled up over the centuries must be attacked with a peculiarly Johannine weapon —that of love.

d) Critical readers will have already noticed that nothing has been said thus far about 8:1-11, the account of the woman taken in adultery. In modern editions of the Fourth Gospel, this passage is ordinarily either dropped into the footnotes or placed within brackets to indicate that it is not part of John's original text. It is missing from our oldest and best Greek manuscripts and seems to have been unknown to the early Greek Fathers, since they did not comment on it. In various old manuscripts it is found either at 8:1, as in our text, or after 7:36, or at the end of the Gospel, or after Luke 21:38. The earliest certain reference to the story is found in a third-century writing on church discipline called the *Didascalia.* In a word, it did not form part of the original Gospel of John.

Notwithstanding the mystery of the story's transmission, and of its insertion into John (because of 8:15?), it contains one of the most striking portrayals of Jesus' mercy and is a strong plea for its own authenticity. It possesses all the signs of historical truth. It must be a story dating back to Jesus that was passed along by oral tradition and used, perhaps, to solve the problem of forgiveness of sin for baptized Christians. It sounds incredibly like a Lukan narrative, dealing as it does with mercy, sin, and a woman.

One of the questions always asked about this beautiful passage is what Jesus was writing on the ground. Two reasonably plausible suggestions are that the doodling indicated lack of interest or that John wished to refer to the Greek text of Jer 17:13: ". . . may those who turn away from thee *be written on the earth,* for they have forsaken the fountain of life, the Lord."

e) The light and water aspects of the Jewish feast of Booths manifest themselves in the significant reference to the living water of the Spirit in 7:37-39, and to Jesus as light of the world in 8:12. It is to that last notion that John will turn his attention in the following chapter.

9:1-10:42 Episode V: Light of the World, Sight and Blindness

This fifth episode focuses on light, on Jesus as the light of the world (prepared for in 8:12), which light can bring sight to those previously blind as well as blindness to those who, confident in their own sight, turn away from the light. The episode does not stop with chapter 9 but continues on into and through chapter 10. It includes three sections: the man born blind (ch. 9); the good shepherd (10:1-21); the feast of Hanukkah (10:22-42). The sections are linked together. Verse 10:21 connects the good shepherd segment to the man born blind, and 10:26-28 connects the Hanukkah segment to that of the good shepherd.

1. The man born blind (9:1-41). We have spoken already of dramatic elements in John: of the technique of ambiguity, misunderstanding, clarification; of dramatic progression of knowledge in the case of the Samaritan woman; of characters, historical though they be, who also have dramatic roles to play, like the "missionary figures" of Andrew and Philip. Chapter 9 is undoubtedly the most dramatic of John's Gospel, and we would like to demonstrate this to an extent by laying it out, word for word from the text, but with the verses divided among various readers as it might be on the stage. Pass out the parts, and *voilà*, instant theater!

[SCENE 1]

Disciples: [1]As he passed by he saw a man blind from birth. [2]His disciples asked him, "Rabbi, who sinned, this man or his parents, that he was born blind?"

Jesus: [3]Jesus answered, "Neither he nor his parents sinned; it is so that the works of God might be made visible through him. [4]We have to do the works of the one who sent me while it is day. Night is coming when no one can work. [5]While I am in the world, I am the light of the world."

[6]When he had said this, he spat on the ground and made clay with the saliva, and smeared the clay on his eyes, [7]and said to him, "Go wash in the Pool of Siloam" (which means Sent).

Blind Man: So he went and washed, and came back able to see.

[SCENE 2]

Neighbor 1: [8]His neighbors and those who had seen him earlier as a beggar said, "Isn't this the one who used to sit and beg?"

Neighbor 2: [9]Some said, "It is,"

Neighbor 3: but others said, "No, he just looks like him."

Blind Man: He said, "I am."

Neighbor 1: [10]So they said to him,

Neighbors 1-2-3: "[So] how were your eyes opened?"

Blind Man: [11]He replied, "The man called Jesus made clay and anointed my eyes and told me, 'Go to Siloam and wash.' So I went there and washed and was able to see."

Neighbors 1-2-3: [12]And they said to him,

Neighbor 1: "Where is he?"

Blind Man: He said, "I don't know."

[SCENE 3]

Pharisee 1: [13]They brought the one who was once blind to the Pharisees. [14]Now Jesus had made clay and opened his eyes on a sabbath. [15]So then the Pharisees also asked him how he was able to see.

Blind Man: He said to them, "He put clay on my eyes, and I washed, and now I can see."

Pharisee 2: [16]So some of the Pharisees said, "This man is not from God, because he does not keep the sabbath."

Pharisee 3: [But] others said, "How can a sinful man do such signs?"

Pharisee 1: And there was a division among them. [17]So they said to the blind man again,

Pharisees 1-2-3: "What do you have to say about him, since he opened your eyes?"

Blind Man: He said, "He is a prophet."

[SCENE 4]

Authorities 1: [18]Now the Jews did not believe that he had been blind and gained his sight until they summoned the parents of the one who had gained his sight.

Authorities 2: [19]They asked them, "Is this your son, who you say was born blind? How does he now see?"

Parent 1: [20]His parents answered and said,

Parent 2: "We know that this is our son and that he was born blind. [21]We do not know how he sees now, nor do we know who opened his eyes. Ask him, he is of age; he can speak for himself."

Parent 1: [22]His parents said this because they were afraid of the Jews, for the Jews had already agreed that if anyone acknowledged him as the Messiah, he would be expelled from the synagogue. [23]For this reason his parents said,

Parent 2: "He is of age; question him."

[SCENE 5]

Authorities 1: [24]So a second time they called the man who had been blind and said to him, "Give God the praise! We know that this man is a sinner."

Blind Man: [25]He replied, "If he is a sinner, I do not know. One thing I do know is that I was blind and now I see."

Authorities 2: [26]So they said to him, "What did he do to you? How did he open your eyes?"

Blind Man: [27]He answered them, "I told you already and you did not listen. Why do you want to hear it again? Do you want to become his disciples, too?"

Authorities 3: ²⁸They ridiculed him and said,"You are that man's disciple; we are disciples of Moses! ²⁹We know that God spoke to Moses, but we do not know where this one is from."

Blind Man: ³⁰The man answered and said to them, "This is what is so amazing, that you do not know where he is from, yet he opened my eyes. ³¹We know that God does not listen to sinners, but if one is devout and does his will, he listens to him. ³²It is unheard of that anyone ever opened the eyes of a person born blind. ³³If this man were not from God, he would not be able to do anything."

Authorities 1: ³⁴They answered and said to him,

Authorities 2: "You were born totally in sin, and are you trying to teach us?"

Authorities 1-2-3: Then they threw him out.

[SCENE 6]

Jesus: ³⁵When Jesus heard that they had thrown him out, he found him and said, "Do you believe in the Son of Man?"

Blind Man: ³⁶He answered and said, "Who is he, sir, that I may believe in him?"

Jesus: ³⁷Jesus said to him, "You have seen him and the one speaking with you is he."

Blind Man: ³⁸He said,"I do believe, Lord," and he worshiped him.

Jesus: ³⁹Then Jesus said: "I came into this world for judgment, so that those who do not see might see, and those who do see might become blind."

Pharisee 1: ⁴⁰Some of the Pharisees who were with him heard this and said to him,

Pharisees 1-2-3: "Surely we are not also blind, are we?"

Jesus: ⁴¹Jesus said to them, "If you were blind, you would have no sin; but now you are saying, 'We see,' so your sin remains."

The preceding lay-out makes the dramatic pattern of the chapter clear. There are six logically successive scenes; brilliant dialogue; characters that are, in turn, merciful, confused, strong, bullying, weak, and self-interested. Playing the major role—even upstaging Jesus—is the intriguing figure of the blind man, courageous and intelligent, counterpunching with success every blow thrown his way. And the play closes with a fine line (v. 41) that gives the gist of the whole story.

The account demands little or no explanation of small details. What is all-important is to capture the deep, underlying truths that our evangelical dramatist has written into it.

a) The story has undoubtedly been used for baptismal instruction. The reader will have noted the happy coincidence of the *blind* man *washing* in a *pool* called *Siloam*, which means *sent*. Having already noted (Episode IV, 5 [a]) that "sent" is a veritable nickname for Jesus in the Fourth Gospel, we can be certain that John is writing of the physical cure in such a way that it reflects and calls to mind the cure of spiritual blindness—from birth—granted to those who wash sacramentally in the pool that is truly Jesus, the "sent one." (It is not hard to imagine that the effect of baptism was explained to catechumens as the immersion in Christ that would provide the insight of reality to which they had been blind from birth.)

Speaking in the same vein, the blind man's progressive enlightenment parallels the progress in knowledge that the catechumens would have followed as they were instructed in the faith. From first knowledge of the fact that there was a man called Jesus (v. 11), they would have advanced to deeper insights into his character as prophet (v. 17), as man from God (v. 33), as the heavenly Son of Man (v. 35), culminating in the final act of worship of Jesus as Lord (v. 38). This progression reflects not only the steps of the catechumen toward complete faith but also an enlivening dramatic technique on the part of the evangelist.

b) The passage is rich in irony, another dramatic touch. The reality of things is just the opposite of what it seems to be. Those who are sure they can see are, in truth, blind, and are so by their own choosing (vv. 40–41). He who starts out blind takes a risk at Jesus' invitation (v. 6) and ends up seeing. He passes from blindness to sight to insight. He is a striking example of the deep theology of which his cure is a *sign*. Jesus is indeed the LIGHT OF THE WORLD (v. 5). The sad foils to this man cured of both blindness and ignorance are the neighbors, who remain in ignorance (vv. 8-12); the parents, who refuse to take a risk—"He is of age; question him" (v. 23); the Pharisees, who cannot make up their collective minds (vv. 13-17); and the authorities and Pharisees, who refuse to believe what their eyes see (vv. 24, 40). No one is so blind as the person who refuses to see. "If you were blind, you would have no sin; but now you are saying, 'We see,' so your sin remains" (v. 41).

c) We find in this chapter the most outstanding example in John of the use of historical bi-levels. The Jesus-level of the cure of the blind has been subtly interpenetrated by the later historical level of John's own community experience. The revealing element in this compenetration is the statement in verse 22 that "if anyone acknowledged him as the Messiah, he would be expelled from the synagogue." And, of course, the cured man was thrown out (v. 34). Such excommunication from the synagogue because of belief in Jesus was not a feature of Jesus' lifetime, nor even of Paul's, whose final trip to Jerusalem found him worshiping in the temple (Acts 21:26). But the relationship between Jewish Christians and the synagogue soured over the decades, and especially with the increasing Christian insight that Jesus was truly God, truly the I AM. Eventually the synagogue prayer was enlarged to include a curse of such heretics as the Christians. No Jewish Christian could, of course, share such a prayer, and that resulted effectively in the excommunication of Jewish Christians.

This whole Gospel, and chapter 9 in particular, reflects this historical crisis. John and his fellow Jewish Christians are angry. They have been thrown out (v. 34). Part of the reason for including this chapter in the Gospel was to strengthen those who had undergone this trauma. Expelled from synagogue, family, and friends as heretics, they were encouraged by this account to fall at the feet of the Lord to worship him (v. 38).

2. The good shepherd (10:1-21). The first question to tackle here is why this section is in this position. Why does it follow the story of the man born blind? There appears to be no connection between 9:41 and 10:1; rather, 10:1 introduces abruptly the shepherd theme, which is totally unexpected after the material of chapter 9. This difficulty has again led some scholars to move chapter 10 to another place in the Gospel. It is, they say, a displacement. Yet it need not be and probably is not. The reference to the cure of the blind in verse 21 ties this segment to the preceding chapter. More to the point, the discussion about the

sheep and the shepherd is probably being used by John as a statement regarding the miserable shepherding being effected by such authorities as appear in the case of the man born blind. Blind guides themselves, they not only fail to recognize the leading light that is Jesus but cast out of the synagogue the one man who does accept the light. Verse 6 insists that they still just do not understand.

Crucial to the identification of the author's purpose at this point is the necessary realization that he is writing about Jesus with the text of Ezek 34 in clear view. In that passage, Ezekiel, speaking God's word, excoriates the authorities of his own time. They had become irresponsible and thieving shepherds, feeding themselves rather than their flock. So God would take away their maladministration and become the shepherd himself. Finally he would appoint another shepherd after the figure of David. John sees all of this coming true in Jesus. God has become the shepherd in Jesus, himself Messiah and Son of David. Jesus' fidelity to his sheep, his sacrifice for them, stands out in contrast to the failure of the stumbling, blinded, bullying authorities in chapter 9.

Metaphors come fast and often in these verses. There are the sheep—easily identified as the flock that Jesus intends to lead into good pasture (v. 9), those whom he knows by name and who recognize his voice (vv. 3-4, 14), those whom he intends to defend against thieves and robbers (vv. 1, 8, 10) and whom he wishes to join together with all others who, listening to his voice, will come into the one fold (v. 16). Jesus will effect all this because he is the GOOD SHEPHERD (vv. 11, 14), loved by the Father because *he will lay down his life for the sheep.* It is this act of total, loving self-sacrifice that is mentioned again and again as the central motif. Appearing first in verse 11 as the good shepherd title is introduced, it occurs again in verses 15, 17, and twice in verse 18. Though the shepherd-sheep metaphor was well known in the Old Testament Scriptures (as in Ezek 34), this laying down of the shepherd's life is something new. It is the characteristic function of Jesus. He is the good shepherd especially because of his willing self-sacrifice.

A final metaphor is that of the gate (vv. 7, 9), also applied to Jesus. He it is who provides safety for the flock by prohibiting entrance to marauders and who provides food by opening out onto good pasture lands. That the two metaphors of shepherd and sheepgate do not co-exist easily may be a sign that they originated separately but have been brought together here for this chapter.

In these verses we have seen two more of John's I AM—plus a following noun—statements. Jesus, who has identified himself as "I am the bread of life" (6:35, 41, 51) and "I am the light of the world" (8:12; 9:5), now says, "I am the gate for the sheep . . . the gate" (vv. 7, 9) and "I am the good shepherd" (vv. 11, 14). And since Jesus is the incarnate-Word revelation of the Father, we recognize in these personal characteristics of the Lord the same loving features of the Father.

Such revelation, as always, is followed by a crisis of faith. Is Jesus a possessed madman or just the opposite? Whose power is it that opens the eyes of the blind (vv. 19-21)?

3. The feast of Hanukkah. This feast celebrated the reconsecration of the temple by Judas the Maccabean (164 B.C.) after its profanation three years earlier by the Syrian Antiochus IV Epiphanes (1 Macc 4:36-59; 2 Macc 10:1-8). This yearly celebration lasted nine days, was a "lights" ceremony like the feast of Tabernacles (7:2), and was celebrated in mid-December. "It was winter" (v. 22). The scene for the present incident in John is set "in Solomon's Portico," a colonnade on the east side of the temple overlooking the Kidron Valley. It was a favorite rendezvous for Christians in Acts 3:11–4:4; 5:12, where it also appears as a place of controversy between Jewish Christians and some of their fellow Jews. Material from such a subsequent argument may well have entered into these verses.

The substance of the dialogue (vv. 24-38) is quite similar to that of chapters 7–8. One question at issue is whether Jesus is the Messiah (v. 24), a possible editorial link to the David figure of Ezek 34, which stood in the background of the preceding section. The other question is whether Jesus is the unique Son of God, whether God is in a very unique way *his Father*. In this brief section, "Father" appears nine times (vv. 25, 29 [twice], 30, 32, 36, 37, 38 [twice]); and "God's Son" is Jesus' claim in verse 36. What more can he offer as proof than his works done through the Father, works that are themselves the Father's revealing words? But Jesus' adversaries will not be-

lieve, as Jesus' divine works indicate, that he and the Father are one (v. 30), that the Father is in him and he in the Father (v. 38).

At one point Jesus almost plays with his opponents over the unique-Son-of-God issue. If Ps 82:6 calls judges "gods" because they share in the divine work of judgment, why should people object if Jesus is called "Son of God," since the Father has consecrated him and sent him into the world (vv. 34-36)? To this do the works testify. The incident ends on a sad note: "They tried again to arrest him; but he escaped from their power" (v. 39).

The final verses (40-42) are a brief presentation of the other side of Jesus' mission. Many came to him, accepted the witness of his signs and of John's testimony (a final reference to the Baptist), and came to believe in him. This paragraph also begins to position Jesus for his move to Bethany (ch. 11) and, in triumph, to Jerusalem (12:12).

John may well have intended a linkage between Jesus as the one "whom the Father has *consecrated* and sent into the world" (10:36) and the feast of the Dedication (v. 22), a memorial of the temple's *consecration* after Syrian profanation. If so, this is another in a line of attempts by John to show how Jesus had replaced the Jewish institutions. We have seen (1) how Jesus replaced *the temple* (2:13-22); (2) how he is a veritable *Lord of the sabbath*, working as does his Father (5:16-18); (3) how at *Passover* (ch. 6) he gives and becomes the manna bread and saves from the water; (4) how in chapters 7–8 at *Tabernacles* he is the living water and the light of the world. And now (5) Jesus replaces *Hanukkah*. He is the consecrated one. As John writes, the temple has disappeared, and Jewish Christians have been expelled from the synagogues. Fear not, says John, Jesus himself is sufficient to replace all these lost and precious treasures.

11:1-54 Episode VI: Life over Death

Jesus is both resurrection and life (11:25), and the restoration of Lazarus is the sign. John has already introduced us to the "life theme" when speaking in Episode I of rebirth (Nicodemus) and living water (Samaritan woman); in Episode II's life-giving word; in Episode III's life-giving bread; in Episode IV's "light of life" (8:12); in Episode V's "I have come that they might have life and have it to the full" (10:10).

Our present episode concentrates on this theme in one well-organized presentation, again one that adapts easily to theater. Pass out the roles—the sisters, Jesus, the disciples and Thomas, Jews/authorities and Caiaphas, a narrator—and the stage is set. It is drama with constant motion. The message of distress goes *from Bethany near Jerusalem* (v. 18) *to Jesus*, a message so simple and trusting that it might well become ours when friends are ill: "Master, the one you love is ill" (v. 3). Jesus and his disciples move *toward Bethany*. Martha and Mary move *to Jesus*. All move *to the tomb*. Lazarus moves *out of the tomb*. Informers move *to the Pharisees*. Jesus and his company move *to Ephraim* in northern Judea.

Mary and her sister Martha are known to us also from the Martha and Mary story in Luke 10:38-42. The personality characterizations are similar in both Luke and John. Martha comes through as the more dominant and active. It is she who is so busy in Luke 10:40 and who moves rapidly at first notice to meet Jesus here in John 11:20. Mary sat at home and later fell at Jesus' feet (John 11:20, 32); in Luke 10:39 she also sat at the Lord's feet to listen to his words. Surprisingly, Luke says nothing about a brother Lazarus, though he does present a parable regarding Lazarus, the poor man who ends up in Abraham's bosom. The Lukan story ends with the provocative conclusion: "If they will not listen to Moses and the prophets, neither will they be persuaded if someone should rise from the dead" (Luke 16:31). This is not meant to insinuate that John has turned the Lazarus of the parable into the brother of Mary and Martha. His characters are real people, and his knowledge of Jerusalem and its environs—which includes Bethany—is trustworthy.

What is truly touching about this incident is the author's insistence on the deep love that Jesus felt for this small family group, within which he must have felt so much at home. This love is evident in verses 5, 11, 35-36. Since Lazarus is the only male disciple of whom Jesus' love is predicated in the Gospel, some commentators have suggested that he is the beloved disciple who will become prominent in our later chapters. This is not probable, since the evangelist goes out of his way to preserve the anonymity of this central character.

There is some evidence that this Lazarus story was a second-edition addend to John's Gospel. This would explain the otherwise odd reference in verse 2 to the anointing by Mary, which will occur only in the following chapter. The oddness would disappear if the author had already included chapter 12 in his first edition and could thus allude to it when adding on what was to become chapter 11.

Our story is rich in the theology it unfolds.

1) Verses 25-26 are the theological center of the whole chapter. Jesus is both the resurrection and the life for all who, like Martha, believe that he is "the Messiah, the Son of God" (v. 27, the same profession that will be found in 20:31). One who has faith, even after death, shall live; one who has faith and is alive will never really die. Of this the restoration of Lazarus is the sign.

2) We find here a stunning example of Jesus' *life-giving word* and are reminded of the sayings in Episode II: "Amen, amen, I say to you, the hour is coming and is now here when the dead will hear the voice of the Son of God, and those who hear will live. . . . the hour is coming in which all who are in the tombs will hear his voice and will come out . . . ." (John 5:25, 28-29).

3) John's salvation theology is voiced in the unintentional prophecy of Caiaphas. "Jesus was going to die for the nation, and not only for the nation, but also to gather into one the dispersed children of God" (vv. 51-52).

4) Deeply hidden in the episode is a further truth: that Jesus' gift of life to Lazarus involves his own death, the offering of his own life. To love Lazarus and give him life, Jesus must be willing to risk and lose his own. This trip to Bethany is shadowed by the approaching cross (vv. 7-8, 16, 50-53).

It is remarkable how the account of Lazarus' resurrection parallels that of Jesus himself in chapter 20. Both accounts speak of:

—a mourning Mary at the tomb (11:31 and 20:11);

—a cave tomb closed with a stone (11:38, 41 and 20:1);

—grave clothes plus a face cloth (11:44 and 20:6-7);

—a special role given to Thomas (11:16 and 20:24-28).

John has written the story of Lazarus in such a way as to prefigure Jesus' resurrection. Chapter 11 is meant to prepare the reader for chapter 20.

We conclude this chapter with a few minor observations. We must be struck by the unexpected delay on the part of Jesus in verses 4-7. Why didn't Jesus prevent the death rather than wait to overcome it? Our author looks at the event from the divine viewpoint rather than the human, and it is this that is promoted by Jesus' words in verses 4, 9, and 15. John, *looking back at the incident*, can now see, and have Jesus proclaim, that it was all for the better. The miracle sign has evidenced God's glory, his presence, and in the person of the Son of God. The miracle was an epiphany. The God of healing love is revealed through the work of his Son. And it is through walking with this Son, himself the light of this world (v. 9), that we are assured of not stumbling.

Caiaphas, whose words unintentionally become so theological in the final verses, was high priest for some nineteen years, from about A.D. 18–37. He was the son-in-law of Annas.

The final verses of the episode (53-54) position Jesus in Ephraim near the desert. From there he will ascend a last time to Bethany and Jerusalem.

11:55–12:50 Episode VII: Life Through Death

This final episode in the Book of Signs will teach not only that Jesus overcomes death (as in the Lazarus story) but that he will give life precisely through death. The text is divided into six clearly distinct but interconnected segments: the introduction; the anointing; the triumphal entry; Jesus' hour; the evangelist's evaluation; Jesus' summary proclamation.

1. Introduction (11:55-57). Our initial verse is almost identical to 6:4, which also introduces Passover material. The double mention of the Passover (v. 55) will lead us naturally into 12:1. The scene is being set as people wonder aloud whether or not Jesus is coming. Meanwhile (v. 57), the trap, too, is being set.

2. The anointing (12:1-11). As we move into material concerning the passion, we find that John's Gospel becomes much more similar to the other three. This story of the anointing, for example, resembles closely that of Mark 14:1-11 and Matt 26:1-16. (Luke 7:36-50 also has an anointing incident, but its time frame and purpose are quite different.) Although Martha, Mary, and Lazarus are prominent, the text definitely avoids saying that the meal was given at their home. Mark and Matthew place it in the home of Simon the leper. John does not disagree.

It is interesting to read, and it seems so correct, that "Martha served" while Mary "anointed the feet of Jesus" (vv. 2-3). The protest by Judas Iscariot allows the evangelist to put at center stage for just a moment this disciple who will be the tragic figure in the drama beginning to unfold. He steals from the poor; eventually he will lose his all. The key expression in this narrative, however, is that of Jesus in verse 7: "Let her keep this for the day of my *burial.*" The ointment is not simply cosmetic perfume; it is not simply preparation for death; it is burial ointment and fills the house with fragrance just as the scent of funeral oils pervades a tomb. This burial motif will surface again shortly.

With verse 9 the "large crowd" moves onto the scene. It will remain throughout, and for a purpose that will appear in just a moment. But for now Lazarus is featured. The authorities plan to have him, like so many later disciples, share Jesus' fate. His very existence is too strong a proof of Jesus' life-giving word.

3. The triumphal entry (12:12-19). The crowd takes over this scene (vv. 12, 17, 18) as Jesus enters Jerusalem one last time. He comes as king (vv. 13, 15), a motif that will become very strong in the passion account. The exultant prayer of verse 13 originates from Ps 118:25-26, a psalm used regularly by pilgrims entering the Holy City. To it is joined a post-resurrection application (v. 15) of Zech 9:9. Zechariah's king, like John's, is humble. Though victorious, he rides, not the stallion of war, but the donkey of service. The crowds that introduce the scene (v. 12) are in strong evidence at its conclusion (vv. 17, 18), where their presence provokes the Pharisees' reaction. Jesus' gift of life to Lazarus is going to demand a frightening exchange: Jesus' life for that of his friend. This segment concludes with the important phrasing: "Look, the whole world has gone after him" (v. 19). Part of this world is the Jewish crowd that we have observed repeatedly.

4. Jesus' hour (12:20-36). This section—a combination of narrative, monologue, and dialogue—is the key to the whole chapter. It follows one narrative (#2) that emphasized *burial* and another (#3) that repeatedly introduced the *crowd*. And now, in unexpected fashion, onto the stage come "some Greeks" (v. 20), who start a move toward Jesus through the aid of our *typical* missionaries (1:41, 45; 6:5-10), Philip and Andrew. Those following Jesus now include both Jews and Greeks, the latter peculiarly illustrative of "the whole world going after him" (v. 19).

In the verses that follow, John begins to pull the whole chapter together—the burial ointment, the large crowd, the Greeks, the whole world. The narratives will now be interpreted by Jesus' words. The HOUR has come (v. 23) in which Jesus will be glorified, that is, in which God will manifest to the utmost his presence in his Son. But this hour entails death: the grain of wheat must fall into the ground if it is to produce fruit (v. 24). Jesus will enter the ground (the burial ointment of verse 7 is an advance statement of that), and his dying will produce much fruit. We have begun to see the whole world going after him—the Jewish crowds of verses 9, 12, 17, 18, 29, 34 as well as the first fruits of the Gentile harvest (vv. 20-22). It is this same teaching, but in different words, that Jesus proclaims in verse 32: "And when I am lifted up from the earth, I will draw everyone to myself." The beginning of this being lifted up will be Jesus' crucifixion.

What Jesus is insisting upon in this episode is that life will be offered to the world *through* his death. If he is buried like the seed, if he is lifted onto the cross, then much fruit will come; then he will draw all to himself. The crowd and the Greeks are simply the initial harvest. And, in a remarkable way, this being buried, this being raised on a cross, is also Jesus' glorification (vv. 23, 28), the manifestation in him of his Father's presence, nowhere more evident than in Jesus' act of self-sacrificing love. (So, too, does Isaiah's servant song join to the death of the servant his glorification and elevation. John's theology flows from Isa 52:13: "See, my servant shall prosper, he shall be *raised high* and greatly *exalted* [glorified].")

As Jesus mentions his own self-giving (vv. 23-24), he joins to it that of his disciples. They are called to identical servant roles (vv. 25-26).

Verses 27-30 are strangely reminiscent of the agony in the garden—missing in the Fourth Gospel, for which it may present a too human Jesus. Yet at this point, as in the garden scene, Jesus' soul is troubled, and he is tempted to pray for the hour's passing— yet he doesn't (v. 27). Rather, reinforcement comes from the Father, who has glorified (manifested) himself through the signs and will glorify himself even further through Jesus' resurrection (v. 28). Lines are being drawn, since the manifestation of God's loving presence at the moment of crucifixion will demand reaction, and the reaction will determine individual judgment (v. 37). The world's prince of darkness will be driven out by the light that is Jesus. The present moment, however, is the hour of Jesus' sunset. "The light will be among you only a little while. Walk while you have the light . . . ." (v. 35). As Jesus leaves the scene (v. 36) and the ministry of the signs ends, some are still stumbling in the darkness: "Then how can you say that the Son of Man must be lifted up? Who is this Son of Man?" (v. 34).

5. The evangelist's evaluation (12:37-43). The signs' ministry has been no great success, neither in Jesus' lifetime nor in the later preaching of them by Jesus' disciples. It is as though Isa 53:1 had been written for this occasion: "Lord, who has believed what has reached our ears?" Paul would have the same feeling with regard to his own preaching ministry (Rom 10:16). It is as though Isa 6:10, too, had been written for Jesus' times. The sad comment of verse 40 was well known and often used in the early church (Mark 4:12; Matt 13:15; Luke 8:10; Rom 11:8; Acts 28:26). It is not a proclamation of predestination. Any blinding and hardening that occur are always seen as a penance that follows personal guilt. Isaiah's text was meant to inform the prophet—and numerous preachers after him—that the comparative failure of his mission entered somehow into God's plan and should not discourage him.

Verse 41 could be clearer for us poor readers in the twentieth century. In what way did Isaiah, living centuries before Jesus, see his glory? This must refer back to the contexts of the quotes from Isa 53 and 6. In the first, Isaiah speaks of the servant; in the second, of his inaugural glorious vision of God as King and Lord of hosts. In God's glory, he has seen that of Jesus, for the Father shares it with him;

and it is with the same glory that the servant has been exalted.

Verses 42-43 introduce us to a fringe group of disciples, crypto-Christians, who hid their feeble faith in Jesus lest, like the man born blind in chapter 9, they be expelled from the synagogue. John is writing now about such Christians of his own generation.

6. Jesus' summary proclamation (12:44-50). There is no attempt here to indicate an occasion or audience for these verses. What we have, rather, is a résumé of the salient points of Jesus' teaching, in his own words, located here by John as a recapitulation before starting the account of Jesus' passion-glorification. Reappearing in summary fashion is the statement of (a) the union of Father and Son (vv. 44-45); (b) Jesus as light of the world, come not to condemn but to save (vv. 46-47); (c) the inevitable judgment that depends on personal reaction (v. 48); (d) the identification of Jesus' word with that of the Father and of the eternal life that it gives (vv. 49-50). These themes have been constantly cycled through these first twelve chapters.

As we come to the conclusion of this first half of John's Gospel, it might be of help to review very briefly what the sign theology has involved. By means of signs—seven of them are miracles—the evangelist has attempted to tell us who Jesus is and what he has effected, so that by knowing Jesus we might know the Father. The seven miracle-signs have taught us that the new era of messianic wine has arrived (Cana); that Jesus' word is life-giving (the official's son, the infirm man at the pool); that Jesus is the bread of life and the saving presence of God (ch. 6); and that he is, finally, both the light (ch. 9) and the life (ch. 11) of the world. If this is who Jesus is and what Jesus does, it is perforce who God is and what God does; for Jesus, by word and action, reveals the Father. Thus far can the signs take us. But if we really want to advance from this position to know Jesus and the Father in the very heart of their being, we must take a further step. Jesus' passion will reveal both him and his Father in their heart of hearts.

C. THE BOOK OF GLORY

John 13:1–20:31

With chapter 13, we turn from Jesus' public ministry and its revelatory signs to Jesus' last days, to the period of his glorification, that is, his death and resurrection, in which God's glory, God's presence, will be manifested. For this reason, this second half of the Gospel is frequently entitled "The Book of Glory." It includes the farewell discourses (chs. 13-17), the passion narrative (chs. 18-19), the resurrection (ch. 20), and the epilogue (ch. 21).

13:1–17:26 The Farewell Discourses

These five chapters veer sharply from the previous presentation of Jesus' ministerial signs to an insistence on the Christian's actual, realized life in Jesus. The emphasis is not on the future but on the present. We hear the voice of Jesus, as though already risen and glorified, speaking to his disciples of present life, of indwelling, of love, of effected judgment, of the Spirit Paraclete who is at once both advocate and revealer. Jesus leaves to go to the Father and, in a little while, to return. The central stress is on union: the union of Father and Son; the gift and indwelling presence of their Spirit; the union of Son and disciples; the union of disciples with one another. The dynamism of all this is *love*, a word that now begins to take over John's good news. If we really want to know who and what Jesus is, so that we might know who and what God is, LOVE is the answer.

1. The opening scene: foot-washing (13:1-30). Again we approach Passover season (v. 1). But this time it will be Jesus' own passover from this world to the Father (vv. 1, 3). In this dramatic scene, Jesus, servant of the Father, becomes the servant of humankind. His hour has come, and he loves his friends "to the end" (v. 1), a Johannine double-entendre that includes both time and measure. Jesus does the servant task (cf. Luke 22:27); so, too, must his disciples serve one another. We are all called to wash one another's feet. All this is clear, and it is enunciated precisely by Jesus to remove any possible doubt (vv. 12-17).

Verses 6-10, however, are confusing. They seem to have a different thrust. What Jesus does cannot be understood till later (v. 7). Peter objects, as he did to Jesus' servant *death* in Mark 8:32; the washing, or rather, the being washed, is so important that without it the disciples can have no part in Jesus (v. 8). This reads like more than a simple example of Christian service and has tempted many commentators to believe that this *servant foot-washing* is also symbolic of Jesus' *servant death*. Moreover, the absolutely essential washing of verse 8 is reminiscent of baptismal teaching.

These clues suggest that the theology here is particularly rich, even though obscure. (a) Jesus' servant foot-washing is symbolic of his servant death. (b) Participation in this salvific death is through baptism, without which "you will have no inheritance with me" (v. 8) and through which we are "clean all over" and need not be washed again (v. 10). The line runs from symbolized salvific death to sacramental participation. (c) All this, in turn, leads to the ethical servant role that we must live with regard to one another (vv. 12-17). Baptized into Jesus' salvific death, we must lead his servant life. "I have given you a model to follow, so that as I have done for you, you should also do" (v. 15). This is a prophetic-action description of the role of all Christians, but especially of authority (like Peter) in the church. This must be exercised on one's knees before the people of God. Peter's difficulty with Christ's servant role—a difficulty felt a million times over by church authorities and ordinary Christians down through the centuries—reminds us of his similar difficulty in Mark 8:32-33.

One disciple is not clean. At this "hour," at this initiation of final conflict, he denies his share with Jesus, he refuses belief in the I AM (v. 19). He too passes over, but into the power of Satan (vv. 2, 27). Judas Iscariot, table companion of the Lord (v. 18, citing Ps 41:9), will now desert the light of the world. As he passes from light to darkness, the evangelist notes significantly and sadly, "It was night" (v. 30).

This insistence on Judas underlines a problem felt by the first Christians and, perhaps, tossed up at them in controversies. What did Judas' act of betrayal say about Jesus' wisdom and knowledge? Could the true Messiah have made so unfitting and fatal a choice? These questions were felt so strongly in the early church that Judas receives special attention in all four Gospels, as well as in Acts 1:15-26. John insists that Jesus knew of the betrayal and that it fit into God's saving plan.

Verse 23 speaks for the first time of the disciple, "the one whom Jesus loved." No name is given, but his function is significant. Close to Jesus' side—as was the Word to the Father's side in 1:18—he mediates between Jesus and Peter; his subsequent appearances will almost invariably be related to Peter.

2. Jesus' departure and return (13:31-14:31). Once Judas has left the light, Jesus begins to speak to his own, his dearest friends. Various disciples—Peter, Thomas, Philip, Judas—carry the discussion forward by the questions they pose. This enables us to break down the whole, hopefully to see it more clearly, by dividing it according to the characters who ask the leading questions.

a) The first section (13:31-35) is simply an introduction. Judas' departure has set in motion the events of the passion. Jesus will be glorified, God will be glorified, since God's presence as infinite love is about to be manifested in Jesus. Jesus will leave, and that absence (or is it presence?) is the problem underlying this whole section. As he leaves, he leaves behind his one essential commandment: "Love one another" (v. 34). It is a *new* commandment because this mutual love must be modeled on something new—on the love that Jesus shows for his disciples. Mutual love must be the sign, the indispensable sign, of their discipleship.

b) *Peter* (13:36-14:4) moves the discussion further: "Master, where are you going?" (13:36). This appearance of Peter permits the evangelist to present a bit of tradition shared, seemingly, by the whole church, that Jesus predicted Peter's denial (13:37-38). Yet, though Peter would deny his Lord, he would also follow him in death (v. 36).

In the subsequent verses (14:1-4), the basic problems that control the rest of the chapter are touched upon. The disciples are troubled (v. 1, as also v. 27)—and so later will be John's own community—because of Jesus' departure. In response, Jesus insists on the necessity of faith, stating that he goes to prepare a place for them and will return to take them with him (v. 3). This sounds very much like a promise of Jesus' future return as visible Lord of the world (the technical term for this is the *parousia* = coming). The early church awaited this with fervent hope (1 Thess 4:16-18). But John's Gospel will now reinterpret such a futuristic approach. Jesus has not passed over a bridge that was subsequently blown up; there is a *way* to him, and they already know it (v. 4).

c) So *Thomas* (14:5-7) asks, "How can we know the way?" Jesus' answer states that Christian hope is not in a method, not in a procedure, but in a person. Jesus himself is "the way and the truth and the life" (v. 6). Through and in Jesus, one *comes to* the Father, *knows* the Father, *sees* the Father.

d) *Philip* (14:8-21) seizes on that final phrase to ask: "Master, show us the Father . . . ." (v. 8). One can hear the sigh of weariness, almost of failure, in Jesus' voice: "Have I been with you for so long a time and you still do not know me, Philip? Whoever has seen me has seen the Father" (v. 9). And the discussion continues, pointing to the perfect union of Jesus with the Father: both his words and his works are the Father's (vv. 10-11). With this, Jesus turns his attention to the disciples. They, too, will do the works that Jesus has done because he will respond according to their petitions, so that God will be manifested in the Son. The disciples' love will bring from the Father another Paraclete, the Spirit of truth, to remain with them always (v. 16). In this sense, Jesus will come back; they will not be left orphans (v. 18).

At this point, the reader's head should be spinning a bit. What is going on? What seemed to be a statement of Jesus' future return to take his disciples to places prepared for them (14:3), a movement carrying believers into some future and unknown paradise, has subtly turned around like a boomerang targeting in on the place from which it was originally launched. Jesus goes, but he returns; and the dwelling places he prepares, which seemed to be located out there somewhere (v. 2), will be found, rather, within the believers themselves (vv. 20-21). In some way, this return is connected with another Paraclete (cf. 1 John 2:1, where Jesus is called the first one) who takes Jesus' place as both advocate and revealer.

It is this boomerang movement—Jesus' departure and consequent return through the Paraclete—that explains the "little while" in verse 19. Just as the disciples see Jesus now,

so they will soon know of his union with the Father, which union he will share with them. The disciples who love will be loved by both the Father and Son, who (through the Paraclete?) will reveal himself to them (v. 21). All they could have hoped for in the future will soon be now.

e) This provokes the *Judas* (not Iscariot) sequence (14:22-31). How strange that Jesus should speak of all this Spirit return, indwelling, union with Father and disciples, when what Judas and the others were expecting was a visible return in majesty accompanied by a fearsome display of celestial fireworks. "Master, [then] what happened that you will reveal yourself to us and not to the world?" (v. 22). Jesus' answer almost avoids the question as it merely insists on what has already been proclaimed. He and the Father will come to those who love and will dwell with them (vv. 23-24). (This, for John, is the all-important coming, *parousia*, of the Lord.) This coming is directly related to the Paraclete whom the Father will send to instruct and to remind. John's community is clearly a Paraclete community, confident that the Spirit, Jesus' Spirit, is with them still, reminding them of, and interpreting, Jesus' words, instructing them with the words and wisdom of the Lord. Surely this Gospel is filled with Paraclete reminders and instruction.

The fear and distress of people awaiting a delayed future return (vv. 1, 27) must give way in John's community to the peace that is Christ's gift, to the joy that is theirs at the knowledge that Jesus has returned to the Father who is his origin, "greater than I" (v. 28).

This discussion, says Jesus, is long enough; now it is time to face the conflict with the Prince of this world (v. 30). The Father has commanded total love, and the world will soon know that this is what the Son will give. "Get up, let us go" (v. 31).

3. Discourse on Jesus and his community (15:1–16:33). There are two major difficulties with this material. The *first* is that it is completely unexpected. Seemingly 14:31 has just set Jesus and his disciples in motion: "Let us go." What would follow naturally after this is 18:1, "When he had said this, Jesus went out with his disciples across the Kidron valley." But between 14:31 and 18:1 we have all the material, almost all discourse, of chapters 15-17.

A *second* difficulty is that chapters 15–16 repeat much of what has already been said in chapter 14. Jesus talks again of indwelling, of the Paraclete, of departure and return, of love, of the "little while." These facts have led numerous students of John to detect here an addition, some kind of parallel to, or alternative version of, chapter 14. This is highly probable. Yet, if chapters 15–16 are an addition, they are surely not an intrusion; they are not a detour, but a circling around the same center. The motifs of chapter 14 appear, disappear, reappear. Not new knowledge, but reinforcement of the already given, seems to be the purpose of these two chapters. They divide themselves into one long monologue, followed by a combination of dialogue plus monologue.

a) *The long monologue* (15:1–16:16)

This is the longest monologue in the Fourth Gospel. It begins with:

i) The allegory of the vine (15:1–17)

The ancient Old Testament allegory of Israel as Yahweh's vine (Ps 80:9-20 is one example among many) becomes deeply Christianized at this point. Jesus is the true vine (vv. 1, 5) of which the Father takes personal care, pruning the barren branches, trimming clean the fruitful. These latter are the disciples who have accepted Jesus' life-giving word (vv. 3, 7). They are invited, encouraged to live on, to abide in Jesus. (The Greek word for "remain," *menō*, occurs eleven times in these few verses, a repeated insistence on the return of Jesus by indwelling. It is, however, translated in various ways in our English text.) The other all-important word here is "love." Just as "remain" is the essential word of verses 1-8, so "love" becomes essential in verses 9-17, while both bring this minor section to its conclusion in the "remain" and "love one another" of verses 16-17. The central teaching of this allegory is clear. *Remaining in Jesus through love* is what this little homily is all about. If this happens, when it happens, the disciple will produce fruit (vv. 5, 8). When it does not happen, the disciple is no disciple at all, but good for nothing but fuel (v. 6).

The love of which Jesus speaks is one, but many. It begins with the Father's love for Christ (v. 9), moves on to Jesus' love for his friends (vv. 9, 12-13), is reciprocated in the disciples' loving obedience to Christ (vv. 10, 14), and radiates out through their love for one another (vv. 12, 17). It is this love that will be the source of their joy (v. 11) and the essential condition of their intimate friendship with the Lord (vv. 14-15). The model of love for all true discipleship is extreme, limitless; for it is Jesus himself who lays down his life for his friends (v. 13), as does the good shepherd of 10:11, 15, 17, 18. Yet it is precisely for love like this that Jesus has chosen them. They will bring forth enduring fruit, their prayers will be answered, to the extent that they love one another (vv. 16-17).

ii) Hatred from a hostile world (15:18–16:4a)

The words of the text are clear, as is the logical progression. The disciples are warned that the price of discipleship will be high. Just as Jesus was hated, as he was persecuted (v. 20), as his words were not accepted, so will it be for his followers—hated, persecuted, unaccepted by the world (vv. 18-20). Such will be the *fact*, a fact seemingly well known in the experience of John's community. The deep-down *crime* is that the adversaries have seen the evidence yet refuse to believe. Jesus has spoken to them (v. 22), he has performed works never done before (v. 24); yet they really know nothing about the Father who sent Jesus (v. 21), and in hating him, they hate the Father also (vv. 23-24). In the words of Ps 69:4, "They hated me without cause." *Witnesses* to the crime will be both the Paraclete and the disciples, who, having seen from the beginning, can bear witness to all (vv. 26-27). The *reason* why this subject comes up at all is that excommunication and even death await the disciples (16:2-3). May their faith not be shattered in such periods of terror (16:1, 4)!

Our text here has been paraphrased easily. Two issues, however, need explanation. The *first* is Jesus' use of the word "world" (vv. 18-19). In the present context, "world" has a strong negative content, quite different certainly from its beautiful appearance in chapter 3: "For God so loved the world that he gave his only Son, so that everyone who believes in him might not perish but might have eternal life. For God did not send his Son into the world to condemn the world, but that the world might be saved through him" (3:16-17). This world that God loves with infinite love, that he saves and does not condemn, seems oceans apart from the hating and persecuting world of chapters 15–16. One identical word is being used in completely different fashions. This is a difficulty in John's Gospel that we must keep before our eyes. The "world" can be the work of God's hands (1:2-4), the object of his love (3:16-17)—that is God's world. But there is another world, too, what we in the twentieth century might call the epitome of worldliness, in which reign darkness and hatred, untruth and death. Of this world, better entitled "anti-world," Satan is prince (14:30; 16:11). John's community has already encountered it.

This brings us to the *second* issue. We find once more a historical bi-level. Expulsion from the synagogue (9:22; 12:42), even death, has touched the Johannine Christians; and this they see as the lot of those who follow the Master (15:18-21). Seemingly, persecution and disbelief have widened in their experience, being found not only in non-Christian Judaism but also among the Gentiles. In this sense, a whole segment of God's world has been transformed for them into a force of disbelief and hatred.

iii) The Paraclete (16:4b-16)

The Paraclete was barely mentioned in the final verses of chapter 15, but will now be the center of discussion. Jesus' departure, followed by persecution, was not a necessary subject of discourse at the beginning of the ministry, since it was not yet imminent (v. 4b). Not surprisingly, to speak of it now brings grief to the disciples. (To record that no one asks, "Where are you going?" [v. 5] ignores that very question raised by Peter in 13:36 and alluded to by Thomas in 14:5, an indication that chapter 16 is of different origin.) Jesus insists that grief is improper, for only his departure will assure the coming of the Paraclete. Into the Jesus-vacuum will come the Paraclete-presence. This divine presence, effectively experienced by John's community, will be proof positive that disbelief was sin, that justice was accomplished through Jesus' passage to the Father, that the prince of evil has been condemned to defeat (vv. 8-11).

The Paraclete will do even more. As the Spirit of truth, he will be the constant guide of the disciples, speaking to them (through inspired preachers and writers like the evangelist) what he *hears* from Jesus, who, in turn,

receives from the Father. The verbal form "he *hears*" (v. 13) is important. It places the Paraclete's function simultaneously in God's eternity and the reader's now. Through the Paraclete, what Jesus says in his Father's realm is *now* transmitted to the disciples. Jesus who once spoke in the flesh now speaks through the Spirit. Much of this present discourse, surely, comes from Jesus speaking through his Spirit to the community. In this sense, Jesus' earthly departure is a gain, for it enables the glorified Jesus to be present. The disciples will lose him in earthly form within a short time but will soon receive him back again in Spirit (v. 16).

b) *From dialogue into monologue into dialogue* (16:17-33)

The long monologue has ended, but there is still more to be recounted in a sort of dialogue between disciples and Master. Jesus' statement about the short time, the little while, brings the disciples back into view. What is meant by this "little while" (vv. 17-19)? Jesus does not answer the question directly but explains instead how grief will be turned into joy (see 20:20 for the actualization of this), like that of a mother once her child is born into the world (vv. 20-22). On that day of birth, to continue the simile, the time of veiled language will be over (vv. 23a, 25), and the time of direct and effective petition to the loving Father will have begun (vv. 23b-24, 26-27) for those who have loved Jesus and believed in his divine origin (vv. 27-28). When the disciples affirm their belief (v. 30b), Jesus gives a final warning. During his hour they will be scattered, leaving him abandoned by all but his Father (v. 32). They will suffer, yet only in Jesus is peace to be found. "Take courage," he says to the disciples of then and now. The glorified Jesus has already overcome the world (v. 33).

4. Jesus' prayer (17:1-26). These chapters of farewell discourse (chs. 13–17), with a precedent in the formal and final addresses of Moses (Deut 29–34), of Jacob (Gen 49), and of Paul (Acts 20:17-38), are brought to a fitting conclusion by Jesus' prayer in chapter 17. This whole chapter is one long prayer directed by Jesus to the Father, his own solemn expansion, one might say, of the simple "Our Father" he taught his disciples in Matt 6 and Luke 11. Positioned between heaven and earth, between his Father and his disciples, Jesus prays for believers present and future. The prayer is often called Jesus' "Priestly Prayer." The title can be justified only if one believes that intercession is priestly, that the union for which Jesus prays is priestly work, that the consecration spoken of in verse 19 deals with sacrifice. Better, surely, to call it simply Christ's prayer for union.

a) Division and content

i) Father and Son (vv. 1-5)

In these five verses, Jesus speaks directly to his Father. The hour has come; the manifestation of the divine presence (glorification) is the task. Eternal life will consist in recognizing this divine presence. As the evangelist puts it in verse 3—and this is his whole Logos, or word theology—"Now this is eternal life, that they should know you, the only true God, and the one whom you sent, Jesus Christ." To know God in the Son whom he has sent is eternal life. Jesus has manifested that presence on earth (v. 4) and will now return to that presence at the Father's side (v. 5). He has finished the work given him to perform (v. 4). The true nature of God, which is love, is about to be manifested in Jesus' self-sacrificing death.

ii) Son and disciples (vv. 6-19)

Jesus' conversation with the Father now turns to the subject of the disciples. To them has Jesus made known the Father's name (presumably the I AM that the Father has shared with the Son), and they have accepted the word (v. 6) and the message (v. 8), believing that what Jesus has comes from him who sent him (vv. 7-8). In a word, they have believed in Jesus' divine origin and divine union.

It is for these disciples that Jesus prays at this moment of departure in verses 9-19. He prays specifically:

—"keep them in your name that you have given me" (v. 11);

—"that they may be one just as we are one" (v. 11);

—"that they may share my joy completely" (v. 13);

—that the Father "keep them from the evil one" (v. 15);

—that he "consecrate them in the truth" (v. 17).

In paraphrase, what Jesus asks for his disciples is that they be protected by the immense power of the I AM (which will be demonstrated graphically in 18:6); that their unity resemble, and be based on, the intimate union of Father and Son; that their sorrow be changed into the divine joy that the Son reflects from his Father; that they be guarded from the prince of this world; that they be truly consecrated—as is Jesus—in complete dedication to God's service, which will be a mission to the world (vv. 18-19).

iii) Son and future disciples (vv. 20-26)

For future disciples, Jesus prays for one central gift—unity: "that they may all be one, as you, Father, are in me and I in you . . . that they also may be in us . . . that they may be one, as we are one, I in them and you in me, that they may be brought to perfection as one" (vv. 21-23). It will be only through this evidence of loving unity that the mission to the world (v. 18) can be effective; for only if the loving union of disciples is apparent can the world believe (v. 21), can the world know (v. 23) that the Father has sent Jesus and that the Father's love can be found in the disciples as it can be found in Jesus himself (v. 23). Where this loving unity of disciples is found, there too will be found the company of Jesus (v. 24), the divine presence (v. 24), the power of the divine name, and the living love of both Father and Son (v. 26).

b) Recurring themes

i) One cannot fail to note the frequent recurrence of "Father," a total of six times (vv. 1, 5, 11, 21, 24, 25). This reflects Jesus' own unique use of the Aramaic *Abba* ("loving Father"), with which he customarily began his prayer. Perfectly joined to the Father in oneness, he remains at all times the obedient and loving Son.

ii) The central motif of the prayer is that of unity—unity of present and future disciples, a unity modeled on that of Father and Son, a union that takes root from the love of Father and Son that is gifted to all disciples (v. 26).

iii) There is strong insistence on love: the Father's love for the disciples (v. 23), the Father's love for Jesus (vv. 23-24), the Father's love for Jesus and the disciples (v. 26). The

Father's love is the supreme revelation of the Gospel. Jesus, the incarnate Word, speaks the Father in one word—LOVE. Throughout this whole prayer, it is clear that the church is meant to be a community of love, the living sign or sacrament of the mutual love of Father and Son.

iv) The "world" is mentioned seventeen times in these verses. It is the world of anti-world, the center of disbelief and hatred and unlove, the contrast and contradiction to what Christian living should be. Judas (v. 12) is an example of one to whom all was offered and rejected, one who experienced light and life but left it for darkness and death. While this world is not here the object of Jesus' prayer, yet it is not a world for which Jesus has no hope or feeling. While the strong emphasis lies on prayer for Jesus' actual and future disciples, verses 21 and 23 do pray that, through Christian unity, the world may *believe* and *know* that Jesus has been sent by a loving Father.

c) *Echoes of the Our Father*

Though the customary "Our Father" is not found in the Fourth Gospel, there are tiny echoes of it that, fittingly enough, appear in this uniquely Johannine prayer. "Father," as we have seen, is found six times as Jesus' prayerful address. Reference to God's name—similar to "Hallowed be thy name"—occurs in verses 6, 11, 12, and 26. Reference to glorification in verses 1, 5, and 24 brings into view the divine presence, the hope of "Thy kingdom come." And the request (v. 15) that the disciples be guarded from the evil one echoes the similar and final request of the "Our Father" in Matt 6:13.

d) *Eucharistic material*

Concluding chapters 13–17, the reader must have noticed the lack of any mention of Eucharistic institution. Seemingly, the evangelist has chosen to locate his Eucharistic material at the end of chapter 6, where it brings the homily on the bread from heaven to a powerful conclusion. The vine allegory of chapter 15, however, may reveal an original Eucharistic setting, especially since its "remain in me" language parallels closely the "remains in me and I in him" of 6:56.

18:1–19:42 The Passion Narrative

We now turn from discourses—at least four whole chapters worth—to narrative. Our feet come back to the ground after a head-and-heart trip through the world above where the Father and Son live in eternal unity and from which they will send the enlivening Paraclete. Here we find the earthly Jesus enroute to the passion and to that elevation on the cross that is the glorification of divine love. It is at this point in the Gospel that John presents material that, in both content and sequence, is quite similar to that of the other three Gospels.

1. The arrest (18:1-11). Jesus and his disciples exit through the city walls, moving eastward a short distance down and across the Kidron Valley to a garden. The name of the garden, Gethsemani, is not given (Mark 14:32; Matt 26:36), nor does John mention the agony found in the other Gospels. John's portrait of Jesus tends to omit characteristics that are, in his judgment, overly human. He must know of the agony, however, since echoes of it do appear, though with changed emphasis and context, in 12:27: "I am troubled now. Yet what should I say? 'Father, save me from this hour'?" and in 18:11: "Shall I not drink the cup that the Father gave me?"

That "Jesus had often met there with his disciples" (v. 2) explains how Judas knows where to find him and agrees with the Johannine insistence on multiple visits to Jerusalem during Jesus' ministry. So it is here that Judas comes with forces from the Romans, "a band of soldiers," and from the Jewish authorities (v. 3). The lanterns and torches provide a stage of light and darkness on which this dramatic scene will be played out. Jesus, armed with divine knowledge (v. 4), confronts his adversaries, including Judas (v. 5), the Satan figure of 6:70-71; 13:2, 27, with the question: "Whom are you looking for?" To their reply, "Jesus the Nazorean," Jesus answers with the majestic and awesome response, I AM—*egō eimi*. In the presence of the I AM, "they [Satan and his assistants] turned away and fell to the ground" (v. 6) in compulsory adoration. Jesus, the one "sent" by the Father, is very much in control of his own destiny. He is in charge, also, of the destiny of his own sheep: "Let these men go" (v. 8). Jesus will not lose any of those whom his Father has given him (v. 9, and see 6:39; 10:28; 17:12).

The violent reaction of Peter's sword is paralleled in Mark 14:47, Matt 25:51, and Luke 22:50, though only John names Peter as the slasher and Malchus as the victim. (Oddly, both John and Luke agree that it was the *right* ear that was affected.) Jesus puts an immediate end to the violence. His food is to do his Father's will (4:34); his drink will be whatever the Father offers.

2. Before Annas and Caiaphas: Peter's denials (18:12-27). From the garden, Jesus is led to Annas, father-in-law of the high priest Caiaphas (whose unintended prophecy of Jesus' salvific death was noted in 11:50). Annas had an extraordinary career in the Jewish hierarchy. High priest himself from A.D. 7-14, he was succeeded in later years by five sons as well as by Caiaphas, a son-in-law. Not surprisingly, he remained a person of substantial power in Jerusalem, even though no longer high priest himself. In these verses the evangelist, as though utilizing a double stage, focuses the spotlight in turn on the Annas-Jesus discussion and then on the nearby encounters of Peter with his accusers.

Peter's first difficulty is at the very gate of the courtyard. Another disciple (the Beloved Disciple?) known to the high priest has used his influence to obtain entrance for Peter also. Peter is a mixture of courage—he is there following Jesus (v. 15)—and intense fear. At the challenge of a servant girl, he capitulates. "You are not one of this man's disciples, are you?" "I am not" (v. 17). The violence of Peter's sword has been transformed into the lying timidity of his tongue. Peter moves to the "charcoal fire" (v. 18). A chill has fallen on both body and spirit.

On the stage of a room apart (vv. 19-24), Peter's fear is being contrasted with Jesus' courage. Jesus' teaching has been "spoken publicly to the world." Why, then, is he questioned as though he were a conniving malefactor? A blow to the face is his answer. Annas, unable to gratify what seems to be cheap curiosity, sends Jesus, bound, to his son-in-law, Caiaphas.

Meanwhile, back at the fire (vv. 25-27), Peter is slipping from bad to worse. Confronted by other bystanders and by a relative of the injured Malchus (v. 26), Peter, so courageous at the supper table (13:37), surrenders completely. "You are not one of his disciples, are you?" "I am not" (v. 25). With the third denial, Peter strikes out—and a cock began to crow.

The details of Jesus' trials vary somewhat in the four Gospels. The arrest in a secluded place outside the city walls is a constant, but there is a variation regarding what happened after that. Where Mark 14:53-65 and Matt 26:57-68 speak of a formal night trial before the Sanhedrin, the religious governance in Jerusalem, Luke 22:54, 63-64 and John describe a less formal meeting that evening at the high priest's house, according to Luke, and with Annas, according to John. These discrepancies are the kind that would naturally arise as the accounts were passed along orally over the years. All four agree on some type of inquisition the following morning and on the definitive appearance before Pilate.

3. Pilate: Condemnation (18:28–19:16). Pilate, as a historical character, is fairly well known. He ruled as Roman procurator of Judea, subordinate to the governor of Syria, for ten years (A.D. 26–36), during which time his chief duty was to administer finances and collect taxes for the imperial treasury. His treatment of the Jews was insensitive, frequently cruel. When his troops marched into Jerusalem with insignia bearing the image of Caesar, the Jews were incensed and persuaded him to have them removed only after a courageous and dangerous confrontation with the procurator in Caesarea, where his official residence was located. He also sequestered money from the temple funds with which he financed an aqueduct for Jerusalem. This caused another protest that terminated with violence as the protesting Jews were scattered by the clubs of Pilate's soldiers. His cruelty to the Samaritans resulted in their appeal to the Syrian governor, the legate Vitellus, who dismissed Pilate and sent him back to Rome to answer complaints before the emperor Tiberius. Tiberius, however, died before Pilate's arrival; and at that time Pilate disappears from history. The date of his death is unknown. (The early church historian Eusebius believed that he committed suicide.) A man of no great talent, he has entered history almost entirely because of his role in the death of Jesus.

Numerous commentators have noted that this trial before Pilate has been organized using the double-stage technique (*outside* with the crowd, *inside* with Jesus) and in the order of inverse parallelism (as was the case with the prologue). Schematically, we find the following seven scenes:

Outside (a) 18:28-32: Jewish authorities demand from Pilate the death of Jesus.

Inside (b) 18:33-38a: First dialogue between Pilate and Jesus.

Outside (c) 18:38b-40: Pilate wishes to release Jesus, since he finds him guilty of no crime.

Inside (d) 19:1-3: Flagellation and crowning with thorns: Jesus as king.

Outside (c') 19:4-8: Pilate finds Jesus guilty of no crime (twice).

Inside (b') 19:9-11: Second dialogue between Pilate and Jesus.

Outside (a') 19:12-16: Jewish authorities obtain from Pilate the sentence of death.

Clearly, and remarkably, (a), (b) and (c) are matched by (a'), (b') and (c'). Section (d) climactically stresses the kingship of Jesus. It is this ordering that we will follow as we study this section.

Outside (a) 18:28-32. John tells us nothing about Jesus' appearance before Caiaphas apart from the fact (18:24, 28). The praetorium (v. 28) was the official tribunal of the procurator while in Jerusalem. It is disputed as to whether it was located at the northwest corner of the temple area (the Antonia) or at Herod's palace on the western hill of the city. Mention of the avoidance of ritual impurity in order that they might eat the Passover supper (v. 28) informs us that John does *not* present the Last Supper as the paschal meal (13:1; 19:14, 31). The other three Gospels do. Commentators are far from agreeing upon any solution to this famous difficulty. The dialogue between Pilate and the authorities makes evident the intent of the latter to do away with Jesus, and it is Pilate who forces this admission (v. 31). The evangelist sees in this a fulfillment of the divine necessity that Jesus be lifted up (3:14; 8:28; 12:32-34) on the cross, a Roman punishment. What evidence we have lends credence to the statement in verse 31 that the Jerusalem Sanhedrin did not have authority to impose capital punishment, and especially while Pilate himself was in the city.

Inside (b) 18:33-38a. Pilate's question, "Are you the King of the Jews?" (v. 33), constitutes the first words of Pilate to Jesus also in Mark 15:2, Matt 27:11, and Luke 23:3. This supposes and constitutes strong proof that

such an anti-Roman claim to kingship was the official accusation made against Jesus by the chief priests. Pilate's question was dangerous—an imprudent answer could bring condemnation as a revolutionary. Jesus' first response, consequently, is indirect, an appeal to Pilate's conscience (v. 34). But verses 36-37 are direct and to the point. Jesus is a king, but of a strikingly different type. His kingdom is not of this world (v. 36), not of earthly origin. In response to Pilate's following question, "Then you are a king?," Jesus answers that his whole mission is to witness to the truth. All who are committed to the truth hear his voice. The question up for judgment, insists Jesus, is whether or not one accepts him, truth incarnate (v. 37). Pilate stands in the shadow. He does not even understand the terms of the question (v. 38).

Outside (c) 18:38b-40. Out Pilate goes again, hoping this time that the choice of the crowd would free him from a decision he fears to make. Surely they will prefer to liberate Jesus rather than the criminal Barabbas (and, in so doing, liberate Pilate as well). But Pilate will not be let off the hook so lightly. "They cried out again, 'Not this one but Barabbas!'" (v. 40). Barabbas, says the Greek text, was a *lēistēs*, probably a political insurrectionist, although the term can also apply to an ordinary robber or bandit. The ball moves back into Pilate's court.

Inside (d) 19:1-3. John stresses here the elements of mockery that echo kingship—a kingship that Jesus truly possesses, but on a different level. Thus come the crown, the cloak of royal purple, the salutation as king. Ironically, notes John, he who was so thoroughly and diversely mocked as a king was truly king. It is this truth, stressed here in irony, that constitutes the theological and structural center of the trial before Pilate.

Outside (c') 19:4-8. This section parallels (c), Pilate's declaration of Jesus' innocence. In this instance Pilate states his opinion twice: "I find no guilt in him" (vv. 4, 6). Verse 6's "Take him yourselves and crucify him" is neither a condemnation nor a permission granted the accusers. A paraphrase might be: "Go ahead. Do it on your own and under your own responsibility, but don't expect me to be responsible for it." The answer to this reveals in all clarity the real reason for the antagonism of the local authorities: ". . . according to that law he ought to die because he made himself *the Son of God*" (v. 7). The Romans became involved because of a false accusation of kingship rivaling Caesar's; the Jewish accusation was that Jesus acted as the unique Son of God.

Inside (b') 19:9-11, the second dialogue. Pilate's reaction to this talk about Jesus' divine sonship is one of increasing fear and wonder. This is further increased, first by Jesus' silence (v. 9) and then by verse 11, the answer of a man confident of his own innocence and destiny.

Outside (a') 19:12-16. The condemnation is finally forced from Pilate by a return to the political accusation: "Everyone who makes himself a king opposes Caesar" (v. 12). This accusation carries the day. The final scene shifts outside before the public, onto the stone pavement called Gabbatha. (An enormous pavement of huge worked stone lies evident today in the excavation of the Antonia at the corner of the old temple area.) The dialogue between Pilate and the crowd is kingly and ironic by Johannine intent. "Behold, your king! . . . Shall I crucify your king?" (vv. 14-15). Back comes the dreadful confession of the chief priests: "We have no king but Caesar" (v. 15). This was blasphemy, for it was religious dogma that Yahweh and only Yahweh was king. John is telling us that those rejecting Jesus cannot have his Father as king. Pilate yields to political pressure and hands Jesus over. "It was preparation day for Passover, and it was about noon" (v. 14). As the Lamb of God (1:29, 36) is sentenced to death, the Passover lambs are being readied for sacrifice. Mutually responsible for Jesus' death are Judas, a disciple; Pilate, a Roman; and the Jewish authorities of Jerusalem.

4. Crucifixion (19:16b-22). Jesus himself carries the cross (v. 17). John is not denying the assistance given by Simon of Cyrene—if, indeed, he knows of it—but is emphasizing the control of Jesus over his own life and death. He accepts his own death; he carries his own cross. He is crucified at the Place of the Skull (in Hebrew *Golgotha* and in Latin *Calvaria*, whence our "Calvary").

The inscription on the cross is mentioned, always with slight variations, by all four evangelists, but only John, who insists so much on Jesus' kingship, tells us of the three languages. Greek was the tongue of the Mediterranean world; Latin, that of the Roman empire. John is saying that Jesus' kingship is universal, proclaimed from the cross to the whole world. Pilate's stubborn insistence on letting the inscription stand as written is his own bit of revenge against those who pressured him to condemn the innocent. Now let them squirm a little at a title that insults them.

5. Christ's clothing (19:23-24). This is the first of a series of incidents in which John sees the fulfillment of some Old Testament prophecy. The pitiful booty of Jesus' clothing is referred back to Ps 22:19, a psalm much used by the early church as a pre-shadowing of Jesus' passion. The reference to the seamless tunic *may* be a conscious parallel between Jesus and the high priest, whose robe was also seamless, but such a possibility is disputed by scholars. John speaks of Jesus, not as priest, but as king.

6. Jesus' mother and the Beloved Disciple (19:25-27). This scene, placed at the most important moment in the Gospel, must have more than simple filial significance, that is, the care of Jesus for his mother at the hour of his death. The only question is: What does this incident symbolize? Suggestions are numerous. Since this paragraph is set in the context of Jesus' delivering over his spirit (v. 30) and of the blood and water flowing from his pierced side (v. 34), I suggest that we find in these few verses John's symbolic picture of the birth of the Christian community. It is the hour of Jesus' glorification—his being lifted up—and as he dies, he hands over his Spirit. Beneath him stand a woman and a disciple, both unnamed as if to emphasize their symbolic character. The woman may well signify mother church, and the Beloved Disciple all disciples called to follow the loving obedience of their Lord. When to the mother-church woman and the Beloved Disciple figure are added the Spirit, which Jesus gives (v. 30) now that he has been glorified (7:39), and the blood and water, signs of the Eucharist and baptism, the Christian community stands revealed. This suggestion, though not certain, is not exaggerated, especially when working with an evangelist so theologically bi-leveled as John.

There may even be a subtle reference to the woman of Gen 3:15 and the enmity between her offspring and that of the Satan-serpent. John shows interest in the Book of

Genesis. Starting his Gospel with the same initial phrase and a reference to creation, he presents a conflict between Satan and Jesus (12:31-33; 14:30), and speaks of Satan's offspring (Judas and the adversaries of 8:44). If the "woman" of 19:26 is, indeed, a reference to the woman of Gen 3:15, then John has reassembled all the elements of the Genesis story for a re-creation event: the serpent, the serpent's seed, the woman, the woman's seed and, perhaps, even the garden locale for "in the place where he had been crucified there was a garden" (19:41). Indeed, the crucifixion account not only ends in a garden (19:41) but also begins in one (18:1); and it is only John among the four evangelists who so locates it.

The Fourth Gospel may be presenting Mary beneath the cross in a double role: .

a) *as feminine symbol of mother church,* caring for, and placed in the care of, Jesus' disciples, who become her children and, consequently, Jesus' brothers and sisters. Relation to Jesus is not merely individual; it includes a community, a family of brothers and sisters;

b) *as woman of the victory,* emphasizing the feminine contribution to salvation. The negative biblical portrait of Eva has been replaced by that of the life-giving Ave.

7. Death (19:28-30). For John, Jesus dies when he is ready to die, at the proper time, when Scripture has been fulfilled. The Scripture "I thirst" may refer to either Ps 69:21 or Ps 22:15. Both psalms are used often in the New Testament. The wine (v. 29) was the thin, bitter drink of the soldiers. The hyssop plant (v. 29) could hardly hold a sponge soaked with wine. It may enter here to recall to John's Jewish readers the plant that sprinkled Israelite doors with the saving blood of the Passover lamb in Exod 12:22. If so, it is intimately connected with what follows. "It is finished" (v. 30)—accomplished is the work Jesus had to do, the will of his Father, the Scriptures, the salvation of humankind. "And bowing his head, he *handed over* the spirit" (v. 30). This wording is unique, proper to the Fourth Gospel. Jesus' death-glorification has released the Spirit into the world (7:39; 19:34; 20:22).

8. The lance (19:31-37). The urgency apparent in verse 31 arises from the fact that it is Friday afternoon, with the Sabbath (also

Passover for John) beginning at sundown. There were but a few hours left for what would necessarily be done to the bodies. The legs of the other two, consequently, were broken to hasten their death, but this was useless for Jesus, already dead. Instead, his side was pierced, releasing a mixture of blood and water, to which the evangelist, or his source of information, bears testimony as an eyewitness. Verse 35 emphasizes this fact. Many of the church fathers have seen in the blood and water signs of the Eucharist and baptism, the life sources of the church, the new Eve, coming forth from the side of the new Adam. John refers again to fulfillment of Old Testament passages. "Not a bone of it will be broken" is a fusion of Exod 12:46, which concerns the paschal lamb, and Ps 34:21, which describes God's protection of the just man. "They will look upon him whom they have pierced" refers to Zech 12:10, where the piercing is joined to God's pouring out on the inhabitants of Jerusalem a spirit of grace and petition. The piercing of Jesus does even more.

9. The burial (19:38-42). All four evangelists mention the participation of Joseph of Arimathea in Jesus' burial (Matt 27:57-60; Mark 16:43-46; Luke 23:50-53). Only Matt 27:60, however, explains how it was that the new tomb was available for use—it belonged to Joseph. And only John introduces Nicodemus. For John, both men were crypto-Christians breaking free from the darkness of their fear. Their courageous act is a verification of John 12:32: ". . . And when I am lifted up from the earth, I will draw everyone to myself."

The huge amount of myrrh and aloes (v. 39) used for the burial may be one final Johannine reference to Jesus' kingship. He receives a regal burial.

20:1-31 The Resurrection

Here, as in chapter 9, the text is arranged in dramatic form, as it might be if performed by actors and actresses. The number of participants could be reduced by having only one angel (A) and one disciple (D). The surprising and challenging fact is that John's text lends itself so naturally to such dramatic arrangement.

[ACT I: The Tomb

Scene 1: *Sunday morning.* Mary Magdalene (MM), Peter (P), Beloved Disciple (BD), Narrator (N)]

N: [1]On the first day of the week,

MM: Mary of Magdala came to the tomb early in the morning, while it was still dark, and saw the stone removed from the tomb. [2]So she ran and went to Simon Peter and to the other disciple

N: whom Jesus loved,

MM: and told them, "They have taken the Lord from the tomb, and we don't know where they put him."

P: [3]So Peter

N: and the other disciple

P and BD: went out and came to the tomb.

N: [4]They both ran,

BD: but the other disciple ran faster than Peter and arrived at the tomb first; [5]he bent down and saw the burial cloths there, but did not go in.

P: [6]When Simon Peter arrived after him, he went into the tomb and saw the burial cloths there, [7]and the cloth that had covered his head, not with the burial cloths but rolled up in a separate place.

BD: [8]Then the other disciple also went in, the one who had arrived at the tomb first, and he saw and believed.

N: [9]For they did not yet understand the scripture that he had to rise from the dead.

P and BD: [10]Then the disciples returned home.

[**Scene 2:** *The same Sunday morning.* Mary Magdalene (MM), Angels (AA), Jesus (J), Disciples, Narrator (N)]

N: [11]But Mary stayed outside the tomb weeping.

MM: And as she wept, she bent over into the tomb [12]and saw two angels in white sitting there,

A-1: one at the head

A-2: and one at the feet where the body of Jesus had been.

AA: [13]And they said to her, "Woman, why are you weeping?"

MM: She said to them, "They have taken my Lord, and I don't know where they laid him."

N: [14]When she had said this,

MM: she turned around and saw Jesus there,

N: but did not know it was Jesus.

J: [15]Jesus said to her, "Woman, why are you weeping? Whom are you looking for?"

MM: She thought it was the gardener and said to him, "Sir, if you carried him away, tell me where you laid him, and I will take him."

J: [16]Jesus said to her, "Mary!"

MM: She turned and said to him in Hebrew, "Rabbouni,"

N: which means Teacher.

J: [17]Jesus said to her, "Stop holding on to me, for I have not yet ascended to the Father. But go to my brothers and tell them, 'I am going to my Father and your Father, to my God and your God.'"

MM: [18]Mary of Magdala went and announced to the disciples, "I have seen the Lord," and what he told her.

[ACT II: The Upper Room

Scene 1: *That Sunday evening.* Disciples (DD), Jesus (J), Thomas (Th), Narrator (N)]

N: [19]On the evening of the first day of the week,

D-1: when the doors were locked, where the disciples were,

D-2: for fear of the Jews,

J: Jesus came and stood in their midst and said to them, "Peace be with you." [20]When he had said this, he showed them his hands and his side.

DD: The disciples rejoiced when they saw the Lord.

J: [21][Jesus] said to them again, "Peace be with you. As the Father has sent me, so I send you."

N: [22]And when he had said this, he breathed on them and said to them,

J: "Receive the holy Spirit. [23]Whose sins you forgive are forgiven them, and whose sins you retain are retained."

Th: [24]Thomas,

N: called Didymus, one of the Twelve,

Th: was not with them when Jesus came.

DD: [25]So the other disciples said to him, "We have seen the Lord."

Th: But he said to them, "Unless I see the mark of the nails in his hands and put my finger into the nailmarks and put my hand into his side, I will not believe."

[Scene 2: *One week later*. Disciples *(DD)*, Jesus *(J)*, Thomas *(Th)*, Narrator *(N)*]

N: ²⁶Now a week later
DD: his disciples were again inside
Th: and Thomas was with them.
J: Jesus came,
N: although the doors were locked,
J: and stood in their midst and said, "Peace be with you." ²⁷Then he said to Thomas: "Put your finger here and see my hands, and bring your hand and put it into my side, and do not be unbelieving, but believe."
Th: ²⁸Thomas answered and said to him, "My Lord and my God!"
J: ²⁹Jesus said to him: "Have you come to believe because you have seen me? Blessed are those who have not seen and have believed."
N: ³⁰Now Jesus did many other signs in the presence of [his] disciples that are not written in this book. ³¹But these are written that you may [come to] believe that
All: JESUS IS THE MESSIAH, THE SON OF GOD,
N: and that through this belief you may have life in his name.

1. Literary arrangement. John has composed this chapter with artistic care. Act I is located at the tomb, where the two different incidents (scenes) occur. Act II takes place in the upper room, the two scenes occurring one week apart. Each scene has two main characters: Peter and the Beloved Disciple; Mary Magdalene and Jesus; Jesus and the disciples; Jesus and Thomas. As we advance through the four scenes, a minor character in one (Mary, then the disciples, finally Thomas) becomes a major one in the following. All is tightly coordinated, neatly orchestrated. In schematic form, with the italicized names being the main characters in the scene, we find:

ACT I—Tomb
Scene 1 (Sunday A.M.)
Mary M., *Peter, Beloved Disciple*

Scene 2 (Same Sunday A.M.)
Mary M., two angels, *Jesus*, disciples

ACT II—Upper Room
Scene 1 (Same Sunday P.M.)
Jesus, disciples, Thomas

Scene 2 (Sunday one week later)
Jesus, Thomas, disciples

2. Theological intent. John's theology becomes evident through observing the reactions of the participants. How do they arrive at belief in the risen Lord? In the opening scene, Mary, a minor character, sees the stone moved from the tomb. Her reaction is the natural one: "They have taken the Lord from the tomb" (v. 2). She does not yet believe.

Peter and the Beloved Disciple, the central actors, proceed to the tomb with haste (and hope). They see the burial clothes and head wrapping. Peter remains perplexed, but the response of the Beloved Disciple is one of faith. "He saw and believed" (v. 8). This loved and loving disciple saw only the minimum yet believed.

In the following scene (vv. 11-18), Mary now becomes a major character. She still holds the natural explanation (vv. 13, 15 repeat the substance of v. 2). She comes to faith only when she has heard (v. 16) and seen the Lord (v. 18). Jesus' sheep recognize his voice (10:4).

The disciples, introduced in Scene 2, become central in the scene that follows (vv. 19-25). Beginning in a state of fear, they pass from fear to joy "when they saw the Lord" (v. 20). For them, too, faith comes through seeing.

Thomas, a minor character in verses 19-25, becomes central in the final scene. His stance is one of extreme incredulity. He will not believe unless he sees and touches (v. 25). And so Jesus invites him to faith through sight and touch (v. 27).

The evangelist is reviewing all these varying reactions and possibilities *for people of his own time*. What will be their reaction, continued reaction, to the resurrection? Will it be the perplexity of Peter? Will it be that of the Beloved Disciple, who, united so intimately with his Lord in love, believed immediately with minimum evidence? Will it be that of Mary Magdalene and the other disciples, who believed only when they saw and heard? Will they be like Thomas, who refused to believe unless he saw and touched, unless placed in a position in which unbelief became impossible? The evangelist is saying to his own fellow Christians: "Those first disciples were by no means exemplary, nor was their situation so fortunate. Faith was almost forced upon them. That is not something to be envied. Our own situation can be more positive, more profitable, more Christian. Let us follow the example of the Beloved Disciple, who believed with such little evidence. We can be gifted with the ninth beatitude: 'Blest are they who have not seen and have believed' (v. 29). And indeed, blest are we who, without seeing, *believe in the risen Jesus, our Lord and our God."*

3. Specific verses. *Verse 2:* "They have taken the Lord from the tomb!" John knows this natural explanation, probably from controversies with non-Christians (Matt 28:13-15). He also denies it. The burial clothes were found, and in order (vv. 6-7), which would hardly be the case if someone had taken the body. These clothes were intentionally similar to those of Lazarus (ch. 11), who, however, came forth still wrapped in his. Resurrection is different.

Verse 8: "He saw and believed." The singular "He" limits this to the Beloved Disciple. Intensity of love leads to instant belief. It is this same love that will enable him to recognize the Lord in 21:4, 7 when the others do not.

Verse 9: This verse alludes again to the process by which the post-resurrection disciples interpreted Jesus' life by means of the Old Testament Scripture (John 2:17, 22; 12:16).

Verse 14: "But [she] did not know it was Jesus." The various resurrection accounts accent this phenomenon, that the risen Lord was truly Jesus of Nazareth, *the same but different.* He passes through locked doors (20:19, 26) and is unrecognized by personal friends (by Mary here, by the disciples in 21:4, by the Emmaus pair in Luke 24:16). The Lord *is* recognized, however, by the sound of his voice (Mary in v. 16); by love (the Beloved Disciple in 20:8 and 21:7); in the breaking of bread (Luke 24:30-31); and in the power of God's written word (Luke 24:32). All these elements are integral to community liturgy.

Verse 16: "Jesus said to her, 'Mary!'" This should remind us of 10:4. Jesus' sheep recognize his voice.

Verse 17: "Stop holding on to me, for I have not yet ascended to the Father." The meaning is difficult to ascertain. Is it that Jesus is at that moment enroute to the Father and Mary is seen to delay the passage? Or that she clings to his feet *in worship* (as in Matt 28:9), whereas Jesus' humanity will become the glorified center of worship (the new temple) only after his ascension, with its fulfillment of his glorification?

". . . to my Father and your Father, to my God and your God" could stress the difference between Jesus' relationship to the Father and ours. But it can also do just the opposite, indicating that Jesus' Father is truly ours, that his God is our God also.

Verse 20: "The disciples rejoiced when they saw the Lord." In the context of the "little while—short time" passage of 16:22, the disciples were told: "So you also are now in anguish. But I will see you again, and your hearts *will rejoice* . . . ." Our present verse, 20:20, is the fulfillment. Jesus has returned, already returned, through his resurrection and through his gift of the Spirit in verse 22.

Verses 21-22 are a key passage in Johannine theology. The disciples receive the Holy Spirit at this second coming of Jesus: the *eschaton*, the final era, is now; future is present. In 7:39, the Spirit had not yet been given, since Jesus was not yet glorified. On the cross, Jesus, manifesting the nature of God, which is love, delivers over the Spirit (19:30), symbolized immediately afterward by the flow of the sacramental symbols of blood and water. And now, at his first encounter with the believing community, he breathes the Spirit again as he celebrates the re-creation of God's people. Simultaneously, he sends out these disciples just as the Father had sent him (v. 21). His mission becomes theirs; his work is placed in their hands. And that mission, that work, is to manifest God who is love in their words and deeds. Through them now, enlivened by the Spirit, will the presence of God become known and seen and felt in the world. If in truth Jesus is God's sacrament, God's exegete, we in turn through the Spirit become Jesus' sacraments, his living exegetes.

Verses 22-23, which speak clearly of the community's share in Jesus' power to forgive sins, can be simply a reference to baptism, the traditional sacrament of forgiveness, or to the church's continuous preaching of forgiveness of sins in Jesus. But this reference to sharing in Jesus' power probably intends more than that. Through the ever-present Spirit, the Christian community can offer a restored union with Father and Son, a divine indwelling that creates peace (v. 21) with God and neighbor. Over the centuries, Christian communities have developed different means by which this unifying power is put into effect.

Verse 24: Only in the Fourth Gospel does Thomas receive any emphasis (11:16; 14:5; 20:24-28; 21:2). A historical character, he also functions in this Gospel as a character type. He is a combination of seeming courage (11:16) and ignorance (14:5), but especially is he a stubborn seeker of manifest resurrection credentials. Surely he calls to mind and reflects, for the evangelist, fellow Christians in the community who, beneath a courageous exterior, manifest both ignorance and lack of deep faith. To all such, Jesus and John say: "Do not be unbelieving, but believe" (v. 27).

Verse 28: "My Lord and my God!" There is no doubt that John intends this powerful phrasing (Ps 35:23-24) as a, or better *the*, Christian profession of faith. For the Johannine disciple, Jesus is both Lord and God. With this profession, John creates his own inclusion to the Gospel, the corresponding covers to his book of good news; for "My Lord and my God" at the conclusion corresponds to the opening ". . . and the Word was God" (1:1). The two statements are intentionally parallel.

Verses 30-31 are quite clearly a conclusion, the ending to the original edition of the Gospel. What the evangelist has written—which is not all that he could have written—is meant to urge and strengthen belief in Jesus as the Christ—and as the Son of God. John has already given us this profession in 11:27 on the lips of Martha in the context of another raising from the dead. To live, to really live, is to believe this: that Jesus of Nazareth is indeed the Messiah. And more, he is truly God's Son, dependent on the Father and obedient to him, yet himself divine. He is the Christian's Lord; he is the Christian's God.

D. EPILOGUE: APPEARANCE IN GALILEE

John 21:1-25

This final chapter is an addition to an original Gospel version that concluded with the magnificent statement of 20:31. It is found, however, in every ancient manuscript of the Gospel that we possess and must have been appended almost with the original publication of the work. Added by an expert in John's thought—surely by one of his disciples, and by one thoroughly conversant with the Gospel material—it is a genuine part of the canonical Gospel.

Chapter 21 has been tied to the previous chapters by a host of literary and theological links. Johannine characteristics found in this chapter are the Sea of Tiberias in verse 1; the names of Simon Peter, Thomas the Twin, Nathanael from Cana in verse 2; the night-day contrast of verses 3-4; the lack of recognition in verse 4; the Beloved Disciple of verse 7, who relates to Peter and who first recognizes the Lord; the charcoal fire of verse 9, together with the image of Jesus as servant and giver of bread to the disciples; the reference in verse 14 to two previous appearances (in ch. 20); Peter's triple profession (vv. 15-17) to counterbalance the triple denial and to reintroduce the shepherd theme (ch. 10); the glorifying aspect of Peter's death in verse 19; the reference to the Beloved Disciple's position next to Jesus at the Last Supper in verse 20. If this chapter is an addition—and it is—it is nonetheless a beautiful addition, and the Christian community would be considerably poorer without it.

1. The catch of fish (21:1-14). This story may well be the same as that recounted in Luke 5:4-10. Luke purposely limits Christ's resurrection activities to the area of Jerusalem, so he placed this Galilee story in chapter 5 of his Gospel for its rich homiletic advantage. Called to be fishers of men and women, the disciples can catch nothing without the assistance of the Lord. And indeed, Peter's confession in Luke 5:8, "Depart from me, Lord, for I am a sinful man," makes more sense if this was originally a post-resurrection story following Peter's denials.

The Sea of Tiberias (v. 1) is a Johannine locale (6:22-23), and the fishing companions are, in general, already known to us, with the exception of "Zebedee's sons," who here make their only appearance in the Fourth Gospel. Among the "two other disciples," seemingly, is the Beloved Disciple, who appears unexpectedly in verse 7. The lack of success during the night, followed by enormous success with the daylight presence of Jesus (vv. 3-6), is a practical application of John's frequent comments about night and day, light and darkness. The disciples' failure to recognize Jesus reminds us of a similar failure on the part of Mary (20:14), and we are hardly surprised when the Beloved Disciple is the first to recognize the Lord (v. 7).

The charcoal fire (v. 9) serves a double purpose. It sets the scene for Jesus' servant role as he becomes giver of bread (and fish) to the disciples and also serves as a stage prop for Peter's profession of love, recalling the previous charcoal fire (18:18), next to which Peter had denied the Lord.

The mention of precisely 153 fish (v. 11) has led to symbolic interpretations of all kinds. And indeed, there must be symbolism involved. John hardly means that the disciples took time out to make a count that then became part of Christian tradition. Saint Jerome believed that the zoology of his time taught that there were 153 different kinds of fish; and the number, as a result, reflected universality. Jerome was probably incorrect about the zoologists of his own day, but his suspicion of some universal symbolism was probably correct. Others have arrived at the same kind of symbolism by pointing out, for what it is worth, that 153 is a "universal" number, the sum of a triangle of increasing lines of dots whose tip is one and whose base is seventeen.

Another symbolic possibility at this point is drawn from the fact that the disciples bring the catch (humankind) to the meal (Eucharist) prepared by the risen Lord.

This appearance is Jesus' third (v. 14), when added to the two "room" appearances of chapter 20.

2. Peter (21:15-19). This encounter of Peter with his risen Lord is filled with beautiful material. Jesus offers Peter a public opportunity to profess repentance through love, surely a striking example of what it is that reestablishes our relationship with the Lord after sin. Peter's threefold denial is balanced by this threefold profession of love (the charcoal fire is the visible stage link). With this, he and his Lord are "at-oned."

This incident is also a continuation of the shepherd theme of chapter 10. There seems to be no real difference between Jesus' three commands:

"*Feed* my lambs";

"Tend my *sheep*," to which is added the composite

"*Feed* my *sheep*."

The function of Yahweh-shepherd in Ezek 34 passes to Jesus-shepherd in John 10 to Peter-shepherd in John 21. It is important to note how Peter's shepherd role is tied to love (vv. 15-17) and to a willingness (like the good shepherd of 10:11-18) to lay down his life (vv. 18-19). Note, too, how Peter's laying down his life glorified God, as did that of Jesus. Love, love to the limit, selfless, life-giving love manifests (glorifies) God because that is God's nature. An act of selfless, life-giving love is God's name published before the world.

When this chapter was written, Peter's death was already an accomplished fact. Like his Lord (note the "You follow me" of v. 22), he had already stretched out his hands (v. 18) to die on Vatican hill. The tying fast (v. 18) would be the fastening to the cross, always accomplished in part by ropes.

3. The Beloved Disciple (21:20-23). This final incident centers, fittingly, on the Beloved Disciple. The question is: What about him? (v. 21). Verse 23 makes sense only if a belief that the Beloved Disciple would live to see Jesus' final coming had been shattered by his unexpected death. As his followers—among whom was the author of this chapter—looked back to recall the source of their misguided belief, they could discover only an ambiguous statement of Jesus upon which this erroneous concept had been based: "What if I want him to remain until I come? What concern is it of yours?" (v. 22). The mystery of the Beloved Disciple's life and death was not theirs to comprehend. His hour, like the Lord's, had come, leaving them behind. The important thing for the moment, says verse 24, is that this disciple remains on as the eyewitness testimony on which the written Gospel is based. It was he who wrote—or caused to be written, like Pilate in 19:22—this version of the good news. The "*we* know" indicates that this chapter itself has been written by others, that it is a God-sent addition.

Verse 25 concludes the chapter with a brief statement that cannot match in content the magnificent original conclusion of 20:30-31. The reader should be encouraged to re-read that beautiful finale as one finishes the reading and studying and praying of this impressive presentation of the Good News that is Jesus, God's revelation, God's love manifested in self-sacrifice, and for us the sole way and truth and life.

Having studied chapter 21, we can now hazard a guess as to why it was added to the original Gospel. There are two centers of attention in the chapter. The first is Peter, who is successively reconciled through his profession of love, then constituted the shepherd, and finally described as a martyr whose death glorified God. The second is the Beloved Disciple, whose death has deeply disturbed the community, but whose eyewitness testimony remains the secure foundation of its faith. This chapter has taken origin from these two concerns: to paint a portrait of Peter as the reconciled, loving, and martyred community shepherd, and to base the faith of the community in the Beloved Disciple on firmer footing. All-important for the Christians is not the Beloved Disciple's visible presence but his life-giving word. And this is enclosed forever in this Gospel.

CONCLUSIONS TO OUR STUDY OF JOHN'S GOSPEL

Now that we have finished our study of John's Gospel, it might be of help to attempt a brief résumé of some of the more important issues regarding the theology, literary origin, and community background of the Gospel.

1. Revelation. John's central theological teaching concerns revelation: God's revelation of himself in his completely unique Son, Jesus of Nazareth, one with the Father, the living and incarnate Word, who in himself bespeaks, proclaims, identifies, immediates the Father. To know Jesus is to know God. And so, too, John gives us the Book of Glory, which climaxes in the ultimate revelation of the Son as self-sacrificing love. It is on the cross that Jesus glorifies/manifests the Father. God the Father, therefore, is love. This will be the final, simple, concise definition of 1 John 4:16, "God is love, and whoever remains in love remains in God, and God in him."

2. Mission. To reveal the Father is Jesus' mission; it is for this that he has been sent. This mission is, in turn, passed to us who believe in him. Our Christian mission is to reveal both the Father and the Son within us. God who is love, the Son who lays down his life, will be known only through us, through our lives of self-sacrificing love. The baton of the Word-made-flesh has been passed to us, who are now called to reveal the Word through our flesh. Only in this way will the world come to know and to believe. Since all

Christians are called equally to share in this mission, John ceaselessly speaks of "disciples—*mathētai.*" John's Christianity is very egalitarian: his challenge is a question to us all. Do we, or do we not, reveal the God who is love?

3. Paraclete. In this mission we are not alone. To us has been given the Paraclete, both to enliven and to enlighten us. As Jesus is God-with-us (Matthew's Emmanuel), so the Spirit is Christ-with-us. He appears as Jesus leaves. He is delivered over as Jesus dies on the cross, breathed upon the disciples at Jesus' first resurrection appearance to them, sent from above as Jesus returns to his Father's side. Every step in Jesus' exaltation is accompanied by a gift to us of his Spirit.

4. The Beloved Disciple. If it is the Paraclete's function to enlighten and enliven the disciples, the community of the Fourth Gospel has experienced this in a particular way through the effect of the Spirit on the Beloved Disciple. It is he who, as eyewitness, provides the firm basis for the belief of the community. As the Word can reveal the Father, since he is at the Father's bosom (1:18), so the Beloved Disciple can reveal the Son, since he rested at the Son's bosom (13:25).

Appearing possibly in 1:35-40 as the anonymous of the two disciples, the Beloved Disciple makes frequent appearances starting with the passion material: at the Last Supper in 13:23-25; very probably in the high priest's courtyard as the other disciple of 18:15-16; at the foot of the cross as Jesus is glorified and the Christian community comes into being (19:25-27); at the tomb (20:1-10); and, finally, during the fishing trip of 21:7, 20-24.

The Beloved Disciple seems to be a Jerusalem disciple with connections to the high priest. His presentation of Jesus—on the solid presumption that he either authored the Fourth Gospel or was extremely instrumental in shaping its literary form (19:35; 21:24)— is so different from that of the other three Gospels that he was hardly one of the Twelve, a title he rarely uses (only in 6:67-71 and 20:24). He is coupled with Peter, over whom he has a certain kind of spiritual precedence. Peter asks Jesus through him (13:24); Peter knows Jesus through him (21:7); Peter believes after him (20:8).

At this present moment of scholarship, it seems best to accept the Beloved Disciple as anonymous, yet as a true disciple and eyewitness of the Lord, connected with Jerusalem, not one of the Twelve, whose different background and different Christian experience led him to produce, directly or indirectly, a version of the Good News strikingly different from that of Mark, Matthew, and Luke.

Historical as he is, the Beloved Disciple is also presented to us as an ideal, a model of what we should be as disciples ourselves—loved and loving.

5. John's community. One very striking facet of the Fourth Gospel is the manner in which the life of John's own community interpenetrates that of Jesus. Since Jesus lives on through and in his Spirit, the Paraclete, the life and history of John's community continue to be the life and history of the risen Lord. What happens to the community happens to Jesus. What is spoken by the Paraclete-enlivened disciples is spoken by Jesus, for the Paraclete transmits what he hears Jesus saying (16:13). Jewish controversies with John's group become controversies with Jesus, and what Jesus says is the community's response. This is Gospel writing and, clearly, not modern history. Let us note three of the most obvious instances. At the end of chapter 6, the sharp discussion regarding the consumption of Jesus' flesh and blood is a later Johannine controversy. In chapter 8, the controversy between Jesus and the Pharisees concerning his unique Sonship and identification as the I AM is, historically speaking, a controversy between the later Pharisees and John's community. A third is apparent in chapter 9, where the blind man excommunicated from the synagogue represents Johannine Jewish Christians of the eighties–nineties, for whom profession of faith in Jesus means radical excommunication from religion, family, and friends. The Jesus of the Fourth Gospel speaks differently than the Jesus of the first three Gospels because his voice is so frequently transmitted through the lips of the Paraclete-inspired community.

If it is true that the Gospel reflects John's own community, we can identify this community as a group that includes (1) true Israelites, such as Nathanael (1:47) and previous followers of the Baptist (1:35) and the man born blind (ch. 9), all of whom have become disciples out of Judaism; (2) Greeks, such as those of 12:20-22; (3) Samaritans who, white

for the harvest, have recognized Jesus as Savior (4:42).

This community is in uneasy relationship with the unbelieving world; with the Pharisees, who reject Jesus' claims (chs. 7–8); even with other Christians who are deficient in their Eucharistic belief (6:66) or who remain crypto-Christians out of fear of expulsion from the synagogue and Judaism (12:42-43).

It is also a community that, while recognizing the importance of the Twelve in general (6:67-70) and of Peter in particular (1:42; 6:68-69; 21:15-19), places its main emphasis on discipleship and the presence of the Paraclete.

6. Dramatic elements. This combination of Beloved Disciple, community, and Paraclete has, for some as yet unexplained reasons, given us a Gospel that is amazingly rich in dramatic techniques. Chapters such as 4, 9, 11, and 20 can be given instant staging. Peter, Thomas, Philip, and Judas (chs. 13–14) are present simply to ask leading questions that help to carry the discussion forward. Other characters, historical as they are, model roles. Nathanael (1:47) is what all true Israelites should be. Andrew and Philip (1:41, 45; 6:5-9; 12:20-22) perform like real missionaries. Nicodemus portrays a person who passes gradually, though with fear, from darkness into light (3:1-10; 7:50-52; 19:39). The Samaritan woman (ch. 4) clarifies the possibility, for a woman as for a man, to move from sin and ignorance into faith and mission. Jesus' mother models Mother Church. The Beloved Disciple portrays what all disciples should be.

The Gospel is filled with other dramatic elements, too: with frequent irony as the obviously untrue turns out to be eminently true—Jesus *will* die for the whole world (11:52) and he really is king (19:19-22); with the use of ambiguity, misunderstanding, clarification to capture the interest of the hearers; with an almost pre-play program description of Jesus in chapter 1; with the stage props of the bucket of the Samaritan woman (4:28) and Peter's charcoal fire (18:18; 21:9).

All of this helps to make this Gospel so rich that a lifetime of study cannot plumb its depths. As Christians of the past twenty centuries have written about the Fourth Gospel without coming close to exhausting its riches, so, it seems certain, will Christians of the next twenty as well.

1 JOHN

Neal M. Flanagan, O.S.M.

COMMENTARY

Tucked far away from the Fourth Gospel in our Bible lie the three writings called the Epistles of John. It is to these that our attention must now turn. As was done with the Gospel, we shall postpone a consideration of what are usually treated as introductory questions (author, occasion, date, community, theological content, interrelationship of the three epistles) until we have actually encountered the material that provides what answers there are to such problems. The only introductory issue we want to face here is that of the possible division of the First Epistle of John. This is a difficult and confusing question, since the epistle is repetitious and circular—like a spiral, suggest some authors, which goes round and round but with a definite, even if not too distinguishable, progression. Though commentators differ in their breakdown of the material, there is sufficient consensus to propose the following division as workable. Though admittedly very general, it will help the reader both to distinguish diverse elements and to synthesize them into an overall unity.

PROLOGUE: 1:1-4 The historical reality of the Christian message

Summary: First John, like the Gospel, begins with a prologue. The entire emphasis is upon the historical reality of what our author and his fellow Christians have experienced. This is the Word of life (v. 1), the message that has been heard and is now to be proclaimed. The message, however, has been incarnated in a human being, the Son, Jesus Christ (v. 3), who was actually heard and seen and touched. In him eternal life became visible so that both he and it might be shared with us (vv. 2-3). This is a fellowship *(koinōnia)* with both Father and Son, and the very act of describing it in writing is, for the author, a source of consummate joy (v. 4).

Comments: This short section is not written with smooth articulation—thus the breaks in continuity, usually indicated in English translations by a dash or parentheses or both. It is almost as though the author were speaking extemporaneously, with the natural breaks in thought that occur away from the discipline of pen and ink. Notable are the phrases reminiscent of the Fourth Gospel, though their content has slight differences from the Gospel meaning. The "from the beginning" of verse 1 is not a reference to eternity (John 1:1), but to the inception of the gospel preaching. The "Word of life" (v. 1) is not exclusively that word which became flesh (John 1:14), but the *gospel message* that became audible, visible, and tangible in the human Jesus.

Does the insistence upon hearing, seeing, and touching demand that the author be an eyewitness to the words and works of the historical Jesus? That, surely, is the most obvious meaning. Yet the words also permit the solid possibility that the author is simply, but forcefully, uniting himself to the actual eyewitnesses from whom he has derived his version of the good news. Through them—and he can summon them up in his memory—he has truly experienced the Lord and his word of life.

1:5–2:2 Walking in the light: the question of sin

Summary: Part of the message for Christians is that there is a sphere of life and righteousness that can be called "light." It is God's sphere, for "God is light" (v. 5). But there is another sphere, too, which is that of darkness, of untruth, and there are those who walk in it. To have fellowship with both God (v. 6) and one another (v. 7), we must walk in the light, cleansed from sin by the blood of God's Son (v. 7). This cleansing demands from us a personal acknowledgement of our sin, which will be answered by the cleansing that comes from God. To pretend that we have never sinned is, in itself, a lie that would continue to bind us to the sphere of darkness (vv. 8-10). Such admission of sin is by no means a suggestion that sin makes little difference in Christian life. Our author's purpose in writing is to keep Christians from sin (2:1). Yet, though living in the light, he is not blinded by it: he can see that Christians can and, on occasion, still do sin. Christ, however, remains effective, both as intercessor (Paraclete) and as sin-offering, and not for us only but for the whole world (2:1-2).

Comments: There are a number of peculiarities in this section. "God is light," says verse 5, a statement that is not too strange after our study of the Fourth Gospel, but yet is a bit different. In the Gospel the emphasis falls on *Jesus* as the light of the world (John 8:12; 9:5).

A second peculiarity is the description of Jesus as a sin-offering (2:2) whose blood not only cleanses *us* from all sin (v. 7) but is effective for the whole world (2:2). This, too, is an emphasis not seen in the Fourth Gospel, for which Jesus' death is not nearly so much expiatory—perhaps only and barely in the Lamb of God statement (John 1:29)—as revelatory of God's love.

The "children" of 2:1 is a third novelty. In John's Gospel the author's posture is egalitarian: the followers of Christ are simply disciples (*mathētai*), and there is little, if any, hierarchy evident. First John makes extensive use of "children" and, in so doing, gives a picture of a person of special responsibility addressing Christians whom he fully expects to listen to his advice and pleading.

Finally, it comes as a surprise for those reading 2:2 in the Greek, or from a literal translation, to find Jesus called "Advocate" (intercessor). John's Gospel reserves that name for the Spirit, though John 14:16 does call the Spirit "another Advocate," thus leaving room for Jesus, too, to fulfill that function.

2:3-17 Keeping the commandments

Summary: Christianity is not simply a "head trip," a question only of knowledge. It demands a life consonant with the God of love we claim to know and experience. Fortunately, we have a human exemplar to follow and thus are challenged (v. 6) to conduct ourselves just as Jesus did.

And this means a challenge to love (vv. 7-11). In a sense, this is now an old commandment, one that Christians have heard from the beginning of their instruction (v. 7). On the other hand, it is still new, for Jesus has given us the abiding newness of his own example, which we renew in ourselves (v. 8). We must live in one of two polarities: in the light that is the sphere of reciprocal love (v. 10) or in the darkness of hatred (v. 11), where one can only stumble blindly in darkness (vv. 9, 11).

Encouragement flows out to the inhabitants of the light: to the "children" (vv. 12, 14), who, though spiritually immature, have, through personal experience of the Father, been freed from sin; to the "fathers" (vv. 13-14), the spiritually mature, whose knowledge of the Father is secure and unmovable; to the "young men" (vv. 13-14), the spiritually proficient, whose strength, rising from the abiding word of God, has conquered the evil one.

All of these Christians are now advised to treat the ungodly world with cautious discernment (vv. 15-17). Passions, greed, wealth and its trappings (v. 16) leave no place for the Father's love to dwell (v. 15). Whereas all things are transitory, the one who does God's will abides forever (v. 17).

Comments: The material in this section has a loose unity, held together by the obedience to the commandments of the initial verses (3-8) and by the doing of God's will (an identical concept) in the final verse (17). The emphasis throughout falls on love. It would be possible to interpret "just as he did" (v. 6) of God the Father, but this expression is uniformly used in 1 John of Jesus. Our author has no difficulty in passing imperceptibly from the Father to the Son, as he does here.

The precise meaning of "children," "fathers," "young men" of verses 12-14 is much disputed. The designations could refer to age groups. Or the "fathers . . . young men" could be officials (like presbyters and deacons) in the community, the membership of which would be referred to in general as the "children." We suggest that these names loosely differentiate states of spiritual maturity. Emphasis—by final position and length of description—falls on the "young men," those advanced in spirituality yet not completely mature, who bear the brunt of the crisis that has occasioned this writing. No one explanation of this terminology has been accepted by all scholars.

Verses 15-17 are surely a pessimistic summation of Christian relationship to the world. As was true in the Gospel, this is largely a question of language. The world of which these verses speak is not God's world, not the "whole world" for which Jesus is an offering for sin (2:2), but the sphere of anti-God, that is, of unlove and untruth. It will be personified in the antichrists of the following verses.

2:18-27 Warning against false teachers, the antichrists

Summary: The appearance of antichrists tolls the final hour (v. 18). Sad to report, they are "of our number" (v. 19), and it is they who now "would deceive you" (v. 26). Protection comes from the divine anointing that provides knowledge (v. 20), that teaches all truth, so that, free from any lie, "you do not need anyone to teach you" (v. 27).

Comments: The "last hour" (v. 18) is a common motif throughout the other New Testament writings, though certainly not central to the theology of John's Gospel, where Jesus' future coming is very secondary to his already experienced presence. The term "antichrists" is found only in this epistle and 2 John among the whole of the New Testament literature. It is similar, however, to the "false messiahs" of Mark 13:22—they, too, are signs of an impending judgment. Cardinal John Henry Newman suggested that the movement of salvation history went along on a straight line up to the brink of the end time, where it changed direction ninety degrees to follow along on the edge of the precipice. Our Christian lives, in this description, would be lived on the brink, just a step away from the plunge into the beyond.

Verse 19 indicates the crisis that has occasioned this epistle. Members have left the Johannine community, members whose very exit proved their insincerity. Like Judas (John 13:30), whom our author may consider as their model, they went out into the darkness. The insistence on knowledge and truth apparent in the following verses (20-27) makes it evident that those who left were faulty in their teaching. Verse 22 is to the point: "Who is the liar? Whoever denies that Jesus is the Christ. Whoever denies the Father and the Son, this is the antichrist." This appears to be an out-and-out denial that Jesus was the Christ, a denial, then, of the central theology of John's Gospel: ". . . that you may [come to] believe that Jesus is the Messiah, the Son of God, and that through this belief you may have life in his name" (20:31). Further passages in 1 John will give us more evidence about the content of this disbelief. The accent in this passage is on faith.

Defense against errant teaching will be provided by the divine anointing (vv. 20, 27) that we have all received, our Christing ("anointing" is *chrisma* in Greek) in baptism with the teaching (vv. 20, 27) provided at that time (v. 24) and our subsequent dwelling in both the Son and the Father (v. 24). This is eternal life, and the promise of an even greater sharing in it (v. 25).

2:28–3:24 Children of God, children of the devil, love versus hatred

Summary: If we but remain in God, our future is without fear, since the holiness of our lives will prove that we are God's children (2:28-29). And indeed, this is precisely what we are now by God's love (v. 1). And we shall become even more intimate children as, seeing him as he is, we meld into his likeness (v. 2). If only we remain pure as he is (v. 3), holy as the Son is holy (v. 7).

The other option is to exist and act in the sphere of sin and lawlessness (v. 4), which is to become a child of the devil, one whose actions are unholy, specifically one who does not love (v. 10).

That we love one another was our first instruction (v. 11), and in this love we have passed from death to life (v. 14). The opposite is to become the devil's child like Cain (Gen 4), who killed his brother in jealous rage, just as the anti-God world now rages against us (v. 13). Not to love is death, the condition of both the murderer and the hater (vv. 14-15). Our call, on the contrary, is to lay down our lives for one another as Christ sacrificed his for us (v. 16). This means, at least, to share what we have with the needy (vv. 17-18). If we do, even though we may be imperfect (v. 20), the magnanimous God will be with us (vv. 20-21), and with him, his peace (v. 19). But all depends on this double commandment: that we *believe* in his Son, Jesus Christ, and *love* one another (v. 23). If we do, God remains in us, evident by his gift of the Spirit (v. 24).

Comments: Verse 2:28 speaks again of Jesus' coming, the final hour of 2:18. As we noted, this is a minor issue in John's Gospel.

The repeated reference to the "children of God" (vv. 1, 2, 10) employs the language and distinction of the Gospel. Christians are God's children, the *tekna Theou;* only Jesus is God's Son, the *huios Theou.* As our author describes the "begotten by God" (v. 9), he slips into strongly figurative language. The Greek of verse 9 speaks of God's seed remaining in his children. John 3:1 has already insisted that this is what we really are—God's children!

The imagery of verse 2 is fascinating. Looking at God as though into a mirror, our own visage is reflected, but with divine configuration. As God's children we will, says the author, bear an amazing family likeness.

Verse 3 is ambiguous. Are we to keep ourselves pure as God is pure or as Jesus is pure? Probably the latter, since in subsequent verses it is Christ who is sinless (v. 5) and the Son who is holy (v. 7).

Verse 4 seems simplistic in stating that sin is lawlessness, but our author wants to insist that there are definitely things that we *should do* and others that we *should not do.* Disobedience is sin, the pattern of the devil (v. 8), who from the beginning fostered disobedience unto death (Gen 3:4-5). John 8:44 concludes in a similar fashion that the devil was a liar and murderer from the beginning. His followers are his children (John 8:44), and for 1 John the murderer Cain is an example (v. 12).

The double reference to the laying down of life in verse 16 recalls the repeated statement in John 10:11-18 that Jesus, as good shepherd, would lay down his life for his sheep.

Verse 23 provides in miniature the theological heart of 1 John: we must *believe* in God's Son, Jesus the Christ, and *love* one another. Belief and love—basically 1 John speaks of nothing else. Where these obtain, the divine indwelling is an accomplished fact, to which the presence of the Spirit testifies. This first mention of the Spirit in 1 John leads us into the following section.

4:1-6 The two spirits

Summary: Be not immediately impressed by a powerful spiritual presence, however, for it may indicate the spirit of antichrist (v. 3), that of the many false prophets who have gone out (from us) into the world (v. 1). The spirits must be tested, and the test is crucial: Do they, or do they not, believe that Jesus Christ has come in the flesh? (v. 2). It is this which we believe and by which we, with the strength of God, have won the victory (v. 4). Those who do not believe belong to the anti-God world that listens to them (v. 5). Theirs is the spirit of deception, ours the spirit of truth (v. 6).

Comments: This question of discernment of spirits comes down to a single practical test: What do the prophets—true or false—believe? What do they teach about Jesus? If they acknowledge Jesus Christ come in the flesh, they are genuine Christians; if they do not, they are false prophets and belong to the world. This test is a clarification of the doctrinal difficulty first expressed in 2:22: "Who is the liar? Whoever denies that Jesus is the Christ." The faith statement "Jesus is the Christ" is nuanced now in verse 2 to insist that Jesus Christ has come in the flesh. *The emphasis falls on the humanity of Jesus.* He in whom we believe, he whose name we bear as Christians, is Son of God, is the Christ, is intimately united with the Father, and is also, and of his essence, *a human being.* It is about this last phrase that the controversy rages, a controversy that, for the author, is absolutely critical for Christian faith.

That the world listens to the opponents (v. 5), to the false prophets (v. 1) with the spirit of antichrist (v. 3), indicates that the opposition is having considerable success. Is our author's group in danger of becoming a minority among what had been a united Johannine community?

4:7-21 God's love inspires ours

Summary: God is love (vv. 8, 16), and he has first loved us (vv. 10, 16, 19). He evidenced this love through the gift of his Son (v. 9), sent as Savior (v. 14). Because God has so loved us, we too must become lovers (v. 9), lovers of one another (vv. 7, 11, 12, 20, 21). Only if we love the visible neighbor can we love the invisible God (vv. 12, 20).

God's love for us and our love for him and for one another should afford us fearless confidence (v. 18), for we have overcome the world just as Christ has (v. 17). It is in him as Savior of the world and as Son of God that we profess our faith through the Spirit (vv. 13-14). On the other hand, sadly and simply, the man without love has known nothing of God (v. 8); his profession of love for God without love for neighbor is a disastrous lie (v. 20).

Comments: This section is a tight unity concentrating without distraction on the one point that God's love generates ours. The verses are linked together by numerous connections: 8//16; 10//16//19; 10//14; 12//20; 20//21, with the whole converging on the central truth that if God has loved us we must have similar love for one another (v. 11). That "God is love" (vv. 8, 16) is now the second description of God given in this epistle; we have already seen that "God is light" (1:5). God is not love in the abstract but in all his

activity. He creates lovingly, he saves lovingly, he judges lovingly. Our God is a God of love.

Reference to the Spirit (v. 13) returns us for a moment to the context of 4:1-6. It is the Spirit, as in 4:2, who enables us to affirm the truth—the truth that Jesus is Savior of the world, that he is Son of God (4:14-15). The basic creedal affirmations of this Johannine community are assuming a more definite shape. For the Johannine Christian, Jesus is the Christ (2:22) come in the flesh (4:2); Jesus is Savior (3:16; 4:14), an offering for the sins of the world (1:7; 2:2; 4:10); Jesus is Son of God (3:23; 4:15).

5:1-13 Faith: conclusion

Summary: All who believe that Jesus is the Christ (v. 1), the Son of God (v. 5), are themselves children of God, to be loved as is their Father (v. 1). In fact, this reciprocal love is the Father's unburdensome command (v. 3), originating from the Christian faith that has conquered the world (vv. 4-5).

Faith is belief in Jesus Christ, who came in essential humanity, in a human ministry stretching from baptism till human death, both testified to by the Spirit (v. 6). Not only does the Spirit testify, but so too do the present-day water and blood (v. 8)—the sacraments of baptism and Eucharist—which bespeak the presence of Christ himself and the eternal life he brings (vv. 11-12). Spirit, water, and blood are part of God's testimony. To deny them is to reject God's own witness and to affirm that he is a liar (v. 10). And, indeed, the purpose of this whole epistle is to help all to realize that they actually possess eternal life—if, that is, they believe in the Son of God (v. 13).

Comments: To the preceding section on love (4:7-21), recalled briefly in 5:1-3, is now added a section on faith. The creedal statement proposed here is that Jesus is the Son of God (vv. 5, 10, 12)—but a Son of God who is also thoroughly human, both at the baptism (at which the Spirit testified in John 1:33-34) that initiated the ministry and in the bloody death that terminated it. Son of God, yes—but a Son of God whose humanity was essential. This is the insistence of verse 6. In verses 7-8 a shift is made. To the Spirit as witness are added both the water and blood. The historical incidents of verse 6 are replaced by the sacraments. The Spirit still testifies to Jesus, and so do the sacraments of baptism and Eucharist. All three give their testimony in the Christian assembly: the Spirit through those speakers who are his inspired mouthpiece; baptism and Eucharist as signs of the eternal life that God gives us in his Son (vv. 11-12), as occasions during which faith in Jesus is solemnly affirmed and strengthened.

Verse 13 looks very much like a conclusion and, indeed, bears striking resemblance to John 20:31, the original conclusion to the Fourth Gospel. Apparently to this conclusion to the epistle have been added the final verses 14-21.

5:14-21 Prayer for sinners, summary

Summary: Our prayer should be made in complete confidence: what we ask for is already ours (vv. 14-15). One specific thing we should request is the conversion of the sinner, except in the case of one sinning in deadly fashion—there is doubt about that (vv. 16-17). We who are begotten by God, however, will not sin, shielded as we are by Christ, part of God's sphere and not of the devil's, to whom belongs the anti-God world (vv. 18-19). Actually we indwell both the Father and the Son, true God and eternal life. One final word—guard yourselves from the idols.

Comments: This short section touches on four different points. The first (vv. 14-15) is simple: Ask and you shall receive (Matt 7:7-8; Luke 11:9-10). God's door is always open. The second (vv. 16-17) is considerably more complicated. We are encouraged to pray for Christian sinners with the promise that this prayer, too, will be answered. But the author expresses serious doubt about the value and efficacy of prayer for those Christians sinning in deadly fashion. He does not say not to pray for them and cautions: "There is such a thing as deadly sin, about which I do not say that you should pray" (v. 16). He must view those whose sin is deadly as ex-Christians who have, with fatal deliberation, moved out into the darkness. Unfortunately for us readers, the deadly sin is not described. Some commentators have suggested murder and adultery, but it seems more in accord with the whole of 1 John to identify the sin as deliberate apostasy—the choice of darkness over light, of death over life, of hatred over love.

The third point (vv. 18-20) presents a rather black-and-white world view. On the one side are ranged the children of God, protected by divine power, dwelling in both Father and Son, graced by divine life; on the other side are the evil one and his anti-God world. For twentieth-century readers the contrast is too strong, too definite. The modern world in which we live specializes in shadows.

The epistle concludes with a terse warning against the idols. These are, in all probability, not false images but false doctrines, especially those that peek out between the lines of this letter—a faulty appreciation of Jesus' humanity and of its saving power.

CONCLUSIONS TO OUR STUDY OF 1 JOHN

This first, and principal, of the three Johannine epistles is elusive. It says nothing about its author, little about his community and about the crisis that occasioned the writing of this epistle. Even the doctrinal elements lack sharp definition. Yet some conclusions can be drawn regarding all of these elements.

1. Occasion. The clearest evidence can be found in 2:19, where we are told that the opponents, the "antichrists," are people who *exited from the author's own community.* They are described as deceivers (2:26) against whom the epistle hopes that the Spirit and instruction received in baptism will provide protection (2:20, 24-27). They are false prophets (4:1) whose spirit is one of deception (4:6). It is their teaching, surely, that constitutes the idols, the false doctrines, of the epistle's final verse. The author has clearly been shocked and offended by this terrible split in the community. He hesitates even to hope that something can be done to repair it (5:16). Whereas the Johannine community of the Gospel has been excommunicated from the synagogue, the community of 1 John has been abandoned by Christians (1 John would hardly call them that) who no longer wish to share belief and life.

2. Theology. (a) The nature and work of *Jesus Christ* is the central issue. The epistle insists, as we have seen, that Jesus is the Christ (2:22; 5:1), come in the flesh (4:2); that Jesus is Savior (3:16; 4:14), an offering for the sins of the world (1:7; 2:2; 4:10); that Jesus is the Son of God (3:23; 4:15; 5:5, 10, 11-13); that

Jesus came through both water and blood (5:6). Although these elements still do not allow us to paint a completely clear picture of what 1 John is arguing for and against, it must be that the opponents are challenging Jesus' humanity and its salvific function. A little later in the history of the church, Cerinthus would teach that the supernatural Christ descended upon the man Jesus at baptism, revealing God during Jesus' ministry, and departed from Jesus before his death. This presented an antiseptic Christ, hardly touched by Jesus' humanity, and not touched at all by his death. If the opponents of 1 John have not quite arrived at the position of Cerinthus, they are well on the way. For them Jesus' humanity was not of salvific importance. And so 1 John insists on the flesh, on the death, on the salvific function, on the offering for the sins of the world. For 1 John, Jesus—the man Jesus—was truly Son of God, but in this unique Sonship the truth and value of his humanity were never diminished. This same insistence on Jesus' humanity may explain why 1 John is considerably more God-centered than the Fourth Gospel. The more emphasis placed on Jesus come in the flesh, the sharper the contrast between him and the eternal Father.

b) The epistle's *moral teaching* is almost too simple. Two verbs describe it all: *believe* and *love*. The author is anguished by those whose belief has been corrupted, by those whose love stands denounced by the very fact of their departure. And so the epistle insists that we believe what was taught from the beginning (1:1; 2:7, 24; 3:11) and that we can only love God if we unfailingly love one another. The core of 1 John's ethics is given clearly in 3:23: "We are to believe in the name of his Son, Jesus Christ, and are to love one another."

c) The position of the *Advocate* in 1 John is subdued in comparison to the importance of this figure in the Fourth Gospel. Actually, the word occurs only once, in 1 John 2:1, where, surprisingly, it is applied to Jesus, who intercedes for us in the presence of his Father.

The entire function of the Spirit gets only brief attention. The references to the anointing in 2:20-27 may refer to the Spirit, but without specification, and the first clear reference is in 3:24, which leads immediately into a warning about testing the spirits (4:1-6). We find other references to the Spirit only in 4:13 and 5:6-7. A scholarly guess is that the opponents have argued so strongly from the supposed presence of the Spirit in bolstering their own positions that the author of 1 John has backed off a bit from a strong Advocate theology, lest he play into their hands.

3. Author and community. The epistle leaves its author unnamed, without even references such as those to the Beloved Disciple that indicate either authorship or original testimony in the Fourth Gospel. The epistle resembles the Gospel in vocabulary and in theological emphases, though these latter show nuanced differences from those of the Gospel. The epistle also seems to be from a later period when the opponents are no longer outsiders, as in the Fourth Gospel, but fellow Christians who have broken unity with the group. These characteristics point with some firmness to a writer different from the evangelist but thoroughly imbued with his theology, writing some years—not necessarily many—after the Gospel was published. About A.D. 100 is a good guess. Some scholars believe that he may have been the writer who re-edited the Gospel by adding on material such as chapter 21. That is possible but not certain, though 3 John 12 must be editorially related to John 21:24. His community is Johannine, related closely in mentality to the Fourth Gospel, with a theology differing from, but not contradictory to, that of the other Gospels. It is a community with little evidence of structured authority, more egalitarian than hierarchical. And it is a community which, perhaps because of that very non-hierarchical structure, has suffered a devastating schism. Unity has been broken. Our author has taken up pen and ink to encourage faithfulness, to protect the truth, to inspire mutual love.

2 JOHN

Neal M. Flanagan, O.S.M.

COMMENTARY

Structure: The Second Epistle of John is a short letter, just long enough to fill one papyrus sheet. It contains the ordinary letter divisions of the time: the introduction (vv. 1-3); the note of happiness or thanksgiving (v. 4); the body of the letter (vv. 5-11); the conclusion (vv. 12-13).

Occasion and contents: The letter fits well into the picture of the Johannine community sketched out at the end of 1 John. Visitors to the author, who now terms himself "the Presbyter" (v. 1), have shown themselves faithful to the truth as he sees it (v. 4). So he writes with joy to the Johannine church (the "Lady" of vv. 1, 5) from which they have come to express his happiness and to tender his advice. The advice, not surprisingly, concerns *love* and *belief.* They are to love one another (vv. 5-6). Equally, they must beware of those who have broken unity, the antichrists who deny that Jesus Christ has come in the flesh (vv. 7-9). They should not even offer them welcome, lest their homes become the pulpits of the evil one (vv. 10-11).

The note concludes with hope for an impending visit and greetings from the members of the author's own church, the children of their chosen sister (v. 13).

1 and 2 John were most probably authored by the same person who in 2 John warns a different Johannine community of the dangers spelled out at length in the first epistle. The two epistles are, consequently, closely related, written because of the same crisis, by the same author, and most probably about the same time, close to A.D. 100.

Comments: (a) Verses 1 and 13, the beginning and the end, use identical terminology. The letter is addressed to the *chosen* Lady and her *children* and encloses final greetings from the *children* of her *chosen* sister. It is ecclesiastical language that is being used. The chosen Lady and her chosen sister are sister churches, of which the children are the members. The "Presbyter" of verse 1 is an ambiguous term. It means more than "older man," since the author calls himself *"the* Presbyter" and addresses the church with some degree of authority. The most probable meaning of the designation is that the author is a second-generation Christian who has known the eyewitnesses of primitive Christianity and can, therefore, testify to what was seen and taught from the beginning.

b) The Johannine polarity between believers and deceivers is strongly phrased. There are those who know the truth, in whom it abides, and who walk in the truth with love (vv. 1-6). And there are the others, antichrists, who do not confess Jesus Christ coming in the flesh (v. 7). The theological framework is clearly that of 1 John. Verse 9 deals with the radical "progressives" who abandoned the traditional truth for novelty. The author has a real fear, reflected in verse 8, that his sister Johannine community might succumb to such novelty. It is that fear which moves him to bar house churches and their pulpits to such false teachers (vv. 10-11).

c) Verse 12 is an affirmation that personal encounter is of more value than literary correspondence.

3 JOHN

Neal M. Flanagan, O.S.M.

COMMENTARY

Structure: The Third Epistle of John is another brief note, slightly shorter than 2 John, and with similar divisions: the introduction (v. 1); the note of happiness (vv. 2-4); the body (vv. 5-12), which centers successively on Gaius, Diotrephes, and Demetrius; the conclusion (vv. 13-15).

Occasion and contents: This letter is addressed to an individual, Gaius, a member of another Johannine church, of whom visitors to the author have spoken well (vv. 3, 6). The purpose of the letter is to congratulate Gaius (vv. 2-4) while encouraging his continued support for Johannine missionaries (vv. 5-8), such as Demetrius, who probably has been sent by the author himself (v. 12) and is the bearer of this letter. The author also wishes to warn Gaius against Diotrephes, who has taken leadership in one of the Johannine groups and refuses to afford hospitality to the missionaries. Even worse, he expels from the church those Christians who do help them.

The epistle, consequently, centers on hospitality and authority, not on the Christological and soteriological problems evident in 1 and 2 John. Yet the same author seems to have written all three, and at approximately the same time. We have already seen how 2 John is linked to 1 John. 3 John, on its part, is linked to 2 John both by the designation of the author as "the Presbyter" and by the close similarity of 3 John 13-14 to 2 John 12. There is a further fascinating similarity between 3 John 12b: ". . . and you know our testimony is true," and the Gospel of John 21:24: ". . . and we know that his testimony is true,"

which provides argument for those who believe that the Johannine epistles were written by the redactor of the Fourth Gospel, whose hand is seen most clearly in John 21.

Comments: (a) About Gaius (v. 1) absolutely nothing is known except what is told us in this letter. That he is one of the author's "children" (v. 4) has suggested to some commentators that he owed his conversion to the author, but "children" is used so often in these epistles that it need not carry such specific meaning.

b) Verses 5-8 give us a picture of early Christian missionaries, whose subsistence depends completely on the hospitality provided by fellow Christians. Those who give such aid should be considered co-workers (v. 8).

c) Most of the scholarly conjecture regarding 3 John concerns Diotrephes. Of him nothing is known except the few particulars given in verses 9-10. His precise position vis-à-vis the elder is uncertain, though there is no lack of suggestions on the part of scholars.

i) Some believe that he had assumed a position of authoritative leadership, much like that of a bishop, and was firmly opposed to the itinerant missionaries deriving their authority from "the Presbyter."

ii) Others suggest that the difficulty concerned doctrine, and that Diotrephes was an innovator and a heretical teacher. In that case, however, it is surprising that the author makes no specific mention of false teaching.

iii) Still others believe that the shoe should be put on the other foot and that the author himself was the innovator.

All that is known for certain, however, is contained in our text: Diotrephes did not acknowledge the Presbyter's authority, claiming precedence for himself; he refused to welcome the missionaries and expelled those who did; he appears to be opposed by Gaius and the others (vv. 5-8, 10, 15) who have welcomed the missionaries. These particulars lead us to support the opinion (i) that Diotrephes had become overly authoritative, challenging the position of even "the Presbyter."

d) Demetrius is evidently one of the Johannine missionaries sent out by the author and probably carrying along this letter.

e) Verses 13-14 are almost identical to 2 John 12, an indication of the same authorship.

f) Verse 15 gives us a view of one Johannine community saluting another. On both sides, the church members are the beloved, the friends, *hoi philoi*. The author has written to keep these friends united and their church intact.

THE ACTS OF THE APOSTLES

William S. Kurz, S.J.

INTRODUCTION

WHAT IS ACTS AND BY WHOM?

1. Importance

Acts is the only book in the New Testament which continues the story of Jesus into the early church. If it were not for Acts, we would have only isolated pieces of information about the beginnings of the church. We would have to dig these bits and pieces out of the New Testament letters, but would have no framework into which to put them. Acts has provided a framework for understanding not only the information it contains but facts gleaned from Paul's letters and other New Testament books.

But Acts means more than this for Christians today. As part of Scripture, we believe it is God's inspired word to us, and therefore it does not just concern the past. As is true of all biblical narratives, the stories in Acts act as models and examples of how God deals with his people. They give Christians of all ages something to imitate and exemplify how God acts in our lives.

Luke wrote Acts to be read in this way. Out of many possible events he could have described, he picked out those which were most important or most able to exemplify Christian living. He concentrated on a few stories and described them in depth. He tied these stories and the speeches that explain them together by means of summarizing passages and travel notices.

Readers today might at first be surprised at such freedom in putting Acts together. But if we put ourselves in the place of the writer, we realize it had to be this way. In both his Gospel and Acts, Luke had many stories from different sources that he had to join together into one continuous narrative. He had to choose which stories he could use and figure out in which order to put them.

Luke is writing not as some kind of "pure historian," but as a pastoral leader to provide his Christian readers with models to follow. His account is a faith account, full of belief in God's action within the events he narrates. It tries to edify or build up the readers' faith as well. In fact, one could describe Acts as a presentation of the Christian way of following Jesus, as seen in the lives of the earliest Christians.

2. Who wrote Luke and Acts?

The author of Acts never gives his own name. Since few historical books of the Bible give the author's name, this is not surprising. Acts is addressed to Theophilus, who obviously knew the author's identity. But today we are not sure who either the author or Theophilus was. Though Theophilus means "lover of God," he is probably a specific person. He seems to have been a Christian leader or a man wealthy enough to have the Gospel and Acts copied and distributed, i.e., the "publisher" or "patron."

There is much debate about who wrote this Gospel and Acts. Traditions from the early church identify him as Luke, which is why we use that name for the Gospel. They say he was a companion of Paul and tend to identify him with the Luke mentioned in some of Paul's letters (e.g., Phlm 24, Col 4:14, 2 Tim 4:11). Since Colossians calls Luke "the physician," he is often called that in tradition.

Many scholars today doubt these traditions. They see too many differences between Luke's and Paul's descriptions of the same events. They wonder why Acts never mentions Paul's letters and consider his theology to be too different from Paul's for him to have been Paul's disciple. For example, the "Paul" in Acts makes little direct reference to Paul's major themes of salvation by faith and being "in Christ." Acts has toned down the clash over whether Gentiles first had to become Jews before becoming Christians.

Others, including myself, do not consider these problems insuperable. Luke and Acts were written in the eighties or nineties, some twenty to thirty years after Paul's death. The controversies that are fresh in Paul's letters are "ancient history" in Acts. So it is not surprising that the tone and outlook are different. It seems historically plausible that the writer was Paul's companion on some of his later journeys, as the narrative use of "we" claims. The writer is less familiar with Paul's early life and controversies, and does not mention Paul's letters that refer to them. His theology is somewhat different from Paul's, as mentioned above, because his situation, audience and purposes are different.

3. Reliability of Acts

Many scholars distrust much of the historical information in Acts. They argue that if the Acts picture of Paul is so different from that in Paul's own letters, then other information is probably also slanted. They consider Acts a glorified picture of the early church that downplays the tensions it had.

Much of this criticism seems extreme, and there is a growing reaction against it. Studies in biblical and Hellenistic historiography have shown that Acts is comparable to the best ancient historical writings, such as the biblical Samuel-Kings and 1-2 Maccabees and histories contemporary with Acts by Josephus and his model, Dionysius of Halicarnassus. All histories had to appeal to a popular audience by rhetorical devices like speeches, vivid episodes, and proofs from prophecy. Luke-Acts

continues the biblical history up to Paul's ministry in Rome, using familiar Hellenistic motifs, as Maccabees had.

Another reason some scholars are skeptical over Acts is its stress on the miraculous. In its extreme forms, rejection of the miraculous exemplifies the pervasive modern prejudice against miracles. Yet since the 1970s there is a widespread awareness of phenomena that defy natural explanations, such as healings through prayer and widely attested phenomena that accompany some alleged apparitions.

Other scholars object to measuring Luke's worth by Paul's theology. The Protestant Reformation sometimes tended to make Paul the standard of genuine Christianity. Acts is often labeled a corrupt "early Catholicism," in which the genuine Paul has been "watered down" to be more acceptable to the "early-Catholic" church. Even that negative term betrays anti-Catholic bias.

Biblical studies are undergoing an important shift from exaggerated historical criticism to more holistic and literary approaches. "Canonical criticism" reads Acts in the context of the whole Christian Bible as it has been appropriated by the church. "Narrative criticism" approaches Luke-Acts with literary questions.

4. Narrative approaches to Acts

Analysis of how Acts is constructed as a narrative considers both the author and readers that the narrative implies, plotting and deliberate gaps to be filled in by readers, and the narrators of the story with their points of view from which it is told. Narrative studies have relativized the dogmatism of some historical-critical conjectures. For example, instead of "seams" and dichotomies between sources, literary critics often find sophisticated "gaps" to engage the reader's imagination. Rather than trying to locate the precise author and historical community for which Luke-Acts was intended, narrative critics investigate what the author reveals about himself in the text (the *implied* author) and the kinds of readers implied by the information that is included in or left out of the text.

Thus: the author implied by Luke-Acts is a Christian follower of Paul, active towards the end of Paul's ministry, who writes in Greek and is aware both of methods of

Hellenistic history and of motifs of the Greek Old Testament. The readers implied by Luke-Acts are familiar with the Greek Old Testament, Judaism, and Christianity. Acts usually has the narrator speaking in the third person ("he," "she," "they") from the common biblical "omniscient" point of view that tells what characters are thinking, in ways that go beyond what an immediate observer could discover. But after Acts 16:10 a "we" narrator describes some events from the perspective of a minor participant. This narrative device claims that the implied author is present at those events and thus sometimes a companion of Paul. Plotting is not purely chronological, but tends to finish treating one character before moving on (e.g., Herod's death in Acts 12). Plotting also illustrates how events fulfill older prophecies. By not stating what happened after the two years of Paul's Roman captivity (28:30-31), the ending of Acts leaves a deliberate gap to be filled by the readers. Mention of "for two full years" implies that the situation changed after that fixed time and that the narrator knows what the change was.

5. The revised New Testament translation of the New American Bible

Revision of the New American Bible New Testament translation on which the Collegeville Bible Commentary is based was one occasion for the revision of this commentary. After comparing the old and new translations of Acts, I find the revised version a significant improvement for liturgical proclamation and for reading and study. Far less idiosyncratic, it has a more traditional "biblical" style and tone.

I have one major objection to the revised NAB translation: it has stopped capitalizing "holy" in "Holy Spirit." I find this uncapitalized "holy Spirit" an uncanonical historicism inappropriate for the Christian Bible. It is true that the Holy Spirit was not defined as one person of the Trinity until well after the New Testament was written. But in the context of the Christian Bible and tradition, as well as in the Western literary tradition, the term "Holy Spirit" in the New Testament has consistently been understood as the Trinitarian Holy Spirit and capitalized. In reading Acts, contemporary Christians encounter the capitalized Holy Spirit of their tradition and experience.

PURPOSE OF ACTS

The preface for Luke and Acts: Luke 1:1-4

Prefaces to a book often state its purpose. The preface in Luke 1:1-4 has stereotyped technical language used in Greek prefaces. Readers expected to find statements about the writer's care and accuracy at the beginning of Greek books, just as readers today expect a "Dear Mr. Smith" at the beginning of a letter. This is true even if the writer hates Mr. Smith and is about to fire him from his job. Despite the conventional style of Luke's preface, however, it does indicate his real purpose. He wrote "so that you may realize the certainty of the teachings you have received" (Luke 1:4).

By "certainty," Luke is not referring merely to how accurate his facts are. He is also showing why these events and developments are legitimate answers to the hopes and promises of Israel. He explains what happens, even the horrible death of Jesus, as according to God's saving plan. In Acts he shows how Peter, Paul, and other Christian missonaries carried on the work of Jesus according to this plan. He demonstrates continuity between what happened to Jesus and the apostles and what the Old Testament had foretold. He also establishes that the traditions he uses are genuine. They go back to eyewitnesses, not mere hearsay, and have been carefully handed down in the church. He shows how God, especially through his Holy Spirit, was active in these events. Thus Luke is not writing the same kind of history as Josephus, a contemporary Jewish historian. Josephus wrote two major histories during the seventies to nineties of the first century, the same time as Luke. Both made more use of Greek conventions than Luke-Acts and had the secular purpose of winning the Romans' respect for Jewish culture and history, despite the Jewish rebellion against Rome in 66–70. Luke, however, writes to build his readers' faith.

A major problem Luke dealt with was the identity question of early Christians. If their founder was the Jewish Messiah, and they were supposed to be receiving the promises made to the Jewish patriarchs in the Jewish Scriptures (Old Testament), why are so many Gentiles and so few Jews members of the church in Luke's time? At the time of Jesus there were several Jewish parties or sects. At first both Jews and Christians considered Jesus' followers to be another such group within Judaism.

Confusion began when this subgroup of Jews, the Christians, started to admit non-Jews as fully equal Christians, without making them first become Jews. Imagine the confusion today if a Catholic parish began a prayer group for its parishioners, and soon admitted so many non-Catholics into the group that the parishioners were outnumbered. Would the group still belong to the Catholic parish? And imagine the trauma if either the parish expelled the prayer group or the group left the parish to begin its own "non-denominational church." Bitterness on both sides would most likely be deep. Certainly people would question how this new non-denominational church could claim to be a continuation of the Catholic parish from which it began. These kinds of questions also were asked about the relationship of the new subgroup from its parent Judaism, especially after it became an independent group. Luke's Gospel and Acts tried to answer some of these questions. He showed how what happened to Jesus and the early church was according to God's plan in the Old Testament. God willed both the restoration of Israel and the blessing of all nations through Christ. Acts 1–6 demonstrate especially the restoration of Israel, through the thousands of Jews who accepted the good news about Jesus and became Christians. The later parts of Acts show how the good news blessed the Gentiles.

HOW ACTS IS CONSTRUCTED

1. Use of the Greek Old Testament

Luke used the Greek translation of the Old Testament, rather than the Hebrew original, as he wrote his Gospel and Acts in Greek. An even more important difference from the rabbis of the first Christian centuries is seen in how Luke used the Greek Bible. Whereas the rabbis tended to treat all of their Bible as law, Luke and other Christians tended to see the Jewish Bible primarily as prophecy. The law approach mined the Old Testament for guidelines and rules of how to live in the daily aspects of one's life. Christians, however,

searched the Jewish Scriptures for prophecies of the Messiah and end times of fulfillment.

Thus, Luke viewed Moses not as "The Lawgiver" but as "The Prophet." Moses was the type and model for other prophets. And since Moses was considered the author of the Pentateuch (the first five books of the Bible, from Genesis to Deuteronomy), these books also could be treated as prophecy. For example, Luke stressed the Genesis promises to Abraham as prophecies fulfilled in Jesus and the church.

2. Speeches and letters

Speeches make up a large part of Acts. Where did they come from? No one had tape recorders when speeches were made. Nor is it likely anyone was taking notes, which Luke then obtained and copied. It is possible that Luke did have some speeches in the material he collected. But we know that even when speeches were available to a writer, Greek training in how to write histories insisted that the author of the history rewrite all speeches in his own words. This would insure that the whole book would have a consistent style. Most scholars think Luke followed this convention. Therefore Luke either composed the speeches in Acts according to what he thought would have been said on that occasion, or he heavily rewrote speeches which he inherited. This is why the speech of Peter in Acts 2 sounds so much like Paul's speech in Acts 13.

The three most important kinds of speeches in Acts are missionary speeches to convert Jews or Gentiles, defense speeches in the trials of Paul, and the farewell speech in Acts 20. Most speeches explain some event which has taken place and give the author Luke a chance to tell his readers the real meaning of that event. Thus the speech in Acts 2 explains the Pentecost event and, in turn, leads to the conversion of thousands. The speech in Acts 3 gives the meaning of the healing of the lame man and leads to further conversions. The defense speeches, as in Acts 22, answer objections Jews had made to Paul and his ministry. The farewell speech in Acts 20 gives insight into what was most important in Paul's ministry and what later concerns would have been most important to him.

Several of the speeches seem to be interrupted, and yet it is clear that Luke has included as much as he wanted. Thus, the speech to the Greek philosophers in Athens in Acts 17 is interrupted after mention of the resurrection, and the Acts 22 defense to Jews is broken up after mention of Paul's mission to non-Jews. This writing technique enables Luke to stop reporting the speech at the most important point and provides dramatic underlining of that main point. In Acts 17 it is resurrection that annoys the Greeks, and the mention of non-Jews in Acts 22 angers the Jewish listeners. This enables Luke to show clearly that Paul's witness to Jesus' resurrection and his mission to the Gentiles were the main reasons he met so much opposition.

3. Repetitions in the story

Readers of Acts may be surprised to find some stories repeated up to three times. Paul's call is described in Acts 9, 22, and 26, for example. Luke repeats some of the key events in Acts to signal their special importance for understanding the rise and spread of Christianity. He tells about the conversion of the Gentile Cornelius three times. This makes clear how it was God's will to baptize non-Jews without making them become Jews first through circumcision. And it was Peter, not Paul, who first endorsed this principle.

The Apostolic Decree from Acts 15 is also repeated, as the compromise that enabled Gentile and Jewish Christians to share table fellowship (and therefore Eucharist) without forcing Gentiles to become Jews. The three versions of Paul's call by the risen Jesus reinforce the fact that Paul saw the risen Jesus and received his mission to the Gentiles directly from him. And three times Luke shows Paul telling Jews that he took the good news first to them, but since they rejected it, he would take it to the more receptive Gentiles.

All these repetitions are especially helpful for explaining how Luke's predominantly Gentile church can legitimately claim to be heirs of the Jewish promises through the Jewish Messiah. They show why and how the shifts from Jew to Gentile were made.

4. Parallelism between Jesus and Christians in Acts

Luke goes out of his way to point out parallels between Jesus and Peter and Paul. All three raised dead people to life, healed, preached, and suffered rejection. Luke often

waits until Acts to mention things about Jesus found in the other Gospels. For example, he does not mention false witnesses charging that Jesus preached against the temple in the Gospel, but he does refer back to this charge during Stephen's trial in Acts 6. And he mentions a slap in the face at Paul's trial before the high priest, but not at Jesus' trial. By stressing parallels Luke shows how Paul and others were following the example and instructions of Jesus. Thus he also defends them against criticism like that in Acts 21:21-24, which seems still to have been current in Luke's time.

5. Humor in Acts

These serious concerns in Acts should not make us overlook how much fun Luke has telling the story. He loves to bring out the humor in incidents. Thus the pagans in Lystra look absurd as they bring bulls to sacrifice to Barnabas and Paul in Acts 14, or those in Ephesus as they keep chanting for two hours, "Long live Artemis of Ephesus," in Acts 19. Such humor reflects Luke's confidence in Christianity and sometimes mocks its rivals.

OUTLINE OF ACTS

1:12–8:3	Birth and growth of the church in Jerusalem through the Spirit
8:4–9:31	Persecution and expansion in Judea and Samaria
9:32–15:35	Gentiles: Peter and Cornelius, Barnabas and Saul, the Council of Jerusalem
15:36–18:23	Paul's mission to the Gentiles: The second journey
18:24–21:14	Paul's destiny in Jerusalem: The third journey
21:15–26:32	Paul as prisoner witnesses to the resurrection
27:1–28:31	"You shall bear witness at Rome."

THEMES IN ACTS

Acts should be studied as a narrative, but several theological motifs continually reappear. They include:

1. The fulfillment of God's saving plan

God's enthronement of the risen Jesus as Messiah in heaven and his outpouring of the

Holy Spirit were the unexpected fulfillment of all Jewish longings for salvation and God's kingdom. The Spirit is the ultimate realization of the promises to Abraham. It would anoint leaders for God's people and empower Christians to preach, heal, cast out evil spirits, and witness even unto death. Thus it would restore Israel and bless all nations by cleansing and incorporating them into God's people without circumcision.

2. The risen Jesus acts through his Spirit-filled disciples

After his ascension into heaven, Jesus continues to act on earth through his disciples by giving them his Holy Spirit and enabling them to preach and heal in his name. Especially through Paul, he will "proclaim light both to our people and to the Gentiles" (26:23). Those who reject his disciples in Acts reject Jesus and are excommunicated from his people (3:23).

3. Continuity amid change: God keeps his promises to his people

Acts reassures Christians facing unexpected changes in God's people. Just as today many Christians are bewildered and dismayed by rapid changes in the church, so it was in Luke's time. Acts shows how God himself initiated the great changes in his people from the Jewish disciples of Jesus to the mostly Gentile church throughout the Roman Empire, as when he had Peter and Paul convert Gentiles without circumcising them.

Other principles of continuity are the Twelve and the many Jews who became Christians. These were the "missing link" between the primarily Gentile church of Luke's day and its Jewish origins. The Twelve were the transitional leaders between Jesus and later leaders like Paul. The Jewish Christians were the restored Israel who continue the people of God's promises (in contrast to Matt 21:43, where Israel is replaced by a new people of God).

4. Healing and restoration of God's people

Acts treats healing as a sign of restoration and salvation. In Acts 3 the healing of the cripple (who was unclean) cleanses and enables him to enter the temple, and symbolizes the restoration of Israel to be able to pray worthily (Luke 1:75). In Luke's Gospel, Jesus often says, "Your faith has saved you." In Acts 4:9-10 Peter uses "saved" for the cripple's healing. Luke carefully distinguishes healing from magic (Acts 8 and 19).

5. Triumph of Christianity despite all obstacles

Frequently Acts remarks that "the word of God continued to spread" (6:7), no matter what persecutions got in the way.

6. God's guidance of the Christian way

All through Acts God guides Christians; they may not go wherever they choose. He refuses to let Paul go into Asia but directs him to Macedonia and Greece instead (Acts 16). God's guidance through the Holy Spirit, appearances, visions, dreams, angels, and prophecies demonstrates for Luke that the decisions and actions of the early church were not human ideas but responses to God's direction.

7. Apologetic for Christianity, especially for Paul

Acts defends Paul and other Jewish Christians from the charge of being Jewish apostates by stressing their fidelity to Jewish law and insisting that the decision to admit Gentiles without circumcision came from God.

Acts also has an apology for Paul's innocence before Roman law like the one Luke's Gospel had for Jesus. The verdicts of "innocent" by Roman judges in Paul's trials in Acts 22–26 show that Christians are no threat to the order of the state.

COMMENTARY

INTRODUCTION

Acts 1:1-11

1:1-5 Foreword. To understand Acts, we must remember that it is volume 2 of Luke-Acts—a continuation, by the same author, of the Gospel of Luke. The way New Testaments are printed obscures this fact because the Gospel of John intervenes between volume 1, Luke, and volume 2, Acts.

Acts tells how Jesus' disciples received his Holy Spirit and continued his work after he ascended into heaven. Much of Acts is a travelog, following the Christian missionaries, especially Paul, as they spread God's word. Similarly, Luke's Gospel had put a unique stress on Jesus' journey to Jerusalem from Luke 9:51 to the end of the book.

Luke begins Acts as he began his Gospel, with a foreword to his patron Theophilus.

Jesus had prepared his apostles for their mission by instructing them during his lifetime. He also appeared to them some forty days after his death and resurrection. The forty days seem the same kind of round number as Jesus' forty days and Moses' forty years in the desert (Luke 4:1-2 and Exodus). The difference between the ending of Luke's Gospel and the beginning of Acts does not seem to have bothered Luke. The Gospel treated the ascension as the last event on Easter Day. Acts dates it forty days later.

The disagreements imply that Luke was less concerned with the date of the ascension than with its importance as the event that closed the series of Jesus' resurrection appearances (except the extraordinary appearance to Paul; compare 1 Cor 15:5-9). Each passage has its own theological message. The Gospel ends with Jesus' priestly blessing as he ascends (Luke 24:51). Acts compares the ascension to Jesus' return from heaven (1:11).

Luke also stresses that the risen Jesus gave the apostles convincing signs that he was alive after his death. He appeared several times and continued teaching them what God's kingdom meant. Since they both saw and heard Jesus risen from the dead, they could be genuine witnesses to his resurrection. Others had only hearsay knowledge about Jesus (e.g., Herod in Luke 9:7-9). Throughout his Gospel and Acts, Luke emphasizes how important it is to both see and hear Jesus. See how Luke contrasts Paul with his companions in Acts 9:3-7.

Luke also underscores how Jesus gave new insights to his disciples after his resurrection. The risen Jesus would give the same kind of instruction to Paul in Acts 9.

The same Holy Spirit who was with Jesus when he chose and instructed the apostles would now be given to them. Both Luke's Gospel and Acts emphasize that being "baptized by the Holy Spirit" is the way God's power is given to humans. The Spirit came upon Jesus and thus began Jesus' mission of preaching and healing (Luke 3:21-22). At Pentecost the same Spirit would be given to the apostles to begin their preaching and healing in Acts. Receiving God's powerful Spirit far surpasses the effects of John's baptism, which had merely used water as a sign of repentance (Acts 11:15-17).

Usually in Acts people receive the Spirit when they are baptized as Christians, like the followers of John the Baptist in Acts 19:1-7. But at the very beginning of Christianity, God gave his Spirit to the apostles at Pentecost and to the Gentiles in Acts 10–11 before anyone could give them Christian baptism with water and the Spirit.

These accounts are meant to show how Christianity began by God's free action, independent of any human cooperation or ritual. The church is not just some human sect, but comes directly from God. The gift of the Spirit which began the church fulfills the Father's promises in the Old Testament, as Jesus had explained them.

1:6-11 Jesus taken up into heaven. In Luke 17:20-37 and 21:7-9 Jesus had to tell people not to listen to those who said the end was near. Nor should they try to estimate when or where the end of the world would come. The same prohibition is repeated in Acts 1:6-7 (see also Luke 12:35-46).

The question about restoring the rule to Israel in 1:6 also shows continued misunderstanding about what the kingdom of God meant. Acts 2:3 will show that God's promise was about the coming of the Holy Spirit, not some earthly kingdom. The prohibition against trying to compute the times of the end is meant to discourage Luke's readers from guessing what cannot be known. Rather, they should focus on the power of the Spirit as the sign of living in the promised final days. Luke says Christians are to use this power during whatever time is left to witness to Jesus to the ends of the earth. They should not waste time (as Christians are still tempted to do) trying to figure out when the end of the world will be.

Verse 1:8 provides a "table of contents" for Acts. The witness "in Jerusalem" is Acts 2 to 7. "Throughout Judea and Samaria" is from chapters 8 to 12, and to "the ends of the earth" from Acts 13 to 28. "The ends of the earth" is an echo of Isa 49:6. Both Acts and the Psalms of Solomon, a slightly earlier Jewish writing, apply the phrase "the ends of the earth" to Rome. Acts ends in Rome. And Pss Sol 8:15 calls the Roman general Pompey "him that is from the end of the earth."

Acts 1:9 mentions that the disciples saw Jesus actually being taken up to heaven to remind readers of 2 Kgs 2:4-15. There, the prophet Elijah told his disciple Elisha that only if he saw Elijah being taken up to heaven would he receive double Elijah's portion of the Holy Spirit. Elisha did see the flaming chariot take up Elijah and therefore received the same Spirit as Elijah. So in Acts 1:9, the disciples saw Jesus being taken up in a cloud and received Jesus' Holy Spirit at Pentecost. The two men in white garments are angels, as in Luke 24:4. Their statement in 1:11, that Jesus will return the same way they saw him leave, refers to his coming on the cloud at the end of the world, as predicted in Luke 21:27.

BIRTH AND GROWTH OF THE CHURCH IN JERUSALEM THROUGH THE SPIRIT

Acts 1:12–8:3

1:12-26 Matthias chosen to restore the twelve apostles. The names of the eleven apostles left after Judas' betrayal come in a different order than in Luke 6:14-16. The Gospel list seems to follow the order in the list as Luke received it. However, Acts adjusts the list in order of importance. It names Peter first, then John (his partner in Acts 3–5), then James, and fourth Andrew. Luke 6:14 had "Peter and Andrew, James and John."

There were at least three important men called James. The brother of John, one of the Twelve, was with Jesus at the transfiguration and agony in the garden and was killed in Acts 12:2. He is often known as "James the Great." The son of Alphaeus also belonged to the Twelve. Tradition calls him "James the Less." And there is the brother or relative of Jesus who had become leader of the Jerusalem church (see Acts 12:17, Acts 15 and 21.)

Little is known about most of the Twelve aside from lists of their names. Most do not appear elsewhere in the New Testament. They are less important as individual personalities than as members of the Twelve. Jesus promised that the twelve tribes of Israel would be restored and that the Twelve would rule them in God's kingdom (Luke 22:28-29). To have twelve rulers, Judas had to be replaced. Acts 1:15-36 shows that all twelve are in place by Pentecost, when the Holy Spirit empowered them to become the new leaders of God's people in Jesus' name.

Acts 1:14 also makes it clear that the Twelve were not the only ones waiting for the Spirit. They were part of a complete community that included both men and women. Acts 2:17-18 shows this fulfills the Joel prophecy that the Holy Spirit will be poured out on "all flesh" in the final days, and both "sons and daughters" will prophesy. Acts 1:14 also stresses the unity in constant prayer of this Christian community. Prayer is a major theme in Luke. For example, of the four Gospels, only Luke 3:21-22 explicitly says that Jesus was praying when the Spirit came upon him.

Luke probably had several reasons for singling out Jesus' mother Mary and his brothers in Acts 1:14. One is the saying in Luke 8:19-21 that Jesus' mother and brothers are those who hear and keep God's word. Another is to draw a parallel between Mary's role in Jesus' birth and her presence at the church's birth on Pentecost, when the Spirit came upon her in a new way. Related to this is Luke's narrative claim that Mary was the ultimate source of information in the infancy narratives ("Mary kept all these things, reflecting on them in her heart," Luke 2:19 [cf. 2:51]) and was present in the Jerusalem church, whose members could pass on to the author traditions about the events in Luke 1-2 (Luke 1:2-3). Another reason is probably the importance of "James the brother of Jesus" in Acts 15 and 21. It is certain the "brothers of Jesus" were considered his blood relatives. Mary's perpetual virginity is church dogma. From New Testament evidence and later church tradition, their exact relationship to Jesus and to Mary is unclear and debated.

Peter continues in Acts 1:15-22 to exercise the leadership role of strengthening his brethren that Jesus had promised at the Last Supper (Luke 22:32). It had begun in Luke 24:34, when he was the first to report that the risen Jesus appeared to him. The round number of "about 120" (12 x 10) is symbolic. It probably alludes to the restored twelve tribes of Israel under the soon-to-be twelve apostles. The community of 120 will be the core of the Spirit-filled Israel at Pentecost.

This is Peter's first speech in Acts. It argues that Judas' betrayal had to happen to fulfill the prophecies in Ps 69:26 and 109:8. Like most of his contemporaries, Luke considered all the psalms as written by David under the inspiration of the Spirit (see also Acts 2:30). Luke usually explains shocking events like Jesus' death and his betrayal by one of his closest followers this way: they are necessary to fulfill God's scriptural plan of salvation (e.g., Luke 24:25-27, 44-47). Even when God seems to be absent, Luke insists he is always in control of events.

One aspect of God's control is his punishing extraordinary sinners like Judas here, and Herod in 12:21-23. God's punishment of the wicked is a common theme in both the Old Testament and in Greek histories. The punishments of Judas and Herod are similar to that of Emperor Antiochus IV, a notorious enemy of the Jews. His death is described in 2 Macc 9:4-10. In the first century both Jews and pagan Greeks and Romans felt that some stress on God's punishment of the wicked was needed to defend God's justice and power. If the wicked got off scot-free, God would seem either unjust or unable to maintain law and order in the world.

The rules for Judas' replacement in 1:21-22 make plain what Luke means by an apostle and witness to Jesus' resurrection. Only someone who knew Jesus before his death could witness that the risen Jesus is the same one who died. According to this strict sense, Luke does not treat Paul as an apostolic witness to Jesus' resurrection. (Acts 14:14, however, calls Paul and Barnabas "apostles," extending the term's meaning.) Thus, Acts 13:30-31 cites Paul as saying the first witnesses to Jesus' resurrection were the Galileans who

came with Jesus to Jerusalem. Paul's own letters were much more insistent that Paul was a genuine apostle and witness to Jesus' resurrection, though not one of the Twelve (e.g., 1 Cor 15:1-11).

Luke distinguishes apostles from Paul because he wants to trace the links from Jesus' earthly ministry, through the twelve apostles, to later missionaries like Paul and Barnabas who did not follow Jesus before his death. Even Paul admits in 1 Cor 15:3-7 that he received from earlier witnesses the message he was passing on.

The community found two men who fulfilled all requirements for joining the Twelve. They left the final choice to God. After praying that God would pick the one he wanted, they drew lots between the two. The one selected by lot was considered God's choice.

2:1-13 Coming of the Holy Spirit at Pentecost. Finally the long-awaited day for the fulfillment of the Father's promise has arrived (see 1:4-5, 8). The community is together, presumably in prayer (1:14), on the Jewish feast of Pentecost. Jewish pilgrims came to Jerusalem on that feast to celebrate God's establishing his people by giving them the law on Mount Sinai. Since early in the Old Testament, Jews had associated wind with Spirit. Both fire and the Spirit were prophesied by John the Baptist in Luke 3:16 (referred to in Acts 1:5 and 11:16). A mightier one than he would "baptize you with the Holy Spirit and fire." There is a strong pattern in Luke and Acts of showing how a prophecy made earlier in the account has come true.

When all were filled with the Holy Spirit, they spoke in the tongues or languages the Spirit gave them (as in 10:46 and 19:6). Both the expression "as the Spirit enabled them to proclaim" (2:4) and the explanation in Acts 2:16-18 seem to envisage a prophetic gift with a missionary aspect. How helpful it would be if missionaries were simply given the ability to speak God's word in many languages! Luke does not seem to be thinking so much of the kind of "gift of tongues" mentioned in 1 Cor 12-14 and common today in charismatic prayer groups.

Paul had described tongues not as human language but as a way to pray to God without words or mental understanding (1 Cor 14:2, 9, 14-19). He said outsiders might think the community was insane if they overheard it (1 Cor 14:23), presumably because tongues at Corinth sounded like incoherent babbling. Even in Acts 2:12-15, the objection that the apostles were drunk seems to indicate they appeared to be babbling. Perhaps the original description of Pentecost that Luke heard treated their speech as babbling. In any case, Luke's version in Acts 2 symbolizes the reversing of the punishment at the Tower of Babel. In Gen 11:1-9, people at Babel who spoke one language became unable to understand one another. At Pentecost, even people of many languages understood the apostles.

There is no need to deny *a priori* that the apostles could have given such a public speech without immediate reprisal from the same authorities who had had Jesus killed. Those authorities later interrupted Peter's temple speech (Acts 4:1-3), but they would not have been prepared for this one. The early church simply could not have spread as fast as it did without some such public preaching.

2:14-21 Explanation of the Pentecost events. In Acts 2:14, Peter acts as spokesman for the Twelve, explaining the sign the people had just seen and heard. For Luke, miraculous events need to be explained, as the empty tomb in Luke 24 and the healing of the lame man in Acts 3. As he demonstrates, miracles in themselves are usually open to either believing or unbelieving interpretations. God does not force people to believe when he provides a miracle. This is why Luke calls them not miracles but signs—signs of God's power and goodness which invite belief but do not force it.

In the beginning of his speech, Peter explains that the apostles' behavior is not drunkenness, but fulfills Joel's prophecy that in the last days God will pour out his Spirit on all flesh. In the Old Testament, the Spirit's coming upon someone was often overwhelming and caused quite different or unusual behavior (e.g., Saul's in 1 Sam 10:5-13).

Luke seems to have added words to the Joel quotation to show more clearly how Pentecost fulfills the prophecy. He changed Joel 3:1, "then afterward," to "in the last days" (Acts 2:17). Acts 2:18 added "and they shall prophesy." Joel 3:3 had "wonders in the heavens" and Acts 2:19 has "wonders in the heavens above and signs on the earth below." This could hint at the wind and fire from heaven and the languages below. But Luke is

probably also trying to echo more closely the "signs and wonders" by which God performed the Exodus of his people from Egypt.

The Joel quotation shows how Christians can be living "in the last days" (Acts 2:17) and yet have to wait for "the great and splendid day of the Lord" (2:20), the final day of judgment. On judgment day, all who call on the name of the Lord (identified as Jesus in 2:36) will be saved (2:21).

2:22-36 Proof that Jesus is Messiah. Messiah and Christ both mean "anointed." Messiah is Hebrew and Christ is Greek. The term originally referred to the king of Israel as God's anointed. When the kingdom was destroyed, Jews hoped God would restore it through a descendant or "Son of David" who would be anointed by God's Spirit as David was. This is how hope for a Messiah began.

Verses 22-36 use resurrection as the identifying sign of the Christ or Messiah. Through an intricate argument, they relate scriptural prophecies to the life of Jesus. The argument is the kind a lawyer in those days would use in court. The speech proves that Jesus, not David, is both the Lord who will rule in heaven and the Messiah sent to save Israel.

The argument in verse 22 begins from "mighty deeds, wonders, and signs" (note the "wonders and signs" in the quotation in 2:19). Those signs showed God's approval of Jesus, as the people themselves witnessed. Yet they rejected the one God approved. Many wondered how Jesus could be the Jewish Messiah if rejected by the Jews themselves. The speech answers that God knew and willed it all beforehand. The sign that God had permitted Jesus' death was his raising him from the dead, fulfilling Ps 16:8-11. The psalm says, "I set the Lord ever before me . . . my body, too, abides in confidence." This might be why Luke's Gospel omits the cry of Jesus in Mark and Matthew, "My God, my God, why have you forsaken me?" (Compare Luke 23:44-49 with Mark 15:33-41 and Matt 27:45-56.) The reason for Jesus' hope is that he knew he would not be abandoned in the nether world, nor would his body corrupt (Ps 16:10 in Acts 2:27).

Verses 29-34 and 36 explain how these psalm verses apply to Jesus. Most people thought David wrote the psalms, so when a psalm says "I" they assumed it meant David. But Luke argues that the prophecy about not corrupting in the grave cannot apply to David himself. For his body never left his well-known tomb in Jerusalem. The argument can only work if Jesus' body, by contrast, is no longer in its tomb. Luke would violently disagree with those who say it would not matter to faith if Jesus' body were still in the tomb. Jesus' empty tomb is the key to Luke's argument. In itself the empty tomb cannot prove that Jesus has been raised (see Luke 24:9-12, 21-27). But if the tomb were not empty, as David's was never emptied, that would end any talk by Luke about Jesus being raised from the dead.

The prophecy that "you will not abandon my soul to the lower world nor let your faithful one see corruption" cannot therefore apply to David as the "my" seems to indicate. When David said "my soul" or "my flesh," he was speaking for the Messiah descended from him. The speech explains that David was prophesying the resurrection of his descendant the Messiah (2:30-31).

David relies on God's promise, given in 2 Sam 7:12-14, in which Nathan prophesies that the throne of David's descendant would stand forever. This promise, repeated in Pss 132:11 and 89:4, became the source of many hopes for the Messiah.

Verses 33-36 use a similar argument from Ps 110:1. The signs that people saw and heard at Pentecost were caused by Jesus, now exalted at God's right hand, pouring out the Holy Spirit. "Sit at my right hand" in Ps 110:1 foretells that David's Lord would exercise the Father's own authority. Since David did not ascend into heaven, this too refers to his descendant Jesus. The conclusion of the whole speech is 2:36: "Therefore let the whole house of Israel know for certain that God has made him both Lord and Messiah, this Jesus whom you crucified."

2:37-41 Response and baptism of three thousand. That the crowd addressed their question to "Peter and the other apostles" indicates that Peter was speaking for them all, as the pope often speaks for the college of bishops today. The reaction to Peter's speech parallels the response to John the Baptist's speech in Luke 3:10-18. Both crowds ask what they should do, both are told to repent, and both are baptized. But John's baptism is only a prophetic sign of the baptism received at Pentecost: "I am baptizing you with water,

but one mightier than I is coming. . . . He will baptize you with the Holy Spirit and fire" (Luke 3:16). The promise of the Holy Spirit was given "to you and to your children" (Acts 2:39)—namely, to Jews from all over the world gathered for the feast and to later generations. "All those far off whomever the Lord our God will call" (2:39) foreshadows the outreach to Gentiles later in Acts. The hearers are to be saved "from this corrupt generation" (2:40). This phrase is from biblical passages about punishment (like Deut 32:5). Luke applies it to the generation that rejected Jesus (Luke 11:29-32, 47-51).

Acts 2:41 mentions the number three thousand to show that a substantial portion of the Jewish people did believe in their Messiah and thus continued as the people of God's promises. This also indicates that salvation has both individual and communitarian dimensions. Each person has to accept his or her salvation, but this is not merely a private matter between the individual and Jesus. One is baptized into God's people and saved as a member of the church.

2:42-47 The Spirit bears fruit in community. Luke gives an idealized picture of the first community, but his message still holds for today. When a Christian community seriously repents of sin and opens itself to the power of the Spirit, this dramatically changes the way Christians live and attracts others to Christianity. The elements of community life Luke highlights are teaching by the apostles, sharing their lives with one another, "breaking of the bread" (Eucharist), and prayer together. They felt the power of the Spirit in many "wonders and signs" (Joel 3:3 in Acts 2:19) through the apostles. This is the first of several summary passages Luke composed to show that the individual stories he reports exemplify more general patterns of behavior.

In 2:44, unanimity and considering all things as common express the ideal of friendship at that time. The point is that all community members had their needs met, and no one hoarded selfishly while others were in want. Luke often stresses another major fruit of the Spirit: the joy and praise of the community. As Jews, the community maintained its links with its Jewish traditions. The first Christians remained faithful to Judaism, were respected by other Jews, and continued winning new Jewish members. Luke emphasizes that people are saved both as individuals and as part of a saved community: "the Lord added to their number those who were being saved" (2:47).

3:1-16 Healing in the name of the Lord Jesus. Peter's speech in Acts 2 foreshadows later events in Acts, as Jesus' speech at Nazareth in Luke 4:16-30 previewed his healings, teachings, and rejection in the Gospel. Thus the cure of the lame man in Acts 3 illustrates the "signs on the earth below" (2:19) that God works through the Spirit's outpouring. It also exemplifies how everyone "who calls on the name of the Lord" will be saved (2:21).

Chapters 3–5 call Peter and John partners, but Peter does most of the acting and talking. Luke seems to be going out of his way to mention John, even when John adds nothing to the action. One reason may be to show that there were two witnesses to the events, since at least two witnesses were needed in some Jewish law cases. Another reason might be Jesus' instruction in Luke 10:1 to go out in pairs. A third might be to bring out the parallel with Paul and Barnabas working as a pair in Acts 13 to 15.

Often Luke shows crowds naturally reacting to miracles by focusing on the human healers, which is still a temptation regarding faith healers today. Both Peter and John in 3:12 and Paul and Barnabas in 14:14-18 corrected the people and told them not to focus on human individuals. The man was not healed because of Peter and John's power or piety but because of faith in the name of the Jesus "you put to death" but God raised. To heal someone by faith does not require power or holiness in the human who prays for healing. It can be done by any Christian who prays in Jesus' name with faith. Today we are witnessing a resurgence of many healings through prayers of ordinary Christians, such as parents praying with their sick children. Sometimes we also hear of faith healers who themselves fall into sin, even though God uses their faith to heal the sick. So in Acts the focus is on God who heals, not on those who pray for healing.

Thus faith healings in Acts are the opposite of magic. They are not a manipulation of power, in which the healer is in control. Faith healing is a form of prayer, as when Peter prayed over the body of Tabitha (Dorcas) be-

fore raising her to life (Acts 9). Healing through prayer and faith, both in Acts and today, is a request of God to heal. It does not force God to heal, but can receive either a yes or no answer according to God's will.

The healing in Acts 3 shows God's vindication of his Servant, Jesus, whom his people had rejected. By healing the cripple when Peter addressed him in Jesus' name, God was showing he had raised Jesus from the dead and was honoring his name (3:13-16).

3:17-26 "Obey the prophet like Moses, that you may be blessed." The speech does not condemn those who rejected Christ. It convicts them of wrongdoing and offers them a chance to repent. Acts 3:17 makes an important distinction between wrongs done to Jesus in his lifetime and rejection of him and his apostles after he was raised. On the cross Jesus had asked his Father to "forgive them; they know not what they do," according to Luke 23:34. Two later speeches differentiate a preresurrection time of ignorance when there was an excuse for not accepting Jesus (17:30 and 13:27). But after God has cleared his Servant's name by raising him from the dead, ignorance is no excuse. Those who reject Jesus a second time after his resurrection deserve to be cut off from God's people (3:22-26). The result for Luke is that Jews who disbelieved that God raised Jesus were "excommunicated" from the chosen people. Therefore only Christian Jews inherited the blessings God had promised his people since the time of Abraham.

The argument in 3:18-21 is similar to those in Acts 2. It claims that God foretold the death of his Messiah in "all the prophets" and used the ignorance of Jews who rejected him to fulfill the prophecies. They can be forgiven if they repent and now accept Jesus as their Messiah (3:19). Repentance can also hasten the long-awaited times of messianic blessings when God will send Jesus back in his second coming. Although the resurrection confirmed Jesus as Messiah, only at the end of the world will his enemies and unbelievers recognize him as Messiah (Luke 21:27). Now he is in heaven from his ascension in Acts 1:9-11 until the final restoration.

The same Greek word can be used both for resurrection and raising up or calling a prophet. Luke puns on "raise up" in Moses' prophecy, "A prophet like me will the Lord, your God, raise up for you from among your own kinsmen" (a loose citation of Deut 18:15 in Acts 3:22). He interprets "raising up" as "resurrecting" the prophet like Moses—that is, Jesus.

Acts 2:23 continues Deut 18:15 with a threat: "Everyone who does not listen to that prophet will be cut off from the people." This verse from "Moses" paraphrases and joins two Old Testament passages, Deut 18:19a, "If any man will not listen to my words which he speaks in my name," and Lev 23:29b, "shall be cut off from his people." It shows how Luke's paraphrasing of Scripture from memory can occasionally make a biblical "point," but in his own wording.

Notice that Luke treats Moses as the first and greatest of the prophets and Jesus as the prophet like Moses. Whoever does not heed the resurrected prophet Jesus (speaking through his apostles) will be cut off from the people (3:23). Acts 3:23 is thus the key to how Luke solves the problem of Jews who do not accept Jesus and how Christianity relates to God's people. Whereas Matthew talks of Christians as a new people replacing the old Israel (Matt 21:43), Luke stresses the continuity in God's people through Jews who accepted Jesus. Thus Acts 2:24-26 announces that Peter's Jewish listeners are parties to the covenant by which all nations will be blessed in Abraham's seed (Gen 22:18). By resurrecting and sending Jesus, God is blessing the Jews as each of them repents.

The introduction mentioned how Acts has a pattern of interruptions that end speeches, but only after everything has been said that Luke wanted mentioned. Those who interrupt Peter in 4:1-3 are Jews who do not believe our bodies will be raised. Acts frequently juxtaposes Jews who believe in resurrection (Pharisees, including Paul) from those who do not (especially the Sadducees, as in 23:6-10). Such unbelievers, who sounded so much like Epicurean philosophers who denied life after death, could hardly be considered good Jews, Luke implies. It is no surprise they did not believe in Jesus' resurrection.

In Acts 4:2, "proclaiming in Jesus the resurrection of the dead" is thematic (see Acts 23:6-8 and 11). Preaching about Jesus as resurrected exemplifies the Jewish belief in resurrection. Though this approach may seem artificial, it is another way that Luke shows the continuity of Christian preaching with true Judaism.

Luke also links Jewish religious leaders with the unbelieving group of Sadducees. Acts 4–5 will show how the apostles take over leadership of God's people from these former leaders.

4:1-22 The apostles obey God, not Jewish religious authorities. Acts 4 focuses especially on the conflict between the old and new leaders of the Jewish people. Luke shows from this incident that the old religious leaders forfeited their claims by rejecting the Messiah God gave them. Since they were disobeying God, the apostles no longer had to obey them but God alone. The apostles replaced them as the new leaders of God's people, in the name of the Jewish Messiah Jesus, who had appointed them (Luke 22:29-30).

The Sanhedrin was the Jewish supreme court and ruling body. The Sanhedrin leaders challenge Peter and John's authority, asking "by what power or in whose name" they have acted (4:7). For this formal charge in a Jewish court, John is needed as a second witness. The confrontation between Peter and John against Jewish leaders who refuse to believe a miracle recalls that between Moses and Aaron against Pharaoh and his magicians in Exod 7–11.

Acts 4:8 mentions Peter received the Holy Spirit for his reply. This fulfills Jesus' prophecy in Luke 12:11-12 that when disciples are dragged before authorities, the Spirit will teach them what to say (see also Luke 21:12-15).

Acts 4:8-12 repeats that the cripple was healed in the name of Jesus, who is "the stone rejected by you the builders which has become the cornerstone" (4:11), as Ps 118:22 had foretold. Salvation comes only through Jesus.

The Jewish leaders were amazed at the boldness of such uneducated and common men (4:13-14). Luke had attributed Peter's boldness to the Holy Spirit (4:8). This boldness is the mark of Jesus' witnesses in Acts (of Peter here and at Pentecost, 2:29; of the community in answer to its prayer in 4:29 and 32; and of Paul at the climactic end of Acts, 28:31). In the helplessness of the Sanhedrin to answer Peter and John, Luke is underlining the bankruptcy of its leadership. Like Pharaoh, the Jewish leaders cannot deny the healing, yet refuse to obey God's will clearly shown in it.

Instead they try to prevent the apostles from spreading the word about Jesus. Peter cannot therefore be considered a rebel when he tells the Sanhedrin he must obey God rather than them. The saying recalls *Antigone*, a play well known in Luke's time, and a similar Old Testament situation in 2 Macc 7:2. The Sanhedrin is helpless to stop the apostles because of the people. In Acts 2–6, "the people" (*ho laos*) is the technical term for God's chosen Jewish people who see the apostolic signs, are impressed with the community, and listen to the sermons, and over whom a contest of leadership is being waged. The Sanhedrin cannot stop the apostles; thus Luke indicates their loss to the apostles of real leadership over "the people."

4:23-31 The community celebrates God's victory through them. The community thanks God for Peter and John's victory, as Moses and the Israelites did after escaping from Pharaoh at the sea (Exod 15). Their prayer celebrates the fulfillment of Ps 2:1-2. According to the Christians' midrashic interpretation, the psalm predicted that kings and rulers, Jews and Gentiles would be helpless against the Lord God and his anointed Messiah. So King Herod and the Jews, and the ruler Pilate with his Gentile Romans, were unable to stop Jesus the Messiah, even though they killed him. In fighting God they fulfilled what God had planned all along (4:24-28).

God's victory even in his Messiah's death reassured the community as they faced new threats from the Sanhedrin. They prayed that as Peter and John had just overcome the Sanhedrin, they could overcome all future threats through God's continued healing, "signs and wonders." God's servant Moses had overcome the Pharaoh by signs and wonders. They pray that new signs and wonders might be done in the name of God's new Servant, Jesus. The community's prayer resulted in a "second Pentecost." The place shook, all were filled with the Spirit, and they spoke God's word with boldness, as Peter had at Pentecost. This was God's stamp of approval on the community despite harassment from Jewish religious leaders. Christians were now as free from the Sanhedrin's leadership as the Israelites had been from the Egyptian Pharaoh.

4:32–5:11 Unity under the apostles, fostered and threatened. The apostles' newly confirmed leadership bears fruit in a community marked by unity of mind and heart and expressed by Christians' putting their possessions at the apostles' disposal. The plot against unity by Ananias and Sapphira is as threatening to their God-given leadership as the revolt of Korah, Dathan, and Abiram had been to Moses' leadership in the desert (Num 16). The death punishment for both groups shows how seriously offensive to God are such threats to community and his appointed leaders. Judas' fate had already illustrated this. As Luke 22:3 says that Satan entered into Judas, so Acts 5:3 asks Ananias, "Why have you let Satan fill your heart . . . ?" Judas bought a field with the money from betraying Jesus and died gruesomely on it (1:18). Ananias cheated on money from the sale of a field and fell dead (5:1-5).

Many find this passage shocking, but Luke would certainly disagree with efforts today to explain away hell or God's punishment. He insists that outrageous and deliberate rebellion against God will be severely punished. God is not mocked. Though this same Luke is known for his stress on God's forgiveness of repentant sinners, we should not overlook his balancing emphasis on a prudent fear of God's power to punish when faced with unrepented sin and rebellion. God will go to any lengths to save sinners who are willing to return to him (Luke 15). But those who refuse to admit their sin and ask forgiveness will suffer the consequences of their separation from God.

In Acts 4:36–5:11, Luke provides contrasting positive and negative examples of surrender of goods to the apostles: Barnabas, and Ananias and Sapphira. Acts 4:36 is the first mention of Barnabas, who later introduces Paul to the apostles (9:26-28). Both the new name he receives from the apostles and his surrendering his money to them signify Barnabas' submission to their leadership. Acts 5:1-11 contrasts Ananias and Sapphira with Barnabas: like him they sold property and ostensibly put the money at the apostles' disposal for the community, but by secretly keeping part for themselves they maintain a hidden independence from the community. In effect, they refused to share fully with them or to submit completely to the apostles' authority. Whether or not unneeded real estate was supposed to be sold for the sake of the community, or goods were to be surrendered before the person's full incorporation, as at Qumran, Ananias and Sapphira did not have to imitate Barnabas' complete submission to the apostles (5:4). By their hypocritical deceit, they "lied not to human beings but to God" (5:4). They sinned against the Holy Spirit (Luke 12:10) in the apostles.

Ananias and Sapphira were in fact challenging the presence of Spirit in the community's midst. Their deaths indicated for Luke that, yes, the Spirit was truly present in the community, and it upheld the apostles' authority. The result was great fear upon "the whole church," the first time this expression is used in Acts.

5:12-16 Third summary: Signs and wonders through the apostles. This is Acts' third summary and linking passage that generalizes from particular incidents to general practices. It brings the apostles' authority to a climax of almost unlimited healing power, like Paul's in 19:11-12. Writing in ways familiar to his Hellenistic readers but sounding a lot like magic, Luke says even Peter's shadow or handkerchiefs that touched Paul's body healed the sick. But 19:13-19 immediately distinguishes Paul's power in verses 11-12 from magic. Likewise, in 5:12-16 Luke expects his readers to remember his careful explanation in 3:12-16 that Peter's healing power was from God in Jesus' name.

Solomon's Portico, where the Christians met, is where Peter had explained the cripple's healing in Acts 3. Some Jews were afraid to join the meetings because they were in direct defiance of the Sanhedrin's order in Acts 4 not to speak further about Jesus. But 5:13-14 stresses that many Jews, both women and men (2:17-18), believed, and that the Jewish people held the community in great respect.

5:17-42 Second confrontation with the Sanhedrin; Gamaliel. The conflict between the old and new leaders of the Jewish people comes to its final head when the high priest and his Sadducee followers arrest the apostles out of envy (5:17-18). Luke shows that God confirms the apostles' leadership by miraculously freeing them from prison and sending them back to the temple to preach to "the people" (5:19-21). Verses 22-26 further mock the helplessness of the Sanhedrin. Its members fear being stoned by the people if they publicly abuse the apostles. When the high priest

complains of their disobedience in continuing to preach Jesus, Peter repeats that they must obey not men but God (5:28-29), who had freed and commanded them to keep preaching about this life (5:20).

Verses 30-32 summarize the Christian witness to God's vindication of the man the Jews had crucified. The words "hanging him on a tree" allude to the curse in Deut 21:22-23 against anyone hanged on a tree. Jews considered that Jesus' crucifixion put him under this scriptural curse and asked how God's Messiah could possibly be cursed by God. In Gal 3:10-14 Paul had had to answer this objection directly. Here in Acts 5:30-32 the response is only indirect, since the curse is not explicitly mentioned. The answer is simply that God raised and exalted the man so disgracefully killed to be Ruler and Savior of Israel. Even though the Old Testament considered people who were crucified as cursed, God willed that his Messiah die this death and then be resurrected. The witnesses for this bold claim are the apostles and the power of the Spirit seen in Jesus' followers.

The high priest and Sadducees, who did not believe in resurrection (4:1-2), are again distinguished from a Pharisee who did, Gamaliel. In 22:3 he is said to be Paul's teacher. The speech portrays Gamaliel as speaking historical wisdom and moderation. It is also an ironic prophecy that opponents of Christianity would be fighting God himself (5:35-39—compare 2 Macc 7:19). Because Luke believes this, he stresses throughout Acts how the Christian cause triumphs no matter what the obstacles. For example, the persecution after Stephen's death in Acts 7 resulted in hastening Christianity's spread in Acts 8. This speech also contrasts Christianity to other messianic movements of the time, which the historian Josephus also mentions, but in a different historical order. The false movements died out with the death of their leaders, but the true one continues to grow because its plan and activity (5:38) are from God.

Luke portrays Gamaliel's advice as an ironic commentary on history, not as advice to be followed by Christian authorities in evaluating spiritual events like apparitions. Gamaliel's principle of having "nothing to do with these men" until their movement either dies out or is confirmed is not a Christian position but that of an unbelieving outsider. One cannot just "wait and see" whether God is acting in or speaking to our time, but must test the fruits and heed those words that correspond to the gospel and church teaching. For example, if God, through apparitions of Mary, is urgently calling Christians to repentance (as many believe he is), a disengaged "wait and see" approach is in effect a negative response to the call. This could be true even though "private revelations" are not binding, as the public revelation of Scripture and tradition is. Genuine private revelations are usually exhortations to live the public revelation more urgently.

The Sanhedrin accepts Gamaliel's "wait and see" advice. They beat the apostles, warn them not to teach, and release them. The apostles' joy at suffering for Jesus is an example for Christians (5:39-41). Obeying God, not the Sanhedrin, they return unhindered to teaching about Jesus the Messiah (5:42). This section of Acts ends with the helplessness of the old leaders of God's people, the Sanhedrin, and the unstoppable preaching of the new, the apostles.

6:1-7 The community needs additional authorities. The apostles have displaced the Sanhedrin as rightful leaders of God's people, but they soon have to expand the leadership. Because of the community's rapid growth, the apostles had to appoint more leaders to help them, as Moses had to do in the desert (Exod 18:17-23). At the same time Luke is showing how church leadership was passed on to a new kind of leader. Like Jesus, the Twelve had all been from Galilee and spoke Hebrew (actually the closely related Aramaic). Jews from all over the world gathered in Jerusalem. Many new Christian Jews were more comfortable with Greek, the international language of that time. The term "Hellenistic" describes people who had Greek language and culture. Jews who used Greek were "Hellenistic Jews," and "Hellenistic Jewish Christians" describes Greek-speaking Jews who became Christians. Just as language group differences have caused friction in French and English Canada, so did they between Aramaic-speaking and Greek-speaking Jews in the Jerusalem Christian community.

The apostles' leadership had been symbolized by their control over the community purse. So this friction is exemplified by charges of unfair distribution of community food between the poor of the two language groups. Although the Twelve speak of praying and preaching while the Seven would wait on tables, that is not in fact what Luke later reports the Seven doing. Stephen has the same gifts of the Holy Spirit, worked similar "signs and wonders," and debated and preached as much as the Twelve (6:8-11 and 7:1-53). Actually, handling the community's goods again symbolizes authority over the community.

The church has added a new set of authorities, Greek-speaking Jews. As the number twelve symbolized the twelve tribes of Israel, the number seven signified universality, since it was considered a "perfect number." The Twelve rooted the church in Israel. The Seven were a sign of the church's outreach to the whole world through those who spoke the world language, Greek. They derive their authority from Jesus' original apostles because they were ordained by them.

Luke ends this account with another summary. Once the church's authority structure has been made more universal, "the word of God continued to spread" and the Jerusalem church "increased greatly" (6:7), beyond the last-mentioned five thousand (in 4:4). Even many priests, who had earlier opposed the Christians (4:1-2), came to believe. On the eve of the church's outreach beyond Jerusalem in Acts 8, Luke pictures the huge Jerusalem community as the restored Israel which was promised in Scripture. It was living the ideal life that Jews since Isaiah had been longing for.

6:8-15 Stephen brought to trial. The new leader, Stephen, soon found himself in conflict with Greek-speaking Jews who did not believe in Christ (6:8-9). They were no match for Stephen's wisdom and Spirit (6:10), as Jesus had promised in Luke 21:15. They falsely accused Stephen of attacking the sacred Jewish institutions of temple and law, and stirred up the people, the elders, and scribes against him (6:11-13). Compare the challenge to Jesus by chief priests, scribes, and elders as he taught the people in the temple (Luke 20:1). Stephen was hauled before the Sanhedrin, as Jesus had been in his passion. The account of Jesus' trial in Luke 22:66-71 had omitted a major incident stressed in Mark 14:55-61 and Matt 25:59-63. It was the false charge by lying witnesses that Jesus had said he could destroy the temple. Now Acts 6:14

mentions that charge against Jesus during Stephen's trial. the temple charge leads into Stephen's speech in 7:1-53.

7:1-53 Stephen's speech to the Sanhedrin. This speech is a major turning point in Acts. The Jewish Sanhedrin rejected and killed the Spirit-filled Stephen, as they had earlier rejected and handed over Jesus. Thus they were rejecting their Messiah a second time, as their ancestors had twice rejected Moses. Stephen's speech presupposes Peter's in Acts 3. Both treat Jesus as "the prophet like Moses" and mention the penalty for rejecting that prophet (Acts 3:23 and 7:39-43). In turn, the Old Testament events mentioned in Stephen's speech are complemented by those in Paul's Acts 13 speech. All this, plus the similar style, structure, and use of the Old Testament, are evidence of Luke's hand in these speeches.

The Old Testament survey pivots around two points. The first is the promise to Abraham that his descendants will be saved from Egypt and receive the land of Israel where they can worship God freely (7:5-7). It is fulfilled in the Moses events (7:17). The second key point is Moses' prophecy, also mentioned in 3:22, that "God will raise up for you from among your kinsmen a prophet like me" (Deut 18:15 in Acts 7:37).

The speech indirectly shows how Jesus is like Moses. It parallels Moses' life to the way Luke's Gospel had described Jesus' life, from their births on. Both grow in wisdom (Acts 7:22 and Luke 2:52) to become "powerful in word and deed" (Acts 7:22 and Luke 24:19). Both Moses and Jesus were disappointed that their own people did not recognize that God wanted to use them as their saviors (Acts 7:25, Luke 13:34-35, and 19:41-44). After Moses was rejected and fled Egypt, God reconfirmed him and sent him back to save them with "wonders and signs" (7:27-36). Acts 7:37 makes explicit the comparison to Jesus' resurrection. After Jesus' rejection and death, God reconfirmed him as Savior. He raised him from the dead and sent him again to save the people from their sins, through preaching, "wonders and signs" (6:8) of Christians like Peter and Stephen, who are filled with Jesus' Spirit and act in his name.

The last part of Stephen's speech recalls the charge in 6:13-14 that he and Jesus were against the temple. It quotes the Old Testament to say that God does not dwell in temples made by hands (Isa 66:1-2 in Acts 7:48-49). It ends by accusing them of being a stiff-necked people (Exod 32:9) who always resisted the Holy Spirit (Isa 63:10). This is what they were doing in resisting the Spirit-filled Stephen. As their ancestors had killed the prophets (Luke 11:47-51), they, the Sanhedrin, had handed Jesus over to be killed (Acts 7:51-52).

These accusations are actually based on the way the Old Testament describes the relationship between God and his people. It emphasizes the people's disobedience, God's long-suffering mercy, warnings through prophets, and the people's refusal to listen (resisting the Holy Spirit, Zech 7:12). Thus it explained why God allowed the chosen people to be exiled. In Acts 7 the accusations explain why many Jewish leaders did not believe in Christ and why they were therefore replaced by the new Christian leaders of God's people.

7:54–8:3 Stephen's martyrdom and the spread of the church. Filled with the Spirit, Stephen witnesses that he saw the resurrected Jesus with God in glory (7:55-56). The reference to the heavens opening indicates a vision, as for Jesus in Luke 3:21-22 and Peter in Acts 10:11. Stephen's reference to the Son of Man at God's right hand (7:56) is the only use of "Son of Man" in the New Testament that is not on Jesus' lips. Casting Stephen out of the city and killing him parallel the casting of Jesus out of Nazareth in Luke 4:29 and his crucifixion outside Jerusalem. Luke draws many other parallels also. Stephen's "Lord Jesus, receive my spirit" (Acts 7:59) is like Jesus' "Father, into your hands I commend my spirit" (Luke 23:46). Both forgive those who kill them: "Father, forgive them; they do not know what they are doing" (Jesus in Luke 23:34), and "Lord, do not hold this sin against them" (Stephen in Acts 7:60). Notice also how Stephen prays to Jesus as Jesus had prayed to his Father.

These prayers of forgiveness are very important for Luke. He links Jesus' prayer for forgiveness to the second chance offered to the Jerusalem Jews in Acts 2 and 3. And Luke implies that Stephen's prayer was responsible for Saul (later called Paul) being forgiven and chosen to preach Christ (9:4-6). That is why he mentions Saul right after Stephen's prayer in 7:60.

It is also one reason he mentions here the resulting persecution that scattered the church throughout Judea and Samaria (as Jesus had predicted in 1:8). The persecution did not force the apostles out of Jerusalem. It only expelled Stephen's fellow Greek-speaking leaders, such as Philip (8:4-5). Saul was also involved in this scattering of the church, but still on the persecuting side (8:3). Thus ends the Jerusalem phase of Luke's account of the growth and spread of Christianity.

PERSECUTION AND EXPANSION IN JUDEA AND SAMARIA

Acts 8:4–9:31

8:4-8 Philip in Samaria. Paragraphs like Acts 8:1-3 are transitional. They both sum up the preceding section and introduce the next one. This notice that persecution scattered preachers throughout Judea and Samaria both concludes the Jerusalem phase of Acts and prepares for Philip's travels to Samaria. At this point Saul (Paul) plays an ironic part as persecutor in the spread of Christianity.

For persecution could not stop the word from spreading. The expulsion of Philip, one of the Seven (Acts 6:3-6), caused him to move on to the city of Samaria. Samaritans were descendants of Israelites and foreigners living in Israel after most of the people were exiled. In Samaria Philip proclaimed the Messiah to that despised "mixed race." He drew crowds by what he said and by signs, especially exorcisms and healings of cripples.

8:9-25: Simon the magician misunderstands miracles. These healings led to the comparison and meeting between Philip and Simon, a practitioner of occult magic. Simon is infamous in later Christian tradition as the head of a sect that combined Christian and pagan elements and became a rival to Christianity. This is the first of several confrontations in Acts between occult magic and Christian healings (also 13:4-12 and 19:11-19).

First-century magicians differed from those today who perform magic shows by sleight of hand and clever tricks. Magicians tried to manipulate life by occult power so as to accomplish whatever they wanted. The magicians themselves were in control, and effects were ascribed to their power. Thus Simon focused attention on himself and not on God.

In comparing Philip and Simon Magus, Luke emphasizes how much more impressed the crowds were by the Spirit-filled Philip's deeds. Even Simon was awed. It is not clear how this account relates to later traditions about Simon as an archheretic. They seem to presuppose some Christian elements in Simon's sect. So this identification of Simon as at least a temporary Christian could account for those Christian aspects. Contemporary cults have a similar mixture of Christian with occult and non-Christian elements.

Acts 8:16 distinguishes the coming of the Spirit from Christian baptism in the name of the Lord Jesus. This has caused much confusion among interpreters and theologians. Usually Luke and the rest of the New Testament (e.g., John 3:5 and Titus 3:5-7) link receiving the Spirit with being baptized as a Christian (Acts 2:38 and 9:17-18). But Luke also mentions receiving the Spirit before baptism (Acts 10:44-48 and 11:15-17) and after (here and in Acts 19:1-7). In these cases Luke is making some other point besides the meaning or practice of baptism. The point in Acts 8:16 is to show confirmation by God and by the apostles of Philip's unexpected outreach to despised Samaritans (see 10:44 and 19:6).

This story cannot be used to prove that a second step of receiving the Holy Spirit must follow Christian baptism before one can become a complete Christian. Nor can it prove the separate sacrament of confirmation, since the church and the rest of Acts and the New Testament teach that Christians receive the Spirit in baptism. Such uses would fail to respect Luke's limited intent. He would not want these stories used to solve problems of baptism, since his only concern was to show that God ratified the church's outreach to the Samaritans and non-Jews.

Though Acts 8:17-19 says only that the Samaritans received the Spirit when the apostles imposed hands on them, Simon the magician wanted to buy this power. The story implies that the manifestations of receiving the Spirit were awesome to Simon. He was even more impressed by what happened through Peter than by the healings through Philip.

The account shows the difference between manifestations of the Spirit and magic and that the Spirit's power is God's free gift for the sake of those who are helped by it. It cannot be bought, controlled, or manipulated as in magic occult arts. Simon the magician becomes an example for Luke's readers (even today) of how we cannot mix Christianity with pagan or occult practices and attitudes. Once that point is made, Luke does not even bother to tell us what later happened to Simon.

8:26-40 Philip and the Ethiopian eunuch. The story of Philip and the African eunuch makes extensive use of Luke's vocabulary for journeying and the imagery of "the Way" to imply the spread of the word and to locate Philip in Caesarea where he next appears in Acts 21:8. Luke uses this story to foreshadow the full-scale turning to pagans in Acts 10–11 and 15. Though 8:26-40 also relates a pagan's conversion, Luke does not stress this event as much as he did the "pagan Pentecost" for Cornelius' household in Acts 10.

As often in Acts, God takes the initiative by directing Philip through an angel (compare Acts 12:7), or a dream or vision (Acts 16:9-10), or the Holy Spirit (8:39). Luke wants to show clearly that God, not mere human decisions, guided the spread of Christianity.

Not only was the Ethiopian a pagan, but he had been castrated. This was an added block to his fitness to enter the assembly of God (Deut 23:1-2). He is another example of the outcasts to which Jesus and his followers reach out in Luke-Acts. As a vision later told Peter (Acts 10:15), "What God has purified you are not to call unclean," that is, unfit to associate with.

Because the Ethiopian was reading from Isaiah, Luke probably considered him a pagan Godfearer (as Cornelius in Acts 10). Godfearers were unable or unwilling to become full Jews, but were attracted by Jewish belief in one God and by their high morality.

Luke also insists repeatedly that the Scriptures need explanation. Private interpretation is not always sufficient. The groups of disciples on the road to Emmaus and at Jerusalem both needed the risen Jesus to interpret the Scriptures for them (Luke 24:25-32 and 44-47). Acts 13:27 says the Jews in Jerusalem and their rulers failed to understand the prophets they read every sabbath. So here Philip has to explain to the eunuch that Isa 53:7-8 referred not to Isaiah but to Jesus (as Acts 2 had explained that Pss 16 and 110 referred not to David but to Jesus) and prophesied his self-sacrificing death (Acts 8:31-35).

The way Philip taught the Ethiopian is un-doubtedly the way Christians taught all their converts, including pagans. Even pagans in the first century put great value on fulfillment of predictions as signs that a religion was true. Beginning from this Scripture, Christians "proclaimed Jesus to" their converts (8:35).

Luke relates the snatching of Philip away after baptizing the eunuch as a further sign that the baptism was God's will.

9:1-9 Saul is called by the risen Jesus. We have said that Luke repeats major events up to three times in Acts, usually with minor variations. He will retell this conversion of Saul (9:1-29) in speeches in Acts 22:3-21 and 26:9-20. He thus underlines its importance and highlights several meanings in it. When we compare the three versions of Paul's call in Acts 9, 22, and 26, the unchanged core has these events. The high priest commissioned Saul to imprison men and women of "the Way," which seems to have been the first name Christians had. On his journey to Damascus he was thrown to the ground, surrounded by a light, and heard a voice saying, "Saul, Saul, why do you persecute me?" Only Paul saw the light and heard the voice. This is similar to modern apparitions: at Fatima, Lourdes, and the reputed apparitions of Medjugorje only the visionaries see and hear the apparition even when others are present. In Acts 9:7 Paul's companions only heard the voice, and in 22:9 and 26:13-14 they only saw the light. (Luke does not seem bothered by this inconsistency.)

All three versions emphasize that Paul is to witness especially to the Gentiles.

Christ's message, "Saul, Saul, why do you persecute me?", clearly shows that Christ is identified with Christians (compare Matt 25:31-46). What is done to them is done to him. Luke mentions this three times, showing how important it is to Acts. This evidence is often overlooked by those who say Luke lacks Paul's teaching that Christ lives in Christians.

The Lord called and appeared to Paul directly. Yet he required his baptism and reception into the Christian community. God overruled Ananias' objections and insisted he go to Saul, just as God would overrule Peter's objections about going to the Gentile Cornelius in Acts 10.

As Luke so often stresses, God's action took place as Ananias, Saul, Cornelius, and

1049

Peter were praying. Even today, Luke-Acts can teach Christians how important it is to let God show us his priorities as we listen to him in private prayer. Often in prayer we will find our own priorities and projects changed by God's different plans for us.

The translation in 9:18, "things like scales fell from his eyes," misses the way the Greek noun for what is peeled off Paul's eyes echoes the verb for peeling off the blinded Tobit's cataracts (Tob 3:17 and 11:13).

9:10-31 Paul switches to the Christian side. It is not easy to harmonize the dates and information about where Paul went after his call that are given in Acts 9 and Gal 1:11-24. Nor are Acts 15 and Gal 2 easy to reconcile regarding the Jerusalem Council. Luke's information cannot be simply dismissed, even when it does not agree with what Paul himself says, for two reasons. First, Gal 1–2 are obviously written in a state of passion and defensiveness. Paul, not Luke, may be going out of his way to prove a point, namely, his independence from and equality with the Jerusalem apostles. Second, it is not always clear how the information given in Galatians corresponds to that in Acts. Nor is it even clear to what extent the same or multiple occasions are meant.

At any rate, Acts 9 focuses on Saul's immediate reversal from persecutor of Christians (see Gal 1:13, 23; Phil 3:6; 1 Cor 15:9) to preacher to the Jews at Damascus about the Christ. What Paul had persecuted the Christians for teaching, he himself now preaches. Luke stresses everyone's amazement at this turnabout. In response to Paul's aggressive witness and arguing that Jesus is the Son of God and the Messiah, the Jews naturally plot against him. 2 Cor 11:33 also mentions Paul's escape over the wall in a basket.

Luke reminds his readers how the Jerusalem Christians realistically feared Paul at first, not believing he was really one of them. Barnabas is the link between Paul and the Twelve. In Acts 4 he had submitted to the apostles. Now he introduces Paul to them and explains Paul's call and his witness to Jesus in Damascus. Because of Barnabas, they accept Paul, who confronts the Hellenistic Jews in Jerusalem as he had in Damascus. The Christians therefore have to save Paul from Jewish plots in Jerusalem also. They send him home to Tarsus.

Usually Acts uses "church" for individual communities, but 9:31 refers to "the church throughout all Judea, Galilee and Samaria." This is another Lukan summary and transition, and describes the church as at peace, "walking [or journeying] in the fear of the Lord," and growing through the Spirit.

TO THE GENTILES: PETER AND CORNELIUS, BARNABAS AND SAUL; THE JERUSALEM COUNCIL

Acts 9:32–15:35

9:32-43 A healing and raising through Peter in Lydda and Joppa. These healing accounts have two main functions in this part of Acts. First, they show how signs helped spread Christianity in Judea and along the Mediterranean coast. Second, they account for Peter's presence in the seacoast town of Joppa when Cornelius in Caesarea (up the coast) sends for him. Thus they set the stage for the pivotal Acts 10–11 report that legitimates the Gentile mission.

Both healing stories use the same command in Greek, "rise" (translated by the NAB as "get up" at 9:34, and "rise up" at 9:40) which recalls Jesus' resurrection. The healing of Aeneas is told simply, according to the basic form of healing narratives. Luke gives the name, sickness, and length of time Aeneas was paralyzed. Jesus had healed paralytics on his own authority (Luke 5:24-25), but Peter tells Aeneas that Jesus Christ heals him and commands him to rise and make his bed. The result is immediate. Whereas Jesus' healings often led to wonder but not to full belief in him, Aeneas' cure resulted in many conversions to "the Lord" (Jesus).

The story of the raising of Tabitha (Dorcas) uses language from Elisha's raising of the widow's son in 2 Kgs 4:32-37. In Kings, the prophet Elisha was alone with the dead person, as Peter was. Each prayed. 2 Kings and Acts 9 both mentioned the dead person opening his or her eyes. But whereas Elisha laid himself on the boy, Peter simply commanded the widow to get up. The resuscitation in Kings was gradual and took two tries by the prophet. Tabitha simply opened her eyes and sat up (as the widow's son did in Luke 7:15). Both Elisha and Peter presented the resuscitated person to the loved ones.

Luke-Acts frequently alludes to the Elijah-Elisha stories. They provide a good model for wonder-working prophets and their disciples that can be applied to Jesus and his followers. And, as Sir 48:15 says, despite two such prophets "the people did not repent . . . until they were rooted out of their land and scattered all over the earth." Luke 21:24 predicts something similar with the destruction of Jerusalem.

Acts 9:36–10:48 thus parallels Luke 7:1-17 in having back-to-back stories about a centurion and raising a widow or her son.

10:1-8 The vision of Cornelius. Acts 10–11 and 15 are major turning points in Acts. They legitimize the Gentile Christian church by grounding it in the approval of Peter and the Twelve. More radically still, Acts 10–11 show that God himself clearly was dispensing pagans from having to become circumcised Jews first before joining his people. The very difficulty Peter had accepting this brings home the fact that it was God's idea. God had made the law that every male of his people must become circumcised (Gen 17:10-14). Now God was repealing that requirement because the final days of fulfillment have come. The expected Holy Spirit is now poured out upon all flesh (Acts 2:17-18 and 10:44-47). This makes the entrance rite of circumcision superfluous, since the Spirit purifies even unclean pagans (see Acts 10:15).

Cornelius' vision is the first of two complementary visions that laid the groundwork for Peter's preaching to him. God takes all the initiative. Luke is defending the church from the charge of human tampering with God's law by letting pagans remain uncircumcised.

Cornelius is like the centurion Jesus helps in Luke 7. He both prays to God and helps the Jewish people (Acts 10:2). Both Cornelius and Peter are praying when this epoch-turning event takes place. Luke again impresses on his readers the importance of prayer. It readies humans for the major events in his Gospel and Acts. Luke implies that if we too are to be able to hear God's call and receive his gifts, we must pray.

10:9-23 The corresponding vision of Peter. The next day Peter is praying and thinking of food. Going into a trance, he has a vision of food that is symbolic. Seeing animals that the Old Testament calls unclean and forbids Jews to eat (e.g., Lev 11), Peter

is told to kill and eat. He protests, like the prophet Ezekiel (Ezek 4:14), that he has never eaten unclean food. The heavenly voice's answer shocks Jewish sensibilities, including Peter's. He should not call unclean what God has made clean. Luke stresses Peter's consternation over the meaning of this enigmatic vision. God had to repeat it three times to get through to Peter. Acts 10:28 shows that the vision refers to admitting "unclean" pagans or Gentiles. "What God has made clean" (10:15) must allude to the Spirit's transforming action upon Gentiles as well as on Jews (10:44-47 and 11:15-17).

10:24-33 Peter goes to Caesarea. This account reminds Luke's readers how hard it was for the original Jewish-Christian church leaders to relate to non-Jews. It gives precedents in Peter's life for Paul's interactions with Gentiles.

Thus Peter rejects the pagan's prostration to him. He tells him he is also human (10:25-26), just as Barnabas and Paul reject the pagans' treatment of them as gods with the words, "We are of the same nature as you, human beings" (14:11-15).

The second apologetic point is in Acts 10:28. It shows Peter's awareness how improper and against all custom it was for Jews to associate closely with non-Jews (the same problem as in Gal 2:12). But the triple vision of "unclean" food had shown Peter not to call any human being unfit for sacred things. Even though Gentiles sullied themselves with idol worship, the Spirit purified them, so that they, as well as Jews, could approach God. Consequently, there was no reason to exclude Gentiles, once they had been made fit to approach God.

This theme of clean and unclean runs throughout Luke and Acts and is hard for us moderns to appreciate. It recalls a more primitive sense of what is sacred and profane than is common today. Recall the former Catholic prohibition against touching the sacred host by hands other than the priest's. Only consecrated hands should touch the consecrated host, it was felt.

In the first century many people were considered profane and unfit to partake in Jewish temple worship and assemblies. They included those who did not keep the purity laws of washing and foods, who were lepers or mutilated or eunuchs, Samaritans or

Roman tax collectors or notorious sinners (like prostitutes), those possessed by unclean spirits, or Gentile idol worshipers. All these people are the focus of cleansing by Jesus in Luke and the Spirit in Acts. They are all invited to God, but first they are cleansed from what makes them unfit to approach God. Luke is famous for his compassion for sinners and outcasts. But neither Luke nor Jesus himself is soft on the presence of sin or on involvement with pagan or immoral practices or the occult. Levi had to leave his tax collecting, the sinful woman her sinning. The possessed were exorcised. Gentiles had to give up both their associations with paganism and their sexual immorality. (That was a major charge both Jews and Christians made against pagans.)

Cornelius recognizes the need to change when he tells Peter that he and his pagan household are ready to obey whatever commands God has for them through Peter (10:33).

10:34-43 Peter's speech to Cornelius' household. The theological core of Peter's speech is from the Old Testament: "God shows no partiality" (as judge—Deut 10:17). As Paul does in Rom 2:11 and Gal 2:6, Luke applies this statement to God's accepting not only Jews but Gentiles who act rightly. Acts 10:34-35 is close to Rom 2:10-16. God is not an unjust judge. He will not favor an unjust Jew over a just Gentile, but in every nation the one who fears God and acts uprightly is acceptable to God (10:35).

Acts 10:36-43 summarizes Christian preaching about Christ to Gentiles. God gave the good news of peace through Jesus Christ (10:36, notice the use of Christ as Jesus' second name). He is "Lord of all" (both Jews and Gentiles, 10:36). Next come Jesus' ministry, death, resurrection, and commissioning of the apostles (10:37-42). Finally the speech recalls the witness of the Old Testament prophets that all who believe in him (Jews or Gentiles) will receive forgiveness through his name (10:43). As the speech began with the Pauline kind of teaching found in Rom 2:10-16, it ends echoing Paul's forgiveness or salvation by faith in Jesus.

Acts 10:39 shows Luke's special focus on the apostles as witnesses. Verse 40 is another allusion to Deut 21:22-23, the curse on him who hangs on a tree (see Acts 5:30). The gospel message continues in 10:40-42 to in-

clude not just the resurrection (where Mark ended) but the command to apostles to witness that God has established the risen Jesus as "judge of the living and the dead" (10:42). Acts 17:31 and 2 Tim 4:1 confirm that preaching to pagans stressed Jesus as ultimate judge of everyone's actions.

10:44-11:18 "Pentecost" for the pagans. The Acts 10 outpouring of the Spirit on the Gentiles strictly parallels the first Pentecost in Acts 2. The Jews with Peter are amazed that Gentiles received the same gift of the Spirit as they. The pagans also speak in tongues and tell of God's wonders, as the apostles had. The difference is that the first Pentecost for the 120 mentioned no water baptism. Everyone after the 120 who received the Spirit were also baptized with water as a reception into the church (10:47-48). God, however, had again taken the initiative. No one baptized uncircumcised pagans until God showed by the visible sign of tongues that he had already given them the Holy Spirit.

The falling of the Spirit on Gentiles is like what happened on Pentecost "at the beginning" (11:15). It also fulfills Jesus' prophecy in Acts 1:5 that "you will be baptized with the Holy Spirit."

11:19-30 Outreach to Antioch and return of help to Jerusalem. After the principle of admitting Gentiles into the church is established, Acts 11:19-30 provides a narrative link back to 8:4 and mentions again the geographical spread of the church that resulted from the persecution after Stephen's death. Whereas Acts 1-8 had concentrated on the Jerusalem church and its missionaries, Acts 11 focuses on the second great missionary church, Antioch in northern Syria on the Mediterranean Sea. The first missionaries to Antioch spoke only to Jews, but Christians from the island of Cyprus and from Cyrene in African Libya won over many Greeks as well. The Jewish mother church in Jerusalem sent Barnabas, who also came from Cyprus, to investigate this unexpected development. Once Barnabas confirmed this new kind of church which included Gentiles, he got Paul to help with it. Antioch is where the name "Christian" was first used, presumably because the influx of Gentiles distinguished that church from Jewish communities.

When Christian prophets warned of coming famine, the Antioch church returned help to the churches of Judea. Thus they showed their gratitude for the missionaries sent to them.

The use of "presbyters" (or "elders") in 11:30 is the first time this term is applied to Christian leaders. Acts 4–6 and 23–25 use it for Jewish leaders, usually members of the Sanhedrin. In the Acts 15 Jerusalem Council, "presbyters" and "apostles" are paired. Here and in Acts 16–21 "presbyters" refers to Christian leaders with no mention of apostles. Luke's only use of "bishop" or "overseer" for Christian leaders is in Acts 20:28 as a synonym for the elders Paul set up in Ephesus. It took until the second century for our standard "bishops, presbyters, and deacons" to become established as fixed leadership terms.

12:1-19 Herod kills James and imprisons Peter. Stephen is the first martyr in Acts 6. James, the brother of John, is the first of the Twelve to be martyred. Herod who killed him also arrested Peter. (This is a different Herod from the one who killed John the Baptist and tried Jesus. That was Herod Antipas; this is Herod Agrippa, the brother of Herodias who married Herod Antipas and caused the Baptist's beheading in Mark 6:14-29.) The portrayal of "the Jews" as hostile in 12:3 is relatively new in Luke-Acts. "The people" in 12:4 and "the Jewish people" in 12:11 are also described as enemies, in contrast to "the church" whose fervent prayers for Peter's escape triumph over Herod's plans and prison and Jewish hostility. The first negative mention of "the Jews" was their attempt to kill the newly converted Paul in 9:23, and "the Jews" will be hostile for much of Paul's career (Acts 14, 17–26, 28). Like Jesus, Peter is arrested around Passover time. God frees Peter as he will later free Paul and Silas (16:25-34).

We see Luke's humor in the spectacle of Peter left knocking at the door while believers inside argue whether Rhoda was hallucinating or seeing an angel. The comic touch emphasizes how unexpected Peter's deliverance was.

James is probably head of the Jerusalem church by now, for Peter says to report his release to James. Herod's execution of Peter's guards underlines his cruelty and prepares for the fear of Paul's Philippian jailer when he thought Paul had escaped in 16:27.

12:20-23 Herod is punished by a gruesome death. Though Herod died later, Luke mentions his death here to show how God punished this persecutor, before Acts turns from Peter to Barnabas and Saul. Luke associates Herod's death with the blasphemy of the people calling him a god and not man. For not giving the glory to God, Herod died of worms. In the Bible worms were the fate of blasphemers and persecutors like Antiochus (2 Macc 9:9). Luke's contemporary Josephus gives a more detailed version of Herod Agrippa's death (*Antiquities* 19:343-50). He too mentions how the people flattered Herod as a god and how he died of stomach pain. Verse 24 is another summary verse and contrasts Herod's death with the continued spread of the word of God.

Acts 12:25 is unclear and the text is uncertain. Perhaps the best translation is to read "to Jerusalem" with the following phrase about completing their mission, instead of according to the more normal word order after "they returned," thus: "After Barnabas and Saul completed their relief mission to Jerusalem, they returned [to Antioch], taking with them John, who is called Mark." For Barnabas and Saul were mentioned in Jerusalem in 11:30; John Mark's mother lives in Jerusalem (12:12); and immediately after this verse, in 13:1, Barnabas and Saul appear in Antioch, from where their first missionary journey began (13:2-4) with John Mark as assistant (13:5).

13:1-12 The Spirit chooses missionaries and punishes a false prophet. When Acts 13:4 says Barnabas and Saul were "sent forth by the Holy Spirit," this does not mean according to their private inspirations. The Spirit worked through the leaders of the community fasting and praying together for guidance. Through a prophecy to these five leaders, the Spirit chose Barnabas and Saul. The leaders then commissioned them, which implies that they were accountable to these leaders for the mission. Their report to the Antioch church on their return confirms this (Acts 14:26-27).

Luke here provides a model for how church leaders should make decisions through fasting and prayer together and be accountable to one another. Thus they will get their decisions from God and not merely human planning. Being answerable to other leaders ensures that a person is really hearing God and not being deceived. A few parishes today have tried to follow Luke's model and have found extraordinary fruit.

On the island of Cyprus, Barnabas and Saul encountered the Jewish magician and false prophet Bar-Jesus (which means "son of Jesus," the Greek equivalent of the common Jewish name Joshua). The magician tried to turn the proconsul away from "the faith." (This is a post-Pauline expression referring to the Christian religion rather than the act of faith, as in Paul's writings; see Acts 6:7 and 14:22). Saul used a punishing sign against him as Peter had against Ananias and Sapphira in Acts 5. Luke mentions that Saul was "filled with the Holy Spirit" and the magician was temporarily blinded. This sign converted the governor. Somewhat surprisingly, Acts 13:12 calls this sign "the teaching about the Lord" (compare Mark 1:27). Teaching involves more than just words. Powerful signs confirm its truth.

This is the first use of the name Paul in Acts. Verse 9 is the transition from the Jewish name Saul to the better-known Roman name Paul: "Saul, also known as Paul."

13:13-43 Paul's first major sermon: Antioch in Pisidia. At the beginning of the first journey, Barnabas is named before Saul, implying he was leader. Already in 13:13, Luke focuses on Paul, merely including Barnabas among "his companions." The John who abandoned them (13:13) is also called Mark (12:12). Mark was his Roman name, John his Jewish (compare the Roman "Paul" and the Jewish "Saul"). Mark, traditionally known as the author of the Gospel of Mark, was Barnabas' cousin (Col 4:10). Barnabas and Paul split up over Mark in 15:36-41, but in Phlm 24, Paul refers to Mark as his fellow worker. Acts 12:12 and 1 Pet 5:14 are evidence that Mark also knew Peter.

Antioch in Pisidia is part of the Roman province of Galatia in Asia Minor. It should not be confused with Antioch in Syria, where the church commissioned Barnabas and Saul. Several Hellenistic cities were named Antioch after the Greek emperor Antiochus. Going first to the synagogue and being invited to preach on the sabbath is Paul's basic approach in Acts, as it was Jesus' in the Gospel (Luke 4:16-21).

As Paul's "inaugural address," this speech is similar to Peter's at Pentecost in Acts 2. It summarizes the main Christian preaching to Jews, which was based on scriptural precedents and arguments. Both Acts 13 and 2 use the same Ps 16:10 text, "You will not suffer your faithful one to undergo corruption" (13:35). They argue that the promises are fulfilled in Jesus who was resurrected, not in David who did see corruption. This further exemplifies how Luke parallels Paul and Peter.

Paul's summary of Jesus' mission begins with John the Baptist (13:23-25) and emphasizes Jesus' passion. It stresses the failure of the people and their leaders in Jerusalem to recognize him, thus unknowingly fulfilling the prophets they read every sabbath. It names as primary witnesses those who came with Jesus from Galilee to Jerusalem as ensuring continuity with Jesus' mission (see 1:22).

Acts 13:38-39 hints at Paul's teaching on justification by faith. Through Jesus, forgiveness of sins is being proclaimed "to you." Everyone who believes in him will be justified from all those things from which "you" could not be justified through the law of Moses. The speech ends with a warning against cynical unbelief, quoting Hab 1:5 (Acts 13:40-41).

The first reaction is positive. Many were converted and the whole city turned out to hear Paul on the next sabbath.

13:44-52 Jewish persecution and Gentile acceptance. But other Jews were jealous and caused trouble. Paul and Barnabas (notice Paul is mentioned first) say they will turn to the Gentiles because of Jewish rejection. Acts reports three such statements, the other two in 18:6 and in the finale at 28:25-28. Repetition indicates emphasis, as we have seen.

Acts 13:47 applies Isa 49:6 to Paul: "I will make you as a light to the nations." Simeon had used this same passage for Jesus in Luke 2:32. Similarly, Acts 26:23 says that the Christ after rising must "proclaim light to our people and to the Gentiles." Christians like Paul and ourselves share in Christ's mission of being God's servant and light to the Gentiles.

This news causes Gentile rejoicing and conversions and the spread of God's word. Some Jews cause Paul and Barnabas to be expelled from the territory. Their gesture of shaking the dust from their feet recalls Jesus' instructions in Luke 10:10-12. The episode ends on the high note of being full of joy and the Spirit (13:52).

14:1-7: Success and persecution in Iconium. In Iconium, about eighty miles from Pisidian Antioch, we find a similar pattern. Through bold preaching, signs and wonders, Paul and Barnabas win large numbers of Jews and Greeks in the synagogue. The unpersuaded Jews then incite the pagans against them. The city divides between those siding with the Jews and those with the "apostles." Some plot to kill them. Luke often stresses how the Gospel divides people into those who accept and those who reject it. Conversion is a totally free response, he thus implies. Persecution again results in spreading the word, this time to Lystra and Derbe, each twenty-five to thirty miles distance. Note also how Acts 14:4 and 14:14 describe Paul and Barnabas as "apostles," a term Luke usually reserves for the Twelve. He may have had the word "apostle" in his source and not thought of changing it.

14:8-18 Healing of a lame man and preaching in Lystra. Paul and Barnabas worked many "signs and wonders" (14:3). Luke focuses on this healing of a lame man to parallel Peter's first healing in Acts 3. Both involved looking closely, faith to be saved, an order to stand, jumping up and walking. Both times the crowds focus on the two "healers," Peter and John or Paul and Barnabas. Both Peter and Paul tell the crowds not to focus on them but on God. The difference is that Jews tended to concentrate on Peter's and John's piety or power, whereas pagans ignorantly treat Paul and Barnabas as gods. Luke again highlights comic aspects of the scene, mocking pagan ignorance and worship of divine men.

The Lystra speech is a good example of typical preaching to pagans by both Jews and Christians. It stresses the folly of worshiping humans or many gods. It emphasizes the one living God who created all things and revealed himself through creation (a kind of "natural theology"). In fact, Jews could have given this speech, since it does not mention Jesus or Christianity. This illustrates how New Testament religion flows from the Old Testament and Judaism. Both have the same basic beliefs about God and creation and prayer and morality. They differ over Jesus as Christ and Savior.

14:19-28 End of first mission and return to Antioch in Syria. With incredible fickleness the crowds turn from worshiping Paul to stoning him. After the Jews incited them to stone Paul, they drag him out of town (cf. Stephen in Acts 7). Stoning is usually fatal. Lest anyone dismiss this as pious legend, 2 Cor 11:25 confirms that Paul was stoned. It also mentions three shipwrecks, which were usually as fatal as plane crashes today.

Paul and Barnabas exemplify remarkable courage by going right back to where they had been beaten. Nor were they irresponsible wandering evangelists. In each town they taught and built up church communities and installed leaders called presbyters or elders. They solidify conversions by teaching and by a community with authority structures that enable it to carry on after the preachers have left. Luke has thus given his readers an example of how evangelism should be done.

Finally, the missionaries return to their home church and report on their mission. This shows that Paul and Barnabas are accountable to the Antioch church. It also puts the prestige of that major missionary center behind Paul's work in Asia.

15:1-21 The Gentile controversy and the Council of Jerusalem. As the mission in Asia Minor was accountable to the Antioch church, it in turn was accountable to the mother church in Jerusalem. Some converted Judean Pharisees objected to the Antioch practice of baptizing uncircumcised pagans. Acts 15 portrays the debate as a question of salvation—no salvation without circumcision. Luke does not cover over disagreements as he is often accused of doing. He shows Paul and Barnabas in violent dissension from this position.

The so-called Council of Jerusalem opens with a report of the fruits of the Antioch practice. The Pharisees insist on circumcision and the law for Gentile Christians. After much argument, Peter recounts (for the third time) how God gave the Spirit to the Gentiles through his ministry, having cleansed their hearts by faith. Therefore they are no longer unclean or unworthy to enter God's presence in worship, as some Jews felt. Peter sounds a lot like Paul: "On the contrary, we believe that we are saved through the grace of the Lord Jesus, in the same way as they" (15:11).

Building on Peter's theological principle, Barnabas and Paul relate their experience. God worked signs and wonders through them among the Gentiles, as he had through Moses in the Exodus. Experience shows this approach bears good fruit.

James gives the clinching argument. He is the brother of Jesus and the leader of the Jerusalem church by this time. He was known as an exemplary Jewish leader. If Luke can show that James approved of Gentile Christianity, he can take the sting out of charges against Paul. For Gal 2:12 proves that people from James' community were the ones who objected to Antioch practices toward Gentile Christians.

Scripture justifies the Antioch practice, according to the James argument. "The words of the prophets agree with this" (15:15). It uses the Greek translation of Amos 9:11-12 to claim that Scripture foretold both the restoration of Israel and then the conversion of the rest of the human race to the Lord Jesus. In other words, Scripture had predicted the events described in Acts 1-6 (Israel's restoration) and 11-15 (Gentile conversions). All are according to God's plan.

Therefore Christians should not put obstacles to Gentile conversions. They should ask only the compromises needed to enable Christian Jews to associate in table fellowship with non-Jewish Christians. Three concern kosher regulations and avoiding meat sacrificed to idols. The fourth has to do with illicit sex (*porneia* in Greek); its import is not totally clear. It probably refers to marriage within degrees of kinship forbidden to Jews, hence "unlawful marriage," as the New American Bible translates it. But others see a reference to ordinary sexual immorality, for which pagans were often criticized by Jews. New Testament letters frequently charge pagan converts to change their sexual ways. Chief among practices condemned were fornication, adultery, prostitution, and homosexual practices, which all undermined the family. New Testament morality was just as countercultural in the first century as it is to popular morality today. But the stipulations asked converts to change only what threatened Christian community or its basic unit, the family.

If the meeting in Acts 15 refers to the same meeting that Paul mentions in Gal 2:1-10, then this compromise (to facilitate table fellowship and community between Christian Jews and Gentiles in mixed churches) may refer to a later problem and meeting. Perhaps it refers to the one about eating with Gentile Christians mentioned in Gal 2:11-16 (whose solution is not stated), which gets linked with the first meeting in this one account. Though Paul makes no mention of it in his letters, the "Apostolic Decree" was in effect when Luke wrote Acts and into the second century.

The reference in 15:21 to Moses read throughout the civilized world probably implies that these basic requirements for pagans who associate with Jews were nothing new. They were probably already accepted by such pagans throughout the empire. Therefore, they would be no obstacle to Gentile conversions.

15:22-35 Letters and delegation to Antioch. Silas is first introduced as a leader and prophet whom the Jerusalem church chose to accompany Paul and Barnabas and to bring the "Apostolic Decree" to Antioch. Only a few maverick manuscripts have verse 15:34, "But Silas decided to remain there," or the like. Later copyists were apparently trying to account for Silas' presence in Antioch in 15:40 when Paul takes him as his new partner from Antioch.

The letter is in the standard Greek style of the time, including its beginning and ending. It does not have the expanded Christianized greetings and endings found in letters that are books of the New Testament. (Many of the expressions are characteristic of Luke's style, e.g., "it seemed good to us having become of one mind," [v. 25 in the NAB: "we have with one accord decided"].) We have mentioned how it was customary for a writer of his time either to reword letters he had into his own style or to compose what he thought would have been written.

The letter recommends Paul and Barnabas, Judas and Silas. They in turn guaranteed that the letter was authentic and explained its meaning. This was necessary because letters were hand delivered. There was no postal system Christians could use.

Acts 15:32 mentions Judas and Silas as Christian prophets. Acts 13:1 had named Barnabas and Paul among the prophets at Antioch. Since little is known about what Christian prophets did or how they spoke, Acts 15:32 is important. It indicates that a major function of prophets in Christian churches was to encourage and strengthen the community (see also 1 Cor 14). Paul and Barnabas belonged to the Antioch community. Judas and Silas remained part of the Jerusalem church and returned there after helping the daughter church at Antioch. The passage provides pastoral wisdom for how an older community can aid a younger one by sending helpers.

PAUL'S MISSION TO THE GENTILES: THE SECOND JOURNEY

Acts 15:36–18:23

15:36-41 Paul and Barnabas separate. Here is another case of sharp dissension among leaders in the early church that Luke is not afraid to report. Acts relates the dispute to the pastoral choice of a helper for their next missionary journey, but the argument over table fellowship with converted pagans reported in Gal 2:11-13 might also have contributed to the rift. Acts reports that Paul objected to Barnabas' selection of John Mark because Mark had deserted them on their first journey. The argument got so heated that Paul and Barnabas parted ways. Barnabas took John Mark with him to his native Cyprus, and Paul took Silas to his home province of Syria and Cilicia (in modern Turkey).

Luke implies that God works even through tragic separations like this. Paul no longer needed Barnabas' guidance as he had at first. Now there were two teams: Barnabas and Mark, Paul and Silas. As an important leader in the Jerusalem church, Silas was Paul's link to that church. Since a respected leader of the Jerusalem church worked with Paul, he could hardly be as disobedient to the mother church as some charged.

Nor was Paul's antagonism toward Barnabas and Mark permanent. Though Gal 2:9 (no later than A.D. 54–55) refers to Paul and Barnabas as co-leaders to the Gentiles, followed by their disagreement in 2:13 over eating with converted Gentiles, 1 Cor 9:6 (about A.D. 56–57) shows Paul appealing to the example of Barnabas as well as of himself, where their common practice differed from Peter's. And in Phlm 24 Paul later refers to Mark as one of his co-workers.

16:1-5 Paul recruits Timothy in Lystra. Because of Paul's statements in Galatians against circumcising Christians, many scholars wonder about the account of Paul's cir-

cumcising Timothy in Lystra in the province of Galatia, now in Turkey. But others point out that Paul circumcised Timothy not because he needed it for salvation but only "on account of the Jews of that region" (16:3). An uncircumcised son of a mixed marriage between a Jewish mother and Greek father would be a stumbling block to winning Jews. Paul himself cited the principle of submitting to the law to win over those under the law (1 Cor 9:20). Paul did not circumcise Titus, who had no Jewish blood, but did circumcise Timothy as a special case to render him acceptable as a missionary to Jews as well as Gentiles.

Acts also notes that Paul promulgated the decisions of the Council of Jerusalem in the province of Galatia in Asia Minor, and not just to the churches in Syria and Cilicia to whom they were originally addressed. This is the last mention of the original twelve apostles in Acts. From now on, Luke traces the spread of the word through Paul. Even his visit to Jerusalem in Acts 21 mentions only James the brother of Jesus and the elders there, but not the original apostles.

16:6-10 The Spirit directs Paul's course toward Europe. Twice Luke says the Spirit prevented Paul from going one direction, but steered him in another. He does not say how the Spirit acted, through prayer or prophecy, for example. He does tell us that it was a dream in the port city of Troas that directed Paul to sail to Macedonia, the province above Greece. In Acts, God's Spirit uses many means to guide Christians. Luke most frequently mentions prayer, visions (including appearances of angels), prophecies, and dreams, and also attributes the church's Jerusalem decision in Acts 15 to the Spirit. The reference in 16:7 to "the Spirit of Jesus" shows the close relationship in Acts between the action of the risen Jesus and of the Holy Spirit (see 2:33).

Acts 16:10 is the first of several passages that use "we," the first person, instead of "he" or "they," the third person. Scholars have noted a convention in ancient Greek histories and fiction, namely, using the first-person "we" when narrating sea voyages to convey the vividness of an eyewitness's account. Therefore some scholars explain the "we" passages in Acts as mere convention and not a serious claim that the author was actually present on Paul's voyages.

However, one must consider not only the presence of a convention but variations in the uses to which it is put. Variations in the use of "we" and "they" in several Acts passages imply that whatever convention may be present is subordinated to the writer's purposes. For example, none of Paul's sea trips in Acts 13–14 have the convention, nor does 18:18-19. Also, the "we" in 20:5-6 distinguishes some companions of Paul from others, and in 20:13-14 "we" refers to his companions but not to Paul. In Luke 1:1-4 the author clearly shows his intention to write what took place, not fiction. This evidence leads me to believe that the author's use of "we" in Acts is meant to imply to his readers that he was present on those sea journeys where "we" is used, and not on other voyages like Acts 18:18-19 where it is not.

16:11-15 Conversion of Lydia's household at Philippi. The first city in Europe that Paul evangelized was Philippi in Macedonia. We know from his Letter to the Philippians that this church remained his favorite. Luke's description of Paul's procedure gives us glimpses of how Christianity spread. Note that Christians did not usually begin from scratch trying to convert pagans who never heard of God. In Athens, Paul began with pagans. But even there he presupposed some knowledge of the one God from popular philosophers, and he had little success.

Usually Christians went where Jews had paved the way before them, to people whom Jews had already instructed about God and morality, but who had remained uncircumcised. Thus, most early Christian churches were in places where there was a significant Jewish population, in cities, not the countryside. Often missionaries began in synagogues.

Here in Philippi they went on the sabbath to a "place of prayer" by the river. "Place of prayer" could be another word for synagogue, but it is curious that only women were there. In any case, the text implies that the women were Jews or "God-fearing" Gentiles. God-fearers were pagans attracted to the monotheism and morality of Judaism but unwilling to become full Jews.

Lydia is the most prominent Christian in this account, but she is not mentioned in Paul's Letter to the Philippians. She seems to have been a wealthy businesswoman and head of a household where a Christian community in Philippi met (see 16:40). Before churches were built, Christians met in larger households, which also provided hospitality to traveling missionaries.

Lydia was probably a widow. Her whole household followed her lead and was baptized, as were the households of Cornelius, of the jailer at Philippi (16:33), and of Crispus in Corinth (18:8). Often whole households were converted together, which provided a solid community base for the local church. We cannot be sure whether the baptized household included children and babies, but many scholars see this pattern as evidence for the beginning of infant baptism. If the church imitated Judaism in this as in so many other aspects of its life, it seems likely that Christians baptized and raised their children as Christians, as Jews circumcised and raised their children to be Jews.

16:16-24 Exorcism and imprisonment at Philippi. At the beginning of Jesus' ministry in Luke's Gospel, demon-filled men named Jesus' identity as Christ and Son of God until he silenced them (4:33-35, 41). Similarly, the Philippian girl with the occult spirit identified Paul and the missionaries as "servants of the Most High God." What she says is true. They are servants of God who teach a way of salvation. As in Luke's Gospel, Acts presents truth in the mouths of evil spirits, who perform for readers of Luke-Acts some of the same functions that the chorus of all-knowing gods have in a Greek play of Luke's time. They state truths that readers know but people in the narrative would not.

Acts clearly shows that the charge against Paul and Silas was false. They were not disturbing the peace or Greco-Roman customs, but had angered the owners of the slave girl by taking away their source of income.

The magistrates had ordered Paul and Silas to be stripped and beaten with rods, which Paul suffered three times (2 Cor 11:25). 1 Thess 2:2 might be referring to this incident as "the humiliation we had suffered at Philippi."

16:25-40 God rescues his servants and converts their jailer. Luke stresses how irrepressible Paul and Silas were. Despite their wounds, they prayed and sang in prison. Luke's humor may be evident in this picture of criminals listening to prayer and singing at midnight.

The earthquake and opened doors and chains are commonly mentioned in other stories of Luke's day. Luke is also paralleling Paul's release from prison with Peter's. Herod had executed Peter's jailers. Fear of execution prompted Paul's jailer to contemplate suicide, but Paul converted him with his whole household. The jailer becomes Paul and Silas' host, cleaning their wounds and feeding them in his home. But they are back in jail the next morning before the magistrates order them to be released. Luke delights in showing Paul insisting on his rights as a Roman citizen, and even rulers quaking before the Christian missionaries. He stresses that Paul and Silas strengthened the church at Lydia's house before they left the city as requested.

17:1-9 Preaching and persecution at Thessalonica. Paul's actions directly parallel those of Jesus coming to Nazareth in Luke 4:16. He journeys, arrives at a city, and teaches at a synagogue on the sabbath "following his usual custom." Jesus had taught that the Scriptures which foretold the Messiah were speaking about him. So Paul gives a two-part proof from Scripture that the Messiah was supposed to suffer and rise from the dead, similarly proving that Jesus was that Messiah.

In all the New Testament only Luke's Gospel and Acts give proof in argument form that Jesus is the Christ. Usually the New Testament merely states that Jesus fulfills prophecies or that the Christ who died for our sins was raised on the third day. In argument form Luke's premise is that the Christ was supposed to suffer and rise from the dead. He implies a second premise that Jesus did so die and rise. The conclusion is that Jesus is therefore the Christ or Messiah.

Luke is using Greek persuasion from his culture to prove and not merely claim that Jesus is the Christ. Eventually this will become a standard argument in Christian apologetics, which is the rational explanation of Christian faith in the face of opposition. Luke certainly sees no contradiction between faith and reason. Nor is he afraid to use reason to explain and defend his faith.

The results of the argument are mixed. Some of Paul's listeners are persuaded. Many God-fearing but uncircumcised Greeks and several influential women join the few Jews whom Paul persuaded.

Such mixed response is a common pattern in Paul's mission. So is the Jewish resentment and stirring up a mob against Paul (for example, Acts 13:45). It corresponds to the different responses by the prodigal and older sons in Luke 15:11-32. The older son in 15:28-29 resents the reception for the sinner, since he, the elder, had always remained home doing the father's will. So Acts shows resentment by Jews, who had always tried to do God's will, against newly converted pagans, whom Jews considered godless and immoral.

17:10-15 Paul in Beroea. Persecution in one city again leads to spreading Christianity to the next. Paul and Silas go to Beroea, about fifty miles southwest of Thessalonica (in modern Greece). The narrator's ideological point of view appears in the aside, "These Jews were more fair-minded than those in Thessalonica, for they received the word with all willingness and examined the Scriptures daily to determine whether these things were so" (17:11). Paul's letters to the Thessalonians confirm that the church there was able to endure without Paul. Another pattern in Acts is how Jewish hostility was so deep that Jews followed Paul long distances (here fifty miles) to cause him trouble in the next city. The hostility seems focused on Paul. Silas and Timothy remain behind to minister to the church before rejoining Paul.

17:16-34 Confrontation with Greek philosophers at Athens. At Athens Paul worked on two fronts: in the synagogues with Jews and God-fearing Gentiles and in the marketplace with pagan passersby. Paul's approach in the market was similar to that of popular philosophers, who preached to whomever they met. Luke tends to parallel Epicureans with Sadducees, Stoics with Pharisees, as does his Jewish contemporary Josephus. Epicureans urged people to ignore the Greek myths about vindictive gods and torments in the afterlife. Stoics, on the contrary, did believe in the providence of the gods and in natural law by which humans are to live.

In the first-century Roman Empire, many new religions and cults were spreading, especially from the East. Paul might well seem to be promoting another Eastern cult, preaching new gods called Jesus and Anastasis (the Greek word for resurrection, which sounds like the name of a goddess). The narrator reveals a negative point of view toward the

Athenians, repeating the stereotype that they have "itching ears" for novelties.

Paul's speech in the Areopagus, the academic meeting place in Athens, sounds quite different from speeches to Jews, which argued from Scripture. Addressed to Greek philosophers, it sounds more philosophical. Nevertheless, it too is steeped in Scripture, but sticks to the parts that sound like philosophy. It is a good sample of the way both Jews and Christians tried to convert pagans by appealing to "natural theology," that is, evidence from nature for the God who created it. Since there are many natural theology passages in the Old Testament, neither Jews nor Christians saw any contradiction between philosophical natural theology and revealed truths about God in Scripture.

Although Acts 17:16 mentioned Paul's annoyance over the many idols in Athens, here Paul praises the Athenians for being so religious! Having gone in their door, he comes out his own immediately by identifying the "unknown god" as the God he preaches. Scholars have found literary references to "unknown gods" but no Athenian inscription to an "unknown god." In any case, such a phrase implied many gods, but both Jews and Christians would reinterpret it as referring to the one God.

The image of all nations groping for God (as a person in darkness) expresses both that all humans are able to know God and how much better off are Jews and Christians to whom he has revealed himself. As in Rom 1:19-20, humans can know God through both nature and revelation. But the resurrection of Jesus is the complete revelation. The ages before the resurrection are the "times of ignorance" when failure to know God could be excused. Revelation brings also the responsibility to repent and believe (Acts 17:30; see also 3:17, 13:27 and Luke 23:34).

Just as the Pharisees and Sadducees listen only until the mention of resurrection in Acts 23:6-8, the Greek philosophers "interrupt" the speech at the same point. Some were intrigued (presumably the Stoics here, the Pharisees in Acts 23). Others mocked and rejected the claim of resurrection (the Epicureans probably, and Sadducees).

18:1-11 Paul founds the church in Corinth. Paul meets Aquila and his wife Priscilla in Corinth. These important co-workers are mentioned in Rom 16:3-5, 1 Cor 16:19, and 2 Tim 4:19. The emperor had expelled them and all Jews from Rome. Acts often demonstrates how Rome did not distinguish between Jews and Jewish Christians. Aquila and Priscilla shared Paul's trade of tentmaker, some kind of skilled craft practiced in cities. Frequently in his letters, and in Acts 20:33-35, Paul stresses how he supported himself and did not drain the church to which he ministered. Scholars also suggest that philosophers used workplaces to teach bystanders and customers, and perhaps Paul also taught while working. But Acts mentions only his teaching on the sabbath in the synagogue, perhaps to accent Paul's similarities to Jesus.

The arrival of Paul's helpers Silas and Timothy from Macedonia changed this (Acts 18:5). It freed him to devote his whole time to preaching. 2 Cor 11:8-9 tells the Corinthians that Paul was supported by churches in Macedonia, which confirms Acts 18:5. It also explains how his helpers coming from Macedonia freed him for full-time ministry, through the money they brought.

Paul's reference to Jews' responsibility for their refusal to believe ("Your blood be on your heads!"—18:6) alludes to Ezek 33:4, and is in turn echoed in Paul's farewell in 20:26. Acts 18:6 is the second of three statements by Paul that since Jews reject the gospel, he will take it to the Gentiles (also in 13:51 and 28:25-28). Yet, though Paul moved from the synagogue to the neighboring house of Titus Justus, a God-fearing Gentile, he did convert Crispus, the ruler of the synagogue, with his whole household (1 Cor 1:14). Thus Jews continued to be an important part of the church at Corinth.

Jesus appears to Paul in Acts 18:9-10 and tells him, "I have many people in this city." This fulfills the prophecy in Acts 15:14-17 that God will acquire "from among the Gentiles a people for his name."

18:12-17 Gallio refuses to judge between Paul and the Jews. Because we know Gallio's term of office at Corinth, A.D. 51-52, we can estimate other dates of Paul's career. The main point of this account is that Roman magistrates found nothing in Christianity to condemn, despite Jewish complaints against Christians. Their differences seemed merely intramural religious squabbling. The story ends with the humorous beating of Sosthenes, implying that the Jews turned on their own leader in frustration.

18:18-23 Return to Antioch and beginning the third journey. Acts 18:18-22 describes Paul's sea voyage from Corinth hundreds of miles back to Antioch in Syria without the use of "we," which disproves any automatic or merely conventional use of "we" for sea voyages.

Acts takes every opportunity to show that Paul remained a practicing Jew. It mentions him shaving his head because of an unspecified vow. This might refer to the ending of a temporary nazirite vow not to cut one's hair, but the details are unclear. The regulations for nazirite vows appear in Num 6:1-21. Also note the expired nazirite vows in 1 Macc 3:49.

That Aquila and Priscilla remained in Ephesus is confirmed in 1 Cor 16:19.

The passage glides almost imperceptibly from the second to the third journey of Paul from his home base in Antioch, back through Galatia to Ephesus (18:23).

PAUL'S DESTINY IN JERUSALEM: THE THIRD JOURNEY

Acts 18:24–21:14

18:24–19:7 Apollos, Priscilla and Aquila, and Paul in Ephesus. These stories raise a lot of questions. How can Apollos teach accurately about Jesus and know only John's baptism? Why do Priscilla and Aquila merely instruct Apollos, with no mention of his baptism and receiving the Spirit? How does this incident relate to Paul's teaching the twelve disciples in Ephesus about the Spirit, then baptizing them so they receive the Spirit?

The story of the twelve Baptist disciples seems to have colored the Apollos account. Luke may have known that Priscilla and Aquila instructed Apollos, but not the content of the teaching. Perhaps Luke added the reason for Apollos' further instruction from the account about the followers of John the Baptist at Ephesus—that is, not knowing about being baptized with the Spirit. The main point is clear: to show that Paul's followers corrected the teaching of Apollos, whom the Ephesian church then recommended by letter to the church at Corinth.

Notice the similarities between Acts 19:1-7 and 8:14-17, where Peter and John confirm and extend Philip's work by laying hands on the Samaritans so they would receive the Spirit. In 19:1-7 Paul brings non-Christian followers of the Baptist into the church. The Spirit leads them, as it led the original apostles, to speak in tongues and prophesy (19:6). "About twelve" recalls the Twelve at Pentecost—otherwise why use "about"?

19:8-20 God's power vs. magic. Paul's arguments with the Jews concerned the meaning of the "kingdom of God." For Paul, it referred to the Messiah's reign from heaven, whereas Jewish concerns were more nationalistic. When Paul could no longer function in the synagogue, he moved his disciples to a lecture hall. This new base was like that of wandering philosophers. Luke continues to stress that Paul and the church fulfilled its obligation to tell Jews of the fulfillment of their promises before offering it to the Gentiles.

The extraordinary miracles through Paul in Acts 19:11-12 parallel those of Peter in 5:12-16. Contemporary experience of some Christians with famous ministries of healing is similar. Such persons, including priests, are not infrequently mobbed. People try to touch them or grab some article of their clothing, despite all their efforts to get people to focus on God and not on them.

Using cloth that touched Paul to heal the sick can look like magic. But Luke stresses its difference from magical practices. He juxtaposes this incident with that of the Jewish exorcists who tried to use Jesus' name magically. He again uses humor to mock these exorcists. The spirit stripping and beating the seven exorcists reads like slapstick comedy. But the crowd's reaction shows Luke's serious purpose. Their awe and reverence for Jesus' name increased. And they repented of their magical practices and burned their magic books (for which Ephesus was well known). The Jewish exorcists failed because they tried to use Jesus' name as magic power, without being personally submitted to Jesus' authority as Paul was. Magic books that survive from Luke's time often try to name as many gods as possible in exorcism formulas, even including Jewish names for God.

19:21-22 Pastoral planning and teamwork. Paul habitually sent disciples ahead or had them stay behind to prepare or finish his work. This might be why only Luke mentions Jesus sending two disciples ahead to Samaria

(Luke 9:51-52). It shows another similarity between how Jesus and Paul used disciples to help in their missions.

19:23-40 Riot of the idolmakers and silversmiths. The statement by the silversmith that Paul had misled many people (19:26) illustrates how every narrative is filtered through a point of view, in this case an ideology hostile to a hero of Acts. Implied readers are to take account of the unreliability of this silversmith as narrator. Luke's humor appears again in the senseless riot and comic two-hour chant, "Great is Artemis of the Ephesians!" The idolmakers' fear of financial loss caused the riot, just as monetary loss angered the owners of the slave girl who prophesied in 16:18-21. Christians are often left alone until they threaten someone's profits. This is why the rich often persecute the church today when it backs land distribution to the destitute in some Latin American countries.

Paul's Macedonian co-worker Gaius is mentioned in Rom 16:23 and 1 Cor 1:14. Paul tells the Corinthians that Gaius and Crispus (converted synagogue leader in Acts 18:8) were the only two besides the household of Stephanus whom he baptized in Corinth. Aristarchus never appears in Paul's letters.

The riot was senseless: most of the crowd did not even know why they were there (19:32), and the two-hour chanting was absurd. The town clerk's decision to break up the meeting provides another example of Roman officials as guardians of order. When Jews had accused Paul, a governor had refused to try to settle that intramural religious fight. Now when pagans riot for religious reasons, the town clerk refuses to get involved in such issues.

20:1-6 Paul's travels in Greece and to Troas. The riot was Paul's signal to leave Ephesus, but first he strengthened the church he would leave behind. His mission in Macedonia was to strengthen churches already founded.

The list of Paul's companions in 20:4 illustrates how Paul attracted followers from most of the churches he founded—from Beroea, Thessalonica, Derbe, and other places in the province of Asia.

20:7-12 Raising of Eutychus to life. Luke is not afraid to use humor even about Paul. In Troas (Turkey) he portrays Paul talking all night long because he had to leave the next day. A young listener fell asleep and toppled off the windowsill to his death. Paul restored him to life, ate, and resumed talking until morning. Thus Paul too raised a dead person, as Jesus and Peter (and Elijah and Elisha) had. This is also the first mention of Sunday rather than the Jewish sabbath (Saturday) as the day for Christian worship (see Rev 1:10).

20:13-16 Paul and "we" journey to Miletus. This time the "we" travel by boat and await Paul coming overland to Assos, a seaport not far from Troas along the shore of the province of Asia (now Turkey). Mitylene is a seaport on the island of Lesbos. Notice how sea voyages were often short hops from port to port. At Miletus, Paul met with presbyters (often translated "elders") who led the church at Ephesus.

20:17-38 Paul's "farewell address" to the Ephesian elders. Luke gives us two farewell speeches—Jesus' at the Last Supper in Luke 22:15-38 and Paul's in Acts 20:17-38. His method was probably to gather information about Jesus and Paul, which he then edited into a farewell address, a kind of writing prevalent in his day.

These elements of Paul's speech in Acts 20 are typical of farewell addresses: (1) he summons the elders, (2) points to his own mission and example, (3) testifies he did not fail in his duty, (4) alludes to his imminent death, (5) exhorts them regarding future problems, (6) prophesies apostasy and false teachers after his death, (7) blesses his followers, (8) prays with them, and (9) exchanges farewell gestures.

The main use of farewell addresses was to lift up a founder as a model to imitate. So Luke 22 does with Jesus, as he tells the Twelve to "do this as a remembrance of me," and Acts 20 with Paul. Paul is Luke's chief model for what a Christian bishop or presbyter should be like. (The word in 20:28 translated "overseers" can also be translated "bishops.") He should serve God and the flock by self-sacrificing labor, authentic teaching, and careful pastoring. He should not look for gain and should be courageous against attacks from both without and within.

The speech also defends Paul. It is not his fault if the church at Ephesus later falls away from what he had tried so hard to teach them. It implies that only after Paul's death did heresy grow as widespread as in Luke's time.

By showing how the presbyters take up where Paul left off, the speech also demonstrates continuity in the church through changes in epochs, such as the passing of the first apostles.

People commonly cherish the last words of someone as stating his or her most urgent concerns. Thus, Jesus' farewell speech in Luke 22 gives us the Eucharist, the leadership of the Twelve over the church, and the true meaning of Christian leadership as service, not domination. Paul's farewell in Acts 20 stresses generous pastoring, care for the poor and weak, courage in facing persecution and apostasy, and the central importance of preserving the true message of Jesus in the face of widespread heresy. Luke presents these to his readers as Jesus' and Paul's chief concerns.

The speech ends with a clear prophecy of Paul's impending death.

21:1-14 Further voyages to Caesarea in Palestine. Paul's sea route went from the port of Miletus to the island of Cos, then the island of Rhodes, next the port of Patara in Lycia in southernmost Asia Minor. The cargo ship they boarded in Patara headed past the island of Cyprus without stopping, straight to the port of Tyre in Palestine.

There were Christian communities at all the port cities of Tyre, Ptolemais, and Caesarea. During the week with the Christians in Tyre, some of them gave him prophetic warnings against going to Jerusalem. The farewell scene highlights the Christians' affection for Paul and his party.

At Caesarea, Paul stays with Philip. He was one of the Seven who were scattered by Paul and other persecutors when Stephen died. Acts 21 calls him "the evangelist" and makes special reference to his four virgin daughters who were prophets. Luke probably mentions them to illustrate the fulfillment of the Joel 3 prophecy quoted in Acts 2, that "your sons and daughters" shall prophesy.

Agabus, the Jewish Christian prophet from Judea (Acts 11:28), performed a prophetic sign of binding his feet and hands, as Jeremiah had worn a wooden yoke to illustrate the slavery he was prophesying (Jer 27:1-15). Agabus' binding of his hands and feet illustrated his prophecy of Paul's arrest. The "we" group joins the Christians of Caesarea in trying to dissuade Paul from going to Jerusalem.

PAUL AS PRISONER WITNESSES TO THE RESURRECTION
Acts 21:15–26:32

21:15-26 James persuades Paul to prove his fidelity to Judaism. The "we" style continues all the way to Jerusalem. Luke wants to imply that his party accompanied Paul all the way to Paul's destined suffering at Jerusalem, as his Gospel had shown the Twelve accompanying Jesus to his capture in Jerusalem. But as the Twelve were not with Jesus in his imprisonment, trials, and suffering, which he bore alone, so the "we" group were not with Paul in his imprisonment and trials in Jerusalem and Caesarea (Acts 21–26) or Rome (28:16-31), though they also accompanied him on the journey to Rome (27:1–28:16).

At this time James is the Christian leader in Jerusalem. The Twelve are not mentioned as even being there anymore. "Many thousands" is an indefinite number. It indicates that a considerable number of Jews believed in Jesus and thus constituted the restored Israel promised by the prophets.

James lists the charges that were frequently made against Paul. This passage answers those charges for Luke's generation also. Rumor had it that Paul taught Jews apostasy from Moses, telling them not to circumcise their children or keep the law. The rumor confused what Paul said to non-Jews with his instructions to Jews. Paul told non-Jews they did not have to be circumcised or keep the law. But Luke here shows that Paul did not turn Christian Jews away from obligations they had taken on as Jews.

The Introduction mentions what a traumatic identity question it was for early Jewish Christians when so many Gentiles joined them. Against that background Paul shares the Jewish ritual with four Christian Jews, laying to rest charges that he forsook the Jewish law.

James distinguished between obligations of Jewish and non-Jewish Christians. The four stipulations from Acts 15:20 and 15:29 recall the obligations of Gentile Christians who share community and meals with Jewish Christians.

For the ritual itself, compare 18:18 and the remarks there.

21:27-40 Jewish rioting against Paul in the temple. Jews and Christians had surprising mobility in the first century. The "Roman peace" (or "law and order") made that possible. Asian Jews (who had caused Paul so much trouble in Ephesus) may have come to Jerusalem on pilgrimage, as did Paul. They charge Paul with the same things James had mentioned (21:21), adding that Paul opposed the temple as well as the people and law. The accusation that Paul polluted the temple by bringing in unclean pagans is a rash judgment. They had seen Paul in the city with the pagan Trophimus (20:4), whom they had recognized from Ephesus.

The charge of profaning the temple stirred up a riot among the Jerusalem Jews. Luke shows that Jewish mob would have killed Paul if the Roman army had not intervened. The mob's cry, "Away with him" (or "Kill him"), is the same as the cry against Jesus when Pilate held him (Luke 23:18).

Acts 21:37 and 21:40–22:2 show that Paul was fluent both in Greek, the international language, and in Hebrew, actually the related Aramaic then spoken in Palestine. Luke may be combining several uprisings in this account, but his main point is clear: Roman officials recognized that Paul and the Christians were not rebels against Rome.

22:1-21 Paul's defense speech to the crowd. This is the first of several apologetic or defense speeches for Paul (Acts 22, 23, 24, 25, 26). Luke rewrote the apologetic speeches, just as he had rewritten earlier missionary speeches in Acts 2, 3, 13, and 17. The beginning is stereotyped: motioning the people to silence, the address "brothers and fathers," the appeal to listen to his defense. (Compare "Friends, Romans, and countrymen, lend me your ears" in Shakespeare's *Julius Caesar*.)

Many commentators doubt that Paul was brought up in Jerusalem under the great rabbi Gamaliel, as Acts 22:3 claims. They cite Gal 1:22, "And I was unknown personally to the churches of Judea that are in Christ," to argue that Paul could not have spent much time in Jerusalem. But that fails to explain the next line: "they only kept hearing that 'the one who once was persecuting us is now preaching the faith he once tried to destroy'" (Gal 1:23). The fact that Paul persecuted Christians in and around Jerusalem makes it likely that he was well respected among Jerusalem Jews. Also, the son of Paul's sister apparently lived in Jerusalem (Acts 23:16). The reasons for doubt-

ing Acts about Gamaliel and Paul seem unconvincing. In its context, all that the Greek of Gal 1:22 states is that *as a Christian*, Paul did not *personally* visit most of the churches in Judea.

Luke's point is clear, regardless. Paul was thoroughly grounded in Judaism, so zealous that he persecuted the Christian sect. This second of three versions of Paul's conversion accentuates Paul's Jewishness, as expected in a speech to Jews.

22:22-29 Paul is imprisoned. This is another apparent interruption that dramatizes the end of a speech and highlights the statement which "causes" the interruption. In 22:21-22 the Jewish mob interrupts when Paul says Jesus will send him to the Gentiles. Likewise, in Luke 4:25-28 the people of Nazareth first erupted against Jesus when he referred to prophets helping Gentiles rather than Jews. Luke-Acts emphasizes Jewish anger at ministry to Gentiles as an explanation why so many Jews opposed Paul.

22:30–23:11 Paul's defense before the Sanhedrin. The incident where Ananias the high priest has Paul struck during his trial is similar to the blow to Jesus before Annas in John 18:19-24. "Whitewashed wall" brings to mind Jesus' expression "whitewashed sepulchers" (Matt 23:27). Has Luke heard of those incidents or sayings and instead of reporting them in Jesus' ministry and trial, as Matthew and John do, alluded to them through similar incidents in Paul's trial? Luke 1:1-4 presupposes that his readers knew other Gospels. He may be trying to describe the trials of Stephen and Paul in ways that remind them of Jesus' trials, referring to details which his implied readers would be expected to know but which were left out from his telling of Jesus' passion.

Luke probably does not interpret Paul's remark in 23:5 against insulting God's legitimate high priest as sarcasm. Even under great provocation, he implies, Paul is careful not to undermine legitimate Jewish authority.

Whatever Sadducees actually believed, the aside in Acts 23:8 reports a widespread stereotype about their unbelief in resurrection, angels, or spirits. Luke treated only Pharisees as Jews with true beliefs. Sadducees were really heretics all along, even though in good standing before the destruction of Jerusalem in A.D. 70. Luke portrays Paul as a true Jewish believer, supported by other Pharisees and persecuted by heretical Sadducees for witnessing to the resurrection.

In the dream, Jesus mentions Paul's witness in Jerusalem. How did Paul do this, since the Acts 23 speech does not even mention Jesus' name? The answer lies in the way Luke equates witness to the risen Jesus with witness to belief in the resurrection held by Pharisees.

23:12-35 Plot against Paul and his transfer to Caesarea. At Jerusalem the son of Paul's sister overhears and rescues Paul from a plot by some forty Jews to kill him. The Romans protect Paul by escorting him out at night with 200 soldiers, 70 horsemen, and 200 light-armed men—quite an expense for one Roman citizen!

Lysias' letter, which is in standard letter form with the ending omitted, states Paul's innocence of anything deserving punishment. He was sent to Felix, the Roman governor of Palestine, to get away from plots against his life.

24:1-21 Paul's trial before Felix. The trial scene gives glimpses into how trials were run in the first century. For the Roman trial Ananias hired a lawyer named Tertullus to argue his case against Paul. After the lawyer's accusation comes the defense by Paul, acting as his own lawyer. First-century lawyers were actually called "rhetoricians." Their training was less in the legal technicalities of modern law schools than in oratorical techniques on how to persuade a judge. Both Paul's and Tertullus' speeches use these techniques.

Tertullus' speech puts heavy emphasis on winning the judge's good graces. It then charges Paul with offenses against the empire. He was a troublemaker stirring up sedition among Jews as leader of the sect of the Nazoreans. Note the parallel false charge against Jesus to Pilate: that he incites revolt, opposes tribute to Caesar, and claims to be king (Luke 23:2). "Nazoreans" was an early Jewish name for Christians. The speech calls Paul, rather than Peter or James, the most influential leader of this worldwide sect. It falsely accuses Paul of trying to defile the temple. The Jewish high priest and leaders supported their spokesman's presentation by vouching for its facts.

Paul also begins his defense by appealing to the judge before refuting the accusations. The only charge Paul admits is that he worships the ancestral God "according to the Way," the name for Christians that even Felix knew. Though the Jews considered the Way a sect, Paul insists that he believes everything in the Jewish law and prophets (= Scripture). He too believes in a resurrection of the just and unjust, as in Dan 12:2.

The speech in fact describes Christianity to outsiders. Christianity is seen as a form of Jewish worship and expectation of resurrection. Jewish presentations to Gentiles usually stressed judgment after death based on how one lived. And Paul's witness to Jesus' resurrection comes under the general theme of resurrection of the dead.

Paul ends by explaining that he was in the temple "to bring alms for my nation" (24:17), which may be an indirect reference to Paul's collection for the Jerusalem church, which Paul's letters emphasize more.

24:22-27 Captivity in Caesarea. The writer Josephus tells us that Felix had stolen his wife Drusilla from her first husband. That probably explains why Felix became afraid when Paul preached to him about sexual morality. The situation reminds one of John the Baptist's rebuke of Herod for his adulterous marriage. Christian preaching to pagans in the first and second century often focused on righteousness, self-control, and the coming judgment, as in Acts 24:25.

Luke has to explain why Felix did not free Paul if he was innocent. He notes that Felix was expecting a bribe, for which he was notorious, and that he wanted to please the Jews. Paul has to suffer years of imprisonment because he would not give a bribe. He is an example for Christians of suffering for refusing to perform an unjust practice, even one that "everyone does."

25:1-12 Trial before Festus and appeal to the emperor. Luke frequently parallels Paul's trials with Jesus'. Only his Gospel mentions all the following: Jesus before the crowd that captured him, the Sanhedrin, the Roman governor (Pilate) *twice*, and the Jewish king Herod (Luke 22–23). Likewise, Paul addresses the mob that seized him, the Sanhedrin, two Roman governors (Felix and Festus), and the Jewish Herodian king Agrippa (Acts 21–26).

With the new governor the Jews again try to have Paul brought to Jerusalem so they can kill him en route. Festus declines to move Paul, but he invites them to accuse Paul at Caesarea. The trial repeats the one before Felix. The Jews "brought many serious charges against him, which they were unable to prove" (Acts 25:7). This echoes Luke 23:10, where the chief priests and scribes accused Jesus vehemently before Herod. Paul repeats the defense he used before Felix. He has done nothing against the law or the temple or Caesar.

Like Felix before him (24:27), Festus curries favor with the Jews by refusing to free Paul. Paul does not acknowledge any authority of the Jerusalem Sanhedrin over him (see 4:18-21; 5:27-29, 40-42). He could not hope for a fair hearing in Palestine, so he appeals as a Roman citizen for trial before the emperor in Rome.

Acts does not focus on Paul's frustration in prison but on how God used these injustices to get Paul to Rome. There he would give the Jews their last chance to accept the message.

25:13-27 Festus invites Agrippa to hear Paul. Only Luke 23:6-12 mentions Pilate inviting Herod Antipas to try Jesus. Luke may mention that as a parallel to Festus' invitation to a later member of the Herod dynasty, Agrippa II, to try Paul. The New Testament tells of four different rulers in the Herod family: (1) Herod the Great (Matt 2, Luke 1:5), (2) Herod the Tetrarch (= Herod Antipas) who killed John the Baptist and appeared in Jesus' passion in Luke 23, (3) Herod in Acts 12 (= Herod Agrippa I) who killed James, and (4) Agrippa (= Agrippa II), son of the Herod from Acts 12 and judge at Paul's hearing in Caesarea in Acts 25–26.

Paul follows closely in the suffering footsteps of Jesus. Pilate in Luke 23:15, 22 repeatedly declared Jesus innocent of charges against him. So Festus and many others assert Paul's innocence in Acts. Festus considers these charges mere intra-Jewish squabbles, "about a certain Jesus who had died but who Paul claimed was alive" (25:19).

26:1-32 Paul's defense before Agrippa and Festus. Acts 26 has been called "the christological climax of Paul's defense" (see Robet O'Toole's book by that name). Christology describes the meaning and identity of Jesus as Christ and Son of God. All the trials from Acts 22–26 culminate in the hearing before Agrippa and Festus, with its verdict of not guilty (26:32). The speech in Acts 26 is interrupted at its climax, according to the pattern seen in Acts 17 and 22. Its final state-

ment is its christological climax. Paul preaches only what the prophets and Moses had foretold. The Christ would suffer, and as first to be raised from the dead, he would proclaim light to both God's people and the Gentiles (26:22-23). All of Acts 22–26 leads up to this suffering witness to Christ's resurrection.

The resurrection hope as God's promise to Israel unites the parts of the speech. The discourse places more emphasis than earlier speeches on how strongly Paul persecuted the church, even unto death. Therefore his about-face when the Christ he rejected called him by name is more striking. Instead of mentioning Paul's blindness, as in 9:8-9 and 22:11, the speech describes Paul's mission as opening eyes and bringing others from darkness to light. Blindness and turning from darkness to light are common themes in both Jewish and Christian preaching to convert pagans.

This is the third time Acts describes Paul's conversion, which puts great emphasis on it. Luke portrays Paul as the model witness to Jesus' resurrection and as fulfilling Jesus' predictions in Luke 21:12-19 and 12:11-12 that Christians would witness before kings and governors.

Acts 26:24-28 contrasts the Roman governor who sees the talk as madness with King Agrippa who understands Jewish controversies and finds it compelling. Luke may also imply that Paul's speech is prophetic. To unbelievers tongues and prophecy can appear madness or drunkenness (Acts 2:13), but they come from the power of the Holy Spirit. Here the power of Paul's speech is almost enough to convert Agrippa!

Acts 26:31-32 ends all Paul's trials saying that Paul was innocent and could have been freed if he had not appealed to Caesar.

"YOU SHALL BEAR WITNESS AT ROME"

Acts 27:1–28:31

27:1-44 Shipwreck on the voyage to Rome. The "we" narrative resumes with Paul's voyage and shipwreck, and is introduced abruptly, without it being clear in what capacity "we" were to sail to Italy with Paul (27:1) or were put on board by the centurion (27:6). This chapter should be read with a map of Paul's journey to Rome and with an appreciation of how risky sea travel was. Boats were unable to tack against the wind, and so were more at the mercy of a fierce storm than sailboats today. In both pagan literature and the Old Testament, the motif of sailing in a storm was quite popular. Acts 27 is as graphic as any such stories.

Paul's effect on his ship contrasts with Jonah's. Whereas Jonah because of his sinfulness polluted the ship and caused its distress, Paul was the salvation of his vessel. Both were prophets. Paul's prophecy that he would stand trial in Rome and his shipmates be saved gave hope to the 276 on board. Paul's prophecy that "not one of you shall lose a hair of his head" echoed Jesus' words in Luke 12:7 and 21:18.

The narrator's point of view, which confidently trusts Paul's opinion over that of the pilot and owner in 27:11, contrasts with normal expectations. The narrator shifts between "we" in 27:15 and "they" in verse 17, and distinguishes between "they . . . took some food" and "two hundred seventy-six of us on the ship" (vv. 36-37). The narrator shows the persuasive power of Paul's example of eating to encourage the others to eat (vv. 35-36).

Paul's breaking bread and giving thanks to God sound Eucharistic, though with pagans this was obviously not an actual Eucharist. As Luke relates the incident, he adds symbolic reminders of Jesus' promise and the Eucharist. When Christians flounder in the storms of life, we should recall Jesus' assurance of protection. And the Eucharist gives new courage in our trials.

28:1-10 Miracles on Malta. The "natives" of the island of Malta are yet another kind of people who respond to Paul. Luke calls them in Greek *barbaroi*, from which "barbarian" comes. The term originally meant non-Greeks. Acts had shown the reactions of Jews, Greeks, and Romans to Paul. Acts 28 and 14 showed how "natives" of Malta (in the Mediterranean) and Lycaonia in Asia Minor (Turkey) responded to him. Both of the latter groups showed much more primitive and superstitious reactions than had Jews, Greeks, or Romans. This could explain why during the Dark Ages, after Rome's fall to primitive western tribes, Christianity became more affected by superstition than during the Roman Empire.

Luke's humor again comes to the fore. In Lycaonia the crowds had comically treated Barnabas and Paul as gods. In Malta the natives wait for Paul to puff up and keel over. Then they decide he is a god. Notice also the popular first-century view of avenging Justice killing a murderer by a snake after he had escaped the sea.

Luke continues the "we" style until Paul's arrival in Rome. In fact, the revised New American Bible translation of Acts 28:16 is misleading: the Greek says "When *we* entered Rome," not "When *he* entered Rome." Luke does not report any preaching by Paul during the three winter months on Malta. But Paul's healing of his host's father led many islanders to bring their sick for healing. The way to win simple people like the Maltese begins with healing. Christians with healing ministries find the same true in travels to less industrialized countries today. In sophisticated countries they report that healings are less common. Among simple peoples they find more openness and cures.

28:11-16 Christians greet Paul and escort him to Rome. Luke reports "brothers," that is, communities of Christians, in the port of Puteoli (near Naples). Other Christians from Rome travel south the forty miles to the Forum of Appius or the thirty-some miles to Three Taverns to greet Paul. Luke is emphasizing that Paul was in very high standing with the church of Rome for Christians to go to such trouble to welcome him.

Some commentators think Luke is trying to downplay the fact that there was a church at Rome that Paul did not found or even to imply that Paul founded the Roman church. But this is not the point of Acts 28. Luke makes clear there were already Christians at Rome who greeted Paul. Christianity is not arriving at Rome for the first time with Paul, nor is his mission to found the church there. In Paul, Christianity is to make one last major appeal and offer of the good news to the *Jews* of Rome. By ending with Paul's conference with leading Roman Jews, Acts makes clear he was not a Jewish apostate. He spoke to the main centers of Jews, even though he was known as "the apostles to the Gentiles."

28:17-28 Paul's appeal to Roman Jews. Paul insists to the Jews of Rome that he had not betrayed the Jewish people or customs, even though it was Jews who handed him over to Rome for punishment. This is Luke's last apology or defense for Paul from the charge of Jewish apostasy. All day Paul witnessed that the kingdom Jews were expecting was becoming a reality. He tried to persuade them from their Scriptures that their promises were fulfilled in Jesus. As often in Acts, some believed and some did not.

The finale of Acts is the third repetition of the theme that Jews rejected the good news, so Paul turned to more receptive Gentiles. We have seen how Acts uses triple repetition to put major emphasis on an event (e.g., Paul's conversion, Cornelius, the Apostolic Decree). The repetition combines with the powerful scriptural quotation in the climactic final position in the book as strong evidence that this is one of the most important themes in Acts. Luke wants to explain how the church of his day is so predominantly Gentile if it is the fulfillment of Jewish promises through the Jewish Messiah. Luke's church is Gentile not because Paul failed to honor God's promises to the Jews. It is so because the majority of Jews, especially those living away from Palestine, rejected Paul's offer.

28:30-31 Through Paul the word is preached without hindrance. Many have wondered why Acts ends without mentioning the result of Paul's two-year Roman imprisonment. Some say Acts was written before Paul died. But most find certain references in Luke to the destruction of Jerusalem in A.D. 70, after Paul's death. Others suggest Luke intended to write a third volume, or that he wrote the pastoral Epistles (to Titus and Timothy). I think Luke ended here because he wanted to end on a high note, as most narratives of his time were expected to. More importantly, he had made the points he wanted to make about how the church came to be as it was in his time. He had kept his promise to Theophilus in Luke 1:1-4. He had shown how the things "handed down to us" have fulfilled God's saving plan found in Scripture. All but one of the prophecies from Scripture, Jesus, and Christian prophets have come true. The church is now living in the final epoch, the "last days" when the Spirit has been poured out as Joel 3 expected. The church is now in the "times of the Gentiles" (Luke 21:24). It is enduring the times after Paul's death when false teachers will arise (Acts 20:29-30). All that must yet be accomplished are cosmic catastrophe and the Final Day when the Son of Man returns as judge.

GALATIANS

John J. Pilch

INTRODUCTION

About ten years ago I wrote my doctoral dissertation on Paul's use of the Greek word *apokalypsis*—usually translated "revelation" —in the first two chapters of Galatians (1:12; 2:2; the verb in 1:16). In the defense of the dissertation, I justified my conclusions by responding with convincing answers to the questions of five examiners.

Now, ten years later, there are some areas about which we know much more than we did then, but there are other areas of biblical study about which we are still undecided. For example, scholars do not agree upon the specific identity of the Galatians, the people to whom Paul wrote this letter. Looking at a map of antiquity doesn't help because the map changed often. Initially, the name Galatia described a north central section of Asia Minor which contained the cities of Ancyra (modern name Ankara, Turkey), Pessinus, and Tavium. In 25 B.C.E. Rome combined this section with southern territories into one province named Galatia, though these latter territories preferred to keep their names. To whom then is Paul writing? Many believe he is writing to inhabitants of the South in places like Lystra and Derbe mentioned in Acts, but others argue for the North. No definite conclusion is yet possible.

The same uncertainty characterizes opinion on the date (sometime between A.D. 49 and 55) and the place from which the letter was written. If I were writing my dissertation today on the same topic, I would still be unable to resolve these uncertainties.

For our purposes, however, the letter itself provides enough information for an adequate understanding of the message. The recipients of the letter are converts to Christianity from paganism (see Gal 4:8; 5:2-3; 6:12-13). Paul converted them, but not too long after he departed Judaizing Christians came along and argued that in order to be a good Christian one had first to be a good Jew by being circumcised and by observing other prescriptions of the Torah.

This, of course, struck at the heart of Paul's conviction that the Torah was no longer binding as law, but continued to be Scripture, that is, story telling how Israel arrived at its present situation. News of the wavering faith of his converts prompted Paul to write this very polemic letter.

Moreover, the contents of the letter and the force with which it is written clearly demonstrate that the letter does not stem from that period (the forties) during which Paul was an apostle "dependent" upon Antioch like Barnabas, but rather from that period (the fifties) when Paul was an "independent" apostle. This is very clear especially in the first two chapters of Galatians.

These aspects of our knowledge about Paul's Epistle to the Galatians have remained basically the same over the last ten years. On the other hand, my rather unusual position as a trained biblical scholar engaged for the most part in medical and health-care settings has made me sensitive to certain new developments in biblical study over the last ten years.

1069

One such development is the increasing application of insights from sociology and cultural anthropology to biblical texts with refreshing results.

For instance, the fine literary and theological analysis of Paul's "conversion" told three times by Luke in the Acts of the Apostles (9; 22; 26) can now be *supplemented* with interesting and plausible conjectures from the modern medical understanding of temporary blindness. In addition, the social and cultural meaning or interpretation of blindness, sight, darkness, and light highlighted by sociology and cultural anthropology suggests still other ways of reading those three accounts. If I were writing my dissertation on the same topic today, I would definitely include these new data.

The present commentary therefore blends some of these innovative insights with the traditional and time-tested interpretations of Paul. In addition to gaining a basic understanding of his Epistle to the Galatians, the reader will also learn some fundamental principles of the exciting and ground-breaking social science approach to interpreting Scripture. One precious result of such a combination of the old and the new is a better grasp of Paul's original meaning. Such knowledge will make it a little easier to uncover the contemporary relevance of our ancient texts.

OUTLINE OF GALATIANS

COMMENTARY

GREETINGS AND INTRODUCTION

Gal 1:1-10

1:1-5 Paul greets the Christians in Galatia. When I attended Mass as a youngster in Brooklyn, New York, the priest who read the Scriptures to the congregation in the vernacular (Polish) would always begin with the excerpt from the epistle with the phrase "Dearly beloved (*Najmilsi*)." Until I began reading the Bible myself, I believed that Paul began every letter with this same simple phrase.

The introductions to Paul's letters are, of course, more complex than "dearly beloved." They more or less follow the basic format of letter introductions in antiquity, identifying the sender and the recipients and including expressions of greetings. Yet each letter's introduction is different.

Paul begins Galatians with an uncharacteristically strong declaration of his apostolic authority—an authority not so much due to human appointment or commission, but rather to Jesus Christ and God his Father. Since Paul himself founded these churches (perhaps together with the brothers or fellow believers who are with him), the specific aspect of authority he uses in his letter is an appeal to the Galatians' loyalty, an appeal hoping to reactivate their previous commitment. He plays on their emotionally anchored sense of duty to God's activity in Christ (v. 1) as well as to the gospel Paul preached to them (v. 9).

The special description of what God accomplished in Jesus tips off the thrust of the letter to follow: Jesus died for our sins to free, deliver, and rescue us from the present evil age, that is, Jesus' redemptive death has made it possible for believers to pursue a different life-style than that of some other people in this present age.

1:6-10 Paul defends his doctrine and authority. Just where Paul ordinarily writes a prayer of thanksgiving (see 1 Thess 1:2-10), he launches straightway into the body of his letter with a resounding criticism of the Galatians calculated to "shame" them, shame (not guilt) being the core emotion among his readers. The first words, "I am amazed," express intense disbelief that the Galatian Christians are willfully forsaking previous loyalty and commitment to God and choosing some other good news. But no other news is good news!

As a matter of fact, Paul has specific culprits in mind whom he holds responsible for confusing, troubling, and unsettling the minds of the recently (about five years ago) converted Galatians. His shocking statement against the very thought of an "angel from heaven" (v. 8) attempting to preach a different gospel suggests that the troublemakers are Judaizers, that is, Christians who believe and insist that converts to Christianity should also (or continue to) observe certain Jewish ritual practices as well, for instance, circumcision and dietary restrictions.

Paul is quite blunt. Those who are presently daring to present a gospel different from the one Paul preached on his first and founding visit to these churches deserve to be abandoned, indeed, condemned by God.

PAUL, HIS GOSPEL, AND PETER

Gal 1:11–2:21

1:11-17 How Paul learned the good news. Though he is quite serious and perhaps even angry, Paul nevertheless begins his comments with an affectionate address of fellowship, "Brothers" (which would also include sisters). The term is an appeal to their emotion-laden loyalty and again illustrates the style of authority Paul exercises in this letter. He reminds his readers of his thoroughly Jewish background, his way of life prior to his category-shattering experience on the road to Damascus. He was both an ardent student of Judaism and a persistent and thorough persecutor of Christians. Indeed, he was recognized by fellow Jews as far advanced among his peers in practice as well as in zeal.

But just as God did to Jeremiah (1:5) and Isaiah (42:1), he chose Paul for a special task, called him, and then revealed to him who the Son really is so that he might tell this good news about him to the non-Jewish world.

Paul's response could well shame a modern believer: it was immediate, unquestioning, and intense. He went immediately to Arabia, that is, the region west and south of Judea known as the Nabatean Kingdom and began preaching at once.

The repeated declaration of independence by Paul from all other apostles or teachers (v. 12) is as puzzling as it is strong. How can he insist that he did not receive his gospel from any person (v. 12) when in 1 Cor 15:3 he admits: "I handed on to you first of all what I myself received," using Greek words that are technical vocabulary for receiving and handing on tradition in a reliable and trustworthy fashion? It seems best to interpret the Galatian statement as saying that Paul received his understanding of the good news "not so much" from any human person or schooling, *"as rather"* through God's gracious revelation about who Jesus really is.

1:18-24 First meeting with Peter. The remainder of chapter 1 and most of chapter 2 describe three meetings with Peter. Having just boldly announced his independence of people (teachers, authorities), Paul now vigorously strives to associate himself with Peter (and the "pillars" with him) in a relationship of equality!

The underlying dynamic is different from what the ordinary, natural born citizen of the United States might expect. Our strong sense of individualism ("rugged" at times), unsurpassed in the history of humanity, as well as our readiness to offer introspectively generated explanations for the behavior of *others*, tempt us to interpret Paul as a highly stubborn, strong-willed individualist. Yet Paul's statement reflecting conformity to tradition in 1 Cor 15:3 would challenge our projection of such American individualism on that Mediterranean person.

Like nearly all the people who populate the pages of Scripture, Paul is not an individualist in our understanding of that word. He is rather a "dyadic personality." Dyadic comes from the Greek word meaning "pair," and it describes the kind of person whose self-awareness, self-esteem, and self-fulfillment depend entirely upon relationships with other people and upon what other people—especially a group—think. Our culture would call such people "other-directed." Let's use that word instead of dyadic in this commentary.

In Galatia the struggle took place between groups. The churches or believers of Galatia as a group forged their identity according to the gospel Paul preached to them, a gospel presumed to faithfully reflect the beliefs and practices of the *Jerusalem church group*. The *Judaizer group* which is disturbing the Galatians claimed that Paul's preaching was incomplete and urged the Galatian churches to mold their identity rather according to the Judaizing concept of the good news, which they insisted was a more accurate reflection of the faith of the Jerusalem church group. Thus, in such a culture, Paul can justify or defend himself only by proving his embeddedness in the right group. He will proceed to do this by asserting a position of equality as apostle with Peter as apostle.

Some three years after his 180-degree turn from Pharisaic Judaism to preaching Jesus as Messiah, Paul went to Jerusalem to "get to know" Kephas. The Greek word for "get to know" could also be translated "gather information from." Because of Paul's emphatic insistence that God alone revealed Jesus to him, translators have preferred "get to know." Yet Jewish tradition says that when two Jewish teachers meet in a Jewish context, the word of Torah was between them, that is, they exchanged information about doctrinal statements from their teachers and predecessors. Or in other terms, they "checked each other out" as is the custom among other-directed personalities.

As such an other-directed personality, Peter knew his self-identity in terms of the Jerusalem community, and very shortly in this letter we'll see how much he experienced and yielded to pressures of that group. In his turn as an other-directed personality, Paul's major task is to persuade Peter that his conversion is genuine, that he has really changed group loyalty from Pharisee-persecutor of Christians, to Jewish-Christian preacher of Jesus as Messiah. Paul's group reference point now is Jerusalem.

Paul's successful change of membership and loyalty from one group to another as just described is evidenced in the concluding verse of chapter 1: "He who was formerly persecuting us is now preaching the faith he tried to destroy." The reality of that conviction is reflected in the glory given to God on Paul's account.

2:1-10 Second meeting with Peter. God prompted Paul to visit Kephas and the Jerusalem church leaders again some fourteen years after his first visit. He took along Barnabas and the Gentile Titus, and in a private conference with Peter and the leaders Paul explained the good news which he habitually and customarily had been preaching to the Gentiles all this time. Paul expresses a note of apprehension when he admits that he called this conference "to make sure the course I was pursuing, or had pursued, was not useless."

He had no doubts about his teaching. He was worried about what his converts would do if he could not win support from Peter and the leaders. They would probably be lost to the Judaizers, and the gospel Paul preached would be perverted.

Paul's apprehension was solidly founded. Some sham Christians (literally false brothers, a shocking counterphrase to the emotion-charged title by which he's been addressing the Galatians) spied on Paul and his followers. They hoped to gather enough evidence to show how unfaithful Paul and his kind were to the Jewish law and then to force them once again to submit to the system of Jewish ritual. But Paul resisted that effort to distort—indeed to reject and make null and void—the gospel. Further, the fact that the leaders did not order Titus to submit to Jewish ritual circumcision as a requirement for continuing in Christian belief was living proof of the legitimacy and validity of Paul's work.

The incident is either part of or very close in time to the so-called Jerusalem Council. Acts 15:6-12 is probably a description of the same meeting Paul relates in Gal 2:1-10. The basic decision by Kephas/Peter and the leaders is not to impose any part of the Jewish law on Gentile converts to Christianity, as with Titus.

There is, however, a significant difference in the two accounts just mentioned. In Galatians, Paul creates the impression that independently and on his own initiative (even if prompted by God) he has gone to visit with the Jerusalem leaders. Acts, on the other hand, says that he is *sent* from Antioch to Jerusalem. The truth most likely is that at that stage of his career Paul was not yet an independent missionary but rather indeed an emissary from Antioch. His perspective at the time of writing this letter about five or more years later seems to color his recollections.

The result of Paul's second meeting with Peter is not only that nothing was added to the gospel Paul habitually and customarily preached, but they also decided on a territorial division of labor. Paul would henceforth preach mainly in the dispersion, that is, to both Jews and Gentiles living outside of Palestine. Kephas/Peter and his co-workers would continue to focus their evangelizing activity in Palestine (Jerusalem).

Notice once again how careful Paul has

been to present himself as an apostle completely "equal" with Peter. The fact that the leaders extended the right handshake of fellowship can be interpreted to mean that they accepted Paul as an apostolic partner on equal footing with themselves. The one proviso to which Paul readily agreed was to remember the "poor," that is, God's spiritually privileged (not necessarily economically destitute) followers in the churches of Judea.

The understanding of Scripture personalities culturally as other-directed personalities helps us grasp yet another aspect of Paul's outlooks reflected in these verses. He describes the Jerusalem leaders as "those who were regarded as important" (2:6, 9) and notes that "it makes no difference to me how prominent they were—God plays no favorites" (2:6).

Some readers have considered these statements as a sign of Paul's arrogant independence. That judgment is technically known as eisegesis, that is, reading into a text something that isn't there. These statements of Paul's further mark him as a man of his culture and time, an other-directed personality. The only way other-directed people get to know one another is externally, by appearances, by one's "face." Thus when Paul says the leaders "were regarded as important," he recognizes and admits the cultural limitations. By all outward appearances, these people seem to be important.

The literal statement behind "God plays no favorites" is that "God does not accept or lift up the face of a person." The dictionary says the Greek phrase means to show partiality or preference. That is correct, but God is not an other-directed (dyadic) personality. He can see within a person, beyond the face, and he and he alone can know everything inside and out.

Paul's point is simply this. Both I and my opponents judge by externals; that's a fact. But the leaders agreed with me and we reached a mutual understanding. So we believe God's on our side. Since we are restricted to externals, what more can we do?

2:11-21 Third meeting with Peter. Some time after meeting in Jerusalem (that is, after A.D. 50), but before the writing of this letter (around A.D. 55), Peter came to Antioch and mingled freely with all believers, converts from paganism as well as from Judaism. But when a (Judaizer?) group arrived from Jerusalem, Peter began to withdraw from fellowship and meal sharing.

See once more the strength of group pressure on other-directed individuals in these scenarios. Peter did indeed know and remember his very own decision not to impose Jewish observances on converts to Christianity from paganism. But old allegiances die hard, group pressures continue strong. It seems that Peter's "category shattering experience" of Jesus was not as thorough as Paul's. Peter knew full well that a Christian is made right with God through faith in Jesus and not through accomplishing works prescribed by the Jewish law. But Peter's former group-identity as a Torah-abiding Jew apparently resumed a prominent and directive place in his consciousness when the Jerusalem representatives came. To avoid displeasing them, he acted externally in a way that contradicted what he taught, said, and even practiced when it wasn't uncomfortable.

Perhaps if it were only Peter who changed course, Paul might have been more tolerant and patient. But when the rest of the Jewish Christians and even Barnabas began to follow Peter's example, Paul faced him as an apostolic equal and rebuked him publicly.

Verses 15-21 conclude these first two chapters of Galatians and introduce the next two. Paul now sums up what he has described in the meetings with Peter: we are made right with God by faith (v. 16) and not by legal observances (or in another translation, "deeds of the law"). In order to be fair to Paul, it is critically important to try to understand his use of the word "law" and our common understanding of the word.

When he uses the word translated in English as "law" in Galatians, Paul (with the obvious exception of Gal 3:21 and 5:23) has the Torah in mind. The Hebrew word *torah* means instruction or directive. It is the name given to the first five books of the Hebrew Bible (Genesis, Exodus, Leviticus, Numbers, and Deuteronomy) because they contain instruction and directives given by God to facilitate the achievement of the basic and core value of the chosen people, namely, *shalom* or peace, that dynamic state in which one continues to become and to be what one should be: a limited, finite, free human being.

When the Hebrew Bible was translated into Greek (the version we call the Septuagint), the word *nomos* was used consistently to translate *torah*. Paul, too, used *nomos* in his letters when he referred to the Torah. But *nomos* literally should be translated into English by the words "rule" (*explicit* instruction or directive) or "norm" (*implicit* instruction or directive). It is the historical and literary context that helps decide when *nomos* should be translated into English as "standard" (rules or norms between two individuals), "custom" (rules or norms in society's institutions), or "law" (rules or norms taken from these institutions and raised to the political or legal order).

Thus, *torah* (or *nomos*) can be translated "law" when it pertains to the period of the Jewish monarchy or the restoration after the Babylonian Exile (587–537 B.C.E.). In this period, law should be understood in its strict sense as a body of binding rights and obligations that have been "twice institutionalized" —once in custom, and then once again in the legal or political realm. So when Israel possessed self-rule, autonomy, Torah was law strictly speaking.

But in the Hellenistic period (300 to 6 B.C.E.) and in the Roman period (6 B.C.E. onward into Paul's time), when Israel lived under the law of its victors, Torah was reduced to custom legitimated by God. These various customs were embedded in the basic institutions of society: family, government, economics, education, and religion. They governed life within each institution because they were recognized as binding, legitimated by the Divine Will.

Here in Galatians, Paul says that in his own lifetime (Roman period) he was once a Torah-observing Pharisee, that is, he studied and lived the Torah. He perceived and understood it to be normative Jewish custom legitimated by God. But when he realized that Jesus is Messiah, that God raised Jesus from the dead (Gal 1:1), he also realized that the normative Jewish customs enshrined in Torah lost divine approval.

For Paul, Torah now became a normative story, the Sacred Scripture, telling readers how they arrived at the present, but offering nothing more since God abrogated it as normative custom. We are therefore made right with God by faith and no longer by legal observances. In Gal 3–4 Paul will present Jewish scriptural arguments to buttress his point.

A NEW-OLD WAY TO PLEASE GOD

Gal 3:1–4:31

3:1-5 Faith, not legal observances. The next major section of Galatians begins as Paul asks his pagan converts to reflect upon their experience of the Spirit (v. 4): has that experience come from legal observances or from faith? The only way Paul can understand how they could turn against their own experience is that someone must have momentarily cast a spell on them after the pattern of an evil-eye strategy.

Mention of the evil eye is not just a tolerant nod toward some pagan practice but is actually part of the everyday first-century Semitic understanding of the whole person. Each person is viewed on the basis of "externals," of parts of the body used as metaphors. Thus, a person has a heart for thinking along with eyes that bring data to the heart. The mouth is for speaking while the ears take in the speech of others. Hands and feet are for activity, for "doing." Another way of saying this is that in the Bible, each person is viewed holistically, but in terms of three kinds of interactions with the external world: eyes-heart representing emotion-fused thought, mouth-ears representing self-expressive speech, and hands-feet representing purposeful and effective action.

Notice the complete and total human experience described by John when he mentions each zone explicitly:

This is what we proclaim to you:
what was from the beginning,
what we have heard,
what we have seen with our eyes,
what we have looked upon
and our hands have touched—
we speak of the word of life. . . .
What we have seen and heard
we proclaim in turn to you
so that you may share life with us.
(1 John 1:1-3)

Observe also how the third section of the Sermon on the Mount (Matt 6:19–7:27) concerning the righteousness of the disciples covers the three zones: the first part of the material deals with eyes-heart (Matt 6:19–7:6), the second with mouth-ears (Matt 7:7-11), and the last section with hands-feet (Matt 7:13-27).

The cluster of words in Gal 3:1: "stupid," "bewitched," "eyes," "publicly portrayed" all pertain to the zone of emotion-fused thought. So, like every other-directed person in his culture, Paul doesn't try to guess at internal motivations, but rather lists these external aspects of human existence as one possible explanation for the Galatian turnabout. Moreover, the fact that this cluster of words relates to *emotion*-fused thought demonstrates once again that this letter is Paul's attempt to reactivate the Galatians' emotionally anchored commitment to the gospel he preached to them.

3:6-14 Abraham, model of faith: midrashic homily number 1. If Paul is writing to his pagan converts to Christianity, why does he now proceed to present arguments rooted in and requiring more than a passing knowledge of Jewish interpretation of Scripture? Perhaps because the Galatians needed persuasive arguments to use against the convincing suggestions of the Judaizers.

The modern reader will probably experience difficulty following the logic of these two chapters and may be overwhelmed with the stream of Scripture references drawn from all over the Jewish Bible. The technique is known as stringing pearls and was a common feature of one kind of Jewish homily in Paul's day. Some scholars have even suggested that the early Christians—perhaps even Paul himself—gathered together especially appropriate strings of Scripture references that could be used in preaching and teaching about Jesus.

Thus, this first midrashic (the word "midrash" means explanation) homily strings together Gen 15:6 (see Gal 3:6), Gen 18:18 or 12:3 (Gal 3:8), Deut 27:26 (Gal 3:10), Hab 2:4 (Gal 3:11), Lev 18:5 (Gal 3:12), and Deut 21:23 (Gal 3:13) to demonstrate that Scripture testifies that Abraham was made right with God by faith and not by legal observances. If a person chooses legal observances, then ALL rules must be obeyed. Anything short of that results in curse. But Christ became just such a curse for us by dying a death accursed by the law. Yet God raised Jesus, indicating that he no longer approves the law, but rather the way of faith in Christ Jesus. We ought to be like Abraham.

3:15-18 Midrashic homily number 2. Continuing his reflections on Abraham, Paul notes that God made his promise to Abraham and his offspring about 430 years before he gave the law to Moses. The promise which preceded the law has been fulfilled in Jesus, the offspring of Abraham (see Matt 1:1).

The contemporary reader might find these verses rather confusing, perhaps even nitpicking, and not very enlightening or convincing. Paul's listeners or readers would note at least two things. One, the Hebrew Bible does not speak unambiguously of a 430-year period between Abraham and the law (see Exod 12:40 and Gen 15:13), but the number does appear in a Targum, that is, a paraphrase of Scripture heard in synagogue services at the time of Paul. "But the number of 430 years had passed away since the Lord spoke to Abraham . . . until the day they went out of Egypt" (Palestinian Targum on Exod 12:40).

Two, Paul's insistence on "descendant" (singular) rather than "descendants" (plural) is clear and obvious in the Hebrew Bible. It would strike the modern reader as preacher's overkill. But in the Targums wherever this word "descendant" appears (Gen 12:7; 13:15; 17:7; 22:18; 24:7), the rendition is always plural: descendants, making it impossible to apply the text to a single individual like Jesus.

What is the point? Paul bases himself NOT so much on what his readers (or their antagonists) might have *read* in the Scriptures, but rather on what they would have *heard* in the Targums, the paraphrases, at synagogue services. In one instance Paul agrees with the Targums, in another he disagrees. Ever the masterful pastoral minister, Paul moves from the known to the unknown, but he always respects the experience and abilities of his people.

3:19-28 Why then the Torah? The answer is simple. The Torah was to be like the pedagogue in ancient times (NAB: "disciplinarian"), whose task it was to take children to school, make sure they paid attention, to discipline them when necessary, and to see to their moral and physical safety. The monitor insured discipline and restraint in the young person's life until that individual reached the age or gained the skill of self-discipline and self-restraint. Like the monitor, the Torah provided discipline and restraint until Christ came and made authentic self-restraint and self-control possible.

The direct address in verse 26, "You are all children of God," makes the remarks personal and is also still another appeal to the emotional anchorage these converts used to have to the gospel Paul preached. According to this good news, "You are all one in Christ Jesus" (v. 28). Differences are not important, so don't bother about them. (See 1 Cor 7:17-28 for a repetition of these contrasting pairs with Paul's comments on not bothering about the differences.)

3:29–4:7 Midrashic homily number 3. The word "heir" appears in 3:29 and 4:7, indicating that all these verses constitute a unity and that inheritance is their theme. Indeed, verse 29 boldly and clearly announces that one who believes in Christ is an heir of Abraham (not Moses) and inherits the fulfillment of the promises made to Abraham.

Now, according to Palestinian custom, a father would appoint a guardian for his son in his will who in the event of the father's death would administer the son's inheritance until he came of age. From this perspective, the son, even if entitled to enormous wealth, is no better than a slave.

In the same way, argues Paul, before believers came "of age," that is, before Christ came to take up his earthly mission, they too were no better than slaves. Specifically, the slavery was bondage to the "elemental powers of the world" (vv. 3 and 9). Scholars are divided on the interpretation of this phrase. One very plausible interpretation relates the phrases to astrology and the heavenly bodies which fascinated the ancients. They believed that the heavenly bodies controlled the physical elements of the world and guided human destiny. Modern individuals who check the newspaper daily to determine whether their horoscope is favorable or not are in a bondage similar to the one Paul describes. Evidence of the thorough permeation of astrological beliefs in ancient Judaism can be found in the mosaic on the floor of the sixth-century Beth Alpha synagogue just south of Galilee. The design contains the twelve signs of the zodiac, but substitutes the twelve tribes of Israel for the expected designations.

Christ, who was born under the law, delivered believers from the law as well as from bondage to astrological determinism. He offers the possibility of being daughters and sons, not slaves. And God himself confirms one's status as his child by sending the spirit of his Son who empowers the believer to speak intimately to God as Father, "Daddy."

4:8-20 A personal plea. In this section Paul intensifies his personal and emotional appeal to his readers. Playing on the Semitic understanding of "know" as descriptive of the most intimate possible relationship between people (as when Adam "knew" Eve and she conceived), he asks how they could ever turn away from such a relationship with God to something less.

Why in the world would the Galatian converts want to embrace ceremonial observance of "days and months, seasons and years"? Paul probably has in mind such days as the sabbath, seasons like Passover, months like the "new moon," and years like the sabbatical year (see Lev 25:5). Granted, these Jewish practices are not in the same category as pagan star worship, but Paul's point is almost hidden in verse 9: "Now that you have come to be known by God." In other words, since it is God's initiative that counts, why do you revert to reliance upon human observances, human calculations? That attitude is equivalent to worshiping those "elemental powers."

"I implore you, brothers," pleads Paul pulling out all the emotional stops, "be as I am because I have also become as you are." By this he means: "Adopt my attitude toward the Torah: as law, it is abrogated; we are free!" His plea echoes similar statements in 1 Cor 11:1; 1 Thess 1:6; Phil 3:17, where he offers himself as an example worth imitating.

Finally, Paul resorts to a feminine image (quite surprising for an alleged misogynist!) of labor pains (v. 19) to describe his loving concern for the Galatians. (See also 1 Thess 2:7 where Paul presents himself as a nursing mother.) His point is that he, not the Judaizers, is the more tenderly caring and genuinely concerned for their spiritual welfare.

4:21-31 Midrashic homily number 4. Mention of labor pains may have prompted this final homiletic snippet on Abraham's wives, the mothers, and their children Ishmael and Isaac. Paul identifies this section as "allegory," that is, a creative reinterpretation of scriptural events and personalities as foreshadowing future truths and events. Clearly everything is hindsight in this interpretation and not at all literally in the text.

The point is that "you, brothers" are free children, "children of the promise" (v. 28). You are children of Sarah who can be interpreted as representing the Abraham Covenant, a context entirely free from the Torah's legal prescriptions. You are not slave children, like Ishmael, son of Hagar, who can represent Mount Sinai and all the legal prescriptions of the Torah.

We can almost hear Paul laughing derisively as he writes: "Do you really want to be subject to the Torah?" Then do what the story says: "Drive out the slave woman and her son . . ." (v. 30 citing Gen 21:10). Cast out those Judaizers and you will really be obeying the Torah!

Paul has developed these reflections on the basis of Gen 16, 17, and 21, but nowhere in these or any Hebrew texts is there mention of Ishmael persecuting Isaac (see Gal 4:29). Very likely Paul once again draws on a rabbinic interpretation familiar in his day. The Hebrew text of Gen 21:9 states simply that Ishmael was playing with Isaac. But in the rabbinic commentary Genesis Rabbah, the Hebrew word translated as "playing, joking, laughing" is taken in a bad sense. The tradition then says this: "And Ishmael took a bow and arrows and started shooting them in the direction of Isaac, making it appear as if he was joking." Paul applies this tradition to the experience of the Galatians from the Judaizers.

Is this farfetched? Not really. The Palestinian Targum on Gen 22, that is, the interpretation that might well have been heard in synagogue services, situated the "persecution" notion just mentioned in the context of a discussion on circumcision. "Ishmael . . . said: I am more righteous than you [Isaac], because I was circumcised at thirteen years of age. At that age, if I didn't want to be circumcised, no one could have forced me. But you, Isaac, were circumcised as a child of eight days. Who knows? If you had been older, perhaps you would have resisted circumcision." Isaac, of course, denies this hypothesis and says that now (at age thirty-six in this situation), he'd give all his members to be cut off if that's what the Holy One were to require. Once again, then, Paul uses traditions familiar to his people from the synagogue.

PRACTICAL EXHORTATIONS

Gal 5:1–6:10

5:1-12 Remain free. Having completed his scriptural argumentation in chapters 3 and 4,

Paul now draws practical conclusions in the final chapters. He urges those who have yielded to pressure and adopted circumcision (v. 4 "are separated from Christ" and v. 7 "hindered" both describe accomplished facts) to dig in, to stand firm, to yield no more!

The absolute and uncompromising stance Paul takes in this letter against circumcision may have been a development in his own thinking. True, in Gal 2:3 he is pleased that Titus, at the Jerusalem meeting around A.D. 49, was not forced to accept circumcision. Yet Acts 16:3 (describing a time frame very soon after the Jerusalem meeting) indicates that Paul had Timothy circumcised in order that he might gain increased legitimacy and credibility in his ministry among the Jews. Timothy came from mixed parentage (Jewish mother and Gentile father), and it seems clear that Paul had him circumcised NOT that he might be saved, but rather that his chances of being accepted by Jewish audiences be improved. But this present letter, from a slightly later time frame, shows no willingness to allow even this consideration. We have been freed from the demands of the Torah; we ought to remain free.

5:13-25 True freedom. Earlier (2:4) Paul mentioned the "freedom that we have in Christ Jesus." Now, addressing the Galatians affectionately ("brothers"), he offers a further explanation. Freedom is not unfettered self-indulgence. "Serve one another through love" (v. 13), says Paul. The Greek verb should literally be translated "render slave-service" to one another. That would accurately reflect Paul's Judaism-conditioned understanding that the human person is never absolutely free, subject to no one. Even in the Exodus, the Jews were freed only to be able to serve God more faithfully.

Paul's point is that formerly, that is, before the advent of Christ, we all were slaves to the elements of the world or to all the legal demands of the Torah (see Gal 4:21-31). But when Jesus died the death cursed by the Torah and was raised from the dead by God, it became obvious that Jesus was the individual who pleased God most entirely; he was the perfectly obedient person. By raising Jesus, God abrogated Torah, and in Christ we have a new freedom, a freedom for a new kind of service. In Christ, differences are not important; what really counts is "faith working through love" (*agápē* in Greek, v. 6), through slave-service to other Christians.

How can a believer render this service concretely? Paul summons two favorite images: "flesh" and "spirit" to explain. We must serve believers by fruit of the spirit and not by deeds of flesh. "Flesh" describes the human being as entirely self-reliant, weak, earthbound, unredeemed. "Spirit" describes the knowing and willing core of the individual, that part of a person most suitable for receiving and responding to the Spirit of God. The present tense of the Greek verb "serve" or "render slave-service" to one another describes an enduring line of conduct, a way of life, not just an individual, isolated act.

This is, in fact, Paul's way of life! He likes to describe himself as slave (1 Cor 9:19) or servant for Jesus' sake (2 Cor 4:5). In context, it is Paul's service to other believers that proves that he is slave or servant.

Specifically for the Galatians, Paul lists actions to be avoided (5:19-21) and actions to be done (5:22-23). The deeds to be avoided, that is, the deeds of a way of life rooted in the "flesh" (self-reliance, selfishness) can be clustered into four groups: sexual aberrations (the first three items), heathen worship (the next two), social evils (seven items, many in the plural indicating numerous and repeated occurrences), and intemperance (the last three items). Notice that these are all failures against justice and love. This cannot and should not be the life-style of those who have accepted the rule of God in their lives.

In contrast, Paul proposes for imitation the fruit of the spirit which is love (*agápē*), together with nine other representative desirable qualities that should characterize a believer's relationships with other believers (5:22-23).

Such lists were very common in antiquity. Ezek 18:5-9 is one example in Jewish Scripture; pagan philosophers, like Aristotle, had their own similar lists. But the pagan Plutarch criticizes the virtue list drawn up by Chrisippus as a "creation of a beehive of virtue neither customarily practiced nor well known from experience." What is noteworthy about Paul is that his lists are shorter, and they appear very rarely in his authentic letters. (The Gospels have no such lists at all!)

Paul is not interested in setting up new laws. Throughout his letters he offers a variety of suggestions for appropriate behaviors: sometimes he presents his own life-style (Gal 4:12); at other times he proposes the general notion of freedom that includes slave-service to believers (Gal 5:1-15). The present listing of deeds of flesh and fruit of the spirit (Gal 5:19-26) suggests how believers ought to behave and not behave toward other believers. There is no indication of how the recipients of these deeds should respond. On the other hand, 1 Cor 9:1-14 is an example of a list of reciprocal rights and duties between and among believers. Behind all these Pauline suggestions is Paul's hope that Christians will "be transformed by the renewal of your mind, that you may discern what is the will of God, what is good and pleasing and perfect" (Rom 12:2).

The final verses (5:24-26) of this section sum up Paul's feelings very pointedly. Those who have accepted Christ have definitively, once and for always put aside the way of the flesh and should live, walk, and be led by the spirit.

6:1-10 Final exhortations. Though some have yielded to Judaizing pressures (5:4), there still remain among the Galatians those who live by the spirit. Paul addresses these individuals and urges them to fulfill the law of Christ by gently helping one another bear any problems that may occur. The apparent contradiction in verse 5 ("each will bear his own load") disappears when it is viewed as a natural sequence to verse 4, encouraging personal responsibility for individual conduct.

Verse 6 stands apart from the context because it seems entirely unconnected with what precedes and what follows. Yet the comment is eminently practical. Even in Paul's day, there was no such thing as a free lunch. The verse is addressed to those under instruction (catechumens, to use a later word) and urges that such an individual share all she or he has with the instructor, that is, make a financial or other contribution to the support of the teacher.

The remaining verses exhort the readers once more to be faithful to a spirit-guided lifestyle rather than to a flesh-directed one. The general instruction to do good to all people but especially to fellow believers squares well with the specific suggestions in 5:21-23, all of which are one-sided directives. These instructions do not describe what one can expect in return for such behavior. This is quite normal in the context of the household. Paul's generalization sums it up well here.

CONCLUSION

Gal 6:11-18

6:11-18 Personal concluding comments. As in other letters (1 Cor 16:21), Paul now adds personal comments in his own handwriting. For a final time he repeats his criticism of the Judaizers who continue to pressure the Galatians to be circumcised for failing themselves to obey the entire Torah. They are interested solely in personal satisfaction and in gaining an accomplishment about which they might boast far and wide.

Paul's boast and pride is in the redemption wrought by the passion and death of Jesus. United to this event and embracing its significance, Paul has rejected a way of life measured by external observances of the law and has been created afresh. That's what really counts. Those who accept this kind of life-style as a meaningful way of life are the really chosen people of God, the Israel of God, the authentic Christian community. To them Paul sends wishes of peace (total well-being) and mercy (God's kindness).

His final lines are as terse as the salutation of this letter. His body already shows the physical effects of his labors and sufferings in the ministry (2 Cor 11:23-25). He pleads with the Galatians not to add any more by troubling him. The concluding blessing is unusually brief and formal, though warmed ever so slightly with his affectionate address, "Brothers." Even in closing Paul makes one final attempt to reactivate their emotional anchorage to the gospel he preached.

ROMANS

John J. Pilch

INTRODUCTION

At the beginning of his third missionary trip, Paul wrote his Epistle to the Galatians. Now at the end of this same period of activity, during a three-month stay in the province of Achaia (Greece), he wrote this letter from the city of Corinth to the Christians in Rome. The date is probably very late in A.D. 56, or early in 58, during the winter.

Paul, of course, did not found the Roman church as he did the Galatian churches. It seems that it was established by members of the Jewish-Christian community in Jerusalem who had traveled to Rome. But about A.D. 49 Emperor Claudius ordered the Jews expelled. After Claudius died around year 54, Jewish Christians who returned to Rome were surprised to meet a large number of Gentile Christians. Converts had multiplied. The Roman Christian church, then, to whom Paul sent this letter was predominantly Gentile-Christian.

Now during his missionary activity, Paul encouraged the Gentile churches to take up a collection which he would personally deliver to the poor in Jerusalem (Rom 15:25-27). His plan was to visit Jerusalem briefly and then to set out for Spain and the West with an intervening visit to Rome (15:28).

Paul may well have had some concerns or even apprehension about visiting Jerusalem. Perhaps he even feared for his safety. Yet he hoped that delivering the collection in person would defuse any still-smoldering anger or hostility concerning his preaching. The circumstances surrounding the Jerusalem visit make it quite plausible that Paul wrote this letter to the Romans to achieve a number of purposes.

First, the letter provided an opportunity to introduce himself to a community which for the most part did not know him personally. Second, he could marshal, evaluate, and summarize the arguments he might have to present in Jerusalem if his preaching were still being challenged. Third, he may well have had the Jewish-Christian minority in Rome uppermost in mind when he composed this letter. The section on the Jews (Rom 9–11) and the chapters on living in mutual harmony (especially Rom 14–15) could have been calculated to win the affection of this minority. If Paul were successful, he would have powerful support from them for his anticipated difficulties in Jerusalem.

History records that Paul's fears were realized. He was arrested in Jerusalem, imprisoned in Caesarea for two years, and finally arrived in Rome around A.D. 60 or 61, some three or four years after his letter had arrived.

Has the biblical God of surprises ever acted differently with his people? The old proverb expresses it well: the creature proposes but God disposes!

Yet this same proverb or outlook raises a question about God's fair play. This epistle, and especially chapters 9–11, could create the impression that God is unjust. How can he have made such great promises to Israel, but grant their fulfillment to the Gentiles instead? To understand Paul, remember that he views God's word as promise and gospel or good news. But God's word can trigger two possible responses: belief or unbelief. God is always faithful; he never leaves his creatures without his address or promise. Experience shows, however, that some hear him and believe while others hear him and take offense. Paul believes that some of Israel is in the latter category.

Rom 9–11 stands at the heart of contemporary Jewish-Christian dialogue. It is important for the reader to understand Paul, his sociocultural context (for example, his postconversion attitude toward the Torah), and his attempt to analyze and explain the actions of both God and his creatures. But it is equally important to strive to grasp the Jewish perception of Paul, the Jewish evaluation of and response to Jesus, and the healthy and thriving pluralism in Jewish belief and practice. We are still far from possessing totally satisfying answers to all our questions, but each new effort—like this commentary—is another sure step in the right direction.

OUTLINE OF ROMANS

COMMENTARY

GREETINGS AND INTRODUCTION

Rom 1:1-17

1:1-7 Paul greets the Christians at Rome. In this longest of all greetings in Paul's letters, he adds to the customary wishes of grace and peace six verses that describe the good news he preaches everywhere. This good news concerns Jesus who is both a descendant of David and God's Son as is evident from God's having raised Jesus from the dead.

This last statement is crucial for understanding Paul's Epistle to the Romans because it is central to his new attitude toward the Torah or the Law. After Jesus died a very shameful and dishonorable death—accursed by the Torah itself (Deut 21:23)—he was believed by some Jews to have been raised by the God of Israel. If God so blessed such an individual, then he must have abrogated the Torah. In other words, in Paul's understanding the Torah was no longer "law," no longer normative or obligatory. Instead, Torah became a guiding story, a Sacred Scripture that tells how we all got to the present, but it no longer has any binding rules for the future (see Rom 3:20).

Then, by way of introducing himself to this community which he did not personally establish, Paul declares that God appointed him to preach this good news—even at Rome—so that all people might become completely obedient to God as a result of accepting and believing in Jesus.

1:8-15 A prayer of thanksgiving. Continuing the customary letter-writing format of his day, Paul thanks God for the world-acknowledged progress that the Roman Christians are making in their faith. There is an interesting dynamic underlying this thanksgiving prayer. At least four times in this paragraph, Paul mentions his longstanding eagerness to visit the Romans. The purpose of this thanksgiving and its repeated mention of the desire to visit is that Paul eagerly strives to initiate a personal relationship with people for the most part still strangers to him.

Thus, whereas with the Galatians Paul could reasonably presume to (re)activate commitment to himself, here with the Romans he will have to rely on his powers of persuasion. Note an immediate example in verse 11, where Paul promises to share with his Roman hosts in the future some spiritual gift, perhaps one or more of those mentioned later in Rom 12:6-8.

1:16-17 The letter's chief idea. The theme is announced briefly and pointedly. The gospel itself contains God's power to save. Faith is central: everything starts and ends with it. As Habakkuk (2:4) told his compatriots, the righteous individual lives out personal destiny by faith. It is precisely this human faith which makes it possible for God to exercise his power to the fullest.

I. SUMMARY OF PAUL'S GOSPEL

Rom 1:18–11:36

The Human Condition Without Christ

Rom 1:18–3:20

First, Paul paints a rather gloomy picture of existence without Christ. Neither paganism (1:18-32) nor Judaism (2:1-29) is able to deliver what Jesus can. Throughout this section (as well as the entire letter) Paul uses his ethnocentric Jewish perspective to prove his point. While addressing this letter to a church that was predominantly Gentile-Christian, Paul nevertheless felt very sensitive to the disillusioned Jewish-Christian minority in Rome, and he concludes this section (3:1-20) with the recognition of some special advantage to being a Jew. Nevertheless, in the eyes of God, without Christ no one is innocent.

1:18-32 Paganism without Christ. Here Paul is particularly concerned about the irreligious or ungodly people who do not behave according to God's plan, which is plain as day to everybody in the orderliness of creation.

Paul's perspective is rooted in the concept of God as holy and its logical consequences: all God's creation should be holy too (throughout Leviticus, for example, 11:45). Holiness means wholeness, wellness, personal integrity. Now these irreligious people certainly know what wholeness, wellness, and integrity in human life mean, but they have chosen the opposite. They have substituted parts of God's creation for God himself; this disregards the wholeness and completeness of God.

Further evidence of this distortion is to be found in their sexual conduct. As is clear in the Leviticus (11–15) rules regarding purity, holiness, wholeness, the human body is a symbol of the social religious body or community. These rules seek to protect body boundaries. Notice the high degree of concern about orifices or body openings, both ordinary (like the mouth, genitals) and unusual (like leprosy = skin eruptions). Thus Paul's remarks about "unnatural relations" (vv. 26 and 27) should be understood in the context of his concern for order, for wholeness, and for bodily integrity, which is supposed to mirror the order and integrity of society and the cosmos, viewed, of course, from a Jewish perspective. Hence "natural" and "unnatural" should be more accurately translated "culturally approved" and "culturally disapproved."

Another way of illustrating these irreligious people's disregard for appropriate wholeness, wellness, and integrity in creation is to list their sins, as in verses 29-31. Scholars generally admit that the list is rhetorical, haphazard, and reflective of popular outlooks. Recent research, however, suggests that the list does have a logic of its own.

Throughout the Bible the human person is viewed in terms of three zones of personal activity clustered around heart-eyes, mouth-ears, and hands-feet. These zones describe and symbolize the entire person. When all three zones are mentioned and not criticized, all is well. The person is considered totally good, integral, whole, holy. But when any zone is omitted or criticized, the person is perceived to be incomplete, unwhole, suffering lack of integrity. Here in these verses all zones are mentioned: greed = heart-eyes; murder = hands-feet; deceit = mouth-ears. But the total picture is faulty, undesirable, unwholesome, indicating that the irreligious or ungodly non-Jewish outlook and life-style are thoroughly and completely perverse, fragmented, and incomplete. Well, what else would you expect without Jesus?

2:1-11 Religious alternatives in living. The basic principle which guides Paul's thinking here is expressed in verse 11: "There is no partiality with God" (recall the discussion at Gal 2:1-10 above). Lest anyone feel especially privileged or exempt from God's judgment, Paul reminds the readers that each person will reap the consequences of individual deeds. Those who pursue the life-style described by the list in Rom 1:29-31 will earn God's wrath and fury. Those who seek glory, honor, and immortality by patiently and persistently doing the right thing will gain eternal life. It makes no difference whether one is Jew or Greek!

2:12-16 The Torah is not a privilege. Pagans who of course do not possess the Torah are nevertheless guided by their experience of the transcendent claim of God's will. Their own interior reflections debate the propriety or impropriety of what they seek to do. If they do good, it will be to their credit. If not, it will redound to their judgment. And the same is true for the Jews! It is not mere possession of the Torah that is important and salvific. It is rather obeying or transgressing the Torah that counts. And it is Jesus who will do the judging at the final reckoning. This is part of Paul's good news.

2:17-24 Jews fail to live up to the Torah. Here for the first time Paul's imaginary debating partner since Rom 2:1 is identified: one known as "Jew," the common name by which members of God's chosen people were designated by non-Jews. In a masterpiece of rhetoric, Paul first lists five legitimate claims (verbs) deriving from being a Jew (vv. 17-18); he then switches to four nouns (vv. 19-20) identifying key roles Jews could fulfill for non-Jews.

But in verses 21-22, Paul raises four embarrassing and indicting questions that each point out a discrepancy between claim and performance. The preachers simply don't live according to what they preach!

This segment of the debate is brought to a close with a reinterpreted citation from the Greek version of Isa 52:5: "Because of you (my unfaithful Jewish people), I am continually blasphemed among the Gentiles." It is a stinging rebuke to the imaginary Jewish debating partner who could well be imagined applauding Paul's earlier indictment of the pagans at the end of chapter 1.

2:25-29 Circumcise the heart, not the body. To drive the barb even deeper, Paul criticizes circumcision interpreted as an automatically effective ritual. Quite the contrary, argues the Apostle. What really counts is not a mark on the body, but a changed heart. The true Jew is not one that carries a visible physical credential, but rather one whose inner core, whose heart, has been affected by the Spirit. In a play on words rooted in Hebrew, the true Jew (Yᵉhûdî) is the one praised (hôdāh) by God, not by other human beings.

3:1-8 Paul responds to objections. Continuing the diatribe, Paul anticipates the obvious objection: is there any advantage to being a Jew if the Gentiles can be so well off?

Though his argumentation may suggest a resounding no, Paul says quite definitely yes! Chief among the privileges of Judaism is that God shared his word, the entire Jewish Scripture, with these people.

But the questioner persists: what if some of them (Jews) have proved unfaithful? Will God then break his part of the covenant, renege on his promises? Not at all, replied Paul. God will definitely be vindicated in the final analysis, even though human beings—perhaps every single one—will fall short. Paul cites Ps 51:6 to bolster his point.

Pressing still further, the questioner wonders: if our sole purpose is to make God look good, isn't he unjust in punishing us for our wrongdoing? Again Paul answers firmly in the negative. To support his contention he recalls the very basic Jewish belief that God is indeed the judge of all the world—Jews as well as non-Jews (see Isa 66:16).

Verse 8 appears to suggest that Paul's teaching was misunderstood and considered blasphemous. Some had pushed his views to unwarranted conclusions that individuals should sin freely in order to let God do good things. Paul identifies the charge as a slanderous presentation of his teaching and concludes the verse with "their penalty is what they deserve."

3:9-20 All human beings are under the power of sin. In these concluding verses to the opening section of this letter, Paul continues the line of reasoning he has been pursuing and asks whether Jews might consider themselves in some way superior to all others. His answer is direct and forceful: no, all people are under the power of sin.

Notice that phrase "domination of sin." Literally, the Greek reads "under sin," yet the addition of domination (or power) is a correct and proper interpretation. Paul understands sin as a negative and hostile power permeating society. It is a coercive power that dominates groups (see Rom 6:12, 14). It is also a lawgiver subjecting human beings to itself (see Rom 7:23, 25).

Sin's power is very much like that of a slave dealer (Rom 6:16-19) or like that of sickness, specifically the first-century sickness known as demonic possession (Rom 7:8-24). Thus, three well-known "power" experiences in Paul's social world (empire, slavery, demon possession) provided him with imagery to describe the power of the evil (sin) permeating his groups. Individual sinful actions are merely symptomatic of sin.

Then, following his custom, Paul turns once again to Scripture to support his arguments. Verses 10b-18 string together assorted citations from the Greek translation of the Jewish Scriptures: Ps 14:1-3, or 53:2-4; Pss 5:10; 140:4; 10:7; and Isa 59:7-8. The citations are comprehensive, colorful, and quite varied in detail.

Modern readers are understandably awed by this sweeping knowledge of Scripture. Yet the frequent repetition of certain passages and the regular linkage of certain texts have led scholars to conclude that Paul and other Christian preachers gathered favorite passages into collections of testimonies or "proof texts." As a preacher found a passage which might be applied to Jesus, it was recorded and added to other such passages. These testimonies then served as the basis for reflective and creative meditations on the Scriptures in the light of Jesus. Similar clusters of texts or testimonies are found in Rom 9:25-33; 10:15-21; 11:8-10, 26, 34-35; and 15:9-12.

In the present passage notice that the various citations seem to be linked to one another by references to parts of the body. Superimposing the Jewish understanding of the human body as noted earlier, we observe this concentric arrangement: a (v. 11) heart-eyes; b (v. 12) hands-feet; c (vv. 13-14) mouth-ears; b' (vv. 15-16) hands-feet; and a' (vv. 17-18) heart-eyes.

This deliberate arrangement draws attention to the centerpiece c, which emphasizes mouth-ears. All these verses together describe a totally, comprehensively unrighteous person, but mouth-ears stands out. How cleverly appropriate then is Paul's closing comment that "every mouth may be silenced," and the whole world without exception is totally convicted.

This tissue of texts is identified as pre-Pauline, that is, it was very likely compiled prior to Paul's usage of it. Its obvious purpose is to describe the human being as totally, comprehensively unrighteous. The opening sentence (v. 11) affirms that everyone without exception—non-Jews as well as Jews—falls under this description. Paul may have made the concentric rearrangement, but he clearly has added the pointed conclusion (vv. 19-20).

Actually, the concluding verses of this section summarize the point of the entire discussion since chapter 1. In the presence of God, no one is innocent. Paul's curious reference to what the *law* says in verse 19, following the list of citations from the psalms and a prophet, makes it quite clear that Paul uses law here in a wider sense than Torah/Pentateuch. He means the entire Jewish Scripture. His concluding implicit citation is from Ps 143:2 which he emends by adding "by observing the law." The law is thus a moral informer, that is, it gives a reflective person a real and deep religious awareness and recognition of moral disorder.

SALVATION THROUGH FAITH IN CHRIST

Rom 3:21–4:25

Having painted a gloomy picture of hopelessness for human existence apart from Christ, Paul now shares with his readers the exhilarating and liberating insight that God has a much simpler way of putting people right with himself: namely, through faith in Christ Jesus.

3:21-31 Here's how God does it. Yet another statement of Paul's basic thesis is expressed in verse 28: a person enters into a right relationship with God by faith and not by seeking to observe all the detailed requirements of the Jewish Torah. One must believe rather than achieve. And this thesis does not contradict or nullify Jewish Scripture (v. 31, notice that "law" really refers to all of Scripture). On the contrary, it supports and confirms the basic message of Scripture.

The rabbinic tradition records this opinion: "I am God over all that comes into the world, but I have joined my name only with you. I am not called the God of the Gentiles, but the God of Israel" (Exodus Rabbah 29, Rabbi Simon ben Yohai). Wrong, Paul would say! The one God (an echo of the Jewish prayer "Hear, O Israel") is God of all—Jews and Gentiles.

All human beings have failed God, have not measured up to their potential glory through their individual, personal misdeeds. But God quite freely has made it possible for all people to regain a right relationship with him through a believing acceptance of the redemptive death of Christ.

This, in fact, is the meaning of the phrase "the righteousness of God" in this passage. The words describe not so much an attribute of God as his activity. It is none other than God himself who justifies or renders upright each person on the basis of faith (v. 30).

4:1-25 Abraham, a model for the Christian believer. In the first century there was a popular Jewish opinion that Abraham knew and obeyed the Jewish Torah, even though he lived long before it was revealed to Moses. Paul challenges this opinion on the basis of Scripture itself. He cites two passages in support of his challenge: Gen 15:6 (in vv. 3, 9, and 22) and Ps 32:1-2.

In Genesis it is reported that Abraham believed God and it was credited to him as justice. The key word is "credited" (or "reckoned" in some translations). It is a bookkeeping term applied figuratively in Scripture to the conduct of a person. Here, in Rom 4:3-6, 8, Paul's use of the word means more than that. His point is that Abraham's faith was recognized by God for exactly what it was: namely, a sign of his uprightness, his good standing with God.

Paul quotes Ps 32:1-2 to repeat the idea: truly fortunate is the person to whom God credits or reckons justice or uprightness, apart from the performance of deeds listed by the Jewish Torah.

Arguing according to Jewish rules, Paul has cited two witnesses to support his view: Abraham (Genesis) and David (Psalms). Deut 19:15 required two witnesses in order that any testimony might be considered valid and convincing. But if Paul was truly convinced that the Torah was no longer binding (see commentary on Rom 1:1-7 above), why would he himself try to obey Deut 19:15? Even though the death and resurrection of Jesus have given him a totally new interpretation of the Jewish Scripture, Paul remains in the last analysis a Pharisaic Jew (Phil 3:5) and is best understood as continuing to reason and argue within that cultural mindset.

But Paul's imaginary Jewish opponent is still not satisfied because it would seem as if the psalm declares happiness for the Jew and not for the Gentile. Again Paul looks to Abraham to illustrate his answer. About twenty-nine years after God declared Abraham upright (see Gen 15), Abraham was circumcised (see Gen 17). Clearly then Abraham was reckoned as upright before circumcision, and the psalm's declaration of happiness therefore applies to anyone who like Abraham strives to believe rather than to achieve. In Abraham's case circumcision was a sign or seal that testified to the uprightness gained by faith long prior to the actual circumcision. Thus Abraham is truly the father of all believers whether circumcised (Jews) or not (non-Jews).

In addition, God promised Abraham an heir and a huge posterity (Gen 15:4; 22:16-18), also independently of observing the Jewish Torah. Verses 17-25 play on the word "dead." Abraham was positively convinced that God could realize his promise from the reproductively "dead" bodies of himself and his wife Sarah. Indeed, Abraham is a father of many nations, a father of us all. Three times in this chapter Paul repeats the Scripture that affirms that Abraham's faith was reckoned or credited to him as uprightness, driving home the importance of this fact for his Roman readers, both the predominant Gentile Christians as well as the Jewish-Christian minority.

Both we and Abraham believe in God who can bring life out of death. For Abraham, God brought life out of Sarah's dead womb; for Christians, God raised Jesus from death and thereby restored them to life through the resulting justification.

THE CHRISTIAN LIFE

Rom 5:1–8:39

In chapter 5 a new emphasis emerges. God's love comes to the fore while justification and righteousness recede to the background. Specifically, Paul describes the Christian experience of new life at peace with God.

5:1-11 How it feels to be right with God. Nearly everyone at one time or another has experienced the relief that follows the resolution of a doubt or the solution of a problem. That feeling of relief is very much like the three effects Paul identifies which result when one has a right relationship with God: peace (v. 1), confidence (v. 2), and a present share in the risen life of Christ himself (v. 10).

These effects are all the more impressive when one recognizes that Jesus died for us when we were at our worst! As difficult to believe or accept as that might be, we have the proof of it in our hearts where God's love has placed the Holy Spirit to guide us in the new life.

Small wonder then that Paul "boasts" three times in these few verses. Boasting, in its biblical meaning, is a way of acknowledging one's personal lord and master. The unredeemed person boasts through self-praise, but the person who acknowledges redemption through Jesus boasts in God himself (v. 11; see Jer 9:23) and in the certainty of sharing in God's glory (v. 2).

This understanding explains how in addition to boasting about his hope (v. 2) and God (v. 11), he can also boast about his afflictions (v. 3). Paul is not a masochist. Rather, he describes his newly discovered ability to resist the challenges and risks of *thlipseis* (Greek for "afflictions") that results from following Jesus. The risk they entail is that they could possibly cause an individual to give up on God. Patiently endured, however, these hardships serve to highlight a God-pleasing attitude of openness to the future characterized by great freedom from death and sin (5:12-21), from self (6:1-23), and from the Torah as law (7).

5:12-21 Freedom from sin and death. This passage has stimulated centuries of debate and caused deep divisions among Christians. Catholics have some guidance in the debate from the Council of Trent (1545), which declared that Paul's words in these verses do indeed teach some form of original sin.

Of course, neither Trent nor Paul used that exact phrase, and readers should be careful not to read into these verses of the epistle the fuller understanding which they have gained from modern religious instruction. Trent affirms that Paul declares the reality of the sin and its universal terrible impact upon all creation. The sin is transmitted (or inherited), but Paul does not indicate how.

In reading verses 12-21 it is important to recognize that "sin" and "death" are personifications of forces. Sin in Paul is an active force within and among all human beings. It has been present since the very beginnings of the human race (as this passage asserts) and expresses itself chiefly through the "flesh." Flesh is not a synonym for body. Rather, flesh describes a person from the perspective of unredeemed weakness. Death is also a personified, cosmic (Rom 8:38) force, which not only destroys the human body but causes definitive separation from God as well.

Paul's main interest is not to talk about sin or death, but rather to draw a contrasting picture of Adam and Christ, prominent figures of the beginning and the end time respectively. Adam is a "type" or "prototype" of the person to come, namely, Jesus, who would far surpass what Adam did. The world was changed by both of these individuals.

Adam unleashed an active hostile force into the world (sin), which had the power to cause definitive alienation (death) from God, the source of all life, inasmuch as or because all individuals have sinned through personal, actual deeds (v. 12). Thus death has two causes in human existence: Adam's sin and personal ratification of that deed by individuals who sin. This was Adam's effect on the world.

In contrast, Christ's effect is starkly different. Through the gracious gift, namely, the redemptive death of Jesus Christ uprightness and life superabound for all individuals who accept him.

The far-reaching perverse consequences of Adam's disobedience is reported in rabbinic terms which divided time into three periods: Adam to Moses, two thousand years of chaos; Moses to the Messiah, two thousand years of law; from the Messiah onward there would be two thousand years of blessing. In the first period, Adam to Moses, there was no law to disobey (v. 14), yet definitive separation from God (spiritual death) held sway, so pervasive was the effect of Adam's misdeed.

Jesus changed this dreary situation through his obedience. The contrast between Adam and Jesus not only highlights the tragedy of Adam's failure but also the magnificent plenitude of Christ's redemption.

In the final verses (20-21) law is personified as a force and identified as the cause of sin and its companion death. But law as force has been overcome by grace which now rules through uprightness, which grants a share in the very life of God himself through Christ our Lord.

6:1-11 Freedom from self. Whereas in Rom 3:5-8 Paul explained why a Jew should not continue sinning so that God could "star," here he answers the same question for the Christian. Baptism, he explains, has worked a very real change in the life of a believer. Through baptism, a believer is united very intimately with Christ and his destiny. As Christ has died so too the Christian truly dies or is truly liberated from the hostile force known as sin which alienates a person from God. As Christ was raised by the Father and thereby enjoys a new relationship with his Father, so too the believer now has a very real share in this new way of life, this new principle of vitality. The power of the resurrection already rules in us. How then can anybody deny this reality and return to a former sinful way of life? It's simply unthinkable!

The "sinful body" mentioned by Paul in verse 6 is an instance of a part representing a whole. The body represents the entire person insofar as it is dominated by an almost unavoidable proneness to sin. But this "old self" truly died with Jesus. The sinful inclination has been destroyed. The tyranny of death has been broken. In fact, death has brought a new status. Verse 11 sums up the thrust of this passage with an exhortation to the Christian: consider yourself snatched away from the power of the sinful force and incorporated instead into new life for God "in Christ Jesus." This latter phrase is a special term in Paul's writings that describes the intimate association of a believer with the life and destiny of Christ.

6:12-23 Free to serve. The high number of imperatives in this section characterizes it as a fervent exhortation that flows as a natural conclusion from the truth described in the first eleven verses. Notice how Paul's efforts at persuasion can easily take the form of a command if the premise is clear and convincing.

Don't let that alienating force (sin) govern your living (v. 12). Don't yield to the powerful cravings, desires, and intentions of your natural self which will only pit you against God. Once and for always give yourself over completely to God, literally to slave service of God (v. 22), so he might use you to do what is right. Don't let the force of sin have power over you. You live now under grace and not the canceled Jewish law.

What does this mean? What kind of freedom is a freedom for rendering "slave service"? It is a freedom quite unlike that which

mainstream citizens of the United States are familiar with. They understand freedom in terms of freedom from external obstacles or restraints in order to choose and pursue an individualistically determined goal.

For Paul, it is impossible to live a human life in total independence in the sense of being subject to no one. In these verses he clearly argues that the freedom from the power or force of sin worked by Jesus' death and resurrection does not mean total and complete human independence, but rather acceptance of another master, namely, God (v. 22). This is why the baptized person (slave of God in Christ) cannot continue to sin (be a slave of the power of sin).

7:1-25 Freedom from the law. Having discussed union with Christ (Rom 5) and the resulting freedom from sin and death (Rom 6), Paul now completes his discussion of Christian freedom with still another explanation of how believers are freed from the Jewish Torah understood as law.

In the first six verses Paul organizes his thoughts around the notion of death, suggested by the reflection on baptism immediately preceding. His example drawn from marriage is weak and unfinished, but the general idea is clear: death terminates obligations. When a woman's husband dies, she is free to remarry. Similarly through baptism we have been united to Christ's death which freed us from bondage to the Jewish law so as to be able to belong to Jesus and be productive in the service of God.

As verses 5-6 point out, the "law" here stands for a religious observance as a way of salvation. It involves a legalistic approach to Torah or any other objective norm of good and evil that does not at the same time give an individual the ability to fulfill it. Rather, a person's social and individual attempt to fulfill the law normally ends in nonfulfillment, thus revealing the presence of this powerful force (sin) actively promoting alienation from God. Paul insists that we died to this. Now we can serve God through a dynamic principle of new life (Spirit), whereas before all we had was a dead letter of the Mosaic law as guide.

Now Paul must take up a very painful consideration. The problem is: how is it that something which is good, just, and holy—indeed given by God (namely the Jewish

Torah) failed to bear good fruit but only fostered sin itself?

Paul's answer is that it was not the law that brought permanent alienation from God (death), but rather the power known as sin working through it. The reader must not be misled by Paul's use of "I" in these verses. In the light of his bold affirmation that "I was above reproach when it came to justice based on the law" (Phil 3:6), the "I" cannot be understood in an autobiographical sense. Paul is not talking about himself personally in Rom 7:7ff. Scholars rather identify the use of this personal pronoun as a rhetorical device in order to describe common human experience, an experience with which the readers could certainly identify.

Without the law, a person leads a relative or neutral existence: not in union with God, nor in rebellion either. But when the law was made known, it stimulated and unmasked sin, that pernicious power hostile to God. Upon close examination, we see that Paul is retelling the story of Adam as typifying the common lot of humankind. Though Adam lived long before the Jewish law was given, that first parent did receive a command from God. But sin, that latent force capable of diverting people from obeying God, did just that to Adam. Sin first deceived Adam, and then through the disobedience brought about death, that is, alienation from God. But the law itself is not synonymous with or equivalent to sin; it was rather intended to make people holy and just and good.

Verses 14-20 now describe what goes on inside a pious person, but from a Jewish perspective. Jewish tradition taught that there are two urges or drives in each person: a good one and a bad one. They are constantly at war with one another. The Jewish law derives from God's sphere, the "spiritual," and causes reverberations in the good drive or urge in each person. But experience shows that more often than not "weak flesh" prevails, that is, the natural self, that aspect of human existence that reverberates with the bad drives or urges. It is a natural playground for the force of sin. Hence the internal strife between the urges with embarrassing and discouraging outcomes. Sin as force is the culprit, not the law (v. 20). Our modern focus on sin as a deed or act makes it difficult to appreciate sin as force.

The final verses (21-23) move the picture to a broader horizon and describe every person. Here Paul's use of the word "law" is correctly translated as principles or recurrent patterns of personal experience. Paul says each person has an internal part which desires what God desires. He calls this the "inner self" or "mind" even in the unredeemed person. But there are also negative forces, and the internal struggle that takes place between the two is a frustrating and weakening process. No wonder Paul cries out for relief: "Who will deliver me from this mortal body?" The answer will come in the next chapter of Romans. In anticipation Paul sings a brief statement of praise.

8:1-39 Christian life in the Spirit. Rom 8 is the climax of the epistle to this point. Specifically it answers the question in 7:24: "Who will deliver me . . .?" The liberator is the Spirit (the word, which until now has appeared only five times, occurs twenty-nine times in this chapter alone), which is nothing else but the power or force of the risen Jesus present upon earth. The believer comes into contact with this force by living in union with Christ Jesus, a union already begun in baptism. This Spirit brings a vitality that the Mosaic law never could.

The contrast spirit-flesh introduced in verse 4 is further developed in verses 5-13. The terms represent competing fields of force or spheres of power. Flesh describes the earthbound person left to unaided individual ability. Spirit describes the earthbound person guided by the life-giving force or Spirit of Jesus. The self-centered all-sufficient person leads a life that can only lead to death, that is, definitive alienation from God. Such a person doesn't need God, doesn't submit to God's law in general, can't obey and can't please God.

On the other hand, the person guided by the life-giving Spirit finds both life and peace. Paul uses various descriptions of the Spirit: Spirit of God, Spirit of Christ, Christ—all to express the multifaceted reality of the Christian experience of a share in divine life.

In the final analysis the indwelling Spirit of God who raised Jesus will also raise us in the resurrection. So the inescapable conclusion is that we are in debt to the Spirit. We have an obligation to put to death the deeds, actions, pursuits of a person dominated by the flesh and live instead by the Spirit.

A very important result of being subject to the Spirit is that one becomes a true child of God. This is the first time the concept appears in Romans (8:14-17). The Spirit or force we have received is not one that would cast us back into fear, even a reverential fear. Rather this Spirit says we are dear to God, we are his very own children. Further, not only does the Spirit make this child relationship with God possible, but the same Spirit gives each of us the power to recognize it, that is, to say "Abba, father." Yet, lest anyone get too carried away with all this good news, Paul reminds the readers with two special compound verbs in Greek that we must suffer with Christ in order to be glorified with him.

Suffering, of course, simply can't compare with the glory or intimate share in God's life which is the destiny of each believer. Three things persuade us of the greatness of this glory: the testimony of creation (vv. 19-22), of believers (23-25), and of the Spirit (26-30).

God subjected creation to futility, that is, an inability to reach its goal. But he also left a spark of hope, and for this reason all creation is groaning as it waits for the final removal of chaos and the restoration to wholeness and integrity. We believers also are awaiting final and definitive redemption of our whole selves (our bodies) in confident hope with patient endurance.

Finally, the Spirit is the third witness to our glorious destiny. But the statement "we do not know how to pray as we ought" (v. 26) appears to contradict the one in verse 15 where the Spirit prompts the confident prayer "Abba, father." Perhaps Paul is offering a corrective to enthusiasm, an excessive emphasis on the gifts of the Spirit. The Greek of verse 26 literally says that the Spirit "intercedes over and above" our own intercessions "with ineffable groanings." It is possible that these groanings refer to the "words which cannot be uttered" heard by Paul in the third heaven (2 Cor 12:4).

Observe the plurals in verses 28-30. The statements refer to Christians as a group and not to individual believers. Paul underlines assurance about salvation. God is in control of everything. His will is that we be conformed to the image of Christ by a progressive share (v. 30—predestined, called, set right, given a share in glory) in the risen life of Christ himself. The ultimate goal is to become like the God who revealed himself in Jesus Christ.

The concluding verses (31-39) are a hymn-like celebration of the reality of the victory, the reality of being in the Spirit. The chief message is that God is for us, and the verses describe what "God-for-us" looks like. In a series of five questions, Paul explores how secure we really are, how certain we ought to be. That, of course, does not mean that life is a bed of roses. Verse 35 lists seven dangers or troubles that might separate us from the love Christ has for us. The list is not purely imaginary; it sums up the varied and potentially fatal attacks to which followers of Christ are commonly subject. The citation in verse 36 from Ps 44:23 was used often by the rabbis to describe the martyrdom of the pious. Yet the bottom line is positive, firm, and confidently secure. No other forces or powers (vv. 38-39), not even the personified power of the stars (height . . . depth), can separate us from the love of God that comes to us in Christ Jesus our Lord.

ISRAEL'S HOPE

Rom 9:1-11:36

Throughout this letter Paul has insisted that the Jewish Torah no longer binds as law, is no longer valid except as sacred story to tell how we reached this point in history. Now the time has come for Paul to draw from this story an explanation of how his spiritual and cultural kin have come to a moment of apparent rejection by God in the history of salvation.

9:1-29 God's free choice. The first five verses are quite an emotional statement. They reflect Paul's deep sensitivity in regard to his sisters and brothers, the Israelites (using their God-given title, see Gen 32:38). Proudly he enumerates seven privileges granted by God to the Jews: adoption as children; God's intimate presence; the covenants; the law; beautiful liturgy; the promises; and the patriarchs, from whom descended the greatest gift of all, the Messiah "who is God over all, blessed for ever" (RSV).

But what good is all of this if it proves to be of no benefit to Israel in the long run? Wouldn't we have to admit that God didn't keep his word? Of course not, Paul insists. Yet he will have to do some fancy scriptural footwork to explain his position convincingly to the Jews. Scriptural deftness, however, is no problem for Paul.

Gen 18:10 (or 18:14, or both combined) identifies Isaac as the child of promise (Rom 9:9). And the true children of God or children of the promise are the descendants of Isaac (Gen 21:12). It is faith that counts, not ethnicity. All of this is clear in the Scripture just cited.

Then Paul moves the argument even further to highlight God's free choices, his freedom to make choices. Just as God chose between two mothers, Sarah and Hagar, to find a recipient for his promise, so too does he choose between the two sons of a single mother, Rebekah: Esau and Jacob. Indeed, the choice of Jacob took place while the twins were still in the womb, before they were at all capable of doing anything toward merit or demerit. The scriptural proof is from the Torah and the prophets: Gen 25:23, "The older shall serve the younger," and Mal 1:2-3, "I loved Jacob, but hated Esau." God is entirely free to do what he wills and to choose whom he wills. The obvious application to Paul's discussion of Jews and Gentiles in his day raises a new objection: God is unjust!

Paul vigorously denies any charge that God is unjust. Again he returns to his arsenal of biblical texts to defend God's behavior. Moses and Pharaoh serve to illustrate the point. In Exod 33:19 God declares his free will to Moses. He can show mercy and pity to whomever he wills. Human intentions or activities are not the prime consideration. And Pharaoh illustrates how God can even use an enemy to achieve his will. Pharaoh hardened his own heart, that is, became stubborn and obdurate. God recognized the situation, affirmed and accepted it. In the process he gained salvation/redemption for the Israelites.

The reader can almost anticipate the next objection: if this be the case, how can God blame anybody? How can anyone be held responsible if no one can resist the will of God? Paul never really answers this question in the text. His actual answer is a diplomatically stated "shut up." The tradition of clay and the potter, or moulder of clay in the Scripture (Isa 29:16; Jer 18:6; Wis 15:7), provides the images for his reply. It's unheard of that any creature ever questioned its maker.

Actually God is quite patient. He has tolerated creatures who deserve his wrath in order that he might demonstrate the wealth of his glory to both Jews and Gentiles. This statement helps Paul finally describe quite clearly the present situation. He uses a tissue of texts that once again seem to have preexisted the composition of this letter.

Beginning with a text patched together from Hos 2:25 and 1:9 and originally applied to the ten unfaithful northern tribes, Paul applies them to the Gentiles: a nation not God's people would become his people; a nation formerly unloved would now be loved by God.

Then turning to Isa 10:22-23 Paul finds a bright spark of hope for his cultural and spiritual kin: "A remnant will be saved." Thus, God's promise continues to be valid, continues to tend toward final fulfillment. Without such a remnant Israel would be no better off than Sodom and Gomorrah. But there is hope. Even though God's ways appear arbitrary, he faithfully keeps his promises. Scripture, says Paul, bears witness to that.

9:30-33 Israel's failure is its own fault. Rom 9:30-33 both conclude chapter 9 and introduce chapter 10. The concluding Scripture citation is a combination of two texts. In their original context Isa 28:17 describes the Messiah as a foundation stone, and Isa 8:14-15 marks God as the stumbling stone. Paul's combination of these texts asserts that the Messiah who was intended to be a "stepping stone" for the Israelites became for them instead a "stumbling stone."

10:1-4 Christ is the end of the law. The truth of the matter for Paul is that with the coming of Christ, the time of the Messiah has arrived. The old order exists no more. In this sense Christ is the end of the period in which the Torah was operative and normative as law (review the commentary on Gal 2:11-21). Paul fervently prays for and earnestly desires the salvation of his compatriot Israelites. He knows firsthand that they have a keen zeal for God. But their zeal is not based on true knowledge. They sincerely believe that they can put themselves right with God. That is what they pursue. The authentic righteous relationship with God, of course, comes through faith.

10:5-13 Salvation is for all and is easy. As he often does, Paul adduces scriptural proof for what he has just said in verse 4. This string of texts again appears to be linked on the basis of the tripartite view of person in the Bible: hands-feet, mouth-ears, and heart-eyes. Lev 18:5 refers to hands-feet: the one who observes Torah will live as a consequence. The emphasis is on doing and achieving.

The righteousness that counts, however, is faith. Faith reflects the zone of heart-eyes. Indeed, that is what Deut 30:11-14 reflects as Paul adapts it to his purposes. Though the text originally applied to the Torah, Paul applies it to Jesus. No one need go up to heaven (hands-feet) to bring him down, for Christ came to earth in human form. Nor need anyone go to bring him back from the dead (hands-feet), because he has already been raised. God's salvation is available in Jesus Christ.

The word is on your lips (mouth-ears) and in your heart (heart-eyes). Observe how Paul draws on the two constituent zones of activity that contrast with doing (hands-feet). The emphatic conclusion is that no one who puts faith in Jesus will be confounded or gypped. All will be saved in the same way: Jew and Gentile alike.

The concluding citations (vv. 11 and 13) confirm the Deuteronomy passage in the same pattern of emphasis. Isa 28:16 is a heart-eyes passage: no one who believes in him will be shamed. Joel 3:5 is a mouth-ears passage: everyone who calls on the name of the Lord will be saved. The important thing is to recognize and declare Jesus as Lord, a phrase very likely borrowed from early church worship.

10:14-21 Israel has refused the Messiah. To wind up this discussion, Paul proposes four objections that could remove blame from Israel. The style is that of chain-argumentation. Each question retraces part of the previous one: (1) Perhaps no one preached the new understanding to Israel. No, preachers did come; Paul was one. He very definitely spoke about Jesus-Messiah and concentrated his efforts outside Palestine. This can't be an excuse. (2) Only very few believed (v. 16). True, says Paul, but already Isa 53:1 foresaw that kind of a situation. (3) Maybe the Jews didn't hear the preaching. Paul counters with a resounding "they most certainly did." And he cites Ps 19:5, saying creation itself has proclaimed the glory of God. (4) Finally, perhaps having heard the message about Christ, they didn't really understand it. Paul

denies that. Again he turns to Scripture (Deut 32:21) to show that even this ancient text predicted that Israel will be humiliated. Isa 65:1-2 wraps up the entire discussion, but Paul divides the verses and applies verse 1 to the Gentiles (they found God though they did not seek him), and verse 2 to the Jews (God patiently tried to reveal himself to an unbelieving people).

11:1-10 Israel's disbelief is partial, not total. Paul returns still once more to the nagging question: Has God rejected Israel? Again he denies it most emphatically and points to himself as an example. He is perhaps the most Jewish of all Jews, holding mint-Jewish credentials: he is an Israelite, descended from Abraham, and tracing lineage from the tribe of Benjamin. This was the first tribe to cross the Reed Sea, and it includes among its worthy members both Saul and Jeremiah.

But is Paul alone the "remnant"? No, he's like Elijah. In 1 Kgs 19:9-18 Elijah felt very much alone, but he had about seven thousand compatriots who were faithful to God just as he was. So too Paul is not alone among Jews who believe in Jesus as Messiah. This group of Jewish Christians is a remnant (see Rom 9:27) selected by God not because of anything they have done, but simply because of God's benevolence. Israel as a whole was unable to find what it had sought. Only a remnant succeeded. The rest were hardened as a result of their resistance to the good news.

What's the problem? Paul cites three passages from Jewish Scripture, all linked by the word "eyes." Deut 29:3, Isa 29:10, and Ps 69:23-24 are drawn each from a different section of the Jewish Scripture: the Torah, the Prophets, the Writings. The indictment is severe: the entire Scripture proves that Israel failed to respond appropriately to God's earlier interventions. They also failed to respond appropriately now to the Messiah. God simply seals the situation.

11:11-24 Israel's fall is temporary, not definitive. Israel's stumbling is not definitive or irremediable. Deut 32:21 remains in the back of Paul's mind as he explains how Israel's fall made it possible for the Gentiles to accept Jesus and thereby stir Israel to envy. If the failure of Israel brought such a blessing, imagine the result when they all accept Jesus!

Addressing himself to the Gentiles, Paul describes his own ministry among them as one that is precisely calculated to make his own people jealous. When they finally do accept Christ, the result for them will be nothing less spectacular than a change in status as if from death to life. The influence of the foundation (Judaism) is strong indeed. Since the root is holy (patriarchs), the tree will also be holy (see Jer 11:16-17). If the first lump (the remnant) is consecrated, so too will the entire loaf be (see Num 15:18-21).

A word of caution, however, is directed to the Gentile Christians lest they begin to boast. They have been grafted like a wild olive branch onto a cultivated root. As Israel was lopped off because of disbelief, the Gentiles were grafted on because of faith. If they lose faith, they too can be lopped off.

Paul takes the opportunity to build an even stronger case for hope for his beloved Israel. If they should turn away from their unbelief, it will be even easier for God to re-attach them, the natural branch, to the cultivated root, than it was to attach the wild branch, the Gentiles. Clearly then the rejection of Israel is not definitive or final, but only temporary.

11:25-32 God shows mercy to all. At last Paul speaks plainly because he does not want his Jewish readers to be misguided, misled, or "wise in their own way of thinking" (see Prov 3:7). A partial insensibility has come over Israel until the number of Gentiles determined by God will be saved. Then all Israel will be saved. This concern for numbers is an apocalyptic idea especially familiar from the Book of Revelation. Paul reflects that mentality, though he generally tends to simplify rather than complexify apocalyptic traditions. Notice that he doesn't even guess at a specific number.

To this point having cited their Scripture against them, it is interesting to see Paul quote from Isa 59:20-21 and 27:9 in their favor. While the Jews have ruptured the right relationship with God by rejecting the good news, they are still loved by him because the election of Israel is irrevocable. The promises or covenants with the patriarchs still stand firm. God simply doesn't vacillate about those whom he blesses and chooses. In point of fact, all groups have been disobedient to God at one time or another. This is what allows God to have mercy on all (see Mark 2:17).

11:33-36 Final doxology. Having now completed to his satisfaction an exploration of how Israel fits into God's plans for salvation and redemption, Paul concludes with a brief but marvelous hymn of praise to the all-merciful God. The Apostle has no doubt that God has complete control over history and human life, that is, that he knows its design, purpose, and fulfillment. And who can understand or explain this? After all, no one has advised him (Isa 40:13), nor is he in debt to anyone (see Job 41:3 or 41:11). He is indeed the creator, sustainer, and goal of the universe (characteristically Stoic ideas accepted by Hellenistic Judaism and absorbed by Paul in his education and travels) responsible for its origin, course, and end. To him be glory forever. Amen.

II. EXHORTATION TO HARMONIOUS LIVING

Rom 12:1-15:13

Following the pattern of all his letters, Paul turns his attention in these remaining chapters to practical exhortation. His discussion presumes that the Torah is no longer a norm for conduct. There are, of course, new demands for believers, but these are based on love and not law. These new demands develop in individual instances and are thus by definition standards. A standard is a value applied to a generally recurring interaction between two individuals (review commentary on Gal 2:11-21).

It is Paul's hope that sooner or later these standards might evolve into custom. A custom is an institutionalized set of standards; that means customs inhere in institutions. In Paul's world there were only two formal, or distinct, institutions: government and family. The additional formal, or distinct, institutions known to us, namely, economics, religion and education, were embedded in the two formal institutions. Thus Paul repeatedly calls these believers "brothers [and sisters]" not because he wants them to consider him especially sensitive, but rather because family—even fictive kinship, or extended family—is the arena in which the standards of individuals can become customs of the community. Until this takes place, primitive Christian exhortation often deals with the challenges of daily life more by way of example than by way of precept or command. This is very common in the letters of Paul.

Rom 12–13 spell out general exhortations, while 14–15 speak of a more specific situation centering on the relationship of people who are "weak" in faith with those who are "strong" in faith. The general idea is that Christian freedom should promote life in peace and harmony among all believers. Individuals should mutually strengthen one another. Rom 15 brings the specific example of Jesus to bear on the problems posed by the relationship between weak and strong.

12:1-8 Proper use of spiritual gifts (charismata). The first two verses of chapter 12 open with three appeals to the Roman Christians: (1) they ought to offer themselves in living sacrifice to God; (2) they ought not reflect their culture (rather they should shape it); (3) they ought to let God transform them through his Spirit. The appeals are made on the basis of what has been shared in the letter to this point: namely, a history of God's "mercies" (the Greek is plural reflecting many acts of graciousness) towards his creatures.

How is this done in concrete daily life? Paul's suggestion needs to be understood in terms of his basic cultural values: honor and shame. No one is to increase or augment his or her honor (think more highly of self) at the expense of the honor (or to the shame) of others. Honor and shame are almost understood as concrete quantities which are limited. If one increases honor, someone must have been deprived. That's simply unacceptable.

Applied to the discussion of gifts (v. 6, charismata), honor and shame set limits. Each one must remain in the limit and recognize the complementarity of other gifts. Charisms, of course, are never intended for personal gain or individual benefit. They are by definition concretions or individuations of the Spirit (this means individual people receive them as individual gifts) intended solely for the service and upbuilding of the community.

Jesus is the guiding norm or criterion for how to use the gifts, for we are all one moral body in union with Christ (vv. 4-5). Thus individual members are incorporated into but do not constitute the body. Therefore there is a need for all to cooperate for the common good.

Paul lists seven gifts and suggests how each one should be used for the good (or for

the honor) of the community. Notice once again how the list reflects the tripartite view of the individual person: mouth-ears, hands-feet, heart-eyes. The one who preaches should be faithful to the basic body of tradition. The one who serves ought to faithfully administer material aid and distribution of alms. The one who teaches is to be guided by the subject matter. The one who exhorts should encourage all who need it. Those who share personal wealth with the needy or distribute community alms should do so with generous simplicity. Leaders (note the position in this list of gifts!) ought to fill that position with sensitive care. And those who aid the sick and abandoned ought to do so cheerfully.

Both Rome and Corinth were port cities which had many neglected widows and orphans, had a constant stream of proletarians to their harbors, and many poor and sick. Hence the practical relevance of Paul's advice. Moreover, since the enumeration reflects all three parts or zones of the person, Paul has described how to deliver holistic care to the entire person. His statement looks like yet another effort to curb enthusiasm, that excessive reliance upon the gifts of the Spirit. Clearly Paul urges a sober analysis of personal gifts and an appropriate holistic response.

12:9-21 Love among other-directed persons. These verses appear to be a random collection of maxims, roughly rooted in the notion of disinterested love, *agápē*. Verses 9-10 actually speak of two distinct kinds of love: *agápē* (v. 9) and *philadelphia* (v. 10). The first love is wider in scope than the other one, rather familiar as "brotherly love," but perhaps preferably translated "sibling love." Thus some scholars believe that the verses explain or suggest particular ways of practicing love in general.

A sharper focus might be gained by remembering the discussion in Galatians about dyadic or other-directed personalities as the dominant personality type in the Mediterranean world. Such individuals always need the opinions of others to ascertain self-identity, self-esteem, and indeed, honor and shame! A literal rendition of Rom 12:10b identifies honor and shame as the context of Paul's exhortation: "Outdo one another in showing honor."

Honor is a claim to worth PLUS public acknowledgment of that worth. Hence, the claim to honor is always a communal or public affair, since it relies on the judgment of the public. Honor has to be granted. Shame is an attitude of sensitivity about one's honor, a concern about what others think, say, and do relative to oneself. Thus, shame includes an all-pervading interest in and a desire for a grant of reputation on the part of others.

Paul's remarks all support honorable living. Above all, he says, serve the Lord; do the honorable thing. Have confidence reaching out for your future (rejoice in hope). Don't just suffer your troubles passively (be patient), and remain open to God (persevere in prayer). Remain honorable: meet the needs of all believers (be conscious of their need for honor), both those you know (widows, orphans, prisoners, and needy in your city), as well as those you don't know (traveling Christians need your help).

Do not shame your persecutors by cursing them. Have the same attitude toward all; don't slight the honor of anyone. If you have been shamed (injured), don't repay that shame with an affront to the honor of your opponent (similar to Jesus' advice to turn the other cheek). See that your conduct is honorable to and in the eyes of all.

For the one who believes in God, God will see to the redress of balance in honor and shame. God's wrath is a description of how God restores his honor when it is affronted or shamed by a challenge of one or another kind.

Advice for treating one's enemy is borrowed from Prov 25:21-22. Heaping burning coals on his head appears most likely to derive from an Egyptian penitential ritual in which the penitent carried on his head a dish of burning charcoal to express repentance. So, by returning "honorable" deeds for an opponent's "shaming" deeds, one embarrasses the opponent into repentance before God. In other and final words, don't be shamed into shaming activity; rather, shame evil by your honorable response.

13:1-7 Duties toward civil authority. These verses seem to be a further development of Rom 12:3, which cautioned that no one think more highly of self than is fitting. Paul may have been worried about yet another form of enthusiasm. Some Christians believed they were already citizens of another world, had gained new freedom in Christ, and there-

fore did not have to obey civil authority. Paul feared the anarchy that would result from such an outlook and therefore felt obliged to discourage it.

It is quite incorrect to think Paul intends to spell out a general theory of church-state relationships. He seems to have a specific kind of situation in mind. His Greek vocabulary (for instance, *diakonos* in v. 4 and *leitourgous* in v. 6) is the vocabulary of Hellenistic civil administration. The word translated by the New American Bible as "servant" in verse 4 and "ministers" in verse 6 describes the bearers of civil power with whom the common, ordinary person comes into daily contact. Behind these stand the regional or central administration. His argument is that God ordered all of creation and expects order in the political community as well. Thus his imperative "Do what is good . . . right" means be sure your political conduct is right, proper, fit. The assumption, of course, is that rulers are working for the common good of the subjects (v. 4). To highlight the assumption, three times in the passage Paul highlights the delegated nature of political, civil authority (13:1, 4, 6).

There are two reasons for obeying: to avoid punishment and for the sake of conscience. But Paul's understanding of conscience is not an interior voice independently telling us what is right and wrong, good and bad. The Greek word literally means a knowledge with others, that is, individualized common knowledge and common sense. In first-century Palestine, the word describes a person's sensitivity to his public ego-image and the determination to align personal behavior and self-assessment with that public ego-image. His or her conscience is a sort of interiorization of what others say, do, and think about the person, since these others play the role of witness and judge. Their verdicts supply the grants of honor necessary for a meaningful, human existence.

Notice how on the one hand Paul tells us that he rejects the opinions of others (1 Cor 4:1-4), yet at other times he seeks approval from his significant others for what he does (1 Cor 9:1). Jesus, too, is a man of honor not acting "out of human respect" (Mark 12:14), yet nevertheless concerned about "who do you [people] say that I am" (Mark 8:27). Paul's advice is that one should obey the civil authorities because it's expected. What will the others say? The command to pay taxes merely specifies the general obligation: don't shame anyone to whom honor is due.

13:8-14 Duties to one another. The word "owe" (translated "due" in v. 7) links this passage with the preceding comments. The one thing we owe one another is love. This fulfills the Torah, no matter which of the 613 commandments deriving therefrom appeal to us. Paul sums them all up in the citation from Lev 19:17 about love of neighbor. It was very common among the rabbis as well as in the New Testament, but there is a significant difference, too. In Jewish understanding "neighbor" meant compatriot, kin. In the Jesus tradition neighbor has a much wider scope. Thus, if Jesus is the end of the period of the law (10:4), and his motive for redeeming us was love (8:35), this kind of love now becomes the norm for Christian conduct, and it replaces the Torah.

Finally, Paul concludes these reflections by drawing a notion from apocalyptic outlooks: *kairos*, time. With the death and resurrection of Christ, the *kairos*, the critical moment has arrived. The present moment has a pressing challenge. True to form, Paul phrases the challenge in honor and shame terms, urging, of course, the honorable path. The images of day and night, light and darkness, symbolize good and evil and reflect honor and shame.

Concretely, Paul presents a list of six shameful life-styles to be avoided. Again, they reflect the three zones of the biblical person: eating and drinking excesses (mouth-ears); sexual excess and lust (heart-eyes in the planning, hands-feet in the execution); quarrels and jealousy (mouth-ears and eyes-heart). The point is that each individual person must avoid, completely and entirely, every shameful life-style (as listed), but seek instead total and comprehensive honor, just like the honorable Jesus. Don't give in to unredeemed and misdirected living (flesh), but rather imitate the quality and direction of the life of Jesus.

14:1-12 Accept one another. Though some scholars have proposed that Paul is addressing his comments here to as many as five distinct and specific parties, factions, or groups in the Roman church, it seems more plausible to assume that Paul continues to keep uppermost in mind the Jewish-Christian minority in the Roman community (see introduction to Romans). Paul draws from his general missionary experience to address a recurrent pattern of behavior between various group-types. Perhaps he witnessed it most recently in Corinth (party strife, exclusive allegiance to Paul, Kephas, Apollos), from where he is writing this letter.

The group-types are described as strong in faith and weak in faith. The strong in faith believed themselves to have enlightened consciences, to be progressive. They threw around the slogan "Everything is lawful for me" (1 Cor 6:12) and may have been one of the specific targets of Paul's comment in Rom 12:3. They felt so liberated in Christ that they believed that everything goes. No restraints are necessary or desirable.

The weak in faith were scrupulous in particular observances, conservative, and still troubled with concepts of "clean" and "unclean." Paul mentions three particular concerns: they are vegetarians (vv. 2, 21); they drink no wine (v. 21); and they consider certain days important, perhaps lucky or unlucky from an astrological perspective (v. 6). No one has been able to identify this group with certitude. They do not seem to be Jews. Perhaps these practices and beliefs were retained from some kind of pre-Christian experience and background.

No matter. Paul has only one solution: mutual respect and acceptance. Give room for growth. Arguments, ridicule, judgment over these matters are forbidden.

God has accepted each person. Can we do less? Each individual acts in order to honor the Lord. We are each of us the Lord's and responsible to him. Since we all must be accountable to the Lord's judgment, how dare anyone anticipate that judgment now?

14:13-23 Peace and joy for everyone. It is important to realize that the main thrust of this passage is Paul's wish for all to enjoy justice, peace, and joy. No one should hinder or destroy that. If this point is lost sight of, the passage seems to contradict Paul's preaching.

No one should destroy the joy of another. Paul uses himself as an example. His firm conviction, rooted in nothing less than the authority of the Lord Jesus, is that nothing in itself is unclean. But there are individuals who cluster into groups which hold the opposite opinion. Paul says it would be wrong to impose his views on this group and ruin their peace. It may often be necessary—out of love, which replaced Torah for Christians—to relinquish one's legitimate claim of freedom for the sake of an individual or group that is weak in faith.

Paul's opinion is typical of other-directed (dyadic) personalities. In verse 20 he points out that it is wrong for a person to eat something if it specifically offends his conscience. Conscience, as explained before, is comparable to group pressure. And since Paul's hope is mutual peace, anything that disrupts that peace is wrong.

Accepting God's rule has little to do with eating and drinking, food and beverage. Rather the rule of God should cause all believers to live together in righteousness, in peaceful openness to all, and in joy that comes from standing in a posture of openhandedness in the presence of God. Whoever served Christ in this way wins friends and pleases God.

The Greek aorist tense in verse 21 suggests that the believer needs to make a fresh judgment on each occasion whether or not to live openly with the conviction personally held (whether to eat or drink this or that). The next verse urges the strong in faith to keep that clear conviction between self and God. The rule of peace, however, may require that a person forego that freedom in certain social contexts. The concluding beatitude sums it up well: Happy the one—whether strong or weak in faith—who has no misgivings about personal choices.

15:1-6 Follow the example of Christ. For the first time Paul now openly includes himself in his remarks to the strong in faith. He continues his call for forbearance, but adds a significant twist. The word translated "put up with" literally means "carry or help carry" the burdens of the weak. It is a call to the strong to be willing to experience self-denial for the sake of weak believers.

The challenge to the strong in faith is that they ought to build the community and its members up rather than tear it all down. Look to the example of the Messiah. Christ's sacrifice was motivated by love, and that should become an effective motive for all believers. The citation from Ps 69:10 about bearing the reproaches intended for God is addressed to the strong in faith, perhaps the Gentile-Christian majority at Rome, that they strive to put up with persecution or misunderstanding just as the persecuted psalmist did.

The doxology (perhaps the letter was read publicly at worship?) prays that God cause the recipients to become patient and not to be discouraged. May they learn to live together in harmony, to seek a common viewpoint by following the example of Jesus so that all may give glory to God together.

15:7-13 Final appeal for unity. With one more statement Paul urges mutual acceptance, perhaps acceptance of the majority Gentile Christians by the Jewish-Christian minority. Again Jesus the Messiah is the example for such a minority. Jesus became a servant for the Jews in order to show them that God is faithful to the promises he made to the patriarchs. If such a minority follows this example, they will give glory to God. The Gentiles give glory to God because of the mercy he showed them, a "no-people," a people not deserving mercy (see Rom 9:25).

Then summoning his rabbinical skills one more time, Paul strings pearls from the Torah (Deut 32:43), the Prophets (Isa 11:10), and the Writings (Ps 18:50 or 2 Sam 22:50, as well as Ps 117:1) to emphasize that the entire Jewish Scripture foretold that the Gentiles would become part of God's plan and join his chosen people. The concluding prayer repeats the hope for joy and peace for all (whether strong or weak in faith) and urges the Holy Spirit to give them hope that will continue to grow.

CONCLUSION

Rom 15:14-33

These concluding verses seem to reveal Paul's actual life situation while writing this letter. Perhaps his real motive emerges as well. He opens the section with diplomatic flattery (serving the technique of persuasion suggested in the introduction). Paul confesses his abiding conviction that the Romans are full of goodness (uprightness expressing itself in mutual openmindedness). He also recognizes that they are filled with complete knowledge, that is, insights into the meaning of salvation history. Therefore, they are perfectly capable of giving advice, correction, admonition to one another—as other-directed (dyadic) personalities are accustomed to doing.

But Paul has decided to write boldly in order to remind them of a tradition, taking courage for his boldness from the fact that God has graced him with the office of Apostle to the Gentiles. He sees his ministry as that of serving like a priest of the Messiah in preparing the Gentiles as a worthy offering to God. He has replaced slaughtered animals with a repentant people. And to the extent that he has done this in union with Christ, he is proud of this service for God and freely and openly boasts of it.

Indeed, he has been traveling and preaching from Jerusalem in territories around it, even to Illyria, working mighty deeds in virtue of the Spirit's power at work among those he meets. He remained in these regions because there were always new paths to cut, new lands to visit, and his guiding principle was never to build on the foundation laid by another. He personally preferred to lay fresh foundations for the faith.

But now that there are no more opportunities in the East, Paul turns his attention to the West. It will be possible for him to visit the Roman church on his way to Spain. He hopes that they will be able to spend some time together, and then he will be able to get to know them better personally. By saying that he trusts they will be able to send him on his way to Spain, Paul subtly hints that they might want to provide him with food, perhaps traveling companions familiar with the roads, some means of travel, and other necessities.

Before he can do that, however, there is a pressing matter to attend to. Paul must take a collection to the poor in Jerusalem. He did promise not to forget them (Gal 2:10). Indeed, just as the Jews have shared with Gentiles the fullness of spiritual blessing which had been promised and delivered to them, now the Gentiles ought to share in return a little of the material blessings in recompense. The exchange is not extraordinary. It is a normal transaction in the culture following the rule of balanced reciprocity.

Still Paul is uneasy about the trip. He describes it and its goal as a "struggle" (v. 30) and asks for prayers that he be "delivered from the disobedient in Judea," that is, either non-Christian Jews or Jews who oppose the gospel. Clearly, Paul was still not out of the woods in Jerusalem. So for the sake of the

unity of the church, which was a major concern for him, Paul hopes to accomplish two things with this letter: (1) to rehearse the presentation he would make in Jerusalem and (2) to win to his support the Jewish-Christian minority in the Roman church. The very recent experience of this minority could help them appreciate Paul's plight.

In A.D. 49, Claudius, emperor of Rome, banned and exiled the Jews (and quite likely Jewish Christians) from Rome. When Claudius died five years later, some deportees returned to Rome, not only as a result of his death but also because his decree slipped into insignificance. Yet upon their return, they found themselves a minority in a predominantly Gentile-Christian church.

Writing this letter to the Romans not too long after the return of the deportees, Paul hopes that his pleas for unity, mutual tolerance, peace, and harmony would persuade the Jewish Christians there of the wisdom of such peaceful coexistence. He further hoped it would inspire them to urge their friends back in Jerusalem to give Paul a kind reception when he arrived with the collection.

Paul could not omit delivering the collection because he promised it. If he sent an intermediary, he could not be certain that the collection would not be attributed to another source. At the same time, he couldn't help wonder if his visit would only antagonize hostility in Jerusalem and jeopardize his own future plans. Perhaps he'd even meet his own death because of the still unsettled situation. Jewish-Christian support from Rome would be so helpful.

One can almost hear the sigh of relief with which Paul wrote the final part of his prayer: God willing, after I drop off the collection, I can come to see you with joy. Your company would refresh my spirit. And with one last tug at their help: May the God of *peace* be with you all. So be it.

PHOEBE COMMENDED

Rom 16:1-23

After reading more than one apparent conclusion in the last two chapters (for example, 15:30-33; 15:13; 15:6), it is probably not too surprising that the letter continues. Yet the tone of chapter 16 has raised questions among readers throughout history. Not many have ever doubted that Paul actually wrote these verses. The real question is: were they written to the Romans? Personal greetings to such a large number of people familiar to Paul in a church he neither founded nor yet visited prompts reasonable skepticism. True, these friends and acquaintances could well have moved to Rome. Some of these names, however, are more familiar in the context of the Ephesian church, suggesting that Paul wrote this letter to introduce Phoebe to the church at Ephesus. (One very early manuscript does not include this chapter, but rather has Rom 16:25-27 following immediately after Rom 15:33.) Current scholarship, however, accepts 16:1-23 as an integral and original part of Paul's letter to the Romans.

In antiquity, when communication was rather slow, and travel was difficult and dangerous, letters of recommendation were quite necessary as a person left a familiar place to visit an unfamiliar territory and people. This was especially true for women travelers.

Phoebe is identified as a "sister," another instance in which Paul continues to build extended-family relationships in the early church. She carries her own letter of recommendation (some scholars believe she carried the entire letter to the Romans to that community). Paul also identifies her as a minister (deaconess or auxiliary in the generic sense as in 2 Cor 3:6) in the church at Cenchrae, the eastern seaport of Corinth. The Apostle writes these lines on her behalf and urges that she be welcomed because she belongs to the Lord and because she has been of very special help to him and many of the church members.

Verses 3-16 send greetings to no less than twenty-eight acquaintances, each of whom most probably regularly gathers a group of believers in meeting. Thus, the circle of people to whom Paul actually introduces and recommends Phoebe is very wide indeed.

The first-mentioned couple is very well known and mentioned more than once in the New Testament. Prisca and Aquila were among the leading early missionaries in the Dispersion, that is, outside Palestine. Both had accepted Christianity prior to Paul's conversion. They began their missionary activity independently of Paul, but later consented to work in association with him.

Prisca and Aquila were Jewish Christians who moved to Corinth when Emperor Claudius banished their kind from Rome. At Corinth they engaged in tentmaking and extended hospitality to Paul when he first arrived (Acts 18:1-3).

In time they traveled with him to Ephesus where among others they instructed Apollos (Acts 18:26). To judge from 1 Cor 16:18, which Paul wrote from Ephesus, Prisca and Aquila led a group of Christians in a house-church, for this group sends greetings to the Corinthian church. Paul's greetings in Rom 16:5 to the house church of Prisca and Aquila seem to suggest they were still in Ephesus.

As a missionary couple, Prisca and Aquila seemed quite effective in the early days of Christianity. The wife in such a situation did not simply accompany her husband for moral support (consider the implication of 1 Cor 9:5), but had access to the women's quarters (a special word in Greek), which would not generally be accessible to men. This role played by Christian women in the formation of the first churches has rarely been paid sufficient attention.

Epaenetus, who is mentioned next, was the first convert in western Asia (with its gubernatorial seat at Ephesus). Paul honors him by affirming that through his conversion he consecrated the rest of Asia to Christ.

Andronicus and Junia (the second-named individual could be a woman) were early Jewish-Christian converts who either designated themselves as apostles or were deputized by some community. In any case they were recognized by Paul as eminent apostles, Christians who accepted the faith before Paul did.

The remaining names in verses 8-16 appear to be chiefly slave names. Yet the concluding comment is that all greet one another affectionately with a holy kiss. Paul's added observation that all the churches send greetings is again not only a statement of fact but also a further cementing of the bonds of fictive kinship Paul is eager to strengthen.

Verses 17-20 mark a sharp shift in tone that strongly contrasts with the rest of Romans. Paul warns against those who would destroy the unity of the community. Good teaching (mouth-ears) aligns well with the entire person (hands-feet and heart-eyes). But their teaching (smooth and flattering speech) serves rather their bellies (a distortion of the three zones or possibly a sarcastic reference to dietary narrowness). The God of peace will crush all disorder and dissension in the community (personified by Satan).

The writer of this letter, Tertius, adds his greetings to those of others—unknown to us except for Timothy. Erastus may have been the co-worker of Paul mentioned in Acts 19:22.

Some English translations (like the new NAB) omit a twenty-fourth verse. This is done because our most trustworthy and reliable ancient Greek texts do not contain the sentence "May the grace of our Lord Jesus Christ be with you all, amen," which was very likely added later by a scribe who was copying an original.

One might wonder why all this fuss over a sentence which is relatively harmless. It is neither blasphemous nor theologically inaccurate. The church, however, and its biblical scholars are very interested in determining as accurately as possible the "original" form of the Scripture as accepted and used by the early church, or perhaps even as written by the original author. Our problems are compounded enough by the fact that most of us have to rely on translations. Each translation is in some sense an interpretation. So we need all the help we can get. A reliable text is definitely the first requirement for serious reading and study of Scripture.

CONCLUDING DOXOLOGY

Rom 16:25-27

The final doxology is a glorious hymn of praise to God who alone can make believers firm and immovable in living out the good news Paul preaches. Whether authentically written by Paul or not (a matter of dispute), this doxology is a fitting conclusion to Romans.

1 CORINTHIANS

Mary Ann Getty

INTRODUCTION

If Paul can be compared to a maker of films, his average reader today is like the moviegoer who views only one or a couple of frames at a time. Sometimes we gather at liturgies or classes or study groups and review a passage or section from Paul to the Corinthians. We often feel inspired (for example, read 1 Cor 1:1-13), impressed (2 Cor 12:1-10), challenged (2 Cor 5:11-21), or perplexed and rebuffed (1 Cor 11:2-16; 14:34-35; 15:33-34). Such is the result of viewing the frames separately. Even the fact that each passage can speak to us so powerfully threatens to blur the whole picture which Paul and the Corinthians create. The more we can discover about the Apostle and the Corinthians, the better we can understand the message's relevance for us today who believe that somehow this correspondence contains God's revelation. We are fortunate, for no other New Testament document reveals so much about the writer and his addressees as Paul's correspondence with the Corinthians. We need to know at least a little about the city, the Apostle's experience at Corinth, the church there, and the purpose and occasion of these letters.

The city of Corinth

At the time Paul wrote these letters (about 56–58 C.E.), Corinth was probably the leading Greek city, its rival, Athens, having declined in political and economic importance. Situated on the narrow isthmus joining the Greek mainland to the Peloponnesus, Corinth was a gateway between the East and the West. This city played a significant role in Greek history and in the whole Mediterranean world of the first century. Paul went to Corinth around 51 C.E. during the course of his second missionary journey. There it was that Paul seems to have realized the implications of concentrating on the Greeks in order to win the Jews. Corinth was a remarkably apt testing ground to establish the validity of this mission.

Corinth, the capital of the Roman province Achaia, exhibited all the tough features of an important city of commerce whose population was mixed and mobile. Jews came there from east and west to find a home. Some were displaced by the Emperor Claudius' punitive expulsion of all Jews from Rome because there had been riots among them over a certain "Chrestus," which is probably a mistaken reference for Christ (see Acts 18:1-3). Many Jews had gone to Corinth from Palestine, some no doubt as slaves, others in search of a livelihood, attracted by the commercial possibilities of the city.

As a leading Greek city reestablished by the Romans under Julius Caesar in 49 B.C.E. Corinth had all the best and the worst of a vital, throbbing pagan capital. The high ideals of Greek civilization challenged citizens of Corinth to a certain spirituality, asceticism, and cultivation of the aesthetic. The worst in pagan vices was nourished by the Greeks' scorn of the physical, a scorn that had given birth to such apparent opposite extremes as hedonism and stoicism. Economic and political growth did not necessarily promote ethical development. The Corinthians' reputation for licentiousness was well known. Religious syncretism provided the melting pot for Jewish, Roman, and Greek practices that tended to boil down the precious and leave a residue of counterfeit alloys.

The Apostle at Corinth

Paul is reported to have stayed in Corinth longer (eighteen months according to Luke in Acts 18:11) than in any other place he evangelized. His relationship to the Corinthians was as an artisan-preacher rather than an itinerant. Simply put, he lived and worked among the Corinthians and his whole apostolic relationship as reflected in the correspondence with them is characterized by all the features of a day-in, day-out rapport, shared experiences such as require time, complete with intimacies, strains, disappointments.

According to Luke, Paul in Corinth first tried to evangelize the Jewish population, teaching in the synagogue and enjoying a modicum of success (Acts 18:1-4). He lived and worked with Aquila and Priscilla, his Jewish-Christian friends who were part of his missionary team there. After being continually assaulted by the Jews (Acts 18:5-6, 12-17), Paul reviewed his priorities. He stopped concentrating on the Jews and focused on the Gentile mission for which he was affirmed by a vision of the Lord (18:7-10). Later Apollos himself preached in Corinth. Apollos' eloquence (18:24) contrasted with Paul's having come to the Corinthians "in weakness and fear, and with much trepidation" (1 Cor 2:3). The Corinthians, impressed by this eloquence, became disaffected with Paul. If perhaps there existed a certain amount of human rivalry between Paul and Apollos, there certainly was some overt competition among their followers. And then some of the disciples of the other apostles joined in, so that it was hard to see the unity of the Corinthians for the disparate groups who clustered around the various apostles.

Paul's reaction to such rivalry is characteristically strong. Even if he were not an apostle to anyone else, he is indisputably the apostle to the Corinthians (9:2), and none of their false notions about the superiority of others can alter this fact (see 9:1-18; 2 Cor 10:1–13:21). His authority lies in the very fact of the existence of the Corinthian community.

He knows these people. They are entitled to their opinions about him, but he insists on their unity. He is firm and forceful. Yet he is also kind and pastoral. He certainly has his own opinion about how they should live, but he will not impose arbitrary regulations on them. He will only call them to the unity mandated by the gospel.

About this unity, Paul is adamant. It is not hard to guess reasons for the urgency in his tone. Undoubtedly he was not the only one interested in monitoring the success of the Corinthian mission. Those who had been sent by James to authenticate the Galatian mission, for example, would have found the Corinthian disorders much more potentially damaging to Paul (see Gal 2:12; also 2:4).

The church at Corinth

A Christian group existed in Corinth before Paul came to share their life. Aquila and Prisca were prominent members of that community and already exercised some leadership (Acts 18:2-3). It was this couple who completed the instruction of Apollos after Paul had left for Ephesus (18:24-28).

The church at Corinth seems to have been composed of Christians of both Jewish and Greek origin. Paul frequently uses scriptural references in such a way that familiarity with the texts is taken for granted (see, for example, 1 Cor 10:1-10). Roots in Judaism probably contributed to the scandal that resulted in the eating of idol-meats by some and the controversy over whether women could conduct liturgical service and the appropriate dress and conduct at the liturgy (11:2-34). The influence of paganism, on the other hand, is evident in almost every issue. Paul, who had a hard enough time convincing the Jewish authorities that the mission of the Gentiles was valid and that the Gentiles received and lived the same gospel as the Jews, would have been understandably concerned about the impact of the Corinthian situation not only on his other missions but also on his reputation and credibility among the Jewish Christians. Consistently he preaches unity, but rarely is Paul's message so threatened by misunderstanding and division as it is in Corinth.

For such a complex church, summary is always dangerous. But if we were to risk the danger, we might characterize the Corinthian Christians as "enthusiasts." Although they were zealous, they lacked depth. They were so drawn to certain ministers that they felt justified in outdoing each other to prove their allegiance. They believed so strongly in the spiritual life that they underestimated even their own physical needs or the vulnerability of their young community. They were so zealous for the sacraments and for the spiritual gifts which they admired that they overlooked the most spiritual of all, charity, the one they all received, which could heal their divisions. Vaguely they were aware that their beliefs should be reflected in practice, but they practiced the wrong things, fluctuating between the extremes of asceticism on the one hand and indifference to the seductions of the world on the other. Their misguided zeal had to be tempered and rechanneled, but not abolished. They had to learn the primacy of charity in their relationships with each other and the consequent subordination of what they ate, what they put on at liturgies, or what gifts they possessed. They had to be encouraged to contribute to the support of the saints of Jerusalem, who were suffering a famine, and this support takes on a great symbolic value as Paul links it to the success and acceptance of the entire Gentile mission (Rom 15:25-27).

The letters to Corinth

There is something many people find generally very fascinating about letters. Even though they may represent only one side of a dialogue, many levels of disclosure can be found in letters between people, leaving much that appeals to the imagination. There is, of course, the self-disclosure of the author. In Corinthians we learn more about Paul from Paul than in any other New Testament work. In Corinthians we can even hear how Paul feels. This implies that by the process of identification we can, from studying Corinthians, learn something also about ourselves as we reflect on Paul's example of what it means to be a preacher and minister of the gospel. We also learn much about the lovable and difficult Corinthians whose experience of Christianity is so pertinent to our own. Theirs, like ours, was no simple reading of the gospel. How they seem to have needed to refine their understanding so that their intellectualizing would not inhibit their incarnating the gospel's message! Paul's tone is firm but compassionate, intimate and challenging, authoritative

but not dogmatic. Whether admonishing or cajoling, defending or persuading or correcting, he shows himself as warm and caring toward a community he understands very well.

Paul wrote to the Corinthians from Ephesus. Taken together, the letters we have give a movie-like glimpse into the never dull life of the Paul-Corinthian relationship. The whole is more than the sum of the parts we have to study. At times the strong tone of the letters gives hope that the picture will eventually become very clear. The sequence of the frames, however, threatens to jeopardize the impact of the whole story. We seem to have two letters, but clearly there must have been more. And the order of those we have is jumbled. Finally, never one for oversystematization, even in the most objective of circumstances, Paul seems to invent his own "structure" as he writes this running dialogue with the Corinthians. We need to consider briefly the tone, the number, and the literary characteristics of the overall correspondence of Paul with the Corinthians.

Internal evidence indicates that there were more than two letters to the Corinthians. There must have been a letter before our extant 1 Corinthians. Paul refers to this "precanonical," now lost letter in 1 Cor 5:9-13; this seems to have been Paul's first written response to the Corinthians' questions about how to survive as Christians in an alien environment. Later, "Chloe's people" (1:11) brought the Apostle news of some disquieting disorders among the Corinthians. Perhaps these messengers also brought to Paul a letter (see 7:1) from the Corinthians with some questions about life within the community. Yet no part of 1 Corinthians, however strong, seems to fit the description of the "tearful letter" Paul alludes to in 2 Cor 2:1-4, which he said he previously wrote. This could refer to 2 Cor 10–13 or yet another letter which is also lost. Many interpreters note the detachable character of 2 Cor 10:1–13:9 and the two conclusions in 9:15 and 13:1-13. Further still, 2 Cor 8 and 2 Cor 9 appear as repetitious exhortations about the collection for Jerusalem, as if these reminders were originally self-contained, independent notes on this topic. In other words, what appear as two letters in our Bibles are the remnants of an ongoing dialogue contained in several letters between Paul and the Corinthians. The fact that these were preserved by the community means that they were valued, and probably read and reflected upon frequently whenever the Corinthians met to deepen their faith and their community life.

Our appetite for appreciating Paul is whetted. We are encouraged to lay aside any inhibiting preconceptions to permit ourselves to see a pastor and his people at work integrating the gospel in their lives. We need not be put off by the fact that the originators of these works lived thousands of years ago. Here are sincere people like ourselves in many ways, struggling to live Christian lives with integrity in a complex world. Far from being the egocentric chauvinist he is sometimes portrayed as being, Paul presents himself as vulnerable, compassionate, caring, strong, convincing. Taken seriously, his invitation to "imitate me as I imitate Christ" (1 Cor 11:1) shows truly remarkable transparency which arrogant people are not usually capable of. And considered to be literally true, his reminder that these things "have been written as a warning to us, upon whom the end of the ages has come" (1 Cor 10:11), is challenge, encouragement, and cause for gratitude to both Paul and the Corinthians who go before us. They give us a model—not pat answers to our twentieth-century problems, but a kind of living legacy witnessing to our common call to be true to the gospel.

The occasion, message, and characteristics of First Corinthians

The city before Paul's preaching presents no simple profile. Worldly, successful, sophisticated, Corinth has all the accoutrements of the best and the worst of worlds. Any religion would have had a hard time being taken seriously there. This is especially true of Christianity as preached by a suspect Jewish convert who felt called to the Gentiles, and who hoped, as a result of this mission, that his fellow Jews would become jealous and themselves accept the gospel of Jesus Christ (see Rom 11:25-32). Already impeded by the hardness of the Corinthian shell, Paul seemed weak in appearance (see 2 Cor 10:10) and eloquence (1 Cor 2:1-5), preaching the good news which had as its sole recommendation the message of the cross, its only wisdom (1 Cor 1:17–2:16). Smitten by Greek philosophical

trends, the more spiritually minded Corinthians might have found the tension between the flesh and the spirit which was part of Paul's preaching intellectually acceptable, but for the wrong reasons. Raised on a body-soul dichotomy that was part of the Greek world view, the Corinthians had great difficulty understanding Paul's Semitic perspective. That perspective treated the entire human person from the viewpoint of the body or from the viewpoint of the spirit; either could express the whole person who could not be divided into only one or the other, body *or* spirit. But the Greek viewpoint that influenced the Corinthians was more dualistic. It tended to separate the body and the spirit, claiming superiority for the latter while neglecting the physical. This provided a basis for the Corinthians to create and tolerate a dichotomy between their beliefs and their conduct (for example, 1 Cor 5:1-11). Paul is eager to refute such a gross misunderstanding of his gospel.

This misinterpretation was part of the root cause of the divisions within the Corinthian community. It reinforced the elitist-separatist tendencies that spawned factions based on allegiance to different ministers (1:10-17; 3:1–4:21), on celibate versus married lifestyles (7:1-40), on the dietary practices of the weak contrasted with those of the strong (8:1-13; 10:23-30), the ostracizing of the poor (11:17-34), or on competition for popularly coveted gifts (12:1-31; 14:1-40). Scorn for the body and all things physical likewise produced misunderstanding and even mockery of belief in the resurrection of the body (15:1-58), and, on the other hand, a smug acceptance of certain extremely basic taboos, including incest (5:1-11). Paul has to show the Corinthians that such disorders as suing other Christians (6:1-11), judging the authority of apostles on the basis of externals (9:1-27), downplaying sexual differences (11:2-16) or complacency in possession of the sacraments (10:1-22; 11:17-34), are inconsistent with the real understanding of the gospel message, which has the cross at its center and limitless mutual charity as its measure of authentic expression.

The eighteen months Paul spent living among the Corinthian Christians seems to have done little to alleviate the fear and trepidation (1 Cor 2:3) he experienced when he first came to them. The disquieting if not alarming reports he received from Chloe's people (see 1:11) and the fundamental questions of the Corinthians themselves betrayed insidious divisions and confusions and probably confirmed Paul's fears. Writing First Corinthians from Ephesus during his third missionary journey (ca. 56–57), Paul seems to alternate between pleading and indignation as he tries to introduce some sanity and balance into the contorted Corinthian version of Christianity.

The structure of First Corinthians, compared to Second Corinthians, is relatively simple. In the first part Paul responds forcefully to the reports he has about the divisions in Corinth (1:10–6:20). For him the most absurd divisions are those based on exclusive devotion to the various leaders, devotion that pits one apostle against another, creating chaos of the divided leadership and misplaced fellowship. Paul could hardly be more adamant in his rejection of this abuse, which he sees as a form of idolatry that confuses ministers with the one Lord (1:10–4:21). The immaturity of the Corinthians' faith is evident in the wedge they have driven between their faith and their behavior (5:1–6:20). Paul cites the most blatant examples of their lack of moral authority (5:1-13), their inability to settle disputes among themselves (6:1-11), and their succumbing to the temptation to return to pagan ways (6:12-20; see 10:14-22). Paul's reaction to these reports is stern and demanding.

The second part of this letter consists of Paul's responses to the Corinthians' questions relayed to him by messengers. Paul does not abandon his adamant tone. The questions are related to the Corinthians' struggle to live a credible Christianity. They include issues regarding social status (7:1-40), problems that arise from trying to live as a Christian with integrity within a pagan environment (8:1–11:1), and internal conflicts related to liturgical celebrations (11:2–14:40). It is not certain whether questions concerning the resurrection were actually addressed to Paul by the Corinthians or if the Apostle identified this as the basic misunderstanding that seems to have spawned all their other difficulties. In any case, since the Corinthians display in their many problems a fundamental lack of appreciation for the body, Paul concludes this letter with a presentation of the resurrection as the basis of faith (see 15:1-58).

These two main parts of the letter are enveloped by the customary introductory and concluding sections. Three further elements, characteristic of Paul's style generally, help to clarify the structure and development of the Corinthian correspondence. These three elements are the indicative-imperative method of presenting content, the so-called ABA' schema Paul frequently uses to develop his thoughts, and Paul's adoption of his addressees' own positions in order to correct and admonish them.

One of Paul's most used pedagogical tools is the indicative-imperative schema which underlies his message. This means that Paul's reaction to the disorders and his responses to the Corinthians' questions proceed from certain basic premises. These premises are based on Paul's understanding of the nature of Christian life which itself flows from Christ's action on the cross. For Paul, the gospel is the fundamental reality which provides the measurement for all other reality. Factions in Corinth, for example, should not exist because in Christ all are one. Unity, signified in baptism and in the Eucharist, enables Christians to overcome all their differences. Paul approached the question of how the Corinthians should act by means of his description of the new creation they have become in Christ (see 2 Cor 5:17-20).

A second general remark about the structure of the correspondence with the Corinthians can help us to thread together the sequential frames of Paul's movie. Throughout, Paul uses the ABA' schema, whereby he introduces a subject (A), interrupts discussion of it with another topic (B), and then returns to the initial subject (A'). While this may seem confusing at times, awareness of its purpose and frequency helps us become less distracted by Paul's method and more able to grasp the implications of his whole perspective. So, for instance, in the middle of a discussion of the relationship between the weak and the strong (1 Cor 8:7-13 and 10:23-30), Paul defends his apostleship, pointing out that his own example shows how the Corinthians must be all things to all people (9:1-27). Similarly, he describes the way of love "which surpasses all the others" (1 Cor 13) to make his point about the destructiveness of competition for spiritual gifts (12:1-30; 14:1-40). Especially First Corinthians is full of examples of this ABA' schema at work. We will make specific reference to how it affects and enhances Paul's development as we work through these letters.

In a variety of ways Paul demonstrates the truth of his statement, "To the Jews I became like a Jew to win over Jews . . . . To those outside the law I became like one outside the law . . . . I have become all things to all, to save at least some" (1 Cor 9:20-22). In both 1 and 2 Corinthians Paul frequently quotes the Corinthians themselves (for example, in 1 Cor 8:1: "All of us have knowledge") as if anticipating their challenges based on his real knowledge of them and of the ways they think. These "quotes" help Paul move the argument forward even while he eliminates his addressees' objections. They also provide a way for Paul to identify with the Corinthians without agreeing with their conclusions and while trying to correct or modify their positions. Similarly Paul sometimes betrays his own agreement with the strong, his own ability to speak in tongues, his own preference for celibacy. Paul likewise regularly draws on Old Testament and Jewish images, linking his religious experience and tradition to that of the Corinthians. Yet Paul also draws on athletic imagery and other experiences more at home in a non-Jewish milieu. Thus he is able to describe the church as a body with many members, and Christians together as a new creation, a society never before known but now visible and active in the real world and developing a rich common tradition.

OUTLINE OF FIRST CORINTHIANS

COMMENTARY

I. INTRODUCTION

1 Cor 1:1-9

1:1-3 Greeting. According to the ancient form of letters, authors begin by identifying themselves. Paul follows this custom, naming himself and Sosthenes as the senders of this letter to the Corinthians. Paul's description of himself is brief. He is called by God's will (see Gal 1:15-16). He is an apostle, that is, "one who is sent." As such, Paul represents the One who sends him. Although his authority is challenged, Paul adamantly defends it. It is Paul, rather than one of the Twelve or any of the eyewitnesses to Jesus' life, who first coined the word "apostle" and fashioned it for Christian use.

Paul's vocation is also a mission that is far from being merely an interior, purely personal, individual call. His response is lived in active service of Jesus Christ whose slave he has become (see Rom 1:1; Gal 1:10). Paul's use of "slave" gives that term a kind of honor it did not ordinarily connote. Jesus Christ is almost synonymous with the gospel Paul preaches. Paul has been "grasped" by Christ (Phil 3:12). He pledges absolute, total commitment to Jesus, who changed his life and now not only influences him strongly but becomes Paul's point of identification.

Sosthenes, a "brother," joins Paul in greeting the church at Corinth. A Sosthenes, described as a leader of the synagogue in Corinth, was beaten before the proconsul by the Jews who had first accused Paul and had not been given satisfaction (Acts 18:12-17). It is not certain from Acts whether this man became a Christian or if his punishment had any direct relationship to the accusations brought against Paul. In any case, this was a common name, and Paul's lack of further description implies that he was well known to the Corinthians. The Sosthenes of 1 Cor 1:1 was, of course, a Christian, a "brother," since Christians become kin to one another, sharing through faith a fellowship that compares in depth with family ties.

Paul greets the "church of God . . . in Corinth" (1:2). Drawing on some Old Testament images, Paul suggests already in these opening verses two ideas which will undergird his instructions to the Corinthians throughout this lengthy epistle: their holiness is based on their common call and their unity under the same Lord. Like Israel, the church is a holy people (Exod 19:6). Consecrated in Christ Jesus, the Corinthians rank with "all those everywhere" who call on the Lord (see Joel 3:5), that is, with all the baptized. The fact that they recognize the same Lord means that Christians everywhere are indebted to one another. (See Paul's self-description in Rom 1:14-15; his description of the debt which links the pagans and the Jerusalem Christians is in Rom 15:26-27.)

Characteristically, Paul bids his readers grace and peace (Rom 1:7; 2 Cor 1:2; Gal 1:3; Phil 1:2; 1 Thess 1:1; 2 Thess 1:2; Phlm 3). These gifts summarize the messianic blessings bestowed in Christ. Paul brings together the usual greeting among the Greeks, *charis* (i.e., grace) and that used by the Jews, *shalom*, reflecting the unity of all those who profess to believe in the one Father and in the one Lord. By addressing such a difficult community in this positive way, Paul exemplifies the manner in which the preacher must challenge Christians to possess their legitimate inheritance.

1:4-9 Thanksgiving. The greeting leads Paul to express thanks. Some form of initial thanksgiving is another trace of the ancient custom Paul follows. Yet, normally authors of letters begin by expressing thanks for their own health or well-being, using the occasion, perhaps, to inform readers about their latest accomplishments. Paul, however, gives thanks not for himself but for the Corinthians and for the grace they have received. Paul acknowledges that the Corinthians have been "enriched in every way." But this letter, written in answer to their questions and because of reports Paul has heard, makes it painfully clear that the very gifts they have received, especially the gifts of "all discourse and all knowledge," which they prize so much, are the basis of the divisions that trouble them. Paul reminds the Corinthians that all gifts come from the same Lord (see 12:5).

The community is the credential of Paul's apostolate, living evidence that the gospel has been preached and heard by them (see 9:2). It is not gifts that are lacking. But the gifts' misuse by the Corinthians does not indicate the proper attitude of those waiting for "the revelation of our Lord Jesus Christ." At his coming, the Corinthians will be called to account for how their gifts have nourished love among them.

Paul's prayers are "eucharistic" (that is, a thanksgiving) because they are based on confidence in God, who will assuredly finish the good work already begun. God is steadfast and trustworthy. This is why Paul offers such effusive thanks, despite his realistic outlook on the very serious nature of the church's problems at Corinth. Paul's own testimony to God's fidelity has been received by the Corinthians. They have experienced the grace of the gospel as promise that God will not abandon them. Despite their problems, Paul expresses grateful confidence that they will be strengthened and ultimately judged victorious.

II. REPORTED DISORDERS IN THE CORINTHIAN COMMUNITY

1 Cor 1:10–6:20

The divisions among the Corinthians are the main threat to the gospel. Apparently the Corinthians had their own set of questions they wished Paul to answer (see 7:1). But first the Apostle gives his reaction to the gross disorders reported to him. He attacks the rival groups who oppose one leader to another (1:10–4:21). He shows how these factions be-

tray the Corinthians' grasp of true wisdom. Then he proceeds to list other examples of the Corinthians' spiritual immaturity (5:1–6:20).

A. Divisions in the Church (1:10–4:21)

Christian life is based on the message of the cross. This message is contained in the gospel Paul preaches, which is the only true wisdom. There is only one gospel and its wisdom must unite rather than divide. Its acceptance is signified by baptism. The very fact that there is dissension among the Corinthians surrounding the very symbol of unity betrays the Corinthians' immaturity. Paul cannot be indifferent to such divisions, since they threaten the basis of the gospel he preaches. He deplores the dissensions (1:10-17), presents the paradox of the cross as true wisdom (1:18-2:5), and then distinguishes the lesson of the cross from the false wisdom of the Corinthians (2:6-4:21).

1:10-17 Groups and slogans. The divisions among the Christians at Corinth belie the purpose of their common baptism. "I urge that all of you agree . . . ," Paul begins his instruction in this letter. Using many examples, he will not really say anything more important or complex than this. Paraphrased, he insists that since they are one in baptism, diversity among them must be an expression of community which signifies the action of the Spirit among them.

Paul launches into his main concern, which centers on the news he heard from "Chloe's people" (1:11) about the dissension among the Corinthians. Nothing is known about this woman herself, but she is obviously a leader of the church, well acquainted with the Corinthians, with unquestionable reliability. The early Christian groups often took their name from the heads of the households in which they met. Chloe might well have been engaged in commerce with associates who traveled between Corinth and Ephesus, where Paul was when he wrote Corinthians. Reports from her to Paul described cliques among the Corinthians. Some identified themselves as followers of Paul; others favored the more dazzling eloquence of Apollos. Then there were some who championed Kephas (as Paul prefers to call Peter; but see Gal 2:7-8). And, finally, there seem to have been those who outdid all the rest in their claims of simply being for Christ. But all, through baptism, become members of one body (12:12-30). To Paul it is inconceivable that Christians be divided, least of all on the basis of who baptized them. Some not only asserted the superiority of the one who baptized them but even seemed to assess their own importance in relation to this alleged superiority.

Yet in Christ, in whom they were baptized, Christians have more than a model. More than just giving them an example to be followed, Christ empowers Christians to be "of the same mind, with the same love, united in heart, thinking one thing" (see Phil 2:1-2). It is not the one who baptizes but Christ who, in being crucified for all, unifies all.

The role of the apostle, as Paul describes it, is to create, form, and maintain community in dynamic relationship with Christians everywhere. It is not part of Paul's call as an apostle that he baptize, and for this he is grateful (1 Cor 1:14, 17). But Paul recommends the example of one he did baptize, Stephanas, who heads a house-church and is probably one of those who had brought messages to Paul from the Corinthians (see 16:14, 17). With a tone of urgency, Paul admonishes the Corinthians to repair the damage to the community caused by such dissension and conflict. Baptism is the outcome of the preaching of the gospel which brings all into the community of the sanctified. He begs the Corinthians to come to their senses, to embrace the wisdom of the gospel, lest the union the cross signifies be emptied of its meaning.

The message of the gospel (1:18–2:5)

God's power, which is stronger than any human power, teaches the wisdom of the gospel. This, Paul shows, is the message of the cross (1:18-25), verified in the experience of the Corinthians (1:26-31) and illustrated in their acceptance of Paul's own preaching to them (2:1-5).

1:18-25 The paradox of the cross. The gospel Paul preaches is the power of God (see 1:18; Rom 1:16-17). The gospel is not like any other truth human wisdom can discover. Indeed, human wisdom can obscure the truth of the cross of Christ. The cross *is* the gospel.

The cross divides humankind into two parts, into those who reject it, who are on their way to perdition, and those who accept its message and are experiencing the power of God. In this sense, the cross is the judgment

of God. The cross is also the fulfillment of Isaiah's warning that God reverses the wisdom of the world (Isa 29:14).

Suffering, the message of the cross, is certainly one of the greatest human mysteries. This mystery, expressed in Jesus' passion, is at the center of the gospel preaching. Such preaching rejects two obvious "answers" which make suffering comprehensible, and therefore somewhat acceptable, to human wisdom. These options are either that suffering is punishment for sin or that, in its absurdity, innocent suffering reveals an unjust God. These are the options of the unjust. Both of these possibilities are defied by the mystery of the cross whereby Jesus, the innocent Just One, did not break faith with God.

Since the cross does not follow human reason, it is an obstacle, a scandal, a stumbling block for both the Jews who expect signs and for the Greeks who look for wisdom. Such expectations blind them so that they cannot see what comes to them, but stumble instead against the "scandal" in their path (see Rom 10:1-2). Conventional wisdom, in the light of the gospel, becomes foolishness: "Whoever would save his life will lose it" (Mark 8:35). And the folly of the cross that confounds the wise, empowers the foolish for salvation. Paul describes himself and those who are in Christ as "fools" and "weak" on Christ's account, and for the sake of the community (1 Cor 4:10).

But belief in Jesus is regarded by the gospel Paul preaches as the greatest wisdom. God's folly is wiser than all human wisdom. Not only is the "weakness" of God more powerful than all human strength, but God's strength supplies for all human weakness. (Paul uses a metaphor here because, of course, God is in no sense "weak.") Paul had experienced the truth of this in his own flesh when he begged God to remove from him the thorn that afflicted him and learned the lesson: "My grace is enough for you, for in weakness power reaches perfection" (2 Cor 12:9). Jesus' disciples learned this lesson when they, despairing of being able to achieve salvation, heard Jesus' word: "For human beings this is impossible; but for God all things are possible" (Matt 19:26).

1:26-31 The experience of the Corinthians. Paul returns to the subject of the divisions he described in 1:10-17, excluding competition and divisions on the grounds of the Corinthians' own experience of the gospel. If only the worldly wise and the worldly powerful were to be the receivers of wisdom, Paul argues, you yourselves would never be included. Paul's point is not simply to insult the Corinthians or to make them humble (see 4:14-17). He tries, rather, to show that the Jewish and the Greek conclusions are erroneous because their premise and their boasts before God are absurd (1:28-29).

Paul challenges the members of the Corinthian community to reflect on their own history. Their world exalts the wise, the influential, the highborn. But the Corinthians do not number among these. Indeed, they were called by God, but not because they had anything to recommend them. As a matter of fact, they were mocked by the world, considered unworthy and insincere by religious people, probably even by the more mature and rooted Jewish Christians. They were suspect even by many Christian authorities. Some of them were even considered "weak" by members of their own Christian community (see 8:7-13; 10:23-30). Paul implies that they may be tempted to aspire to acceptance by the world and by other, more settled communities. Yet, he reminds his kin in the faith, God has already begun in them the good work of confounding the strong in order to reveal the foolishness of boastful pride before God. In giving us life, wisdom, justice, sanctification, redemption, God willed that these become ours in Christ Jesus, who eliminates all individual and divisive boasts.

2:1-5 The illustration of Paul's preaching. Paul personally exemplifies the idea of 1:17: "Christ [sent me] . . . to preach the gospel—not with the wisdom of human eloquence . . . ." Paul's own weakness is evidence that what he preaches is the power of God. From the perspective of worldly standards, Paul's mission should be a failure. He cannot rely on what the world values or commends. He is plagued by illness (2 Cor 12:7), his appearance is unimpressive (2 Cor 10:10), his personal delivery weak (1 Cor 2:5). Yet the very existence of the community at Corinth is a powerful argument for the presence of the Spirit, since only the Spirit can create community (see 9:2; 12:1-3). Thus, Paul continues to draw gospel conclusions that defy the human limitations of his own or the Corinthians' experience. A clear result is that faith is built not on the merits of either members or minister, but on the power of God.

True and false wisdom (2:6–4:21)

The gospel shows the difference between worldly or false standards of wisdom and the true wisdom that measures spiritual maturity (2:6-16). The Corinthians, in their immaturity (3:1-4), fail to recognize the true role of the apostle (3:5–4:5) or to employ tools adequate to the true evaluation of an apostle (4:6-21).

2:6-16 True wisdom as spiritual maturity. Paul does not deny that the gospel is wisdom, but he argues that it is a different kind of wisdom than the world understands, one which the world does not recognize. The Gentile Christians at Corinth were tempted by many forms of worldly wisdom. It is difficult to identify precisely which expression or form Paul opposes in 2:6-16 to the real wisdom he describes in 3:1-4. It was probably some form of logic such as was taught by Philo, the Alexandrian philosopher (died ca. 50 C.E.) who attempted to translate Jewish teachings into philosophical categories. Greek philosophy generally held that the spiritual was superior in every way to the physical (see p. 1103). All that pertained to the body could and perhaps even should be ignored. The material is irrelevant. Ethics was often ignored, while what one could grasp with the mind was considered to be of sole importance. Paul is against spiritual elitism because it moves away from everyday Christian life led in the body. Paul warns that such "wisdom," which he characterizes as of this world, breeds division, jealousy, competition. The Corinthians pursued a kind of enlightenment that would give them superiority over those who were considered merely infants. The "rulers of this age" used such ideas to maintain power over others, and even to put Jesus to death (2:8; see Luke 22:25).

But, says Paul, only the Spirit of God can plumb the depths of God and only the truly spiritual person can receive the revelation of God. God's is a revelation summed up in the wisdom of the cross. This is a revelation that changes the criteria for judgment, enabling us to put on the mind of Christ (2:16; see Phil 2:5).

3:1-4 The immaturity of the Corinthians.
After describing what God's wisdom is not
(2:6-16), Paul goes on to say what it is in
3:1-4. Yet, from the perspective of true spiritual wisdom, the Corinthians, especially those
who use worldly standards as a measurement
of worth, are themselves "infants." The barriers they erect and justify convict them of
spiritual immaturity. Although they are in
Christ, they have not yet been able to absorb
anything beyond food appropriate for infants.
Their behavior shows that they have not yet
understood the wisdom of the cross. Such
conceits are absolute foolishness before God
(3:19).

3:5-4:5 The role of the apostle. In the
light of God's wisdom, factions based on the
alleged superiority of one minister over another or of one group over the other are absurd. All are servants of the one Lord, fulfilling the roles assigned for the nurturing of
the community. God does not need human
help (Acts 17:25), but has chosen ministers according to the divine purpose. God's purpose
will not be frustrated.

Using the imagery of farming in 3:5-9,
Paul emphasizes the unity and cooperation
that characterizes the task and common goals
of the ministers. The Corinthians are working against the very plan of God when they
oppose their ministers to one another. Since
the ministers work toward a common end,
their followers must not sabotage this work
by competing against one another.

Whereas unity is the point of 3:5-9, the
complementarity of roles is explained by Paul
using construction imagery in 3:6-23. Jesus
Christ is the one foundation upon which the
new temple of God is built. There are several
examples in Judaism where the dual images
of farming and construction are associated (Jer
1:10; 12:14-16; 24:6; Ezek 17:1-8) in a manner similar to Paul's association here.

Paul underscores the contribution not only
of such ministers as himself and Apollos but
of all the members of the Corinthian community. His emphasis is on the Christians' cor-
porate identity as the temple of God. As
Christians mature spiritually, they contribute
to the upbuilding of God's temple (see 1 Cor
12:4-26). God lives in a temple not built by
human hands (see Acts 17:24). The God of the
Old Testament is reluctant to allow the Israelites to build a temple because they could then

mistakenly conclude that God is more present in one place than in another (see 1 Chr
17:3-10). Proportionate to the people's failure
to remember that God dwells among them is
their insistence that they should build God a
house. Paul echoes a prophetic warning to his
readers: If anyone destroys God's temple (that
is, the unity of the community), God will destroy that person (see John 2:19). If in 1 Cor
3:5-9 Paul seems to subordinate his role as
teacher and leader of the community, he emphasizes its importance here. The early
church, and especially the Corinthians,
seemed to have been plagued with false
teachers who compounded the sin of their
own disbelief by leading others astray. This
was the ultimate scandal in a struggling community, that leaders would misrepresent the
gospel. Better, Jesus warned, that these tie a
millstone around their necks than that they
be the cause of the downfall of one of the
"little ones" (see Matt 18:6; Mark 9:42).

Jesus as Judge is one of the oldest christological images. The image is linked with the
Old Testament concept of the Day of Yahweh
(see 3:13; Amos 5:15, 18), a day of hope for
the remnant, but a day of judgment against
God's enemies. Paul transfers the title "Lord"
and the judgment role of God to Jesus. One
of Christ's main roles as Paul describes it for
the Corinthians is the subjection of all creation under himself and the return of all to God
(see 1 Cor 15:24-28; 2 Cor 5:17-20). This is
the work of salvation or reconciliation. In carrying out this work of the reconciliation of the
whole world, Jesus reevaluates all creation,
determining what will be saved. All is therefore judged in view of Jesus' action on the
cross. Paul reiterates his conviction that the
cross of Christ brings to an end and destroys
all human wisdom.

Paul attests that his conscience is clear.
Nevertheless, he continues, this is not enough
to convict or acquit him. His conscience is
subject to the higher authority of the Lord
who judges the hearts of all. Thus, even his
own spiritual maturity, his role as leader in
the community does not give him the right to
judge. He is not merely imposing his own convictions on the Corinthians. Nor is he subject
to any other judgment than God's own.

4:6-21 The true evaluation of an apostle.
When Paul uses himself as an example to be
followed, he could be misinterpreted as dis-

playing the epitome of pride. But Paul avoids all boasting, cogently showing that Christians have nothing that they have not received. His transparence as an apostle fixes him always under the scrutiny of others. He renounces the right to a private, unexamined life. His apparent arrogance is, in reality, a marvelous humility and integrity that allows others to observe all his actions, his words, his very life, and thus learn what it means to imitate Christ (see 11:1). Paul has effectively shown the absurdity of claiming self-importance over others. Now he proceeds to contrast such attitudes with the role of the apostles which causes them to be considered foolish on account of Christ (4:10).

Still Paul does only what he invites the Corinthians to do. He suggests that they consider their own experience, the gifts they have received. Without cost to them, he argues, they have, as believers, been called to reign over the world. This authority they have received from God's mercy.

B. Other Examples of the Corinthians' Immaturity: Moral Disorders (5:1–6:20)

5:1-13 A case of incest. Pride has tempted the Corinthians to take an "enlightened" view of a very basic disorder, namely, incest. They are "inflated with pride," no doubt thinking themselves possessed of a knowledge that transcends ethical norms (see 8:1-2; also 4:6-18). They consider themselves above the ordinary taboos related to marriage and family, taboos which characterize even the most primitive civilizations. The Corinthians rejoice in their own broadmindedness. Paul forcefully admonishes that the man guilty of incest must be excluded from the community and thus "delivered to Satan." Impressed that they are already living a supernatural life that frees them from sin, they seem to delight in the sophistication that suggests that they cannot be harmed by the desires of the flesh. Behavior to the Corinthians does not seem important; only spiritual enlightenment matters.

Paul is undoubtedly reacting against the Corinthians' blatant rejection of common moral standards. He upbraids them for their lack of moral authority and courageous leadership (see Gal 6:1). Yet it is the context which betrays Paul's even deeper concern. The fledgling Corinthian community is not capable of discerning conduct consistent with commitment to Christ. Nor do the Corinthians even seem to think that it is necessary to bring behavior into line with beliefs. Paul has already stated in the preceding chapters that the Corinthians are spiritually immature and have failed to grasp true wisdom. Such failure is evidenced in this separation of beliefs and practice. Their obligation to the offender is to separate him from the community and thus, hopefully, be a means of his coming to repentance.

Paul's own preaching may have inadvertently contributed to the Corinthians' misunderstanding. The Apostle ascribed to the view of humankind that saw people as being under some force, either for good or for evil. In order to emphasize the difference, Paul often speaks of the dichotomy between the spirit and the flesh (see, for example, Rom 8:1-13). He also insists that in Christ we are dead to the law (Rom 7:1-6) and to sin (Rom 6:1-14). Enthusiasts already, the Corinthians would have easily fallen prey to one extreme of this thinking which would suggest that since they have been saved, they are no longer subject to the flesh with its taboos. Paul the realist, however, knows how susceptible this community could be to eliminating all standards. Although he does not explicitly include here the problem of scandal in his instructions to the Corinthians, the fact that they were ignoring ordinary taboos recognized by both Jews and pagans would have provoked negative criticism from Paul. The Corinthian community had enough problem being accepted by the Jerusalem authorities and by the other, more exemplary communities. But Paul is reacting against anything which would cause sufficient scandal to inhibit others, and especially other Gentiles, from accepting the gospel. For this is his mandate—to make the gospel accessible to all the Gentiles.

The image of the leaven, borrowed from the Passover liturgy, reveals Paul's real emphasis as he proceeds to address the immorality which plagues the Corinthian community. This emphasis is twofold: first, conduct must be consistent with Christian commitment and, second, an individual's behavior has implications for others. Just as the Jews rid their homes of all leaven to celebrate the Passover, so Christians must rid the community of the corruption and wickedness that contaminates it, guarding their consecration and call (see 1:2) with the leaven of "sincerity and truth" (5:8).

Besides ignoring the universally recognized laws of decency, some of the Corinthians are guilty of another extreme. Taking literally Paul's instructions in a letter now lost (see 5:9) about not associating with sinners, they were becoming judgmental and elitist. Corinthian extremists were all too ready to escape from the world by rejecting it. Paul tries to help them live with the tensions of the world. Paul's comments here and in the next chapter about different life-styles are primarily intended as a corrective against this kind of extremism. Paul reminds the Corinthians of their missionary obligations to the pagans. They are not to judge the outsiders, but leave them to God. But they are to correct the erring within the community (see Gal 6:1-5). Their responsibility is to develop faith and to reflect this faith in their conduct as members of the community of the justified. Paul concludes the chapter with another reference to the incestuous man, quoting the law (Deut 13:6) to reinforce the order to expel him from the community.

6:1-11 Lawsuits before unbelievers. Paul's reference to judgment in 5:12-13 provokes him to set aside the issue of immorality for the moment and consider another abuse in Corinth that has been reported to him. Christians are betraying their own members by bringing their disputes before pagan courts. Paul reminds them that the world itself, indeed, even the angels, are to be judged by those who believe in the gospel. Christians recognize a morality more binding than that which characterizes pagan courts which, at best, may claim to arbitrate right and wrong. Christians recognize the law of love which qualifies all other judgments. Is it not then absurd, a scandal even, that petty quarrels among believers be brought before pagan courts? When such quarrels occur, Paul insists, they must be settled within the community (6:1-6). Yet the Apostle, before he returns to the issue of sexual immorality in 6:12-20, denounces the fact that disputes even arise (6:7-11).

It is to the Corinthians' shame that they do not acknowledge one among them who is wise enough to give sound judgment in these everyday matters. At the close of this epistle (16:15-18), Paul will recommend the leadership of Stephanas, Fortunatus, Achaicus, who could have been the very bearers of the reports of this abuse. The Corinthians dispute among themselves even about leadership roles while failing to recognize in their leaders the authority to help them reconcile their differences.

Paul denounces the fact of lawsuits among the Corinthians as no less than tragic. The power of the gospel mandate is that Christians would willingly allow themselves to be cheated rather than retaliate (see Matt 5:21-26, 38-42; Rom 12:14, 19-21). God's grace attained through baptism enables Christians to act toward each other in the same gracious way that God acts toward them (see Matt 5:45). If, however, Christians merely repay evil for evil and thereby cheat their own, they will be judged by their own baptism and fail to inherit the kingdom of God. Paul lists the vices that characterized their pre-baptismal, pagan existence. But *now*, having been baptized, Christians already have begun to share in the blessings of God's kingdom, made accessible through Jesus (see Rom 5:1-11; 8:1). Formerly pagan sinners, they now have a new identity, having been washed, consecrated, justified.

6:12-20 The idolatry of sexual sins. Paul tries to be especially careful when speaking to the Corinthians, who seem to be so quick to misinterpret his words. In 6:10-11, Paul contrasted the former life of paganism with the "now" of the Christian who has been justified through baptism. Paul's own teaching insists that the baptized are free from this former sinful condition. But Paul's anthropology also suggests that, freed from one master, we are made subject to another. If, in freedom, we do not live for God, we risk falling back into the slavery of sin.

Paul's teaching on freedom had been abused to legitimize the sexual licentiousness of the Corinthians. The same extremism that prompted their complacency regarding incest in their midst is used to justify their sexual conduct. They seem to argue that since sex is natural, it is necessary. Paul, who develops his theology of the resurrection in more detail in chapter 15, now grounds his comments on the dignity of sexuality in the resurrection and in his introduction of the image of the body to describe the union between Christ and the faithful (see 12:12-30).

Through baptism we have become members of Christ's body. The image of marriage is used to express how perfect then is the union between Christ and the baptized. Sin prompts us to prostitute ourselves, giving ourselves over to the false gods of pleasure and promiscuity. Drawing on a long Old Testament tradition, Paul identifies idolatry and adultery. He refers not only to sexual sins but to any pact with evil which desecrates the Christian committed to God (see 10:21). Any return to paganism is a form of prostitution, since by baptism we belong to God.

Finally, Paul caps the chapter by returning to the image of the temple of God. Fornication defiles the one who has, through baptism, become the sacred dwelling of the Spirit. This Spirit, given to us by God, is the pledge of our inheritance (see Eph 1:14). Therefore, we no longer belong to ourselves or to sin. We have been purchased at the great price of the death of Christ who reconciled us to God (Eph 2:4-10; Col 1:19-20).

Paul thus concludes his reactions to reports he has heard about the Corinthians. Continuing his straightforward, blunt approach, he now addresses the questions the community has posed to him (1 Cor 7:1–11:1).

III. ANSWERS TO THE CORINTHIANS' QUESTIONS

1 Cor 7:1–11:1

The young Corinthian church posed several questions to their pastor. Paul's responses to these questions comprise most of the next major part of the epistle (1 Cor 7:1–11:1). To these responses Paul adds his reactions about other problems in Corinth: appropriate behavior at the liturgy (11:2–14:40) and a true understanding of the fact and manner of the resurrection (15:1-58). So important is this last doctrine and so central to all comprehension of the gospel, Paul implies from this structure, that all the other misunderstandings and problems of the Corinthian community hinge on the fact that they do not grasp the resurrection and its implications.

Paul sorts out the questions posed to him by the emissaries of the Corinthians. They fall, the Apostle suggests in his response, into two general categories: questions concerning social status such as marriage and slavery

(7:1-40), and the survival and identity struggles experienced by the minority Christian mixed community within a hostile pagan environment (8:1–11:1). Probably nowhere in Paul are both the complexity and the simplicity of the Christian message more evident than in this section of 1 Corinthians. Clearly Paul had opinions on how the community was to act, but never does he impose his own style of conclusions on his churches. Rather, he calls them to a new level of awareness of the implications of doing whatever they do with love, for the glory of God (see 10:31; 16:14).

A. Questions Concerning Social Status (7:1-40)

Some of the Corinthians' questions arose from debates on the relative significance for the life to come of one's social status in this world. The Corinthians' spirituality caused them to disdain human institutions, including marriage. On the other hand, however, the institution of slavery, prevalent in Paul's day, seemed to validate discrimination against the slaves. Paul's emphasis on freedom could have been understood to support the Corinthians' disregard of the obligations incurred by human institutions. At a time when wives and slaves were expected to follow the religion of their husbands and masters, Christianity could have been considered dangerously subversive by outsiders and as an opportunity to avoid responsibility by insiders. Paul first addresses the question of marriage and obligations to one's spouse (7:1-16) and then returns to basically sexual issues in 7:25-40. He inserts within this discussion some comments on other social issues, especially slavery. This is an example of his use of the ABA' schema where he teaches the implications of a guiding principle (usually expressed in "B") by introducing an example, enunciating the principle, and then returning to his initial example. In this case, Paul's basic argument is that no change in status should be sought in view of the imminence of the parousia (see 7:17-25).

7:1-16 Advice concerning marriage. Paul begins his reactions to their questions by quoting the position of the Corinthians themselves that it is well for a man not to touch a woman. This quotation tactic occurs rather frequently in First Corinthians (for example, 10:23; 14:34-35). Concerning celibacy, the Corinthians' position is basically one which Paul can identify with. But while he himself admits his preference for celibacy, he also recognizes the serious errors involved in trying to legislate this as the life-style for everyone. The Corinthians view celibacy as a preferred state. Some seem to be even using their baptism as an excuse to escape commitments already made. Just as they had tried to escape reality in shunning all sinners (see 5:10-11), now they wish to use baptism as an escape from the burdens of married life, under the pretext of asceticism. They seem to have devalued marriage on the assumption that it has no place in the eschatological kingdom of God (see Matt 22:30; Mark 12:25; Luke 20:35). Further, the degraded status of women in the society of Paul's day provided good reason, especially for women, to look for excuses to escape the oppression of marital responsibilities. Christian converts in Corinth argued that since they already lived in Christ, they were exempt from their pre-baptismal commitments, including marriage, which they saw as only concerned with life in the flesh. Considering the spiritual to be higher and therefore better, they denied their own sexuality as expressed in marriage.

The realist, Paul, corrects this tendency and invokes reasoning similar to that which he uses to resolve the conflict between the weak and the strong (see 1 Cor 8:1–10:33). One's choice for abstinence, although admirable, cannot be unilateral or absolute. Christians live out their baptism in this world, respecting their commitments, subjecting their decisions to the demands of mutual love. Christians consider Jesus' new law of love not only one command among many but primary. Nor is it merely an external demand, but empowerment for fidelity. Paul reminds the Corinthians to honor commitments already contracted. Marital relations are a "duty" owed to one who has authority over the other's body mutually. This dutiful view may at first appear negative and legalistic, and it has been interpreted historically as such. Actually, however, in comparison to the Corinthians' view, Paul's is quite positive.

Paul goes on to justify marriage by reasoning that marital fidelity is better than sexual promiscuity (7:9). One's choice of life-style is based on faith in the Lord and the coming of the kingdom. Those who choose celibacy must be faithful and vigilant. Likewise, those who choose marriage are to be faithful to and respectful of one another.

Jesus' approach to this question as recorded in the Gospels should be compared to Paul's (see Matt 19:1-12; Mark 10:1-12; Luke 18:15-17). In answer to a question about divorce, Jesus pronounced on the indissolubility of marriage. This is his instruction, by which believers are expected to be able to make lasting promises. When his disciples learn how seriously Jesus views the marriage contract, they reply that it might be better not to make such promises (Matt 19:10). Jesus' response is that celibacy is a gift not given to all (Matt 19:11-12).

Husbands and wives belong to one another (1 Cor 7:4). Such union reflects the order of creation (Matt 19:4-6). In the positive perspective, then, marriage thus provides a model for the kind of union attainable for Christians. Paul often exhorts Christians to obey one another, carry one another's burdens, support, love, challenge one another. Christian love requires that all selfish ambitions be subordinated to love.

Thus, even though there may be a legitimate personal desire for periodic sexual abstinence to enhance prayer, such a decision ought to be mutual and limited. All the decisions of a Christian are based on mutual love and responsibility, so that whether a believer chooses to marry or not to marry, to abstain or not to abstain, there is no superior rule, no other absolute than charity.

Jewish law made no provision for a woman's divorcing her husband, since only men were responsible for the marriage contract. In a sense, then, Paul's reflections on marriage represent progress regarding the mutual obligations of both wife and husband for fidelity in marriage. Paul recognizes a woman's obligation regarding marriage and insists that baptism does not provide an excuse for women to evade such responsibility.

The Corinthians' situation also involved questions concerning their obligations to unbelievers, especially in marriage. Customs in the society required that wives and slaves adhere to the religion of their husbands and masters and that all citizens fulfill the religious obligations dictated by the state. This requirement put believing wives of unbelievers in a particularly vulnerable position, and Paul responds to the Corinthians' questions regarding this vulnerability. 1 Cor 7:15 has been interpreted as the basis for the so-called Pauline privilege to provide for the necessity of divorce under certain circumstances. But originally Paul addressed the particular needs of married believers living in tension with unbelieving spouses. As long as the unbeliever tolerated the faith of the believing spouse, the marital union existed. But since the commitments of baptism were primary and could not be jeopardized, if the unbeliever was not willing to live with a believer, the couple must separate. It is God's will that a couple live in peace.

7:17-24 Against change in believers' social status. Paul's ideas on the desirability of marriage reflect the general rule of 7:17 about Christians continuing in the state in which they were called. Paul undoubtedly believed that the parousia was imminent. His letters therefore address problems as they arise, providing solutions to questions within the context of living in the "in-between" times, which are shortened and which will be ended with the sudden coming of the Lord (see 1 Thess 5:1-11; Rom 13:11-14). Thus, Paul's personal preference for celibacy is reinforced by his conviction that the end times relativize the value of all human institutions, including marriage, circumcision, and slavery.

Believing that the time before the parousia is short, Paul says that each should continue in the state he or she was at baptism (7:17, 20, 24). The Apostle has just addressed the issue of sexual differences in marriage. Now he reflects on two other divisions that threaten Christian unity—the differences between Jews and Gentiles, slave and free (see Gal 3:28). Although baptism does not overlook these differences, it renders them impotent to divide people. It is not necessary, then, or even desirable that one's state of life be changed after baptism. Christians must only live their baptismal commitment in an exemplary way. This means that because of the union established among believers through baptism, there can be no discrimination or inequality due to sexual, religious, or social differences.

While Paul denies that any social change should be sought on principle, he does consider that changes may be necessary to accommodate weakness. And, if they are necessary, they are acceptable. This applies not only to changes in marital status but to any social or legal change, including whether one is circumcized or not or whether one is slave or free. God's call is gratuitous. It is independent of a person's standing in the eyes of the world. By the same token, a convert cannot argue that this call demands an upgrading or change in status. Paul is less interested in the revolutionizing of the institutions of the world than in challenging Christians to live out their Christian commitment in the particular situation in which they were called. If, for example, the nonbelieving master frees the believing slave, this change may be acceptable. But, in view of the imminent parousia, this change should not be sought by the believer.

Neither circumcision nor non-circumcision counts before God. Apparently some tried to reverse the operation of circumcision. Nor does God regard one's status as free or slave. Paul could have stated his own preference here as he does in the case of marriage. In his letter to Philemon, for example, he argues that Philemon may not exercise the ordinary recourse that would be followed by a wronged head of household toward a runaway slave. Yet Paul himself refrains from commanding Philemon, with one result that it remains unclear what exactly Paul was asking of Philemon. An authoritarian, doctrinaire statement, however tempting to Paul or to us, would have been a contradiction of all Paul is trying to teach about the relative value of any principle except love. Paul concludes his advice concerning social status with the admonition not to return to the slavish ways of thinking merely in human categories. All are subject only to the one Lord who is soon to come.

7:25-40 On virgins, widows, married life. Paul now considers the relative freedom of the unmarried (7:17-35). He regards virginity as preferable since the "time is short" and marriage tends to scatter one's energies. Paul's thinking is shaped by his conviction that the Christian has already begun to live a heavenly existence and therefore should not become more ensconced in this world. In heaven there is no marriage, so marriage is not necessary for Christians. It is irrelevant to inheriting the kingdom of God (see 15:50).

The Corinthians, in their enthusiastic extremism, seemed to even suspect that marriage is sinful (see 1 Tim 4:1-5). On the contrary,

Paul responds, marriage is the chosen life-style of the majority and its obligations cannot be avoided on the pretext that now one is Christian. Marriage is not sinful. Indeed, it is better to marry than to ignore the needs of the flesh. Since Paul's society considered women the property of men, the Apostle addresses men when he advocates marriage rather than irresponsible and promiscuous sexual behavior.

Paul is against change in marital status, not only for virgins but also for widows. This represents another departure from Jewish tradition which advocated remarriage after the death of a spouse. Paul reinforces this opinion by expressing the belief that he is guided in this by the Spirit of God.

B. Struggles Within a Pagan Environment (8:1–11:1)

8:1–11:1 forms a unit manifesting Paul's typical method of dealing with the everyday problems that arose in the Corinthian community as a church struggling within a pagan environment. The ABA' schema is operative. In 8:1-13, Paul deals with the question of food offered to idols (A). Then, in 9:1–10:22 (B), Paul turns to some of the underlying principles which must influence the Christian judgment of behavior. Finally, Paul returns in 10:23–11:1 (A') to the issue of idol-meats, stressing charity as the motivating power behind any decision about which foods to eat.

8:1-13 The idolatry of knowledge. Among the issues that threatened to divide the Corinthians was the issue of food offered to pagan idols. Just as the community was divided on the basis of ministers (1–4), and life-style (7), so the advanced "knowledge" of some (that is, the strong) separated them from others whom they considered to be weak and unenlightened. The language of love which upbuilds (13:4) is exactly the opposite of knowledge which inflates the ego (8:1; see 4:6, 18; 5:2). Those who consider themselves enlightened presume superiority over those who are scandalized by the eating of meat offered to idols. The enlightened ones argue that since idols do not exist, there can be no harm in eating meat which had been offered to them and which was often served at public banquets. Since these gatherings had religious meaning for most participants, many Corinthians shunned them and were shocked at the par-

ticipation of the strong. The gist of Paul's response is that although the enlightened are actually objectively correct, they are not therefore justified in wounding the consciences of the weak. What Paul says here is actually very startling. In effect, he asserts that even the profession of faith that there is one God who is Father and one Lord, Jesus, is not enough. This faith has consequences in one's acceptance of the sensitivities of others. No believer may give offense to others and exclude them without sin (see Rom 14:23). There are many "gods" and "lords"; some people even deify certain practices which they claim lead to self-righteousness. But the one true God who is Father calls us to subordinate all things, including knowledge, to the reign of Christ which is love.

There are many who do not possess knowledge of certain things, and so responsibility in the one Lord is to act out of love. The actions of a believer are not merely private as if salvation depended on the enlightenment of individuals. Paul reminds the Corinthians that many of them have so recently converted from the worship of idols that their consciences are weak and immature. Subordinate your knowledge to love of the weak and to the whole community, he admonishes.

Principles of Christian behavior (9:1–10:22)

Paul is no stranger to the difficulties involved in the Corinthians' struggle for integrity within a hostile environment. He draws principles for Christians, not *a priori* but from his own apostolic vocation and from the example of Israel as recorded in the Scriptures. In 9:1-27, Paul gives some reflections on being an apostle, suggesting that his own life can serve as a model for the strong to study in reconciling themselves with the weak. In 10:1-22, Paul warns the Corinthians, and especially the strong, to learn from the Israelites not to become complacent.

The example of Paul (9:1-27)

Paul's call from God gave him an authority he does not hesitate to defend. It is clear that especially in Corinth he must defend it. With their propensity to misunderstand, at least some in Corinth, noting that Paul did not exercise the same rights as the other apostles, argued that he must not have these rights, that he is an inferior apostle (see 2 Cor 12:11). There are two main issues Paul introduces in 9:1 which he will develop in this chapter—his freedom and his rights as an apostle. He will defend these in reverse order, beginning with his rights (9:1-18) and then explaining the terms of his freedom (9:19-27).

9:1-18 Paul's rights. Paul's response to his detractors is more than a justification of his own life. It is significant that his defense occurs in a context of admonishing the strong to consider the needs of the weak (see 8:7–10:33). Paul defends his apostleship because it is the authority upon which his gospel preaching is based. This apostleship carries rights and privileges that Paul clearly recognizes. Yet he renounces certain of these for the sake of the community. In other words, he himself provides a model for the strong to follow in subordinating their course of action to the needs of the weak.

Paul is an apostle no less than any others because he has seen the risen Lord (see 15:3-5). This is the fundamental criterion for being an apostle. Yet even if he cannot prove that he has seen the Lord, the very existence of the Corinthian community is ample testimony that Paul is indeed an apostle. His poignant statement that even if he is not an apostle for others, he is certainly one for the Corinthians, indicates how deeply Paul is affected by the criticism he hears from the community. Yet his defense goes beyond personal hurt or self-justification, revealing how fundamental is his conviction that his apostleship must be recognized. It is imperative that the questions of rights and their use not inhibit the spread of the gospel.

The other apostles accepted support from the community. This included food and drink, not only for the apostles but for their families. The reference to marriage might seem strangely out of place, except that it appeared as a problem in chapter 7. The fact that the apostles married might have given further authority to Paul's attempt to curb the Corinthians' disdain for marriage. Paul might also have been inspired by the threefold proverbial connection made by the unjust whose motto is to eat, drink, and be merry, for tomorrow we die (see 10:7). The last, of course, is a euphemism for enjoying the pleasures of the flesh. Thus, Paul includes this in the list of the rights of an apostle, a right, he

has already indicated, that he renounces. The Corinthians who may have been sympathetic to his decision not to marry, then, should not criticize his apostleship for that very reason. Nor is it legitimate to criticize him for not exercising the rights generally recognized as belonging to an apostle.

Four arguments to justify the support of the preacher by the community are furnished by Paul in 9:6-14. First, in 9:6-7, Paul argues from common sense, citing examples from ordinary life, like that of the soldier, the farmer, the shepherd, all of whom are supported by their trade. Second, these examples from common experience are supplemented by the teaching of the law (9:8-9): Moses prescribed even the care of animals. Paul's readers are not to surmise that this example is farfetched. There is a parable in this, a lesson in the respect due to all creatures.

Paul draws the third argument (9:10-11) from a Greek philosophical tradition which influenced the Corinthians' thinking. The Corinthians recognize the superiority of the spirit over the flesh. Paul uses this spirit-flesh tension to his advantage. Since he has shared spiritual blessings with the Corinthians, he is clearly entitled to expect from them the less significant blessings represented by their material support of him (see the commentary on 2 Cor 8:1–9:15 for Paul's description of the collection as a "debt"). Paul's apostolic service has directly benefited the Corinthians. The other apostles have had a less direct impact on them. If these others are supported by the Corinthians, how much greater are Paul's rights! So far, apostle and community agree.

Yet Paul interrupts the chain of arguments to remind the Corinthians that he has not used these rights among them. They can recall the months he stayed with them, working at his tentmaking trade, preaching to them while he worked with his hands. The Apostle says repeatedly, "Imitate me" (for example, 11:1; 2 Thess 3:7). He has renounced his right to support precisely so that his life-style will not be an obstacle to the message he preaches. This decision has meant that he has endured every manner of hardship and sacrifice. Just such a model is now needed by this very community that criticizes him. Paul himself dredges up the very criticism that has so pained him as an example of how the strong must act. The Apostle incarnates the primacy of love to provide an example of how the Corinthians are to address the issues which threaten to divide them.

The fourth argument (9:13) in favor of the support of the preacher by the community is well rooted in both Jewish and pagan religious practice. Moreover, the Lord himself ordered that all who preach the gospel should live by it (see Matt 10:14). This last argument seems to be so conclusive that Paul's unwillingness to be ruled by it is all the more surprising and calls his position into question. He reasons that even the Lord's command can be set aside for the sake of the community. With similar freedom and conviction, the Apostle had justified his exception to the commands of the Lord regarding divorce while he defended, on the other hand, his own decision not to marry despite having no command from the Lord. In other words, for the Apostle, even the sayings of Jesus himself cannot be applied in any literal, legalistic way, disregarding the discerning role of the community. Such an application would effectively relativize or nullify the only absolute command, which is love. All of the commands, even the sayings of the Lord, are summed up in this, for love alone cannot hurt another (see Rom 13:8-10).

Paul's mission as Apostle to the Gentiles revealed that the gospel has no limits. He has made a rule for himself not to limit the gospel by preaching only to the communities which support him. Thus he opts to preach while supporting himself, not only to avoid scandal but to insure that the gospel be independent of a community's wealth. This has been his practice since the beginning, although he does accept financial aid from communities after he has left them. This practice gives him the freedom needed to speak prophetic, challenging words without either jeopardizing his livelihood or incurring a financial obligation to certain people.

The reasons Paul gives in 9:15-18 for renouncing his rights bridge the preceding consideration of an apostle's rights and his description of freedom in 9:19-27. Paul lives by his convictions and would rather die than be deprived of his role as an apostle who preaches without condition. Yet he does not boast because he preaches the gospel. This he is compelled to do because Christ has grasped him (see Phil 3:12). If Paul preaches willingly, that is his recompense. If he is unwilling, the obligation nevertheless remains. Since he accepts this commission, he exemplifies freedom all the more in not accepting material support.

Freedom is never an absolute for Paul. It is always described as freedom from something (sin, death) for other service (to God, to Christ). For the sake of the gospel, Paul becomes free for the service of all. He is not limited to serving either Jews or Greeks. Once more he is describing his own experience by way of example to challenge both the strong and the weak. Although he is not bound by anyone, he serves everyone so as to bring the salvation of the gospel to as many as possible (9:19-23). At the same time, Paul runs the race as if to win, and his zeal for the goal involves renunciation (9:24-27).

9:19-23 Paul's freedom to serve all. Paul respects the traditions of the Jews. He himself lives according to these traditions when he is among the Jews. Although he knows he is not bound by the law, he imitates, for their sakes, those who think they are. Likewise he acts with those who are not bound by the law, not assuming erroneously that mere knowledge will free them or change them. In this reference to "those not subject to the law," Paul includes both Jews and Gentile Christians, whom he previously designated with the title "the strong." Paul also identifies with the weak, lest his freedom regarding the law be an obstacle to them. By making himself "all things to all," Paul diminishes the possibility of being one by whom the least are scandalized and fall (see 8:11-13).

9:24-27 Zeal for the gospel and renunciation. The Greeks were renowned for their games. His readers' familiarity with sports makes Paul's athletic illustrations appropriate for suggesting the proper motivation to inspire a healthy Christian self-discipline, sacrifice, and renunciation. The Corinthians had a special need for balance, being too prone to become extremists, either in overindulgence or in asceticism. Paul uses images from two of the more popular sports, running and boxing.

Paul compares Christian life to the disciplined runner who keeps focused on the goal and thus subordinates all other desires to the attainment of the prize. To the winner the Greeks awarded crowns which symbolized victory and supremacy. Paul's argumentation implies that if single-mindedness and self-renunciation are necessary to gain a perishable reward, how much more important these are in the pursuit of the imperishable crown. Paul "fights" in like manner. The contest is real and often the enemy is within. Paul alludes to the Greek boxing practice of completely vanquishing and humiliating the opponent. Paul's own experience showed him the need to deal the decisive blow to give him mastery over himself. Occasionally in this correspondence (see 2 Cor 4:8-10; 6:4-10; 11:23-29), he rehearses the sufferings he himself has endured for the sake of the gospel. Predictably and for the sake of balance, Paul situates his self-discipline, his asceticism and willingness to suffer, in the context of service for others. He not only accepts hardship but even seeks it in order to provide a more credible witness to the gospel and to transform his own life into the kind of Christian witness others can imitate (see 11:1).

Caution against complacency (10:1-22)

Paul continues to reflect on the principles of Christian behavior which will help to reconcile the weak and the strong. Having reflected on his own experience as an apostle, he widens his circle of examples, appealing to the lesson of Israel and the circumstances of the Corinthians before he returns in 10:23-11:1 to the question of idol-meats and his warning against scandal, which is a fundamental threat to the community (see 8:1-13). The Israelites, Paul reminds the Corinthians, became complacent and were punished (10:1-13). Paul warns against likewise incurring the wrath of a jealous God by the idolatry of participating at sacrificial banquets while also assisting at the Eucharist (10:14-22). He contrasts such recklessness with the love and mutual respect characteristic of the Christian who does all out of love for the glory of God (10:23-11:1).

10:1-13 The lesson of Israel. The reality of grace, which is an expression of God's mercy, is an antidote to complacency. Having invoked athletic imagery to emphasize the necessity of self-discipline and vigilance, Paul warns his fellow Christians against pride, using the example of Israel. The Old Testament is full of examples of prophetic utterances against the infidelity of God's people. Israel is the spiritual ancestor of the Christians. Paul presupposes that his audience is very familiar with the story of the Exodus. He uses events from that story in the same order in which they appear in the Old Testament—the cloud, the sea, the manna, water from the rock. All the Israelites, Paul reminds the Corinthians, as a warning, were under the cloud that represented the presence of God. All of them passed through the sea that symbolized for them God's mighty deeds.

Paul continues to draw parallels he hopes his readers will identify with. He helps them to this end by presenting the passage through the sea as being "baptized into Moses." There is no direct Jewish precedent for this phrase. Paul may have coined it himself and used it to evoke a parallel between the Israelites' perception of the Exodus and the Christians' perception of it. Baptism literally means "immersion" and signifies belonging to the one in whom they are baptized.

Instead of referring explicitly to the manna and the water, Paul alludes to the spiritual food and spiritual drink. This allusion could allow his readers to relate not only to baptism but to the Eucharist. A Jewish tradition, popular in Paul's time, was that a stream of water accompanied the Jews through the desert. Another tradition was that a well from which they drank followed them. Paul's point is that even these signs did not insure the Israelites against God's wrath or envelop them in a protective covering. They displeased God and their rebellion was punished.

The Scriptures were written for our instruction (10:6; 11; Rom 15:4; 2 Tim 3:16). Our ancestors became idolaters, erroneously assuming that these signs were gods who would protect them. They had no concern for the context in which the meaning of these signs would be made clear.

10:14-22 Participation at sacrificial banquets. Paul reminds the Corinthians of his love as if to indicate that this is basic to understanding what he is about to say. Avoidance of idol worship is fundamental to true faith. The cup of blessing makes all Christians sharers in the blood of Christ. The bread they share binds them to Christ and to one another. As the body of Christ they are nourished by this sharing. This is no empty symbol.

"Israel according to the flesh" represents the community's link with the history of Israel and serves as a lesson for us (see Rom 9:6; Gal 6:16). All those who participate at one altar share in the eating of what is sacrificed. Paul, like the strong, denies the existence of the idols whom the Gentiles honor by their sacrifices. But this denial does not bring with it license for idolatry. Once converted, Christians must guard against any return to paganism. All actions must proceed from faith in the one Lord. One cannot serve God and mammon (see Matt 6:24), nor can we assist at the altar of Christ while simultaneously condoning divisive practices. The unity represented by the Lord's Supper is desecrated by the idolatry of ideas and practices that scandalize and divide. It is not possible to eat at the Lord's table and to disregard the consciences of some Christians. If one eats at a sacrificial banquet, one is united in some way to the god in whose honor the sacrifice is offered and to those who honor this god. When Christians do this, they risk the anger of a jealous God whose will it is to bring all to unity and fellowship with one another in Christ.

10:23–11:1 Seek the good of others. Paul accepts the slogan of the strong that "all things are lawful" in Christ. But this does not imply that all things are good or constructive to community, which is the one "law" or goal binding all Christians. Whereas public ritual banquets are excluded on the basis of the scandal and division they might provoke, Paul grounds the Christian's freedom to eat anything that is served at private meals in the love command. Christ put an end to the law (see Rom 10:4) that distinguishes between clean and unclean foods. Love alone is the absolute enabling the believer to eat of the fullness of creation. Food is irrelevant. Just as charity gives the believer the freedom to eat anything, it may also, in some instances, require abstinence. Charity links and rules Christian consciences.

Christians submit to each other's consciences in charity, as to the Lord. The only sufficient motivation for Christian action is charity which is neither self-seeking nor slavish scrupulosity. Love is sincerely interested in the welfare and the edification of others (see 1 Cor 13). Freedom in Christ enables Christians to be subject to one another in faith. Thus, like Paul, who himself imitates Jesus, all seek the salvation of the many (see 9:19-23). This is why Christ came to give his life (see Mark 10:45; 14:24).

IV. PROBLEMS IN LITURGICAL ASSEMBLIES (11:2–14:40)

Paul has been told of some of the disorders in the Corinthian community's celebration of the liturgy. He has heard that there is confusion about liturgical dress, a topic he addresses in 11:2-16. More serious are the abuses against communal charity, which deny the very meaning of the Lord's Supper (11:17-34). Likewise, Corinthian Christians are competitive and divisive about the place and the importance of some of the more dazzling spiritual gifts such as speaking in tongues, and this attitude of superiority leads to violations of charity (12:1–14:40). Since all these disorders occur in liturgical celebrations, Paul considers them together despite the disparity of their importance.

A. Liturgical Dress and Behavior

11:2-16 Liturgical dress. This is a topic that, according to all evidence, almost had to have been introduced by the Corinthians themselves rather than by Paul. Paul, who chided his readers for being divided on the basis of what ministry itself means and who their valid ministers are, would apparently have considered liturgical dress a relatively insignificant matter. This section is sometimes mistakenly described as addressing the issue of *women's* attire and appearance at liturgies. This is misleading in that Paul comments on the appropriate appearance of both men and women who both pray and prophesy (11:4-5). It is clear that Paul recognized the possibility of liturgical leadership roles for both men and women.

Many problems among the Corinthian Christians arose because of their disregard for the physical and for legitimate mores. Paul characteristically argues for a correct appreciation of sexual differences, depicting failure to honor these differences as foolish, a sinful rejection of the order that God intended in creating male and female (see Rom 1:24-27). His comments to the Corinthians regarding liturgical dress are in this vein. Failure to respect the wisdom of common practice regarding dress could lead to more serious abuses of authority and Christian freedom, and undermine the real purpose of coming together in liturgical assembly to worship. Just as Paul argues for peace and harmony in the regulation of spiritual gifts (1 Cor 14:1-40), he similarly instructs both men and women in the appropriate decorum and attire at liturgical celebrations for the sake of offering fitting worship to the God of peace.

First, he praises the Corinthians for holding fast to the traditions he has taught them, thereby cleverly reminding them of his own authority and supporting the instinct which moved them to submit this issue to him for comment. Despite the apparent insignificance of the issue of attire, Paul commends the Corinthians. But for the more gross and more threatening violations of charity even at the Lord's Supper, he does not commend them (11:17).

The subordinationist view some interpreters see in 11:3 is excluded by Paul's reasoning in 11:11-12. Paul's opinion, supported, he says, by the order of creation and by common sense, reflected in the practice of all thinking people and all the churches, is that there should be a difference between men and women. This difference is not in role, for he talks about their both having the same role, that is, to pray and prophesy. The point of 11:3 is that all comes from God, who is the source (= head) of all life. This implies recognition of the order of creation (see Rom 1:20-32), which imposes responsibility for the mutuality of men and women. Although deutero-Pauline writings sometimes do *appear* to support the subordination of wives to their husbands (for example, Eph 5:22-24; Col 3:18–4:1), this is clearly not the point of our passage, which makes no reference to relationships between married people, but speaks of the dress and appearance of both men and women while they perform identical liturgical roles. Further, it would be a mistake to propose that "headship," an image used to describe unity in Christ, could be interpreted to support a subordinationist-domination mentality, especially when it is precisely just such misinterpretations that Paul attacks.

Paul argues from creation in 11:3-9. Christ is the first-born of all creation (Col 1:15). Man is the image of God and reflects God's glory. It would not be appropriate, then, for man to pray with his head covered, Paul contends, lest this glory be concealed. Paul argues that the custom of the day for men to wear their hair short is authoritative. Women, however, wear their hair long and cover their heads as a sign of God's authority over them as medi-

ated by men. For women, then, as for men, Paul accepts the custom of the day as authoritative, reflected also, Paul suggests, in the order of creation of the sexes. Women without veils implied availability. The whole of 1 Cor 11:2-16 represents Paul's elaborate way of warning the Corinthians against divisions and competition that may arise at other gatherings, but which are intolerable for the Christian community in a liturgical context.

The veil is to be worn by women because of the angels (1 Cor 11:10), who were considered the guardians of the liturgy. This could be a scriptural reference to Gen 6:1-4, which describes the desecration of the design of human creation, when the sons of God lusted after the daughters of men and produced a race of giants. This atrocity prompted God to regret having created the world and to vow to destroy it with the flood. Thus, Paul reasons, in preserving the customary "sign of authority on her head," women assume their rightful place in the liturgy, subordinate to the angels who guard its order. In this way there is no danger of women's being a distraction to either men or angels. Since a woman's long hair is her glory, it would be her shame if she would have to have her head shaved. The long length is perhaps in contrast to the practice of prostitutes and lesbians to wear hair cropped short. Shaving a woman's head could refer to a punishment sometimes mandated for prostitutes. But a woman cannot use the liturgy for her own glorification, so she must cover her hair lest she provide a distraction at the liturgy. However unconvincingly, Paul is trying to give scriptural and authoritative reinforcement for customs that prescribe differences between the sexes while also maintaining women's right to "pray and prophesy" at the assemblies. In short, appearance must be conventional so that decency is respected and the liturgy does not occasion perversions.

Also, the element of scandal is to be avoided. Women played major roles in the rites of pagan religions, but only men presided at the Jewish liturgies. Paul advocates that the freedom of men and women alike to celebrate in Christian communities composed of both former Jews and Greeks should not be a cause of scandal to either the former Jews of Corinth or to the Jewish-Christian authorities, who would have been shocked had they themselves heard the reports Paul had received. As is the case throughout the epistle, the spirit of charity governs even the freedom won through Christ.

B. Celebration of the Lord's Supper (11:17-34)

Paul begins this section emphasizing that he cannot commend the Corinthians for the very serious abuses he now addresses. Paul is unambiguous. Proceeding according to his typical ABA' pattern, he outlines the abuses in Corinth, focusing on the way social and economic differences are allowed to inhibit appropriate celebration of the Lord's Supper. First he details these abuses and these differences (11:17-22). Then he focuses attention on the memory of Jesus' action and command in the institution account (11:23-27). Finally, he returns to the abuses and recommendation for healing the Body (11:28-34).

11:17-22 Reported abuses. Perhaps the Corinthians had implied in their letter to Paul that although they experienced some conflicts, such as what is appropriate liturgical dress (see 11:2-16), they nevertheless prided themselves on dutifully and regularly meeting to celebrate the Lord's Supper. Paul is not impressed. Such meetings as are described to him are not profitable but harmful. The really faithful tried and true, those interested in deepening their faith, are challenged to "stand out clearly," distinguishing themselves from the factious members.

The Corinthians are not assembling for the Lord's Supper. They have ulterior, destructive motives. Two meanings are suggested. First, it is not their *intention*, when they get together, to celebrate in remembrance of the Lord (11:24-25), and second, in fact, this is not the *result* of the Corinthians' gathering. In other words, from what Paul says, it is clear that the intention of many Corinthians is more divisive than reflective of the Lord's command, with the result that they do not carry out this command in their meetings.

Reports allege that the many divisions among the Corinthians are allowed to be part of the Eucharistic celebrations. Violations of charity, directly opposed to Jesus' command, are flagrant. Some are gluttonous, eating their own food, unmindful of the needs of others. On the other side, "one person goes hungry," even in the midst of the assembled commu-

nity whose obligation it is to provide for the needs of all, especially the poor (see Gal 2:10). Some people become drunk, dramatizing the inability of the self-centered to contribute to building community. If it is only for eating and drinking that they assemble, the Corinthians would do better not to risk the judgment of God by assembling without a willingness for conversion, as if the Eucharist were magic. The Corinthian temptation to be overconfident seems to need correction once more (see 1 Cor 10:1-12). Their coming together, when not motivated by charity, shows contempt for the community. By embarrassing them rather than showing hospitality to those who have nothing, some members test God and court judgment against themselves (11:29).

Paul cannot avoid his pastoral responsibility to condemn the disorder rather than overlook it. Paul will not condone the Corinthians' gross misinterpretation of the real meaning of the liturgy. Apparently they mistakenly assumed that it was sufficient to come together regularly, and they seemed to have prided themselves on observing a ritual which brought together people of every walk of life or social standing. Nothing commendable in this, Paul says. In fact, such hypocrisy, while failing to reconcile the differences among them or make charity really practical, is, in fact, testimony against them. Even though in other parts of this letter Paul betrays a deep sensitivity to his fragile popularity in Corinth, he is not willing to soft-pedal his reaction to these abuses.

11:23-27 Tradition of the institution. Without suggesting that they have neglected the literal practice of the Lord's Supper, Paul inserts in his general instruction on the liturgy an account of the institution of the Eucharist. For emphasis, Paul enhances this account with a repetition over the cup as over the bread of the words "do this in remembrance of me." The memory of Jesus, who offered himself and whose death Christians proclaim in their liturgy, is the antidote to the factions in Corinth. Jesus' life and death is more than a memory. It effects unity among all those who recognize him as Lord.

Paul begins his institution account using technical language of receiving and handing on the Christian tradition (see 15:1-3). The phrase "from the Lord" does not necessarily mean that this tradition was part of the revelation of Paul's initial vision of Jesus which Luke describes as occurring on the way to Damascus. The tradition was an essential part of the gospel which Paul identifies with Christ. Even if the account was mediated by the Christian community, its authority, like the word prohibiting divorce (see 7:10), was the Lord's.

Paul rarely refers to the earthly life of Jesus. But this account of the action of Jesus, specified as happening the night before he died, is particularly significant because of its uniqueness. The aspect of betrayal on the part of Jesus' followers, which is part of the synoptic account (see Mark 14:17-31 and parallels), is accentuated in Paul's account, too. Betrayal and human weakness provide the context for the Eucharistic institution account (see 11:17-22 and 27-32), wherein Paul describes the abuses surrounding the memorial celebration in Corinth. Similarly, the gospel reports the betrayal and denial of the disciples at the Last Supper. Luke, in particular, stresses the constant misunderstanding of the disciples who, even at the moment of the Eucharist, argued among themselves over which one was the greatest in the kingdom of heaven (see Luke 22:24-30).

Jesus took ordinary bread and gave thanks for it. After it was broken, he identified it with his body. In contrast to the more original account of Mark, Paul has the words "which is for you." This addition emphasizes at once the timeless but very real significance of the Eucharistic celebration. Whenever believers share this bread and this cup, they recall the Lord's command to do this in memory of him. In so doing, they recall his death as they await his coming in glory. Three stages of time, the past (the original Last Supper and Jesus' death), the present (the community's celebration), and the future (the parousia) are brought together in this action. Anyone who performs this action unworthily, that is, separating one of these aspects from the other, sins in not fulfilling the Lord's command.

11:28-34 Practical recommendations for healing the body. To avoid this sin, one must examine oneself, recollecting, in the literal sense, the necessary faith to transcend all that would prohibit a realization of the implications of eating and drinking as a disciple of the Lord. Such a self-examination allows one to recognize oneself as a member of the body. Anyone who eats and drinks without this recognition sins against the body and blood of the Lord, thus calling a judgment down upon oneself. This accounts, Paul says, for the suffering so many of the Corinthians experienced through sickness and death. These are the punishments of the Corinthians' disbelief, most of all in the body, which is the church. Like the Israelites, who were chastised in the desert (10:5-12) for their complacency, the Corinthians are witnessing God's displeasure.

Nevertheless, there is still hope that they will be converted and saved if they consider these chastisements as a warning. For Paul, Christ's judgment is salvation for all who believe, but it is condemnation for disbelief (see 1:18). Paul's stern words, then, are actually a loving admonition urging the Corinthians to show that they are different from the nonbelieving world. This difference can be expressed in very significant, concrete ways that will demonstrate for all to see that participants recognize the real meaning of the Lord's Supper. When Christians assemble, they are to be considerate, waiting for one another. The hungry are to eat at home so that it is clearly not for selfish reasons that they gather. Since they will not be gathering merely to obtain food, there will be no danger of selfish motives prohibiting the genuine communal celebration.

The community must have raised other questions about the celebrations of the Lord's Supper, but Paul defers instruction in these matters until he comes. This is the essential. The rest can afford to wait (see 4:19; 16:5-9).

C. Spiritual Gifts and the Community (12:1-14:40)

The Corinthians' lack of appreciation for the body affected more than their liturgical celebrations. It permeated their understanding of all things Christian, including the basic profession of faith. Paul's attempt to correct this continues in 12:1-14:40, where he shows how the use of even the most spiritual of gifts is meant for the edification of the "body," the church (see 12:12-31). For example, the elementary saying "Jesus is Lord" (12:3) is a confession of faith in the bodily resurrection of Jesus (see Rom 10:9). The opposite, which says "Cursed be Jesus," attacks and weakens the body and is therefore a grave sin against the Spirit. All gifts with which the community is richly endowed (see 1 Cor 1:5), must be valued in proportion to their role in the building up of the body. Paul now turns to a discussion of the relative importance of such gifts in 12:1-14:40.

Yet there are still some pressing liturgical matters that Paul must address at this time. Again we find him using the ABA' schema in the next three chapters, which discuss the spiritual gifts and their use in the community. This discussion is highlighted by his main idea, which is a development of the notion of charity (12:31-13:13) (= B). Charity must become practical by effecting unity and enabling those with gifts to serve the whole body, the church. There was much confusion in Corinth, particularly over the apparent superiority of the gift of tongues, and this led to dangerous competition (chapter 12) (= A) and even to chaos (chapter 14) (= A').

Paul acknowledges that no spiritual gift is lacking in this community (see 1:5, 7). He readily admits that speaking in tongues, so coveted by the Corinthians, is among the spiritual gifts they possess. Indeed Paul himself exercised this gift (see 14:18-19) and may have introduced it into the community (14:6-14). Paul discusses the relative significance of various gifts, warning against ignorance of the purpose of all spiritual gifts. Clearly knowledge is especially cherished by the Corinthians. The Apostle would have their appreciation of spiritual gifts based on Christian wisdom, which has unity as its goal.

12:1-11 The Spirit's gifts. When they were pagans, the Corinthians were easily led by all kinds of false ideas. Driven by compulsion, they did not hear God's revelation but were led by mute idols. Paul refers to the powerful idols such as Elijah opposed (see 1 Kgs 18:21-40). Again he takes for granted his readers' acquaintance with the Old Testament Scriptures (see 1 Cor 10:1-13).

Apparently the Corinthians tended to consider any persuasive speaker or collective impulse as evidence of the possession of the Spirit. Perhaps this explains why Paul's own lack of eloquence in comparison, for example, to the silver-tongued Apollos caused some in Corinth to disregard Paul while exalting Apollos (see 1 Cor 2:1; 3:5; 4:6; 2 Cor 10:1-2, 9-10; Acts 18:24). The point of all Christian speech, Paul maintains, however, is not eloquence, but the proclamation of the lordship of Christ. No one who "curses Jesus" can be moved by the Spirit. Paul may be referring to those who tear down the community by nurturing divisions. The Apostle might also envision the more flagrant apostasy of those who failed to sustain their faith in Christ and actually returned to Judaism or paganism. At a time of increasing antagonism with Judaism, for example, some Christians continued to worship in the synagogue, where gradually phrases condemning Jesus and his followers were introduced and became more bitter. This was obviously intolerable to the early Christians who considered themselves rooted in Judaism. Paul emphasizes that the proclamation of Jesus as Lord can only be made through the Spirit, and that this proclamation cannot be divisive. The same Spirit who gives the gift of faith distributes all other gifts. The Spirit brings the variety of gifts into a marvelous unity. Experience shows that even gifts can be divisive if faith, not only in Christ but also in the church, is not strong. Gifts can result in envy, pride, arrogance, exclusiveness. The Spirit is required for the church to use gifts to effect unity.

Similarly, the talents of ministers who provide needed services sometimes induce people to make them lords. Yet since all Christians acknowledge the same Lord, they recognize all ministries as subordinate to one Lord over all. All are brought into unity and harmony by the same God, source and goal of all that is. Each manifestation of the Spirit is designed not for the promotion of the one who administers the gift but for the good of all. The idea of the "common good" described in 12:7 is a prelude to Paul's description of the community as a body (12:12-31). This draws on the analogy of the Stoic politic as a commonwealth.

Paul proceeds in 12:8-10 to give several examples of the variety of the gifts before reiterating in 12:11 that all gifts are manifestations of the same Spirit. The list is not exhaustive. Similar, but not identical, lists occur elsewhere (12:28-30; Rom 12:6-8; Eph 4:11). One may be a great rhetorician, another a great scientist or teacher. Clearly Paul does not mean that faith is necessary only for some. All who are justified share a common faith. Yet, in some, this faith is a visible evidence of things unseen (see Heb 11:1). In others, the predominant sign is their ability to heal physical and spiritual ills. Some even have the ability to perform miraculous deeds. The list is not intended to be a comment on the respective value of each of these gifts. Prophecy, which elsewhere Paul describes as having greater value than tongues (14:1-3), is simply listed as one of the manifestations of the same Spirit. Each gift is distributed, not according to individual merit, but according to the will of the Spirit.

12:12-31 The analogy of the body. The Corinthians exalted spiritual gifts and did not sufficiently respect the body. As part of his corrective, Paul describes the Spirit as the unifying power making all one. He uses the analogy of the body to teach this lesson. According to Paul, all reality is reevaluated in the light of Christ. Thus, even the "inferior" body (see 12:24-25) provides the most appropriate image to describe the work of the Spirit. Paul borrows the image of the body from the Stoic philosophy popular in his day. The Stoics presented the state as a commonwealth, a body with many members. This image was forcefully suggested by Paul's application of the meaning of the Eucharist for the Corinthian community (see 11:17-34). The body represents the unity and the diversity of the community. The body needs the diversity of many members, just as each member depends on the cooperation of the other members to function as part of the body. The interrelationship is symbiotic.

So it is with Christ. Paul nowhere says explicitly that the church is the body of Christ. But he does apply this image to the communities he addresses. Through baptism, believers participate with Christ in his dying and rising. Through the Eucharist they are joined to one another in his body. Thus, all natural distinctions which may have tended to divide people are eliminated through these sacraments. The Spirit enables us to transcend racial or national (Jewish or Greek) or social (slave or free) differences. Gal 3:28 adds to these the unity of the sexes. The discussion of 1 Cor 11:2-16 already spoke of this relationship (see 7:17-40).

The body is not identified with any one member, but needs many members cooperating as one. Each believer is a member of the body of Christ; the believer's body is also called a temple of the Holy Spirit (see 1 Cor 6:19). The body, the church, gathers the members and all belong to one. All the parts contribute essentially to the building up of the body. The differences of the members contribute to their unity. One cannot become the other, nor can one inhibit the function of the other. If one member suffers, every other member suffers, and all other members instinctively supply for the hurt member. Similarly, if one member is given special recognition, all members are more animated because they share in this honor.

The Corinthians naturally valued the things of the mind and of the spirit more than the physical. Yet they realized that the mind had influence on the body and vice versa. Regarding the whole person, then, the "less important" or less "honorable" members are given propriety by the more honorable members. In other words, just as our minds govern our passions so that there is no contradiction in ourselves, so, too, the Spirit brings together in harmony the less and the more honorable members of the body. Thus, too, for example, the "weak" and the "strong" can be reconciled (see 1 Cor 8:7-13; 10:23-30).

So it is with the body of Christ, the church. Each Christian finds a new identity in relationship to other Christians of the same body. The gifts of God bestowed upon the church range from apostleship to the gift of tongues. The apostles here seem to be ranked first, yet they are considered the "last of all" (1 Cor 4:9). They qualify as apostles by accepting the wisdom of God, which makes them appear foolish to the world (4:10). Their function, as Paul describes it, derives from the vision of the risen Lord (9:1; 15:8-10). The apostle's task is to preach the gospel, form communities (9:2), maintain the local churches in harmony with the greater church, notably the authorities in Jerusalem (see Gal 2:1-10). The apostles are not synonymous with the Twelve. Nor does Paul, who fashioned the term "apostle" for Christian use, describe apostles as followers of Jesus during his earthly life. Their mission is from God and not necessarily subject to the qualifications the community might wish to impose.

After the apostles come the prophets. Paul defers his description of the function of the prophets to 14:1-5. Then come the teachers who explain the gospel's implications and thus strengthen faith. It is not clear that for Paul there existed a real hierarchy. Yet, as a corrective for the Corinthians, who believed that speaking in tongues was of utmost importance, Paul mentions this gift last. His emphasis is that there are many ministries to be performed, and so there should not be competition. While each one has a gift, not all have the same gift. The greater gifts are not necessarily the most dazzling. The greater gifts are those which best serve the needs of the community. So, Paul concludes, set your hearts on the greater gifts, and the greatest of these is charity.

13:1-13 Love, the more excellent way. In understanding this very famous passage, we need to bear in mind Paul's description of charity as the gift of the community. It is the more excellent way, which is also the more fundamental way, the way for all. The "love of God," Paul says, "has been poured out into our hearts through the holy Spirit that has been given to us" (Rom 5:5). Any gift without love is really nothing. It is allusion. Paul's audience at Corinth would understand this as an absolute statement of futility. The Apostle has just finished discussing the variety of spiritual gifts. Now he considers three of the more extolled. And without love, they amount to zero.

Paul considers first the gift the Corinthians favored, eloquent speech, the ability to express oneself in human or even superhuman tongues. Without love, this is a senseless void. In fact, lovelessness, according to Paul, makes *me* nothing. In 14:7-8, Paul uses a musical example. In 13:1, he seems to anticipate this analogy. A gong or a cymbal, while capable of enhancing the harmony of other instruments, are mere loud noises themselves. So it is with eloquence devoid of love.

Even prophecy, which Paul himself exalts above tongues (14:1-5), is nothing without love. So also with faith. Too often faith seems to pertain exclusively to one's relationship to God. For Paul, however, without faith in the community, nourished by love, there is nothing. Even almsgiving and martyrdom are nothing without love.

The characteristics of love are the opposite of the self-seeking, competitive characteristics of knowledge. The Corinthians' hierarchy of values fostered factiousness. But this is opposed to Christian community. Un-

like the strong who anathematize the weak, love is patient. Unlike the weak who condemn the strong, love is kind. The enlightened or the celibate may put on airs or expect certain honors, but this is not the way of love. The poor, the outcast, or the neglected may brood over their injuries, but love will teach them to forgive without limit and hope without condition. It cannot be love that prompts the Corinthians to rejoice over wrong, as in the case of the incestuous man, for example (see 5:1-13). Perhaps Paul did not really intend his description of love to be applied to each of the matters brought before him by the Corinthians. But clearly the Apostle stresses that the divisions in Corinth would not exist if the community had been mindful of the primacy of love.

Love does not run out. Prophecies, tongues, knowledge, have limits, but love does not. The chapter begins and ends with a list of these three gifts that are reduced in 13:9 to two (prophecy and knowledge). Paul will compare prophecy and tongues in chapter 14 to show the superiority of prophecy. Thus, he concentrates for the moment on the remaining gift, knowledge, which decreases in importance in proportion to love.

The perfect eliminates the imperfect, which it fulfills. Love perfects knowledge, which is imperfect. The Corinthians strive for knowledge, but Paul tells them that this is symptomatic of their immaturity. Even the clearest knowledge is like a shadow compared to love, which sees face to face. The Corinthians reason like children. As they grow in Christian wisdom, they will learn to put aside childish ways and pursue love as the greatest wisdom. They despise what they do not love, but when they become mature, they will see that only love lasts. Of the three realities which endure, the greatest is love.

There are other spiritual gifts, but love is the one essential gift that characterizes the community worthy of the name Christian. Love is the criterion for judging the relative value of all other gifts, since all gifts are given for the sake of building up the community (14:1-5). Paul then develops this understanding, using the example of sound without intelligibility being like tongues without love (14:6-19). Admissible evidence for the presence of love in the community is the impact and witness value of that community upon the non-believer (14:20-25). Paul proceeds, then, to prescribe concrete rules for order which will help the community make love practical in the building up of the community (14:26-40).

14:1-5 Prophecy, a most desirable gift. True wisdom seeks love, realizing that if the community possesses this greatest gift, all the rest can have meaning. Paul considers prophecy next to love. In this section he contrasts this gift with the gift of tongues preferred by the Corinthians. One who speaks in tongues communicates with God, but not with others, whereas the prophet speaks for the sake of others. Rather surprisingly, perhaps, communication with God alone is not better than communication with others. On the contrary. Because the prophet's words are for the community, the gift supersedes the gift of tongues.

Influenced by pagan mystery religions, perhaps, the Corinthians erroneously considered the gift of tongues to be superior. Paul shows the extent and the implications of his preference for love. Tongues can separate one from the community and may be used to promote oneself. Whatever builds up the church is the greater gift. Paul recognizes tongues as a spiritual gift, but the criterion for evaluating all gifts is the edification of the community. This is the same criterion by which, Paul has insisted, all actions of the Christian, such as the judgment of personal life-style (7:1-40), of conscience (8:7-13), of whether one has the right to eat meat offered to idols (e.g., 10:23-30), or conduct at liturgies (11:17-34) must be made.

14:6-19 A comparison of gifts. Paul continues to develop the topic of the importance and function of the gift of tongues and of prophecy. Clearly appealing to the Corinthians' practical sense, Paul asks what good he would be to them if he were to come to them speaking a foreign language they did not understand. Perhaps, Paul reasons, the Corinthians would understand his point if they considered themselves as the outsiders, those who would be frustrated by his use of tongues rather than as ones who possessed this gift. Tongues without revelation, knowledge, prophecy, or instruction are useless.

Next Paul borrows an image from the world of music. The arrangement of different notes gives meaning to the sounds produced by a flute or a harp. If the notes are indistinguishable, the instrument is useless. Similarly,

the bugle has to produce the expected sequence to call an army to battle. Otherwise, not only confusion, but even disaster, could result.

So it is with speaking in tongues. As long as these remain unintelligible sounds without the essential complement of interpretation, they are useless. It is absurd for the Corinthians to be impressed with futility and nothingness. Even the laws governing human languages teach us this. Unless we can interpret the sounds of others' languages, they remain strangers to us, outside the possibility of our communicating with them. But languages are designed to be a means of communication, making possible bonds among people. Language needs intelligibility, however, to become the communication it was meant to be. Tongues without interpretation are not what they are meant to be. If the Corinthians are serious about spiritual gifts, they should enrich themselves with those gifts that edify the church.

And so, the one who speaks in tongues, recognizing that this gift needs its complement, should pray for the gift of interpretation. The Greeks made a distinction not only between the body and the spirit but also between the spirit and the mind. The mind grasps intelligible things. Although with the gift of tongues we may pray with the spirit, the gift of interpretation helps us also to pray with the mind.

The mind (*nous* in Greek) or intelligibility and harmony can control even the spirit. Paul challenges the Corinthian view that speaking in tongues is more excellent because it withdraws one from the body and *nous*. Rather, Paul argues that the more excellent way is charity by which all gifts, including those of both body and spirit, work in harmony for the building up of the church and the glory of God who is peace (see 12:31–13:13).

The traditional response of the community to the words of the leaders in prayer is "Amen," which means to accept something as steadfast, to proclaim faith that what is said is true (see 2 Cor 1:20). For this "Amen" to mean anything, the members of the community must understand the reality they accept. If tongues only praise God but fail to speak to other people, then the community need not answer "Amen." Such praise could be given to God in private. Unless the community understands, its "Amen" does not signify a common prayer of the church. Paul's last comment is *ad hominem:* he gives thanks that he excels any of the Corinthians in the gift of tongues. But he far prefers the gift of instruction which serves the community.

14:20-25 Another measure of the Corinthians' immaturity. The Corinthians are childish in their conceit. With a touch of irony Paul admonishes them to be childish so far as evil is concerned, but to grow up mentally and spiritually. Such instruction echoes Jesus' words: "Be shrewd as serpents and simple as doves" (Matt 10:16). The Corinthians' competition for spiritual gifts shows how immature they are (see 3:1-4; 13:11).

Once again Paul assumes a certain knowledge of the Old Testament when he quotes Isa 28:11-12, implicitly threatening the proud Corinthians with the punishment of unbelievers. Paul seems to want to penetrate their complacency and to shock them into looking closely at how similar they are to unbelieving Israel, which did not heed God. Then Paul plays on the idea of unbelief. The nonbeliever may be attracted or impressed with the gift of tongues, just as the Corinthians were. Thus, in a sense, tongues is a gift for unbelievers. It dazzles and attracts them. But if they enter a whole assembly speaking in tongues, the nonbeliever could become indignant and judge that the whole community was out of its mind. If, however, an unbeliever enters where believers are prophesying and speaking for the upbuilding, encouragement, and consolidation of all (14:3), he or she will be confronted with the truth and given an example of love in practice. They will be led to worship God and to acknowledge that God lives among people. Thus the church functions as a prophet bringing God to the world.

14:26-40 Some rules order. Paul now lays down some rules of order in the use of the variety of spiritual gifts by the community. Having shown the propensity on the part of the Corinthians for abusing even the spiritual gifts, Paul makes some practical suggestions that could help the Corinthians avoid further confusion and make love effective in strengthening the community. Having already acknowledged that all have some spiritual gifts, Paul says that now the point is to use these for a constructive purpose.

Since the gift of tongues seems to be the most troublesome, Paul begins there. This gift must be controlled in a variety of ways—by the number of those permitted to speak, by the order in which they speak, and by requiring them to be interpreted. If there is no one with the gift of interpretation, there should be silence, since God does not require that the word be externalized and spoken. At most two or three should speak and then two or three interpret. Part of the problem of the Corinthian assembly is that the extravagant length of the services contributes to disorder and competition. The services would be limited to a reasonable length of time. Even the number of prophecies spoken are limited. The "two or three" may have reflected the promise of Jesus: "Where two or three are gathered in my name, there am I in their midst" (Matt 18:20), and "If two of you join your voices on earth to pray for anything whatever, it shall be granted you by my Father in heaven" (Matt 18:19).

It is for the assembly to decide upon the impact of the prophets' words. If one who had not even prepared to speak should receive a revelation, this one should take precedence and those who had planned to speak should listen to that one. Eventually all the prophets may speak, but only one at a time. Even the prophets themselves need to be advised and encouraged. Therefore, they must listen to the others.

The idea of control of the spirit was probably repugnant to the rambunctious Corinthians. But Paul's reasoning leaves no room for rebuttal. God is a God of peace, not of chaos. God does not inspire disorder and dissatisfaction, competition and empty rhetoric.

1 Cor 14:34-35 expresses a viewpoint which apparently contradicts what Paul had said earlier about women's prominent role in worship (see 11:5, 11-12). Moreover, Paul's use of the law to support the submission of women is contrary not only to what he says elsewhere on the subject of women (see Gal 3:28) but also to the legitimate role of the law for Christians (see Gal 4:10; Rom 10:4). Two ways of reconciling the contradiction between 1 Cor 11:5, 11-12 and 14:34-35 have been proposed.

According to one view, 14:34-35 represents an interpolation dating from the end of the first Christian century and expressing a heretical view such as the one challenged in 1 Tim 2:11-15. A problem in the early church was that women, particularly vulnerable and susceptible because of their general lack of education, fell prey to heretical teaching about sexuality and marriage. Given the propensity in Greek cultures to deemphasize the body, teachers easily went one step further, asserting that marriage was evil and abstinence better. Women themselves began to perpetuate this by believing and teaching it to other women and to their children. The author of 1 Timothy responds that women must not teach but listen, and that, far from being sinful, childbearing is for the salvation of woman (1 Tim 2:11, 14).

The second solution to the contradiction between 1 Cor 11:5, 11-12 and 14:34-35 is this. Paul is quoting the slogans of the Corinthian male elitists in 14:34-35; 14:36 is his rebuttal to this viewpoint. His sarcastic tone can almost be heard: "Did the preaching of God's word originate with you? Are you [that is, males] the only ones to whom it has come?" In a similar way he quoted and then corrected the negative view of some of the Corinthian males on marriage: "A man is better off having no relations with a woman" (7:1). Such quotations of the Corinthians' positions which Paul challenges punctuate this letter (see also 8:1; 10:23). Having discussed the appropriate way for both men and women to pray and prophesy in 11:2-16, Paul could not now be denying this liturgical or some other leadership role to women in the church. Especially at the close of this section (12:1–14:40), where Paul argues for peace and harmony in the exercise of divinely inspired gifts, it is not possible or reasonable to assume that Paul is now siding with the elitists, excluding women and alleging male superiority.

First Corinthians represents Paul's attempt to reconcile rather than aggravate factions in Corinth. 1 Cor 14:34-36 must be interpreted in the light of the reconciliation Paul tried to effect, and any interpretation of these verses has to consider the overall conciliatory tone of the entire epistle.

V. The Resurrection (1 Cor 15:1-58)

By adding his instruction on the resurrection, Paul implies that the Christians in Corinth would not have experienced so many problems and conflicts if they had under-

stood—or better, if they had really accepted—the ramifications of the resurrection of the body. Almost all the Corinthians' misunderstandings were related to their failure to correctly appreciate the physical. All Christian faith depends upon acceptance of the reality of the resurrection (see 15:17). Paul concludes and summarizes his entire message to the Corinthians with a review of the foundations and the implications of this basic teaching. First, he presents the basic traditional elements of belief in the resurrection of Christ (15:1-11). He then addresses the Corinthian hypothesis that there is no resurrection, but dismisses this as hopeless nonsense (15:12-24). Paul goes on to try to explain the manner of the resurrection (15:35-58), concluding that this mystery can only be grasped through faith.

A. The Resurrection of Christ (15:1-11)

Paul reminds those who have become family through baptism and the gospel they have heard preached to them, which they have received, that the gospel is not mere catechetics or doctrine; it is the power to save (see Rom 1:16). And it is even now saving the Corinthians if they remain committed to what they have learned from Paul. If they do not persevere in the same gospel, they will have been converted in vain.

Again employing technical language for tradition ("I handed on to you . . . what I also received"), as he did when he spoke of the Eucharist (1 Cor 15:3; see 11:23), Paul bases the gospel on the firm ground of the tradition reaching back to Jesus' life on earth. At the center of Christian teaching is Jesus' death and resurrection. For this tradition, Paul borrows from an existing creed, which he quotes in 15:3b-5. The creed professes four elements: Christ died, he was buried, he was raised, he appeared. The Old Testament Scriptures had promised one who would save us from our sins. This is what Christ's death accomplished.

Christ's burial emphasizes the reality of his dying. In Jewish thought, burial is the final stage of death. The three days in the tomb signify the reality of that death and burial. Jesus is not presented by Paul as the agent of his resurrection. God is the judge of the living and the dead. Christ was raised by God, Paul says (see Rom 10:9). Christ truly lives. Then Christ appeared to many leaders of the church. They had no hallucinations. The Christians expressed their own consciousness that what happened was something objective, namely, Christ appeared, rather than merely "was seen." These appearances ground the Christian faith.

Paul proceeds to list some of the resurrection appearances that are important to his development here because they are foundations of the church. Some of the appearances Paul mentions are not in the Gospel accounts (for example, to the five hundred). On the other hand, all four Gospels record appearances first to women, which Paul overlooks. Paul's selectivity here betrays his motive for appealing to the resurrection appearances. Paul is reinforcing his own apostolic authority and referring to the resurrection appearances as the basis of the faith he shares with the Corinthians. Paul's own vision concludes the list. His point is that an appearance of the risen Lord gives his apostolic work its authority. Although he is the least of the apostles (Paul's name means "least"), he has been called not because of his own merit but because of God's grace in him. This grace has produced fruit, a reference to Paul's missionary activity. By the grace of God Paul preached, and by grace the Corinthians believed.

B. The Resurrection of the Dead (15:12-34)

15:12-19 The absurdity of the Corinthians' denial. In this section Paul entertains, for the sake of argument, the Corinthian hypothesis which leads to absurdity. The Corinthians who have already demonstrated certain false assumptions about the significance of the body, deny the resurrection of the dead and, with it, Christ's resurrection. Paul asks: Then why has Christ been preached as raised from the dead? Is this a lie? Is faith in vain? The resurrection of believers hinges on the resurrection of Christ. If those who have died do not have hope, believers are the most pitiable of all people, because they would be the most disillusioned. Paul's Corinthian audience would appreciate the hopelessness of such a fundamental ignorance. And without hope, what do we have? If we have this life only, we are doomed to despair and absurdity. The Corinthian hypothesis leads to no solution at all. It is a dead end.

15:20-28 Paul's alternative. Paul dismisses the Corinthian hypothesis as false, since it is based on the falsehood that Christ is not raised. Paul proceeds to review his own conviction. Christ is now already raised. His resurrection is a promise for all those who die, which, of course, includes everyone. His resurrection already has an effect on our lives of faith. As the first fruits, Christ represents the promise that all others will become as he is. This is so because Christ is the antitype of Adam, whose sin brought death to the world. How much more effect for life does Christ's resurrection have!

Paul's anthropology here is christological. The universal consequences of Adam's sin implied a universal need for salvation. Sin brought death to all. Christ's resurrection, which saves all from the reign of death, brings life to all. As the first fruits, Christ's resurrection in the past is a promise for the future.

In the end Christ will have subjected all things, spiritual and physical, to himself. His role is to destroy all disbelief and then to hand over all who are under his lordship to God the Father. The final enemy is death. Death has been vanquished in Christ, but not yet in all creatures everywhere. Paul invokes the Old Testament Scriptures to validate his point. The word of God says that all things will be placed under his feet. Christ's death began the process of overcoming the enemy powers of sin and hostility. But Christ's death is not fully accomplished even in the believer. Similarly, the author of Colossians says, "In my own flesh I fill up what is lacking in the sufferings of Christ for the sake of his body, the church" (1:24). In Christ, God has given us a part of the work of reconciling the world to himself (2 Cor 5:17-20; Col 1:20). Christ is the pledge of our inheritance, the first payment against the full redemption of a people God has made his own.

By his resurrection Christ became Lord. He was exempted from the subjection of all things, since all was to be subjected to him. He obediently subjects himself to the Father, emptying himself, taking on the form of a slave. Therefore he is exalted, and given a name above all other names (see Phil 2:9), so that always and everywhere, God is all in all.

15:29-34 The Corinthians' ignorance attacked. Having shown the absurdity of the Corinthian hypothesis in contrast to the obvious validity of his own convictions, Paul resorts to *ad hominem* arguments. He begins by asking what would be the point of some of the practices of the Corinthians themselves if Christ is not raised. He ends this section, begging them to return to reason, concluding by saying that they are ignorant.

If the dead are not raised, the custom, apparently popular in Corinth, of being baptized on behalf of the dead is absurd. Some interpreters have taken reference to this practice as evidence that the Christian community in Corinth might have modeled itself along the lines of a burial society, a voluntary association common in Paul's day that had as its goal the burial and memorial of its members.

Paul continues with an example from his own life. Continually he puts himself in danger, facing death. What wisdom could explain his being so willing to face the "beasts at Ephesus," a probable reference to the strong hostility he encountered there (see 16:8; Acts 18:19-21; 19:1-12).

If death is the last word, then the only wisdom is that of the unrighteous who preach, "Let us eat and drink, for tomorrow we die" (1 Cor 15:32; see Wis 2:6-9). This motto summarizes the selfish, unethical, purposeless existence of those without hope. Paul has already implied that some Corinthians have fallen prey to such a philosophy. The real bait of his argument is that they who are so zealous for wisdom are, in fact, ignorant of God. Because of this lack of faith in the resurrection, they are being counted with the unbelievers whom they despise.

C. The Manner of the Resurrection (15:35-58)

15:35-49 The reality of the resurrection. The skeptics among the Corinthians, because they could not describe the manner of the resurrection or the appearance of the body at the resurrection, challenged the very idea that there is a resurrection. Again Paul deals critically with these opponents. What nonsense! They pose the wrong questions. An ordinary example from agriculture demonstrates their error. The seed must die to produce the full-blown plant. The mystery of the resurrection is an everyday occurrence, and yet humans could not predict this or make it happen.

God gives to each the body he pleases, but even this cannot be fully understood. The terms "flesh," "body," and "glory" have several meanings. Simply put, Paul suggests that

the term "body" after the resurrection could have a meaning we do not yet know. The body that is put in the earth is corrupted; the body that rises is incorruptible. The Corinthians certainly believe that the present body is inglorious; what rises is glorious. Many Greeks considered the body as the weaker element; what rises is strong. The physical body pulls downward, but the risen (spiritual) body ascends.

Even more sure than the existence of the "natural body" is the existence of the "spiritual body." This phrase is not intended to detract from the real aspect of the risen body. Rather, for the Corinthians with Greek philosophical tendencies, the spiritual is more real than the physical. Thus Paul cloaks his arguments in terms that those with a Greek philosophical bias will appreciate.

Next Paul introduces the Jewish conception of the two Adams made pouplar by Philo. The first man was created alive, even though he was to bring sin and death into the world. The last Adam, Paul argues, is so fully alive, so fully spiritual, that he passes on life. As the archetype of all humans, even the first Adam is the image of God. As the originator (rather than the goal) of human life, Adam was formed from dust. Earthly people are like this Adam. But spiritual people become more and more like the image of God. As we all resemble the earthly Adam, so we shall resemble the spiritual Adam (Christ). But this will require a transformation such as Paul describes in the concluding section of this chapter.

15:50-58 The resurrection as a mystery of faith. What is most clear about the resurrection is that it is based on a faith conviction rather than empirical data. We experience the body as corruptible. This universal experience demonstrates the necessity of the resurrection. The body requires a transformation before it can inherit the kingdom of God. By "flesh and blood," Paul refers not to the body per se, but to the as yet unredeemed part of our humanity. The whole argument of this chapter has been that indeed there is a resurrection of the body. Thus, it is not possible that Paul could deny the body's inheritance of the kingdom of God. Now Paul merely wants to emphasize that this is based on grace rather than on any merits inherent in the human condition.

All of this is a mystery. Paul seems only to begin to realize that there might be an extended time before the return of Christ. Many may die before this return, but not all, he thinks. Nevertheless, by the power of God, all of us will be changed. Paul uses conventional apocalyptic signs—quickly, at the sound of a trumpet (1 Thess 4:16), the dead will be changed to incorruptibility and so will those who are alive. This new incorruptible body will be necessary in the new life we will lead.

VI. CONCLUSION

1 Cor 16:1-24

Paul concludes this letter somewhat abruptly, probably because he intends to visit the church soon (16:5-7). He refers briefly to the collection (16:1-4) which he considers in much greater detail in 2 Corinthians (see 8:1–9:15). He presents his own and his companions' plans for the immediate future (1 Cor 16:5-12). He then closes with remarks about union and charity and with personal greetings (16:13-24).

16:1-4 The collection. An essential part of the gospel is the effort to relieve the needs of the poor (see Gal 2:10; Luke 4:18-19). As Apostle to the Gentiles, Paul was particularly sensitive to the possibility of making the Corinthian collection to help the starving in Jerusalem a symbol of the unity of the whole church. For Paul the collection came to represent the "debt" which the Gentile Christians owed their Jewish-Christian brethren because they reaped the benefits of the more important spiritual inheritance (see Rom 15:27). To Paul the collection also came to represent the full acceptance of the Gentiles into the church by the Jerusalem church authorities (see Rom 15:31).

Nevertheless, Paul is careful especially with the Corinthians to be completely above board and obviously free of any possible criticism about his own interest in the collection. Like the discussion on the resurrection, the collection is probably part of Paul's own agenda. The Corinthians are to follow the instructions Paul must have already issued to the Galatians, but which are not known to us. The Corinthians are to set aside whatever they can afford "on the first day of the week." This could indicate the incipient custom of Christians' gathering on Sundays, although this is not self-evident.

Paul asks that the collection be taken up before he arrives, either to avoid the time-consuming work of gathering it, which anyone could have done, or to anticipate any criticism about any particular method of collecting. Paul suggests that if the community wishes to choose its own emissaries without his personally accompanying the money, he will provide the necessary letters of introduction (see 2 Cor 8:16-24). The issue is expedited quickly, as if lingering on the details could become too painful.

16:5-12 Paul's plans. Paul speaks of his own and of some of the others' plans. He desires to visit Corinth. He thinks his business in Macedonia will not require much time, yet he needs to pass through that region before visiting the Corinthians.

Then he speaks of the others, Timothy and Apollos. He is uncertain whether to send Timothy, whom the hard-to-please Corinthians may disdain. In Paul's name the author of the Pastorals admonishes Timothy himself not to allow anyone to look down on him because of his youth (1 Tim 4:12). Apparently Paul had sent a message which he feared the younger man had not received. He wanted Timothy to return to him in Ephesus via Corinth. In any case Paul reminds the Corinthians to be instruments of peace. He concludes this section with a telling reference to Apollos, whom the Corinthians did revere. Paul heads off any suggestion that he himself may have prevented Apollos from visiting them, as if motivated by rivalry. It was Apollos' idea not to go, Paul says, despite Paul's own strong urging. No reasons are given for this disappointment. But Paul adds a promise that they will see Apollos when circumstances favor a visit.

16:13-24 Directions and greetings. Finally, typical of Paul's style and following the ancient letter form, the epistle concludes with directions and greetings. Again he warns: "Be on your guard, stand firm . . . ." This is a gospel watchword, and one Paul repeats (see Mark 13:32-37; Rom 13:11-12; 1 Thess 5:4-8). Be courageous. Be strong. Do all out of love. These sentences summarize the whole epistle.

Paul reminds the community that there are some exemplary Christians among them. He likewise calls on Stephanas, Fortunatus, and Achaicus to be models of service to the community. Perhaps these were the bearers of the Corinthians' letter and questions to Paul (see 7:1). The enthusiasm with which Paul wrote this letter suggests that he might have sent them back with many spoken and unspoken messages which a mere written response could not contain. Their example will be their most eloquent statement.

Part of Paul's mission is to maintain communication among the churches. Thus he includes greetings from the believers in Asia. Aquila and Prisca had lived with Paul in Corinth where they met and shared his means of livelihood after the couple had been expelled from Rome (Acts 18:1-3). Now they are presented as leaders of the church at Ephesus from where Paul writes.

Paul instructs that the letter be read during the liturgy and that Christians make the kiss of peace the sign of acceptance of the contents and the lessons. Paul seals the letter with a postscript in his own handwriting. The Old Testament idea of a choice of ways, one leading to life and the other to death, lies behind Paul's curse of all who do not love the Lord. The Lord's favor and Paul's are one. He ends with a profession of his own great love for the Corinthians.

2 CORINTHIANS

Mary Ann Getty

INTRODUCTION

Nowhere else in Paul's writings is the passionate human character of this great apostle more evident than in Second Corinthians. Here we have the personal testimony of Paul, his ardent reactions when distrusted and accused and concerned about a community he loves deeply. There in broad strokes Paul paints his own profile and, at the same time, gives us a look inside himself, at his vulnerability and strong feelings for others. Second Corinthians conjures up that part of Paul which most attracts us—his depth, his affection. Second Corinthians also provides the focus on what readers most dislike and suspect in Paul and what they are most likely to misunderstand and reject. Some of the outstanding qualities of this letter are related to three focal points on very sensitive issues: Paul's apologia and self-defense, his stress on suffering, and his insistence on the importance of the collection.

In a sense, this appears as a very harsh letter, punctuated with solemnity and oaths (for example, 1:3-5, 23), issuing corrections and warnings (see 2:9-11, 17; 11:18-23), spotted with threats of severity, self-justification, and complaints (for example, 10:3; 13:2). The frequent appearance of the term "boasting" suggests that the charge of egoism often levied against Paul is well-founded (see especially 10:1–13:10). Paul is hardly mild in his reaction to the challenge that he is not a true but an inferior apostle, and he turns sarcastic in his references to the "super-apostles" (see 11:5; 12:11). The Corinthians, for their part, seem to be incorrigible in their need to measure and control love as they demand proof that they are loved by the Apostle (see 12:15-16). Paul counters their skepticism and competitiveness with reminders about the only evidence admissible to the only court he recognizes as valid. Before God and before the tribunal of Christ, the faith of the Corinthians provides the irrefutable witness of the Apostle's authority and integrity.

In Second Corinthians Paul stresses the value of suffering as a witness to the truth of the gospel, the power of God (especially 10:1–13:10). So powerful is this witness that suffering is transformed from an evil into the most eloquent testimony of faith. In First Corinthians, Paul presented the cross as the decisive truth, folly for those who were perishing, but salvation to those with faith (1 Cor 1:18). In Second Corinthians, Paul describes his own suffering as indisputable evidence of his call as an apostle, of his authority to make all things subject to God in Christ, of his mission to share the ministry of reconciliation with others. An experience of suffering and of receiving God's healing mercy qualifies the minister of the new covenant (see 2 Cor 2:16; 4:1, 7-15). This is a ministry Paul shares with the recalcitrant Corinthians (5:17-20).

Finally, in Second Corinthians, Paul gives a theoretical, theological basis for the very practical collection (8:1–9:15). Although he himself rejects financial support and downplays the value of this support as a sign of his apostolate, he insists on the importance of the Corinthians' generous giving as a symbol that they accept kinship with the starving saints in Jerusalem. Although he himself is criticized precisely because he refuses personal support, he warns the Corinthians that their willingness to contribute liberally is essential, not secondary, to their full participation in the spiritual benefits of the gospel.

Second Corinthians contains many unique allusions to events we cannot corroborate with any other New Testament writing. This observation underscores another reason tradition has so highly valued this letter. Further, there are in 2 Corinthians sporadic changes of mood, sudden shifts of emphasis, changes of subject, disruptions and resumption of topics already presumed to be settled. These may tempt us to despair of ever trying to fit together the pieces of the puzzle which would elucidate the reasons Paul wrote and give us a clear picture of the unity of this letter. Most scholars concur that this canonical letter is a composite of possibly as many as four separate letters or fragments of letters. The most readily separable parts are 2 Cor 6:14–7:1; 9:1-15; and 10:1–13:10, each of which we can briefly introduce in anticipation of our commentary.

The warning against pagan contacts (2 Cor 6:14–7:1) appears suddenly and intrusively within the context of Paul's personal appeal to the Corinthians to widen their hearts (7:2) as he has done in their regard (see 6:11-13). This suggests that 6:14–7:1 is an interpolation or a digression. The hypothesis that this is a fragmentary interpolation representing what remains of a pre-canonical letter referred to in 1 Cor 5:9 is attractive, but it lacks sufficient hard evidence. Since Paul is completely capable of whimsical digressions whenever he happens to think of a topic, the more reliable possibility is that, while speaking "frankly" (2 Cor 6:11), he could have digressed to the topic of the undivided devotion required of the true believer (6:14–7:1). Paul's language and ideas in this digression are not only foreign to this context but even unique in Paul's writings. On the other hand, they are familiar in Qumran literature, and Paul could have drawn on this contemporary source to give another dimension to his notion of the community as the temple of God.

2 Cor 9:1-15 is a kind of doublet compared with chapter 8 but with another perspective and reasoning. Both deal with the collection for the poor. The introductory statement (9:1) about how it would be superfluous to mention the collection is particularly strange in view of the preceding chapter. Possibly chapter 9 was originally a separate letter to the churches in Achaia. It might have been written as a letter of introduction for the delegates, who would use it as credentials for their mission of actually taking up the collection. The early church, which would have wanted to make sure that it was not lost, probably inserted it here because of the congruity of content with chapter 8.

Finally, 2 Cor 10:1–13:10 does not seem to be part of the original unity of this epistle. Again, there is an abrupt, unexpected change of tone and return to some issues already presumed to be settled in the preceding chapters, especially compared to the first seven chapters (for example, the charge of Paul's recommending himself, of his not accepting support for his mission from the Corinthians, of his credentials compared with the "superapostles," etc.) Further, it seems surprising that Paul would relegate to the end of this epistle these important reflections on how he authenticates his apostleship through sufferings. The apparent self-contained, detachable qualities of these chapters make it questionable that they originally belonged precisely here, at the end of Paul's highly charged letter.

OUTLINE OF SECOND CORINTHIANS

COMMENTARY

I. INTRODUCTION

2 Cor 1:1-11

Paul's introduction to Second Corinthians is brief, as if superfluous. The Apostle begins with the customary self-introduction and greeting (1:1-2), which is markedly abbreviated. The usual thanksgiving is replaced with a benediction for the blessings Paul has received, especially for the hardships he has been able to endure (1:3-11).

1:1-2 Greeting. Characteristically Paul identifies himself as an apostle, one sent by Jesus Christ, called by God's will. On that call his authority as an apostle rests. He is joined in sending greetings by Timothy, a Christian whose brotherhood also is recognized both by Paul and by the Corinthians. Timothy, trusted by both, acts as mediary, facilitating the difficult relationship between the Apostle and this troublesome community (see 1 Cor 4:17; 16:10; 2 Cor 1:19; Acts 18:5; 19:22). The Corinthians, regardless of how quarrelsome and sinful, are identified as "holy ones." Paul greets the church of Corinth, capital of the Roman province of Achaia. Recognition of the mixed character of the church is implied in Paul's joining of the Greek "grace" to the Jewish "peace."

1:3-11 Paul's hardship and blessing. The usual thanksgiving found in all Paul's letters, except in 2 Corinthians and Galatians, is replaced by a benediction calling for praise of God, Father of our Lord, of mercies, and of consolation. According to the ancient custom, letter writers begin with thanks for their own good health. Paul's implication is that his recent suffering and hardship that even threatened death (1:8-9) do not nullify his thanksgiving but cause him to offer praise to God. The suffering of a believer can actually contribute the dimension of conviction and credibility to ministry. The strengthening of having suffered that God communicates to a disciple through afflictions is not merely a selfish, interior thing. It is passed on to others. Sharing the suffering of Christ means having the hope and consolation he brings through his victory over suffering and death.

The Apostle sees in his own experiences an opportunity for encouragement of others. Indeed, this can be the salvation of others, who see his patience as a testimony against despair. Thus Paul fulfills the role of the prophet (see 1 Cor 14:3). Paul, the consummate optimist, holds on to his belief in the fidelity of God. Jesus' own death experience, although it threatened to break the thread of hope that bound him to a faithful God, only served to provide the source of life for all believers after him. Similarly, Paul acknowledges to the Philippians that even the great suffering of his imprisonment is turned into the good of encouragement for the sake of other believers (Phil 1:12-14). Paul himself provides a model of a believer for whom there is no comparison between the sufferings of this world and the glory as yet to be revealed, but all things work together unto good (see Rom 8:18, 28).

The Corinthians are Paul's kin because of their common faith. He shares with them his hardships so that they will be strengthened. This encouragement will come not because they will either understand suffering better or somehow be pleased to know Paul's recent struggle has been so excruciating. Nor is Paul merely wanting to rehearse his trials to impress the Corinthians. It is not certain exactly what suffering Paul refers to here, but clearly it was some adversity that went so far as to confront him with death. The experience of suffering, so threatening to faith, deepens in Paul not only his own faith convictions but his credibility as a minister of the gospel which has the cross at its center. Having faced even the possibility of death, the Apostle now manifests a new dimension of compassion, a new appreciation of life, a new level of confidence. Having been rescued from death, the Apostle recognizes how God continually sustains him in life. His hope having thus been strengthened, Paul asks for the aid of the Corinthians' prayers. These prayers express Paul's and the Corinthians' thanks to God, who is recognized not only as the originator of life but as a sustainer and consoler in trials.

II. THE CRISIS BETWEEN PAUL AND THE CORINTHIANS

2 Cor 1:12–7:16

The charges of the Corinthians draw from Paul a self-defense poignant in the depth of human feeling it betrays while it is balanced by Paul's confidence in ultimate reconciliation. Paul defends his sincerity when it is attacked by the Corinthians, whose confidence has been strained by the Apostle's change of plans (1:12–2:13). He then presents his ministry of the new covenant and his own suffering as qualifying credentials (2:14–7:4). Finally, Paul returns to the strained relationship between himself and the community, expressing the basic conviction that they will be reconciled (7:5-16).

This structure is determined by the general ABA' schema characteristic of Paul's style. According to this schema, Paul typically introduces a topic, suddenly abandons it for another idea, and then returns to the original subject. Often his emphasis is expressed through the middle or "B" section (in this case, 2:14–7:4), where Paul states principles and gives further illustrations of their implications. Thus, Paul's divinely inspired ministry is the basis on which he defends his sincerity (1:12–2:13) and expresses confidence in eventual reconciliation with the Corinthians (7:5-16).

A. Past Relationships (1:12–2:13)

Paul undertakes a self-defense, noting his sincerity and trustworthiness (1:12-14), despite his change of plans (1:15-24). He then refers to a previous letter written with many tears (2:1-4). He does not specify why he had to thus justify himself and his change of plans, and this section of the letter was apparently written before he received good news from Titus regarding the compliance of the Corinthians (see 7:6-7).

1:12-14 Paul's sincerity. Paul calls on his own conscience and, later, on God (1:23), as witness to the truth he speaks. He is absolutely sincere. His behavior is motivated by the call and authority he has from God. Holiness as described here by Paul is relational, given by God and certified in the actions of a legitimate apostle. Such Paul is. His is a true channel for God's holiness to be read and understood by God's people, the Corinthians. Paul refers to their past experience together. His comparatively long stay with them means the Corinthians are acquainted with him. A better knowledge will bear out the truthful sincerity of Paul's words.

Paul's boast before God and the indisputable evidence of his apostleship (see 1 Cor 4:15; 9:2) are the Corinthians themselves, who in the flesh of the life of their community, are writing a letter of recommendation to God on Paul's behalf (2 Cor 3:3, 6). The judgment which will vindicate the truth of this will come on the day of our Lord Jesus when the only legitimate boasts will be the works done in the service of the Lord (see 1 Cor 1:31). These alone lead to salvation.

1:15-24 Paul justifies his change of plans. Apparently Paul's detractors have undermined the Corinthians' confidence in him, so that he must justify why he has delayed so long in visiting them. It appears that a promised visit never occurred. Paul reviews his plans so that they will understand why some changes were made rather than accuse him of insincerity in raising their expectations for that postponed visit. Originally Paul had hoped to go to Corinth twice, once in passing on the way to Macedonia, and then to stay longer on his return (see 1 Cor 16:6-7), before he would travel on to Judea. The implication of insincerity pains him deeply. He pauses in his review of what unexpectedly intervened to emphasize how fundamental he considers the trust which is threatened by the Corinthians' charge.

Paul is true to his word. Jesus' injunction against oath-taking might have inspired Paul's insistence that there is no need among believers to be more emphatic than a simple yes and no. Nevertheless, to reinforce his point, Paul implicitly makes reference to the law which demands at least two witnesses for the admission of valid testimony. He then calls on the witness of his co-workers Silvanus and Timothy who, together with Paul, preached Jesus as the faithful Son who fulfilled God's trustworthy word. The faith of the Corinthians rests on this same preaching. Thus the Corinthians must believe Paul.

Both the Corinthians and Paul express their Amen to Jesus in worship (see 1 Cor 14:16). Paul's solemnity is extreme because of the seriousness of the charge against him. His testimony rests on God's word which, above all, established the relationship between the Corinthians and their apostle. God anointed Paul an apostle, and the Corinthian ministry sealed this apostleship (see 1 Cor 9:2). The love of God poured into human hearts by the Holy Spirit (Rom 5:5) will enable the Corinthians to accept Paul. The Spirit is the first fruits, the payment or pledge of our final inheritance (see Eph 1:13-14).

Paul's word can be trusted. But it was out of love for the Corinthians that Paul's plans were changed. The Apostle is convinced that love is the only thing that cannot hurt another (see Rom 13:8-10). Thus, charity is the only

thing that offers adequate explanation of Paul's change of plans. Charity qualifies and relativizes even the most cherished projects such as Paul's ardent desire to see the Corinthians. When Paul decided that a visit to them would suggest that he was trying to dominate the Corinthians' faith, he abandoned his plans for the time being. His physical presence with them was relatively unimportant; the only essential was that they stood firm in their faith. Paul abrogates the role of domination for himself, preferring to work side by side in equal and reciprocal partnership with his communities (see Phil 1:3-8). His goal is their happiness. As long as their faith is firm, he is willing to forego his own projects.

2:1-4 The tearful letter. Paul returns to the fact that, indeed, he decided not to visit them "again" (see 1:23) under painful circumstances. On a former visit, he had to admonish and punish them. He resolved not to further undermine their relationship with him by appearing again in this role he now repudiates. He adds that just as he is capable of making them sad, so is he affected by them. And he can only be made glad again by the repentance of those he had to punish. Paul explains that his letter was intended to provoke the conversion upon which both the Corinthians' and his own happiness depends. Formerly he chided them for their failure to correct an erring member (see 1 Cor 5:1-11). Now he shows his willingness to follow his own advice while recognizing how dearly he pays for chastising those he loves. His copious tears testify to the great love he bears for the Corinthians. He is not indifferent to them. That they are saddened must be transformed into gratitude for the love that binds apostle and community.

2:5-11 The offender is forgiven. The community could not smugly overlook blatant offenses. It had a responsibility to promote justice. Paul had instructed the community to judge and punish the offender, as in the case of the incestuous man. It is possible but not certain that this is the same person whom Paul now advises the community to readmit lest he be crushed by his sorrow. It is futile to try to identify the person in question on the grounds of the offense he has committed. Paul's point is that he himself takes no pleasure in that man's punishment. Nor is Paul's issue that he himself was personally offended, so that restitution has to be made to him. The offense injured the community, which explains why the community who punished him could and should now be reconciled to him. Jesus entrusted the power to bind and to loose to his disciples (see Matt 18:15-18), who are contrasted with the scribes and the Pharisees who bind but do not loose (see Matt 23:4). The community's authority is exercised in healing and reconciling. Its goal (i.e., the repentance of the sinner) has been achieved. Now the community must show itself capable of integrating the offender within the unlimited boundaries of forgiveness.

Just as the community had shown itself faithful to Paul in punishing the offender, now it must believe that reconciliation is possible. Paul's instruction serves also as evidence of the Corinthians' loyalty to him. His own forgiveness of the offender represents an example for their sakes. This he also swears before Christ. One of the functions of forgiveness is that it is a weapon against Satan, who tries to divide and overcome the community. The incestuous man had been expelled from the community and delivered over to Satan only so that his spirit would be saved (1 Cor 5:5). Such exclusion must be temporary and ultimately replaced by reconciliation, so that evil will not triumph.

2:12-13 Paul's anxiety and relief. Paul's change of plans involved skipping Corinth and traveling on to Troas where there was ample need and opportunity to preach. But his concern for the Corinthians impeded him so that he continued on to Macedonia, where he encountered Titus fresh from Corinth. Titus' news included the report of the Corinthians' passing the "test" Paul administered. The Apostle, heartened by the fact that they had obeyed his instruction and punished the offender, now implies his confidence in their forgiving his own change of plans and acceptance of his loving motives.

God's ways are mysterious, but the believer does not let sorrow, incomprehension, or despair darken the heart. No pain endured or length of time passed without understanding should cause a believer to lose faith. There seems to be a complete break between the poignant pain expressed in 2:13 and the mood expressed in the hymn of praise that erupts in 2:14. But this is not atypical of Paul (see Rom 7:24 and 25; 8:35-39 and 9:1-5). The experience of the cross strengthens Paul's faith in the provident wisdom of God to whom he offers thanks.

B. Paul's Ministry (2:14–7:4)

Having been assured by Titus' reports about the Corinthians, Paul embarks on a series of reflections on his apostolate (2:14–7:4), testifying that his mission is an extension of Christ's own. As he did in 1 Cor 1:18, Paul identifies the two divisions among people that are effected by the judgment which the cross of Christ represents. There are those who are being saved and those who are headed for destruction. The distinction is made by faith (2:14-17).

Paul continues his defense of his ministry of the new covenant (3:1-18). He identifies the divine origin and power of his ministry (4:1-15) and looks to the everlasting recompense for his fidelity (4:16–5:10). He goes on to describe the ministry of reconciliation which excludes no one, but includes all who are in Christ (5:11–6:10).

2:14–3:3 Ministers of a new covenant. No mere human qualifications can prepare a person for such a mission as this. Paul's authority and motivation come from God. As an apostle, Paul represents the One who "sent" him, for this is the meaning of his apostolate. His very lack of human credentials testifies to this authority. No one will accuse him of gaining personally from preaching the word.

Paul refutes a double charge of the Corinthians. First, they accuse him of arrogance and boasting. In addition, they point out that he bears no letters of recommendation such as were customary to expect from a messenger. These might have testified to Paul's credentials, his gifts, the authorities' approval of him. The Corinthians valued such things. Paul's rhetorical question suggests incredulity and sarcasm. Others might need such letters. But the Corinthians themselves are all Paul needs to recommend him. Even if he were not an apostle to anyone else, he is to them (see 1 Cor 9:2). They are his letter, written by Christ. The whole world can read this recommendation. The letter is written on the Corinthians' hearts.

The letter is not written in mere ink but by the spirit of God. Paul combines the allusion to the stone tablets of Exod 31:18 to the new covenant written on human hearts of Jer 31:33, and to the spirit God promises, who will change hearts of stone into hearts of flesh (Ezek 11:19; 36:26). This combination prepares the stage for Paul's contrast between the "new covenant" (3:6) and the "old covenant" (3:14), which the rest of the chapter develops.

3:4-18 The contrast between the new and old covenants. Continuing his response to the charge of arrogance, Paul describes the basis of the confidence of the minister of the Lord (3:4, 12). The only legitimate boast is in the Lord (see 1 Cor 1:31). Interested in external, superficial qualifications, the Corinthians continually erect false standards for judging the apostles. Paul resists the claim of entitlement. The same God who called him when he was a persecutor of the church (see Phil 3:3-7) is faithful. Although no one could conceivably be qualified for this mission (see 2 Cor 2:16), the God who created and who made the covenant written in stone, now recreates and qualifies ministers for the new covenant. The purpose of the law was to define sin which kills. But the spirit of God gives life.

Paul's argumentation in 3:7-8 should not minimize the power of his contrast between the old and the new. Not only the former Jews among his readers would affirm the first "conditional" clause. Indeed, the entire early Christian community, which adapted the titles originally claimed by Israel for itself, recognized the glory that went with Israel's being chosen as God's people. Indeed, Exod 34:29-35 describes how Moses had to cover his face with a veil when he descended the mountain to talk to the people after speaking with God, so great was even the mere reflection of God's glory on Moses' countenance. If such be the force of glory that fades, of a covenant that condemns and that had the knowledge of sin (see Gal 3:19), how much greater will be the glory of the spirit and of the ministry which gives life? The former covenant is characterized by a fading glory, limited and condemning. In comparison to the new covenant, the former glory is no glory at all.

The glory of the new covenant, which far surpasses and relativizes the glory of the old, gives Paul full confidence. In the following chapter he will describe the trials he has endured (2 Cor 4:8-12); here Paul reveals the reason for his boldness and assurance. "We are not like Moses." Whereas Moses hid his face and the glory that shone on it, Paul announces the unveiling of the covenant of the Lord.

The metaphor of the veil becomes confused in the transfer from Moses' face to the minds of the Israelites. Paul alludes to the blindness that prevents them from recognizing the true meaning of the law (Rom 10:1-3), namely, its passing nature. The law has been both abrogated and fulfilled in Christ who is its end and in whom there is justification for all who believe (Rom 10:4). A quotation that originally referred to Moses and God is applied by Paul to the Christian who recognizes Jesus as Lord.

In Paul we can trace only the faint beginnings of a Trinitarian conception. Here he equates the Lord (usually a reference to Jesus) with the Spirit. In the Lord we are given the spirit of freedom. This freedom makes us children of God, capable of saying, "Abba, Father" (see Rom 8:15; Gal 4:6). In freedom, believers are transformed into the image of God. All are thus transformed, growing in likeness to the Lord through the Spirit. Just as Paul's confidence develops from great (2 Cor 3:4) to "full" (3:12), so Paul expands his consideration from his own ministry to that of all believers.

4:1-15 Paul's versus his detractors' ministry. Paul continues to contrast his view of the gospel and his mission with the views of his opponents. He is undaunted, not because he is indifferent to the charges made against him but because his confidence is firmly rooted in God's mercy, which never changes (see Gal 1:15-17). This experience of mercy qualifies Paul as a minister (see 2 Cor 2:16-17). Because his ministry is based in God rather than in his own merits, he is enabled to repudiate every falsehood and to proclaim the truth with disarming boldness.

Paul's detractors accuse him of exercising cunning and of not being trustworthy (see 1:17-18; 12:16). They add that he does not show the recognizable signs of a true apostle (see 11:13; 12:11-16; 1 Cor 9:3-18), signs they themselves have deemed necessary, such as letters of recommendation (see 2 Cor 3:1-3). Paul's disclaimer is that since his ministry is based on an experience of God's gratuitous predilection and mercy, he has nothing to hide. Indeed, with startling transparency, he continually invites his readers to scrutinize all of his actions and words and his entire life and to imitate him (see 1 Cor 11:1; Phil 1:27-30; 4:9). Paul shows little interest in the external criteria of "true apostleship" invented and recognized by the Corinthians. He adamantly denies that he falsifies the gospel message, although he accuses his opponents of doing just that (see 2 Cor 2:17), probably because they make it dependent on other things besides God. He has repeatedly taught that there is only one gospel, and even if he himself tried to change it, he would be anathema (see Gal 1:8; 2 Cor 11:4). Yet the truth persists.

Paul concedes that he does commend himself. This for several reasons. Certainly he needs no other recommendation than that he introduced the Corinthians to the gospel. He completely identifies himself by the gospel he preaches and places himself at the service of those to whom he preaches (see 1 Cor 9:19-23). He is, then, in a sense, the gospel link between Jesus Christ and the Corinthians. This is the truth, plainly revealed and recognized by all except those on their way to perdition.

Continuing his use of the image of the veil, Paul also tentatively and provisionally concedes that there is, for some, a veil over the truth he preaches, but this is due to their unbelief rather than to his cunning. Paul has no false humility which would obscure the gospel. Those headed for destruction ally themselves with the god of this age. Possibly Paul refers to Satan who, for a time, appears to dominate the world. Or Paul could be adapting the traditional Jewish teaching of the successive aeons of the world: chaos, which reigned before the law; the period of the law, which previously separated the just from the unjust; and finally the coming of the messianic age, when the observance of justice would be perfect and universal. The relationship of this messianic age to the present time was disputed by the rabbis. Paul presents Jesus as ushering in the final, decisive time and thus makes the gospel the new basis, replacing the law, for distinguishing between the saved and those who are not.

The exact charge of Paul's detractors is unclear, but the context suggests that they refer to Paul's personal weaknesses (see 10:10) as disqualifying him from the apostolate. Paul himself recites the history of his suffering, not as a detraction but as proof that his ministry is rooted in God's own power. Such a ministry reflects the witness of Jesus as the image of God manifest in his sufferings on the cross (see Gal 3:1). Paul uses the reference to the image of God in Gen 1:26-27 to complement his very powerful paradoxical image of the treasure carried in earthen vessels. Jesus is the image of God and, through the cross, Jesus revealed the power and the wisdom of God. This is scandal for those who do not believe, but salvation for those who do (1 Cor 1:18). By referring to Christ as the image of God, Paul implies his preeminence (see Col 1:15-20) and his obedience to the point of death on the cross (Phil 2:6-11).

Just as Jesus' own ministry is reflected in Paul's life, Paul's ministry is bearing fruit in the believing Corinthians. The contagious character of the Christian mystery teaches that life comes through death and the sharing of faith. This mystery begins with the power of the resurrection already taking place among believers. The power of grace is that through faith God is glorified, and thankful praise is offered by the many who believe.

4:16–5:10 Suffering as the credential of the Apostle. The sting of suffering is the severe strain it puts on faith. It tests belief both in a just God and in the efficacy of redemption. Paul reiterates his own faith while at the same time inviting others ("we") to dispel discouragement. Even while his body is being spent in ministry, his inner being is being daily renewed. Paul adapts a Greek philosophical idea about the tension between the body and the spirit. This section employs several images (the inner being, a house, clothing, exile) to describe Paul's apparently just dawning realization that the in-between times, that is, the lapse between Jesus' promise to return and the final judgment (see 5:10), may be prolonged. Even the most firm belief in the resurrection does not detract from the poignancy of the sufferings of this life. Paul describes salvation generally in terms of fixing our gaze, not on the here and now, but on what is unseen and hoped for.

This hope is a form of firm knowledge. We live as in a tent, preparing for the eternal dwelling God is providing for us. No believer is really at home in the world. Attempts at comprehending the relationship between this life and that which is to come constitute mere groanings of the spirit, such as the Israelites in Egypt uttered even before they knew the name by which they could call upon God (see Exod 2:23-25). Nakedness is a symbol of shame and depravity in the Old Testament (see Gen 3:10; Isa 33:11; Ezek 16:7, 37-39). Christian life clothes us with armor to guard us against such evil (see Rom 13:12-14; 1 Thess 5:8). Yet so helpless and overburdened is the human condition that we depend completely on what is immortal to save and envelop us. Paul's language reflects his resurrection teachings: "This corruptible body must be clothed with incorruptibility" (1 Cor 15:53). The mortal must be absorbed and transformed by the immortal, death is transformed by life. What we see only leads us to hope, since despair renders all absurd. God has fashioned us for life and God does not repent of his creation. The pledge of this life is the Spirit who has been given to us.

In the Spirit is our confidence. While we are still in the earthly body, we groan awaiting the full redemption of the children of God (see Rom 8:14-27). Faith is not a static condition but a dynamic life in which we walk. Faith tells us to be full of confidence as we acknowledge our desire to be already with the Lord. This desire makes life in this body seem like an exile, while we long to be at home. Yet we subordinate personal desire to the will of the Lord. Imprisoned and frustrated, Paul himself felt this same tension and he wrote to the Philippians: "To me, 'life' means Christ; hence dying is so much gain" (Phil 1:21). The purpose of the life of faith is not to completely understand God's will but to acknowledge that such a will exists, that it is provident, and that it includes a ministry for all believers. All of this can be fully revealed only at the tribunal of Christ. Christ is perceived as a judge (1 Thess 1:7-10) whose gospel reevaluates all things, giving a new basis for distinguishing between good and evil.

5:11-21 The ministry of reconciliation. Placing himself constantly before the tribunal of Christ (see 5:10), the sole arbiter of his sincerity, Paul continues his self-defense (see 1 Cor 4:1-5). At the same time, he continues to demolish the false standards by which the Corinthians judge their ministers. Paul's accountability is to the Lord, but he wishes that his integrity would also be recognized by the Corinthians. He refers again to the charge of recommending himself (see 2 Cor 3:1). Vow-

ing that he will not repeat this offer, Paul now invites the Corinthians to revise their negative judgment and, on the basis of the qualifications Paul has described, not only to accept him and his ministry, but to take pride in him. This will enable them to respond to those who falsely pride themselves on externals.

Paul's own life is a parable of the way God works, which reverses human standards. Paul seems to alternate between mystical or ecstatic experiences and the very down-to-earth experiences of his weakness. And this is also because he is a minister of the new covenant—on the one hand knowledgeable in the ways of God, and on the other a servant to all people. It is God's own charity that impels him. Grace (charis) provides the guiding conviction of Paul's life, which says that since Christ died, all have died—to sin, to self-seeking, to any need for self-aggrandizement. Christ's death for our sins was also a promise that with him, all will truly be raised up.

The resurrection provides a new perspective, a godly vision that restores all things. If, before the conversion effected by the resurrection, we judged Christ and others from human standards such as the Corinthians counted important, now we see everything differently. All is new in Christ. Priorities have changed. All that matters is that one is created anew (see Gal 6:15). The same God who created out of nothing is certainly capable of recreating and of making us, however poor, unpromising, and undeserving, sharers of his work. God reconciled the world to himself in Christ. Further, in Christ, God overcame the obstacle of our transgressions so that we are enabled to become partners in the ministry of reconciliation. And not only the apostles, but all who are in Christ, have been sent out into the world with a single message: Be reconciled! This is both imperative and empowerment. For our sakes God made the sinless one sin so that redemption could penetrate the darkest, most forbidding, isolated, and inhuman part of our human experience. This was so that God, in Christ, could bring us to holiness.

6:1-10 A description of Paul's apostleship. Paul describes the ministry of all believers. Paul identifies the Corinthians as his co-workers, detaching himself in his role as apostle from any claim to power or domination over others. The optimism of Isaiah's promise is already fulfilled today, Paul insists. Paul calls us to the now moment. His primary motivation is the spread of the gospel. He wishes to do nothing that would impede that ministry. He does not wish to be an obstacle so he struggles to liberate the gospel from any binding circumstances of his own life and actions. He reflects Jesus' beatitude: "Blessed is the one who takes no offense in me" (see Luke 7:23).

Paul proceeds to give a description of that ministry which already in his life has manifested itself as "much endurance" through every kind of adverse condition—afflicted by nature and accidents, maligned by others and subjected to self-imposed discipline. The mettle of his sincerity has been tested by fire. He is not a victim of circumstances but a warrior who sharpens his "weapons of righteousness." While the war imagery is decidedly objectionable to many Christians today, Paul's use here underscores the realism and vigilance required of the minister of reconciliation who struggles for serenity and integrity, not only when honored but when dishonored, not only when assailed by outside opponents but also when experiencing inner conflicts and fears, not only in favorable but in unfavorable circumstances, too. The "gospel" has effected a reversal of values. The most blatant dichotomy exists between how the apostles were viewed and the real meaning and experiences of being an ambassador of reconciliation (see 1 Cor 4:9-13). Accounted as fools, having nothing, the ministers of the gospel are rich and wise in the only reality that matters.

6:11-13 A personal plea to the Corinthians. Paul pours out his heart. He makes an appeal to all the sympathy that characterizes the relationship between apostle and community. Having spoken personally (see 4:8-15; 6:4-10), he now reminds the Corinthians of the grandeur of their calling in God and then urgently, passionately exhorts them to manifest this identity in their relationship and acceptance of him.

Paul has defended his sincerity and he invites the Corinthians to witness the openness of his heart. He refers to himself as a parent to the Corinthians, to whom he has given birth in Christ. With disarming tenderness, he begs them to reciprocate his sincerity. He does not ask of them more than he has already done by way of example (see 1 Cor 11:1).

6:14–7:1 A digression: You are the temple of God. It is entirely possible that this apparent digression was originally part of another letter, perhaps the pre-canonical, now lost letter written in tears (see 1 Cor 5:9-11; 2 Cor 2:3-4; or 7:8-9 or a combination of these). But even though it appears abruptly, without transition, with ideas and vocabulary somewhat foreign to Paul, this section serves as an appropriate reminder to the difficult Corinthians of their real identity in God and their need to reevaluate all things in relationship to this identity.

The Corinthians were continually in danger of succumbing to the pagan environment in which they lived. There was a traditional religious connection based on the Old Testament between idolatry and adultery, and Paul uses this to form a graphic link between the Corinthians' well-known reputation and their tendency to be easily misled. Although he does not allude to the questions of false credentials or to the Corinthians' charge of recommending himself in this passage, Paul's warning about a mismatching between God and idols does qualify this section as a particularly apt illustration of the dangers of misinterpreting the real purpose of ministry and failure to recognize the true ministers. Several antitheses serve Paul's point. Light has nothing to do with darkness (see John 3:19-21; 11:10), just as righteousness is opposed to lawlessness. Christ opposes all that is evil, personified as Belial, as the evil one or Satan is called in some Jewish writings. Faith is the valid criterion for salvation. There is no common ground for worship of idols alongside worship of the one true God (see also 1 Cor 10:21-22). The God of Israel is a jealous God, as the Old Testament teaches.

Paul identifies the community as the temple of the living God, drawing on a collection of references from the Scriptures (see Lev 26:12; Ezek 37:27; Isa 52:11; Jer 31:9). Whereas in 1 Cor 6:19 Paul presented the individual Christian as the temple of God, his meaning here is collective, depicting the bonds between believers as sons and daughters of God which distinguish them from those who follow idols. Paul's inference is that the Corinthians risk falling back into paganism when they erect false criteria by which to judge true apostleship. Paul concludes this section with a reminder of the promises which define the goal of all believers. "Fear of God" does not reduce the believer to abject servility. It describes the virtue of singleminded awe that recognizes only God's own judgment as operative in our decisions (see 2 Cor 5:10-11).

7:2-4 Paul resumes his plea. Paul reiterates his sincerity and openness, dispelling any notions of either blame or guilt. He has harmed no one, another way of saying that he has acted out of love. Nor does he condemn anyone. He emphasizes the positive. He speaks openly and honestly, joyful that he still can, as before, so completely trust in the Corinthians, his boast in the Lord (see 1 Cor 1:31). He is full of confidence that his trust will be vindicated (see 2 Cor 7:14-16). Paul's joy is disproportionate to his afflictions (see Rom 8:18). Indeed, because it is based in God rather than in human limitations, Paul's joy knows no bounds (see Rom 15:13; Phil 1:18-21).

C. Resolution of the Crisis

Having treated the apostolic ministry in an objective way (2:14–6:10), Paul returns to a description of the strained personal relationships he has with the Corinthians (6:11–7:4). He inserts a reference to them as the temple of God (6:14–7:1), within his personal appeal to them to open their hearts to him as he has to them (6:11-13; 7:2-4). Paul concludes these reflections on their rocky relationship with a confident, almost exultant celebration of the good news Titus bore and the hope it inspires in his apostolic heart (7:5-16).

7:5-16 Good news from Titus. The good news of Titus' report on the Corinthians is part of Paul's gospel. It refreshes his spirit and removes the shackle of sorrow, timidity, and fear. This is a particularly sensitive section that shows Paul's reaching for some ways of expressing the care he has for the Corinthians and the boundless joy he feels from hearing of their loyalty. He is like a parent who forgets her own pain and apprehension at the successful achievement of her child. The story line, interrupted since 2:13, refers to the occurrences after Paul's departure from Troas, as he awaited word from Titus.

Paul's description of his exhausted depression echoes the plight of Elijah who complained, even after his victory over the false prophets of Jezebel, that the loneliness of the true prophet was intolerable (1 Kgs 19:1-13).

Even if it is possible to accept suffering for the sake of a just person, as Paul says of Christ in Romans (5:7), it is particularly painful to persevere when one is opposed by others and fearful within. Yet God, who does not test us beyond our strength, consoled the hearts of both Elijah and Paul in the form of tangible ordinary human signs that revealed his presence and providence.

Titus' report included the affirmation Paul needed. Paul refers to the kind of reaction that must have endeared the Corinthians to him all along. He hears of their longing, their remorse, their concern for Paul, and he is heartened. Although he regrets the grief his letter reportedly caused them, he happily acknowledges the affection that this grief betrays. If grief can produce such zeal as Titus describes, he is more than comforted. His letter was not inspired by pettiness nor a desire for vengeance. It verifies before God, whose judgment alone is significant, the loyal devotion between Paul and the Corinthians.

Paul's personal consolation, and the evident zeal of the Corinthians, are the fruits of this strained time between them, but not the only fruits. Because of this Titus has experienced an invaluable lesson in apostolic ministry. Common faith does not exclude nor even, perhaps, erase the strain among Christians or the pain they might experience individually. But faith makes tensions relative and subordinate to the common bonds of love. Faith ultimately transforms misunderstandings and doubts into manifestations of the fidelity of God for all. Paul's faith in the Corinthians is vindicated. Not only has he saved face but, indeed, God is shown at work reconciling all, and this grounds Paul's faith.

II. THE COLLECTION FOR JERUSALEM

2 Cor 8:1–9:15

Once reconciled with the Corinthians, Paul presses on to the topic of the collection which, in the context of his whole perspective on the gospel, is of singular importance as a manifestation of faith. While remaining sensitive to the fragility and intricacies of his relationship to the Corinthians, Paul makes no apology for the significance he assigns to generosity in the giving of alms. The collection becomes for him an essential element of the gospel as evidence that it has been completely accepted. Thus, Paul considers worthwhile the risk of instructing even the skittish Corinthians on this delicate issue as if to suggest that it cannot be avoided simply because the matter is so sensitive.

A. Appeal to the Corinthians' Generosity (8:1-24)

After setting the Macedonians up as an example of liberality for the Corinthians (8:1-5), Paul explains the spiritual motivation for almsgiving and then recommends the delegates who will actually pick up the collection (8:6-24).

8:1-5 Example of the Macedonians. Paul presents the Macedonians, who provided hospitality for him while he wrote to the Corinthians, as an example of extreme generosity. They gave not only out of their abundance but out of their poverty. They were not responding merely to a concept of justice that could be considered natural. Nor were they motivated merely by so lofty an ideal even as the equitable distribution of resources to all. They had a deeper source of motivation and power. Grace combined their own deep poverty with overflowing joy to enable them to perform a service that would be a sign to all. Beyond all hopes, the Macedonians actively searched for the opportunity to reach into their own experience of poverty in order to testify to their dependence on God and their joy in being Christian. Their surrender in faith was expressed in astonishing liberality.

8:6-24 Titus' role and motives for generous giving. Paul reintroduces Titus, already known as bearer of good tidings about the Corinthians. In addition Paul identifies Titus' role as initiator and delegate in taking up the collection. This is a work of grace which binds rich and poor, making them one.

Paul had testified that the Corinthians are rich in every conceivable blessing (see 1 Cor 1:5, 7). For him this is a sure sign of their "debt" (Rom 15:27; see 1:14-15) to those with whom and because of whom they share in the blessings of salvation. The intended beneficiaries of the collection are the starving saints in Jerusalem, who were suffering the effects of persecution and deprivation (see Rom 15:25-27; also 1 Cor 16:1-4).

Paul reasons that since the Corinthians are rich in spiritual benefits because they are identified as heirs to the promises originally made only to the Jews, they owe the Jewish-Christians a share in their abundance. Paul capitalizes on the Greek notion that spiritual benefits have priority over the material, so that the Corinthians' own integrity would make them see how generous they should be in sharing their material goods.

One of the real effects of the gospel is that faith makes believers responsible to one another. If the gospel is really preached and really believed, it has practical effects for the betterment of all. The same faith that eliminated the spiritual barriers between Jew and Gentile now acts as an equalizer, expressing itself in acts of justice and mercy toward the poor. The collection, for Paul, represents acceptance of mutual responsibility. The Israelites' confidence in God was similarly tested when Moses required that they collect only as much manna as was needed for one day. This was to prevent them from letting greed cause divisions among them and to allow their dependence and equality before the Lord to be manifest in their daily actions.

Paul recommends Titus as his trusted co-worker and as someone as zealous for the good of the Corinthians as he himself is. Paul is grateful to God that he did not have to convince Titus to undertake this mission but that Titus freely accepted it. Like the Macedonians, he seeks to do more, not less (see 2 Cor 8:2-4). Titus is Paul's delegate; two other delegates are chosen by the faithful, but their exact identity is not known. Tradition presumes one to be Luke, but positive identification is impossible.

Paul seems exceptionally prudent with regard to this collection, unlike his sentiments in Romans where he sees his role as one of those who will actually make the delivery in Jerusalem as essential (see Rom 15:28-33). The issue of money is at best delicate, but probably even more so with regard to the Corinthians who are still prone to suspicion. Paul relinquishes his own role in making the collection so that there can be no criticism of him. Whereas he is sure of his own motives and does not require the approval of others (see Gal 1:7-10; 1 Cor 4:1-5), he is sensitive to the need for complete trust between himself and the Corinthians and does not wish that anything, least of all money, interfere with that. He seeks, then, on this one issue, their good esteem as well as God's approval. This admission underscores the importance of the collection as a symbol for Paul.

B. A Second Appeal Addressed to the Churches of Achaia (9:1-15)

Chapter 9 is a doublet that seems to have originally been composed as a separate note to serve as an introduction to the collectors. As capital of Achaia, Corinth might have been included in the wider appeal Paul extended to all the churches of the province. Paul's motivation and language are a little different in this second appeal where he concentrates on the need for promptness (9:1-4) and then enumerates the blessings of liberality (9:5-15).

9:1-4 Exhortation to promptness. The first sentence, protesting that it is superfluous to write about the collection, suggests that this chapter was probably a separate missive originally sent as a letter of introduction to the delegates to the churches of Achaia. Paul admits that he uses the Corinthians as a model for the Macedonians, just as he portrayed the Macedonians as generous to the extreme for the edification of the Corinthians (see 2 Cor 8:1-5). Paul supports this challenge with a reminder of his confidence and his boasting because of the Corinthians. His reputation and theirs are at stake.

9:5-15 The blessings of liberality. Paul's reputation is all the more important because acceptance of the gospel itself hangs in the balance. Although Paul is not explicit here, the urgency of the collection as evidence of the sincerity and good will of the Corinthians was probably heightened by a certain amount of understandable skepticism on the part of Jewish-Christian authorities, and especially those in Jerusalem. Paul has had to confront certain of these authorities on the issue of the Gentile Christians' equality in the church (see Gal 2:11-21). The flagrant abuses in the Corinthian church might have threatened Paul's position and made his mission there vulnerable. Apparently Paul hoped a generous response from the Corinthians to his appeal about the collection would have appeased these Jewish-Christian critics.

In 9:5-15 Paul provides a theological and scriptural basis for his financial appeal. Generosity is its own reward. Anyone who gives liberally will benefit from this same gift. Paul reflects the teachings of Jesus on the use of talents and on the measure with which a believer is asked to share. God is infinite in gifts, so that there is no need to covet or hoard those entrusted to us. The role of the believer is to reflect the richness of God in concern for the poor while acting as God's steward. This form of justice requires faith in the unlimited resources of God. All of this sharing is motivated by a desire to proclaim God's name and to render the thanks which is God's due.

The practical outcome is that the Jewish Christians will be helped in their need. But this is not all. They will also be prompted to give thanks in recognizing that the same God is working now through the Gentile believers who have the gospel preached to them. The gospel leads to the obedience of faith of both Jew and Gentile in Christ through whom all are reconciled (see Rom 1:5; 16:26). Thus all join in a common prayer of gratitude and praise not only for the gifts accorded each one personally but for the community of believers. This grateful community is evidence of the surpassing grace, the indescribable gift.

III. PAUL'S DEFENSE OF HIS MINISTRY

2 Cor 10:1–13:10

These chapters probably comprised a separate letter. The abrupt change of tone and the return to the defensive topic suggest that Paul did not originally intend these to follow chapter 9, or chapter 7, which showed how Paul resolved similar questions and seemed to have cooled his emotions. With chapter 10 the Apostle strongly refutes the charges made against him by his detractors at Corinth (10:1-18). Then he indulges in some boasting, allowing us an intimate look at his feelings, vulnerability, and strength (11:1–12:21). Paul ends the epistle with a solemn warning (13:1-10) and farewell (13:11-13).

A. Paul Refutes His Enemies (10:1-18)

The Corinthians deride Paul by saying that he is forceful with words on paper, in letters, but not so impressive in the flesh. This particular charge of weakness Paul refutes with a warning to his detractors not to push him to show just how severe he can be when he is with them (see 1 Cor 4:21). Rather, Paul urges, may they be inspired by the meekness and kindness of Christ himself to relinquish such foolish standards for judging his power.

Paul insists that he does have power. He evokes his familiar battle imagery to express its nature and uses. While he admits ordinary human frailty, he identifies his weaponry as spiritual, possessing God's own power. Although his enemies are spiritual, too, they are mere creations—sophistries, pretensions, thoughts. However strong they may seem, they are nothing compared to the power of God, who in the process of reconciling the world is subjecting all to Christ. As minister of the gospel which proclaims this truth, Paul has and will use the power to destroy all that is an obstacle to the knowledge of God. Once these obstacles are overcome, all will recognize God's wisdom in the cross of Christ. The Apostle expresses confidence in the Corinthians' ultimate submission while he declares war on all that threatens to prevent their obedience.

The Apostle blames their susceptibility to false teaching and their false standards on their own superficial perspective. Believers must judge themselves as well as their ministers in Christ. This will bring about unity among them. If Paul needs to, he can make further claims about his power. He has been restrained thus far so that the Corinthians would not be intimidated. There is no real dichotomy between his letters and his actions. Forced to, he will act more severely.

Sarcastically, the Apostle pokes at the opponents he will face head-on shortly (see 11:1-15). These, he says, futilely erect the standards by which they compete and judge themselves and one another. Their ignorance is abysmal. He will not fall prey to the temptation to imitate them by comparing himself to them.

Rather, he stays "within the bounds" of the same God who led him to the Corinthians in the first place. His apostolate with them is the only limit he will accept. His boasts about the Corinthians are justified, since they are his work in the Lord (see 1 Cor 1:31; 2 Cor 10:17). Further, his evangelization of the Corinthians provides a legitimate basis for boasting because he is respecting his own personal vow not to build on another's foundation (see Rom 15:20). This was also the agreement of the church, that he go to the Gentiles while the others concentrate on the Jewish mission (see Gal 2:9). As the Corinthians grow strong in their faith, Paul can relax a little his need to nurture and sustain them. Paul hopes that his influence on them will overflow to others. He probably refers not only to the hope that he will be able to give his energies elsewhere but that the Corinthians themselves will be able to help in the work of evangelization. The closing line of this section contains a warning that the ultimate judge is the Lord whose verdict or recommendation alone counts.

B. Paul's Cause for Confident Boasting (11:1–12:21)

The Corinthians are impressed with ostentatious qualifications. Paul challenges them to review some of his own credentials. Paul contrasts himself to the "super-apostles" (11:1-15). Then he reminds the Corinthians of the suffering that gives him the right to speak (11:16-33). Finally Paul speaks of his ecstasies and visions (12:1-4, 7) before concluding with an impassionate testimony of his concern for the Corinthian church (12:11-21).

11:1-15 Paul versus the super-apostles. Since the Corinthians appear only too willing to listen to the credentials of others, Paul invites them to tolerate his own "folly," by which he means his comparing "degrees" in the school of Christ's apostleship. He is prompted to do this by God's own jealousy. Paul's apostolic role is to present the church as a chaste bride for her husband only. His fear is that the too impressionable Corinthians will be seduced by the same evil one who seduced and corrupted Eve.

Paul interprets the image of Eve in a traditional way, that is, as the more susceptible, weaker element of humanity in comparison with Adam. This traditional male-biased interpretation is elaborated upon in other New Testament writings (for example, 1 Tim 2:13-14; see 1 Pet 3:7). Here Paul simply uses Eve to explain his concern for the Corinthians, whom he sees as easily seduced by errant teachers, and to warn them to be cautious in their evaluation of the gospel and its true ministers.

Jealousy is an attribute of the unique relationship of one God with the chosen people. The one gospel Paul preaches is authorized by God. A single gospel was endorsed by the church (see Gal 2:1-10). Paul's apostleship, no less than that of his antagonists, sarcastically called "super" here and "false" in 11:13, is based on the call of God and a vision of the risen Christ. He may be lacking in eloquence compared to the others, but he is equal in the authority based on his knowledge of Christ crucified. This is evident in his relationship with the Corinthians. His frustration with their challenge is hardly veiled in 11:6.

Paul refers to the old charge that he must be inferior, since he does not accept financial support. Whether they brought up the charge again or whether some simply remained unconvinced is not clear. With impressive simplicity, Paul indicates the absurdity of the charge. Are the Corinthians so senseless as to use his independence in their regard as an accusation against their minister? Paul testifies that he does not believe in being a burden to the communities he evangelized. He only accepts support for communities after he has worked among them. So, for example, he refers with gratitude to the support he received from the Macedonians (2 Cor 11:9; see Phil 4:10-20). But he does not want to allow money to in any way inhibit his work of evangelization. He struggles to free himself and to be self-supporting so that he will not be restricted by or dependent on only those churches capable of financing his mission. This would limit the gospel and Paul's role in its spread. Paul also seeks to be above suspicion personally and especially in his use of money so as to incur as little legitimate criticism as possible. Thus he chides the Corinthians' insincerity in suggesting that such independence implies his inferiority to the other apostles.

Paul goes so far as to say that not only is this not reprehensible, but he swears in Christ's name that he will continue to be able to boast about this fact. Not that he does not love the Corinthians enough to become indebted to them. They and God witness his love. He only wishes to forestall any possible reason for maligning and criticizing his ministry. And the Corinthians have given Paul adequate reason to be this prudent. Paul's anger is provoked against those who disturb the precarious balance of the community's faith. Satan disguised himself as Lucifer, an angel of light. It follows, then, that Satan's ministers claim to serve the justice of God. The ominous threat of Paul's last line should haunt his detractors. Their end will correspond to their deeds.

11:16-33 Paul's experience of mercy and healing. Paul and the Corinthians had two different ideas of foolishness. Paul bases his in the wisdom of God and reckons anything wise by worldly standards as vain, futile. Such, for example, are the Corinthians' criteria for an apostle. But since the Corinthians respond to such foolishness, Paul indulges in boasting of his own qualifications. He is impelled to do this not by values the Lord recognizes, but by the ways of the foolish Corinthians. They even, he says, tolerate those who exploit them and impose upon them and those who use brutality and force to show their strength. If these are what is necessary to convince the Corinthians, Paul confesses that he is indeed weak. Yet he will have his say.

Are qualities of birth and religion admitted? Paul has these no less than his opponents. Ethically and religiously he is credentialed (see Rom 11:1; Phil 3:3-7). Whereas Paul's Jewish past was privileged, he is a minister of Christ only by his sufferings. There are no other New Testament parallels for many of the hardships Paul mentions. His point is that if others gain recognition because of their witness in suffering for the gospel, their trials would seem insignificant in comparison to Paul's own.

Luke tells us some of the hardships of Paul's litany. According to Luke, Paul was scourged once at Philippi and stoned once at Lystra (see Acts 16:22-23; 14:19). Luke records that in the course of his three missionary journeys Paul faced opposition and trials from accidents and nature, from both Jews and Greeks, and from rivals within the church. Further, Paul endured the physical hardships of his labors and his voluntary act of self-discipline. But without furnishing the details, Paul recites the continual adversity he suffered from five times enduring the maximum number of lashes the Jews permitted within their law and the three times he was beaten by the Romans. He adds the shipwrecks and the horror of being adrift in the open sea. He recounts the explicit opposition and the inner doubts, tensions, and fears. He cannot refrain from adding his anxiety over the churches he has founded, suggesting not too subtly that the Corinthians will be able to appreciate that point.

There is left no weakness Paul cannot identify with. Surely no one can be scandalized by the mounting indignation of his tone on needing to remind his own churches of this painful history. He qualifies himself as one who has experienced weakness, mercy, and healing. When he mentions God as his witness, he cannot help but add a prayer of praise. Finally Paul concludes his litany of sufferings with an incident that might seem surprising in its detail, but which actually shows better than any other that the mighty providence of God protects Paul from all the powerful forces that militate against him.

12:1-10 Ecstasies and humility. The charges of Paul's detractors and the Corinthians' susceptibility have combined to compel him to be so foolish as to imitate them on their own terms. If they are impressed by visions and revelations, he says, then he can add these to his credit. He refers to a revelation he received in about 42–45 c.e. that transported him to paradise. He speaks of himself in the third person as if to emphasize more strongly the gift quality of this experience which was completely undeserved. Paul gives a classic description of an ecstatic, mystical experience. He was so caught up in the divine that he lost consciousness of himself and of his body. He was absorbed in God.

Until driven to this extreme by the Corinthians, he had refrained from speaking about this experience, which is not recorded elsewhere. His witness to the gospel requires only the truth of what others can see and hear of his life. Yet, in order to prevent him from becoming proud, he was gifted, too, with a "thorn in the flesh" (see Phil 1:29). Exactly what Paul means is uncertain, but the function of this affliction is clearly to humble Paul. It serves as a weapon of Paul's perennial enemy, Satan, and reminds Paul that he is vulnerable. Paul's temptation is to not accept this, and he persistently asks that it be removed. His threefold request reflects Jesus' prayer in the Garden (Matt 26:39, 42, 44).

Paul's answer reveals the truth that divine power is made more evident in human frailty. When Paul is most empty of all human cause for boasting, he is able to identify and testify to the source of his power and strength. This amazing reversal of all earthly wisdom transforms weakness, distress, and mistreatment into powerful evidence of God's presence.

Stepping back, Paul appears to be almost shocked to find that he has been driven to the epitome of foolishness in recounting God's favors to him. Yet the good he draws from this foolishness, as he reminds the Corinthians, is the consciousness that since all apostleship comes from God rather than from himself, he is not in any way inferior to any other apostles who, if they are sincere, claim the same source of their apostleship. These others Paul labels the "super-apostles." And if apostolic signs are the only credentials the Corinthians recognize, then they should be commending Paul, for he has worked signs and wonders among them. But, less foolishly, the real "signs" of Paul's apostleship are the very existence of the Corinthians' faith and Paul's willing endurance of sufferings and hardships for the faith.

12:13-21 Paul's apprehension regarding the Corinthians. Two recurrent, apparently related charges remain to be answered. The fact that Paul did not accept support for his apostolic work prompted the Corinthians to accuse him of deceit. Paul has already responded to these charges, but a residue of distrust remains. The Corinthians' competitive spirit even goes so far as to charge that Paul is in some way rejecting them in not accepting their support. They mistakenly search for reasons to explain Paul's gratuitous faithful love for them. No wonder he refers to the consummate patience he has had to manifest in working with them. Perhaps the Corinthians are even beginning to imagine that Paul considers them inferior to the other churches. Paul stands firm in his decision not to burden them financially. His frequent and prolonged visits are the most telling evidence of his love for them. If they must rely on external signs to reassure themselves of Paul's love, they need look no further than his willingness to be spent for their sakes. His is a parent's love which is provident and generous in its concern for the children. His love is no less strong because it is not self-seeking. Because it is a gift, his love should not be considered undeserving of love in return. There is no craftiness or guile in this. He has no ulterior motive. He has never deceived or taken advantage of them, either personally or through his envoys.

Paul swears that he had done everything possible and necessary for the edification of the Corinthians he finally addresses with a note of endearment. He expresses his apprehension about their imminent meeting and the petty obstacles that threaten to make it disastrous for the community. Paul fears this. The Corinthians need to be fortified and encouraged, yet he fears that, finding them divided and not really corrected from their former pagan ways, he will have to act severely with them and increase the tension among them. Paul's apprehension makes him ambivalent about the visit he desires so much.

C. Final Warnings (13:1-10)

Paul will come a third time. By quoting Deut 19:15 he ominously warns the Corinthians of the significance of a third visit being as painful as the first two. If he again finds the Corinthians guilty, that would constitute a third and therefore complete testimony against them. His actions will follow his own counsel. The unrepentant must be judged and punished by the community. If the Corinthians want proof that Christ is working and speaking through Paul, they can expect a powerful manifestation in Paul's dealing with sin in the community.

He returns to the paradox he first raised in the beginning of First Corinthians. God's wisdom is in what is humanly regarded as weakness and folly. In his crucifixion Jesus appeared to be weak, but God showed his power in him by raising him from the dead. Paul compares the Corinthians to himself. They, like him, experience this paradox of their weakness being the manifestation of God's power in them.

Paul, then, warns: Test yourselves. They know the criteria for judgment. It shall not come as a surprise. They must realize that Jesus Christ works in them, unless, of course, they have not surrendered themselves to him in faith. Without faith, they would fail the challenge. But Paul has not failed.

Paul's prayer is that the Corinthians do no evil. He has no ulterior motive for this, such as his own approval. Rather, doing no evil, they will only do what is true and good. This is its own reward. The Apostle is not self-seeking, nor is he jealous if they seem strong while he is weak. He neither fears their mistakes because they redound on him, nor does he look for credit. His prayer is that they will be strengthened by the finding of what God has begun in them.

V. CONCLUSION

2 Cor 13:11-13

Paul writes as he does so that his visit will not bring unexpected and unwanted severity. The Lord has bestowed on him the authority to build up the community, and he hopes that will not involve destroying any of the confidence that links him to them. He abruptly brings the letter to a close, repeating his hope that they will mend their ways. He admonishes them to live in peace and love. He expects the letter to be read at the liturgy and encourages the Christians to let the kiss of peace signify their acceptance of the difficult and the easy suggestions he makes. He includes the greetings of all the Macedonian Christians who are called to the same holiness as the Corinthians are. Paul's blessing is unusually solemn. The Trinitarian formula is odd in Paul, who usually ends with some reference to Christ and then to God, but who does not suggest such a developed understanding of the three Persons. Yet this solemn formula is particularly apt for the Corinthians. Paul includes them all in his heartfelt prayer that their divisions and misunderstandings will be healed by the grace of our Lord, the love of God, and the fellowship of the Holy Spirit.

1 THESSALONIANS

Ivan Havener, O.S.B.

INTRODUCTION

Until fairly recently Paul's First Letter to the Thessalonians was largely neglected by biblical scholars, but that is no longer the case. Two key factors are responsible for this change. The first is the recognition that this is the earliest writing in the New Testament and, therefore, the oldest extant document of Christianity. The second factor is a better understanding of the Book of Acts that views it less as a series of objective historical accounts about the beginnings of Christianity and more as a theological interpretation of those beginnings.

In the past 1 Thessalonians had been interpreted in the light of what Acts had to say about Paul's missionary involvement at Thessalonica. But since 1 Thessalonians is a first-hand document written by the apostle who was himself present and since Acts was written thirty to thirty-five years later and after Paul's death and is primarily a theological rather than a historical work, it has become increasingly clear that 1 Thessalonians should not be read in the light of Acts but just the opposite. This is especially important in the case of this letter, for the account of the founding of the Thessalonian church as given in Acts 17 is quite different from the information we receive from the letter itself. It is questionable, therefore, whether the two accounts can be or should be harmonized.

With 1 Thessalonians freed from the interpretation of Acts, the way has become clear to study the letter on its own merits. This has led to a rigorous investigation of the letter's form and content, a study yielding new insights into the development of the Christian letter form and into Paul's early ministry among the Gentiles.

When Paul wrote 1 Thessalonians, his letter-writing style was not yet fixed. He was in the process of breaking with some literary conventions of his time and forging a new means of communication, the Christian letter. Therefore, the form of this letter is somewhat different than the Letter to Philemon, which is more typical of Paul's later letter form, as this comparison shows:

1 Thessalonians	Philemon
Introduction 1:1	Introduction, verses 1–3
Sender	Sender
Recipient	Recipient
Greeting	Greeting
Thanksgiving 1:2–3:13	Thanksgiving, verses 4–7
Instructions 4:1–5:22	Body, verses 8–21
Conclusion 5:23–28	Conclusion, verses 22–25
Prayer	Announcement
Greeting	Greeting
Blessing	Blessing

In 1 Thessalonians the thanksgiving section is the largest part of the letter, whereas it usually consists of only a few verses in Paul's later letters, and the instructions are often found to be only one small section of the body of later letters rather than a large section by itself. The remarks Paul makes about the senders and recipients in the introductions and the form of the initial greeting break with the usual pattern found in Graeco-Roman letters of the time and with Aramaic letters, too. Likewise, the concluding blessing is an innovation. In a sense, then, we may speak of

1 Thessalonians as an experiment in Christian letter writing. Its form is refined in later letters.

The content of 1 Thessalonians reveals a Paul more closely associated to other Jewish-Christian missionaries to the Gentiles and to a more Jewish-Christian theology than in his later writings. For instance, the place of God (the Father) is more prominent in this letter than is the naming of Jesus (the Lord). Even what Paul says about Jesus here has a different emphasis than in his other letters. Thus while Paul stresses the significance of the death and resurrection of Jesus in his later writings, here the primary saving event is seen as the coming of the Lord at the end time. This may seem strange to us because that truth, while still present, is not at the center of contemporary Christian thought. For the Thessalonians, however, it was a major concern because they expected that event to occur yet in their lifetime.

Paul gently encourages this congregation to have confidence as the day of the Lord approaches and that they should go about their everyday lives in a calm, responsible, and loving manner. This is advice valid for all times, and in this regard Paul points out the importance of Christian example. How one lives one's Christian life affects others, Christians and non-Christians alike. For Christians, it is a means of strengthening one another in faith and in our common commitment to serving God as we await that final glory promised to us. For non-Christians, our example bears witness to the radicality of our commitment to a God who wills that we live as God's children, that we owe allegiance to something beyond ourselves which is one, true, and living.

Paul worked for his keep while he proclaimed the gospel to the Thessalonians, but the primary motivation for this work may have been for another reason than the poverty of the congregation, rather, to distinguish himself from other traveling preachers (usually non-Christian philosophers) who often had a bad reputation for preaching for personal gain and also to give an example for the Thessalonians to follow, so that they not cause scandal to their non-Christian neighbors and therefore place barriers to the spread of the gospel. The congregation is located in the port city of Thessalonica in Macedonia, the modern city of Thessalonike in northern Greece, and it appears to be primarily, if not entirely, a Gentile congregation. Most likely the letter was sent from Athens or Corinth about the year A.D. 51.

COMMENTARY

INTRODUCTION AND GREETING

1 Thess 1:1

The senders of this letter are Paul and two of his fellow workers, Silvanus and Timothy, who are mentioned together also in 2 Cor 1:19 and 2 Thess 1:1. While all three preached "Jesus Christ as Son of God" among the Corinthians (2 Cor 1:19), we never hear anything else specifically about Silvanus in Paul's letters, whereas Timothy appears very frequently with Paul and is his righthand assistant. While all three have sent the letter, Paul himself is responsible for its writing (3:5a; 5:27), though he often speaks in the plural and thereby usually includes his helpers in his thoughts (1:2; 2:1). In contrast to his other letter introductions, this one is unique for its simplicity. Paul uses no title as "apostle" (Gal 1:1) nor any other designation such as "slave" (Phil 1:1) or "prisoner" (Phlm 1) to describe himself.

The letter is addressed "to the church of the Thessalonians"; it is meant to be read before the assembly of the Christians at Thessalonica, who probably gathered in homes for worship, since there were no church buildings at this early time.

The community is greeted more simply here than in Paul's other letters. Paul probably abbreviated the usual liturgical formula (see Phil 1:2), since he has already mentioned God the Father and the Lord Jesus Christ in the previous sentence.

THANKFUL REMEMBRANCE—PART I

The Gospel Comes to Thessalonica

1 Thess 1:2-10

1:2-3 Thanksgiving for an active faith. As Paul and his helpers give thanks to God for all the members of this community, they remember them in their prayers for the way they are showing themselves to be people of faith, hope, and love, the Pauline triad of Christian virtues (1 Cor 13:13). Their manner of life bears witness to their Christian calling and points to the power of example.

1:4-5 The gospel takes root. Paul looks back upon his initial preaching at Thessa-

lonica to account for the fact that the Thessalonians have become God's chosen people in Christ. The word of the gospel that he proclaimed to them was not just ordinary speech, but was filled with the power of the Holy Spirit and was, therefore, convincing to the hearers. The word of God was effective because the Holy Spirit was operative in it. The other factor in the success of the gospel among them was the example given by Paul and his companions in their actions on behalf of the community.

1:6-8 The Thessalonians as imitators and models. Upon hearing the preaching of the gospel and experiencing the example of Paul and his fellow workers, the Thessalonians became imitators of them and of the Lord, whose example Paul was following. To follow this example was no easy task for the Thessalonians who had to endure suffering and persecution, when they accepted that word which Paul preached, but they received it anyway, filled with the joy coming from the Holy Spirit. This all-pervasive joy, this divine power, gave them peace in the midst of opposition.

As imitators of Paul and of the Lord, the Thessalonians themselves have become models to believers in their own and neighboring regions. In fact, their example of faith has become renowned even beyond these areas, so clearly has the word of the Lord reverberated from them.

1:9-10 Content of the gospel. What exactly it is that others in Macedonia and Achaia have found so praiseworthy in the Thessalonian example is now spelled out. First is the reception that they gave to Paul and his fellow missionaries. Evidently, unlike some others, the Thessalonians welcomed Paul and readily listened to him. Second is their turning to God and away from idols. Apparently the Thessalonians have been able to make a clean break with their former pagan past, whereas their neighbors are having more difficulty doing that, as reflected also in Paul's comment to the Corinthians (1 Cor 10:14).

Then quoting from a catechetical formula used by Paul and by other missionaries before and alongside him, Paul repeats the gospel message given to the Thessalonians. According to this formula conversion to

Christianity involves two simultaneous processes: (1) a service of worship and obedience to the living and true God, instead of the dead and false gods of paganism, and (2) an awaiting of the arrival of God's Son from heaven, who will effect salvation by delivering us from condemnation at the last judgment. The mention of Jesus' resurrection in this context, the first time it appears in extant Christian literature, serves the purpose of showing why the historical person of Jesus can be expected to come as God's Son from heaven—because God raised him from among the dead.

How and when Jesus will come as Savior in the end time and what effect it will have on believers dead and alive is a key theme of 1 Thessalonians, as indicated by the numerous references to his coming: 1:10; 2:19; 3:13; 4:15; 5:23.

THANKFUL REMEMBRANCE—PART II

Paul's Stay in Thessalonica Explained and Defended

1 Thess 2:1-12

2:1-2 The favorable reception. Referring back to the good reception which the Thessalonians had given him (1:9), Paul notes that his presence among them was not in vain, a welcome change from the stormy reception he had received in Philippi, where he had suffered and been maltreated. In Thessalonica, however, God had given him courage to proclaim the gospel with good results despite the strain he was under from others in the city who were not so receptive (see 1:6).

2:3-7a Paul's defense against assumed accusations. Drawing upon the language of contemporary wandering Greek philosopher preachers, Paul makes a defense of his ministry among the Thessalonians. There is no evidence here that he has been personally attacked for the issues he raises, but he is aware of the general mistrust that local people often had against such outside preachers because so many of them were, in fact, charlatans. Paul wants to distinguish himself from them and therefore takes up the accusations usually leveled against these preachers. His motives for preaching are not for any other reason than to do what God has entrusted him

to do, namely, to preach the gospel. In doing this he has sought to please God, not his audience, and he is confident that God will rightly judge his motives, for it is God himself who has commissioned him.

Calling upon the knowledge of the Thessalonians themselves, as well as God as his witness, Paul also denies that he has been guilty of certain other charges often raised against wandering preachers: flattery, greed, and seeking of praise. On the contrary, he and his missionary helpers have not even claimed what they could rightly expect as apostles of Christ. This use of the word "apostles" is unusual in 1 Thessalonians because it is the only time in this letter that Paul refers to himself as an apostle and because Paul includes his companions among the apostles. In other letters he frequently refers to his apostleship, but does not give that title to his fellow workers. There seems to be a narrowing of the meaning of "apostle" as the New Testament writings are composed one after another.

2:7b-12 Paul's presence among the Thessalonians. After countering the charges that might be leveled against him, Paul summarizes what his presence among the Thessalonians was like in order to underscore the groundlessness of any such accusations. He does this by means of two parental images.

First, he describes himself and his companions as displaying the gentleness of a nursing mother caring for her children. These apostles are so full of love for the Thessalonians that they not only want to share the gospel message with them but also to give of themselves for the sake of the community. Paul cites the example of their working for their keep. In this way they encouraged the Thessalonians to do the same, but at the same time showed that they proclaimed the gospel free of charge and did not want to become a financial burden to the congregation. (Actually, it may not have worked out as ideally as it sounds, for in Phil 4:16 Paul thanks that community for the financial aid he twice received from them during his stay at Thessalonica.) Paul probably worked as a tentmaker (see Acts 18:3) from sunrise to sunset (= during the "night and day"; see 3:10 where Paul also prays "night and day") and may have preached even while he was employed in his workshop. The reference to individual attention in verse 11 easily fits into this workshop setting. Again both the Thessalonians and God are named as witnesses to Paul's integrity with regard to his conduct among the community (see 2:5).

Second, he describes the apostolic trio, as exhorting in the manner of a father concerned about each of his children. Therefore, the Thessalonians were encouraged and pleaded with to lead lives acceptable to the God who has called them into God's kingdom and glory.

Thus Paul and his fellow missionaries have been both mother and father to the Thessalonians, not only in begetting this church through the preaching of the gospel but also by expressing their love and concern for their "children," bringing them up in the Faith. It would be a misapplication of Paul's intention, however, to see in this family-life imagery a model for family life today, in which mothers are to be warm and loving, whereas fathers are to be stern disciplinarians. Paul is merely describing his concern for the Thessalonians using two aspects of family life, both of which are applied to himself.

A NON-PAULINE ADDITION

1 Thess 2:13-16

At this point, the flow of Paul's letter is surprisingly interrupted by a second thanksgiving that disturbs both the continuity of what precedes and follows it. The authenticity of this second thanksgiving is frequently questioned because the content of the passage conflicts with what we know about Paul and the historical circumstances in which he lived. It appears to be an interpolation or an addition to Paul's original letter; and its non-Pauline use of Pauline language suggests that an editor is trying to copy Paul in order to have the Apostle address himself to issues that are a matter of concern to the editor in a period after the Apostle's death.

Borrowing terminology especially from 1 Thess 1:2, 5, the editor writes a second thanksgiving section of the letter. Convinced by what Paul and his fellow workers had to say and by their example among them, the Thessalonians have accepted their message not as human words but as the word of God. This word has become operative among these Thessalonian believers, and because of this, Paul constantly gives thanks to God.

The Thessalonians are said to have become imitators of God's churches in Judea (see 1:6 where the Thessalonians are "imitators" of Paul and his helpers). These Judean churches are described as being "in Christ Jesus." (The Greek text of 1:1 speaks of "the church of the Thessalonians in God the Father and the Lord Jesus Christ.") The Thessalonians have suffered at the hands of their pagan neighbors like the Judean Christians suffered at the hands of the Jews. These Jews are charged with having done three things: they killed the Lord Jesus, they killed the prophets, and they persecuted "us" (= Paul and his fellow workers?). Furthermore, they are said to be displeasing to God, hostile to all people, and trying to prevent the preaching of salvation to the Gentiles. By doing such things and having such attitudes, the author says they are meeting their limit of sin and, therefore, wrath has already come down upon them.

This anti-Semitic sentiment can hardly be attributed to Paul, who even in his last letter still proudly speaks of himself as an Israelite (Rom 11:1). He never attributes Jesus' death to the Jews but only to "the rulers of this age" (1 Cor 2:8). Far from being despised by God, the Jews have not been abandoned by him, for "all Israel will be saved" (Rom 11:26), and according to 1 Thess 1:10 the wrath of God is still to come; it is not something that has already shown itself.

How then do we account for this addition to 1 Thessalonians? Most likely, the editor is reflecting on the fall of Jerusalem in A.D. 70, which is interpreted as God's wrath that has descended on the Jews. The editor is living at a time after that event, when Jews and Christians are in conflict, with the Christians being expelled from the synagogues. Therefore, the editor writes in a polemical spirit against the Jews because he or she has personally tasted the hostility of this persecution. To counteract it, the editor projects the situation of the present back into the time of Paul and states his or her own observations and comments through the mouth of the Apostle, thus giving them apostolic authority.

In making use of this text today, it is important that we keep in mind the stressful situation which gave rise to its composition and to its author's polemical generalizations. In highly emotional situations, such as this, overstatement and lack of proper perspectives often go hand in hand. Therefore, the claims of this passage must be tested in the light of historical evidence. According to the gospel passion narratives, *some* Jews conspired with Roman officials to put Jesus to death, but Jesus died directly at the hands of the Romans. *Some* Jews were responsible for the death of *some* prophets, a tradition common to Christians and Jews alike. We have no record from Paul's early missionary experience that he was persecuted in Judea. If the "us" in verse 15 refers to Christians in general, rather than specifically to Paul and his companions, it is possible that *some* Jews may have persecuted Christians, like Paul himself had done (Phil 3:6), but there is no evidence of a widespread, systematic persecution of Christians in Judea before the fall of Jerusalem. In any case, it would be wrong to condemn all Jews because of the actions of some. There is no place for anti-Semitism in Christian teaching.

THANKFUL REMEMBRANCE—PART III

Paul's Current Situation

1 Thess 2:17–3:13

2:17-18 Paul is orphaned. Paul turns now to the present situation in which he is physically but not spiritually separated from the community. Continuing to speak in familial terms, he describes that separation as temporarily being bereft, that is, "orphaned." This orphaned condition has led to an intense longing to be reunited with the community. Although all three missionaries have tried to visit, and Paul himself has tried more than once, these attempts have always failed because Satan has prevented it. What exactly the situation is that Paul attributes to Satan's activity is unknown to us, though it may refer to some problem that has arisen in Thessalonica itself (3:5). The reason for Paul's longing to be with the community is due to his deep love for them. It will be the Thessalonians who will give him cause to exult before the Lord at his coming. He later says very similar things to the Philippians whom he describes as his "joy and crown" (Phil 4:1) and who give him cause to boast on the day of Christ (Phil 2:16).

3:1-8 Timothy's mission to Thessalonica.

Because of the Thessalonians' special place in Paul's heart and his genuine concern for their welfare, Paul could wait no longer to hear about them, so he decided to send Timothy to them while he remained behind in Athens by himself. It is not clear whether Silvanus was still with Paul, since the "[we] sent Timothy" in verse 2 becomes "I sent" in verse 5. This may indicate that Paul is merely using the convention of the epistolary plural, that is, he is speaking in the plural when it is really only himself who is meant. Certainly, Timothy was already known to the community, so what appears to be a misplaced introduction here is really an explanation of why Paul has sent Timothy as his representative. Paul considered him to be eminently qualified for this role, for he is "our brother" in Christ and preaches the gospel of Christ as a worker through whom God is operative. As God's fellow worker he is sent by Paul to strengthen and encourage the Thessalonians with regard to their faith, so that they would stand firm in the persecution they are currently undergoing. Such persecution should have come as no surprise to them, however, since Paul had told them, while he was still with them, that this was a common fate for believers. Now Paul's words have been proven true, and the Thessalonians are experiencing that bitter reality. Paul was anxious to know how their faith was bearing up under this pressure, and when he could no longer endure the suspense, he decided to send Timothy to find out. Paul's concern derives, in part, from his own experience during persecution; he is aware of the danger to faith, and for this reason he expresses some fear that the tempter may have tried them beyond their endurance, with the result that all his work among them may have been in vain.

Happily, Paul's fear was not very well grounded, for Timothy's report upon his return from Thessalonica was the good news that the Thessalonians had remained steadfast in faith and love and that they were constantly thinking well of Paul and wanted to see him as much as he wanted to see them. Their faith is so consoling to Paul in the midst of his own distress and tribulation that he will flourish despite those troubles, and this will continue to be the case as long as they remain firm in the Lord. Thus a mutual strengthening in faith is one effect of Christian example.

3:9-13 Thanks and prayer. Paul concludes this section of the letter with a prayerful reflection. It begins with a rhetorical question which indicates that it is virtually impossible to adequately thank God for the joy that Paul has received in God's presence because of the Thessalonians. He prays constantly—night and day—that he will be able to see them personally and to supply them with whatever is still lacking in their faith. In this gentle way he lets them know that Timothy's report included some areas of Christian life and understanding that need work and development. Since he cannot yet visit the Thessalonians in person, this letter will have to serve as his apostolic presence among them and be the means for addressing the faith issues he has just alluded to.

The prayer itself consists of two parts. In the first petition Paul asks God the Father and the Lord Jesus that he may be able to visit the congregation without further delay. This invocation of Jesus, together with God, the first to be recorded in Christian literature, shows the intimate relationship of Jesus to the Father, for he shares in God's ability to answer prayer.

The second petition goes a step further, when Jesus alone is addressed in prayer, another first in Christian literature. Paul prays that the Lord may increase the Thessalonians' capacity to love and that they may overflow with that love not only for one another but for everyone, like the example of Paul's love for them. Paul prays, in effect, that they become imitators of himself (1:6). The purpose of this petition is that the Lord may also strengthen their hearts so that they are spotlessly pure in the presence of God the Father on judgment day, when the Lord Jesus comes with all his holy ones (see 1:10). The meaning of "holy ones" is uncertain. Paul usually means "Christians" when he uses the term (Phil 1:1), and thus he may be anticipating his discussion about the dead being raised on the day of the Lord (4:13-18), or the "holy ones" may refer to the angels who accompany the Son of Man at judgment (Matt 24:30-31). The awkwardness of the Greek text of verses 12-13 suggests that Paul is taking over a traditional expression which he had not coined and which may, therefore, have used the term "holy ones" in a way different than Paul uses it himself.

INSTRUCTIONS

1 Thess 4:1–5:22

4:1-2 Introductory exhortation. Paul begins the second part of the letter with a general introductory exhortation, given "in the Lord Jesus," that is, he speaks as the Lord's representative to them. He admonishes the Thessalonians to continue to conduct themselves in a manner pleasing to the Lord. When Paul was with them, he and his companions had taught them to do this; the Thessalonians are, in fact, doing it, but Paul encourages them to make even greater progress. They should act confidently, for they know what instructions had been given to them.

4:3-8 Negative admonitions. Instead of speaking directly to problem issues at Thessalonica, Paul draws upon a traditional catalog of vices as the basis of his instruction with regard to sexuality. Perhaps Timothy has reported that such a general reminder would be in order and helpful. These are things the Thessalonians are to avoid: sexual immorality, passion, desire, greed, and impurity (this is exactly the same list of sins as in Col 3:5, except that "idol worship" is not mentioned in 1 Thess 4).

Growth in holiness, which is God's will, requires abstention from sexual immorality. This means honorably acquiring a spouse with pure motives and actions and not living like the Gentiles, who do not know God and who give their bodies up to their passions and desires. It also means not overstepping oneself into sin and greedily taking advantage of one another in this matter, because the Lord punishes all such actions. Again, this is not new information, for Paul had already given it to the Thessalonians. The goal of God's call is holiness, not impurity; therefore, God has given the Holy Spirit to us that we may grow in holiness, and to reject what Paul has instructed is not merely to reject him but God, whose word Paul makes known.

4:9-12 Positive admonitions. After this general reminder of what to avoid in sexual matters, Paul exhorts the Thessalonians, once again in a general way, to make greater progress in the expression of mutual love. They certainly know that they are to love one another. God himself has taught them this through Paul, who has proclaimed God's word among them, and they have, in fact, responded by their love for their fellow Christians in Macedonia (see 1:7-10). Such a love should also be reflected in a quiet life and the minding of one's own business instead of meddling in the affairs of others. As Paul had directed before, they should continue to work despite the nearness of the Lord's coming and thereby take care of their material needs and at the same time be an example to their non-Christian neighbors. The power of Christian example is not only important, then, for inter-Christian growth and strengthening but is important also for non-Christians to see and experience.

4:13-18 Day of the Lord as a consolation with regard to the faithful departed. At this point Paul introduces into his creation of a Christian letter an element not found in typical pagan letters of the time, namely, teaching concerning the end time. Since Paul treats this subject in the context of general exhortations, it may be that he is not presenting something new nor taking up an issue that was especially troubling to the Thessalonians, but was merely repeating for them a part of his teaching from the beginning. In this section he reviews for the congregation what will happen to those members whose deaths have occurred before the coming of the Lord. Paul assures his readers that these dead Christians have not missed out on the deliverance which the Lord is to effect when he comes. Therefore, Christian grief over one who has died in the faith is not the same as that of those who have no hope.

To show why Christians are hopeful, even when saddened by the death of fellow believers, Paul draws upon a creed that was familiar to the congregation: "We believe that Jesus died and rose." This belief is important because what happened to Jesus will analogously happen also to those who die believing in Jesus. God will take them up from among the dead even as God raised Jesus.

Paul also makes use of an early Christian prophecy, through which the risen Lord has spoken. According to this prophecy, those who are alive at the Lord's coming, and Paul seems to include himself among them, will not be any better off than those believers who have died. This is clear from the prophecy's description of what will happen to believers on the day of the Lord. It is told in vivid apocalyptic imagery, as we find in Mark 13, 1 Cor 15:24-28, and throughout the Book of Revelation. With spectacular sound and glory the Lord will come down from heaven (see 1:10), and those who have died will rise up to meet him first; then the living will be swept up, too, and all believers will meet the Lord in the clouds to begin an eternal existence with him in glory. Less important to us is how this is done than the fact that all believers, dead and alive, will share in the glorious presence of the Lord forever.

While Christians certainly grieve when their fellow believers die, their grief is tempered by the hope of the resurrection and eternal life. Therefore, Paul exhorts the Thessalonians to console one another with the message of hope.

5:1-11 Day of the Lord as a consolation to the living. Because the day of the Lord is the primary saving event according to this letter, those Christians who are still alive at its arrival have no need to fear either in regard to how or when it takes place. The Thessalonians already know that the Lord will come at a time when he is least expected, like a thief in the night (Matt 24:42-44), and that no one will be able to escape the judgment that will take place at that event. For some it will be a day of God's wrath, a time when they will experience sudden ruin and destruction, but for Christians it will be a time of deliverance and salvation (see 1:10).

Even though the Lord is described as coming like a thief in the night, Christians do not fear this darkness, for they are children of light and day. Through baptism, which seems to be alluded to here, they have become illumined and have no part with darkness or night. Thus they are not like their non-Christian neighbors who sleep at night unprepared for the coming of the Lord or who waste their time carousing around in the same unsuspecting darkness. Instead, Christians must be alert by their very nature, clothed in the triad of faith, hope, and love (1:3), which is the armor of salvation (see Eph 6:11, 14-17). The reason for this Christian optimism is God's saving activity; God has not destined Christians to wrath but for that future salvation that comes on the day of the Lord. Despite that future notion, however, salvation has already begun through the agency of the Lord Jesus Christ, "who died for us." This is a short creed, appearing frequently in Paul's writings (Rom 5:6; 8:3; 14:15 etc.), but given here for the first time in Christian literature. Through baptism this saving death takes its effect among Christians, who then become children of light. Therefore, whether Christians are physically awake or asleep at the Lord's coming, or even dead or alive, they will live with him.

With this complete confidence in their salvation, the Thessalonians are to encourage and console one another, even as they have been doing.

5:12-22 General admonitions on Christian conduct. In a final series of instructions, Paul gives another table of Christian duties that are so general that the list could be used for almost any community of his.

With regard to church order, it appears that some provision has been made for the administration of the community. Therefore, the Thessalonians are asked to respect and honor those in the community who have the job of exercising authority and admonishing. Harmony among the members is to be maintained.

Four brief exhortations then follow, all of them addressed once again to the whole community: to admonish the insubordinate, to cheer the discouraged, to support the weak, and to show patience to all. Vengeance is to be avoided, and the good of all, whether Christian or not, is to be sought.

Paul calls on the Thessalonians to do what he has done—to rejoice (3:9), pray, and give thanks (1:2-3) always and constantly. He asks them to do this because that is God's will in Christ Jesus.

Finally, since the Spirit manifests itself in many ways (1 Cor 12:4-11), care should be taken that its gifts are properly used and ac-knowledged. Prophecies are singled out for special attention and respect. But everything is to be tested whether it is of the Spirit or not. That which is of the Spirit, that is, the good, is to be retained. On the other hand, evil is to be avoided in all its forms because it is devoid of the Spirit.

CONCLUDING PRAYER AND BLESSING

1 Thess 5:23-28

Paul's concluding prayer underscores the reality of the Thessalonians' Christian existence. They can be exhorted to do all the things mentioned in the whole letter because through Jesus Christ, God has made it possible for them to do so. For this reason Paul addresses his prayer to God and asks that they may be made perfect in holiness. Earlier Paul had stated that it was God's will that they grow in holiness (4:3, 7) and that they dwell in peace (5:13). Only this God of peace can bring them to perfection, for it is God who preserves their total being (spirit, soul, and body) blameless at the Lord's coming (3:13). It is God who calls them (2:12) and is trustworthy (5:9) and will complete their salvation.

Paul also asks the congregation to continue to pray for him and his companions and to greet one another with a holy kiss, a ritual sign of Christian fellowship. Then speaking in the singular, he asks them to swear by the Lord that his letter be read to all in the congregation. This request may indicate that there was more than one house church in Thessalonica at which the letter was to be read. The letter concludes with a liturgical blessing that the grace mediated by the Lord Jesus Christ be with them all.

PHILIPPIANS

Ivan Havener, O.S.B.

INTRODUCTION

The Letter to the Philippians shows Paul at his pastoral best—at one moment he is praising the community, then teaching, then encouraging, then admonishing, then warning, but always clearly loving the members of this community as he gives it advice and direction. He speaks to this community of Philippians with the pride of a founding father and frequently associates the words "joy" and "rejoicing" with it.

There is a complex set of circumstances in which the community is living. On one hand it is struggling against hostile neighbors, and on the other it is troubled by visiting missionaries who, in one case, say things differently than Paul does, but still preach the gospel and yet, in another case, directly contradict Paul's presentation of the Christian message. Besides this, and perhaps also because of it, the community itself is beset with disharmony and bickering, the sort of troubles that have plagued Christian communities throughout the centuries.

At the time that Paul was writing to this community, Philippi was a Roman city located in Macedonia (part of northern Greece today) along a major Roman military and trade road, the Via Egnatia, and only nine miles from the port town of Neapolis. Despite its Roman background, the city had a mixed population, as the names given in the letter indicate. For example, "Clement" is a Roman name whereas "Epaphroditus" and "Syntyche" are Greek names. While Acts 16:11-40 records the initial visit of Paul to Philippi, almost none of this bears upon the information provided in the Letter to the Philippians itself. According to Acts, this was Paul's first mission foundation on European soil.

Although the Letter to the Philippians looks like one document, a closer inspection of the text shows that three originally separate letters of Paul have been welded together to form our present text. While we cannot be sure why this was done, it may simply have been a more adequate means of preserving these apostolic writings, especially when they were passed on to other Christian communities for their edification. Since two of these three letters were written on a single sheet of papyrus apiece (or on a part of one sheet), less space was taken up and some of the repetition removed, like the introductions and thanksgivings, when all three letters were combined together. The editor placed two truncated letters into the framework of a larger letter, where he or she thought they fit best. Since the editor was reluctant to change any of the material, the seams of the editorial work are relatively easy to find. Most likely this editing was done at Philippi itself, where the community's high regard for Paul, inspired by his love for them, found expression in the desire to preserve and pass on his writings.

By looking at each of these letters separately and noting how they relate to one another, we are better able to understand what was going on at Philippi and what the situation of Paul was on three different occasions.

Letter A (4:10-20) is a fragment of a thank-you note to the Philippians for the monetary aid which the community had twice given to Paul when he was at Thessalonica (4:16) but especially now for their aid when Paul is suffering from distress (4:14). The "distress" probably refers to his imprisonment, a situation which continues and is spoken of at greater length in Letter B. The gift for which Paul gives thanks has been brought personally by Epaphroditus, a member of the Philippian community who has also been given a charge to stay with Paul and help him (2:25). The place of Paul's distress is not mentioned, though it is probably not far from Philippi, as Epaphroditus' travel suggests. Perhaps the place of imprisonment was Ephesus, where we know that Paul spent a lengthy period of time.

Letter B (1:1–3:1a; 4:4-7, 21-23) is a lengthier letter to which the other two letters were added. Paul has been in prison for some time, but expects to know soon what the outcome of his trial will be. Although he is anxious about the result, he has come to find a deep joy in the Lord which he can share with the Philippians and which he encourages them to share with one another. He has time to reflect on the news he receives about the Philippian community, and he speaks concretely to them about their situation, as he also reflects on his own. He is concerned about the advent of other Christian missionaries among the Philippians, but is not upset. He gently encourages the community to unity, especially in the face of the enmity of their neighbors. His cheerful attitude is seen even in his admonitions, where he cites a hymn about Christ (2:6-11) as an example for the community. Epaphroditus had fallen ill during his stay with Paul and nearly died, but now he is well enough to be sent home and look after Paul's concerns for the Philippians till Timothy comes and, perhaps, even Paul himself.

Letter C (3:1b–4:3, 8-9) is written after Paul's imprisonment has come to an end—at least, he makes no further mention of it. In this letter he is responding to two immediate needs: to counter the infiltration of the community by false teachers and to settle a particularly destructive quarrel between two leading women in the community. Evidently, the good news which Paul expected to receive from Timothy was not so good after all. The teachers he spoke of in Letter B (1:15-18) were more disturbing to him after he learned more about them, and his previous calls to unity were not heeded, a situation especially grievous to Paul, since the quarreling women were his helpers in the gospel. This letter fragment is especially treasured for its autobiographical material in 3:4-11 and its short summary of Paul's attitude toward the keeping of Jewish law by Gentile Christians, along with his understanding of what salvation is.

All three letters were written close together. If Ephesus was the place of imprisonment, they can be dated somewhere between A.D. 55 and 57.

In the following commentary the three letters will be presented in the order in which they apparently were originally written.

COMMENTARY

LETTER A: A THANK-YOU NOTE

Phil 4:10-20

When this letter was edited into the present text of Philippians, it lost at least its introduction. What remains is the body of a short letter, together with its conclusion. It was written early in Paul's imprisonment, perhaps, the same trouble he refers to in 2 Cor 1:8.

4:10-14 Joy in the midst of distress. The first phrase preserved for us in the Philippian correspondence speaks of "rejoicing," the term so characteristic for Paul's attitude toward the Philippians. Paul rejoices in the Lord because they have now been able to express their concern for him, a situation which had not been possible before this and the absence of which had made life more difficult for him. But Paul does not complain, for experience has taught him to be content both in good and bad circumstances, in times of poverty and abundance, in facing plenty and hunger, wealth and want. The secret for his success in these situations is the strength he receives from the Lord (4:10). Nonetheless, he is grateful for the kindness of the community for sharing in his troubles.

4:15-19 The generosity of the Philippians. What exactly the Philippians had done for Paul becomes clearer in the following verses. Paul reminds them how they alone among those churches which had received the gospel from its introduction into Macedonia had shared in giving and receiving. In fact, the Philippians after receiving the gospel had twice sent monetary aid to Paul while he was staying in Thessalonica and had need of their help, despite his attempt to earn his own way there (1 Thess 2:9). In his thankfulness Paul does not seek more of this gift; rather, he hopes for the result of this generosity which redounds to them. He has been so richly paid back that he abounds with the gift that he has received from Epaphroditus, who has personally brought it from the community. Paul describes this gift in worship terminology, as a fragrant sacrifice, pleasing and acceptable to God. Even as they have been generous, so also God will fulfill their every need according to God's glorious riches, which are found "in Christ Jesus."

4:20 Concluding doxology. This letter fragment concludes with a liturgical doxology, glorifying God the Father unto the ages of ages, together with the acclamatory "Amen!" which means "So be it!"

LETTER B: THOUGHTS FROM PRISON

Phil 1:1–3:1a; 4:4-7, 21-23

This is the only letter of the three which comprise our present text of Philippians which has come down to us in its complete form. Since it is the longest and most important of the three, the other two were incorporated into it.

INTRODUCTION AND GREETING

Phil 1:1-2

1:1 The senders and recipients. Paul and his fellow worker Timothy are the senders of the letter. They are slaves of Christ Jesus, for he is their Lord and master. This slavery leads to life (Rom 6:22-23) and requires obedience. The Christians at Philippi, together with their overseers and ministers (the respective terms for bishops and deacons), are addressed. The mention of bishops and deacons is striking, since Paul never speaks of them elsewhere in his genuine letters, though he does mention the woman deacon Phoebe in Rom 16:1-2. It is, perhaps, a sign that he is concerned that his community have administrators in his absence and that he is coming to grips with the possibility that Christ will not return during his own lifetime (see the contrast with 1 Thess 4:17); the bishops and deacons will continue to lead the community after Paul is gone.

1:2 The greeting. The community is greeted with a stereotyped liturgical formula frequently used by Paul (Phlm 3), which is more elaborate than greetings found in ordinary Greek letters of the time (for example, Acts 23:26). It incorporates both Greek and Hebrew elements, but becomes specifically Christian with the naming of the Lord Jesus Christ.

THANKSGIVING AND INTERCESSION

Phil 1:3-11

1:3-8 Joyful thanks. Though Timothy was mentioned as one of the senders of the letter (1:1), it is clear that Paul has actually written it himself, when he writes, "I give thanks . . . ." He begins his thanksgiving to God in this generally cheerful letter with an emphasis on completeness: *"every* remembrance," "praying *always*," "in my *every* prayer." While he certainly means what he is saying, he enjoys this play on words, and in this light-hearted mood he first speaks of "joy," a theme occurring more frequently in the Philippian correspondence than for any other community. Paul is thankful, in part, due to the Philippians' openness in sharing the gospel—something begun when Paul founded the community and something they have continued to do up to the present. He is also thankful that the God who worked through him in the establishment of the community and in its mission of sharing the gospel will bring that good work to completion on the day when Christ Jesus returns, that day which brings final deliverance (1 Thess 1:10). A third reason for giving thanks is the mutual affection between Paul and the community; he has them in his heart, and they are partners in God's grace. While he is imprisoned, they share in the task of defending and establishing the gospel. Paul's warmth and depth of feeling for this community is underscored when he names God as witness to his longing for everyone of them with the affection of Christ Jesus.

1:9-11 Intercession. From thanksgiving Paul moves into intercessory prayer, asking that the Philippians' rich love might continue to increase in knowledge and experience for the discernment of that which is truly valuable. He asks this so that they arrive at the day of Christ pure and blameless, filling themselves up with the fruit of righteousness which comes through Jesus Christ and redounds to the glory and praise of God.

SPREAD OF THE GOSPEL DESPITE OPPOSITION AND RIVALRY

Phil 1:12-18a

1:12-14 Imprisonment aids gospel. Paul begins the body of this letter by pointing out to the Philippians that the circumstance of his imprisonment has actually been advantageous for the spread of the gospel, and this is clear in two ways. First, Paul's imprisonment has been made known "in Christ," probably through testimony at his trial, to the whole household of the political officials in charge and to "all the rest." Second, Paul's imprisonment has also been a source of encouragement for the majority of his fellow Christians to proclaim the gospel further without fear, but he does not explain why. Perhaps his fearless testimony in the midst of oppression has influenced other Christians to do the same.

1:15-18a Rivals preach Christ. This mention of Christian witness reminds Paul of some inter-Christian difficulties with regard to the preaching of the gospel. As elsewhere in his letters, Paul speaks here of Christians who are his rivals and, perhaps, even opponents. While admitting that they proclaim Christ, Paul questions their motives, claiming that they do so out of envy and contention. He is probably referring to how they seem to react to him and his influence on the Christian mission; there is an obvious disagreement. On the other hand, some proclaim Christ from good will, their motive being love; such as these are in agreement with Paul and see the value of Paul's role in the defense of the gospel. In Paul's view, however, his rivals proclaim Christ out of selfish ambition and from impure motives, even hoping to add affliction to Paul's imprisonment. In fact, they may see his imprisonment as a sign of weakness. While this clearly disturbs him, nonetheless, he remains in a cheerful mood and rejoices, because no matter how it is done and whatever the motives, the main thing is that Christ is preached. He has, of course, already pointed out that his imprisonment, far from being a sign of weakness, has been a means for proclaiming the gospel (see 1:12-14).

PERSONAL FATE OF THE APOSTLE

Phil 1:18b-26

Looking on the bright side, Paul says that he will continue to rejoice, for what he is doing and undergoing will lead him to deliverance, in the sense of release from prison but, perhaps, also in a broader sense of salvation as well. This will occur through the intercessory prayer of the Philippians and the support of the Spirit of Jesus Christ, that is, with Christ's dynamic presence as an aid. Therefore, Paul rejoices in this eager expectation and hope that the Spirit will not let him be disgraced and that Christ will in all boldness be publicly praised now and always in Paul's body, whether through his life or through his death. He cannot lose in either case, for Christ is associated both with life and death. But if he continues to live in the flesh, that is fruitful work for him. What he will prefer he does not make known, since the choice is so difficult: he has a longing to depart from life and to be with Christ, for that is a much better situation; yet other considerations are in order. For the sake of the Philippians, it is more necessary at this time for Paul to continue in the flesh. Confident in this greater necessity, he knows that he will remain and go on living with all of the Philippians so that they might progress and have joy in their faith. This will result in their abundant boasting in Paul's presence again with them, but all Christian boasting is done "in Christ Jesus" (1 Cor 1:31).

CHRISTIAN LIFE AS IMITATION OF CHRIST

Phil 1:27–2:18

1:27-30 United in Suffering. Paul reminds the congregation that while they bear witness to the gospel of Christ, they should also lead lives worthy of it. He mentions this because of some inter-Christian squabbles in the community about how Christianity is to be expressed. They must not only proclaim the gospel but also live according to it. If they do this, then it makes no difference whether Paul visits them or only hears about them in his absence, which in this case is his imprisonment. He will learn of their firm stance in the one Spirit as they bear their struggle with one mind in the faith that is called forth by the gospel. Given this threefold unity of Spirit, mind, and resolve to lead lives worthy of the gospel, they will not be intimidated in any way by their non-Christian opponents. They will form a united front. All of this is an omen of destruction to the gospel's opponents, but

for the community it is a sign of their salvation which comes from Christ, even as he was their source of boasting in verse 26. Paradoxically, however, this life for Christ which has been granted the Philippians to lead involves not only belief in Christ but also suffering because of him and undergoing themselves the same kind of struggle which they have seen in Paul's example before and what they are currently hearing about. Christian life means suffering, the taking up of one's cross (Mark 8:34-35).

2:1-5 Christian characteristics. Again addressing the unity of the congregation, Paul lists a number of characteristics that he thinks are part and parcel of being a Christian. The Christian should have consolation in Christ, encouragement in love, sharing of spirit, compassion and mercy. If the Philippians have these characteristics, Paul wants them to manifest these qualities and thereby complete his joy, for then they will be of one mind with Paul and one another and possess the same love. As a result they will treat one another not selfishly and with haughtiness but with humility, considering others to be better than themselves and looking after the concerns of others rather than their own. The supreme example of this way of life is Christ Jesus himself, and Paul exhorts the community to be disposed to this example, which Paul explicates by quoting an early Christian hymn about Christ.

2:6-11 Christ's example in a hymn. The first part of the hymn (vv. 6-8) deals more directly with some of Paul's immediate concerns with regard to the Philippians, for we find a portrayal of Christ who did not selfishly cling to his exalted position of being "in the form of God." A contrast seems intended here between Jesus and Adam who was made in the likeness of God (Gen 1:26-27), but tragically succumbed to the temptation to grasp at equality with God. (In Gen 3:5 the serpent says, "You will be like gods.") Rejecting Adam's sin, Jesus freely emptied himself from his exalted position and took on Adam's condition of slavery to sin and corruption; he accepted "the form of a slave." Then being found in this corrupt, human-like condition, which we all have a share in, Christ completed the way of Adam by humbling himself even further in obedience to God by undergoing death. Paul probably selected this hymn because of the emphases of selflessness and humility which ultimately meant death itself. These are precisely the matters he has been instructing the Philippians about. Paul may have added that this death was "on a cross," since the earliest credal formulas and hymns, otherwise, generally avoid mention of the cross. For Paul, however, the cross is not a symbol of shame but of glory (1 Cor 1:18).

Although Paul may have been more specifically interested in the first part of the hymn, nonetheless, the second part (vv. 9-11) is also significant, for what has happened to Christ Jesus, who humbled himself and died, is important as an example of what will also happen to the Philippians, who humble themselves and, perhaps, even undergo death in bearing witness to the gospel. As God exalted Jesus, the second Adam, so Christians who suffer and die for the faith may expect to be raised to new life when the exalted Lord returns (1 Thess 4:13-18). The remainder of the hymn discusses the exaltation of Jesus and his uniqueness: he has been given a name which is above every name, so that when it is pronounced the whole cosmos responds by kneeling and glorifying God the Father by confessing and praying, "Lord Jesus Christ!" It is both an invocation of the name of Jesus and a profession of who he is.

Thus this hymn that emphasizes the uniqueness and importance of Jesus also provides Paul with the example he wishes the Philippians to follow.

2:12-18 More admonitions to Christian conduct. Continuing in his own words, Paul refers back to the Christ hymn by taking up the concept of obedience, recognizing that his beloved Philippians have been ever obedient, not only as in the case when Paul is himself present but even now that he is imprisoned and is, therefore, absent from them. Their obedience is to Christ who, in turn, was obedient to God, even unto death. With this obedience he urges them to play an active role in the working out of their salvation in awe before God, not in the sense that they can add to the salvation won by Christ, but they can make that salvation come to effectiveness among themselves as a community, because God in his good will is at work among them producing both their desire and action.

Once again referring to some dissension in the community, Paul admonishes them to do everything without grumbling and questioning so that united in the midst of their non-Christian neighbors, whom Paul describes as a crooked, perverse generation, the Philippian Christians will become blameless and innocent, unblemished children of God radiating like stars of the universe among those neighbors and clinging to the word of life. They will become a reason for Paul to boast on the day of Christ's coming and at the same time prove that he has run an effective race and his difficult labor has been vindicated by the results. Then moving abruptly from these images to cultic imagery, Paul says that even if he is offered as a libation on the sacrifice and worship service of their faith (that is, if his death is required in behalf of their faith), that is reason for him to rejoice, indeed, to rejoice together with them all, and vice-versa, they also should rejoice and especially rejoice with Paul. Togetherness in witness and Christian community means rejoicing, even in the face of death.

ARRIVAL OF TWO FELLOW WORKERS

Phil 2:19-30

2:19-24 Paul hopes to send Timothy. Still cheerful despite his imprisonment, Paul continues to hope in the Lord Jesus. This hope has two aspects in this context—first, that after a short while Timothy will be sent to the Philippians as Paul's representative and, second, that Timothy will report good news concerning the community when he returns to Paul. Timothy is praised by Paul for his trustworthiness and his genuine concern for the Philippians, attributes not found among all whom Paul could also send but does not, because they are more concerned about their own interests than for those of Jesus Christ. The Philippians, too, know Timothy's value when he served with Paul like a child with a father for the sake of the gospel among them. As "father" Paul is the leader, the one in charge. He it is who sends others and who hopes to send Timothy, as soon as he finds out what the outcome of his trial will be. Paul expresses some confidence that even he himself may be able to come soon.

2:25-30 Epaphroditus returns home. In trying to decide when to send Timothy, Paul has found it necessary to send Epaphroditus on ahead, probably as the bearer of this letter. He is described as Paul's brother, co-worker and fellow soldier, ministering to Paul's need, especially acute while he is in prison. Besides this, he is the Philippians' apostle who was sent by the community to help Paul. Therefore, he is not only known to them but was one of them (4:18). They have heard of his near fatal illness, and Epaphroditus is eager to return home and put their distress over him to rest. God was merciful both in restoring him to health and in not adding the death of a fellow worker to Paul's present sorrows. Epaphroditus' arrival in Philippi should, of course, be a source of rejoicing to the community, even as it is a source of relief to Paul, that his anxiety over them will be alleviated. Therefore, Paul asks the Philippians to receive Epaphroditus with joy, honoring people of his sort, who are willing to give all, even to die for the work of Christ. Epaphroditus has risked his life in carrying out the community's commission to serve Paul in his mission work.

ADMONITION TO JOY

Phil 3:1a

3:1a Call to rejoice. Paul admonishes the community one last time to rejoice "in the Lord," even as he hopes "in the Lord" (2:19). At this point the text is abruptly interrupted with a fragment of another of Paul's letters (3:1b–4:3), but Letter B continues again in 4:4 where the admonition to rejoice is taken up again and emphasized.

FINAL ADMONITION AND ASSURANCE

Phil 4:4-7 = Letter B

At this point Letter B resumes, repeating the call to rejoice that was begun in 3:1a. The community is also encouraged to reveal its considerateness to all, even as it has done so to Paul. Since the Lord is not far away but is nearby, the community need not be anxious about anything, for it can turn to God in prayer with petitions and thanksgiving and be assured of his care.

4:7 Assurance of God's peace. The main body of Letter B ends with Paul's final assurance that God's peace, which is beyond all human understanding, will preserve their hearts and minds "in Christ Jesus." Once again Letter B is interrupted by fragments from other letters (4:8-9 = conclusion of Letter C; 4:10-20 = Letter A).

CONCLUSION OF LETTER B

Phil 4:21-23

4:21-22 Greetings. Picking up on the phrase "in Christ Jesus" from 4:7, Paul sends his greetings to each of them "in Christ Jesus" (they are members of the church because Christ has made them holy, setting them apart, and because they are one with him). Those with Paul also send greetings, as do all the brothers and sisters in Christ, especially those who are in the service of the government, probably in Ephesus.

4:23 Final blessing. Letter B concludes with an abbreviated liturgical blessing upon the entire community, the phrase "with your spirit" virtually interchangeable with the phrase "with you" (cf. Gal 6:18; Phlm 25 with 1 Thess 5:28).

LETTER C: AN APOSTOLIC SALVO

Phil 3:1b–4:3, 8-9

This letter fragment says nothing of Paul's imprisonment and contrasts in tone with his otherwise cheerful disposition in the previous two letters. The major portion of Letter C clearly intrudes between what is said in 3:1a and what is said in 4:4; therefore, it appears to be another letter of Paul altogether and is addressed in more forceful and sharper terms than we find in Letters A and B.

POLEMIC AGAINST FALSE TEACHERS

Phil 3:1b–4:1

3:1b-2 Speaking out against false teachers. This letter no longer contains an introduction and thanksgiving, but begins with a statement about Paul's fearlessness to speak out on an issue which he finds very troubling. The primary purpose of his writing is to protect the Philippians against an assault on the gospel which he has proclaimed to them.

Paul launches into a frontal attack on the false teachers who have infiltrated the community, telling it to be on the watch for them. His choice of unflattering names for these false teachers suggests that he is arguing against a Jewish-Christian group. "Dogs" is a term that Jews used for Gentiles; thus Paul is especially insulting to his opponents by using this term to designate them. "Evil-workers" is just the opposite of what the opponents claim for themselves as they demand others to keep Jewish law. "Mutilation" is the unflattering term Paul uses to describe circumcision when they require that of Gentile Christians.

3:3-11 The value of gaining Christ. In contrast to these false teachers, Paul points out that the Philippians are already a chosen people, the spiritual circumcision, for they worship in the Spirit of God and boast in Christ Jesus and, therefore, do not need to place confidence in the marks of a physical circumcision in order to gain entry to God. Then Paul digresses into some autobiographical material, noting that if anyone has reason for confidence in the marks of this physical rite, he certainly has and even more so than others. He proceeds to list his Jewish pedigree, which shows that he was completely a Jew, faithful in religious observance, a Pharisee so zealous that he persecuted the church and kept the law blamelessly. Yet as good as all this was, in comparison to having gained Christ, it can only be seen as a loss for Paul. Indeed, everything else must be seen as loss in view of gaining Christ; everything else must be seen as so much garbage which can be thrown out.

Paul's understanding of Christ has changed his whole value system. Because righteousness comes from God through Christ, it is faith in Christ which saves—not a self-gained righteousness by the keeping of the law. And this salvation means a participation in the power of Christ's resurrection, even as it also means sharing in his sufferings and becoming like him in death. It is an imitation of Christ which Paul hopes will be completed by his resurrection from the dead, even as Christ also was raised.

3:12-16 The goal of perfection. Now Paul's argument takes a new twist; he points out that he has not yet reached his goal, that is, he has not yet been raised and is not yet perfect—the same kind of issues he needed to deal with in 1 Cor 2–4, 15. Resurrection and perfection are goals which are pursued, not that which we already have. The Philippians are urged to pursue these goals to make them their own, even as Christ has made the Philippians his own, but Paul relates this in the first person, giving himself as the example (see v. 17). This goal becomes so all-consuming an ambition that all else recedes into the background and lies forgotten, as in an athletic contest the runners strain forward to attain the prize, not concerned with what they have passed by. The prize of which Paul speaks is "God's upward calling in Christ Jesus," that is, knowing and experiencing Christ (v. 10). Those who are really perfect should think the way Paul has just suggested, but if not, God will still reveal it to them anyway. But in the light of the current missionizing by Paul's opponents, it is at least necessary to hold firm to what has already been attained.

3:17-21 Citizenship in heaven. The Philippians are not left to drift along on their own, however, for Paul calls them to imitate himself and others in the community who live like him. These examples of Christian life are important, especially when, as Paul claims in tears, there are others present who live as enemies of the cross of Christ, who downplay the significance and embarrassment of that instrument of torture and death, who are wrapped up in their dietary laws, making a god of rules and thereby showing concern only for the things of this earth, whereas the true Christian citizenship is in heaven. It is from there that Christians await the coming of the Lord Jesus Christ as Savior. At this future coming, this Savior will transform our bodies to be like his glorious body with his all-encompassing power (see 1 Thess 4:16-17). Paul's view is not that this world is evil, rather, that there is more to Christian life than this world offers, a point which he feels that his opponents are not taking sufficient stock in.

4:1 Appeal to stand firm. Paul concludes this section of Letter C with an appeal to the Philippians, his fellow Christians, loved and longed for by him, his joy and crown, that they not give way to his opponents but stand firm "in the Lord."

PHILEMON

Ivan Havener, O.S.B.

INTRODUCTION

Paul's Letter to Philemon is the shortest complete letter of the Apostle which has come down to us. It provides us with a good example of how Paul could bring his apostolic authority to bear upon a member of one of his communities in order to encourage him to act in a responsible, Christian way. It is a masterpiece of persuasion, a kind of letter writing which was frequently done in the Graeco-Roman world of Paul's time.

While we may admire and even enjoy Paul's power to persuade, the timelessness of the letter lies in its primary message of how we treat our fellow Christians. That ultimately has some implications for how Christians view the social system of slavery, but Paul was not addressing himself to the issue of slavery, even though it provided part of the context out of which he wrote. Paul's concern is simply that conversion to Christianity places Christians in a new relationship to one another. They are brothers and sisters in Christ or partners, as it were, in the Lord, and this relationship transcends all other relationships, such as master and slave. This Chris-

tian existence does not, however, automatically do away with other relationships, though in the course of time it should certainly affect them. Paul does not deal with this latter concern, because in his excitement to proclaim the gospel before the coming of Christ or his own death, he has not worked out the social implication of the message. That has been left to us.

The letter itself does not indicate when it was written nor where Paul was imprisoned nor where Philemon's home was. If we accept as historically accurate the information from Colossians, it is likely that Philemon's home was in Colossae, a small town in the southwestern part of what is today modern Turkey, and that Paul's imprisonment was not far away, perhaps, in Ephesus. Since Paul expected to be released from prison soon, the letter may have been written around the same time as the Philippian Letter B (1:1-3a; 4:4-7, 21-23) or shortly thereafter, if, indeed, the same imprisonment is being referred to as in Philippians. In that case the date of composition was close to the year A.D. 56.

COMMENTARY

INTRODUCTION AND GREETING

Phlm 1-3

1a The senders. Both Paul and his assistant Timothy are senders of this letter, though Paul himself has actually written it (see v. 19).

Because Paul likes to play on words, his self-designation in the Greek text as "a prisoner of Christ Jesus" probably refers not only to his physical confinement but also to his commitment to Jesus. He is Christ's prisoner, even as he describes himself elsewhere as Christ's slave or servant (Phil 1:1).

1b-3 The recipients and greeting. The primary recipient of the letter is Philemon, whom Paul addresses in glowing terms—the first step in the process of encouraging Philemon so that he will eventually meet his Christian responsibilities as Paul will point them out. Instead of sending this letter privately to Philemon, as he could have done, Paul chooses to send it to the whole community which meets at Philemon's home; thus he also addresses two other members by name, Apphia and Archippus, about whom we know nothing. (At this early date, the Christian communities were often quite small, perhaps no more than thirty people, and they were not yet worshiping in church buildings but in private homes.) The whole community, in whose presence the letter is to be read, is greeted with a blessing which may have been a liturgical formula, since it appears so frequently in Paul's writings with exactly the same wording (Phil 1:2). The remainder of the letter, with only a couple of exceptions, is addressed to Philemon alone. This is a brilliant ploy on Paul's part, for by writing to Philemon via the community, Paul has made it difficult for Philemon to turn down his request without public embarrassment to Philemon. Paul has also given the community a chance to plead his cause should Philemon hesitate to fulfill Paul's request.

THANKSGIVING AND PRAYER

Phlm 4-7

4-5 Thanks to God for Philemon's example. After Paul tells Philemon that he is continually remembered in his prayers, he mentions why Philemon is the object of thanksgiving to God: Paul has heard of Philemon's love and faith for the Lord and his fellow Christians. Thus by letting Philemon know that he considers him to be a model Christian, Paul has set the stage for this good Christian person to listen to the request of an apostle, and this becomes obvious when he reveals the contents of his prayers on Philemon's behalf.

6-7 Paul's prayer for Philemon. Paul prays that Philemon's sharing of faith will be effective when it is accompanied by the knowledge of the good which Paul and Timothy have for Christ's sake. Before Paul tells Philemon how to share his faith more completely, he expresses his joy and comfort in the way Philemon is willing to be of service to his fellow Christians. The path has now been paved for Paul to make his request.

THE APOSTOLIC REQUEST

Phlm 8-21

8-12 Paul appeals for his child out of love. Paul reminds Philemon of his apostolic right to command Philemon to do what he wants, but says that he prefers, instead, to make his request out of love. Although Paul is no doubt sincere in making this claim, he has, in effect, really underscored the impact of his apostolic authority by the mere fact of bringing it up.

As an old man and a prisoner of Christ Jesus (see v. 1), Paul invites Philemon's sympathy, while he makes his request on Onesimus' behalf. Paul speaks of the runaway slave Onesimus as his child, whom he has "fathered" into Christianity. Before Onesimus' conversion to Christianity, Paul notes that the slave was, in fact, useless to Philemon (was he disloyal or slothful or a thief?), but now he is useful both to Philemon and Paul. Paul makes a word play on the literal meaning of Onesimus ("useful"), but in what way Onesimus is useful is explained later. At this point Paul acknowledges his reluctance to send Onesimus back to Philemon, since the relationship between the slave and Paul has become so close that Paul considers Onesimus a part of himself.

13-14 Philemon owes Paul a debt. Paul takes the argument one step further and expresses the desire he has to keep Onesimus to serve him in Philemon's place, especially while he is in prison for the sake of the gospel. Paul implies that Philemon owes him something, but he is not asking for Onesimus' freedom from slavery, rather, suggesting that Philemon may possibly place his slave at Paul's disposal. Paul would not take it upon himself to do this without first asking Philemon; otherwise he might appear to be forcing Philemon to do "the good" when Paul prefers that Philemon would make that decision of his own free will. For Philemon not to do what Paul wants, however, would be the opposite of "the good," something not worthy of a model Christian.

15-17 Paul's specific request. Paul suggests that Onesimus' separation from Philemon for a time may have taken place so that Philemon will receive him back forever, not merely as the slave he used to be (and still is) but also as a beloved fellow Christian, a state much more important. In this capacity Onesimus is especially beloved by Paul, but Philemon is twice blessed because he will be receiving Onesimus back both in the flesh as his slave and also as a brother in Christ.

The letter reaches its climax with a deceptively simple request that Philemon receive Onesimus back, as if the slave were Paul himself. But Paul is once again subtly persuasive, since he assumes that this will follow naturally, if indeed Paul and Philemon are partners, something Philemon would be loath to deny. Paul is not asking for Onesimus' freedom from slavery, but that Philemon accept this slave back without meting out the harsh punishment or penalties usually imposed on runaway slaves.

18-21 Philemon asked to be useful. Paul offers to correct any wrongs or pay any bills which Onesimus may have been responsible for, and his concern is highlighted by the fact that he has written this letter himself and repeats his offer to pay any damages. This is a generous offer, in Paul's view, since Philemon himself owes his very Christian existence to Paul. Therefore, Paul feels justified in asking that Philemon now be of some profit, that is, "useful" (another reference to the meaning of Onesimus) to him and do this favor in the Lord. In this way Paul's anxious heart can be put to rest in Christ.

All suspicions that Paul is hardly giving Philemon a free choice in this matter are proven correct when Paul says that he has written to Philemon trusting in his compliance (literally "obedience") and in his willingness to do even more than Paul says. Paul has let his apostolic authority weigh heavily on Philemon, but not for mere manipulation. He has sought to show Philemon the necessity of responding in a Christian manner to a matter having serious social consequences. How one receives a brother or sister in Christ cannot be a matter of indifference, but requires action that may go beyond secular conventions and laws, because life "in Christ" is of a new order. This is the abiding message of Philemon for every generation of Christians.

CONCLUSION

Phlm 22-25

22-24 Announcement and greetings. Having finished his major reason for writing, Paul asks Philemon to prepare a room for him and then announces to the whole community that he hopes that through their prayers he will be able to come to them, evidently expecting his prison term to come to an end soon.

Greetings are sent to Philemon from Epaphras, who is a prisoner with Paul, as well as from other fellow workers: Mark, Aristarchos, Demas, and Luke. This is the only time Paul himself names these persons, though later traditions mention all of them again, as in Col 4:10-14, or some of them, as within scattered references in Acts.

25 Blessing. The letter concludes with the same liturgical blessing upon the entire congregation that we find in Phil 4:23.

2 THESSALONIANS

Ivan Havener, O.S.B.

INTRODUCTION

Second Thessalonians is a pastoral letter which addresses a number of problems that have arisen in a Christian community jolted by the claim that the "day of the Lord" has come upon them. Some in this community have reacted in terror, quit work, and are making a general nuisance of themselves to others within the community as they await the full effect of the Lord's coming.

The author seeks first of all to comfort the agitated and disturbed with the message that the day of the Lord is not yet here, for certain events have to take place yet before that happens. Meanwhile, the community is to continue going about its everyday existence as usual, calmly exercising its Christian responsibilities and earning its own keep. The author is concerned that the faith itself, as well as individual members of the community, may come into disrepute and disbelief if fanatical doomsday preachers are listened to. Therefore, the author suggests an appropriate sanction against those who are unwilling to follow this teaching.

Who is this author? What is the community that is being addressed? Which circumstances have led to the claims that the author attacks? In one sense we do not know the answers to any of these questions, but an explanation for this state of affairs is necessary because of the claims of the letter itself.

The author claims to be Paul and is writing to the Thessalonians, but there are a number of indications in the letter which suggest that the author of 2 Thessalonians is actually writing under Paul's name but is not Paul and that the letter has nothing to do at all with the Christian community at Thessalonica but to an unknown community or communities which know about Paul and respect his place in the early church. In other words, the author wants Paul to speak authoritatively on the crisis that the author's community is currently facing, so he or she writes fictively as the Apostle to the Thessalonians. The author may have chosen "the Thessalonians" because in 1 Thessalonians the coming of the Lord was also an important issue. Also the author is very familiar with 1 Thessalonians, frequently borrowing phrases, terms, and ideas from that letter but ingeniously using them in a new context. Therefore, while the vocabulary of 2 Thessalonians is heavily Pauline, the author often uses that vocabulary in a non-Pauline manner both with regard to the combination of ideas and sentence structure.

A comparison of the arrangement of the two Thessalonian letters reveals some similarities that cannot be overlooked. While the parts of 2 Thessalonians are more distinctly separate units than their counterparts in 1 Thessalonians, there is a clear literary dependence of 2 Thessalonians on the first letter (minus the later addition of 1 Thess 2:13-16, which 2 Thessalonians shows no clear signs of knowing):

1 Thessalonians

Introduction and Greeting 1:1

Thanksgiving Section 1:2–3:13
a. Thanksgiving and Prayer
   1:2-4

b. Past and Present Mission
   (main issue) 1:5–3:8

c. Thanksgiving and Prayer
   3:9-13

Instructions 4:1–5:22

Conclusion 5:23-28
   Prayer 5:23-24
   Admonitions and Greetings
   5:25-27
   Blessing 5:28

2 Thessalonians

Introduction and Greeting 1:1-2

⌈Thanksgiving 1:3-4   Thanksgiving
| Comment 1:5-10   Section I
⌊Prayer 1:11-12   1:3-12

Lord's Coming
   (main issue) 2:1-12

⌈Thanksgiving 2:13-14   Thanksgiving
| Comment (admonition) 2:15 Section II
⌊Prayer 2:16-17   2:13-17

Instructions 3:1-16
   Admonition 3:1-4
   Prayer 3:5
   Admonition 3:6-15
   Prayer 3:16

Conclusion 3:17-18

Greetings 3:17

Blessing 3:18

While the precise situation which gave rise to the claim that the day of the Lord has come upon the author's community cannot be found in the letter, the references to "persecutions and the afflictions" (2 Thess 1:4) may indicate that a major pogrom was underway within the Roman Empire. The intensity of such persecutions as well as their widespread nature may have been interpreted by some Christians as a sure sign that the world was coming to an end and that judgment day had fallen upon them. The dating of the letter could fall anywhere then between A.D. 70 (the fall of Jerusalem) and the early years of the second century. Two widespread persecutions took place in this period: A.D. 81–96 under Domitian and A.D. 98–117 under Trajan. Since the effectiveness of a writing written under Paul's name would be questionable in areas where Paul's genuine letters were well known, the author's community is probably to be found in Asia Minor instead of Macedonia or Achaia and almost certainly not in Thessalonica itself.

Although 2 Thessalonians hardly stands in the forefront of our theological interests today, its message (despite the strange apocalyptic imagery) has a peculiarly contemporary cast in the light of numerous modern doomsday preachers. No doubt, dire predictions of the end time will be stated even more frequently and stridently as the end of the twentieth century approaches. Thus 2 Thessalonians may speak even more directly to us in the near future, as it spoke to those living near the end of the first century.

COMMENTARY

INTRODUCTION AND GREETING

2 Thess 1:1-2

The naming of the senders and recipients of this letter is given in almost exactly the same wording as 1 Thess 1:1, the only difference being "God *our* Father" instead of "God the Father." This is already a sign that the author of 2 Thessalonians is copying from 1 Thessalonians, since Paul does not elsewhere use such fixed wording in his introductions. Unlike the greeting of 1 Thess 1:1, however, the greeting of 2 Thess 1:2 is not abbreviated, but it presents the full liturgical blessing which Paul often does repeat with exactly the same wording (Phil 1:2; 1 Cor 1:3; Phlm 3). This indicates that the author of this letter is familiar with Paul's writings beyond 1 Thessalonians, especially (but perhaps only) with 1 Corinthians.

THANKSGIVING AND PRAYER

2 Thess 1:3-12

1:3-4 Thanksgiving. The thanksgiving is introduced with a somewhat impersonal tone, "We ought to thank," suggesting that the author is following a literary rule, already a traditional convention, rather than Paul's more spontaneous and personal thanksgivings (see 2 Thess 2:13 where a second thanksgiving is introduced in a similar manner). The author, writing fictively in Paul's name, gives thanks to God unceasingly for the Thessalonians (1 Thess 1:2) because they are growing in faith (1 Thess 1:3) and their love for one another is increasing (1 Thess 1:3; 3:12; 4:9-10), but the author omits any specific mention of "hope" (1 Thess 1:3). This faith and love of the Thessalonians is reason for Paul and his companions to boast of them—not before the Lord Jesus Christ at his coming as in 1 Thess 2:19-20—but "in the churches of God" (1 Thess 2:14; 1 Cor 11:16, 22), so exemplary is their steadfastness (1 Thess 1:3) and their faith during persecutions and afflictions (1 Thess 1:6-8; 3:3-5).

1:5-10 Judgment and the Lord's coming. Sandwiched between the thanksgiving and prayer is a short excursus on judgment and the Lord's coming, which are really the key concerns of the author. What the Thessalonians have had to endure at the hands of others points to God's just judgment in the future when the wrongs done to them will be rectified; they suffer in order to worthily share in God's reign (Phil 1:28-29; Acts 14:22; 1 Thess 2:12). Justice seems to require also that their persecutors be paid back by God in such a way that these persecutors will become the persecuted. The relief that is promised to all believers is seen as a future event; it will be provided by God first at the revelation of the Lord Jesus from heaven together with his mighty angels (1 Thess 1:10; 3:13; 4:16). This revelation of the Lord Jesus (1 Cor 1:7) which is the same as his "coming" or "presence" (2 Thess 2:1, 8) is described in 2 Thessalonians not only in terms of what will happen to believers, the primary concern in 1 Thess 4:13-18, but also what will happen to those who do not acknowledge God (1 Thess 4:5) nor listen to the gospel of the Lord Jesus. 1 Thess 1:10 mentioned this latter aspect only briefly as God's wrath, but in 2 Thessalonians we receive a more detailed account, steeped once again in apocalyptic imagery. Those who have rejected God and God's message will suffer the punishment of eternal ruin (not annihilation!), separated from the Lord's presence and the glory of his power, when he comes to judge in flaming fire (1 Cor 3:13, 15). At the same time, that day will include the glorification of the Lord among his holy ones and adoration by all who, like the Thessalonians, have believed in the message of Paul and his companions. The "holy ones" and "all who have believed" may mean the same group, or the "holy ones" may refer to the angels who have accompanied the Lord (2 Thess 1:7; see comment on 2 Thess 3:13), so that we have here a scene of cosmic worship (Phil 2:10-11) on the day of the Lord.

1:11-12 Prayer. The single Greek sentence which began with verse 3 is now concluded with a prayer that borrows a number of words and ideas from the long thanksgiving section of 1 Thessalonians but in the same impersonal tone as in 2 Thess 1:3 (see the same phenomenon in the prayers of 2:16-17; 3:16). The author, writing as Paul and his companions, says that they "always pray for you" (1 Thess

1:2), that the Thessalonians be made worthy of God's call (1 Thess 2:12), and that with God's power (1 Thess 1:5) they fulfill every good purpose (Phil 1:15) and effort of faith (1 Thess 1:3), that is, that they live upright lives. The result of such Christian living is, first, the present glorification (in contrast to the future glorification spoken of in v. 10) of "the name of our Lord Jesus" (Phil 2:9-11; cf. Rom 15:6) and, second, their glorification by him (Rom 8:17) according to the grace of God (1 Cor 9:13-14) and of the Lord Jesus Christ. God's initiative is preserved throughout this prayer, for it is God who empowers believers to conduct their lives according to God's will.

THE COMING OF THE LORD JESUS CHRIST

2 Thess 2:1-17

2:1-2 Admonition to remain calm. The author returns to the topic of the Lord's coming, also described here as the assembling of believers together with him (1 Thess 4:17), in regard to a different concern. The author begs (the same term as in 1 Thess 5:12) the Thessalonians not to be easily shaken in their understanding of that coming nor to be intimidated by a claim that the day of the Lord has even now come upon them, a claim that they may have heard attributed to the Spirit, or to a saying (1 Thess 4:15 refers to a saying of the Lord and 1 Thess 4:18 refers to sayings [NAB: "words"] taught by the Apostle), or to a letter supposedly from Paul and his companions. Prophecies said to be uttered under the influence of the Spirit, sayings ascribed to the Lord or to other important figures, and letter forgeries were common problems to early Christians; they had to try as best as they could to determine what was authentic and accurate information. The development of the New Testament itself was, in part, an attempt to fulfill this need for a rule, a canon, by which the reliability of claims could be measured. There is some irony in the mentioning of forgeries, since the author of 2 Thessalonians claims to write as Paul himself. While the author may believe himself or herself to be doing this honestly, others who say things differently than the author does may also believe themselves to be mouthpieces for the Apostle in a new age. Therefore, the problem of deciding who was right was a real one for these early Christians.

2:3-4 Signs of the Lord's coming. The author warns the community not to be taken in by the claim that the day of the Lord is already taking place; the author seeks to allay their terror at the thought of it by pointing out that certain events must occur before the Lord comes. To do this, apocalyptic traditions that were probably first formulated around 167 B.C.E. when the Syrian ruler Antiochus IV Epiphanes imposed Greek culture and customs on the Jews and rededicated the Jewish temple in Jerusalem to Zeus Olympius are drawn upon. Reacting violently to this blasphemy and the apostasy of some of their fellow Jews (2 Macc 5:8), the Maccabean revolt broke out, in which the Jews gained control of Palestine and saved the integrity of their religion. (The story is related in rich apocalyptic language in the Book of Daniel.) Before that "time of salvation," terrible events took place, so now before the day of the Lord, there will first be a mass apostasy. It is not clear whether the author is referring specifically to Christian apostasy in a time of persecution (see 1:4) or just to wretched circumstances in general, that are interpreted as rebellion against God. A massive Christian apostasy hardly fits the time of Paul's ministry, since there were only a few Christians then. It does fit, however, a later period when widespread persecution was taking place and when Christians were rapidly growing in numbers. Second, "the lawless one" will be revealed before that day. This mysterious figure is also described as "the one doomed to perdition" and as an "opponent" who is self-exalted above other false gods, seating itself in God's temple and proclaiming itself to be a god. This figure is the embodiment of evil but is a human and not a demon or Satan (see v. 9). Since mention of the temple belongs to the tradition which is cited, it cannot be used as evidence that the temple was still standing in Jerusalem at the time 2 Thessalonians was written.

2:5-7 Author's commentary. At this point the author interrupts his telling of the apocalyptic tradition about the lawless one to address the community directly, using the first person singular (also in 3:17). The author reminds them that they were told (oral tradition) about these things when the author was still with them, but this still does not resolve the conflict between this information and what Paul says in 1 Thess 5:1-12, where he repeats what he had told them before, namely, that no one knows when the day of the Lord will come and that the Lord will come like a thief in the night. Having reminded the community of the past message given to them, the author of 2 Thessalonians adds what they also have learned since then: they know what is preventing the appearance of the lawless one. Unfortunately, the author does not identify this positive power for us, though it provides a helpful function of restraining the lawless one until the proper time. Perhaps the delay of the Lord's coming itself, as part of God's plan, is meant, so that ultimately it is God who is restraining the lawless one. It is God who can remove the delay which restrains this evil character. Even though the lawless one is currently restrained, nonetheless, the mystery of lawlessness is at work, a mystery which is revealed completely only at the release of the lawless one. With the assurance that God is still in control, however, the author seeks to calm the fears of the readers or audience.

2:8-10a The lawless one overcome. Returning to the apocalyptic tradition of verses 3-4, the author states again that the lawless one will be revealed, but only after the restraining power is removed. The author comforts the community by announcing that this evil revelation will be countered by the presence of the Lord Jesus, who at his manifestation will utterly destroy the lawless one "with the breath of his mouth" (Isa 11:4b). The lawless one will appear as a tool of Satan, having power to do signs and wonders which lead to deception and to exercise every manner of wicked seduction.

2:10b-12 Condemnation of those who reject the truth. Those who give in to the seduction of the lawless one are destined to ruin because they have not accepted the love of truth, which is the way of salvation. This rejection does not first occur when the lawless one appears but in the present when the mystery of lawlessness is at work (v. 7). Since they have chosen the way of falsehood instead of truth, God sends a deluding influence to lead them further into falsehood, the final result being condemnation on the day of the Lord. This harsh statement concerning God's activity preserves the integrity of God's sovereignty as also in Rom 1:24, 26, 28.

2:13-14 Thanksgiving for those chosen for salvation. Having discussed the condemnatory side of the Lord's coming, the author turns attention to the saving side of that event. Using almost the same wording as in 1:3, the author gives thanks a second time, even as Paul does in 1 Thess 3:9. This thanksgiving draws heavily upon Pauline language scattered throughout 1 Thessalonians; therefore, the author addresses the "brothers loved by the Lord" ("brothers loved by God" in 1 Thess 1:4) in giving thanks to God, because God chose them as the first fruits for salvation through sanctification by the Spirit (1 Thess 3:2, 4, 7) and belief in truth (see vv. 10-11). Then the author paraphrases what Paul said in 1 Thess 5:9, that God has called them "through our gospel" (Paul says "through our Lord Jesus Christ") unto the possession of the glory of our Lord Jesus Christ (Paul says "to gain salvation").

While at first glance it might look like God predestines some to destruction (2:11-12) and others to glory (2:13-14), it is clear from 2:10 that the destiny to ruin is not God's will but the choice of those who did not believe in God's truth when it was offered to them. God wills the salvation of all people, but does not force anyone to accept it.

2:15-17 Concluding admonition and prayer. In language reminiscent of 1 Cor 11:2, 23; 15:1-3, the author exhorts the readers or audience to stand firm (1 Thess 3:8) and to hold fast to the traditions they were taught by word of mouth or by letter (see 2:2). These traditions are not necessarily different in one form or the other, nor is the intention of the author to present a two-source theory of revelation.

This portion of the letter concludes with a prayer patterned after 1 Thess 3:11-13. The author prays that both the Lord Jesus Christ and God the Father will encourage and strengthen their hearts (1 Thess 3:13) for every good deed and word. While this prayer begins structurally in a manner very similar to that in 1 Thess 3:11-13, the naming of Jesus and God the Father are reversed. God is described also as the one "who has loved us" (1 Thess 1:4) and "given us everlasting encouragement" ("who [also] gives his holy Spirit" in 1 Thess 4:8) and good hope through grace.

With this prayer the major concern of the author is brought to a conclusion. The day of the Lord is not yet breaking in upon the community, and the author has consoled them in their time of persecution that other events must first take place and that as long as they love and believe in the truth, they need not fear the events that will occur on that day.

INSTRUCTIONS

2 Thess 3:1-15

3:1-5 Admonition to prayer. The set of instructions which makes up the last major section of the letter begins with a request for prayers which repeats the wording of 1 Thess 5:25 but, in this case, names specific petitions. The first petition asks for the success of the mission preaching of Paul and his companions, that the word of the Lord may be effective and glorified by others, even as it has been so received by the Thessalonians (1 Thess 1:8-9). The "word of the Lord" presents the Lord himself who is effective and, therefore, he is glorified by those who willingly receive him; a similar idea was expressed in 1:12, where a prayer is made that the "name of our Lord Jesus" might be glorified, that is, that the Lord himself be glorified. The second petition asks that the Apostle and his companions be saved from wicked and evil opponents because faith does not belong to everyone. Since these petitions are directed fictively to the Thessalonians, they are not addressed to a concrete situation and thus they speak in imprecise and general terms. (Who are these opponents? What are they doing?) Though some people are without faith, the Lord is faithful nonetheless, and the author assures the readers or audience that the Lord will strengthen them (1 Thess 3:2, 13) and protect them from the evil one. The "evil one" is probably Satan (2:9), but in this context could also refer to the lawless one who is being restrained (2:6-7). "Confident of you in the Lord"—terminology frequently found in Paul (Phil 1:14; 2:24; Rom 14:14; Gal 5:10) but not in 1 Thessalonians—the author is assured of the community's obedience in continuing to do what is asked of them (Phlm 21; 1 Thess 4:11), and he prays now for them that the Lord will direct their hearts (in 1 Thess 3:11 the Lord directs "our way") into God's love (1 Thess

3:12-13; Rom 5:5; 8:39) and into Christ's endurance (1 Thess 1:3 speaks of "endurance in hope").

3:6-16 Admonitions to proper conduct while waiting for the Lord. The author commands (1 Thess 4:11) the community to avoid a fellow Christian who goes astray and departs from the apostolic traditions that have been given to them (1 Cor 5:9-13). This matter is taken up again in verses 14-15 after the author has shown what the proper conduct should be based on Paul's example and Paul's rule in this regard and after the author has admonished the readers or audience to do what is right.

The author underscores the community's knowledge of what it takes to be imitators of Paul and his companions (1 Thess 1:6; 4:1) and repeats several facts from 1 Thessalonians which are worthy of imitation: Paul and his fellow workers lived orderly lives among them (1 Thess 2:10), worked for their own keep, so as not to be a burden (1 Thess 2:9). They did not exercise their apostolic rights (1 Thess 2:7) because they were more interested in providing a good example to be imitated. (Specific commands to imitate Paul, however, are found, for instance in 1 Cor 4:16; 11:1 but not in 1 Thessalonians.)

This example of the orderly, hard worker is based not only on Paul's own activity but also on a rule he laid down "in the Lord Jesus" (1 Thess 4:1). According to this rule, which has become the basis for the so-called work ethic, no one should eat who has not worked. This rule is not stated in 1 Thessalonians, though Paul encouraged the Thessalonians to work with their hands and thereby give an example to outsiders and at the same time provide themselves with their own material necessities (1 Thess 4:11-12). In 2 Thessalonians the author speaks of some different reasons for working. If the Thessalonians are working quietly, they are keeping themselves busy in a useful way. They are avoiding rowdy behavior and keeping themselves from being a nuisance to others. The author seems to be counteracting those who were so upset at hearing of the Lord's coming: they stopped working and became busybodies, running about in their frenzy and also sponging off others for their food.

In view of these "judgment jitters," the author feels compelled to state that proper conduct continues on and is not to be set aside; those who do so are to be considered wayward fellow Christians (v. 6) and are to be marked out for separation from the community. This exclusion is meant to make the wayward ashamed of their faulty behavior, but this punishment is to be carried out in the consciousness that fellow Christians are being dealt with rather than enemies (1 Cor 5:9-13; 2 Cor 2:5-8; Rom 16:17-18).

Like the sets of instructions preceding it (2:15-17 and 3:1-5), this set also concludes with a prayer. The author asks that "the Lord of peace" (1 Thess 5:23 has "the God of peace") bestow peace on the community in *every* way through *every* time and that the Lord be with *each* of them.

GREETING AND FINAL BLESSING

2 Thess 3:17-18

While Paul does write his own greeting in some letters (Phlm 19; Gal 6:11; 1 Cor 16:21), he does not say that he does so in Romans, 2 Corinthians, Philippians, or 1 Thessalonians. Therefore, it is an exaggeration by the author of 2 Thessalonians to claim that Paul does so in "*every* letter" he writes. This raises the suspicion that the author "protesteth too much" about the authenticity of this letter (2 Thess 2:2) in the attempt to secure apostolicity for this message.

The concluding blessing is the same liturgical formula that is found in 1 Thess 5:28, except that the word "all" (that is, "*every* one of") has been added to 2 Thessalonians. The author has consciously used the word "every/each/all" several times in verses 16-18 for emphasis and for rhetorical effect as the letter comes to a close.

COLOSSIANS

Ivan Havener, O.S.B.

INTRODUCTION

In many ways the Letter to the Colossians is a mysterious document. We do not know precisely who the author is, nor do we have a clear picture of the doctrines of the false teachers that the author is arguing against, nor do we even know if the letter is actually written to the Christians living in Colossae, a small town in the southwestern area of modern Turkey near the neighboring towns of Laodicea and Hierapolis. Despite these uncertainties, however, the overall theological message of the letter stands out clearly enough, with its striking presentation of Jesus as the cosmic Christ and what it means for us as Christians to be free to serve him alone.

While the author claims to be Paul (1:1; 4:18), he or she is in reality someone unknown to us but clearly standing within the Pauline tradition. The author is familiar with a number of Paul's writings, especially Philemon, and with some important Pauline concepts, such as the body of Christ (3:15), the formula "in Christ" (1:2, 4, 28), dying with Christ in baptism (2:12), the triad of faith, hope, and love (1:4-5). But how the author makes use of these concepts and terms often moves in a new direction and away from Paul's understanding. In this respect the author of Colossians is a more theologically creative disciple of Paul than is the author of 2 Thessalonians, who ingeniously reuses Pauline terminology, but does not provide any significant theological developments beyond Paul.

That Paul is not the author of Colossians is supported also by the style of the letter. How sentences are formulated and the use of rhetorical devices and words, like conjunctions and prepositions, clearly breaks with Paul's style, despite the presence of many Pauline phrases and words and allowing for incorporation of blocks of traditional liturgical material.

But even more telling is the fact that Colossians simply does not fit into what we know of the biography of the Apostle. The letter purports to be written in the same situation as Philemon—Paul is imprisoned, probably at Ephesus, and sends greetings from the same large number of people. This means that Paul would have written Colossians some time before his Letter to the Romans, creating the difficulty that Romans often betrays less development than Colossians with regard to some key concepts such as "body of Christ," the relation of baptism to resurrection, and emphasis on Christ's future coming.

Because Colossians is probably not written by Paul, the question arises whether the letter is meant to specifically address the Christian community in Colossae or whether the author indirectly addresses his or her own community, which is completely unknown to us, through the fiction of a letter supposedly sent to the Colossians. This latter possibility seems more likely because the omission of Philemon's name in the greetings, when he is clearly a key figure in the Colossian congregation (Phlm 2), is unthinkable if the author is truly writing to that community. If the author is only writing fictively, then specific names are not so important. Since the author is familiar with almost all of Paul's letters, including Romans, it is clear that Paul's letters have already been collected together, a fact attested also in the last of the New Testament documents to have been written (2 Pet 3:15-16). Allowing for some time to have elapsed while these letters were being gathered together, it is probable that Colossians was written after the Apostle's death, which reduces the possibility that it was actually written to the Colossians.

When was Colossians written? There is a broad range of possibility, for if the author is dependent upon Paul's letters, there is no reason at all to assume that the author must be temporally close to the historical Paul. Therefore, the letter was written somewhere between A.D. 63 and 90.

We are never directly told who the author's opponents are; yet, most of the author's theological thought is developed in argumentation against them. Terminology dealing with "wisdom" and "knowledge" plays a significant part in the presentation. While this kind of language was common to Jewish literature of the time, it was part of Gentile modes of thought as well. The author tries to show against the rivals, who apparently have combined elements from Judaism, Christianity, and paganism, that wisdom and knowledge can only be interpreted properly when they refer to Christ. His unique position as the agent and Lord of creation, the conqueror of the elements and cosmic powers, is to be acknowledged. Through him alone comes redemption, the forgiveness of sins. Christians, as members of his body, the church, are freed by their baptism from any sort of submission to regulations and ascetical acts which are meant to serve these inferior elements and powers. Anyone who tries to impose such restraints on the Christian's freedom to serve Christ alone must not be listened to; such teaching falls outside the apostolic tradition. Therefore, the author by writing in Paul's name underscores for the author's own community the apostolic teaching—what Paul would say if he were addressing the same situation himself.

This freedom attained by Christ must, in turn, be exercised in his service. Freedom in Christ brings with it certain responsibilities. Therefore, the letter includes several instructions on what to avoid or what to strive for and specific instructions for Christian households. The whole manner in which Christian life is lived is characterized by the author as "giving thanks."

COMMENTARY

INTRODUCTION

Col 1:1-2

The senders of this letter and the words that describe them are found with exactly the same order and wording in 2 Cor 1:1a (see similarly 1 Cor 1:1). Paul is singled out for special honor as an "apostle," whereas Timothy is given a secondary position with his designation as "our brother." This distinction between Paul and Timothy was not so marked in 1 Thessalonians, where titles were avoided in the introduction (1 Thess 1:1) and where Timothy is included, later, among the apostles (1 Thess 2:7). As Paul's understanding of the nature of his apostleship deepened, he seems to be responsible himself for this distinction. The author of Colossians, writing in Paul's name, preserves this heightened understanding of Paul's apostleship. Paul is the "one who is sent" by Christ Jesus in fulfillment of God's will. As such, he plays a leading role in the early Christian mission to the Gentiles.

The letter is addressed to Christians in the town of Colossae. They are described as "the holy ones" (typical Pauline expression) and "faithful brothers [not found elsewhere in Paul] in Christ." The "in Christ" phrase is an important Pauline concept, used here to reflect the grounding of the community's life in the saving activity of Christ. The greeting appears in an abbreviated form, with the concluding words "and the Lord Jesus Christ" being omitted. This expression has been left out due to the mention of "Christ Jesus" and "in Christ" in the preceding verses; therefore, the present text does not reflect an earlier Jewish or Jewish-Christian formula to which mention of Jesus Christ was later added on.

THANKSGIVING AND PRAYER

Col 1:3-20

1:3-8 Giving thanks. Despite some unusual features, like the complicated Greek style, this thanksgiving section begins in a typical Pauline fashion. The author gives thanks (in plural, as in 1 Thess 1:2) to God who is described as "the Father of our Lord Jesus Christ" (2 Cor 1:3; Rom 15:6). The prayer on behalf of the community and the giving of thanks to God are simultaneous actions, and the author is engaged in this unceasing practice, having heard of two things—their faith in Christ Jesus and their love for all the holy ones (Phlm 4-5). The reason for their faith and love is the hope stored up for them in heaven. In this way the Pauline triad of faith, hope, and love, first stated in 1 Thess 1:3; 5:8, again comes to expression, but hope is the guiding principle in Colossians, whereas love is singled out in 1 Cor 13:13, and the relationship of faith to hope is different than in Rom 5:1-5. This hope was heard through the preaching of the gospel, which is the word of truth that had come to them. Even as that gospel has borne fruit and grown among them (see the parable of the mustard seed, Mark 4:30-32) from the day they first heard it and came to know God's grace in truth, so also this same phenomenon has been taking place in the whole world—something of an exaggeration, even for this post-Paul author, but a hyperbole which expresses the exuberance of the author's own hope. The Colossians learned this message from a certain Epaphras, who is called "our beloved fellow slave," a faithful minister of Christ on their behalf. He—not Paul—has first preached the gospel to this community, but his reporting of the results back to Paul indicates that his ministry has Pauline approval, that he is subservient to the Apostle and has probably been given the commission to preach as Paul's representative. Through this legitimation of his ministry by Paul, Epaphras comes to stand within a line of apostolic succession, a matter of increasing concern toward the end of the first century and throughout the second. The language of "hearing," "learning," "coming to know" suggests a community familiar with the terminology of a nascent Gnosticism, whose teachers are combatted in chapter 2 through "apostolic" teaching.

1:9-14 Prayer. This summary of the content of the author's prayer concludes the thanksgiving section of the letter. It consists of another very long, complicated Greek sentence, which begins with verse 9 and continues on through verse 20. Due to the special nature of the material in verses 15-20, however, we will treat that part separately.

In response to Epaphras' report, Paul continues to pray and intercede for the community (see v. 3). He takes up language familiar to this community, giving the terms an apostolic interpretation and thereby also countering some who interpret them differently. He prays that the Colossians "be filled" with "knowledge" of God's will in "all spiritual wisdom" and "understanding." The real meaning of these terms becomes obvious by the community members' manner of life, when they lead a life worthy of the Lord completely pleasing to him, shown by "every" good work, bearing fruit and growing in "knowledge" of God (see v. 6), empowered by "every" power according to the strength of his glory unto "all" endurance and patience with joy. By emphasizing the "all/every," the author makes clear what a total commitment Christianity demands of its members and what a complete "knowledge" entails.

All of this includes giving thanks to the Father, because it is God and not themselves who empowers the community to share in the inheritance of the holy ones in light (1 Thess 5:5). Then the author continues to speak of God's saving activity in hymnic language; the shift from "you" in verse 12 to "us" in verses 13-14 also indicates that traditional liturgical material is being employed here. Because the Father has delivered us from the power of darkness, it is clear that salvation is already present; God has already brought us into the kingdom of God's beloved Son. (The "beloved Son" phrase occurs in the accounts of Jesus' baptism and transfiguration, as well as in the parable of the wicked tenants; see Mark 1:11; 9:7; 12:6.) Paul himself, drawing upon traditional apocalyptic, also speaks of the kingdom of the Son, but this contrasts with the usage in Colossians, where the kingdom is present and where no emphasis is placed on the future. By the saving action of God's Son, we already have redemption, which is described here as "the forgiveness of sins."

1:15-20 The Christ hymn. At this point in the discussion of Christ's role in God's plan of salvation, the author adds a whole block of hymnic material concerning Christ. Because the style of this material is different from that in verses 13-14, it is a hymn which the author takes up and quotes more fully, probably adding some of the author's own comments and interpretations as he or she does

so. Like the Christ hymn of Phil 2:6-11, this hymn is one of the most important theological statements about the person of Christ in the New Testament.

Christ is praised as the icon or image of the invisible God, that is, he manifests God's presence in his person. He is called the first-born of all creation because everything else was created through his mediation. Therefore, he existed before all creation and is preeminent among all creatures. The author of Colossians adds some phrases to show what the full scope of creation is. The author begins with the antitheses—heaven and earth, visible and invisible—and continues with synonyms for power and might, especially with regard to spiritual beings—thrones or dominions, principalities or powers. All of this was not only created in him and through him but also for him. (This kind of terminology, borrowed indirectly from Stoicism, appears in other liturgical formulations: see Rom 11:36; Eph 4:6; 1 Cor 8:6.) Everything is subject to him, and it is through his continuing creative power that creation itself continues on. Nothing is left to chance, all is in Christ's control.

That Christ is also head of his body, the church, is a development of the body of Christ concept which goes beyond Paul's notion, for Paul himself never distinguishes between head and body in this regard. The mention of the church here, without elaboration and without close connection with what precedes and succeeds it, suggests that the author has added it to the hymnic material because the author wants to discuss the matter later (see 2:9-19). The author's understanding of "church" here, as in 1:24, is a universal entity, whereas for Paul "church" usually refers to the local community. ("Church" in 4:14-16 means "local community.") In the original hymn, "head" probably referred to Christ's role as leader of the universe.

The second major portion of this hymnic material speaks of Christ as the beginning—he is the starting point of redemption. He is the first to experience the resurrection life and is, therefore, the first-born from among the dead. Once again he is preeminent in "all things" even as "all the fullness" of God's presence was pleased to dwell in him, to reconcile "all things" through him and for him. By the frequent use of the word "all," the cosmic dimensions of Christ's power and effect are emphasized. The reconciliation which he brings about is the peace-making accomplished by the shedding of his blood on the cross, and this, too, has cosmic proportions, for this reconciliation applies to everything, whether on earth or in heaven.

APOSTOLIC MINISTRY TO THE CHURCH

Col 1:21–2:3

1:21-23 Gospel of the Apostle. The author underscores the significance of the Christ hymn by reminding the community of their own pre-Christian, pagan past. They were once alienated from Christ and were hostile in attitude, reflected by their evil works. But this former existence has given way now to a new one through Christ's action in reconciling them by his death "in his fleshly body" (literally "in the body of his flesh"). This last phrase is peculiar to Colossians (see 2:11), not being found elsewhere in Pauline literature. "Body" is a broader term than "flesh," which in this case means the physical, mortal flesh; therefore, the church can be described as his body (v. 24). The purpose and effect of Christ's reconciliation is to present the community's members to God holy, without reproach and blameless (1 Thess 3:13), but the future concern with judgment so apparent in 1 Thessalonians has almost completely receded into the background in Colossians. Instead, stress is laid on the present state of holiness and blamelessness in view of Christ's past action of reconciling and on the preservation of this new state. Therefore, the community is admonished to hold fast to "the faith" (see 1 Cor 15:1-2), which is here almost synonymous with the gospel itself, and to remain unshaken in the gospel hope they heard, when the gospel was preached in all of creation under heaven. This is the gospel whose minister the Apostle is.

1:24-2:3 Apostolic revelation of a mystery. The author of Colossians, speaking as Paul, tells of the nature, content, and perils of the ministry of the gospel. The author presents an idealized picture, vaguely placed within the historical setting of Paul's ministry. Thus, ministers who suffer for the Christian community do so with joy, following Paul's example (Phil 1:18; 2:17). They continue to experience in the flesh the tribulations which

Christ experienced before his resurrection, for these tribulations did not end with his death. Therefore, it can be said his ministers fill up what was missing yet in Christ's suffering. As with Christ, so their suffering is undertaken for the sake of his body, the church (see v. 18a). Ministers of this universal church, steeped in the apostolic tradition—the very reason for writing under Paul's name—are given the commission by God to make known the fullness of God's word. (Paul could hardly say he was commissioned to preach "for you" if, as he claims in 2:1, they have never seen him!) This word of God is called a "mystery" that is revealed now to the holy ones (see v. 2) but formerly was hidden. More specifically, the mystery is Christ himself who through the preaching becomes present among the hearers, the Gentiles, according to God's plan. God wanted to make known the wealth of glory, the hope for glory, which is Christ. This is the same Christ whom the ministers proclaim, and this is done by admonishing and teaching "every" person in "all" wisdom, so that "every" person is made perfect. (Similar terminology is used in vv. 9-11.) Perfection comes only "in Christ," that is, within his body and not apart from him (Phil 3:12-15a). Perfection in Christ is the goal of ministry, which itself is both work and a struggle, but which must be done under the powerful force of Christ's energy that is operative within his ministers.

After this generalized picture of apostolic ministry, the author briefly touches ground historically by referring directly to the Colossians, Laodiceans, and many others who have never met Paul in person (1:7-8). The impersonal tone reappears almost immediately, however, when the author wishes "their" (instead of "your") hearts to be strengthened and that this strengthening be accompanied with their unification in love and entrance into "all" wealth of assured understanding. Ultimately this is knowledge of the mystery of God which is Christ, for it is in him that "all" treasures of wisdom and knowledge are hidden.

THE PROBLEM OF FALSE TEACHING

Col 2:4-23

2:4-8 Remaining faithful to apostolic teaching. Addressing the community directly again, we are told why the author has spoken of the things he has mentioned so far. The author is trying to prevent the community from being deceived by false teaching. At the same time, the author is encouraged by their good order and the steadfastness of their faith in Christ. While the reference to "absent in the flesh . . . am with you in spirit" (1 Cor 5:3) is a return to the literary fiction of the author, it also points to the unity of Christians in the body of Christ, the church.

The author's community is admonished to lead lives in accord with the Lord Jesus Christ whom they have come to know through apostolic teaching. They should have their roots in him, building on the apostolic foundation, growing stronger in faith just as it was taught to them, and abounding in thanksgiving (cf. 1:9-12). They are told to be on their guard against anyone who seeks to captivate them by a false wisdom and empty deceit proceeding from human tradition, a wisdom based on cosmic elements instead of on Christ.

2:9-15 The preeminence of Christ. Returning to some earlier statements, and especially developing some of the themes mentioned in the Christ hymn of 1:15-20, the author once again speaks of Christ's saving role. The author states in even clearer terms than did the hymn, that the "fullness" of deity dwells bodily in Christ (see 1:19); Christ is the head (1:18) of every principality and power (1:16), and all of this has consequences for the author's community. They "share in this fullness" in Christ (1:9) because they are his body. Even as circumcision is a sign of God's covenant with the Jews, so in baptism Gentile Christians have become a covenant people. Baptism for Gentiles is, then, a type of non-physical circumcision in which they are so identified with Christ that they share in his circumcision and the baptism of his death, having been buried with him and also having shared in his resurrection (Rom 6:3-5). Here baptism and the credal formula that "God raised Jesus from the dead" (1 Thess 1:10) are closely associated with one another, even as the present rite of baptism includes a profession of faith in Jesus' resurrection.

In this discussion of baptism, two significant differences between Paul and the author of Colossians become apparent. In Galatians and Romans Paul argues so strenuously against the need for Gentiles to be circumcised

that it is unlikely that he would use the rite of circumcision as a positive parallel to baptism, as the author of Colossians has done. Second, there is a greatly reduced tension between the present and future in Colossians in comparison to Paul. Both authors say that Christians have been buried with Christ, but for Paul the resurrection remains a future reality, even though baptism leads to a new life now (Rom 6:4-5). In Colossians, however, we have already been raised in baptism with Christ, and Paul's future concern is virtually missing here.

God's role in the redemption by Christ is shown in that while the community was still pagan—spiritually dead and uncircumcised—God brought them to life together with Christ, pardoning all their spiritual debts (and letting them share in Christ's circumcision—2:11). God has done away with this bill of debts by nailing it to the redemptive cross together with Christ. In this way the armor of the cosmic principalities and powers was stripped off, and these cosmic forces were publicly ridiculed as they were paraded as captives in the triumphal procession of the victorious Christ. The imagery here is typical of the triumphal return of a military victor publicly humiliating the conquered foes by having them march in the conqueror's victory parade.

2:16-23 Freedom in Christ. As members of the body of Christ, the author's community is not subject to regulations concerning food, drink, festivals, new moons, and sabbaths which are associated with cosmic powers and astrological signs. Therefore, they cannot be condemned for not following such rules, despite the claims of some false teachers. In fact, the community must not let itself be robbed of its freedom in Christ by becoming subject to lesser, angelic powers and worship of them. Those who teach differently than the author are the victims of their own self-deception and pride because they have not maintained contact with Christ who is head of his body, the head from which the whole body with all its parts is given growth by God.

If the community has died together with Christ and has thereby shared in Christ's victory over the cosmic elements, then it makes no sense for them to follow regulations which serve these elements and to live as though Christ has not conquered. That would be giving up the freedom of Christ to become servile to merely human prescriptions and teachings. These rules and doctrines may appear to have the trappings of wisdom, but are really only a show. Pious religiosity, humility, and bodily asceticism are expressions of human pride, when Christ, the source of true wisdom, is not accepted for who he really is.

INSTRUCTIONS

Col 3:1–4:6

3:1-4 General admonition. Since the community has been raised with Christ and freed by baptism from serving cosmic powers, this new-found freedom requires responsibility in its exercise. Therefore, the author provides several admonitions, beginning with one to seek out those matters which pertain to spiritual life, where Christ has the place of honor next to God. Their concern should not be over matters pertaining to a worldly, non-spiritual life because they have died to that in baptism. Now their life is hidden in God together with Christ. When Christ, their life, becomes manifest at judgment, then, they also will be manifested in glory with him. This is the only specific reference in the letter to the hope of Christ's future coming; it is important, however, because we see that this expectation remains part of Christian belief, even though it is no longer given the emphasis it had in Paul's genuine letters.

3:5-11 Negative admonitions. Those matters which pertain to worldly life and which are to be put to death are now specified in a catalog of vices—the same list as in 1 Thess 4:3-8 but with the addition of "idolatry" here. The author has merely taken over this traditional listing without defining the terms; the only comment of the author is that these are sins which provoke God's wrath (1 Thess 1:10). These sins were part of the community's everyday life in their pagan past, but since they are now Christian, these sins are to remain in the past. Instead of immediately countering these vices with a catalog of virtues, the author adds yet another catalog of vices to be avoided. As with the first set, these are sins which were set aside when they became Christian, when they put on a new person who is renewed in knowledge according to the image of the Creator. They have put on Christ, the new Adam. This new existence is not de-pendent upon one's former religious background or ethnic origins or social status, for what is important in each, what is, in fact, everything in each is Christ himself.

3:12-17 Positive admonitions. God's chosen ones are those who are in Christ, holy and beloved, even as he is, and this requires putting on the clothes of virtue. The author cites a catalog of virtues which should be the dress of Christian life. In addition to this, the author names specific admonitions to patience and forgiveness, singling out love as the highest virtue, uniting and perfecting the rest (1 Cor 13:13; 1 Pet 4:8). Peace is the calling of Christians as members of Christ's body, the church. As such, its understanding cannot be limited only to a private spiritual state; it has communal implications, too. Finally, the community is urged to be givers of thanks (3:15b), a theme mentioned again with greater precision in 3:17b. What is mentioned between these verses, however, are ways in which thanksgiving is to be done: letting Christ's word dwell in them richly, teaching with all wisdom according to apostolic understanding, admonishing one another, worshiping and singing to God from the heart in gratitude, doing everything in word and deed in the name of the Lord Jesus. Seen in this light, thanksgiving to God the Father through Christ becomes a whole way of life. Christian life is eucharist, that is, it is thanksgiving.

3:18-4:1 Household duties. Writing at a time when Christian communities were beginning to settle down in the world and Christ's coming was seen as an event in the more distant future than was true for Paul, the author of Colossians wants the community to make a favorable impression on its pagan neighbors so that no unnecessary stumbling blocks stand in the way of the gospel's proclamation. Therefore, the author admonishes the community to follow the conventions of that society with regard to family relationships. In a patriarchal society it was the duty of wives to be obedient to their husbands, so the author admonishes the community to do the same, as their duty in the Lord. In our society, however, where the patriarchal system is breaking down and where other social practices based on Christ's teaching have taken on greater importance, equality in the Lord needs to be more seriously incorporated into the husband–wife relationship; we do better to speak of mutual obedience today, as well as mutual love and mutual avoidance of bitterness. Also, both mother and father should not nag their children, even as children should obey both parents.

Similarly, what is said here about slaves and masters must be interpreted in view of the circumstances of the time in which it was written, for once again the author is speaking to a social setting different from ours. Instead of arguing against the system of slavery, the author encourages slaves to be good slaves and masters to be good masters. At this point in time, the radical social implications of Christ's teaching, which would eventually lead to condemnation of slavery, had not yet been noted and acted upon. Nonetheless, the individual admonitions of how to serve one another—whether those addressed to slaves or to masters—are valid for all Christians also today: mutual justice and fairness, all being slaves of the Lord, reverently serving him as they carry out their various activities.

The teaching concerning reward for the good which is done and punishment for the evil, while found in Paul (1 Cor 3:8, 14-15), is not emphasized by him, especially in view of his teaching on justification by faith.

4:2-6 Final admonitions. Prayer is a key term in these closing admonitions: the community is encouraged to persevere in it, to be attentive in it with thanksgiving (see 3:15b-17), praying together in behalf of the apostolic ministers, that God open the way for them to speak the mystery of Christ, to make it known, even as these ministers are under compulsion to proclaim it (1:24-29). The reference to imprisonment is probably to be understood in two ways: Paul is writing from prison (part of the author's literary fiction), and he is a prisoner to revealing the mystery of Christ, that is, he is not free to do otherwise (Phlm 1a).

The concern for not offending outsiders, implicit in the formulation of household duties in 3:18–4:1, is stated explicitly in the admonition to be prudent in dealing with them, in making the most of each situation, and even by their manner of speech and their response to anyone who speaks with them.

CONCLUSION

Col 4:7-18

4:7-9 Announcement of the arrival of Tychicus and Onesimus. The conclusion of the letter shows that the author is familiar with the names of several of Paul's companions and friends. The author names Tychicus first (Acts 20:4), describing him warmly in three ways: "beloved brother," "trustworthy minister," and "fellow slave in the Lord." He is being sent to tell the community about Paul and thus put their anxiety over him to rest. He is accompanied by Onesimus (Phlm 11), a "trustworthy and beloved brother" from Colossae. Together they will fill the community in on events concerning Paul.

4:10-14 Greetings from Paul's fellow workers. The Apostle also sends greetings from his fellow workers. This is an attempt on the part of the author of Colossians to give this letter the appearance of authenticity, whereas in reality the author has merely taken over a list of names from Philemon, especially verses 23-24, and fleshed them out with brief comments. Also, the author knows some names of Paul's companions who appear in Acts. Aristarchus, Mark, and Justus are the only circumcised among those working with Paul for "the kingdom of God" (see 1:13, which speaks, instead, of "the kingdom of his beloved Son"). As earlier in the letter (1:7-8), Epaphras is given special attention here, as well. He is a Colossian himself and a slave of Christ Jesus, whose pastoral concern for the community is apparent by his solicitude and continual prayer on their behalf, that they stand firm as "perfect ones" (1:28) who "are filled up" with every desire of God (1:9). Epaphras' activity as Paul's representative extends beyond Colossae to the neighboring towns of Laodicea and Hierapolis. Luke, who is described here as a doctor, and Demas, who is simply mentioned by name, are both named also in Phlm 24.

4:15-18 Final comments and blessing. The Christians in Laodicea who meet at Nympha's house church (see Phlm 2) are also greeted, and this letter is meant for reading at their worship assembly as well. A textual problem in the Greek manuscripts makes it difficult to know whether the owner of the house in which the Laodicean community met was a woman (Nympha) or a man (Nymphas). The exchange of letters between communities reflects the common practice of early Christians and helps to explain how some writings in the course of time became well known over a wide geographical area. Finally, Archippus (Phlm 2) is asked to carry out the ministry the Lord has commissioned him to do.

The letter concludes with a reference to Paul's own signature (Phlm 19; see comment on 2 Thess 3:17) and a request that he be remembered in his imprisonment—a point not explicitly asked in Philemon but made obvious there by Paul's numerous references to his imprisoned state. The concluding blessing is an abbreviation of the liturgical formula: "The grace of our Lord Jesus Christ be with you all." Only in Colossians is mention of the "Lord Jesus" omitted entirely in this formula, though it is probably understood even without it being stated.

EPHESIANS

Ivan Havener, O.S.B.

INTRODUCTION

While the Letter to the Ephesians shares an interest with Colossians in the portrayal of the cosmic Christ, Ephesians is unique among New Testament writings for its description of the church as one, holy, catholic, and apostolic. It is this teaching on the nature of the church that is the key contribution of Ephesians.

The understanding of the church which Ephesians sets forth has developed out of and built upon the Pauline tradition and, therefore, goes beyond Paul's own teaching. Paul tended to speak of "church" primarily in terms of the local community, whereas the author of Ephesians, writing at a later period, has seen the churches develop into an institution which he calls "the church." For the author of Ephesians, the church is the cosmic (that is, the catholic or universal) body of Christ, with Christ himself being its head.

Although Paul made no distinction between the head and body when he spoke of the "body of Christ," he did stress the unity of the whole, while noting the diversity of the parts. The author of Ephesians applies these insights to the concept of the cosmic church, but the emphasis clearly falls on unity. The author stresses, in particular, the oneness of Jewish and Gentile Christians in the body of Christ, the church. They are united through the reconciling peace of Christ which has been attained by the redemptive shedding of his blood on the cross.

Cleansed by this redemptive action of Christ and sharing in that redemption through the washing of baptism, the church has been made holy, blameless, spotless, and without wrinkle. This has already happened, so the notion of the imminent end of the world has receded into the background and is of little concern in this letter.

Finally, the church is also apostolic. The author looks back with reverence to the time of the "holy apostles." Using building imagery, the author speaks of their role as the foundation upon which the church is built, with Christ as its capstone. At the time that the author is writing, toward the end of the first century A.D., it was important to stress continuity with the apostolic tradition and origins of the faith in the face of some esoteric, revelatory forms of Christianity which departed at key points from traditional teaching. By writing in Paul's name, the author clearly wanted to anchor his or her own teaching in the apostolic tradition.

In the light of the subsequent history of the church, it is significant that the author of Ephesians saw no conflict between the existence of an institutional church and the work of the Holy Spirit. In fact, the Spirit is mentioned more frequently in Ephesians than in many other writings within the Pauline tradition. Even as there is one body, the church, so there is one Spirit. Despite this frequency of the Spirit's presence in Ephesians, however, the author has not yet developed a systematic understanding of what the Spirit is and what its role is.

Much of Ephesians is based directly on material borrowed from Colossians, though the author has frequently given a new or expanded interpretation of that material. The two letters even show many points of similar-

ity in structure, as the following comparison indicates:

Colossians	Ephesians
Greeting 1:1-2	Greeting 1:1-2
	Benediction 1:3-14
Thanksgiving 1:3-14	Thanksgiving 1:15-23
Hymn 1:15-20	
Gospel of the Apostle 1:21-23	God's Plan for Gentile Christians 2:1-10
Apostolic Revelation of a Mystery 1:24–2:3	Role of the Apostle 3:1-13
The Problem of False Teaching 2:4-23	
	Apostolic Prayer 3:14-21
	Unity of Body and Diversity of Gifts 4:1-16
Various Admonitions Based on Catalogs of Vices and Virtues 3:1-17	Various Admonitions Based on Catalogs of Vices and Virtues 4:17–5:20
Household Duties 3:18–4:1	Household Duties 5:21–6:9
	Preparation for Battle with Cosmic Forces 6:10-17
Prayer 4:2-6	Prayer 6:18-20
Announcement of the Arrival of Tychicus and Onesimus 4:7-9	Announcement of the Arrival of Tychicus 6:21-22
Greetings from Paul's Fellow Workers 4:10-14	
Concluding Comments and Blessing 4:15-18	Final Prayer and Blessing 6:23-24

Sometimes Ephesians quotes verbatim from Colossians as in 6:21-22 (= Col 4:7-8) but more frequently uses blocks of material, like the catalog of vices and virtues and the table of household duties, from Colossians and expands upon them.

The tone of the letter is, for the most part, quite impersonal. If the formal letter structures of the document were to be stripped off, the remaining material has all the characteristics of a theological treatise, eminently suited for widespread circulation. Almost certainly

the letter was not intended for the sole use of the Christian community at Ephesus, a major seaport on the southwestern coast of Asia Minor (present-day Turkey). In fact, in some of the earliest extant Greek manuscripts of this letter, the city of Ephesus is not mentioned at all. This fact lends support to the possibility that the document was meant from the beginning to be a circular letter, or, more precisely, a theological treatise in a circular-letter form. It was written by an unknown author standing within the Pauline tradition.

COMMENTARY

INTRODUCTION AND GREETING

Eph 1:1-2

Paul, the sole sender of this letter, is described in exactly the same wording and word order as in Col 1:1; only the reference to Timothy has been omitted. This omission heightens the importance of Paul even more, with emphasis falling on his apostleship—a matter of significance in this letter. The recipients of the letter are, likewise, designated by some of the same terms as in Col 1:2: "to the holy ones . . . in Christ." The modifications in the phrasing show that the author of Ephesians is familiar with other writings of Paul, where Paul, for instance, also uses the phrase "in Christ Jesus" in a similar way (1 Cor 1:2; Phil 1:1b). The phrase "at Ephesus" is printed in brackets in our text because it is missing from several important manuscripts and may not, therefore, belong to the original letter. This is significant, since no other letter of the Pauline tradition is addressed so vaguely. The author intends the letter to be imprecise, for it is destined to be read in several communities—not really to the specific community at Ephesus. The reference to Ephesus was added at a later time to give the letter the appearance of greater authenticity and was possibly added under the influence of someone from Ephesus. The greeting repeats the usual liturgical formula but without abbreviation (unlike Col 1:2b).

BLESSING GOD

Eph 1:3-14

1:3-12 A Jewish-Christian benediction. Even as the author of Colossians incorporated a hymn into the thanksgiving section of that letter (Col 1:15-20), so the author of Ephesians places a benediction, written in highly poetic style, at this point in this letter. This material comes completely before the thanksgiving section, however, and is independent of it; the opening words have a precedent in 2 Cor 1:3 which begins similarly, "Praised be God, the Father of our Lord Jesus Christ . . . ."

This poetic material differs from that in Colossians in that it emphasizes God's action

in Christ and speaks of the role of the Holy Spirit as well but always for the praise of God's glory (vv. 6, 12, 14). Thus God is "blessed" for having "blessed" us with every spiritual "blessing" in the heavens. This is a Jewish-Christian manner of speaking, a "benediction," which names God first and is addressed directly to God. Christ Jesus is the agent of God's plan of salvation to such a degree that despite the cosmic proportions of this plan, all is done "in Christ."

God's saving plan began before creation itself, when God chose us "in Christ" to be holy and without blemish in love before him. Therefore, what 1 Thess 3:13 envisioned as preparation for judgment at Christ's coming and what Col 1:22; 2:12 saw as happening already in baptism by dying with Christ is here seen in the mind of God before the world began. Already then we were destined to be God's children through Jesus Christ in accord with God's will, so that the gloriousness of God, manifested by this free gift of our adoption through God's beloved (Col 1:13), might be praised. This tremendously generous gift from God is defined as "redemption," that is, a release through the blood of Christ and the forgiveness of trespasses. (Similar terminology appears in Col 1:14, 20 and Rom 3:24-25.)

God, the source of all wisdom and understanding, has taken the initiative in making the mystery of the divine will known to us. Wisdom, understanding, and knowledge (similar concerns in Colossians) are seen in proper perspective only when seen in the light of God's role. God wanted the divine plan, this mystery, to be carried out in Christ at that grand climax of history when all things whether in heaven or on earth (Col 1:15) are united under the headship of Christ. It is in Christ that we were called to be partakers in God's plan, so that in Christ we might be the first to hope (similar to "first-born" in Col 1:15, 18) unto the praise of God's gloriousness.

1:13-14 Inclusion of the Gentile Christians. There is a shift at this point from the confessional "us" to the direct address of the readers as "you." What was professed in the Jewish-Christian benediction applies also to the author's Gentile-Christian audience. In Christ, the readers have also heard the word of truth (Col 1:5), which is here defined as the gospel of salvation. Having believed in Christ they were sealed by the promised Holy Spirit, probably a reference to baptism. This Spirit is the guarantor of the inheritance God had planned for them, the attainment of their redemption—all to the praise of God's gloriousness.

THANKSGIVING

Eph 1:15-23

1:15-19a Thanks and intercession. The author, writing as Paul and evidently considering Colossians to be a genuine letter of the Apostle, continues to draw heavily upon the wording and ideas of Colossians. In verses 15-16 there are only a few minor variations from Col 1:3-4; for instance, Ephesians uses the phrase "in the 'Lord' Jesus," whereas Colossians has "in 'Christ' Jesus." (The "Lord" title appears twice as often in Ephesians as in Colossians.) God is named in two ways—as "the God of our Lord Jesus Christ" (similar to Col 1:3) and as "Father of glory," an expression unique to Ephesians. The purpose of the prayer is that the baptismal event referred to in the benediction will take effect in the lives of the readers. Therefore, the author prays that they be given the Spirit of wisdom and of revelation which are to be found in God's knowledge (see Col 1:9, 26-28), the Spirit proceeding from the Father as in the language of the Hebrew Bible (Isa 11:2). The "revelation" suggests the "mystery" of verse 9 which needs to be revealed. Given this Spirit, the author prays that they will be illumined (see 1 Thess 5:4-5), so that they will know three things: what the hope of their calling is (1 Thess 5:8-9), what wealth of gloriousness God's inheritance among the holy ones is, and what the immeasurable greatness of God's power is for us who believe, according to the effect of his great strength.

1:19b-23 Confessional formulation. Drawing upon traditional credal and hymnic formulations, the author concludes the thanksgiving section with a brief summary of Christian belief. The greatness of God's power is shown by the effect of God's strength exercised "in Christ," when God raised Jesus from among the dead (Col 2:12; 1 Thess 1:10) and seated him at God's right side in heaven (Col

3:1; Rom 8:34). There Christ reigns over all the cosmic forces (Col 1:16) and has a name exalted above all others (Phil 2:9-11). God has placed all things in Christ's control and has made him the head of the church, which, as his body (Col 1:18), completes his being; he it is who fills all that exists, the whole cosmos (Col 1:19).

GOD'S PLAN FOR GENTILE CHRISTIANS

Eph 2:1-10

2:1-3 Present and past. The author reminds the readers of their present Christian way of life by contrasting it with their pagan past. Now they are dead to their trespasses (1:7) and sins, which characterized their former way of life. At that time they were under the influence of worldly existence and the satanic ruler (Col 2:10, 15; 1 Cor 2:6, 8) of the air, who is also described as the spirit who is now active among the children of disobedience. (This contrasts with the adoption spoken of in 1:5.) The author says that "all of us" lived at that time according to (physical) passion, giving in to the desires of the flesh and evil thoughts and, like the rest, were by nature children of wrath, that is, were deserving of God's wrath (1 Thess 1:10). While the author's inclusion of himself or herself among sinners of this sort is usually interpreted to mean that Jews and Gentiles alike were under the domination of sin (Rom 3:9), it is not likely that Paul would have spoken in quite this way because the sins named here are those specifically associated with paganism and hardly fit the situation of Jews in general nor of Paul in particular; Paul even boasted of how well he kept the Jewish law (Phil 3:3-6). Therefore, the "all of us" may be a slip of the tongue which betrays the real author's distance from the historical Paul.

2:4-10 God's mercy in Christ Jesus. Because God is rich in mercy, God did not leave the Gentiles to suffer divine wrath. God's great love for them was manifested, when God quickened them from their death in trespasses (2:1) to live with Christ, to be saved with Christ by God's favor, to be raised with him and to be seated with him in the heavens (1:20). As a result of this merciful action in Christ Jesus, the immeasurable wealth (cf. 1:19) of God's free gift will also be manifest to the ages to come. (The author clearly does not expect Christ's coming in the near future.) This saving action is a gift from God which comes through faith and is not something that can be attained on one's own. Good works, therefore, do not in and of themselves save, so that no one can boast of attaining salvation through self-effort. On the other hand, as the product of God's creative hand, we have been made "in Christ Jesus" for good works. The doing of good works was planned out by God before creation and is an integral part of Christian life.

ONE CHURCH IN CHRIST

Eph 2:11-22

2:11-13 Gentile Christians belong to the promise. Without polemic and arguing rather matter of factly, the author begins the discussion of the relationship of Gentiles and Jews in Christ. Before they were Christians, the readers, who were Gentiles by birth, were derisively given the epithet "foreskin" by the Jews who had entered God's covenant with Israel through the rite of circumcision. Because of their lack of circumcision, these Gentiles were excluded from the community of Israel, had no part in that covenant relationship with God, and so did not share in the promises associated with that covenant. Their existence in the world was without hope, without God, and at that time also without Christ. But now in Christ, this has all been reversed—they who were so far away from hope have been brought near through the shedding of Christ's blood.

2:14-18 Jews and Gentiles united in Christ. In elevated language and perhaps drawing upon hymnic material, the author takes up the theme of peace (2:14, 15, 17a, b) in order to show the unity of the relationship of Gentiles and Jews in Christ. Christ who is our peace has also effected peace by uniting Jew and Gentile. He did this by breaking down the barrier wall of enmity separating them, that is, through his death he abolished the law with its commands and prescriptions as a divisive factor. The purpose for doing so was to create one new being in himself from the two groups, Jews and Gentiles. In this way, through the cross, he reconciled both to God in one body, having put the enmity between them to death. The one body is a pregnant term referring both to Christ's physical body which was put to death and to his body, the church, which consists of Jews and Gentiles. Therefore, through his coming and by his action, he proclaimed peace to both—to the Jews who were near and to the Gentiles who were far away (2:13). As a result, both have access to the Father in one Spirit (4:4); the Spirit is at work in the body of Christ, is active in the church.

2:19-22 Place of Gentile Christians in the church. Because of the reconciling action of Christ, the author's Gentile readers are no longer outsiders (2:12) but are fellow citizens of the church with Jewish Christians, having equal rights with them, and they are fully members of God's family. Abruptly switching imagery, the author notes that they have been built up into the church on the foundation of the apostles (Rev 21:14) and prophets. This departs from Paul's statement that Jesus Christ is the foundation (1 Cor 3:11) and reflects the concern of Christian writers toward the end of the first century and into the second to show a continuity with apostolic tradition in order to stand up against false teachers, some of whom claimed special revelations from Jesus himself. The "apostles" spoken of here are certainly not limited to the Twelve, for Paul, who was not a member of that group, was still an apostle (1:1). The "prophets" do not refer to the Old Testament figures but to a specialized group of Christians whose ministry is still attested in Christian literature long after all the apostles had died (*Didache* 10:7; 14:1-3). Paul speaks of the gift of prophecy as one of the manifestations of the Spirit (1 Cor 12, 14).

For the author of Ephesians, Christ is not the cornerstone on which the church is built but the church's capstone, its crowning glory. Yet, despite this somewhat static image of the church as a building already built, an enclosed entity, the author still speaks of its "growth," thus combining "body of Christ" imagery with building construction. The whole structure, having been fit together in Christ, grows into a holy temple. In Christ, these Gentile readers are built into this temple, too, the place where God dwells in the Spirit (2:18).

APOSTOLIC MINISTRY TO THE GENTILES

Eph 3:1-21

3:1-13 Role of the Apostle. By placing emphasis on the figure of Paul, the author shows how the message preached to the Gentile readers is based on apostolic tradition. As a prisoner of Christ, Paul's incarceration is an example for these readers, a notion more fully explained in 3:13, but as a prisoner of Christ, he is also in Christ's captivity for their sake in that this captivity includes a stewardship of making known to them God's mystery which had been revealed to him. They stand in continuity with apostolic tradition, for they have already heard this message before when it was preached by the Apostle, and they will recognize it again when they read this letter. The Apostle Paul, as the representative of apostolic tradition, has become himself a part of the catechetical teaching.

The mystery, of which the author speaks, is no longer hidden as it was in the past (Col 1:26), but has been made known because of the activity of the Spirit working through the holy apostles and prophets, who are the foundation of the church (2:20). The word "holy" in this context (3:5) is evidence of an aura of piety and reverence that is already surrounding the apostles and prophets, as figures in a past that is now becoming legendary. The content of the mystery revealed by the apostles and prophets is different from the meaning given to the term in Rom 11:25 and Col 1:26-28; in Ephesians, "mystery" refers back to 2:11-22, where "in Christ Jesus" the Gentiles share in the inheritance that God has promised the Jews. They are all part of the same body, that is, Christ's body, the church. This mystery has been revealed through the preaching of the gospel, but "gospel" and "mystery" are not clearly differentiated here.

Again, reverence for the person of the Apostle is coupled with the importance of his apostolic mission. God's gracious gift was given to Paul so that he might minister. God's exercise of power, in this regard, is virtually synonymous with the phrase "in the Spirit" (2:22). That God chose Paul to preach to the Gentiles, despite his earlier persecution of the church, was a paradox to Paul himself, who said that he was the "least of the apostles" (1 Cor 15:9; see 2 Cor 12:11); in Ephesians, however, he is described in even more lowly terms as "the very least of all the holy ones." (This may also be a word play on the name "Paul" which in Latin means "little.") This heightened contrast enhances the portrayal of Paul's humility, but it also underscores the astounding magnanimity of God's grace which the Gentiles are heir to through that apostolic ministry of his.

This ministry is described in terminology similar to that in Rom 11:25-36 and Col 1:25-28, as proclaiming the gospel of the inscrutable riches of Christ and enlightening of all with God's mystery. Here "mystery" and "riches of Christ" are one and the same. In continuity with this ministry of the Apostle, the ministry of the present (therefore, in the time after Paul) is being carried out "through the church." It is the church which continues the apostolic ministry, making God's wisdom known to the cosmic powers in accord with God's eternal plan. Thus, "in Christ," the church has taken on Christ's cosmic role! It is in him and by faith in him that we can confidently and freely have access to God (2:17-18).

This section concludes with a reference back to Paul's imprisonment in 3:1. The Apostle's tribulations are for the sake of the readers of this letter; these tribulations are their glory and not reason for being disheartened. Suffering (and martyrdom) have apostolic approval and example (Phil 1:29) and their own peculiar power of proclamation.

3:14-21 Apostolic prayer. In a profound posture of worship, the Apostle kneels (Phil 2:10; Rom 14:11) before the Father of the cosmos and prays for his readers. From the Father, every family of heavenly and earthly beings has received its name, and from the Father with his wealth of glory, the Apostle prays that his readers will be strengthened inwardly in power through the Father's Spirit. As in the case of 2:22 and 3:7, power and Spirit are closely related. Second, he prays that Christ dwell in their hearts through faith, faith being the means for this indwelling. This second petition makes precise what was meant in the first. Then he asks that they, being rooted and grounded in love, may fully understand with all the holy ones (that is, also with Jewish Christians) what the full dimensions of Christ's love are. But to know the love of Christ is paradoxically to know a love which surpasses knowledge itself. Finally, the prayer comes to a climax in the petition that they themselves be filled with all the fullness of God, the same which is attributed to Christ in Col 1:19.

The prayer concludes with a doxology, a liturgical formula in praise of God. In this case, the Father, whose ability to act far exceeds anything we are able to ask for or even think of and who lets his power operate in us, is to be glorified forever in the church and in Christ. The church and Christ are intimately related, as the author of Ephesians has sought to point out from the beginning.

INSTRUCTIONS

Eph 4:1–6:20

4:1-6 Unity of the body. The author exhorts the readers to lead lives worthy of their Christian calling (1 Thess 2:12; Col 1:10) and names a catalog of virtues borrowed from Col 3:12-15 which they should practice. Unity of the Spirit, however, is unique to Ephesians and reflects the author's greater interest in the role of the Spirit. A whole series of "one formulas" are introduced to further describe the components of the Christian calling: one body, one Spirit, one hope, one Lord, one faith, one baptism, and one God. Since the sole ritual action in this list is baptism and because eucharist is not mentioned, it is possible that such "one formulas" were used as liturgical shouts during the baptismal rite itself. The formula which speaks of "one God" appears to be a unit in itself, a Jewish formulation which has been incorporated into Christian teaching. It consists of the additional designation of God as the "Father of all," plus the three prepositional phrases—over, through, and in all. This is a Stoic manner of speaking, taken up and transformed by Greek-speaking Jews and Christians. See the "one formula" of 1 Cor 8:6 and the similar use of prepositions there.

4:7-16 Diversity of gifts. Each individual in the one body of Christ has been given grace according to the measure of Christ's gift. While Paul speaks of similar subject matter in 1 Cor 12 and Rom 12:4-6, he refers to "charisms" (gifts) instead of "grace," and these charisms come from the "Spirit," instead of "Christ." Both Paul and the author of Ephesians emphasize, however, the diversity of gifts within the one body.

Ps 68:19 is quoted directly by the author as scriptural support that Christ has given gifts, but this passage also enabled the author to take up the notion that the cosmic powers have been taken captive in the person of Christ (Col 2:15). By arguing that "ascent" requires a previous "descent," the author seeks to show that the passage really refers to someone other than Moses. The descent into the lower regions of the earth probably refers to Christ's victory over the realm of the dead (1 Pet 3:19-20), which prepared the way for his ascent high above the heavens as the cosmic conqueror to fill all. Thus, he is the source of gifts.

It is Christ who has given the leaders of the church. This list of leaders is similar to that given by Paul (1 Cor 12:28), but the Pauline triad of apostles, prophets, and teachers is interrupted here by the addition of evangelists (2 Tim 4:5) and pastors (1 Pet 5:2-4), roles that took on greater importance as the apostles died. These are not just random examples but roles essential to the life of the church; those who exercise them are responsible for equipping the holy ones for ministry, that is, for service, and thus for the upbuilding of Christ's body (2:20-22). The goal is the future unity of us all in faith and knowledge of the Son of God (this is the only time in this letter that Christ is given the Son of God title), the formation of a perfect, mature person, completely grown in the fullness of Christ.

Since the goal is perfect adulthood in Christ, the author exhorts the readers not to act then like children, when false teaching is being bandied about. Because Christ has bestowed on them church leaders steeped in the apostolic tradition, they need only heed that message alone, that is, to profess that truth in love which has already been taught them and thus continue the process of growth toward maturity in Christ, the head. It is through Christ that the body grows. With all the members working together, doing their proper function, it builds itself up in love. There is unity in the attempt to attain unity in Christ.

4:17-24 Discontinuity with the past. Solemnly invoking the apostolic role "in the Lord," the author declares that the readers must no longer live as pagans. As in 2:13, the author describes again the worthlessness of paganism: pagans have purposeless dispositions and darkened understanding; they are separated from the life of God (2:12; Col 1:21) on account of the ignorance and hardness of their hearts, and they have given themselves over to immorality (Col 3:5). This manner of life contrasts starkly with what had been taught to them when they learned about Christ, for in Jesus they heard and were taught truth itself. Therefore, they were taught to set aside that former manner of life, that old person corrupted by seductive passions and to be renewed, instead, in the spirits of their disposition, putting on a new person, that second Adam who, like the first, was created in God's image. This new person's attributes are justice and holiness, which come from Christ who is truth.

4:25–5:7 Community rules. Since Christians are members one of another in Christ's body, there are certain vices which need to be avoided and certain virtues which need to be practiced for the body to function properly. Therefore, lying is to be supplanted by speaking the truth to one's neighbor; the sun should not set on a sinful anger; the devil should be given no opportunity to act; stealing is to be replaced by honest labor, so that what is obtained from it can be shared with the needy. Evil talk should give way to constructive talk that builds up and imparts grace on the hearers. The readers should not trouble God's Holy Spirit in whom they were sealed (1:13) for the sake of their redemption on the last day. In 4:31, the author cites a whole catalog of vices (Col 3:8) which should be removed from them. Then follows a catalog of virtues as a replacement. Among these virtues, forgiveness is singled out, in view of God's forgiveness of them in Christ (Col 3:12-13).

As Paul asked his readers to be imitators of him (Phil 3:17) and as he himself was an imitator of Christ (1 Cor 11:1), so now the author of Ephesians asks his readers to be imitators of God. As God's beloved children, they should conduct their lives in love, like Christ did for "us" when he offered himself up as a sweet-smelling sacrifice to God. (The change from "you" to "us" suggests that a traditional confessional formula has been taken up here.) This way of love excludes a whole series of vices which are incompatible with the life of the "holy ones." Their life should be characterized, instead, by thanksgiving, for the practitioners of the vices listed here do not have an inheritance in the kingdom of Christ (Col 1:13) and of God (Col 4:11). It is important, therefore, not to be led astray by teaching to the contrary and not to participate in such vices, because these sins bring the anger of God upon the children of disobedience (Col 3:6).

5:8-20 Living in the light. The readers of this letter were once Gentiles without Christ and were darkness itself, but now as Gentiles in the Lord, they have become light. Their new identity as children of light requires that they live in a different way. The fruit produced by this light-life is all goodness, righteousness, and truth, considering what is pleasing to the Lord. Therefore, instead of participating in the unproductive works of darkness, they should condemn such deeds. It is even shameful to speak of the deeds done in secret by the children of darkness. Such deeds condemned, however, are illumined by light, and everything so illumined becomes light. To underscore the point, the author quotes a passage from an unknown source, probably a fragment of a baptismal hymn. It challenges the one to be baptized to wake up from the sleep of a spiritual death and to arise from among the spiritually dead. Resurrection is conceived here as entry into newness of life, permeated by the light of Christ.

Those who have been so enlightened are also "wise" and should take care to live accordingly—not as the foolish do. They should make the most of the opportunity (Col 4:5) during these evil days, being alert to discerning what the will of God is—not unthinking. Drunkenness with wine is to be avoided because it hinders that discernment process and is yet another indication of base, pagan life. In contrast to being filled up with wine, they should be filled up with the Spirit. This Spirit-life is expressed in community by psalm and song to the Lord which proceeds from the heart and also is manifested in giving thanks constantly to God the Father in the name of our Lord Jesus Christ (Col 4:17).

5:21-33 Household duties—wives and husbands. Another manifestation of being filled in the Spirit is mutual obedience out of reverence for Christ who is himself the prime example of one who is obedient. By incorporating and explaining the household duties of Col 3:18–4:1, the author develops this concept of mutual obedience.

While the author takes up the same exhortation as Col 3:18, that wives should be obedient to their husbands, the statement is modified to the effect that such obedience should be like that given to the Lord. The author's explanation for this follows this line of argumentation: as Christ (masculine) is head of the church (a feminine word in Greek), so the husband (masculine) is head of his wife (feminine), and as his body, the church (feminine), is obedient to Christ (masculine), so wives (feminine) should be completely obedient to their husbands (masculine).

This interpretation, sexist by our standards today, is balanced in part, however, both by the call to mutual obedience in 5:21 and by what husbands are admonished to do in verses 25-33. Care must be taken, therefore, not to lift verses 22-24 out of context, as though it were meant to be a put-down of women; that would be a clear distortion of the author's purpose.

As in Col 3:19, husbands are exhorted to love their wives, but unlike Colossians this is explained in Ephesians in terms of the church. As Christ (masculine) loved the church (feminine) and gave himself up for it, so completely should husbands (masculine) love their wives (feminine).

The line of thought is interrupted by a brief explanation of the ecclesiastical significance of Christ's self-sacrifice. Christ acted in this way in order to make his church holy, purifying it with the baptismal washing and the proclamation of the word, and thus to present "to himself" (1 Thess 3:13 has "before our God and Father") a glorified church, holy and spotless. With this description of the church as "holy," the author of Ephesians completes the naming of the four characteristics of the church, summarized later in the Nicene Creed: one, holy, catholic, and apostolic church.

Returning to his discussion about husbands, the author continues to argue in a similar vein: like Christ loved his body, the church, and as husbands love their own bodies, so they should also love their wives. When they love their wives, they are, in fact, loving themselves. The author cites a common proverb about not hating oneself, which is thought to lend support to the author's argument. Love of self (a positive virtue here) is shown by our concern to feed and care for our bodies, something which Christ does for his church and which we experience as members of his body. (The feeding may be a reference to the Eucharist, which is not otherwise spoken of in this letter.) The author adds scriptural support by quoting Gen 2:24 to show the unity of husbands and wives in the one body of Christ which is his church. Therefore, every husband is exhorted to love his wife, and the wife is admonished to revere her husband.

6:1-4 Household duties—children and parents. Exhorting children to obey their parents (Col 3:20), the author of Ephesians quotes another passage from the Hebrew Bible (Exod 20:12) and notes the unique promise of long life associated with that commandment. This command is to be carried out "in the Lord" for the simple reason that it is the right thing to do, whereas Col 3:20 says, with a slightly different emphasis, that "this is pleasing to the Lord."

Fathers are admonished not to anger their children, but no explanation of this is given here. In Col 3:21, however, they are warned not to nag their children "so they may not become discouraged." Instead of this explanation, the author of Ephesians adds another admonition to fathers: that they rear their children in Christian discipline and instruction. This is yet another indication that the imminent end of the world has receded from consciousness.

6:5-9 Household duties—slaves and masters. Slaves are exhorted to obey their earthly masters with reverence and awe (Phil 2:12), as if they were obeying Christ himself. (Similarly, Col 3:22 notes that when slaves obey their masters, they are by that very fact showing reverence to the Lord.) These "slaves of Christ" (see commentary on Phil 1:1) do the will of God when they carry out their duties responsibly and willingly, doing them to please the Lord rather than their earthly masters and, perhaps, even in spite of them. Unlike Col 3:25, Ephesians speaks of a positive reward: everyone will be rewarded by the Lord for the good that is done. It is meant to be a message of comfort to slaves.

Some of the material used to address slaves in Colossians is employed with better effect by the author of Ephesians in applying it to masters. Both master and slave have one and the same Lord who shows no favoritism due to one's higher (or lower) rank in society. Masters are to act with the same knowledge as their slaves, namely, that they also have the Lord over them, and they must serve him. They have the specific obligation not to threaten their slaves. What is revolutionary in this teaching is that masters not only have rights but also have obligations with regard to their slaves.

6:10-20 Preparation for battle with cosmic forces. Although Christ has already triumphed over every cosmic principality, authority, power, and domination (1:21), and even though believers are freed from bondage to the ruler of the power of the air (2:2), nonetheless, these cosmic forces still maintain a threatening influence. The author of Ephesians, therefore, takes up military imagery to describe how Christians should stand firm against these powers. They are exhorted to be strengthened "in the Lord" (NAB: "from the Lord") and in the power of his strength as they prepare to do battle. They are to put on the armor of God in order to stand firm against the devil's own military strategy. This armor of God is necessary because the battle is not with mere flesh and blood (2 Cor 10:4) but with cosmic forces; this armor will enable them to stand their ground on the evil day and consists of truth as a belt, righteousness as a breastplate, gospel of peace as footgear, faith as a shield, salvation as a helmet (1 Thess 5:8), and the Spirit (described as the word of God) as a sword.

Thus armed, the readers are to keep a persevering watch, praying and interceding at all times in the Spirit on behalf of all the holy ones. The author, writing as Paul, adds the more personal note that they should also pray for him that he will be able to speak the word, to make known with courage that gospel mystery for which he is now Christ's imprisoned envoy.

CONCLUSION

Eph 6:21-24

6:21-22 Announcement of the arrival of Tychicus. The letter concludes with an announcement of the sending of Tychicus to the community to tell them how Paul is and what he is doing and thus put their anxiety over him to rest. This seemingly personal announcement has, in fact, been quoted directly from Col 4:7-8. Of the thirty-four Greek words in the Colossian passage, thirty-two have been repeated here verbatim and in exactly the same order. This is the clearest sign of a direct literary dependence of Ephesians on Colossians.

6:23-24 Final prayer and blessing. Both the final prayer and blessing have an impersonal tone, the readers being referred to in the third person. This indicates that a wider audience is meant than a single community. In the prayer, "peace," a major theme in this letter (2:14-18; 4:3; 6:15), has replaced "hope" in the Pauline triad of faith, hope, and love. The blessing is addressed generally to "all who love our Lord Jesus Christ in immortality." It is unclear whether the phrase "in immortality" belongs with "love," or belongs with "grace," or refers to Jesus Christ who reigns in immortal glory, or refers to those who love the Lord and, therefore, have a share now in immortality. All of these are grammatically possible.

THE PASTORAL EPISTLES

Jerome H. Neyrey, S.J.

INTRODUCTION _____

Author

Modern biblical criticism has seriously challenged the claim that Paul wrote the so-called pastoral Epistles—1 Timothy, 2 Timothy, and Titus. The vocabulary in the Pastorals differs from that in the undisputed Pauline letters. The bold themes in Paul's letters are only formulae here, but above all the view of the church is significantly different from that found in Paul's letters. The question of authentic authorship, while important for historical studies, is distracting here. The letters are not less valuable for faith because Paul probably did not write them, nor more valuable if authentic. Their value for us as Christians comes from the fact that they are inspired by God and important for the church's self-understanding. It was common, moreover, in the Old Testament to attribute later psalms, prophecies, and bits of wisdom to earlier noted authorities, such as David or Solomon. The same procedure was common also in many New Testament writings. Since it is unlikely that Paul wrote the Pastorals, an early date for their composition is unwarranted. It is generally agreed that they stem from the last decades of the first century.

If the historical Paul did not actually compose these letters, they were, nevertheless, intended by their genuine author to be taken as Pauline statements, in accord with Pauline traditions. And I will regularly point out the many similarities between Paul's undisputed letters and these pastoral Epistles.

Form and function

In many ways these letters, at least 1 Timothy and Titus, seem to be extended codes of "household duties," a common form of exhortation in pagan, Jewish, and Christian literature. The Pastorals are, moreover, collections of very traditional moral materials, echoing not only gospel sources but Pauline advice to his churches and Petrine materials as well. Most importantly, in all three letters we find a formal written document which certifies the present status of Timothy and Titus as church leaders and which subsequently authenticates their successors. These letters, then, stress church order and morality and so function as official constitutions for their respective churches.

Changes in the early churches

Comparing the view of the church in the Pauline letters with that in the Pastorals, we note many significant changes which are characteristic of "early catholicism." This concept is a useful historical label for indicating just the shift in the church's profile mentioned above: (1) *Leadership*—no longer does Jesus commission apostles, nor is leadership designated by God's Spirit, but volunteers arise and are validated by the church. (2) *Doctrine*—the great, dynamic themes of faith, righteousness, and grace are now reduced to slogans and formulae; more stress is placed on correctness of doctrine than on the dynamics of conversion and allegiance to Jesus. (3) *Church* —the freely elected group of Christians enflamed with charismatic gifts and waiting for the parousia has quieted down to a group of second-generation believers who are urged to be exemplary citizens and to live long and full lives. (4) *Equality*—the freedom and equality of men and women, so strong in the Pauline churches, is moderated here; conformity to local cultural norms is urged.

"Early catholicism" is a useful historical tag for pointing to this clear shift in the early churches, but it is open to considerable misunderstanding. For some, this shift is interpreted as a corruption of the Pauline genius and as an indication of the smothering institutionalization of the church; still others find in the shift a quasi-warrant for later authoritarian and doctrinal controls. Here is the crux— we should neither overly depreciate the shift nor unduly celebrate it. It is not true that the church went to ruin after Paul due to compromises within it, nor is it accurate to champion later developments as divinely ordained evolutions, necessarily good.

The pastoral churches were seriously adapting the gospel to their unique situations. As they grew from small groups into large urban churches, they suffered the stresses and pains of any growing religious group. And herein lies their importance for us, the warrant to adapt and develop in the face of new cultures and situations. It would surely be a mistake to expect our church to look and feel like the Pastorals; we must preach the gospel to our own world, not simply cling to old traditions and formulations which suited a world long since passed.

Conservatism and tradition

How frequently the Pastorals speak of the "deposit of faith," of "sound teaching," of the gospel of truth. How often Paul tells Timothy to adhere to the gospel and resist false teachers. This sounds conservative and traditionalistic, but the needs of these churches were such that they had to clarify many important things: (1) the orderly succession of leaders, especially where there are competing claims; (2) the orthodoxy of teachers, especially when there are radical differences of opinion; and (3) the central tenets of the gospel faith, clearly expressed and without excesses. These problems were especially acute as the older leaders of the young church died and the church spread and matured socially. The crisis called for firm decision-making, for saying: "This is the gospel! That is heresy!" and "Here is our leader, not that one!"

The stress on tradition does not mean that all new ideas or developments are corrupt; this would be naive and clearly wrong. The Pastorals do not formally address the issue of valid development of gospel teaching, for they merely identify certain erroneous teachings about the law, ascetical practices, and the resurrection. To read them as a charter for freezing church teaching and becoming doctrinally conservative, afraid of change or development, is a misinterpretation of them. They are "pastoral" in the rich sense that they squarely address problems troubling the life of their churches and offer novel solutions and solid advice to the developing churches. For all their formalism, they are vitally alive with the love for God's church and with a keen sense of the total conversion to which the gospel calls us. They are "pastoral" in the way they call upon their foundational traditions about Jesus and how these theological ideas intimately structure and enrich the way we live. They are "pastoral" in the demand they make on the church to become acculturated in pagan society and yet to be distinctly faithful to the gospel. They are "pastoral" in the practical development of church offices to ensure stable succession, fidelity to the gospel, and fresh leadership in a church in transition.

1 TIMOTHY

Jerome H. Neyrey, S.J.

COMMENTARY

1:1-2 Letter opening. All ancient letters begin with a notice of sender, recipient, plus a short greeting. The author typically begins by stating that he is an official "apostle" of God and Jesus Christ, thus underscoring his authority, as is the case here. He calls Timothy his "true child in faith," just as he spoke of himself to Christians as their "father" (1 Cor 4:15; 1 Thess 2:11). This way of speaking illustrates the church's understanding of itself as a genuinely new family, especially reflecting warmth to those who may have sacrificed natural family ties for Christ (see Matt 10:34-39). The greeting here expands the typical Pauline greeting ("grace and peace") to three items ("grace, *mercy*, and peace"), perhaps to signal the stress on "mercy" shown to Paul in 1:13.

1:3-7 Defender of the faith. Verse 3 alludes to the command that Timothy take his place in Ephesus and become an "overseer" of that church. Ephesus was a church particularly important to Paul. He spent two years there (Acts 19:1-10), where he met both great success and hostility (Acts 19:11-20; 1 Cor 15:32). The great Alexandrian preacher Apollos became a convert there (Acts 18:24), and Paul summoned the elders of Ephesus to himself for a farewell speech (Acts 20:16-35). This was obviously an influential church, for we have one long letter addressed to it (Eph) and a shorter one as well (Rev 2:1-7).

Timothy's commission was to guard the faith, which means here to charge other would-be teachers to cease from propagating deviant doctrines. It is impossible to know just what these "myths and genealogies" were, but we know what was wrong about them: they did not promote integrity of faith and life. Here we touch the heart of the author's concern for these churches, that their lives be worthy of their calling. He sees that true doctrine leads to good morals and to a religiously integrated life. The would-be teachers promote only mere speculation but not "training" in faith, that is, ordering of lives in the wholeness of faith. In contrast, Timothy's task is an active one—practical love which comes only from what is pure, good, and sincere. In this concern for the inner relationship of faith and life, the author echoes the gospel charge that "by their fruits you shall know them" (Matt 7:16). The inner person, totally caught up in the gospel, will express itself richly in a morally upright life, but the inner self must be formed in truth. So Timothy stands confronting would-be teachers of religion, not only in their conclusions about the validity of the law but especially in the emptiness of their understanding of the relationship of faith to life.

1:8-11 The value and function of the law. It is not clear just what the would-be teachers of the law are proposing: either abolition of all law (libertinism) or imposition of esoteric laws (Jewish gnosticism). Either way the author will have none of this excess. He rather asserts the essential worth of the law, just as he did in Rom 7:12, 16; after all, God revealed it and his word is true (see 2 Tim 3:16). In his

1200

genuine letters Paul claimed that the law had various functions: (1) to increase trespasses (Rom 5:20), (2) to act as guardian or educator (Gal 3:23-24), and (3) to restrain wickedness (Gal 3:19). Here in verse 9 the last reason is stressed; obviously not all "need" a law if they are truly led by the Spirit and have been totally converted to God. Because of sin and error, some need to have the implications of Christian faith spelled out for them, hence the list in 1:9-10. It is a common feature of popular moral preaching that teachers would remind their audiences of typical moral virtues and vices by citing lists of such, which Paul regularly did (Gal 5:19-21; 1 Cor 6:9-10). The list here is special, for it is based on the core of the Old Testament covenant law, the Ten Commandments, much the same way that the list of virtues cited in Matt 15:19 is also based on the Ten Commandments. Despite Christian arguments that Jewish law was no longer binding, the Ten Commandments always remained a central part of Christian moral teaching, probably because they are the essential covenant law which spells out the implications of our covenant faith. The great love command of Jesus (Matt 22:36-40) is in fact the covenant code found in the Ten Commandments; this is what covenant love means (see Matt 19:18-19). The law is intended to restrain whatever is contrary to "sound" teaching, a common phrase in these letters which suggests that the author's doctrine is both healthy (accurate) and health-giving (1 Tim 6:3; 2 Tim 1:13). After all, good theology leads to good morals. The measure of what is "sound" is determined by what is in accord with tradition, i.e., the gospel entrusted to Paul and the church, which is another indirect polemic on the would-be teachers with their speculation on myths (1:3-7).

1:12-17 Prayer of thanksgiving. It is typical of Pauline letters to contain a thanksgiving prayer at the beginning of the letter, usually in gratitude for God's gifts to the church addressed (see Rom 1:8-10; 1 Cor 1:4-9). Here the author gives thanks for the grace shown him, which he does in characteristic fashion. He notes his former sins (see 1 Cor 15:9; Acts 8:3) and his call to repentance and ministry (Gal 1:13-16; Eph 3:8). Stories about Peter always seem to remind us of his weakness or his denial of Jesus, just as accounts of Paul's commission retain the fact

that he formerly persecuted the church. The point of this is to underscore the kernel of our faith, which is confessed clearly in verse 15, "Christ Jesus came into the world to save sinners" (see Mark 2:10; Luke 15). So Paul's total conversion from sin to ministry becomes the moral example for Timothy and for all of us (v. 16)—leaders were not always perfect when called, but they are expected to be totally converted to God, a theme developed in chapter 3 where the rules for bishops and deacons appear. It is characteristic of Paul to tell the church: "Be imitators of me" (1 Cor 4:16; 11:1). This pastoral repetition of Paul's election is climaxed with a typical Jewish blessing or act of praise to God (see Rom 16:27); another beautiful prayer will close the letter in 6:15-16.

1:18-20 Timothy's difficult duties. Timothy's general task, which was described earlier (1:3-7), is repeated in specific terms. Like Paul, he was entrusted with a mission by the church's prophets (Acts 13:1-3), a mission "to wage warfare" on error in the church; this is a common metaphor for popular preachers and one that will be repeated again and again in these letters (6:12; 2 Tim 4:7). Even Paul saw his task occasionally as warfare (2 Cor 10:3-5). The weapons are "faith and good conscience," which apply equally to orthodox teaching and to constancy in faith. Two deviants are cited as examples of those who have turned away from the truth: Alexander, who is said to have harmed the author (see 2 Tim 4:14), and Hymenaeus, who distorted the meaning of the resurrection (see 2 Tim 2:17-18). These two, like the incestuous man in 1 Cor 5:1-5, have been temporarily expelled from the group for lives that are radically incompatible with the ideal of sound faith/good morals. A similar procedure is reported in Titus 3:10-11. This excommunication is not punitive, but educative, as it should lead to a reconversion (1:20). This process is not taken lightly, and it indicates that the church is *not* unsure of itself but vigorously witnesses to the gospel even at the cost of causing separations from the group.

2:1-7 Christians and the secular world. Here begins a long exhortation to the church, spelling out "household duties." In earlier Christian writings, these duties are restricted to those of husband/wife, parent/child, and master/slave (Col 3:18–4:1), but here the whole church is addressed (see 3:15, what kind of conduct befits a member of God's *household*, "the church of God").

A typical assembly is envisioned in which "supplications, prayers, petitions, and thanksgivings" (2:1) are made. Paul regularly enjoined his churches to pray for civic rulers; here the aim of prayer is religious toleration for the new religious group. This presupposes, however, that the church will live "quiet and tranquil lives" in full accord with the gospel, "in perfect piety and dignity" (v. 2). Implicit in this advice is the call to be exemplary citizens, as well as complete Christians. This appeal has a missionary edge to it; prayer for the civic rulers pleases the Christian God who is thoroughly ecumenical in his plan of salvation and "wills everyone to be saved and come to knowledge of the truth" (v. 4). Hence the traditional confessional formula cited in verse 5 (God is One! Jesus ransoms all!) suggests that the church is praying as well for the rulers to share its faith. These few verses suggest a view of this church that is clearly not sectarian or world-denying but ecumenically open to all and which sees Christian life as fully compatible with good citizenship in the empire.

2:8-15 Husbands and wives. The exhortation then addresses the family unit, in particular husbands and wives; such advice is common in Christian moral teaching (see Eph 5:21-33). Men (husbands) should lift holy hands in prayer—again a community meeting is envisioned which is *not* filled with factions and quarreling, as were many of the Pauline communities (see 1 Cor 1:11-12). The oneness of God (2:5) should be reflected in the oneness of the church.

Comparably, women (wives) are instructed to appear in the assemblies clothed not in wealth and fashion but in "good deeds" (see 1 Pet 3:1-6), advice which was common fare even in pagan exhortations. The instruction that women should keep silent is very problematic: (1) In the Pauline churches there are women prophets (1 Cor 11:1-13) and deaconesses (see Phoebe, Rom 16:1). (2) Paul's churches experienced a remarkable degree of equality among men and women (Gal 3:28), equality based on the gospel that Christ has redeemed *all* people and that God has called *all* to grace. Here, however, we see a community which professes the same equality of call

from God (2:5), but the social structure is considerably more restrictive and the implications of the gospel in this regard are muted. The reasons for women's silence in 2:11-14 are based on bizarre exegesis of Genesis: (1) Because Eve was created *after* Adam she should listen to him (yet both accounts of Eve's creation indicate her equality with Adam: Gen 1:27; 2:18, 23). (2) Because Eve seduced Adam she should not advise her husband ever again (yet biblical theology clearly speaks of *Adam's* sin, not Eve's: see Rom 5:12-19). The church here seems to be mirroring the typical social patterns of the world around it in restricting the role of women in the church assemblies. But evidently in its desire to accommodate itself to the local culture an important aspect of the gospel message is forgotten, an ironic feature of a letter which defends the old traditions so carefully. There is, however, a sense in these letters that women are especially prey to the would-be teachers who are disturbing the churches (5:13; 2 Tim 3:65; Titus 1:11). Hence, the concern for women probably represents a genuine pastoral concern which was unfortunately smothering and unenlightened. Would that Timothy had been more traditional in this regard!

One final note: the concern in chapter 2 seems to be with the visible side of the church, the public, assembled community; for the advice in 2:1-7 concerns public prayer, as does the exhortation to husbands in 2:8; and women's silence makes sense primarily in the context of the assembled church. This concern for the orderly face of the church has its missionary side. Paul can even enjoin silence on prophets and those who speak in tongues for the sake of its mission (1 Cor 14:23-25).

3:1-7 Qualifications for bishops. The list of household duties is extended with a list of qualifications for bishops and deacons in 3:1-13. Although there is no clear job description here, we are told of the qualifications for this position. The list of 3:2-7 is typical of pagan as well as Jewish lists of qualifications for office; in fact, there is hardly a hint of anything distinctively Christian about this list. A good leader is typically without reproach, respectably married, temperate. He should be noted for hospitality—for as Christians traveled more widely, it was necessary to welcome them (see the notice of travelers in Rom 16) as well as traveling prophets and missionaries

(3 John 5; Rom 12:13; 1 Pet 4:9). Besides being a figure of good personal character, the bishop should be a unifying social force. His motive for service should not be mercenary, like the false teachers (6:5; Titus 1:11). In the world view of the pastoral Epistles, proper order is most important, hence the bishop's right ordering of his family according to recognizable standards will qualify him to order the church. As in Paul's case, a suitable apprenticeship is fitting after conversion (see Gal 1:17). And the bishop, because he is a public figure, should be a person of character and respectability in relationship to the secular world.

So many questions are raised by this passage for which there are no clear answers: (1) What is the role of the bishop? Economic assistance? Yes, and probably clear teaching of the tradition as well (see Titus 1:9). (2) How does one become a bishop? Timothy was prophetically designated (1:18), but the figures here seem to be volunteers. (3) What is the nature of their authority? The very fact that we have letters confirming Timothy's position suggests that legitimation of bishops was becoming increasingly important. Even Timothy is seen here as authorizing other bishops and successors. (4) What is the status of the office? We have no clear sense that "bishops" here are different from "elders"; both are mentioned interchangeably here and elsewhere (see Jas 5:14; 1 Pet 5:1); they are surely not the monarchical bishops, such as Ignatius of Antioch. This new office is still developing and adapting to the pastoral needs of the church members.

3:8-13 Qualifications for deacons. In Phil 1:1 Paul addressed "bishops and deacons," and it is hard to distinguish them clearly at this early stage of the church. Deacons served the poor (Acts 6:1-6) but they preached as well (e.g., Philip in Acts 8:4-8, as well as Stephen's great speech in Acts 7). It is simply unclear in 1 Timothy what ministry deacons performed, although we are probably safe in seeing them as performing broad and varied tasks such as in the Pauline churches. For example, there are people who do teaching, helping, and administering (1 Cor 12:28); Rom 12:7 speaks of those who do serving, teaching, and helping.

The list of qualifications is similar to that of the bishop: the deacon is a person of good character and standing, but he is noted in verse 9 as singularly orthodox—he holds fast to "the faith with a clear conscience," which implies that he is somehow responsible for correct teaching. Does verse 11 refer to deaconesses? We know of Phoebe the deaconess from Cenchreae (Rom 16:1). But most probably verse 11 speaks to the wives of the deacons.

3:14-16 The church of God. Brief mention is made of the author's travel plans and the possibility of his delay, a common theme in his letters (1 Cor 4:19). In the event of his inability to visit, the letter will function as a type of church constitution (v. 14). All of the preceding and subsequent lists of household duties serve one purpose—to inform the community how to behave as a Christian church (3:15). The images of the community here are an important clue to how we should understand "church" in these letters. It is "the household of God which is the church of the living God." The last image stresses the free yet universal call of God to all people (see 2:4-6), while the first image touches on the orderly structure of the new temple, the community of God. Neither image implies that the church is set against the world or is exclusivist or world-negating.

One of the distinguishing characteristics of this church is its possession of truth, the "mystery of devotion" (v. 16). What this means is immediately demonstrated in the hymn to Christ in verse 16; the pastoral Epistles are full of such fragments of hymns and confessions (see 2 Tim 2:11-13; 4:1). Two questions need to be answered: (1) What does the hymn refer to? (2) How is it functioning in 1 Tim 3? As regards its meaning, it is best to compare it with a similar hymn in 1 Pet 3:18-19, 22. (For a full discussion of its meaning, see the commentary under that passage.) It is sufficient to note here that "manifested in the flesh" probably refers to Jesus' public crucifixion, not his incarnation. Indeed this hymn encapsules various aspects of Jesus' paschal mystery. As regards its function in 1 Tim 3, inasmuch as Jesus is heralded as the one "mediator between God and the human race" and as the "ransom for all" (2:5-6), the Jesus of this hymn is also the universal Jesus "proclaimed to the Gentiles . . . believed in throughout the world." The universality of Jesus' role is stressed in his resurrection visitation to angels as well as to humans and in his enthronement as Lord of the church. A catholic church has a catholic Savior.

It is often said that the Pastorals reflect a time when Christian faith was becoming frozen in dogmatic propositions. It is true that "the faith" of this church is remarkably clear and can be stated in brisk formulae, but this was true even of the Pauline churches, which knew of hymns (Phil 2:6-11) and confessional touchstones (Rom 10:9). The Pastorals evidently are concerned with false teachers and deviant doctrines, and so it is pastorally appropriate to point to the clear core of Christian faith. The traditions about Jesus' paschal mystery are the central aspects of the church's faith in him: he died for all, was vindicated by God, was enthroned as Lord of the church, and will come to judge the living and the dead.

4:1-5 Errors in the church. The mention of explicit errors in the church is prefaced by a "prophecy" about heretics arising in the community. This is a very conventional phrase, found especially in literature which purports to leave the "last will and testament" of an apostolic figure. Hence Paul predicted heretics attacking the church like wolves (Acts 20:29), just as Peter did (2 Pet 3:3). Yet differences of opinion existed even in the earliest Christian groups, so heresy is not a late event in the history of the church. It might be said that doctrinal pluralism has been with us from the beginning. False teachers will arise, possibly the same figures mentioned in 1:3-7. Here they are said to forbid marriage and impose dietary restrictions. Paul encountered similar problems at Corinth about marriage (1 Cor 7:1) and food (1 Cor 8, 10); rigorous dietary rules are noted in Rom 14 and Col 2:16-23. Although we know there are would-be teachers of the law expounding on the Old Testament, the situation here requires further clarification. There are strains of Judaizing concern for law observance which may be linked with claims that the resurrection has already occurred in the lives of authentic believers (see 2 Tim 2:18). This would imply that we are already "spiritual" and should abstain from physical pursuits such as sex, marriage, and food. Some claim that even this early we find the roots of a later heresy, gnosticism, which took a negative stance toward the world (see the mention of "gnosis"/knowledge in 6:20). Those most affected by this radical

error seem to have been certain women in the church who are described as easily deceived (5:13; 2 Tim 3:6). It is not surprising, then, that we find considerable favorable attention given to marriage: the urging of young widows to remarry (5:14) and instructions about married women (2:11-14; Titus 2:4).

The response to the errors is straightforward: all God made is good and for our use, which was also Paul's answer in 1 Cor 8:6 and 10:26. There is certainly nothing world-negating in this posture, and it accords with the view of God calling all people into this catholic church. A word of thanksgiving before meals reminds us of God's creative word and how all was made good and good for us (Gen 1:29-31). Like the prayers mentioned in 2:1, 8, this word of thanksgiving may well be a public blessing before a community meal (see 1 Cor 10:30-31).

4:6-10 False vs. true teachers. Ostensibly we have an exhortation to Timothy, but the content and context suggest that Timothy is contrasted with the false teachers of 4:1-5. A set of contrasts seems to structure the passage: false teachers busy themselves with myths and tales (4:7; see 1:4); true teachers are concerned with "the words of the faith and of sound teaching" (4:6). False teachers promote eccentric asceticism (4:3); true teachers admit the need of genuine spiritual discipline (gymnasia), but without excess. False teachers boast that they are already experiencing the resurrection (see 2 Tim 2:18); true teachers admit that future life is still a promise (4:8, 10). This last item, the promise of future life, is called in the Greek "a word of faith"; it represents a central item of early Christian belief, a clear tenet of faith touching on our relationship with God and Christ.

4:11-16 Timothy's duties. When bishops were discussed in 3:1-7, no specific duties were mentioned. Now we are told of Bishop Timothy's duties, which may conveniently serve as the job description for typical bishops in these churches. This is one more example of the list of "household duties" which extends from 2:1-6:2. Although young, Timothy is not to be overlooked in deference to "elders" in the group. He is to be a living example of full Christian faith—in the way he behaves, in what he believes, and in whom he loves. The advice in 4:12 is remarkable in its sense of how Christian faith should touch every aspect of our lives, moral and social as well. His specific task is to read the Scriptures accurately, unlike the false teachers of the law (1:7). Preaching and teaching indicate that his work is not simply missionary but full care of the church as it grows in time. Verse 4:14 speaks about Timothy's vocation in such a way as to undergird the authority he has in the church; God's grace to minister was given him through prophetic recognition (see Paul's calling in Acts 13:1-3); and this very letter serves as confirmation of this. Finally, Timothy is strongly encouraged to be constant in faith and labor, to persevere. The duties of bishops are, then, twofold: they are the church's authorized teachers and guardians of the faith, but they are also the living witnesses of their faith both in the integrity of their lives and in the perseverance in their tasks.

5:1-2 Respect for elders. Two more instructions are given to Bishop Timothy that are very appropriate for ancient cultures. As well as the Ten Commandments prescribe care for aged parents (see Sir 3:3-16), there is in the ancient world a deep respect for the elderly, which is reflected in the advice that Timothy deal gently with older men and women. Those more equal in age are treated as equals, as brothers and sisters in Christ. Although for conversion's sake one may be asked to "hate" parents (Luke 14:26), Christianity reinforced family social structures.

5:3-16 Rules for widows. Still more parts of the church's list of household duties are mentioned, this time rules concerning widows in the church. The first and most noteworthy rule is that Christian families should support widows—a point so important that it is mentioned three times (5:4-5, 8, 16). Popular biblical tradition speaks of God defending widows (Ps 146:9) and commanding their protection (Exod 22:22; Deut 16:14), and it may be that certain Christians expected God to provide miraculously for their own widows. But like Jas 1:27, true religion shows practical covenant love in care for the aged. In 5:5-6, true widows are contrasted with false ones; a true widow is first of all a religious woman who depends actively and totally on God, whereas a false widow is self-indulgent. Verses 9-10 lay down specific qualifications for true widows, qualifications not unlike those for bishops and deacons: age minimum, marital stability, a tested character, ability to manage

one's own family, and hospitality. The key test is her life of service, a life which she will continue to exercise much like a deaconess, although she is called "widow" instead.

In contrast to rules for including true widows, Paul gives rules for excluding others (vv. 11-13). Young women especially are urged to remarry, which probably should be seen in connection with the false teachers' attack on marriage in 4:3 (see also 2:15). The great danger of early widowhood is the time it gives for idleness and curiosity which Timothy sees as the soil sought out by the heretics (5:15). Far from rejecting God's gifts of family and marriage like the heretics, the author supports them and sees them as an important public witness to the church's world-endorsing attitude.

What is important in this archaic list of rules? Pauline churches celebrated the liberation and equality of women in Christ (see the discussion on 2:11-14), a thrust which appears to be muted in these very letters. The rank of widow may well be the last vestige of the public ministries which women were allowed to perform and of their free and independent lives in the church. There is no question here of eliminating this tradition, but one senses a move toward limiting the role of women in the public life of the church, both in scope of their actions and in the number of women who will perform these tasks.

5:17-22 Church elders. Chapter 5 began with concern for how Timothy should treat older men and women (vv. 1-2) and continued with questions of support for older women/widows (vv. 4-5, 8, 16). Now rules for dealing with the "elders" of the church are stated, another item in the list of household duties. Like the widows, the elders seem to be an important group in this church; they are probably to be distinguished from the bishops, although they too share the duty of preaching and teaching. They also are responsible for authorizing bishops, such as Timothy (4:14). There is no doubt that Bishop Timothy is the leader of this church, but his ministry seems to be in collaboration with a variety of elders, bishops, deacons, and widows. The first item in the rules for overseeing elders is their remuneration. Obviously "preaching and teaching" are the most important tasks in this group, a point made evident in the special double payment for this service (v. 17).

Although some Christian traditions speak of "giving freely" of what the preacher has freely received (Matt 10:8), yet as verse 18 states, there is biblical warrant for support. The text almost insists too much, for it cites the Old Testament (Deut 25:4) as well as the Christian tradition (Luke 10:7). Paul has attacked the false teachers as being money hungry, so one is surprised to find this seeming over-insistence on financial matters here.

Correct procedures are established for processing complaints and accusations against an elder. According to biblical tradition (see Deut 19:15; Matt 18:16), unless an accusation can be substantiated, it must be discounted. In Matthew, a church council rebuked an erring member (5:22; 18:17), a procedure also found in 1 Cor 5:1-5. Since an elder is a public figure and his sin is scandalous to the church, a public reprimand is in place. This is obviously a task as necessary as it is unpleasant, for the author practically requires a special oath on Timothy's part to carry this out (v. 21). The sense of holiness as well as fairness in the church demands no less. Finally, Timothy is warned not to be hasty in laying hands on any elder, implying that a period of testing is appropriate; the same advice is given in regard to deacons (3:10) and widows (5:10). This may stem from the confusing situation of the church with so much divergent teaching.

5:23-25 Miscellaneous remarks. Inasmuch as a strange form of diet and asceticism was wrongly urged in 4:3, the encouragement to drink wine is probably a further counter to that false teaching. Verses 24-25 present a typical exhortatory contrast between bad and good deeds. Some evil deeds are so flagrant that they call for present judgment (see the judgment of the elders in 5:19-21), and others will be revealed at God's judgment (see 2 Tim 4:1). Likewise some good deeds shine like lamps (see Matt 5:16) while others will be revealed later. Although this is reminiscent of the warning in Matt 10:26 that God's judgment will prevail, it seems to stress the importance of good deeds to promote the church's standing and the harm which evil deeds do to its mission (see 1 Pet 2:12). This should be linked with the concern for the public face of the church, which was treated earlier in regard to 2:1, 8 and 3:1-7.

6:1-2 Advice to slaves. Typical of Christian lists of household duties is advice to slaves and masters (1 Pet 2:18), but oddly only slaves' duties are mentioned here, although some of their masters are Christians. The early church proclaimed "freedom" in Christ, a bold proclamation which evidently led to considerable misunderstanding about the social status of slaves even in the Pauline churches. Most of the early churches did not see themselves as radically countercultural groups and thus did not promote slave liberation (1 Cor 7:20-22) or the abolition of all cultural customs (see the problem of women's veils in 1 Cor 11). Surely in the Pastorals the issue is: Can a Christian be a good citizen? In its struggle for toleration in ancient society, the church did not regularly see the world as an evil to be avoided or condemned. It urged its members on to civil obedience and civic responsibility as well as to moral excellence. The motive in 6:1-2 for slaves' behavior accords with this; failure to be responsible brings abuse upon the name of the Christian God and upon the Christian faith. Remember that bishops, who represent the church publicly to the world, should have a good public reputation (3:7). Christian slaves, especially those of Christian masters, should be responsible persons. Their tasks are not just menial for their "good works" are virtuous acts as well (the Greek *euergesias* implies an "act of kindness").

6:2-10 The evils of false teaching exposed. Verses 2-16 contrast two kinds of teachers: false teachers (2-10) and good teachers (11-16). In this first part the root causes and the final results of evil teachers are exposed. By definition a false teacher is one who does not adhere to the sound teaching proper to religion; he is rather inclined to speculation, polemics, and controversy (see 1:3-4). And since by their fruits you shall know them, they are shown to be false from the list of vices to which false teaching traditionally leads. The vices are just those which fracture a community, not unlike the problems which Paul confronted in 1 Corinthians. The sense of morality here is fully in keeping with the large sense of the church and its role in the world as light, example, and truth. The author imputes mercenary motives to the false teachers, a traditional charge in such debates (see 2 Pet 2:3). Once on the topic, the author contrasts the avaricious false teachers and anyone else lusting after money with the correct Christian appreciation for moderation and sufficiency; this contrast sounds similar to the gospel warning that we cannot serve two masters (Matt 6:24). The polemical attacks on the false teachers are rather traditional and stereotyped, but they serve to point out how false teaching is totally wrong—wrong in its motives, sources, and consequences.

6:11-16 Good teachers and their accountability. We now come to the last of the household duties mentioned in this letter. In contrast to the false teachers is Timothy, a man of God. Instead of seeking money, he should seek after virtue, especially virtues which build up the church, such as piety, faith, loving service, perseverance, and gentleness (see 1 Cor 13:4-7). True teaching does not fracture communities and lead to factions and arrogance. Timothy's task is faithful witness to Christ and the gospel, just as Jesus bore faithful witness before Pilate (see Luke 21:12-13). So difficult a task has a special reward, everlasting life (see 2 Tim 2:11).

Timothy is charged with keeping the "commandment," which may be the general covenant law required of all (see 1:8-11) or his own special commission from God. At any rate, he is called to be blameless and irreproachable, code words in this letter for faithful, persevering, and wholehearted service. Like Paul, the exercise of his commission is linked with the coming of Jesus and the divine scrutiny of human lives, especially those of leaders (1 Cor 4:1-5; 1 Thess 2:4). The solemn injunction to Timothy is closed by a typical benediction, calling upon the Christian God and acknowledging his uniqueness and sovereignty (6:15-16). The function of invoking God's judgment in regard to one's commission is common in the Pastorals (see 5:21 and 2 Tim 4:1). And the substance of the benediction is typical of the monotheistic doctrine of God characteristically preached here as well (see 1:17; 2:4-5). The benediction underscores the importance of the task entrusted to Timothy. And so ends the extended exposition of the household duties of the church.

6:17-19 A last word to the wealthy. A few last remarks are addressed to wealthy church members to be generous in their use of wealth and not to be proud of it nor trust in it. This advice is typical of the exhortations found in Luke that Gentiles who had no previous traditions of almsgiving and covenant charity should see that wealth is good only when generously used in service. Treasure in heaven has nothing to do with treasure laid up on earth (Luke 12:32-34).

6:20-21 Final advice to Timothy. This letter curiously closes without any mention of travel plans, greetings, etc., so typical of other letters. It ends, rather, on an anxious note. Final reminders are given to Timothy to guard the deposit of faith and to shun the useless speculations and myths of his rival teachers which pass as "gnosis"/knowledge. This is virtually the same advice given Timothy throughout the letter, but its repetition here seems urgent, suggesting that the crisis in the church is rather inflamed.

2 TIMOTHY

Jerome H. Neyrey, S.J.

INTRODUCTION

The basic introduction to 2 Timothy is well covered in the earlier general introduction to the pastoral Epistles. But certain important features of 2 Timothy deserve to be highlighted for they will help us to read the letter more sympathetically. Compared to 1 Timothy, the second letter is quite personal: The author complains of loneliness and abandonment; he relishes the kindness of fellow Christians (1:15-18; 4:9-13). Whereas 1 Timothy contains an extensive list of household duties for the diverse members of that church, the second letter addresses Timothy personally as a distinct individual, sympathizes with his difficult job, and encourages him in many touching ways to persevere. The list of greetings at the letter's close also points to a more familiar and personal ambiance for the letter.

The letter frankly acknowledges the plight of Timothy and his church. The bloom is surely off the rose in this church; day-to-day problems plague Timothy; unpleasantness (see "persecutions" in 3:12) besets him. His is not a glamorous job, hardly one to be ambitioned, for it is a thankless job of patient correction and guidance.

Some changes are noticeable in the theological contents of 1 and 2 Timothy. 1 Timothy was enormously rich in christological hymns and confessions, celebrating Christ's death and resurrection, his ransom of all people (1:15-16; 2:5-6; 3:16; 6:13-14). The second letter confesses Jesus primarily as Judge of the church, who rewards fidelity and faithful service and requites evil and error (1:18; 4:1, 8, 14). In 2 Timothy, Christ is still the

pattern to be followed: endurance with him means that we shall reign with him (2:11-12). The christological teaching of 1 Timothy was functionally integrated into the exhortation of that letter, which is also the case in the second letter, although the stress on Jesus as Judge is intended to support Timothy in hard times with promises of reward and success (see 4:6-8). The doctrine about the Christian God was so much fuller in the first letter than in 2 Timothy. Rich benedictions (1:17; 6:15-16), assertions of God's oneness and his universal salvific will (2:4-5), appeals to God's creative goodness (4:3), all point to a conscious reminder to pagan converts of the excellence of their faith in the God of Jesus Christ. This thrust is muted in the second letter, where there is only casual and passing mention of God as the one who chooses and commissions the church's leaders (1:6-8, 9; 2:10). God is likewise witness to the ministry of Paul and Timothy and will reward them accordingly. The shift obviously is a pastoral concern to call attention to Timothy's authority and the seriousness of his task.

So much attention is given to Timothy's role as protector of the faith that one might feel that only conservatism befits church leaders. Timothy's church surely faced serious and pressing problems with the orderly succession of its leaders, a problem commonly experienced by all religions. Its solution was to see succession validated in a living chain of witnesses from Paul to Timothy to others (see 2:2). Paul's sense of his impending death motivates him to confirm Timothy and to

1208

authorize him to appoint successors. The Spirit is less the designator of new leaders in the church than the abiding strength and support of the church (1:6-7) and the source of its fidelity to the gospel (1:14).

If the conservation duties of Timothy are so heavily stressed, this should be seen in the light of the churches of that period. They were beset with serious doctrinal problems which threatened the gospel (2:18); some of its leaders had quit the ministry (4:10); others seem to be advocating unacceptable doctrines (2:23; 3:6). Love seems to have grown cold (4:16). The leadership is disbursed (4:9-12). This was a time to strengthen the internal character of the church, to solicit and confirm new leaders, to clarify the faith of the developing church, and to keep firmly rooted in the tradition. Less exciting than a letter to a new church full of charismatic converts, 2 Timothy is a window into a church in an age of transition, in a confusingly pluralistic society.

COMMENTARY

1:1-2 Letter opening. Like typical letters, the opening of 2 Timothy indicates the sender (Paul), the addressee (Timothy), and a greeting. Although 1 Timothy suggested that the author's vocation comes from Jesus (1:12), here it is God who "wills" Paul to be an apostle, a theme repeated in 1:9. The purpose of the author's calling is unusual here: it is to proclaim the promise of life, which is explained more fully in 1:10.

1:3-8 Thanksgiving. Typically Pauline letters contain thanksgiving prayers right after the letter opening (see 1 Cor 1:4-9), and these thanksgivings typically function as summaries of the main themes and issues of the letter. Such is the case here also. The thematic items are introduced in verse 4 where Timothy's "sincere faith" (v. 5) is prayed over; this faith was evidently handed on from grandmother Lois to mother Eunice to son Timothy, a living and faithful chain of believers, which is just how Paul sees his relation to Timothy and to Timothy's successor bishops (see 2:2). Second, "faith," the central theme of the letter, has many meanings; it is helpful to distinguish them early in the letter. "Faith" may mean: (1) *fidelity* to duty or tradition (2:22; 3:10; 4:7), or (2) *orthodoxy* of belief (1:13; 4:7; negatively expressed in 2:18-19; 3:8), or (3) *personal bond* with Jesus (3:15). Third, Timothy's vocation is celebrated in such a way as to evoke faithfulness in him, a theme continually recurring in the letter (2:1-2; 4:2-5). Whereas, according to 1 Tim 4:14, the elders laid hands on Timothy, Paul claims that distinction here, perhaps to stress the clear chain of authority and correct teaching from Paul to Timothy and to his successors. Timothy is indeed charismatic in his vocation, for he has God's Spirit; but the function of the Spirit here is more structured as the guardian and support of God's chosen members than as the source of their appointment. The Spirit here gives "strength," evidently a code word for perseverance and fortitude in a difficult job rather than a power for charismatic signs and miracles (see 1 Cor 12:9-10). In fact, the fourth theme in the thanksgiving points to the hardships which Paul, Timothy, and their successors must endure in their jobs, a theme developed in 1:11-12; 2:2-7, 8-10; 3:12; 4:3-5. So the thanksgiving prayer calls immediate attention to the themes of the letter: vocation, fidelity, orthodoxy, and hardships.

1:9-14 The Pauline model of vocation. Paul regularly tells communities to imitate him (1 Cor 4:16; 1 Thess 1:6), and here the author says the same to Timothy (v. 13). Paul recalls that his vocation was a gift of God's grace (v. 9; see 1 Cor 15:10). This grace was already active "before time began," which is a typical Jewish statement about pre-existence which stresses how holy or important something is. In Eph 1:4 the church is said to be already chosen in Christ for redemption before creation. Paul himself saw his vocation as naturally linked to the appearance of Jesus, his Savior (see Acts 9:4-6; 1 Cor 9:1). Both 1 and 2 Timothy interchangeably designate God and Jesus as "Savior" (1 Tim 1:1; 2:3-4), which title in verses 9-10 speaks of Jesus' achievement as the vanquisher of death and the bringer of life and immortality. Typical Jewish-Christian references to our eschatological future speak of resurrection, but here a Greek phrase is used, "immortality" (of the soul), which may be just one more of the pastoral adaptations of the gospel message characteristic of these letters; after all, Paul used this language also with the Corinthians (1 Cor 15:42, 50-54). The pastoral thrust of this advice is centered in verses 12-14, where Timothy is commanded again to "guard this rich trust." The role of Timothy, then, is seen as custodian of the tradition, as one who faithfully hands on the gospel (see 2:2; 4:3). He does this with the strengthening power of God's Spirit who dwells in the church (1:7). It is not uncommon for Paul to speak of the Spirit in the church as a spirit of holiness (1 Cor 3:16-17) or as the holiness in individual Christians (1 Cor 6:19). Here the Spirit has a more structural role as the preserver of the gospel's integrity, very much the way we tend to understand the promise of infallibility to the church in contemporary theology.

1:15-18 False and faithful friends. Twice in the letter the author laments that church members appear to have failed in charity to him, first in Asia (1:15) and then in Rome (4:16). He contrasts these false friends with Onesiphorus, who literally fulfilled Jesus' command to visit those in prison (Matt 25:36); hence he prays for his reward on the day of judgment. The "Lord" spoken of here is surely the Lord Jesus, who is characteristically described as overseer of his church, who rewards the good and faithful servant at his return (see 4:1, 8, 14; Matt 24:45-47).

2:1-7 The hardships of ministry. The topic of this exhortation is summed up in 2:1, "Be strong in grace." As we have seen, Timothy's "strength" comes from God's Spirit who supports him daily in his difficult tasks. The prime task of his ministry is to "hand on" what he received, which is a technical formula in Jewish writings for indicating both that the material handed on is of prime importance and that its accurate transmission is a sacred enterprise. Paul prefaced his "handing on" of both the Eucharist and the resurrection traditions with just this tag (1 Cor 11:23; 15:3). This official handing on parallels the domestic handing on of faith from Lois to Eunice to Timothy (1:5). And this verse may be especially important as a clue to the function of this whole letter. As Paul laid hands on Timothy and confirmed his authority, so Timothy is empowered to do the same. This letter, then, serves as a source of authority both for the post-Pauline churches and beyond, for the chain of valid ministry is established through a correct "handing on" of the gospel and authority. The ministry of Timothy seems quite unenviable, for it will entail hardships (v. 3), singleness of life (v. 4), rigorous athletic training (v. 5) and simple hard work (v. 6).

2:8-13 Endurance and victory with Christ. The high point of this exhortation is the hymnic passage in 2:11-13 which invites us to conform to Jesus' paschal mystery and so to share his victory. This presumably is a popular hymn in Timothy's church and the appeal to it reflects the pastoral sensitivity of the author to explain his exhortation in terms meaningful to his hearers. Although addressed to Timothy, the invitation is open to all Christians. In substance, those who suffer hardships with Christ and for him, who die (v. 11) and who hold out to the end with him (v. 12) will live and reign with him. This clearly should be linked with the mention of "Jesus . . . raised from the dead" in 2:8 (1:10) and the suffering which Paul and Timothy experience for the gospel (2:9). Fidelity with Christ means victory with the Lord, a theme repeatedly stressed in the letter, especially in terms of the reward for faithful service (1:15-18; 4:1, 8, 17-18). But there is a problem in verses 12b-13. One verse says that denial of Jesus will be met with denial by Jesus, a common gospel warning (Matt 10:32-33). But verse 13 contradicts that and says that even "if we are unfaithful, he remains faithful." God's faithfulness is constantly noted in Paul's letters (1 Cor 1:9; 10:13; 1 Thess 5:24), in regard to God's promise of election and justification by faith, but not in regard to God's indifference to human sinfulness. This letter, however, which stresses the rewards and punishments for service and failure, would seem to suggest that verse 13 is somehow an addition to the text and that the theological stress is on verses 11-12—the appeal to conformity to Jesus as the source of life.

2:14-19 Why the job is so hard. Preaching the gospel of Jesus would be a serious enough task, but Timothy's job is complicated by the fact that his church seems to be beset with conflicting teaching on very crucial points. He, of course, should follow the straight course in preaching the truth (v. 15), which echoes the earlier command to "hand on" the truth (2:2) and to "take as your norm the sound words that you have heard" (1:13). Others in the group are seen to be engaged in disputes over words (v. 14), disputes which spread like a plague through the church (v. 17). One such error is pointed out: Philetus and Hymenaeus claim that the resurrection has already taken place, probably an overstatement of the proclamation that in baptism we die and rise with Christ (see Rom 6:3-5). It seems that certain charismatics in Paul's Corinthian church began to say the same thing (see 1 Cor 4:7), which led them to despise flesh and body in favor of "spiritual" existence, to feel superior to all authority, and to reject all rules in the name of resurrected freedom (1 Cor 6:12). Even this letter implies that we are to share with the risen Jesus "life and immortality" (1:10), and if we die with him we shall live with him (2:11-12). But the author never meant such confessional language to be taken so literally, for he constantly preaches in this letter the future scrutiny of all, even of heavenly appointed apostles (see 4:1, 8). He surely implies that we are indeed already justified and saved in Christ, but he equally insists that we will render an account to the Lord of how we have lived a life worthy of our calling (see Rom 14:10, 12). Because literalist and fundamentalistic interpretations can be very distorting of the truth, the church needs learned and authorized teaching.

2:20-26 A pure life of service. In contrast to false teachers, Timothy and other bishops must cooperate with God's calling and so cleanse themselves of evil things, to be fit and faithful ministers of the gospel. The differences in gold, silver, wood, and clay realistically point to people in the church variously gifted, similar to Paul's body metaphor in regard to diverse gifts in the church (1 Cor 12). What counts is not the material of the vessel but its holiness, its being set aside exclusively for the Lord's work. The contaminations to be avoided are twofold: (1) youthful passions, and (2) senseless disputations. But what positively consecrates a minister is the pursuit of the Christian virtues of righteousness, loving service, peace, and faithfulness. After all, the object of ministry is "every good work" in the service of the gospel. Likewise, a minister must guard the rich deposit of faith (1:14) and teach with clarity and charity, "correcting opponents with kindness" (v. 25). In short, he is the shepherd of God's flock (see Matt 18:12-14).

3:1-9 False teaching in the church. This passage follows up the exposé of the false teachers in 2:14-19, giving not so much a refutation of their doctrinal errors as the inevitable consequences of wrong teaching. A prediction is made by Paul that in the future ("the last days") false teachers would arise; this is a common convention in New Testament writings; e.g., in 1 Tim 4:1 the Spirit says that "in later times some will turn away from the faith," whereas in Acts 20:29-30 Paul predicted the same in his farewell address to the church of Ephesus. The function of this convention is to take the horror out of finding God's holy church split into factions and gangrenous with heresy; to lessen that shock the future horrors are artificially predicted. The danger to this church, nevertheless, is genuine, and the harm to it no less real. No specific identification of the false teachers is given, again a convention, for it does not make sense to give false ideas free publicity (yet see 2:18). Rather, the pattern here is to argue that false doctrines must be wrong, to judge by their evil results. Bad theology leads to bad morals. So we have a brief and stereotyped list of vices. Vice lists are a common feature of New Testament moral exhortations (1 Cor 6:9-10; Gal 5:19-21); Paul even used one in Rom 1 to show how wrong theology leads to base morality, the same point made here. The converse of this tactic is also true: good teaching leads to good morality. In 2:21-25 the good vessel, full of truth and gospel, is also full of virtue.

It is noted that these false teachers prey on women in the church (v. 6), which should not automatically be dismissed as an anti-feminist remark. After all, Lois and Eunice are noble evangelists (1:5) of their families; widows are virtuous and exemplary (1 Tim 5). But it would seem that Christianity was as vulnerable as the rest of the Graeco-Roman world to novelty in religion, a novelty especially attractive to women. Hence the Pastorals are quite sensitive to groups of women who do not find an ordered place in church and family (see 1 Tim 2:10-15; 5:12-15). Like the parable of the wise and foolish virgins (Matt 25:1-13), there are obviously two classes of women in these churches: the wise, faithful, upright and the foolish, unstable gadabouts. Although no specific identification of the false teachers is given, they are described as contentious people, constantly quarreling with the church's leadership. They oppose the truth (v. 8), like the two magicians of legend who argued against Moses when he tried to lead Israel out of Egypt (see Exod 7:11). This brands them as the ultimate opponents of the church's freedom in Christ.

3:10-17 The author's example as teacher. In contrast to the false teachers who oppose the truth, Timothy is praised as one who has "followed my teaching" (v. 10; see 2:2). The emphasis here is squarely on the fidelity needed in a burdensome job. Timothy is explicitly told that his task is not simply to guard the rich deposit (1:14), but gently to correct his "opponents" (2:25) and to correct, reprove, appeal "through all patience" (4:2). The firm but patient exercise of authority by the bishop entails hardships, which is why Timothy is reminded of Paul's conduct as well as his teaching (v. 10). Persecutions come with the job—not political harrassment from state officials but hostility from within the church. Hence the prized virtues are those which support one in such difficulties: "purpose, faith, patience . . . endurance" (v. 10). The foundation of this good behavior is adherence to the truth, so Timothy is urged to be faithful to the belief of the church, to the authentic chain of its teaching (1:5; 2:2).

Special mention is made of Timothy's acceptance of the Scriptures—surely the Hebrew Bible, which is read in the light of faith in Jesus. The Scriptures alluded to here may well be the Pentateuch, the way of covenant living; for the author notes that these Scriptures lead to salvation those who believe in Christ. Hence, they do not prophetically point so much to Jesus himself but to how Christians live. We know of a debate in 1 Timothy over interpretations of the Old Testament law (1:7) and erroneous attitudes to marriage, diet, and other ascetical practices. The author indicated there (1:8-11) that the Ten Commandments are the covenant code of the Christian church, suggesting a Christian insistence, not on Old Testament laws and legalism but on the expressions of the law of love as found in the essential covenant code.

The early church was beset on both sides by erroneous attitudes to the law. Some would throw out all laws and live as libertines and antinomians, freed from all authority and order; they based this stand on the radical freedom they experienced in sharing Christ's resurrection and in the possession of God's Spirit (see 1 Cor 6:12); this line of thinking may be reflected in 2 Tim 2:18. Others would reimpose Judaism on Christianity and demand strict observance of the law (Acts 15:1, 5; Gal 5:1-2); they based their arguments on the lasting importance of God's revealed word as Scripture. The early churches saw dangerous excesses in both directions and tried to insist both on the essential end of the law in Christ and freedom in the Lord, yet freedom which was understood as complete obedience to the Lord Jesus and the living of a life worthy of one's calling. In 3:15-16, the lasting value of Scripture is maintained. It is, after all, the inspired Word of God. Unlike Marcion and other early heretics who would completely dispense with the Hebrew Bible, this author insists that the Jewish Scriptures remain the Bible of the church. Nor were they merely spiritualized, as a collection of prophecies about Jesus. For as verse 16 shows, they are useful for "teaching—for refutation, correction, and training in righteousness." Yet for all this concern for the permanent validity of the Old Testament, there is relatively little of it explicitly cited in the Pastorals (see 1 Tim 5:18; 2 Tim 2:19), although these letters are incredibly rich in allusions to the Scriptures and to the traditional moral teaching of late Judaism.

4:1-5 Timothy's solemn commission. The author invokes a most solemn setting to confirm Timothy's commission. God is called to witness that Timothy is duly commissioned with this office, as is Jesus who is the Lord of this church and its Judge. A similar formula was used in 1 Tim 5:21 to undergird Timothy's teaching of church order. Here the solemn appeal not only confirms Timothy's commission but reminds him of the importance of his task, one which Christ will evaluate at the church's judgment, a familiar theme in the synoptic Gospels (see Matt 24:42-51). Paul frequently invoked the final judgment in his letters as an appeal to the churches to cease judging him and to let God's true judgment prevail (1 Cor 4:1-5), but here the appeal is made for another purpose, to underscore the importance of this job.

The tasks of this office are many and varied: Timothy is evangelist (4:5), teacher (2:24), and guardian of the deposit of faith (1:14). But his job has many unpleasant aspects as well, for his leadership will entail correction (2:25) and rebuke (4:2). The author never ceases to warn of the hardships of this job (1:12; 2:3; 3:11-12); to be forewarned is to be forearmed (see 2:2-7). Obviously Timothy's greatest trial is dealing with the opponents described in 2:18 and 3:7-8, some of whom are seen as rejecting all law and order in the church while others seem to be bent on binding the church with rigorous laws and customs. They are the ones preoccupied with myths and speculations (4:4; see 1 Tim 1:4; 4:7; Titus 1:14). They will not tolerate "sound doctrine," which is a favorite phrase in these letters, "soundness" being a quality of *teaching* (1 Tim 1:10; 2 Tim 4:3; Titus 1:9), *words* (1 Tim 6:3; 2 Tim 1:13), *preaching* (Titus 2:8), and *faith* (Titus 1:13). Soundness reflects both on accuracy of teaching and the correct morality to which it leads. Evidently the church is struggling to find some accepted mechanism within the group to solve doctrinal problems and so avoid schisms and heresies. This effort put great burdens on Timothy and his successors, as well as it demanded great loyalty from church membership.

4:6-8 Farewell. Often in his letters Paul warned that he was about dead in Christ's service (Phil 1:21-23; 2 Cor 5:2), a topic which seems to be more seriously treated here. In fact, this letter is often cited as an example of Paul's farewell address, his last will and testament, which was a common enough convention in the early church. We have Jesus' farewell addresses in John 13–17 and Luke 22:14-38, Peter's in 2 Pet 1:12-15, even Paul's in Acts 20. Typical of such literary forms are: (1) acknowledgment that death is near, (2) warnings about the coming of false teachers, (3) the appointment of successors to carry on the tradition, and (4) correct interpretation of disputed points. The language here is typical of Paul's farewells; he is a libation already poured out (Phil 2:17); he has fought the good fight (1 Tim 6:12), run the race (2 Tim 2:5; 1 Cor 9:24). His crowning achievement is: "I have kept the faith" (v. 7), which means both his careful handing on of the gospel to his successors (2:2) and his faithfulness in his office as evangelist and teacher. Like Paul in 1 Cor

4:1-5, he looks forward to God's judgment to prove him worthy and to reward him with the traditional crown of success. Crowns of laurel go to athletic champions (1 Cor 9:25), to church leaders (1 Pet 5:4), and to typical Christians (Rev 2:10). Here the phrase stresses the crown of life, the immortality which Jesus won for us (see 1:10). The letter, moreover, emphasizes that death endured with Jesus will result in life with him (2:11-12). This stress on eschatological reward (4:1, 8) is not accidental, especially in light of those who would deny a future reckoning with Jesus in their insistence that the eschatological event has *already* come, since they are *already* sharing in Jesus' resurrection (2:18). In this modest way, the letter reinforces a disputed aspect of the gospel tradition about Jesus by affirming him as Judge and Lord of the church.

4:9-13 Loneliness in ministry. Just as the author complained of loneliness in 1:15-18, he again gives us a very personal statement. But this passage is equally remarkable for the window it gives us on the geographical spread of the early church: Thessalonika, Dalmatia, Galatia, Troas, and Rome. Travel was relatively easy; journeys were frequent, and Christianity moved easily and quickly in this mobile society.

The list of persons mentioned is difficult to evaluate. The names themselves are very common in the ancient world, and they may be related to known figures of the Pauline communities. Demas, Luke, and Mark all send greetings with Paul to Philemon (v. 24) and to the Colossian church (4:14). Luke may be the traveling companion of Paul in Acts 16 and 20–21; Mark may be the co-worker of Paul in Acts 15:37-39; and Tychicus of Acts 20:4 may be the same faithful figure whom Paul regularly sends as his personal emissary (Col 4:7; Eph 6:21; Titus 3:12).

4:14-18 Trials and rescues. Faithful and false friends were contrasted earlier in 1:15-18, and as Onesiphorus was commended to God's blessing judgment for visiting the author in prison, now Alexander is commended to God's severe judgment for harming him. His harm, however, is compounded by his having "resisted our preaching," which makes us think of Alexander in 1 Tim 1:20 who made a shipwreck of his faith. The notice of escape from the lion's jaw need not imply his imprisonment under Nero and the threat of exe-

TITUS

Jerome H. Neyrey, S.J.

COMMENTARY

1:1-4 Letter opening. The letter opening contains the typical note about the sender (Paul), addressee (Titus), and a greeting ("grace and peace"). The author is both an apostle and "slave of God," which was a common biblical description of one commissioned by God (see 2 Sam 7:5), a description used by James (1:1) and 2 Pet (1:1). What is unusual about this letter opening is the lengthy remark about the purpose of the author's commissioning. It is not only to bring pagans to faith but to promote "the recognition of religious truth," suggesting a more long-term, settled role than the picture of Paul in Acts and his letters, dashing from city to city, making converts, and moving on. Obviously for pastoral reasons the author is calling attention to his new role as one who teaches the fine points of the gospel faith, with special attention to the proper understanding of Jesus' resurrection and second coming and the Christian's relationship to these.

1:5-9 Qualifications of presbyters and bishops. Structurally 1:5-9 balances 1:10-16, contrasting good leaders with bad teachers in the church. Here we find a list of qualifications for the good teachers, the bishops, which list probably tells us about the prime purpose of the letter: the authorization of both Titus and his successors. And in its list of qualifications, Titus shows greater affinity to 1 Timothy than to the second letter; not only do they have a list of qualifications, but the items in both lists are almost identical.

The qualifications of church leaders do not seem to differ from those one would expect of a reputable city official: a person of good character, experience, probity, whose upright life is an excellent argument in support of his good advice. In short, he must be a responsible public figure. The duties and tasks of bishops, however, are only mentioned in passing in verse 9, where they are expected to be orthodox in preaching, both to encourage and to rebuke. The virtues of bishops are the same as those expected of all church members. But what makes this list important for contemporary readers is the window it gives us on the church at that time and place, a church realizing that its leaders are as important as witnesses to the secular world of Christianity's excellence as they are internal guides and models of the power of the gospel to permeate and shape full, responsible life.

1:10-16 In contrast, false teachers. Titus is warned about false teachers, especially converts from Judaism. Now Paul and the early church were beset with a similar and persistent problem, whereby new converts were required to be circumcised and otherwise made to live like Jews (Gal 5:1-2; Phil 3:19). Evidently this erroneous movement in the early church lived on, for it is addressed harshly in 1 Timothy where some would reimpose on converts the Old Testament law (1:7) and Jewish dietary restrictions (4:3-4). Here it is a threat to the church at Crete, imposing on converts "rules invented by men" (see Mark 7:7-8, 13), especially dietary laws. The statement in verse 15, "to the clean all things are clean," is similar to Paul's argument against clean/unclean foods in Rom 14:20, a function

1215

which it has here as well. The fuller response, of course, is found in 1 Tim 4:4, where God's creative goodness touches all creatures and so there can be no unclean (or "bad") creature, especially in the new creation begun in Christ's resurrection. The Judaizing dietary observances are evidently based on bad theology, or "Jewish myths," as they are called in the Pastorals (1:14; 1 Tim 4:7, and 2 Tim 4:4).

Asceticism and a strict moral life are *not* the issues here. Titus is hardly liberalizing the life of this church. These Judaizing problems threaten the core of the church's life and so must be taken seriously. If successful, the Judaizing threat from the right would reduce Christianity from a religion open to all (see 2:11; 1 Tim 2:4-6) to a mere splinter Jewish sect. If the strict keeping of Jewish customs was *necessary* for being a Christian, then this challenges the absolute redemption effected in Christ's death (see Gal 2:21). Either we are saved entirely by Christ or we save ourselves by observing laws and customs. When the issue is put this starkly, the church has always maintained that redemption is a gift of grace from Christ, not our own doing. While resisting these Judaizing tendencies, the author is no less emphatic that true Christian faith must subsequently flower in a life of uprightness and integrity. Morality is no less important for him than it was for the Judaizers, but the understanding of its place in relationship to Jesus' saving death is radically different.

2:1-10 The church and social structures. Like the list of domestic duties urged upon the church in 1 Tim 5:1-16 and 6:1-2, we find a similar list here. Unlike 1 Timothy, there is no concern for widows in Titus' church, nor is he instructed how to deal with older Christians. The focus is typically on the responsibilities of recognizable social groups, a pattern of exhortation found in many New Testament writings (Col 3:18–4:1; Eph 5:21–6:9; 1 Pet 2:18–3:8). In a chiastic form, older men (A), older women (B), young women (B'), and young men (A') are addressed. They are all called upon to be good family examples, self-controlled, steadfast, and loving. The importance of these exhortations lies not in the list of virtues or vices, which are rather obvious, but in the sense of the public face the new religion must have. Could Christians be good parents and raise honorable families? Would

Christianity so liberate people from former ties and structures that the social fabric would be destroyed (see Mark 10:29 and 1 Cor 7:10-15)? Would Christians be loyal and upright citizens? Verse 5 clearly tells us of the church's public concern: If families are authentically Christian, then "the word of God may not be discredited." This same concern stands behind Titus' own charge that he be sound in faith and practice; if he does, "the opponent will be put to shame without anything bad to say about us" (v. 8). Likewise, by honest lives slaves will "adorn . . . the doctrine of God our savior" (v. 10). Thus there is a strong evangelizing thrust to this teaching. The best apology the church had for its new doctrine was the probity of the lives of its converts and the result of this good theology in exemplary moral lives. By their fruits you shall know them.

2:11-15 Faith and moral living. We noted above that good theology leads to good morals, which axiom serves as the link between the previous list of duties and the present passage. "Grace" is proclaimed (v. 11), which if authentic "trains us to reject godless ways and . . . live temperately" (v. 12). But what is the faith of the church? In verses 11, 13-14 we are reminded of the basic kerygma in crisp, clear terms. God has appeared in our history to save all people (v. 11), which plan was realized in Jesus who redeemed us by his sacrifice (v. 14). Already justified, we wait for our sanctifying confirmation at "the appearance of the glory of the great God and of our savior Jesus Christ" (v. 13). The gospel kerygma is not at all theoretical, for it is told in a way that stresses how it is the pastoral foundation of the church's ethical exhortation. We were redeemed from "lawlessness" and cleansed from sin and made eager to do what is right. Our redemption was both a radical change of life from sin to grace and also an instruction and empowerment by God's Spirit in integrity (see "training," v. 12). If this conversion of mind and life is authentic, then we will stand confidently on the day of God's scrutiny.

3:1-2 Citizenship and Christianity. These are the final bits of exhortation in the church's list of "household duties." It is not uncommon in Christian exhortations to encourage prayer for the emperor (1 Tim 2:1-3); here obedience to legitimate civil authority is praised as a

Christian virtue, as was the case in Rom 13:1-7 and 1 Pet 2:13-17. The church does not see itself as a sect opposing the state or the world but indicates that Christians belong to that world and should be exemplary citizens. Part of that citizenship is "to be open to every good enterprise" (v. 1). The text literally says "ready for every good," which may refer equally to virtue as to employment. Perhaps "employment" is valid, for in 3:14 the church membership is encouraged to live lives of "good works to supply urgent needs." And in 2 Thess 3:6-11, we find a lengthy exhortation to avoid idleness and pursue an honest day's work, climaxing in the famous saying that "anyone who would not work should not eat" (3:10). Since Christian citizenship is the topic in 3:1-2, it is probably safe to interpret verse 1 as urging Christians to a full civic life—respect for government, full employment, and a neighborly avoidance of quarrels and slander.

3:3-8 The difference Christianity makes. This paragraph tries to spell out the difference Christianity should make in the lives of believers by contrasting former lives of sin with new lives in faith; the same pattern may be found in Eph 2:3-10 and 1 Pet 4:1-3. The argument is one we have already seen in the letter: good (i.e., Christian) theology leads to good morality. Hence good citizenship is not only compatible with Christianity but enhanced by it. Former pagan lives were typically characterized by slavery to passions— malice, envy, hatred of self—hardly a commendation for good citizenship.

The contrast between former pagan lives of vice and present Christian lives of virtue rests not on a strenuous moral effort on the part of Christians but on God's action of grace. And given the tendency of the Judaizing members of this church to exaggerate the meaning and importance of law observance (1:14-15), the theological foundation of the Christian's new life is explained. Excellent is the Christian God, a God of kindness and philanthropy (v. 4); God's excellence is not abstract but historical; it has "appeared" (see 2:11) in time and history; and it is active—it saved us. Salvation, however, does not come from the Judaizing perfection of law obedience but rather from God's mercy (v. 5). This is vintage Pauline teaching, which occurs also in Eph 2:8-9 and in 2 Tim 1:9. We saw earlier in 2:14 that God's salvation was realized in

Jesus' sacrificial death, and Christians personally participate in that salvation when they receive the cleansing of a new birth and the gift of God's Spirit.

Both of these items are standard elements in Christian preaching: conversion is often described as a new birth (see John 3:5; 1 Pet 1:3, 23; 2:2), a baptism of cleansing (Eph 5:26), and as a gift of a new spirit (Gal 4:6). Just as God gave a spirit of life to Adam's lifeless clay body and made him alive, and as God put a new and holy spirit in Christ's body at the resurrection and made him alive (Rom 1:4), so in our sharing in Christ's death and resurrection God made us alive by putting a new and holy Spirit in us, a Spirit which allows us to love and acknowledge God as "Abba" and to walk blamelessly in our new lives (Gal 4:6; Rom 8:14-17). Far from being God's enemies, we become God's children, even heirs (Gal 4:7; Rom 8:17). Our life does not end in death, as pagans believed, but we have in God a hope of eternal life (see 1:2; 2:13 and 2 Tim 2:10). So Christians are radically changed because God has entered their lives, and to the pagan world the Christian God is proved to be true Lord and Savior of all. Faith in this God, far from corrupting us, perfects us for a full and responsible life.

3:8-11 Final directives to Titus. Timothy certainly had ample instruction concerning his duties (see 2 Tim 4:2-6), but only here does Titus receive a brief set of "dos and don'ts." Titus should "insist" on what has been said (v. 8), that is, both the truth about the free gift of salvation from our God and the new moral lives to which our faith leads us. This is not only true but is a selling point for Christianity in the religious marketplace (v. 8b). Titus is *not* to be like the false teachers who were exposed in 1:10-16. He must shun arguments like theirs over "genealogies" and abstain from controversies, especially quarrels over the law (see 1:14-15). This point has been adequately thrashed out in the early church, and there can be no going back on the issue of law vs. grace. It is useful ("advantageous") to insist on the truth (v. 8), but Judaizing insistence is definitely not useful (v. 9).

Like Timothy, Titus is to rebuke and correct the wrong-thinking members of the church (v. 10; see 2 Tim 2:25; 4:2). Two warnings, in fact, are given, which in some way resemble the gradual process of correction in

Matt 18:15-17. If the warnings fail, then the "heretic" would appear to be censured with some form of social correction, seemingly a form of excommunication (see 1 Tim 1:20). The severity of the action is in proportion to the danger perceived. Not only was this false doctrine a contradiction of the cross of Christ, its proponents were apparently avid proselytizers (see 1 Tim 5:15; 2 Tim 3:6), and so were becoming like gangrene in the church (see 2 Tim 2:17-19).

3:12-15 Final directives. The mobile state of the first-century church is well reflected in these final directives. Messengers are to be sent, presumably from Rome or the western Mediterranean eastward to Nicopolis. Tychicus must do a lot of traveling for the author claims to be sending him to Ephesus in 2 Tim 4:12. And missionaries, it would seem, are also being dispatched: Apollos, who may be the famous Alexandrian scholar known from Acts 18 and 1 Cor 1-4, and Zenas, who is otherwise unknown. It is interesting to note that Zenas is a "lawyer," not a Jewish scribe but a jurist; he is evidently a figure of considerable education and social standing, like Erastus, the city treasurer mentioned in Rom 16:23. They are to be equipped for their journey by the host community, a procedure typical of Paul's own missionary practice (see 2 Cor 11:8-9; Phil 4:14-16). Verse 14 is a general summary exhortation to the church to be good citizens, taking care of their own needs and not being idle or lazy (see 3:1 and 1 Tim 5:8). The letter concludes with a typical epistolary greeting and farewell.

JAMES

Jerome H. Neyrey, S.J.

INTRODUCTION

Author

There is considerable scholarly debate over the authorship of this letter. If James is truly the author, then he could be "James, son of Alphaeus" (Matt 10:3) or more probably "James, the brother of the Lord" (Gal 1:19; see also Mark 6:3). This James, moreover, was a major figure in the early church; the risen Jesus appeared to him (1 Cor 15:7); he became second head of the Jerusalem church (Acts 12:17), and he was a leading figure in opening the church to Gentile membership, both in his guidance of the Jerusalem conference in Acts 15 and in his confirmation of Paul's ministry to the Gentiles (Gal 2:9). He is the figure Paul visited on his last trip to Jerusalem (Acts 21:17-18). But as is the case with the pastoral and catholic Epistles, there is a solid argument that the letter is pseudonymous, only attributed to James. The material in James is very common hortatory material and does not demand an eyewitness either for its source or value. The vision of the church is that of a more developed group than the apostolic churches. The debate over authorship eventually is irrelevant to a pastoral understanding of the text, for the letter is transparently rich with traditional New Testament materials. It does not need genuine authorship to secure its authority or the worth of its contents. To judge from the pseudonymous character of the letter and its developed view of the church, the date of James' composition is judged to stem from the late first century.

Genre and thrust of James

Although it is loosely put in a letter form, the genre of James is more accurately that of exhortation or popular moral teaching, which was common in Jewish wisdom literature, in the Sermon on the Mount (and 1 Pet), and in Graeco-Roman writings as well. Characteristically there is a frequent use of imperatives and a persistent urging to excellence. The exhortation typically consists of a chain of smaller items, sometimes connected (especially by catchwords), but often haphazardly strung together. The main topics typically include concerns for perseverance, proper speech, prayer, practical charity, avarice, pleasure, etc.—all standard items in exhortatory literature. The exhortation is laced with vivid metaphors and pointed citations from the Scriptures.

The author delights in sharp contrasts between good/evil and alive/dead to highlight his point. One must insist on the very traditional character of all of James' material, for he serves as an excellent window on the preaching of the church to converts on the need for perseverance and for a thorough conversion of their lives to God. James represents the pastoral concern of the early church to lead the flock of God into greater and greater possession of its gift of salvation. Far from overturning the advances in Pauline theology, as some have contended, James' concern for the moral life of the church really takes seriously Paul's basic exhortation "to live a life worthy of the calling you have received" (Eph 4:1; see also 1 Thess 2:12; Phil 1:27; Col 1:10).

1219

Major themes

While there is surprisingly little material about Jesus (1:1 and 2:1), there are extensive reminders about the Christian preaching about God. After all, pagans were regularly converted to faith in the one true God (see 1 Thess 1:9-10) as well as to faith in Jesus. The rich portrait of God in James is, of course, traditional and is based on biblical sources: God is "compassionate and merciful" (5:11), Lawgiver and Judge (4:12); God is one (2:19), creator (1:18), constant and unchanging (1:17).

James' main concerns are for perseverance in conversion to God and growth in the living of gospel morality. He sees the intimate relationship between faith in God and love of neighbor, for both are characteristic of cove-nant faith. The integrity of the moral life is maintained: one cannot pick and choose among God's covenant laws (2:10-11). James never tires of pointing out the roots of disorder in our lives and urging us to control them lest they devour us like a forest fire. James' sense of church constantly dominates his writing to remind us that religion is not a private affair between us and God but a covenant relationship between God and his covenant people; hence love of neighbor (2:8) as well as the foregoing of judgment are persistent themes. One cannot but be impressed by James' pastoral sense of the wholeness of Christian life, the maturity to which the gospel must grow in believers, and the active relation between religion and life. No part-time Christians in James' churches!

COMMENTARY

1:1 Letter opening. The work begins with the most unexciting of letter openings. The sender is identified as James, "slave of God" (see introduction). The addressees are the "twelve tribes in the dispersion," which probably means the church at large in the pagan world. The fact that the twelve tribes are addressed suggests the catholicity of James, that it was written not just to one church (e.g., Corinth), or to seven churches (Rev 1–3), or to the regional churches of Pontus, Asia, and Galatia (1 Pet 1:1), but to Christian churches everywhere.

1:2-4 Perseverance. Where typical letters start with "thanksgiving prayers," James begins with an exhortation to persevere. Instead of being depressed by difficulties or thinking that trials give a lie to the Christian proclamation of Jesus' victory, we are to count trials as "all joy." In 1 Pet 1:6-7 trials are deemed valuable because they test the gold of faith in fire; here they are acceptable because they lead to worthwhile ends: endurance, perfection, and maturity (v. 4). The chain effect of one virtue leading to another is a common feature in this type of literature (see Rom 5:3-5 and 2 Pet 1:5-7). Obviously this is addressed to people who have been justified in Christ and for whom sanctification (i.e., endurance and growth toward maturity) is now the dominant task.

1:5-8 Prayer and faith. The catchword linking verses 4 and 5 is "lacking": the perfect Christians lack nothing, but if anyone lacks something, let them pray. So the new topic is introduced. Perseverance will lead to maturity in which we lack nothing, but a shortcut to supply what is lacking is prayer. Typical of this author is the use of contrasts in describing what is right/wrong. Here we find contrasting "pray-ers": true believers ask in faith (Mark 11:24) but false pray-ers are doubters or "split persons" (see v. 8). The advice is less a word on how to pray than it is another call to completeness and maturity as Christians. And for the first time we find one of the vivid images used by James: a doubting pray-er is like surf tossed by the wind.

1:9-11 Rich and poor. We are introduced briefly to a theme which James will develop more at length later. This terse word only stresses the contrast between right and wrong behavior: the poor of the community are correct to boast in their exaltation which eventually comes from God; the rich are wrong to boast for they are as fragile and short-lived as flowers which the sun scorches. This image reminds us of God's fiery and discerning judgment (see Matt 3:11-12). It is assumed that the rich are somehow split persons (see v. 8) for they are described as "fading away" because they are involved "in the midst of pursuits" (v. 11) besides God and the gospel.

1:12-16 Temptation. James returns to the theme with which he began the letter in 1:2-4; temptations befall converts to Jesus. But blessed is the one who endures such temptations, a phrase resembling the beatitudes in the Sermon on the Mount (Matt 5:3-11). Many themes and terms return for fuller consideration: temptation, endurance, testing (1:2-3, 12). Whereas endurance led to maturity, now we are told that it leads to a crown of life, which is a traditional statement of God's saving judgment (see 1 Cor 9:25 and 2 Tim 4:8). The source of temptations remains a problem; the author insists that God does not bring them upon us but that we are tempted by our own lusts and desires. But all of us, nevertheless, are subject to testing. The speculative aspects of this problem are less important than the pastoral contrast between two possible results: the one who endures temptation is blessed (v. 12) but others when tempted give birth to a chain of evils leading to death (v. 15).

1:17-18 God and God's gift. James returns to God's giving (see 1:5-7), but now to remind the converts about the God whom Christians worship. God gives good gifts (1:5, 17) impartially to all. God rewards (v. 12) and punishes (v. 11); God does not tempt us (v. 13), nor is God changeable or fickle (v. 17). What this means is that God is a moral God. He purposefully made the world and chose us (v. 18), and his moral purpose pervades the universe of his chosen ones. Hence, those who commit themselves to a moral God must be moral as well. As God is steadfast, so should we be.

1:19-25 True vs. false believers. Two different contrasting pieces of advice are contained here: we are to be swift to listen (v. 19) but woe betide the listener who is slow to act (v. 22). The first advice contrasts patient with quick-tempered people (vv. 19-21); the second comment contrasts believers who only listen with believers who act on their faith (vv. 22-25). The term "word" is the catchword linking verses 18, 21, and 22-23: God's word created us, resides in us to save us, but must be acted upon. The emphasis here is on verses 22-25; what one does and how one lives out the faith is the moral concern of this author. Typically he uses a contrast to get his point across about what the true Christian is like. The false Christian only glances at the mirror and has no perseverance, no memory, no moral response to the gospel. The true Christian looks, sees, remembers, and acts. The seed of faith is alive and active (see the parable of the seeds again, Mark 4:14-20). According to verse 25, the true Christian is not lawless but shoulders the yoke of Christ (Rom 6:18, 22) and so the law is a law of freedom from evil, a perfect law which does not enslave. James labels this person with the traditional tag for success, "such a one shall be blessed" (v. 25). Some commentators see here an attack by James on Paul's "works vs. grace" principle, but that is unjustified by the text. What we have is a contrast between two types of believers, between true and false believers. For while all are freely justified by God through faith, our sanctification demands that we live a life worthy of our calling.

1:26-27 True vs. false religion. In still another contrast, James tells us what is true/false religion. False piety, like faith without action in 1:22-23, is religion which has no ramifications in the life of a believer. Anyone who professes love of God yet whose tongue is abusive of the neighbor is empty and misguided (see Matt 5:22)—the theme of correct speech is both a common topic in this type of literature (Sir 28:12-16) and a topic which will be developed later in 2:16; 3:1-12; 4:11 and 5:13. True religion acknowledges the bridge between covenant faith and covenant love, for it manifests itself in concern for "orphans and widows," the traditional people in the community most in need of covenant support (see Deut 27:19; Ezek 22:7 and Acts 6:1; 1 Tim 5:3-16). True religion also abstains from worldly self-seeking and self-assertion (see 4:2) and so is unstained and purehearted before God.

Chapter 1, then, presents a wide sample of small bits of exhortation. In general, James addresses the developing life of Christians, reminding them of the moral God who redeems them and calls them to a wholehearted and faithful life. His favorite technique is to describe right and wrong in vivid images (waves, burning sun, mirrors) and by means of sharp contrasts between good and evil, true and false.

2:1-7 Favoritism in the church. A community meeting is described where two clients come to the elders for a judgment (see 1 Cor 6:1-6). James attacks the favoritism that is naturally shown to successful and influential people, arguing that such is wrong. In a different context Paul insisted on God's lack of favoritism, both in judgment (Rom 2:11) and in election (Rom 3:22; 10:12); this impartiality destroyed the privileged position of the Jews as God's favorites and led to a radical sense of egalitarianism in the Pauline churches (see Gal 3:28). This is probably the basis for James' attack on favoritism here: God's impartiality to us and our equal status in the church. The attack again centers on the way Christians evaluate rich and poor; in the Old Testament literature, wealth is seen as a sign of God's blessing and favor (Ps 128), but not so in the Christian tradition which calls the poor "blessed" (Matt 5:3) and sees them as God's favorites (Luke 1:50-53). So James argues in verse 5 that God's election is to the poor as well, to make them rich (and equal) in faith (see 1:9). The church is called to witness to its faith: as God is impartial, calls all to life, and even favors the poor, orphans, and widows, so the church must mirror God's actions in its structures, lest it be like the person of shallow faith without works (see 1:22-25).

2:8-11 Love as the key to faith. In contrast to the favoritism condemned in 2:1-7, true religion is described in verses 8-11. One acts rightly if one keeps the law of the kingdom, to love one another. Ordinarily in the New Testament this command occurs alongside the command to love God with all one's heart (Matt 22:37-39), but here it is presumed that one is a believer in (and lover of) God. The problem is: How does faith/love of God show itself practically in our lives? Hence, the stress in 2:8-11 is on love of neighbor as the demonstration of the one who hears and acts (1:22-24) and of the one whose faith is alive (2:14-17).

Covenant love excludes favoritism (v. 9) as well as aggression against a community member. The argument insists that we are to keep the whole law, probably the Ten Commandments as covenant law (see Matt 15:19; 19:18-19). To fail in covenant love in one area is to fail completely. This demand for completeness in the Christian moral life is quite characteristic of James, who repeatedly calls upon us to be mature and perfect (1:4), faultless (3:2), and spotless (1:27). Religion, then, is not a part-time, selective, compartmentalized activity. This exhortation ends with the call to expect moral scrutiny from God for our lives. Merciless people, who show favoritism or neglect widows and orphans, will find little mercy with God (see Matt 7:2; 25:33-46); but in typical Christian fashion, mercy will cover many sins (see 1 Pet 4:8). Typical also is the idea found even in the Our Father that what we do to others will be done to us (see Matt 6:14-15).

2:14-17 Dead and live faith. In another series of contrasts, James juxtaposes active faith with verbal faith, live faith with dead faith. The passage begins and ends with the same phrase, "faith that does nothing in practice" (vv. 14, 17), which controls the discussion and highlights the central theme. The focus is on how one shows covenant faith to a community member; if one sees a naked, hungry person and only *says:* "Keep warm and well fed," then one does not "love your neighbor as yourself" (v. 8), and so faith in God cannot save (v. 13). This sounds similar to the parable of the sheep and the goats in Matt 25:31-46. The concern for practical faith here simply continues the stream of arguments in 1:22-25, 26-28, and 2:1-8 on how Christian faith, if real, permeates one's life. In 2:14-17 James makes a bold demand which requires some theoretical justification, which follows in 2:18-26.

2:18-26 Two kinds of faith. The echoes of Paul's teaching on "works vs. faith" are strong, but it is not correct to argue, as many do, that James is attacking Paul or radically disagreeing with him. They are discussing two different issues (see the discussion above of 1:19-25). Paul opposed Jewish claims that the principle of salvation is the keeping of the law. By evangelizing Gentiles he came to realize that God was impartial in selecting all to salvation—all who believed in God and Jesus Christ. So, as regards basic justification before God, Paul saw that not just a few law observers were justified, but all who believed God's promises were invited to life. Hence, *law vs. faith.* James is dealing with a different problem; he presupposes justification through faith and treats of two kinds of faith: *active vs. dead faith.* He is consistently trying to show that true religion is not just a right confession of words, which a convert makes initially and forgets later. But true religion is covenant faith in God and covenant love of neighbor which lasts, which realizes itself in deeds of love, and which is alive and active.

In 2:19 James repeats the traditional Jewish-Christian formula about God which was the foundation of the new faith of converts from polytheism: God is One. Demons acknowledge this principle of faith, but do not act on it; hence, adherence to an idea is not itself salvific, no matter how important it is. Professing the right creed is not the same thing as living one's faith. Abraham is cited because he is the traditional witness Christians summon in their arguments on these matters (Rom 4; Heb 11). Whereas Paul contrasted Abraham's naked belief in God's promise of a son with Moses' doing of the law, James shows that Abraham's faith has a history—it was tested and showed itself as genuine covenant obedience in the episode where Abraham was commanded to sacrifice Isaac. The contrast is not between works and faith but between enduring, active faith and transient, verbal faith. Abraham's faith was "perfected" only when he acted upon it (2:22). The example of Rahab proves a different point, namely, that covenant faith, if real, must lead to covenant love. Rahab showed hospitality to strangers, giving food, shelter, and clothing (v. 25). She exemplifies the one who acts in love toward widows and orphans (1:27-28), who acts to feed, warm, and clothe the needy (2:16). Together, Abraham and Rahab complement one another and show that genuine faith is faith that has a persevering and active history, faith which is faithful when tested, faith which is not just verbal but active, faith which is obedient and loving. And so, James shows that religion either deeply penetrates our lives or it is not true religion.

3:1-12 Control of the tongue. This lengthy passage on control of the tongue begins with a command that there be few teachers in the group. Teachers are mentioned as officials in the early churches (Acts 13:1; 1 Cor 12:28; Eph 4:11). Different from prophets, teachers may be thought of as people who give new insights into old materials, as people who guard and reinterpret the tradition. James surely functions as a teacher himself in his reinterpretation of the law (2:8, 10), in his reapplication of the Scriptures (1:10; 2:23), and in his reuse of Jesus' teachings (1:5, 17; 4:3). It is not clear why there should be few teachers (3:1), for this group does not seem to be particularly threatened by false teachers. James only says that teachers face a stricter judgment, a theme he has repeatedly stressed (see 2:12-13).

Concern for teaching is only the preface to the major discourse on controlling one's tongue (vv. 2-12). Although we are warned that we must perfectly keep *all* the commandments (2:9-11), here it is admitted that we are all still sinners, failing in one or another thing. Yet the one who controls the tongue is a "perfect" person, perfection being the completeness or totality of one's growth in faith, not simply sinlessness. "Perseverance" brings perfection (1:4); the hearer who practices faith is likewise perfect (1:25); Abraham's faith was perfected by his faithful actions (2:22). Again we have the ideal set before us: a great value put on careful speech. Now control of the tongue is a standard topic in traditional moral exhortations (see Sir 14:1), which tradition James echoes not only in his advice but also in the metaphors used to dramatize its importance. As a bit can control a powerful horse, so guarding the tongue serves to control the whole person (see Ps 32:9). Likewise a huge ship is controlled and guided by a small rudder, just as we are by our mouths (see the Egyptian counterpart of this by Amen-em-Opet: "Steer not with thy tongue alone; if the tongue of a man be the rudder of a boat, the All-Lord is its pilot"). Still a third example is used to stress the importance of this virtue: a spark can set a forest ablaze, so a small tongue can wield great destructive power.

In 3:6 the importance of control of the tongue is repeated, in terms used earlier in verse 2. The whole person and the whole body depend on this one organ for their integrity. This idea resembles the gospel description of the eye which is evil darkening the whole body and vice versa (Matt 6:22-23). The danger of an unbridled tongue is perhaps exaggerated when James calls it a "world of malice" which is always endangering us from birth (3:6), but this is probably traditional language used to describe the importance of this. Surely charity (2:8) is more important to

James. As dangerous and as extensive as is the damage which an unbridled tongue can bring, it is also uncontrollable (v. 8) and demands constant attention. James' concern for the tongue pervades the exhortation: on the one hand he is worried about faith which is only verbal, without action (2:15); he warns against oath-taking (5:13); he warns that speaking ill of one another brings judgment (4:11); and here he stresses the constant need to control an organ which potentially can set forests ablaze and kill with poison. Obviously the early church prized charity and brotherhood, and was fiercely on guard against anger and factionalism. Lest anyone think they are keeping the law by avoiding murder, Jesus told them that name-calling and slander come under that prohibition as well (Matt 5:22).

In a final argument, James maintains that as judgment belongs to God (see 4:11-12), our speech should never be cursing but only blessing. And he employs once more his vivid metaphors: blessing and cursing are as incompatible in one mouth as finding fresh and foul water in the same spring, as gathering grapes and figs from the same plant.

3:13-18 True and false wisdom. Verse 13, the introduction to this presentation of true and false wisdom, is James' typical demand for a living and practical faith which shows itself actively in deeds. An appeal is made for humility, which links verses 13-18 to verses 1-10, for the control of speech will mean a nonaggressive behavior which avoids bitter jealousy and selfish ambition. The community focus of this advice is clear in the appeal for unity of heart and speech, which clearly is prized over against arrogant and false claims to individualism. Typically James contrasts true with false wisdom, wisdom from above with earthbound wisdom. Earthly wisdom promotes the self (see v. 14); it is concerned with earthly matters, such as riches, power, and prestige; it is not spiritual but material; it is devilish, just as was the unbridled tongue (see 3:6). In 1 Corinthians, Paul also found a community split into factions, seeking self-interest, full of strife and jealousy (see 1:11; 3:3), just as James describes here. In general, James is showing how false theology (false wisdom) leads to false morals, a typical argument in the ancient world for showing the evils of heresy: it leads surely to division and immorality.

In contrast to false wisdom is wisdom from above. It is pure and spotless, James' favorite concepts (see 1:27; 3:6). True wisdom is community-building: it makes peace (Matt 5:9), is forebearing and willing to give in to teachers and group leaders. Typical of James, it is full of mercy (2:13) and good works (2:18-26), it shows no favoritism (2:9), nor is it pretentious (2:2-3). In short, "wisdom" for James is not esoteric knowledge or gnostic secrets but the traditional Jewish notion of correct behavior and moral uprightness. Again James shows his hand in exalting the living out of the Christian faith over merely knowing its tenets or simply confessing its creed. Wisdom, like faith, is practical, active, and community-oriented. In listing the contrasting results of this prime value, James mirrors Paul's similar list of typical vices and virtues which stem from true freedom in Christ (see Gal 5:16-26). He concludes his exhortation here with another typical saying: As you sow, so you reap (see Gal 6:7). Here he stresses again the moral character of the Christian universe, just as he did earlier in 2:13. Our actions have consequences and the harvest is the judgment time of God when we will reap what we have sown.

4:1-3 The arch-vice and its cure. This passage is structured in three parts: the prime vice is identified (4:1-3), its incompatibility with God is described (vv. 4-7), and the cure of the vice is indicated (vv. 7-10). As regards the identity of the vice, moralists in the ancient world traditionally reduced wickedness to four prime vices (desire, pleasure, fear, and grief). James already identified "desire" as the root of temptation in 1:14-15 (the translation here is "covet," but the meaning is "desire," one of the four cardinal sins), and in 4:1-3 he returns to that theme. Where there is a lack of heavenly wisdom, conflicts abound (3:14, 16) and these conflicts James says stem from "desire," which cannot yield anything good: "You covet but do not possess. You kill and envy but you cannot obtain." It is, of course, a popular saying even in the Bible that "money (desire) is the root of all evil" (see 1 Tim 6:10).

James keeps insisting that the roots of evil and sin are within us. Temptation comes, not from God but from deceiving hearts and passions (1:14-15); anger and hostility, which reside in the passion with which we were born, flame out in an unbridled tongue (3:6). Despite conversion and baptism, Christians are not perfect yet and must strive to let God's grace rule their hearts progressively in every way. Here James is content to show the wickedness of "desire" by dramatizing its evil results: desire and envy lead to murder and quarreling, just as an uncontrolled tongue leads to a blazing rage (3:5-6). Vices, moreover, are interrelated: "desire" leads to other vices, such as "passion." Just as "covet" means "desire," so "passions" mean "pleasure," the second of the four cardinal sins. People covet goods for the sake of pleasure (4:3) and not for the sake of sharing them with others (see 2:14-17).

4:4-6 God vs. world. Christians still under the dominance of "desire" and "pleasure" are friends of the world and so enemies of God (4:4); they have broken the covenant and so are "adulterers." Typical of James is the contrast between friends of the world and enemies of God. As the gospel says, one cannot serve two masters (Matt 6:24), and James indicates in 4:5 that God is a jealous God. Another contrast is stated between proud and lowly: as Scripture says, God resists the proud (the desirous) and gives grace to the lowly— a very traditional principle in the Bible (see Job 22:29; Prov 3:34; 1 Pet 5:5). "Proud" and "humble" are surely code words for desirous pleasure-seekers and for total Christians.

4:7-10 The cure of the vices. The antidote to these cardinal vices is to wage war on sin, a traditional metaphor in moral exhortations (1 Pet 2:11; Rom 7:21-23). The sides are clearly drawn: God versus the devil. James has already called earthly wisdom "demonic" (3:15), and he stated that an angry tongue was kindled from hell (3:6). Yet the reader knows as well that evil and vice are not simply the devil's doing but reside in human hearts (see 4:1). The cure of vice is metaphorically described as a battle, but James clarifies that by saying the real cure is to "draw near to God" (v. 8), to let God be Lord of our hearts and lives (see Matt 22:37; Rom 6:22). The reconversion of our hearts is described in the Old Testament language of repentance which does not mean that Christians are gloomy or guilt-ridden (see Jer 4:8; Joel 2:12-14); along with that is the advice to "cleanse your hands . . . purify your hearts"—spotlessness, which in James refers to the completeness of Christian conversion. And "those of two minds" in 4:8 are the double-minded people who pray falsely in 1:7-8 (the Greek term is the same in both cases); they are people who have two Lords and hedge their bets. Hence a *total conversion of heart and life* is the remedy for vice which James urges. His exhortation concludes with the traditional appeal for a complete change of mind, heart, and action: Be humble and God will raise you up. This is a popular saying found in Matt 23:12; Luke 14:11 and 18:14. Here it refers less to humility than to the complete reversal of direction of our lives from vice to God and to the comprehensiveness of our conversion to the Lord.

4:11-12 Do not judge. These verses continue the earlier themes of correct speech (3:1-12) and the warnings about conflicts and fights (3:14-15; 4:1-3). In essence they proscribe slander as well as private judgment of a community member (group judgment, reflected in the courtroom setting of 2:1-7, is approved). This is typical of moral exhortations and is found even in the Sermon on the Mount (Matt 7:1); it reflects the principle behind the gloss on the Our Father in Matt 6:14-15 to forgive and so be forgiven. Slander and judgment are contrary to "the law," that is, the royal law of love mentioned in 2:8. They are condemned for good reason: all judgment belongs to God, a traditional belief which is found also in Paul's exhortations (Rom 12:19). The simple mention of judge and judgment are essential elements in the religious world of James: God is a moral God and our lives must be moral as well. This requires a clear sense of what is enjoined and what is proscribed, which is the whole point of James' letter. This also implies that the moral God will scrutinize the moral lives of his creatures, and so James reminds us periodically in the letter about judgment. Our actions count (2:12-13); God both rewards and requites (4:11-12); the Judge is genuine and his coming is imminent (5:9). Let no one take God's role!

4:13-17 Total trust in God. This advice, while it sounds as if it is addressed to merchants, is really a statement of a general Christian principle. It calls for a radical reorientation of the whole of our lives in the light of conversion to the one true God. Hence, our lives, whether we live one or a hundred years, whether or not we succeed in our undertaking, are all under God's providence and not

1225

our own control. Again James stresses that Christianity requires a sweeping and pervasive change in our lives which are totally caught up in God. The contrast is clear: God is Lord, not we. This extends the polemic against radical self-assertion, which is condemned throughout the letter (see 1:11; 4:1-3). The point is not quietism or passivity but completeness of our conversion to God with our whole heart, mind, and strength.

5:1-6 Woe to the unjust rich. A vigorous condemnation of the rich occurs here which echoes New Testament attacks on unjust wealth and Old Testament prophetic charges as well. Like Matt 6:19-20, the unjust wealth is shown to be ultimately profitless, for it is rotted, moth-eaten, and rusted. No lasting gain there! It is, moreover, lethal to be its owner for it bears testimony against its possessor, probably in the sense that it was not spent on orphans, widows, or the needy as was urged in 1:27; 2:14-16 (see Sir 29:10). It witnesses rather to the vice "desire" (see 4:1-2). Fiery punishment is a common biblical description of judgment (see Matt 18:8-9); and it is common in New Testament eschatological discussions to speak of wrath "treasured up" in heaven (see 2 Pet 3:7). The rich are not condemned simply for being rich (see Luke 6:24) but for their injustice. The stated cause of condemnation in James is the withholding of wages from workers, a thing proscribed by the law (Lev 19:13). Remember how the owner of the vineyard in Matt 20:8 paid his workers promptly at the end of the day! This crime is considered so serious that it cries to God for redress (Deut 24:15), as did Abel's blood (Gen 4:10), and the sin of Sodom (Gen 19:13). Again James calls attention to the role of God as judge, to remind the church of God's moral lordship over all people (5:4). Like the rich man in Luke 16:19-31, the rich in James are accused of using wealth only for their pleasure, a major vice (see 4:1, 3). Using another vivid metaphor, James describes how these sinners bring ruin upon themselves as though they were cattle fattened for slaughter through constant feeding on injustice and pleasure. It is unlikely that the rich are seen as murderers in verse 6; rather, the extreme extent of self-seeking is projected, showing how evil self-centered vices are. The rich, nevertheless, are said to harass the poor (see 2:6-7).

5:7-11 A persevering life. As in 1:2-4, James again puts great stress on a full and faithful Christian life. Difficulties will surely beset Christian converts (see 1 Pet 4:4), so they are urged to be faithful and patient. In another vivid comparison, Christians are to be like farmers waiting for the early and late rains. Genuine Christians are not afraid of God's coming; they long for it and even hasten it (see 2 Pet 3:12). In the meantime they are not to grumble, presumably against those hostile to them (4:11-12), but to leave justice in God's hands, for he is the judge at the gate (see Matt 24:33). As models they take the prophets who suffered for God's word, which bears close resemblance to one of the traditional beatitudes (Matt 5:11-12). "Blessed" are they (5:11), a cry of praise reserved in 1:12 for the one "who perseveres in temptation." As James would say, this one is a mature, complete Christian. In support of this advice, another biblical precedent is cited: Job, who was a paragon of patient endurance and an example of God's generous rewarding (Job 42:10-17). Although James has stressed God's judgment to the wicked, the moral God of Christians is especially a God of mercy and compassion (v. 11), the very self-description given by God to Moses (Exod 34:6). God truly is judge, who both saves and requites (4:12).

5:12 Oaths and speech. As well as Christians avoid judgmental speech (4:11), and angry speech (3:5-6), they are to avoid swearing, just as the Sermon on the Mount indicated (Matt 5:37). The only proper speech is blessing (3:10) and praise—speech which builds up the community.

5:13-18 Prayer, healing, and forgiveness. The common thread holding verses 13-18 together is the concern for prayer which appears in every verse. The structure, however, is complex, for we move from the injunction to pray always (v. 13) to what to do when a community member is ill (vv. 14-16) to the example of Elijah, the model of powerful and persistent prayer (vv. 17-18). In verse 13 James again expresses his sense of the completeness of faith permeating our lives; whether things are going well or ill, we should "draw near to God" in prayer—a good general principle (4:8). A more specific situation is next envisioned, the illness of a member of the community. Obviously misfortune and illness are *not* signs of divine displeasure, and so the leaders of the group are urged to show charity and to pray over and anoint the sick with oil (see 2:14-17). This procedure seems to presuppose gifts of prayer and healing in the group, not unlike Paul's Corinthian church (1 Cor 12:9, 28). It was common Jewish practice as well to ask that holy figures of the synagogue officially pray for the needy. As we were instructed in 1:6, the prayer must be made wholeheartedly and this prayer of faith will not only restore bodily health but lead to forgiveness of sins. Again James stresses the influence of grace on the whole person.

The introduction of "forgiveness" in verse 15 leads James to further general advice to the church in verse 16 that in its common meeting it develop a procedure of confession, prayer, and forgiveness. It was expected of Christians that they break with their former sinful lives through baptism. Ever the realist, James addresses throughout the letter the unfortunate fact that even believers fail and sin, and so the church must take that into account. The procedure James suggests is hardly an inquisition or a courtroom scene, but a structural way of living out the Our Father, which calls upon us to forgive one another. His letter has stressed this over and over (see 2:13; 4:11). It is passages like verses 14-16 that suggest the roots of later Christian practices such as the anointing of the sick. In his final remarks on prayer, James cites Elijah's persistent prayer: "He prayed . . . and prayed again" (vv. 17-18). And in accord with God's will, this prayer was powerful for it could mean drought or life for the people.

5:19-20 More on community prayer. The final verses of the letter continue the theme developed in 5:13-18; now the sick person is the one who has strayed away from the group. Lack of perseverance is the worst thing James can think of. This one deserves the same attention as the physically sick person in 5:14; the community should act vigorously to save him. This is what James means when he speaks of love of neighbor (2:8) and of doing something concrete for the needy (2:14-17). And the healing this produces will "save his soul" from death, from the moral judgment of God. James echoes popular tradition when he notes that such kindness "covers a multitude of sins" (see 1 Pet 4:8). Thus the errant sister or brother, as well as the shepherd who goes in search of the lost, will find favor with God (see Matt 18:12-14).

1 PETER

Jerome H. Neyrey, S.J.

INTRODUCTION

Author

An uncritical reading of 1 Peter would innocently say that Peter the apostle wrote this letter on the occasion of his martyrdom at Rome under Nero, exhorting other churches to prepare for the great Roman persecutions. But martyrdom is not the topic of the letter, although there is much language about suffering; no formal persecution of Christians occurred until the last decade of the first century. Although we cannot prove who did or did not write the letter, the church addressed looks very much like the churches of the pastoral Epistles and Ephesians and Colossians—late first-century churches concerned with household duties and with the church's relationship to the pagan world. The letter is no less valuable for faith if Peter did not write it, nor more precious for faith if he did. It speaks for itself.

There is no solid reason to date this letter to the sixties if it does not speak of Nero's persecution. Rather, scholars tend to date it late in the first century, probably in the nineties.

Occasion

It was once fashionable to see 1 Peter as a martyrdom exhortation, a trend which has prudently faded. Nor is it a Passover baptismal liturgy, although there is much baptismal material in it. Rather, it is very similar to typical Christian exhortations with its stress on traditional morality, lists of household duties, concern for the public face of the church in relation to pagan society, and appeals to recognizable traditions. The audience is very general and broad: Christians in Asia Minor who live as "sojourners" among their pagan neighbors. Included in the audience is a spectrum of social classes: slaves, families, leaders. Great concern is given to the issue of how a Christian can also be a good citizen. While a certain emphasis is put on conversion and the new status of converts, the letter addresses a variety of people on a wide range of topics. Less dramatic than martyrdom, perhaps, but more practical and easier to identify with!

Major themes

The letter develops two major ideas: (a) church, and (b) God and his Christ. As regards church, the letter reminds Christians of their free election by God, their conversion, and their noble and rich life in Christ. Great stress is put on the wonderful character of the church and how superior life in Christ is to pagan religion. Whence the church came about, how God founded it, its structure, its dignity, its call to holiness, its relations with pagan society—these are all treated carefully in the letter. The character and history of the church, then, are major themes.

Alternatively, the church is reminded of its new Christian God. He cares for them, chooses them, exalts them, and judges them. The Christian God is so far superior to their former pagan gods! Correspondingly, God's actions on Jesus are retold, how Jesus was vindicated from his sufferings and became a living spirit. The retelling of Christ's paschal career serves a very pastoral purpose in 1 Peter, for Christian experience is interpreted in the light of that pattern. As we shall see in regard to chapter 2, the career of Jesus is the career of the church, with special emphasis put on suffering and vindication. As God raised up the suffering Jesus, so God will sustain and vindicate all converts who suffer for their new faith in God and Jesus.

A pastoral letter

1 Peter is a very pastoral letter, for it aims precisely at encouraging Christians in the face of real problems and crises which beset their daily lives. The letter is pastoral in the choice of exhortation materials, nothing less than the kerygma of faith. Since that faith is called into question by the crises of life, the author tries to show how Jesus is the sure pastoral pattern of life, how God is involved in the daily lives of Christians, and how God saves us precisely insofar as we are like Christ, sufferings included. The letter does not ignore problems or minimize them, but calls us to see our lives more clearly in the light of the truth about a redeeming God and Jesus, the proof of God's power and plan.

COMMENTARY

1:1-2 Letter opening. Like typical ancient letters, 1 Peter begins with the formula "X to Y, greeting!" The sender identifies himself as "Peter, an apostle of Jesus Christ," and his audience as "sojourners of the dispersion." The greeting ("grace and peace be yours in abundance") is likewise typical (see Rom 1:7; 1 Cor 1:3). The address highlights the free gift of grace to these Gentile communities, for they were "chosen . . . in the foreknowledge of God the Father," a phrase suited to stress the full inclusion and equal status of Gentiles in the early church (see Eph 1:3-5); in fact, their divine election will be stressed throughout the letter (see 2:4, 6, 9), for one of the purposes of this letter is to celebrate God's gift of grace to them. Although the recipients are strangers of the Diaspora, they are not from the Jewish dispersion, for this phrase stresses their separation from their pagan neighbors which conversion to Christ has caused (see "sojourners" in 1:17; 2:11). This separation, in fact, has occasioned suspicion and hostility, which may account for the letter's stressing how Christians are now different from their pagan pasts (see 2:11-12; 4:2-4, 16). By identifying the church as the Diaspora, there may be an implied remark that the church is the new Israel (see Gal 6:16; Phil 3:3; Jas 1:1), scattered as was the old Israel.

In the popular mind it is generally thought that the twelve apostles went out on missionary journeys all over the world, but oddly, we have little literary evidence for this, and only fragments of Peter's journeys to Lydda and Joppa (Acts 9:32ff.), Antioch (Gal 2:11-14), Corinth (1 Cor 1:12; 9:5), and finally Rome (see "Babylon" in 1 Pet 5:13). His preaching to these churches is otherwise not known.

Although God, the Spirit, and Jesus are mentioned in verse 2, we should not rush to identify this text as a dogmatic Trinitarian formula. It is typical of other places in the New Testament where God acts on the world by the power of his Spirit to create a new Israel in Christ (see Rom 8:11). This letter focuses on God's activity first on the church (1:3-5, 13-21), then on Christ (2:20-24). After all, pagans were converted from their many gods to the one true Christian God (see 1 Thess 1:9-10), and this is surely stressed even in 1 Peter where God is judge (1:17) and midwife (1:23). The "obedience" to Christ is the obedience of faith, the taking of a new Lord whose rule is so much better than service to old pagan gods which led to decadent morality (see Rom 1:22-32). The call to obedience (1:14, 22) is a call to holiness and responsibility, which will be treated in detail later in the long list of household duties (chs. 2–4). The letter greeting, therefore, sounds the two dominant themes of the letter when it identifies the awkward situation of the pagan converts and the grace of God calling them to a new and consecrated life.

1:3-5 Thanksgiving. Typical of ancient letters, a thanksgiving prayer follows the greeting. This one is unusual for it praises God rather than "thanks" God, which may indicate a more Jewish form of greeting (see 2 Cor 1:3; Eph 1:3). Typical New Testament thanksgivings tend to serve as a summary of the main themes of the letter, which seems to be the case here: (1) God gave us a *new birth* (see 1:22–2:3), (2) this birth leads to a *hope* (1:8, 21; 3:15), (3) which is based on Jesus' *resurrection* from the dead (3:18–4:6), and (4) Christians have a heavenly *inheritance* which is incapable of fading (1:7-8). Our new birth is through faith in the gospel (3:18-22). New birth and faith correspond to the conversion experience of this group; the future hope and inheritance to be revealed at the last day surely urge perseverance in one's conversion.

1:6-12 Grace and yet suffering. The letter immediately addresses a real issue for this church. How great and exhilarating was their conversion, but how odd and incomprehensible are the difficulties and suffering which accompany it. The author often speaks of the dislocation that conversion has caused in the lives of these pagan converts (2:12; 4:4, 16), which might call in question the value of the new faith. So repeated attention is given to this theme, at least to show that it is appreciated and what it might mean. The best possible interpretation is given in 1:6-9: the new faith is more precious than gold, but like gold it is put in a furnace and proven true only after much testing. This view attempts to make sense of their experience and to evoke sentiments of perseverance and hope. Like Christ's suffering, their conversion dislocation leads to glory (1:11).

Another way of shoring up the new faith is to stress its antiquity and uniqueness. No, Christian faith in God and Christ is not a recent invention, a fad. It is found in the Old Testament where prophets foretold its unfolding; hence, it is an ancient faith whose antiquity gives great respectability to it in the eyes of the pagans. But it is also new and precious, for those prophets did not know the riches which the converts now know, nor were the angels in the know either. How wonderful, then, that the converts possess this knowledge of God and Christ. Christian faith, then, is more precious than gold, ancient, and specially revealed—all of which support the value of the new convert's faith.

1:13–2:3 Response of faith. But it is not enough simply to have converted; so great a faith requires a special response. So converts are urged to live a life worthy of their faith: "Live soberly . . . like obedient children, do not act in compliance with desires . . ." (1:13-14). Ideally they are to be like God, holy as "I am holy" (1:16). This passage also reminds the converts that as great as was their conversion, they must persevere; so "set your hopes completely on the grace to be brought to you at the revelation of Jesus Christ" (v. 13). And the gracious God whose foreknowledge chose them will judge them impartially (v. 17). Hence, their conversion faith must be supplemented by hope in God who will raise the dead and judge them.

Delivered by God from the futile ways of their ancestors, they are expected to be out of step with their former pagan culture; so they are exhorted: "Conduct yourselves with reverence during the time of your sojourning" (v. 17). Purchased by the priceless blood of Christ, they are to live like that, spotless and unblemished. In this way the author acknowledges their experience and pastorally addresses them with a word of encouragement, reminding them of their grace-filled past, and with a word of exhortation, calling them to responsibility.

Several postscripts are added to this long celebration of their new faith. By conversion, they may have suffered the loss of kin and clan (see Mark 10:29-30), for they seem alienated from their former culture and are now sojourners and exiles among their former neighbors. But Christians gain a new family by their conversion, new brothers and sisters (v. 22), and the church becomes a new family in which genuine love is shown (see 3:8-9). And so their conversion is celebrated as a new birth into a new family, and it entails a new way of living. Finally, the author touches on a sensitive point: If Christianity is so new, might it be just a fad? Might God be fickle? Is this for real? Most emphatically the converts are told that their rebirth comes from an imperishable seed, that is, through God's word which is living and trustworthy. To support that encouraging idea, the author cites Isa 40:6-8, which contrasts human frailty and mortality with the word of the Lord which "endures *forever*." Hence, their faith, as ancient as the prophets, will endure forever, for God is forever faithful.

2:4-10 Christ and church: Precious to God. This passage is very rich with Old Testament texts which bear on our confession of Jesus and our knowledge of the church. The key to these riches is to remember that this is the last and most glorious reflection on the church, which is meant to serve as a foundation stone for the exhortation which follows. So, all the rich images here serve two purposes: they tell the story of a holy church and conclude to a holy way of life worthy of that identity. The passage is structured around two Old Testament images, "stone" and "people," both of which are interpreted in terms of the church. "Stone" is the catchword common to verses 6-8; those verses, moreover, speak about Jesus, "the stone": he is "the stone" which God laid in Zion, a cornerstone, chosen and precious (see Isa 28:16); he is "the stone" rejected by some but important to God (see Ps 118:22); finally, he is "the stone" which is an obstacle and scandal to some (see Isa 8:14). This Christ-stone is the pattern for the church; like Jesus, we are chosen and precious to God; we are also rejected by pagans and unbelievers. But as Christ is the cornerstone, so we are being made into a household, a holy body of priests. Hence the stone image does two things: it first explains our situation in the world, how we share the pattern of Christ (suffering/election) and then how we join Christ in becoming a new and holy dwelling place of the holy God.

"People" is the catchword linking verses 9-10. The church is a "people of his own," and so it is a chosen race, a royal dwelling place, a holy nation (see Exod 19:3-6); the church has gone from being "not my people" to being "my people," from "not having received mercy" to "having received mercy" (see Hos 1:6, 9; 2:1). Both the "stone" and "people" images speak, then, of our election by God and of our holiness. And they point to what this means in our lives: as a household of priests we offer "spiritual sacrifices," that is, a holy way of life characterized by faithfulness and obedience (2:5). And as a holy nation we tell the story of the holy God and his saving deeds (2:9). So our "priesthood" is a way of being called to a holy status before a holy God and an exhortation to do holy things like acting holy and speaking about the holy God. These images, then, do not reject formal worship in the church, nor do they argue against liturgical leadership for this group; their sole purpose is to tell the church of its exalted status as "chosen" and "holy."

2:11-12 The Christian way of life. These verses begin the extended exhortation to the various constituencies of this church. As general as these initial remarks are, they are thematic. Christians have left paganism and its vices, so they are spiritual exiles and strangers (v. 11; see 1:1). Hardship will surely follow conversion, for pagans will view Christians with uneasiness, even hostility. Because they are truly different in so many ways, Christians will be perceived as troublemakers (v. 12). So the best apology for this suspicion and hostility is a blameless life which will convince the neighbors of the church of its rightness and so lead to praise of God.

2:13-17 General civic duties. The list of community duties begins with a general exhortation to all Christians to be good citizens, which advice is made concrete in the exhortation to respect civil government. Emperor, governors, and officials of the city, state, and empire legitimately command Christian obedience (vv. 13-14). This advice makes concrete the statement in verse 12 that an obedient Christian life is the best apology for hostility to the church (v. 15). Christians by baptism are made free in Christ; among Christians there is no slave or free, no Jew or Gentile (Gal 3:27); nevertheless, Christian freedom is hardly lawlessness or opposition to responsible living in society. So, Christians are encouraged to have a positive attitude toward society, i.e., love of the brethren as well as respect for the emperor (v. 17). Even if strangers in exile, Christians are called to responsible civic life.

2:18-25 Christian advice to slaves. The specific constituencies of the community begin to be addressed here, the first being Christians who are slaves. There is a typical form of exhortation in Christian moral teaching called a code of household duties, which addresses the mutual responsibilities of husband/wife, master/slave, and parent/child (see Col 3:18–4:1 and Eph 5:21–6:9). This standard form is evidently being used here, but in an adapted way. Carrying Christian civil responsibility one step further (2:13-17), slaves are called to obey masters "with all reverence" (v. 18). The focus of this exhortation differs from typical advice to slaves, for here the difficult plight of the slaves is fully recognized and their suffering is the center of the exhortation. Suffering, especially for those of the slave class, is a bitter fact of life, but the letter attempts to interpret that experience in the light of the Christian kerygma about Jesus: he too suffered, albeit unjustly. Slaves, like all Christians, are called to moral excellence, and thus Christians will eliminate suffering from their lives as a just retribution for irresponsible behavior. And so slaves will come to be more like Christ, whose example is presented through the reference to Isaiah's Suffering Servant in verses 21-24 (Isa 53:1-12). Christ was truly innocent, no deceit was found in his mouth; and when he suffered, he did not counter with threats. So Christian slaves are called to imitate Christ, living out the pattern of their baptismal likeness to Christ in a special way. And it is implied that as Christ by suffering won healing for us, the slaves by their honest suffering might also win converts to Christ or at least end hostility (see 2:12, 15). Oddly, this part of the code of household duties addresses only the faithfulness of slaves and strangely omits any mention of the duties of masters.

3:1-7 Advice to husbands and wives. The bulk of the advice is to wives, especially wives of pagan husbands, and their excellent behavior is seen as a strong missionary ploy (3:1). Hence, Christian wives are called to be different from pagan wives in not being fashion-crazy; they are to shun the extravagant ornamentation, clothing, and hair-styling which seemed to be the passion of that day. Their beauty is in the purity of their "chaste behavior" (v. 2), an interior beauty of the heart and a gentle disposition (v. 4). Typical also of household codes is the repeated exhortation to wives to be obedient to their husbands (3:1, 5-6). This obedience is probably to be understood as part of the Christian apology that church members are not lawless citizens, destructive of their cultures in their claims to freedom in Christ. Probably 1 Cor 7:12-16 reflects a comparable fear that some new Christians are abandoning former marriages and corrupting the social fabric under the guise of the new freedom they have gained in Christ.

The duties of the husbands reflect the cultural bias of their time, for they are to recognize woman as the weaker sex; yet the Christian note of equality in Christ is also struck: they are "joint heirs of the gift of life" (v. 7), an idea commonly tied to the understanding of baptism ("in Christ there is no male or female"; see Gal 3:28). This advice

would seem to have a definite propaganda bias: such good behavior will put an end to suspicion and hostility about Christians being free and irresponsible vis-à-vis civic institutions.

3:8-12 General advice to the whole church. Where typical codes of household duties next treat the reciprocal duties of parents and children, this letter departs from the tradition and gives advice to the whole church. The community is called to a great ideal: not friction but rather sympathy and love for one another (v. 8). Especially are they called to bear up well under suspicion and hostility from their neighbors. They are to bear insults and evils, and to give blessing in return (v. 9; see Matt 5:38-48; Rom 12:14-21). Moreover, Christians are once again called to an excellence befitting their Christian call (vv. 10-11). As the psalmist says: "Keep your tongue from evil and your lips from speaking guile; turn from evil and do good; seek peace . . ." (Ps 34:14-15).

3:13-17 Christian realism: Election yet suffering. The difficulties which beset Christian converts are pastorally dealt with once more. By living exemplary lives, Christians will not be persecuted for doing what is wrong. But even virtue has its costly price, hence this intensified exhortation on how to interpret suffering and how to see it in the light of one's baptismal conversion.

Christians will evidently be the focus of public controversy, but that is no cause for fear (v. 14). When questioned or accused, Christians should readily witness to the truth and proclaim their faith (see Mark 13:9-11; Matt 10:16-21). But the best witness is an honest life which refutes defamation and libel by its evident goodness (v. 16; see 2:12; 3:2). The sufferings of converts are real, but the author repeatedly calls Christians to suffer for their good deeds, like Jesus (v. 17; see 2:19-23), and not for their sins.

3:18-22 The example of Jesus. The warrant for the advice to suffer nobly has been the example of Jesus, known through the church's preaching and ritualized in the baptismal catechesis of the converts. At this point in the letter, the author appeals to another source of the Jesus tradition to ground the exhortation, in this case a creedal formula, a confession which is quite similar to that in 1 Tim 3:16:

1 Pet 3:18, 22

put to death in the flesh
made alive in the Spirit
to the spirits in prison he preached
at the right hand of God
having gone to heaven
angels, authorities and powers subject to him

1 Tim 3:16

manifested in the flesh
vindicated in the Spirit
seen by angels
preached among the nations
believed on in the world
taken up in glory

The pastoral use of this confession of baptismal faith goes in several directions: (1) Christ's death (v. 18) is life-producing, just as Christian suffering can be. (2) Baptism, which is our spiritual coming to life, is our way of ritually participating in Jesus' death. (3) As Christ died in the flesh and was made alive in the spirit, so converts likewise put off fleshly sins in baptism and live irreproachable lives through Jesus' resurrection (v. 21). So 1 Peter is emphasizing the baptismal situation of these new converts, reminding them of the gift of liberation which baptism was to the few—to Noah and his seven companions and to the few Christians as well. Baptism, likewise, is a sharing in Jesus' paschal mystery: we share his new life, but we share also his suffering. So Christians are reminded of the roots of their moral newness of life in Christ's passover through the catechesis of their baptism.

4:1-6 Conversion and alienation. A further appeal is made to Christ's paschal transition, once more to his suffering. "Christ suffered in the flesh." This is literally applied to converts who, because of conversion to Christianity, will suffer after baptism. But this suffering is proof that converts have in fact "broken with sin" (v. 1). There can be no thought of lapsing from Christian holiness back into vice; enough time was spent on vice in former pagan lives; Christianity means a death to that old way, a radical break with the past. But such a break brings down suspicion and hostility (v. 4) from former comrades who do not understand the excellence of the new religion. Christians have passed through judgment into life by baptism; not so their pagan comrades who will be judged according to their deeds (v. 5; see 1:17). Chris-

tians once were dead in their sinful flesh, but through baptism they are made alive in the Spirit, like Jesus (v. 6; see 3:18). Converts, we are reminded, have radically broken with the past and are conformed in baptism to Jesus, dead in the flesh, alive in the Spirit.

4:7-11 More general advice. The code of household duties is evident again in this general community exhortation. God's judgment was mentioned in 4:5 and now becomes the background to this part of the letter ("the end of all things is at hand," v. 7). Living in the final age of God's grace, Christians are called to display distinctive virtues: constant love (v. 8), hospitality, and generosity, especially to those who suffer economic hardship because of conversion (vv. 9-10). Christian duties within the church are singled out for special emphasis: speakers in the assembly and servers of the group are exhorted to fidelity and generous service (v. 11; see 5:1-7).

4:12-19 Our trials and Christian future. Ever the realist, the author returns to the theme of suffering and the difficulties which befall the convert. Faith, baptism, and conversion do not mean that Christians are somehow "out of this world," immune to flesh, suffering, and sin. So it is necessary to identify and interpret correctly the disturbing areas of Christian life. Suffering is unfortunately a fact of life. But what does it mean? Verse 12 speaks of a general trial of the church which the author interprets as a test, much like the testing of gold in a furnace (see 1:6-7). Gold will survive! Hope-filled optimism is part of Christian faith; so we can rejoice in the measure in which we share in Christ's sufferings. Happy are we, for as Christ was made alive in the spirit by God's Spirit (Rom 1:4), we who are conformed to Christ are given the same gift of Spirit. But as we were told earlier and often, Christian suffering must be in innocence, not as a just punishment for an immoral life (v. 15). The tone of the exhortation shifts in verse 17. Optimism is tempered; because the church is the elite, the testing of God will begin with it. And how difficult it will be for the church to survive. This somber note serves to underscore the importance of fidelity to baptismal ideals. But we are reminded here of how our lives are totally caught up in God's providence: our suffering is mysteriously part of God's will and we should, like Jesus, totally entrust our lives to our faithful God (v. 19; see Luke 23:46).

5:1-5 Advice to church leaders. The code of household duties now explicitly extends to the mutual duties of leaders and members of the church. The elders of the church are addressed first, and their dealings with the church are clarified: their ministry should be done with eager service; their motives should be noble, not mercenary; their exercise of leadership should be supportive, not authoritarian. In this typical advice 1 Peter reflects the common tradition in the New Testament about the quality of leadership, which is prized in the church: the Gospels give us Jesus' advice to be servants of one another (Mark 10:42-45); the duties of a bishop in 1 Tim 3:3 warn against avarice as a motive for ministry; Eph 4:11-16 likewise instructs us that leaders are indeed called to special tasks, but ones which do not negate Christian equality in baptism. Evidently the early church was sensitive to the shambles which authoritarian leadership could make of its baptismal catechesis of the freedom, dignity, and equality of all Christians (Gal 3:28). Leadership was and is no easy charge in the church, and so special mention is made of the concerns of the chief shepherd for his flock. Faithful service will be recognized by a special recognition (v. 4; see 2 Tim 4:1; Matt 19:28 and 24:45-47).

Church rank and file are alternately reminded to have respect for the tasks and authority of their shepherds (v. 6), otherwise their ministry of leadership would be impossible. Although we are all free and equal in Christ, it behooves us to show how as a free people we serve God in orderly and responsible lives (see Rom 6:16-18). Thus our freedom leads us to humility and to close bonds with the church. The call to obedience and humility echoes the tradition of Jesus' words to would-be masters in Matt 23:12. This appeal to order and obedience should be seen in conjunction with advice given throughout the letter: how Christians are to be good citizens of the state, good members of family households, and responsible members of the Christian church. A certain propaganda appeal is made in this exhortation to upright and orderly living, implying that Christians make very good and unselfish members of every part of society.

5:6-11 Faith in God. As the letter draws to a close, the church is called once more to faith, this time to know their God more clearly. Unlike impotent pagan gods, the God of Jesus is truly powerful and genuinely faithful. We remember the great emphasis put on the right knowledge of God in this letter: in chapters 1–2 we were reminded of God's free and generous call, even of pagans; God's exaltation and vindication of Jesus was stressed in chapter 3. Now the letter emphasizes how we are to place our total trust in God; we do this safely because God "cares for you" (v. 7). No adversary can withstand our God—not sin, nor death, nor Satan (vv. 8-9). The "God of all grace" wants us to be happy and he will vindicate us from suffering, just as he raised up his son, Jesus (v. 10). Our God is loving, powerful, trustworthy, and faithful. And to him we give dominion forever and ever (v. 11).

5:12-14 Letter closing. The author indicates that he is using a secretary to write this letter, an important point for our understanding of early Christian literature. It does *not* mean that the author is illiterate. It was typically the task of educated slaves to act as secretaries, for they were trained in formal correspondence, which fact accounts for the good Greek style of the letter. See Paul's use of secretaries in 1 Cor 16:21 and Gal 6:11. Typical of Christian letters, we find a formal greeting at the end of the letter: the churches of the East are greeted by the church of the West (Rome; see "Babylon," v. 13). East-West, Jew-Gentile—all people are freely and equally chosen by God. "Mark" also sends greetings, a figure often said to be Mark the evangelist, who was reputed to have edited Peter's recollections of Jesus. But "Mark" is such a common name, and this link between Peter and Mark's Gospel is very doubtful. Despite the great social diversity of the early church, it functioned as a close family, for members greeted one another with the sign of intimacy, the holy kiss (v. 14), a gesture common in the ancient churches (see Rom 16:16; 1 Cor 16:20; 2 Cor 13:12).

2 PETER

Jerome H. Neyrey, S.J.

INTRODUCTION

Author

Despite the claims of the letter (1:1, 12-15; 3:1), modern scholarship considers 2 Peter a pseudonymous letter, not written by Peter but attributed to him. The evidence for this judgment includes the following: (1) 2 Peter virtually incorporates the letter of Jude, which casts doubts on the authenticity of 2 Peter itself. (2) It alludes to several of Paul's letters, which further argues for its lateness, since these were scarcely known that early nor collected until the end of the first century. The appeal to Peter, then, reflects the growing tradition in the early church of ascribing theological as well as missionary and administrative leadership to Peter.

Topics

The figure of Peter is important as a spokesman for the traditions which the letter defends. Opponents are attacking the parousia (Jesus' return to judge), prophecy of the parousia, and theodicy (God's providence to reward and punish)—all traditional topics which need support from people who had firsthand experience of Jesus and his words. The author's testimony is intended to ground these issues at a much later time. Probably 2 Peter was written about the year 100, long after the deaths of Peter and Paul. It looks back on the church's early days from a much later time (see 3:1-2) and is concerned with orthodoxy in the church.

Church

The church of 2 Peter reflects a mixture of Jewish-Christian and pagan converts; all of the biblical examples cited in chapters 2–3 have close parallels in pagan literature as well as in the Bible. For example, Noah's flood is mirrored in the pagan accounts of Deucalion; the fall of the heavenly angels (Gen 6) is reflected in the casting of the Titans into Tartarus (2:4). This pastoral concern to make the traditions of eschatology equally understandable to Jew and Gentile alike suggests an urban church setting, of mixed ethnic and religious backgrounds, in dialogue with the surrounding pagan culture and very reflective of the church's long heritage. This letter is unusual in the number of biblical authors it acknowledges: it claims to know 1 Peter (3:1-2), gospel traditions about the transfiguration (1:16) and the parousia, some of Paul's letters (3:15-16), Jude's letter, as well as an extensive knowledge of biblical traditions. We would say that the author is a sophisticated churchman who argues against heresy in ways which reflect the best of Jewish-Christian and pagan culture.

COMMENTARY

1:1-2 Letter opening. Like typical New Testament letters, 2 Peter opens with a greeting: (1) The sender is Symeon Peter. (2) The addressees are "those who have received a faith of equal value to ours" (oddly, no place designation is given). (3) To the typical wish ("grace and peace") is added here the desire for correct acknowledgment of God and Jesus, the Lord, which is probably a clue about the central problem of the letter, the denial of God's judgment. So the letter is addressed to orthodox Christians who have a correct confession of God. When Peter calls himself "slave," he is echoing a common title in Jewish and Christian literature for designating an official person (see "Moses, the slave of the Lord," Deut 34:5; and "James, a slave of God and of the Lord," Jas 1:1).

1:3-4 Main theme introduced. At this point letters typically have a thanksgiving prayer, which is absent here. Substituting for this is the statement about God's power which providentially bestows life and piety on the church through the correct acknowledgment of God. Moreover, God has given the church great and precious promises, promises which 2 Peter will defend against heretics and scoffers, promises about the parousia (3:3-4), a new creation (3:10-12), and even a share in God's own nature to those who flee the corruption of this world (1:4). The correct acknowledgment of God and God's promises, then, is the focus of the letter. The hopeful promise is fulfilled by Christians who act in accord with it: they see the moral implications of the prospect of a future with God and so act honorably on earth in accord with that future, thus showing the close link between doctrine and life.

1:5-11 Religion and life. We find here a typical list of virtues (see Rom 5:1-5) which illustrates the goodness of the promises by showing how this correct doctrine leads to correct moral life. But whoever disregards this teaching on God and God's promises is blind and myopic (v. 9). In contrast, Christians will hasten to confirm their vocations by proper thought and behavior and so richly secure their entrance into Christ's kingdom. The dominant theme of 1:1-11, then, stresses three points: (1) There *is* a future, (2) which is the everlasting kingdom of Christ, our Savior and Lord, (3) where the ultimate promise is a share in God's own nature. God's promises, power, and providence are the key topics which are being attacked by heretics but which are likewise vigorously defended by 2 Peter.

1:12-15 Last will and testament. Peter tells us of a revelation from Jesus that he would die soon (see John 21:18-19), which prompts him to give us his last will and testament. There is a common tradition in biblical literature that patriarchs and leaders on the occasion of their death gave special teaching and even prophecies of the future to their disciples, a convention found in John 13–17 and Acts 20. Our author uses this convention to give us the definitive word about the church's eschatological tradition. He consciously intends to set down for all time the authentic memory of the promises and prophecies which he alluded to earlier (see 1:4, 11). But before he can do this, he needs to attend to a pressing problem—his reliability to give authentic heavenly teaching.

1:16-21 Defense of the parousia prophecy. This is the first explicit mention of problems in this church. Heretics are maligning the traditional teachings about Jesus' parousia by claiming that these teachings are not heavenly revelations but only human concoctions, made up to control naive Christians. In reply, 2 Peter denies this charge and cites his eyewitness experience of Jesus' transfiguration as an event which foreshadowed the parousia. Jesus' honor and glory, then, were prophetic of his status when he would return in glory to judge the living and the dead. The author did not make up the transfiguration event, nor does he pass on secondhand material, for he was an eyewitness there: he heard God's voice (1:17-18). Hence, the future coming of Jesus at the parousia (which the transfiguration foreshadows) is grounded on God's own word.

The appeal to the transfiguration, then, serves several apologetic purposes in response to the slander in 1:16: (1) The parousia prophecy is *not* humanly concocted, for it has God as its author, and (2) Peter has firsthand experience of it, and so the tradition about the parousia is not a rumor or an unverified event. In verse 19 the author can then claim that the "prophetic message" about the parousia has a very firm foundation, which phrase refers to the transfiguration-as-parousia prophecy in 1:16-18. Such an authentic prophecy is a lamp shining in Christian hearts until Christ, the daystar, dawns and the fulfillment of the prophecy is wonderfully realized. But even 2 Peter's interpretation of the transfiguration is open to dispute by the heretics. They argue that his interpretation is farfetched and fantastic—a point he denies in 1:20. He argues that just as humans do not originate prophecies on their own (see 1:16), so they do not interpret prophecy on their own, in esoteric ways. *God* gives prophecy to prophets (see God's voice at the transfiguration in verses 17-18); and *God's* Spirit inspires correct interpretation of those prophecies as well.

Peter, we will recall, is often cited in the New Testament as a recipient of special revelations (Matt 16:17; 17:26-27; 28:16-20) and special prophecies (Mark 13:1-3; 14:27-31; John 21:18-19). So at the end of chapter 1, Peter has laid the foundation for his defense of the eschatological tradition of the church. He defends the prophecy of the parousia in its formal aspect as prophecy: God is its author, not Peter; he is its authentic recipient and he is its inspired interpreter. Now that the groundwork of Peter's knowledge of the parousia is laid, he can get on with his plan in 1:12-15 to leave a solid and lasting exposition of the eschatological tradition.

2:1-3 Exposure of the false teachers. Whereas Peter claimed to write this letter on the eve of his death (1:12-15), that was only a literary convention, a convenient occasion to stress the importance of the topic at hand and to lay out the truth of the matter. The real occasion of 2 Peter is the presence of heretics and scoffers in the church. We saw earlier that they rejected the parousia prophecy as a human concoction (1:16), and they will further scoff at the parousia in 3:3-4, 9. In 2:1 they come in for criticism as false teachers. They are compared with the "false prophets" of the Old Testament, who were called false precisely because they preached peace and security when God's prophets preached judgment and imminent ruin (see Jer 4:10; 5:12; 6:14; 14:13-14). This is an important clue, for by comparing his own false teachers with false prophets, Peter alerts us to their opposition to God's judgmental action on the world, especially as this is developed in the church's es-

chatological traditions about the parousia. When he claims that they deny the Master (2:1), this means that they are practical atheists—they do not deny that there is a God, but they deny that God notices or cares about us: *God does not judge us.* The psalms often tell us about sinners who say "there is no God" (see Pss 10:11, 13; 14:1, 73:11) and because they fear no judgment, they live sinful lives. So the opponents of 2 Peter are false prophets who deny the Lord's judgment. But like the false prophets, they will meet ruin, for God's judgment does not sleep *nor* is it idle (2:3).

2:4-9 Proof of God's judgment. To prove that God acts with judgment on the world, the author cites three examples. While this material is borrowed from Jude 5-7, 2 Peter has changed the examples to tell a new message:

Jude 5-7

desert generation
angels
Sodom and Gomorrah

2 Peter 2:4-8

angels
Noah
Lot and Sodom and Gomorrah

Whereas in the examples of the desert generation and the holy angels Jude warned of the danger of lapsing from faith and salvation into destruction, 2 Peter argues more simply that God knows how to rescue the devout and to guard the wicked in punishment (2:9). 2 Peter rearranged Jude's list (substituting Noah for the desert generation); his list is more clearly following the events of Genesis. The reason for these changes is the purpose of 2 Peter to support the fact of God's judgment (rescue of the godly, ruin for sinners); the changes also stress how God has already acted on the world by water and by fire, a point he will return to in 3:7. And the focus is clearly theological, for as 2:4, 9 state, God does act in judgment! And so he answers the false prophets who "deny the Master," proving that our sacred traditions prove that God acts in the world, with judgment and power. The heretics are surely wrong.

2:10-16 Immoral consequences of wrong doctrine. After this theoretical argument in support of God's judgment, the author begins to point out other disturbing aspects of the scoffers, again showing how bad doctrine leads to bad morality. He warns that God especially judges those who are at home in a corrupt world, who live lustful lives and who show contempt for lordship (especially God's). In 2:10-11 the author points out that the scoffers even deny that God's angels participate in the judgment of the world, which is contrary to the tradition of the early church (see Matt 13:41-42). Their rejection of judgment is total—neither God, nor Jesus, nor even the angels exercise judgment.

Such heretics are like brute animals, born for capture and destruction; what they do not understand they scoff at (see 3:3-4). But these denials bring ruin (2:12); and they will receive an appropriate reward for their wickedness (2:13). It is typical of aggressive writers to see opponents in the worst possible light, envisioning the ultimate consequences of their errors (see Rom 1:29-31); 2 Peter sees the heresy of the scoffers as leading to sexual depravity (2:13-14), a typical polemical charge against heretics. Another typical vice credited to heretics is greed (1 Tim 6:5; Titus 1:11), of which 2 Peter accuses his opponents in 2:3, 14.

Borrowing the example of Balaam from Jude 11, this author finds in Balaam not only an example of greed repaid but, more to his point, an example of a false prophet who wandered away from the way of truth, who was rebuked by his donkey, and who ultimately received a terrible recompense for his wickedness in a violent death. Balaam, then, is another example of a wicked person who met judgment, and so he stands as a rebuke to the heretics who by denying judgment bring ruin on themselves.

2:17-22 From grace to slavery. Borrowing again from Jude 12, 2 Peter charges his opponents with being empty and directionless like waterless springs and mists whipped by the wind. Worse than that, they corrupt new Christians, leading them right back to the immorality from which they fled at conversion. As in 2:10, 13-14, the charge of sexual immorality is probably a stock accusation against heretics, showing the ultimate depravity to which false teaching inevitably leads. Just as the scoffers mock Christians about unfulfilled prophecies of the parousia (3:3-4), the author accuses them of unfulfilled promises: They promise them freedom, not only from restricting laws (1 Cor 6:12; 10:23); but especially from fear and judgment. Hence, the heretics are accused of denying the Lord (2:1), i.e., denying divine judgment as well as the moral laws of the group. Their promise of freedom from judgment ironically leads to slavery, just as their denial of punishment leads to swift ruin. Far from liberating their converts, the heretics lead them to a worse state than their previous paganism, for now they know the truth about God but spurn it for false doctrine. The author compares them to a sow, after being washed, returning to wallow in mire, and to a dog going back to its vomit (2:21-22).

All of chapter 2, therefore, is a polemical portrait of 2 Peter's opponents: (1) He accuses them of teaching evil practices and charges them with traditional vices; (2) their doctrine is evil; (3) they are mercenary; (4) they corrupt God's church. Their doctrine is wrong in itself and in its effects, for it leads to immorality and ruin. The author has said the worst he could about them. The fact that so much of chapter 2 is borrowed directly from Jude's letter and that so many of the charges against the heretics are standard polemical materials suggests that 2 Pet 2 is not a vivid historical portrait of these opponents. Rather, it is a stereotypical attack on the enemy, using easily recognizable and traditional accusations to point up the error of the false doctrine. What is distinctive, however, about chapter 2 is the careful identification of the false teaching: the denial of judgment, the rejection of all judgmental agents, even angels, and the freedom from fear and punishment.

3:1-2 Foundations of the doctrine of judgment. The author begins the main part of his letter by linking this work to a previous letter, presumably 1 Peter. As he said in 1:12-15, his task is to remind the community and to give them the correct interpretation of the tradition. (Perhaps *eilikrinē dianoian* in 3:1 might better be translated as "correct interpretation" than as "sincere disposition.") The tradition he is interpreting is nothing less than the teaching of the holy prophets and of Jesus. In 1:16 his opponents accused Peter of fabricating the prophecies of the parousia; but as he did there, he also insists here that the source of his teaching is God's and Christ's word. *His* teaching is authentic! His constant "reminding" the church of the truth (3:1-2 and

1:12-15) is in stark contrast to the willful forgetting of the same by the opponents (see 3:5, 8).

3:3-7 Opponents scoff at the tradition. When the author alerted us to his impending death in 1:12-15, he invoked the last-will-and-testament convention, a typical element of which is the prediction of future false teachers. The future heretics (3:3) will scoff at the church's traditions about the parousia: "Where is the promise of his coming?" (3:4). When biblical texts cite questions which begin with "Where is . . .?" they imply ridicule and skepticism on the part of the questioner (see Judg 6:13; 2 Kgs 18:34; Isa 36:19); hence, these scoffers are calling into question the truth of the parousia prophecies. The ground for their skepticism is the apparent permanence of the world; from time immemorial the world has remained and so it will always be. But this argument implies several things: (1) The scoffers doubt that God has ever been actively involved in the world, so why should God suddenly become active? (2) The concern about the parousia here is narrowly focused on cosmology, the destruction-renewal of the world. For the time being the questioning of God's judgment is put aside and the brunt of the attack is on the predictions of the end of the world (see Mark 13:24-25).

The author's response to this scoffing meets the criticism head-on in support of (1) God's *constant* activity in the world, (2) the *reliability* of God's word/predictions, and (3) the *judgment* of God which awaits the wicked. Inasmuch as the author's task is "reminding," he accuses his opponents of willfully forgetting ("they deliberately ignore," 3:5) their biblical history. By God's word the heavens and earth were fashioned out of water (v. 5), by God's word the world was judged and destroyed by water (v. 6), and by God's word the heavens and earth are reserved for fire and judgment (v. 7). This response parallels the argument in 2:4-6 where we were told of Noah and Lot, whose worlds were destroyed by water and fire respectively; those stories proved that God knows how to rescue and requite (2:9). So in 3:5-7, God's judgmental activity in the world is defended and the reliability of his word is assured, even the promises of the parousia. The scoffers are wrong, then, when they question God's prophetic word about divine involvement in the world and about the parousia. Biblical history is proof against their objections.

3:8-14 Defense of God's delay in judging. The author continues his defense of the parousia traditions here. For a second time he accuses the scoffers of willfully overlooking biblical truths (v. 8); so, apropos of the delay of Christ's coming, he reminds them of the scriptural saying that one day with the Lord is like a thousand years (Ps 90:4). Since God's timetable is mysterious to us and virtually incalculable, the scoffers are erroneous in harping on the delay of the parousia. It was common knowledge that God told Adam that "the moment you eat from it [this fruit] you are surely doomed to die" (Gen 2:17), but still Adam lived on for many hundreds of years after his sin; this "delay" was interpreted as a gift of grace to Adam to allow time for repentance before judgment. In 3:9, when the heretics accuse God of being slow about his promise, they imply that slowness to them is evidence that God has no intention of judging. According to them, God has never acted previously to judge the world, and every day is further proof that God will not. This fact of delay is disturbing, to be sure. But the author treats it positively in a traditional fashion as a sign of God's forbearance in giving sinners time to repent before judgment comes (see Rom 2:4-5).

The author draws out the moral implications of the doctrine he has defended. Since God will judge the world at the end of the age, we should live godly lives of holiness (3:11) and be found without spot or blemish (3:14; see 2:13). Our goodness is the logical consequence of our correct theology. This world is corrupt and passing away; so believers are invited to a pure future life, even a sharing in God's nature (see 1:4). Those who accept God's promises of the parousia live accordingly and so flee immorality and prepare for the end of this age. Their destiny is a new heaven and a new earth where righteousness resides. Not so the heretics; they think that this world is all and everything. They are at home in this world's corruption and expect nothing further from God. Making no preparation for the future, they are headed for genuine and permanent ruin.

3:15-18 Even Paul agrees with Peter. When the author appeals to Paul, he shows acquaintance with some of Paul's letters, which for him are inspired. Paul's teaching on God's universal judgment is found in Rom 2 and 14:10-12. The delay of judgment as a gift of time for repentance is found in Rom 2:4-5, and the depiction of Jesus' coming as a thief in the night is treated in 1 Thess 5:1-7. Paul was divinely inspired in these teachings (3:15) just as the present author claims to be (see 1:12-15, 16-21). So the teaching is authentic, even if it is hard to understand. Implicit in this is an appeal to the church to accept the normative teaching on the parousia as genuinely "traditional" in the sense that God is the ultimate source and Christian teachers like Peter and Paul are divinely authorized to teach it; thus it was always taught everywhere in the church. Let the scoffers realize how out of step they are with God's Scripture and God's authorized tradition.

As ancient letters do, this one ends with a typical letter closing (3:18). There is a special note in this closing, however, which seems to sum up the letter: the author wishes the church to grow "in the knowledge of our Lord and savior," and the insistence on "knowledge" echoes the wish he made at the letter's beginning for the same (1:2). This suggests how dominant in the letter is the concern for true teaching and orthodox knowledge of Jesus, especially in regard to Christ's parousia and the eschatological tradition of the church.

JUDE

Jerome H. Neyrey, S.J.

INTRODUCTION

Author

The stated author is "Jude . . . brother of James." It is probably not the case that Jude is the same figure as the Apostle Jude/Thaddeus (Mark 3:18; Luke 6:16; Acts 1:13). He claims blood ties with James, who was himself "the brother of the Lord" (Gal 1:19) and leader of the Jerusalem church (Acts 15:13-21). Such ties, if authentic, would serve as excellent credentials, placing Jude in the mainstream of early Christian orthodoxy. But modern scholarship is critical of this for several reasons: (1) the seemingly late date of the letter (e.g., verse 17 speaks of "the apostles of our Lord" as figures of the distant past); (2) the sense of "the faith, delivered once for all" as representative of thinking in the late first century; (3) the typical convention of validating later orthodox teaching by linking it with known earlier authorities. For internal reasons, the letter of Jude is judged to come from the late first century and is pseudonymously attributed to Jude.

Occasion and contents

The church addressed is disturbed by conflicting teachings, and appeal is made for fidelity to "the faith, delivered once for all," which is somehow under attack by members of the church. The nature of the doctrinal disagreement is extremely difficult to describe, for there are no firm clues, only hints and suspicions recorded. The very silence about the heretics is itself typical of anti-heretical literature, where the author avoids giving more free publicity to the errors under attack by not mentioning them further. The charges of moral libertinism are not so much descriptions of the heretics' actual positions but the author's interpretation of the direction in which their errors will lead. What we are certain of is a wrenching internal conflict, as much over the leadership of the church as over traditional issues.

Unusual features

Jude quotes several ancient writings which were not admitted to the Christian canon: 1 Enoch in verses 14-15 and the Assumption of Moses in verse 9. He surely saw great value in citing them as authoritative arguments on his side and that may be the point: they do reinforce and echo traditional statements about God's judgment and Christ's coming. The use of these unusual writings may indicate the scope of the theological discussion in this church when the group is sifting out the main points of its faith, "delivered once for all," and the foundations of that faith. Use of these unusual writings, as well as extensive use of the Old Testament and popular Jewish traditions, may indicate the author's sense of the truth of Christian faith, supported by such diverse and respected sources. It has long been recognized that most of Jude's letter reappears in 2 Pet 2. And it is generally accepted that 2 Peter borrowed from Jude and reworked that material to fit his situation.

Pastoral importance

The relevance of Jude does not seem to lie in its moral exposé of the heretics or in its simple demand to fight for the faith. Although Jude pleads with his church to remain faithful to its tradition, it would be unfair to the letter to translate this advice into a modern plea to hold on to our tradition without further ado. This would be traditionalism of the worst sort and unfaithful to the gospel which must be preached anew to every culture in every generation. The pastoral importance of Jude is the window it offers on the church struggling to recognize its roots, traditions, and faith, but not in a fearful or defensive way. Differences of opinion *within* this church go back to its very beginning, and addressing new peoples with different cultures has challenged the church from the days of the apostles. Jude's church is not unlike ours: a church with a rich tradition, but one sailing through a pluralistic sea of many different religions and even indifference to religion. The pastoral importance lies in the image of a church trying both to recover the roots of its faith and yet attempting to speak to a different culture.

COMMENTARY

1-2 Address to the church. Jude opens the letter with a typical letter greeting. The sender is Jude, "slave of the Lord" (see Jas 1:1; Titus 1:1). Since this Jude seems to be relatively unknown to this audience, he is further identified as "brother of James," presumably "the brother of the Lord" (Gal 1:19). This type of identification serves as Jude's credentials to represent the orthodox tradition of the church. The addressees are not said to belong to any specific church (such as Corinth, Thessalonika), but are general members of the church, hence Jude's "catholic" or universal character. These Christians are said to be "kept safe," but this is perhaps a bit ambiguous. The verb used here (*tereō*) can mean "kept safely" as in verse 1, but it likewise means "kept locked up" as in a prison—the meaning it has in regard to the sinful angels (v. 6) and the deviant heretics (v. 13). So the church is guarded by God in the truth, which ironically contrasts it with the heretics who will be locked up in judgment. The greeting ("mercy, peace and love") is a typical letter greeting (see 1 Tim 1:2 and 2 Tim 1:2).

3-4 Occasion: The arrival of heretics. The letter lacks the typical prayer of thanksgiving found in Paul's letters or the typical commendation of the recipients. Instead, there is an immediate note of urgency: the author claims that his eagerness to write about their "catholic," or common, faith was supplanted by an urgent sense of crisis. Rather than merely discussing their common faith with them, Jude exhorts them to fight for the faith, which was handed on accurately once for all. The fight is necessary because heretics have entered the church, heretics whose coming was predicted (v. 18) and whose judgment is likewise noted (v. 4).

Who are they? What was their heresy? As was noted in the introduction, these are difficult questions to answer because the language in verse 4 is quite general and could apply to any person the church considered deviant: (a) They pervert grace (freedom?) to licentiousness, and (b) they deny the Lord and Master Jesus. These two comments probably reflect the typical view of heretics as people whose doctrine is so perverse that it leads to the worst type of sexual immorality. Their "denial" is the author's perception that the heretics dispute some important items of faith and so are seen as rejecting Jesus' teaching (see Matt 10:33). This type of general language would make sense in a church which was cruelly split over doctrinal matters, for the hearers would surely know who the enemy is. Moreover, it is typical of attacks on heretics *not* to keep mentioning their errors as a way of denying them further publicity for their false teaching.

5-8 Warnings from the past. A series of biblical examples is immediately brought forward as a "reminder" to the church. The common thread running through the three examples is the warning that ancient figures who experienced God's grace/favor fell from that position and were destroyed in their sin. Baptism and initial conversion do not automatically protect a Christian, for living in faith and truth is essential to life. So we are told of the Exodus generation, once sacred, but which fell from grace and truth and was destroyed (v. 5). Some angels fell from heavenly grace and are kept for judgment (v. 6). Sodom and Gomorrah are included because their sin was "unnatural"; literally, they were after "other flesh," thus abandoning former grace and bringing upon themselves ruin. Three examples of falling from grace into judgment are sobering indeed!

The three biblical examples are brought to bear on the heretics who are charged with polluting flesh, spurning dominion, and reviling angelic beings (v. 8). The Exodus generation broke God's covenant and so proved adulterous (Num 14:35); the angels refused to serve God and were cast down. And Sodom and Gomorrah defiled the angels sent to warn Lot and his family (Gen 19:1-11). The heretics are said to be doing the same thing and so are inviting a comparable judgment.

9 Judgment pronounced. An obscure writing (The Assumption of Moses) is cited here. As the heavenly angel Michael did not dispute with Satan but left all judgment to God ("May the Lord rebuke you," v. 9), so Jude will not wage war on the heretics but leave their judgment in God's hands (see vv. 14-15). The obscure writing is probably cited because it is seen to endorse traditional statements of God's judgment of sinners.

10-13 General description of the opponents. More general errors of the heretics are pointed out. Of course, it is assumed that the heretics are ignorant, a point stressed in verse 10 where they are said to revile what they do not understand. But even what they know is only the passion of brute animals which is leading them to ruin. Like verses 5-7, three more biblical examples of sinners who were requited are cited in verse 11: Cain, Balaam, and Korah. In Jewish traditions these three are characterized as figures who reject God's judgment, act contrary to divine directives, and rise in rebellion against God's established leaders. They are even commonly linked together as people who lead rebellions or who lead Israel into error ("The following have no share in the world to come: Cain, Korah, Balaam . . . ," *The Sayings of Rabbi Nathan*, 41).

More polemical charges are leveled against them which are typical of this type of literature. The doctrinal errors of these heretics lead them into immorality; hence, they soil and pollute some solemn Christian assemblies. Is this a hint that they should be expelled? (see

1 Cor 5). Their errors are easy to spot: they have no direction or substance—they are like moistureless clouds blown this way and that; they are fruitless trees which should be uprooted (see Matt 3:10; 7:19; 21:19); like wild waves they splash their immoral foam everywhere; like stars without direction they will never see light. So will the heretics of this church fare: they will be locked in the gloom prepared for them.

14-15 Another warning of judgment. Another esoteric writing (Enoch) is cited by Jude to the same purpose as the earlier one (v. 9). The Lord will come with his holy ones (see Matt 16:27; 25:31) to judge sinners, especially ungodly sinners who rebel against God. This echoes the charges in verse 4 that the heretics deny the Lord and in verse 8 that they deny authority. This citation of Enoch probably serves to emphasize the traditional character of divine judgment rather than to identify the heretics more fully.

16 More charges. This string of charges interprets the behavior of the heretics in the worst possible light, pointing out how they have always been mavericks in regard to doctrine, following passion rather than truth, prone to boastful claims, and with an eye to the profit such behavior might bring. These charges are general in character and do not help us identify the heretics with any greater precision.

17-18 Prophetic warnings. The author appeals to well-known traditions that on their deathbeds prophets and apostles predicted the future for their followers, a common element of which was the warning about heretics entering the group (Acts 20:29; Matt 24:11-12; 2 Pet 3:2-3). This warning serves to defuse the shock of finding division in the church. It was expected! predicted! But the same warning serves to identify false parties: the traditional faith, given once for all (v. 3), is authentic; not so the errors introduced later.

19-21 Who has God's Spirit? The heretics are called "sensualists," which means that they are living in the flesh as opposed to a spirit-filled life (see Gal 5:16-25). Their morality is fleshly because bad doctrine leads to nonspiritual or fleshly morality. Their doctrine is also wrong because they are not led by God's Spirit but by error and deceit. The heretics, of course, probably claimed divine inspiration for their ideas, so discerning God's Spirit became important in the early churches as a test of truth. Certain statements can never be inspired by God's Spirit, such as "Cursed be Jesus" (1 Cor 12:3) or "Christ did not come in the flesh" (see 1 John 4:1-3). Paul claimed that genuinely spiritual people do not cause divisions (1 Cor 3:1-4), which is the same charge here. The church, on the other hand, is characterized by union and love, upbuilding in shared faith, and prayer in the Spirit. In this way the church will "keep itself" (i.e., continue) in God's love (v. 21); we recall here that they were called in love and urged to persevere in that love (v. 1). Their steadfastness in love contrasts the church with the heretics who wander in lust and turn aside into error (vv. 12-13). So their future is one of eternal mercy and salvation, whereas the wandering heretics face eternal ruin.

22-23 A saving hand extended. The church must do more than guard itself against heresy. Like a physician, it should act to save those being led astray by the heretics. This means trying to convince some who are wavering (v. 22) and snatching others from ruin, even some of the most depraved who soil in lust their baptismal garment of grace. This is not unlike the advice to Timothy and Titus to argue the church's case with conviction and charity (see 1 Tim 4:1-2, 11-13; 2 Tim 4:2-4).

24-25 Farewell and conclusion. The letter closes with a characteristic farewell greeting. God is named as the one who keeps the church upright and pure, because right theology leads to right morality. And uprightness in faith and morals leads to joy and glory. A formal benediction ends the letter in which God is acclaimed by the church for his glory, power, and authority—items which Jude insists that heretics deny (vv. 4, 8).

HEBREWS

George W. MacRae, S.J.

INTRODUCTION

This eloquent document, one of the best written works of early Christianity, has its origin shrouded in mystery. In antiquity as well as in modern times, there has been a great deal of inconclusive speculation about its author, place of writing, and destination. Traditionally it has come down to us in the New Testament as "The Letter of Paul to the Hebrews." But this title does not belong to the original writing. All the elements of it are suspect, and modern scholars agree that the work is not a letter, it is not by St. Paul, and it is not addressed to "Hebrews." Such a negative conclusion should not leave the reader with a negative impression of Hebrews, however. On the contrary, this is a magnificent work, treasured for centuries in the life of the church and well worth our effort to read and study it carefully.

A literary sermon

Hebrews is clearly not a letter, even in the rather broad category of New Testament letters. It has no letter greeting and is not directed to any particular church or individual. Its conclusion contains some elements typical of early Christian letters (see especially 13:18-25), but these seem to be added merely because the writing was circulated. They testify to the authority of letters as a means of communication among early Christians. Instead Hebrews is a written sermon, and it is important as one of the very earliest Christian sermons on record. It combines theological explanation, most of it based on inter-

pretation of the Bible, the Old Testament, with exhortation to persevere in hope and faith. The passages of exhortation are scattered throughout the sermon, and it becomes clear to the reader that these are the main focus of the work as in any good sermon. This commentary will highlight these passages.

The fact that Hebrews is a sermon may help us to understand one of its classical problems for the interpreter. It is the problem of the thought world of the document. Two different, and somewhat conflicting, views are present in it. One is the common expectation that the world is about to come to an end. God will resolve human history by intervening in it to send Christ again and establish his kingdom. This kind of thought, which we call apocalyptic, is oriented to the future and has a certain urgency about it. With many variations of detail it is characteristic of much of Judaism in the time of the early Christians and also of much of early Christianity itself. The other view is one that is much more concentrated on the present than on the future. It makes a distinction between the heavenly world of true reality and the earthly world of copies. It has its roots in popular Greek thought as interpreted by such thinkers as the Jew Philo of Alexandria of the early first century A.D. In this view God's promises are already realized in heaven. The saving work of Christ has already taken place there, and faith is insight into its reality.

Both of these views are prominent in Hebrews, and modern interpreters have tended to stress one or the other as the dominant view of the author. The situation may be more complex, however. The preacher does not always have the very same presuppositions as his hearers, but he does not always want to do away with them either. Hebrews makes the best sense if we suppose that the hearers are oriented toward traditional apocalyptic thought, and the author seeks to reinforce that orientation with the assurance that the future hope is already grounded in the present. We shall see the interaction of these two perspectives as we read Hebrews carefully.

Authorship

Like many other New Testament writings, Hebrews is anonymous, and all attempts to identify the author are ultimately guesswork. Before Hebrews was accepted widely as part of the canonical Scriptures, in the second to the fourth century, the Christian church in the East was convinced that Paul was the author, and this view finally won out. But it was clear then to many Christians that in style, vocabulary, and theology, this sermon was not written by Paul. The great theologian Origen, early in the third century, discussed the question and concluded, "Who really wrote the letter, God knows." Ancient speculation tended to concentrate on Luke, or Barnabas, the missionary companion of Paul according to the Acts of the Apostles, or Clement of Rome. Later writers, starting with Martin Luther in the sixteenth century, suggested the name of Apollos, another associate of Paul (see Acts 18:24-28 and 1 Corinthians *passim*). Apollos has won a wide following since, and if any known Christian leader was the author, he would be the best candidate.

To Hebrews?

It is by no means clear to whom this sermon was addressed. It makes various references to the lives of the Christians it speaks to, but these are all of a rather general kind and do not permit us to draw a very specific portrait. The ancient designation "Hebrews" is itself not very clear, but it probably refers to Christians of Jewish background. Because Hebrews uses the Old Testament so extensively, it was thought in antiquity, as well as by many modern interpreters, to be addressed to former Jews who were in danger of losing their hope in Christ and slipping back into Judaism. Such a situation is possible, of course, but not easy to demonstrate. We must remember that intense familiarity with the Old Testament, which was readily available in its Greek translation, was common among all Christians, whether Jew or Gentile in background (see, for example, Paul's letter to the Gentile Christians of Galatia). And there is nothing in Hebrews that clearly suggests the danger of a relapse into Judaism. It is therefore probably best to assume that the sermon is addressed to Christians in general and not merely to former Jews. It would be interesting to know where they were, but we could only guess.

It is more interesting to speculate where the sermon was written. Because of the similarity of its thought to that of Alexandrian Judaism, people have thought of Alexandria as its origin. That is possible but not essential, since philosophical thought of the Alexandrian type was fairly widespread over the ancient Mediterranean world. Hebrews has some ideas in common with the First Letter of Peter, which purports to come from Rome. Even more significantly, it is related closely to the non-biblical First Letter of Clement, the reputed bishop of Rome near the end of the first century. These contacts suggest that Hebrews shared a kind of Roman theology and was most likely written from Rome.

Date

The question of when Hebrews was written is also controversial. The sermon itself hints that it was written some time after the first generation of Christian preaching (see 2:3 and 13:7). Some interpreters have understood it to refer to contemporary Jewish temple worship, since it uses the present tense to describe Jewish sacrifices. But they fail to recognize that Hebrews is essentially biblical commentary, using the accounts in the Pentateuch of ancient Israelite worship in the wilderness tabernacle or tent to interpret the supreme sacrifice of Christ. Because the author believes that the biblical word of God is still "living and effective" (4:12), it is appropriate to use the present tense. In fact, Hebrews never mentions the Herodian temple or its ritual. That temple was destroyed by the Roman army in A.D. 70, and there is no evidence on this ground that Hebrews was written before or after the destruction.

The First Letter of Clement of Rome, generally thought to have been written in the nineties of the first century, contains several passages that seem to quote or allude to Hebrews. This would suggest that Hebrews was circulating at that time. Yet Clement does not indicate that he is quoting, as he does for example with 1 Corinthians or the Old Testament. The similarity to Hebrews may mean only that he shares with it some common ideas and formulations of Christian thought in Rome. In this case Hebrews itself might be dated late in the first century.

The issue of Hebrews' dependence on the text of the Old Testament has broader significance than merely the question of date, however. It reminds us that the theology of this work is primarily a matter of interpretation of the Bible. That means that the reader of Hebrews should first look to Old Testament passages to understand the author's reasoning. The argument is sometimes complicated, but almost always it can best be understood as interpretation of the word of God expressed in the early Christians' Bible.

Structure

It is always useful to discuss the literary structure of a work in order to understand it better. With Hebrews this is difficult, not because it is badly structured, but because it is so carefully crafted with the techniques of ancient rhetoric. Key words and phrases are used to sum up themes and to introduce new ones, sometimes with interlocking references that make outlining the work very complex. For example, one can note how the subject of angels is introduced in 1:4, to be discussed in 1:5-14, and how the whole passage is held together by the use of the word "inherit" in 1:4 and 1:14. In a brief commentary such as this one, it is not possible to point out the many structural elements, but the careful reader will notice them in the text.

The main body of the sermon (chapters 1-12) may be understood best as making three points, which constitute the major divisions of the work. Since this is a sermon, these divisions should be understood as exhortations, even though the bulk of the text is devoted to theological explanation. The first section, 1:1-4:13, deals with the word of God spoken in his Son and exhorts the hearers to pay attention to this word more carefully than to God's word communicated through angels or through Moses, that is, the word of the Mosaic law. The second, and the principal, section, 4:14-10:31, interprets the saving death of Jesus against the background of the Israelite priesthood. Jesus is the eternal high priest whose sacrifice does away with sin once and for all and establishes a new covenant relationship between God and humanity. Christians therefore have grounds to persevere in their hope. The third section, 10:32-12:29, seeks to bolster this hope by the concept of faith as insight into the heavenly world of reality where Jesus' work has already been accomplished. The work concludes (chapter 13) with some practical instructions and some letter features.

The importance of Hebrews

This New Testament document is important in more than one way. First, it is a completely self-contained theology of salvation in Christ. It is somewhat surprising in the fact that it does not lay emphasis on the resurrection of Jesus or on the liturgical side of Christian life. Indeed, one might have expected some attention to be given to the Eucharist in such a sermon. But Hebrews shows us a dimension of early Christianity that is entirely centered on the death of Jesus as the saving act. Second, the sermon is important because it shows us more clearly than any other New Testament writing the extent to which the interpretation of the Old Testament played a role in the development of early Christian thought. Such a role can be seen in most New Testament books, and it is important for the Christian belief in the continuity of salvation history from creation to redemption, but Hebrews illustrates it in a special way.

We might sum up the theology of Hebrews in a threefold statement of the function of Christ, corresponding to the three main divisions of the sermon. First, Christ is seen as the new word of God, the communication of God to humanity in a new idiom that is personal. It is a word spoken in the life and death of a human being who is also God's Son. Second, Christ functions as the unique, eternal high priest whose self-sacrifice in death finally atones for sin, inaugurates a new covenant, and provides a new and open access to God.

And third, Christ's own insight into the heavenly world of God is the model of faith that Christians need to persevere in their hope. This is a remarkable sweep of Christian faith focused on the person and role of Christ himself.

How to study Hebrews

The sermon to the Hebrews is so carefully written that it deserves to be studied carefully. Some suggestions may be helpful toward that end. To begin, it would be useful to read the whole sermon quickly in order to have an overview of its message and its structure. In such a reading one should note the main divisions of the book, for in detailed reading it is easy to lose sight of the forest while examin-ing the trees. Then, when reading the text slowly along with the commentary, one would do well to have a copy of the whole Bible at hand in order to look up the many Old Testament and occasional New Testament passages referred to. Studying Hebrews this way is a good method of integrating the Old Testament with understanding Christ's saving work. The reader should be aware that Old Testament passages in our modern Bibles will not always make the point that Hebrews wants to stress. This is because modern Bibles usually translate the original Hebrew and Aramaic of the Old Testament. The author of Hebrews used the Bible in its ancient Greek translation, which sometimes differed from the Hebrew.

COMMENTARY

THE WORD OF GOD SPOKEN IN HIS SON

Heb 1:1–4:13

1:1-4 Prologue: God has spoken. Hebrews shares with the Gospel of John and the First Epistle of John the fact that it begins with a prologue focusing on the idea of word (John 1:1-18; 1 John 1:1-4). As we shall see, the term "word" is applied rather differently in these three New Testament books, but in all its meanings it is important to the beginnings of Christian thought.

Prologues are a kind of introduction to literary works, and Hebrews is one of the most literary pieces in the New Testament. This prologue serves two functions. First, it introduces the first major division of the sermon, which has to do with the appropriate response of the hearers to the new mode of God's speaking in a Son. After showing the superiority of this kind of divine word, the author will sum up his statement in 4:12-13, thus indicating one of the structural principles of his rhetorical style, namely, enclosing units of thought within clearly related statements. Second, the Hebrews' prologue functions like a kind of "text" on which the preacher-author bases his sermon. In content these few verses range from a brief interpretation of the word of God in the Old Testament to a summary of what has been accomplished in the event of Jesus Christ.

The underlying idea is that of "word" as God's revelation to humanity. In the Gospel of John, "Word" is a personification of Jesus himself; in the First Epistle of John it is the gospel message preached in the author's church. Here it suggests the broader concept of all God's dealings with humanity, starting with the Bible and extending to the significance of the divine Son. The theme that permeates the whole sermon is how to hear and respond to God's revelation. Of old, God spoke variously in the Bible; now, in the "last days," he has given a new message in his Son Jesus. But it is the same God who has spoken, and therefore the Old Testament may be used to interpret the person and work of Jesus.

The style and content of verses 2-3 remind us of the hymns of early Christianity, of which we have examples in Phil 2:6-11, Col 1:15-20, and elsewhere. These tend to emphasize the divine closeness of the Son to God the Father, even his preexistence and role in creation. Such a series of statements was made possible by applying to Christ features of the personified figure of God's "wisdom." For a good parallel to our passage, one should read Wisdom of Solomon 7:25–8:1, where even the Alexandrian Jewish vocabulary is similar.

The second half of verse 3 refers to the saving activity of the Son, his sacrifice of himself for sins and his exaltation into heaven, which will be the subject of the second major division of Hebrews. Verse 4 both announces the theme of the section to follow and concludes the preceding statement (it is part of the one Greek sentence formed by verses 1-4). The name that Christ has inherited is that of Son, and the superiority of that name to the name of angel is yet to be shown.

1:5-14 Jesus, superior to angels. Even given the transitional statement of verse 4, one cannot help asking, Why the comparison with angels? It has often been thought that the author wanted to argue against a view, seen in some strands of second-century Christianity, that Jesus was an angel, not a real human being. But there is little evidence of polemic in these verses. Instead there are two considerations to bear in mind. First, the angels were thought in some sense to be the mediators of God's word in the law of Israel (see 2:2; Acts 7:53; Gal 3:19), which was superseded by the Christian gospel. Second, the scene introduced already in verse 3 is that of the heavenly enthronement of the Son (see Ps 110:1) beside God in heaven, reminiscent of frequent Old Testament conceptions of God and reflected in the imagery of the Israelite king enthroned in the psalms. The one who is enthroned is clearly superior to the angels who are in attendance before the throne.

This passage is a very important introduction to how Hebrews interprets the Old Testament, and three points need to be clearly understood. First, the Old Testament is taken to be God's word. This is a clear doctrine of inspiration, shared by all of early Christianity, and it matters little whether God, the Holy Spirit, or even Christ is understood as speaking the words of Moses or David or others. Second, passages are used in isolation, without any necessary regard for their context, though the author can sometimes allude to more words of them than he actually quotes. Third, and most important, the Old Testament can be seen as speaking about or to the divine Son Jesus. This last point is significant, for it reveals one of the most important constitutive elements of early Christian theology, namely, the reinterpretation of the Scriptures of Israel as a way of understanding the person and meaning of Jesus.

It is possible that at this point the author was not simply combing the Old Testament for suitable passages, but that he had a collection of passages used for messianic preaching. That such collections existed is no longer a mere conjecture; we have Jewish examples among the famous Dead Sea Scrolls.

Despite the lack of emphasis on original context, the reader would do well to refer to the passages cited in their own Old Testament settings. There is a pattern in the seven citations in these verses, referring to son-son-angels, angels-son-son, son-angels (the last statement without a citation, v. 14). The general point is to suggest that the angels are subordinate and impermanent, while the Son is exalted and enduring. In chapter 2 we shall see a much more radical statement, that the angels are subordinate to human beings as such (already hinted at in verse 14).

The citations of biblical texts are often familiar to readers of the New Testament because some of them are used elsewhere pertaining to Christ. Verse 5 cites Ps 2:7 and 2 Sam 7:14, well-known messianic passages. Verse 6 is problematic; it cites something like Deut 32:43, but the introductory formula, "And again when he leads the first-born into the world," might refer to the second coming of Christ (see 9:28). By a slight twist of interpretation, verse 7 makes Ps 104:4 refer to the impermanence of the messengers (angels), and verses 8-9 refer to Christ (Ps 45:7-8). Verses 10-12 (Ps 102:26-28) contrast the permanence of the Son with the impermanence of the heavens, which are perhaps a category of angels or at least the place where they dwell. Verse 13 refers to Ps 110:1, which is an important proof text both in Hebrews and elsewhere in the New Testament.

2:1-18 The humanity of Jesus. Chapter 2 begins with the first of the many exhortations of the preacher to his congregation. The danger they face is called that of "drifting away." We are not yet told exactly what this means, but we shall see that it involves abandoning faith and especially hope, in effect ceasing to be true Christians. This exhortation draws the conclusion from the first chapter: since the Son is superior to the angels, the message of salvation he brought is even more to be obeyed than the law of Moses, which came through angels. Verse 3 clearly implies that Hebrews is being written in a second- or third-generation church, but one which has experienced miracles and gifts of the Holy Spirit as evidence confirming the message (v. 4).

The author again takes up the argument

that Christ is superior to the angels, but from a new angle. In chapter 1 Christ was superior as the Son of God; here he is superior because he is a human being. The argument again is based on Scripture as verses 6-8 quote Ps 8:5-7, but this time the author explicitly interprets the text he quotes. Two features of his interpretation are important. First, he understands the passage as referring not to humanity in general but to Jesus the man. And second, he reverses the meaning of the original psalm, which had said that God created human beings "a little lower than the angels." For Hebrews, Jesus the man is superior to the angels but was made "for a little while lower" than them in that he suffered death (v. 9). The subjection of all things to Christ still belongs to the future, but the process has begun with Jesus' exaltation to heaven after his death.

What is of most interest to the author in declaring the true humanity of Jesus is the fact that he shares that humanity with all human beings, who in verse 10 are called God's "children." In order that Jesus' death might be *for all* a liberation from slavery to the power of death (vv. 14-15), Jesus had to share their human nature fully. Verses 12-13 quote Ps 22:23 and Isa 8:17-18 with the supposition that Christ is speaking the inspired words. He is a brother to human beings, and like them he praises and puts his trust in the Father. Jesus' solidarity with humanity is also brought out in their common origin in the Father (v. 11), their sharing in flesh and blood (v. 14), and above all their sharing in death itself.

The last verses of the chapter perform the typical Hebrews' function of announcing new themes to be taken up. Jesus must share fully in humanity because he is to take on the role of high priest offering himself for the sins of his fellow human beings (v. 17). In particular he is a merciful and faithful high priest. His merciful character, suggested already in verse 18, will be spelled out further in chapter 5; his faithfulness is the subject of the next paragraph.

3:1-6 Jesus, superior to Moses. The paragraph begins with an exhortation to reflect on Jesus the faithful one. The readers or hearers are addressed in a lofty manner: they are holy because they have been consecrated by Jesus' sacrificial death (see 2:11), and they share in a "heavenly calling" to follow him into heaven. Only here is Jesus called an apostle, that is, one who is sent on a mission. There is no reference to the way the New Testament customarily uses the word to identify various Christian leaders. It is normal to think of a "confession" of faith (3:1), but we shall see that Hebrews is distinctive in referring to our "confession that gives us hope" (10:23). Moreover, the context here is one of hope, not of faith (v. 6).

Why the comparison with Moses? For one thing, Moses was the model of faithfulness and thus a good Old Testament foil for Jesus. But, in addition, Hebrews seems to be concerned with showing Jesus' superiority to various figures who functioned as intermediaries of God's word (such as the angels), and Moses, who received the law, was such an intermediary (see v. 5).

Most of the arguments of Hebrews are based on the interpretation of Scripture, and this one is no exception. Only this time the passage is not formally quoted but merely alluded to. It is Num 12:7-8 in its Greek version: "Not so with my servant Moses. He is faithful in all my house. With him I shall speak mouth to mouth . . . ." Two elements of the passage are contrasted with Jesus. Moses is only a servant in God's "house," the people of God; Jesus is God's own Son, not *in* the house but *over* it. In addition, the Son ranks with the founder of the house in the sense that Jesus establishes a new "house" of God, namely the Christian community, which must cling to its hope in order to remain God's house.

3:7–4:11 Entering God's rest. All of chapter 3 and most of chapter 4 are dominated by the theme of faithfulness: first the faithfulness of Jesus the Son compared with Moses (3:1-6), then the unfaithfulness of the Israelites in their desert wanderings (3:7-19), then the faithfulness required of Christians (4:1-11), and implicitly God's faithfulness to his word in Scripture.

What we find in this section is an extended commentary on Ps 95:8-11, quoted, with some slight modifications, in Heb 3:7-11. It is a preacher's use of the text—not merely an exegesis of it but an application to the lives of the hearers. Thus it shows us yet another facet of Hebrews' varied scriptural interpretation. Underlying the whole passage there is a carefully structured argument which supports the exhortation summed up in 4:11. With some simplifying we can restate the argument this way. As Psalm 95 shows, God created a "rest" for his faithful followers to enter (3:11). But the Israelites, who were repeatedly unfaithful in their Exodus journey, were excluded from entering it (3:16-19). Yet that rest was a part of God's creation, and it remains for those who are faithful to him to enter it (4:1-6). God reminds us of the continuing openness of this promise by saying through the psalmist David, centuries after the Exodus, "Oh, that today you would hear his voice" (4:7-10). Therefore Christians have the opportunity to enter God's rest and must strive to do so by being faithful.

The failure of the Israelites to enter the Promised Land, the rest after their journey, hinges on a particular passage of the Bible, Num 14, which is clearly alluded to in 3:16-19. According to this version of the Exodus story, only Joshua (see 4:8) and Caleb, and presumably their extended families as well as the women and youth of Israel, actually entered the land of Canaan.

The emphasis on the presentness of the word "today" is important to the argument (3:13; 4:7), for it shows how the word of God in Scripture is regarded as effective in the present (see 4:12-13 below), speaking to the reader now and not just then.

It is also worth noting how the author blends three different notions of God's "rest" in this passage. The first is the rest of the Promised Land, rest at the end of the desert wanderings of Israel, as implied by the literal meaning of Psalm 95. The second is God's own sabbath rest from his labors in the creation story; Heb 4:4 quotes Gen 2:2 (and see Heb 4:10 in particular). The third, and most fundamental for the purposes of Hebrews, understands God's rest as the ultimate destiny of his faithful followers in heaven. The idea of entering God's rest as the goal of Christian life implies an image of that life as both labor and a pilgrimage or journey toward a heavenly homeland, a metaphor which will be picked up again in Hebrews (for example, in chapters 11–12).

What is the danger of unfaithfulness for the Christians? We learn a little more about their situation from this passage, in which exhortation dominates. The danger is one of succumbing to "the deceit of sin" (3:13) in such

an extreme way as to "forsake the living God" (3:12). It is the risk of apostasy, of so losing faith and hope in God as to abandon him and the promises he made—by implication to cease to hear the word of his revelation in Scripture or in his Son. Deep-rooted discouragement might motivate such an attitude, and that would be consistent with the emphasis in Hebrews on clinging to hope and confidence (see 3:6). In this light, perhaps one should translate the second part of 4:1 in more directly personal terms: "we ought to be fearful lest any one of you think he has missed his chance of entering."

4:12-13 The living word of God. The first major division of the sermon began with a very rhetorical, almost poetic, statement about the modes of God's speaking in the Bible and in his Son, and it continued with emphasis on both the Old Testament and the salvation announced by Jesus. It is appropriate that the section should end with another carefully composed, again almost poetic, statement about the power of God's word. In its immediate context this statement sums up the argument based on Psalm 95, but it also extends to the broader concept of God's word as revelation introduced in 1:1-3. Thus, typically of Hebrews, this statement looks backward to the scriptural arguments and forward to the interpretation of Jesus as high priest.

The language of this short passage is in fact rather conventional, particularly in Alexandrian Judaism or Christianity. One can find some close parallels in the writings of the Jewish philosopher and biblical interpreter Philo, though he personifies God's word in a way that Hebrews does not. The author's intellectual background nevertheless is reflected in passages like this.

According to verse 12, God's word is alive (v. 7: "Oh, that *today* you would hear his voice") and so effective that it penetrates to the innermost parts of a person, forcing one to come to grips with what really matters. Verse 13 is less than completely clear in the original Greek and has been translated in many different ways. As an alternative to the New American Bible translation, we might suppose that it refers not to God but still to God's word, and that it makes a transition to the main division of the sermon that is about to begin. In Greek this short paragraph begins with "God's word" and ends with "our word."

So we might translate the verse: "Nothing is concealed from it (God's word); all lies bare and exposed to the eyes of that (word) toward which our word (or message) is directed."

HOPE IN THE SACRIFICE OF JESUS

Heb 4:14–10:31

4:14-16 Confidence in our high priest. The theme of the second major section of Hebrews is the role and activity of Christ as unique high priest whose once-for-all sacrifice of himself for the sins of humanity accomplished what the elaborate sacrificial ritual of the ancient Israelites could not do. Consequently, the sacrifice of Christ inaugurates a new covenant and replaces the entire old order described in the Old Testament. Yet the Old Testament is still the word of God, and therefore it will still be used to interpret the meaning of Jesus' death in this section.

Just as the first major section of the sermon was enclosed between two passages on the word of God, so the second is bounded by two passages of exhortation (4:14-16 and 10:19-31) that have many similarities, even verbal ones (see especially 10:19-23). We shall note some of them in discussing chapter 10 below.

Jesus had been introduced as high priest for the first time in 2:17, where he was called merciful and faithful. Having discussed his faithfulness in chapter 3, the author turns now to his quality of mercy, first in the transition passage 4:14-16 and then further in 5:1-10. His mercy is rooted in his sharing of human nature, to the point of being tempted in every way that all humans are, yet without yielding to sin (v. 15).

Jesus' passage "through the heavens" (v. 14) perhaps reflects the common Jewish view of a series of heavens above the earth, in the highest of which God dwells. His successful entry into God's presence grounds the hope and confidence of his followers, as will be repeatedly stated in the sermon. The reference to "our confession of faith" in verse 14 leads us to the same caution made in the commentary on 3:1. The text literally says only "let us hold fast to the confession." As the parallel verse 10:23 will show, it is a confession of hope, not faith.

This short passage introduces us to an important shift in the imagery of exhortation in Hebrews. It is the shift from holding fast to hope and confidence, or the confession (see 3:6, 14; 4:14), to moving forward: "approach the throne of grace" (4:16). The imagery of forward movement was already anticipated in 4:11 and will be prominent from now on. It has three dimensions, which we shall note as they occur: continuing on the journey toward God's rest, approaching God as worshipers approached the altar of sacrifice, and growing up in one's understanding of Christianity.

5:1-10 Christ as high priest. By this point the author has identified Jesus as high priest several times (2:17; 3:1; 4:14-15), but he has not explained or justified this notion. Now he does so in a classic rhetorical way by defining what a high priest is and showing how the definition fits Jesus. For these ten verses it is important to recognize the structure used by the author. He first defines a high priest by stating three qualifications, which he derives from interpretation of the passages relevant to Israelite worship in the Pentateuch. The high priest is the descendant of Levi described there, and though historically Jesus does not qualify (see 7:13-14), nevertheless he fulfills the proper conditions. The qualifications are stated in verses 1-4: (1) the high priest is chosen from human beings and represents them in the sacrifice he offers; (2) he can perform his representative function because he shares in human weakness; and (3) he is called to this office by God and not by his own choice.

Verses 5-10 show how Christ meets these qualifications, but in reverse order. In addition, they introduce a new element of comparison, the priesthood of the shadowy figure Melchizedek, who will be dealt with formally in chapter 7. First, Christ did not assume the office of high priest, but he received it from God, as the Scripture attests, understanding Pss 2:7 and 110:4 as addressed to him. One should note that the latter passage speaks only of a priest, not a high priest. Melchizedek will be "elevated" to the high priestly status starting with verse 10 because this status is important for the author's argument. Verses 7-9 demonstrate the solidarity of Christ with human beings in weakness, but the argument is a subtle one because Jesus has been declared to be sinless (4:15) and thus cannot offer "sin offerings for himself as well as for the people" (v. 3). This nuance will continue to be a delicate issue.

Verse 7 in particular has long been a focus of interest. Traditionally it has been taken to be a reference to the prayer of Jesus in the Garden of Gethsemane, as reported in Mark 14:32-42 and parallels. But two factors make one hesitate to understand it in this way: it has nothing in common with the Gethsemane story from a language point of view, and also this would be the only reference in Hebrews to a specific Gospel passage. The alternative is to suppose that the verse is a depiction of the typical Jewish hero, such as Abraham or Moses, who prays demonstratively to God, and the language used has notable parallels in Philo's description of such persons. If there is any reference to the Gospel story, it is very indirect.

Verses 9-10 clearly illustrate the role of Christ as the representative of the people for whom as high priest he offers sacrifice. His intercession was so effective that he became a source of salvation for others. The transition from a priest like Melchizedek to a *high priest* like Melchizedek takes place quietly, but the reader will have to wait until chapter 7 before perceiving its significance.

5:11–6:20 Exhortation to hope. This rather long section, dominated by exhortation, seems to interrupt the author's flow of thought. Instead of going on to explain what it means for Jesus to be a high priest like Melchizedek, the author both reproaches his hearers for sluggishness and encourages them to hope. But the passage looks much less like an interruption if we bear in mind that Hebrews is a sermon, not a treatise. Here especially the art of the preacher comes through skillfully. Before entering into a rather detailed and complicated explanation, he pauses to motivate the hearers to follow it. Again, the underlying theme is that of moving forward, growing in mature understanding of Christian life (6:1) and in hope following Jesus the forerunner (6:18-20).

The preacher begins by using a metaphor that must have been familiar to his congregation, that of milk and solid food, little children and grownups (5:11-14). St. Paul uses the same metaphor in a very similar way in 1 Cor 3:1-2, and there are examples of it in such more or less contemporary Jewish writers as

Philo of Alexandria. The problem is that the hearers are refusing to grow up in their understanding of Christianity. They are stuck at the level of the ABCs; the Greek word translated "basic elements" means exactly that. We must pause for a moment over the word "mature" or "adult." In Greek it is the same word that is often translated "perfect" in Hebrews, and it is an important theme of the sermon as a whole. In Greek, "perfect" does not mean not having any defects, as we often use the word, but it means being complete, being all that one is supposed to be. Repeatedly Hebrews says that Jesus was made perfect in this sense through his suffering and death (2:10; 5:9), thus becoming a source of salvation for others. Christians too must share in this salvation; they must become complete and mature and eventually partakers of the same heavenly destiny as Jesus.

Chapter 6 begins with a list of the "foundations," elementary Christian teachings that one must go beyond in order to grow up. They are not of course to be abandoned, but the Christian cannot stay at that level. To use our language, Hebrews is a work of adult education. Nothing in the list directly concerns Christ, and most of the rest of Hebrews does. We can conclude, therefore, that for Hebrews adult Christian education focuses on understanding the person and saving work of Christ the high priest. The modern reader cannot be certain of the exact meaning of each item in the list given in 6:1-2. For example, "baptisms" probably does not refer to Christian baptism as such but to some kind of ritual washings which Christians inherited from their Jewish background. "Laying on of hands" might mean commissioning members of a community to perform certain functions—what we would call ordination.

The danger for those who refuse to advance toward maturity is that of losing hope, of turning away from God (see 3:12). In 6:4-8 the author sternly warns his hearers of the consequences. One who has become a Christian, been enlightened, shared in the Holy Spirit, tasted God's word, and yet has rejected it all can even be said to participate in responsibility for the death of Jesus. Hebrews is often said to take a hard line on the matter of penitence and forgiveness (see also 10:26-31), but note that the author is careful not to say that God does not forgive, but only that personal repentance is beyond the reach of one who definitively rejects the Son of God. Verses 7-8 make use of a biblical metaphor that is quite clear in its application here. The language is partly drawn from Gen 3:17-18, but there is no allusion to the Genesis context here.

The good preacher does not leave his hearers with a strongly worded warning ringing in their ears, but goes on to encourage them. The remainder of chapter 6 is a reassuring exhortation to hope marked by the decided change of tone in verse 9 and the commendation of the hearers' love and service to one another (v. 10). As a basis for perseverance and progress in hope, the author refers to God's oath and promise to Abraham that he would bless Abraham's descendants (6:13-18; see Gen 22:16-18). The argument supposes that the promise made to Abraham applies to all Christians and therefore gives them confidence. The famous example of Abraham is often used in a similar way in the New Testament. Verse 15 may mean only that Abraham obtained the promise; what was promised was to come later, only with the saving work of Christ.

Verses 18-20 perform several functions, as most transitional passages in Hebrews do. They summarize the theme of hope; reintroduce the next topic, a priest like Melchizedek; and give advance warning of a new topic, which reaches "beyond the veil." That phrase refers to the Israelite high priest's entry into the inner shrine of the tabernacle, the Holy of Holies.

7:1-28 A priest like Melchizedek.

Chapter 7 deals in reality with three priesthoods, and it is helpful for the reader to keep them distinct. First, there is the priesthood of Melchizedek, an ancient and somewhat mysterious figure from the time of Abraham. Second, there is the high priesthood of the Israelite tribe of Levi, legislated for in Num 18. And third, there is the priesthood of Christ himself, which resembles that of Melchizedek in its perpetuity and also has the function of that of Levi.

The author has built up to the comparison of Christ and Melchizedek by referring three times to Ps 110:4: "You are a priest forever, according to the order of Melchizedek" (5:6, 10; 6:20). We know of no *order* of Melchizedekian priests, and we should probably understand this expression to mean simply "a priest *like* Melchizedek" (see v. 15). But how is Christ like him? Indeed, why the comparison with Melchizedek at all? Several answers are possible. For one thing, Christ is an eternal priest, not a merely mortal one like the levitical priests, and Melchizedek is a priest forever. And as we have already seen more than once, passages from the psalms such as this one are often understood as speaking about or to Christ. In addition, there is some evidence that in Judaism even earlier than Hebrews, namely, in the Dead Sea Scrolls, there was some speculation about Melchizedek as a heavenly figure, perhaps even a saving figure. It may have been natural to compare the exalted, heavenly Christ with him.

In this chapter we have another excellent example of the biblical interpretation and exegetical reasoning of the author. The reader needs to be reminded that Hebrews has no interest in Melchizedek as a historical figure; the entire argument is an interpretation of Old Testament passages. Besides Ps 110:4, only one other Old Testament passage mentions Melchizedek—the brief and somewhat obscure story found in Gen 14:17-20. It would be useful to read that story in its context when reading Heb 7, since the author uses it to interpret Ps 110:4. His interpretation of it may seem fanciful to us, but it is typical of his own day.

Popular explanations of Melchizedek's name and kingdom enable the author to associate justice and peace with him and, by inference, with Christ (v. 2). Since the Genesis text says nothing of Melchizedek's personal background or even his birth and death, the inference is that he is a priest forever (v. 3). The two elements of the story that are most important are the facts that Melchizedek blessed Abraham and that Abraham gave a tenth of his spoils of war, a "tithe," to Melchizedek. Both of these demonstrate Melchizedek's superiority, and since Levi and all the levitical priests to come were to be descended from Abraham, they too are placed in a position subordinate to Melchizedek (vv. 4-10). The conclusion will be spelled out further: a priest like Melchizedek is superior to the Israelite priests.

The argument of verses 11-17 becomes clearer if we understand the "law" in question as the law of Moses regarding the levitical priests, their right of inheritance, their right to tithes, and other matters, found in Num 18. We should then translate the parenthesis in verse 11: "concerning which the people received a law." The argument runs as follows. If the priesthood of the law were not inherently deficient, there would have been no need for God to appoint a priest like Melchizedek (v. 11). But Christ could not have been a levitical priest because he was of the tribe of Judah, not of Levi (vv. 13-14). And he was appointed as an eternal priest like Melchizedek, not by a law of physical descent (Num 18), but by the living word of God addressed to him in Ps 110:4 (vv. 15-17).

One should note how the theme of perfection, including the sense of completeness, pervades this discussion (vv. 11, 19, 28). The law has been incapable of bringing the priesthood to perfection. But the appointment of Jesus as high priest was in Ps 110:4 accompanied by a divine oath, "the Lord has sworn," and thus was made more sure (vv. 20-21; compare 6:13-18). The basic reason why the Israelite priesthood was deficient was that it resided in mortals whose death terminated their priestly activity (vv. 23-24). This point will be spelled out further, as well as the relationship between priesthood and covenant. As an eternal priest, Christ offered a once-for-all sacrifice which did away with sin forever (v. 27). Having established the eternal character of Christ's priesthood, the author can leave Melchizedek behind and not mention him again.

8:1-6 Old and new ministry. Chapter 7 introduced the theme of contrast between the priesthood of the Old Testament and that of Christ. The next three chapters will extend that contrast to the priestly ministry, the covenant which it implies, the sanctuary where the priest functions, and the sacrifice which he performs. We begin with a short passage on priestly ministry, and the main thrust of the preacher is his assertion in verse 1 that Christians *have* such an eternal high priest as he has described, namely Christ, who has been exalted into heaven, as Heb 1:3 had already declared. There he exercises his unique priestly ministry, which takes place only in heaven, since on earth Jesus, not being a Levite, would not be a priest. Verses 4-5 do not really imply that the Jewish sacrificial ritual is still going on, that is, that the temple has not yet

been destroyed in the war with Rome, for the basis for the argument is the text of the Bible, not observation of current practice.

Underlying this paragraph is a principle of the author's thought that will remain important for the next few chapters of the sermon. It hinges on the notion that the superiority of Christ's priestly work lies in the fact that it is performed (eternally) in heaven. Verse 5 quotes Exod 25:40, recalling that Moses was instructed to build the wilderness tabernacle according to a divine plan or pattern revealed to him. The preacher to the Hebrews has his background in the popular philosophical ideas of the day, which held that the true realities were in the heavenly world of God, and the earthly ones were merely copies or shadows of them. Thus the divine plan for the tabernacle has become the "true tabernacle" (v. 2) in heaven as opposed to the shadowy imitation on earth. Christ's ministry is superior because it is exercised in the world of true reality. Verse 6 summarizes this point while at the same time introducing the next comparison.

For centuries Christian theological interpretation of Hebrews has been fascinated with the question of whether Christ's sacrificial act took place on earth, on the cross, or takes place in heaven, in his entrance into the sanctuary of the true tabernacle. The question may be impossible to answer, and perhaps unnecessary to ask, since the author shows no awareness of it. For him the sacrificial death of Jesus *was* his entry into the sanctuary of God, and the transition between the historical and the eternal was instantaneous. We shall see later that Hebrews does not simply assume that the present world is not the real arena of human salvation. It is indeed, and almost despite the interest of the author in the heavenly realities above, it is on earth that human beings associate themselves with the suffering and death of Jesus.

8:7-13 Old and new covenant. This section of Hebrews merits little comment, for it consists mostly of a rather long Old Testament quotation, the majestic passage from Jer 31:31-34, which will be commented on more thoroughly in 9:15-22 and especially 10:9-18. This unique announcement of a *new* covenant in the Old Testament itself obviously invites comparison with the old covenant, which is here limited to the covenant with Moses on

Mount Sinai. It also suggests a rationale for the new relationship between humanity and God inaugurated by Christ. The minimal comment of the author (v. 13) emphasizes the theme of replacement.

The idea of covenant dominates much of the Old Testament. Set against the background of treaties between kings or kingdoms in the ancient Near East, the biblical idea of covenant suggests a kind of legal agreement between God and his people setting forth the duties and responsibilities of each party. Basically the people of Israel must obey God's will, and he will in turn be their protector. Jeremiah's vision of a new covenant in the future portrays a somewhat less legalistic and more personal relationship between God and his people. It is hardly surprising that the Christians should have seen this prophecy fulfilled by the mediation of Christ.

The link between priesthood and covenant, or priestly sacrifice and covenant, is important for the thought of Hebrews. According to Exod 24:3-8, Moses had ratified the Sinai covenant with the blood of sacrifice, a passage which will be referred to in 9:19-22. The hint is already present in our passage that the sacrificial blood of Jesus will be the ratification of a new covenant. The most important feature of the new covenant, as we shall see, is that God will forgive the sins of his people (v. 12).

9:1-10 The old sanctuary. In preparation for describing Jesus' death as a sacrifice for sin, the author first gives a very concise and stylized description of the wilderness tabernacle of Exod 25–26 and other passages, as well as of the ritual that went on in it. Again it should be noted that there is no allusion to current practice in the temple of Jerusalem, which probably no longer existed when Hebrews was written. The basis of the description is biblical interpretation, even if we cannot verify all the details in our texts of the Pentateuch. It is possible here that the author was familiar with some Jewish tradition about the furnishings of the tabernacle. He refers to the tabernacle furnishings and ritual as regulations of the first covenant, since the prescriptions for worship were part of the law given at Mount Sinai. Verses 2-5 describe very concisely the two divisions of the tabernacle— the essential structure of ancient Near Eastern temples—and what was in them. The

golden splendor of the Holy of Holies contrasts vividly with the fairly austere outer tent.

Verses 6-7 describe the ritual, highlighting the once-a-year entrance of the high priest alone into the Holy of Holies. This is the ritual of Yom Kippur, the Day of Atonement, and since it was a blood sacrifice, it serves the author's purposes as the model for the sacrificial death of Jesus. There is, as we shall see presently, a spatial imagery here: Jesus enters heaven (or the innermost sanctuary of heaven) as the high priest enters the Holy of Holies. But verses 8-10 also introduce a temporal dimension which complicates the picture. Perhaps we can make the best sense of the complication by taking "the present time" (v. 9) to refer to the time contemporaneous with the sacrificial ritual of Israel described in the Old Testament. The ritual of this time does not get to the heart of the matter, the conscience of the worshipers. But when the time of "the new order" has come, that is, the time spoken of in verse 11, sacrifice has a wholly new significance.

9:11-28 The sacrifice of Jesus. After setting up the Old Testament contexts of priestly ministry, covenant, and sanctuary ritual, the author finally turns to an application of these categories to the saving death of Christ. It may be helpful to the reading of this and the following section to realize how the author envisions the heavenly temple or tabernacle, which is the scene of Christ's sacrifice. He draws on two somewhat different pictures, both of them known in contemporary Jewish thought, without always clearly distinguishing them. One is the picture of a complete tabernacle in heaven with its outer court and its inner sanctuary beyond the veil where God dwells. This seems to be the picture presupposed in verse 11. The other sees the universe itself structured like a tabernacle in which the earth is the outer court and heaven itself is the inner sanctuary. Entering heaven, by death, is passing through the veil into God's presence; this imagery seems to underlie verse 24.

The important point of this passage is that the death of Christ is interpreted as the one really effective sacrifice that atones for the sins of humanity (vv. 14, 26, 28). The principal underlying image is the ritual of the Day of Atonement as described in Lev 16. But the author blends with it two other pictures. Verse 13 refers to the sacrifice of the red heifer, a sin offering, described in Num 19. The ashes of the heifer had the power of making holy again persons who had incurred various forms of ritual defilement. Thirdly, verses 19-22 refer to the sacrificial ratification of the Sinai covenant described in Exod 24:3-8. What all three of these rituals have in common is that they involve the shedding of blood and thus can be applied symbolically to the death of Jesus. Sacrificial blood is a powerful and pervasive theme in ancient Israelite worship. It could be used as a petition for the forgiveness of sin, as a means of purification, and as a way of sealing a covenant with Yahweh. In all these respects the one effective sacrifice of Christ replaces the old ritual. To understand the details of this passage better, the reader should look up all three Old Testament passages.

Verse 15 begins the author's commentary on the new covenant prophesied by Jeremiah. What is essential is that it involves the definitive forgiveness of sin. Since Christ has accomplished that in his sacrificial death, he is the mediator of the new covenant. The following verses 16-18 are puzzling until one realizes that in Greek the words "covenant" and "testament" (in the sense of last will and testament) are the same. By a play on the two meanings, the preacher finds another way of showing how the covenant involves death. A will is executed only after the one who made it has died. St. Paul uses the same play on the word in Gal 3:15-18.

The main force of the contrast between the sacrificial death of Christ and the Day of Atonement sacrifices of the Israelite high priest is brought out explicitly in verses 25-28. The latter sacrifices were inadequate to take away sin in a definitive way because they had to be repeated every year. Sin continued to be a part of peoples' lives. But Christ's death was a once-for-all sacrifice that took away sin for good. To understand Christ's saving work this way means for the Christian to renounce sin completely. The terms "once" and "once for all" are important for the theology of Hebrews and are used frequently.

The passage ends with a rather clear reference to the second coming of Christ which is not wholly consistent with the author's own viewpoint in other passages. Through his once-for-all sacrifice Christ has effectively made salvation available already (compare the language of verse 11). It may be that the preacher mentions the second coming because he knows that it is part of the belief of his hearers.

10:1-18 Old and new sacrifice. The author concludes the argument of the main section of the sermon with a summary comparison of Christ's sacrifice with those of Israelite ritual, to be followed by further exhortation. Verses 1-18 contain a certain amount of repetition because the passage is a summary, but they also contain some new ideas. The picture they portray of the levitical priests and their sacrifices is sad (for example, v. 11), but we need to be reminded that Hebrews is not making an anti-Jewish statement. The superiority of Christ's sacrifice, and consequently of Christianity itself, is not being established at the expense of the author's Jewish contemporaries. He does not speak of current or recent Jewish practices, but only of the ancient Israelite tabernacle ritual as it is described in the Pentateuch. It is God's word in the Bible that indicates the limitations of this ritual and at the same time points toward the meaning of his word spoken in the Son.

The passage begins with several contrasts between the sacrifices in question. First, there is the inherent imperfection of the law of Moses, which is described as being at two removes from the divine reality (v. 1). The background is that of popular philosophical thought, which distinguished between reality which is spiritual, the visible image of that reality, and the shadow cast by the image. Since the law pointed toward the future, it was only in the realm of shadow. Verses 2-3 make explicit the argument we have already seen that repeated sacrifices for sin are ineffectual precisely because they have to be repeated. But verse 4 introduces a new idea, that it is impossible for animal sacrifices to take away sin. The proof lies in the quotation of Ps 40:7-8 (in its Greek translation), in which, as often is the case, the speaker is understood to be Christ. There God is said to reject animal sacrifices. The author then interprets the psalm as a displacement of the law, the old covenant, by the sacrifice of the body of Christ, which was God's will for his Son (vv. 9-10). Verses 11-14 repeat the contrast between multiple sacrifices and the once-for-all sacrifice of Christ, emphasizing the eternal effects of the latter. Verses 12-13 refer again to

Ps 110:1, which has been used several times from 1:3 on.

Some final comments on the new covenant passage of Jer 31 round off the argument (vv. 15-18). This time the Holy Spirit is said to be the speaker of God's word, but the quotations are in fact the author's paraphrases of the text. The conclusion is that since the new covenant mediated by Christ has achieved the forgiveness of sins, on the authority of the word of God himself, all other sacrifices for sin have come to an end.

10:19-31 Confidence and judgment. The final passage of exhortation in the second major division of the sermon, which, as mentioned above, counterbalances the opening one (4:14-16), contains both encouragement (vv. 19-25) and dire warning (vv. 26-31). But warning is not the last word, since the exhortation continues to the end of chapter 10. The resemblance of verses 19-23 in particular to 4:14-16 is striking, and one should at this point read again the earlier passage. In the discussion of that passage, it was pointed out that many of the hortatory passages of Hebrews take the form of "holding fast" and "moving forward." Both appear here also: "let us approach" (v. 22) and "let us hold unwaveringly" (v. 23). The former is the language of approaching God in worship as in 4:16. The latter finally identifies the Christian confession as a confession of hope ("our confession that gives us hope" is literally "the confession of hope"). It is hope that really defines the basic Christian attitude for Hebrews, hope in God's promises of salvation through Christ. Unlike many other New Testament writings, Hebrews makes faith subordinate to hope in the sense that faith provides the grounds for hope. We shall see this more clearly in chapter 11. Here verse 22 expresses the idea in that "the fullness of faith" (the literal translation of the words "absolute trust" in the New American Bible) is not the goal but a necessary condition for reaching it. Note that our passage also mentions love in verse 24, thus taking up and using in its own way the familiar Christian grouping of faith, hope, and love.

Verse 20 contains a famous difficulty of translation from Greek that has occasioned much discussion. Literally it speaks of "the new and living way he opened up for us through the veil, that is, his flesh." The New American Bible understands the veil, the curtain that separated the Holy of Holies from the outer sanctuary in the tabernacle, as symbolic of Jesus' physical existence, and it has translated the verse accordingly. It is equally possible, however, to read the verse in such a way that the path of access to God is symbolic of the physical existence of Jesus. This would mean that the sacrifice of the body of Jesus (see 10:10) is the way to God that is now open to Christians. It would imply that Jesus' "flesh" was not an obstacle to approaching God but the very means of doing so. The important point in any case is that followers of Christ now have access to God himself in the heavenly sanctuary, thanks to the sacrifice of Christ. One is reminded of John 14:6: "I am the way . . . no one comes to the Father except through me."

It is often the case that the Greek of Hebrews lends itself to more than one translation. Verse 25 affords another example. In the New American Bible translation the issue is that some of the congregation addressed have been neglecting to attend community gatherings, perhaps as a symptom of their abandoning hope in God's promises. This may well be the case, for the preceding verse seems to deal with practical matters also. But the word for "assembly" in verse 25 is unusual in the New Testament, and in its only other use there, 2 Thess 2:1, it clearly refers to the gathering of Christians about the Lord at his second coming, on the "day of the Lord." In this sense verse 25 would be a warning against giving up on the idea of a future gathering with the Lord, that is, a warning against abandoning hope.

Verse 26 begins a very solemn warning about deliberate sin—turning away from God, as we have seen—by referring back to 10:18. If one turns his or her back on the atoning sacrifice of Christ, there is no other sacrifice for sin to appeal to. The warning is made sharper by comparison in verse 28 with the fate of the Israelites who turned away from the law of God (see Deut 17:6 and especially its context). Such persons were subject to death by stoning. What will be the fate of those who reject the salvation that comes in God's Son (recall the similar argument in 2:2-3)? Verse 30 is a reminder that judgment by God is inescapable; the evidence is from Deut 32:35-36.

THE POWER OF FAITH

Heb 10:32–12:29

10:32-39 Living by faith. The third major division of the sermon begins with a continuation of the preacher's exhortation to his hearers, again softening the rigor of his warning with a reassuring note. Yet this is an appropriate place to see a new section beginning because the passage is a typical transition in Hebrews, shifting the focus from hope and confidence (vv. 35-36) to faith (vv. 38-39).

Verses 32-34 seem at first glance to tell us something concrete about the background of the congregation to which Hebrews is addressed. They are people who, having become Christians, have suffered for their Christian identity and willingly sympathized with other Christians who suffered even more. The passage mentions public exposure to insults, imprisonment, the confiscation of property. But all of these things are expressed in very general terms, and there is no way to draw from them specific conclusions regarding the history of a particular early Christian church. They sound like the typical things various early Christian communities may have had to confront, and that may be precisely the author's intention—to be universal rather than particular. The main point is implicit in verses 35-36: you have made a heavy personal investment in following Christ; much is at stake for you. To give it all up now is an alarming prospect.

What do such people need to sustain their hope? The author finds the answer in the text of Hab 2:3-4 (mainly in its Greek form): it is by faith that the just one shall live. St. Paul quotes this famous line of the passage (Rom 1:17; Gal 3:11), but in a different way. The faith that he has in mind is faith in the person and work of Christ. As we shall see, that is not what Hebrews understands by faith. But it is those who have faith who are able to maintain their confidence and hope (v. 39).

11:1–12:2 A cloud of witnesses to faith. The main component of the third major section of Hebrews, and by far the best-known passage in the work, is the long list of examples of Old Testament models of faith, culminating in the example of Jesus, the new and supreme model, in 12:1-2. The literary form of this passage is well known. Lists of figures from the Old Testament whose lives illustrate some virtue or quality are not uncommon, in the Jewish wisdom literature especially. One can find good examples in Sir 44–50 or Wis 10.

The passage begins with something like a definition of faith that deserves careful attention. For centuries there has been a tradition of interpretation of verse 1 that emphasizes faith as a subjective attitude on the part of the one who has it. This is often reflected in the translation of the verse that is made to speak of "confident assurance" and "conviction." (It is interesting that the older Catholic translations from the Latin of St. Jerome were more objectively oriented, translating the words as "substance" and "evidence.") In fact the Greek text uses very objective language and should be translated more literally: "Now faith is the reality of things hoped for, the evidence of things not seen." Of course faith is personally appropriated, but it is first of all an objective quality. We might well describe it in modern terms as insight into the reality of the invisible divine world. It is related to hope, to be sure, but as a motivation that sustains hope when the goals hoped for are not visible. Since such faith is characteristic of the heroes of the Old Testament (v. 2), it is obviously not oriented toward Christ but toward God and his promises. Verse 6, speaking of Enoch, gives a kind of minimal description of the object of faith: belief that God exists and that he rewards those who follow him. The faith of the Christian will be informed by the word of God spoken in his Son, but it is not really qualitatively different from the faith of the biblical heroes. Perhaps we could preserve a little of the objective character of faith if we substituted the phrase "in faith" for the translation "by faith" in each of the examples to follow.

Verse 3 surprises us. Expecting examples of the "men of old," we first meet a statement in which "By faith we understand that the universe was ordered." If the author wishes to begin at the beginning with creation (Gen 1), there were no witnesses to respond in faith. But perhaps he wants to suggest that there is in fact a continuity between the faith of the ancients and that of his contemporary Christians, for whom faith in God's creation is fundamental to everything else. The examples to follow are not museum pieces, but are illustrative of the same faith demanded of and implicit in the very existence of Christians.

Ideally it would be good to have the space to comment fully on each of the Old Testament examples in this long litany of people who acted in faith. To appreciate the chapter properly, and to enjoy reading it, the reader should be sure he or she has a fresh memory of each story referred to. That involves more "homework" than can be done here. Instead we shall point out some individual instances of exactly what actions were performed in faith, and marginal references in most modern Bibles will provide information about the relevant Old Testament passages to look up.

The story of Cain and Abel (v. 4; Gen 4:1-16) naturally highlights Abel as the example of faith. The fact that Abel "still speaks" may be a reference to his blood crying out to God from the soil (Gen 4:10; see Heb 12:24) or a general reference to the example of Abel still speaking in the Scripture. The faith in which Enoch lived (vv. 5-6; Gen 5:21-24) is deduced from the fact that he was pleasing to God (the Greek version of Genesis) and therefore did not suffer death. Contemporary Jewish literature was fascinated with the idea that Enoch, like Elijah long after him, was "taken up" without experiencing death. The example of Noah (v. 7; Gen 6-9) is clear. Abraham (vv. 8-12; Gen 12-25) was a prime example of faith even for New Testament writers such as St. Paul (see Rom 4:13-25). Verse 11 is notoriously hard to translate. In the Revised Standard Version, Sarah, taken as the subject, tends to interrupt the example of Abraham and is in conflict with a key word of the passage referring to male begetting. Another translation is possible and perhaps preferable: "In faith—though Sarah herself was sterile—he received power to beget even when he was past the age, since he thought that the One who had made the promise was worthy of trust."

The eloquent verses 13-16 sum up the examples of the wandering patriarchs by recalling the theme of pilgrimage in search of a permanent home, thus linking the faith of the patriarchs to that of the Christians. The extended example of Abraham ends with reference to the so-called sacrifice, or "binding," of his son Isaac (vv. 17-19; Gen 22:1-18). This is the supreme example of Abraham's insight into the invisible world of hope. Confronted

with the promise that he would have descendants through his only son Isaac and with the paradoxical command to sacrifice Isaac, Abraham could only act with the insight that God could raise from the dead.

Isaac (v. 20; Gen 27) acted in faith when he gave his blessing to Jacob instead of to the older son Esau; subsequent events justified his action (see also Heb 12:16-17). Jacob (v. 21; Gen 48) also reversed the blessing of the sons of Joseph and was vindicated by the history of Ephraim. Joseph (v. 22; Gen 50:24-26) in faith foresaw the Exodus from Egypt when he asked to be buried in the land of promise.

The story of Moses and the Exodus (vv. 23-29; Exod 2-14), given its prominence in the tradition of Israel, naturally provides another extended list of examples of faith. Most of them are clear if one refers to the Book of Exodus, but two details may be mentioned here. In verse 26 God's "Anointed" might be a reference to the Messiah (Christ), which means "the anointed one," but it may equally well refer to Ps 89:52, where "the anointed" means the people of God. Second, Moses' departure from Egypt (v. 27) could refer to his flight to Midian (Exod 2:15), which is more likely, or to the Exodus itself, as many interpreters understand it. The occupation of the land of Canaan is represented by only two allusions: the fall of Jericho (literally "By faith the walls of Jericho fell"; v. 30; Josh 6) and the incident involving Rahab (v. 31; Josh 2:1-24; 6:22-25).

In good rhetorical style the author concludes this long list with a series of summary statements without identifying specific persons with specific events (vv. 32-38). With some detective work one can recognize the Judges, Daniel, the Maccabees, the fate of the prophets (for example, legend had it that Isaiah was sawed in two, v. 37). Appreciation of the passage depends in part on one's knowledge of the biblical and also non-biblical traditions about more recent heroes, but the thrust of the paragraph as a general summary of examples of faith does not depend solely on such knowledge. The main point of the whole list is in verses 39-40: though all the above are valid examples of faith, God deferred the content of his promises until the present time when the Christians respond in faith to the saving work of Jesus Christ.

Although 12:1-2 changes in style to exhortation, it nevertheless functions as the climax to the list of examples of faith and therefore may be included in the same section. Jesus is seen as the supreme example of faith—in the particular sense of Hebrews, in which faith does not have Jesus as its object—with which his followers can identify. Verse 2 speaks of him as what one could call "the leader and perfecter of faith." Christ is thus not only the high priest whose sacrifice finally achieves salvation, but he is also the supreme model of the faith that enables his followers to sustain their hope in the promises of God.

12:3-17 Divine discipline. The long passage of exhortation that follows actually is begun in 12:1-2, and these two verses, besides forming a climactic ending to the list of examples of faith, are the transition to exhortation. The whole passage makes use of an elaborate set of metaphors, some of them developed at length. The first is an athletic one, "running the race that lies ahead" (v. 1), and it is picked up again in verses 12-13. Second is the metaphor of the father disciplining his children (vv. 5-11), and third, that of the "bitter root" (v. 15).

Verses 3-4 continue the metaphor of the Christian life as an athletic contest. The example of Jesus' suffering as a man of faith can help to sustain the Christian in the ongoing struggle. The struggle is against sin, and human suffering is interpreted as the price one must pay to avoid sin. It is not certain whether persecution of Christians is hinted at here, or even martyrdom, though 10:32-34 clearly implied opposition to Christians from outside their own circles. Resisting "to the point of shedding blood" might be a vivid description of the athlete's exertions, perhaps those of a wrestler rather than a runner.

Verses 5-6 quote a well-known passage from Prov 3:11-12, and verses 7-11 are the preacher's homiletic interpretation of it. Among the many ways he understands the word of God in Scripture—the Holy Spirit speaking, Jesus speaking, God speaking to or about his Son, and the like—we meet a new one here. This time the word addresses the Christian hearers directly as sons of the Father (compare the direct address in Psalm 95; Heb 3:7). The designation of Christians as sons or children of God is not frequent in Hebrews (recall 2:10), but it is important. Because they share in the saving work of the divine Son, they share in his sonship also. The

application of the metaphor of discipline is clearly presented. This time human suffering is interpreted as evidence that God is disciplining the children he loves to bring them to maturity. Like the divine Son, they too must learn from their suffering (see 5:8). Verses 12-13 return to the image of a runner who, weary and sore, is tempted to give up the race.

The next exhortation is of a somewhat different kind, resembling more what we will find in chapter 13. But the author turns it to a familiar theme in verse 17. There is in verses 14-16 a concern for what we might call the integrity of the Christian community: peace with all, holiness, the absence of any notorious sinners who might lead others astray. The "bitter root" in verse 15 refers to Deut 29:18, a warning against the harmful effect on the Israelite community of people who turn to the worship of idols. Gen 25:27-34 tells the story of how Esau gave up his rights as the elder son of Isaac in exchange for a meal. In later Jewish interpretation Esau was accused of many kinds of evil, and that is probably why Hebrews makes him an example of a fornicator and a godless person. Verse 17 has caused difficulties for interpreters. It refers to the story in Gen 27 of how Esau's younger brother Jacob received the blessing of his father Isaac instead of Esau himself (see 11:20). Esau becomes an example of a person who renounced his salvation (by selling his birthright) and was unable to repent afterwards. The example is, of course, a warning to the Christian community not to abandon their salvation, a warning familiar to us from such passages as 6:4-6.

12:18-29 The unshakable kingdom. There seems to be an abrupt change of thought as we begin to read verse 18, but actually this is not the case. The verse begins with "for." The example of Esau was a warning, but it was not really a threat. Christians do not have to live in fear of imitating the failures of certain figures in the history of salvation, real as the danger is, for they have advantages which the ancients did not have. In a truly eloquent passage the preacher contrasts the ancient Israelite's approach to Mount Sinai, the place of the law and the old covenant, with the Christians' approach to the heavenly Jerusalem on Mount Zion, the "place" of the new covenant mediated by Christ (v. 24). At issue are two fundamental theological questions. First is that of access to God. The

Israelites' access, according to the Exodus story, was at best indirect and at worst reluctant. They experienced it in an atmosphere of fear and trembling (v. 21). The Christians by contrast, thanks to the saving sacrifice of Christ, approach God in confidence and splendor. The second theological question has to do with time. The Christians' access to God has been made possible by Christ's entrance into the heavenly sanctuary, but for individual Christians this entrance, following the forerunner, is still in the future. We encounter here the poles of the "already" and the "not yet," which also characterize the thought of other New Testament writers such as St. Paul.

The picture of the Israelites at Mount Sinai in verses 18-21 is drawn with details derived from Exod 19 and other Old Testament passages. It is obviously selective, designed to emphasize the gloomy and fearful aspects of the old covenant experience in contrast to the picture of Mount Zion (vv. 22-24). In the latter we again find a scene of God enthroned in heaven, with the angels in attendance. The groups mentioned in verse 23 have been interpreted in different ways. Perhaps the "assembly of the firstborn" refers to Christians of an earlier generation, and the "spirits of the just made perfect" to the Old Testament heroes of faith, who now have access to God along with the Christians (see 11:39-40). The "sprinkled blood" of verse 24 connotes the death of Jesus interpreted as a covenant sacrifice (see 9:15-22). Speaking from heaven, it is contrasted with the blood of Abel already alluded to in 11:4 (see Gen 4:10), which cries out from the earth.

Verse 25 repeats a now familiar argument (see 10:26-31) warning that Christians who do not listen to God speaking through the sacrifice of Christ in heaven risk an even greater punishment than the Israelites, who refused to obey God speaking on Mount Sinai. The importance of heeding God's word recalls the beginning of the sermon. God's voice was accompanied by an earthquake (v. 26) at Mount Sinai (according to Ps 68:9). He has promised in Hag 2:6 to shake the world once more in the time to come, and there will remain only an eternal, unshakable kingdom for those who are faithful to him. Because Christ has already made access to God possible, the preacher can reassure his hearers that they are in the process of receiving that kingdom. The main part

of the sermon ends (v. 29) with a quotation from Deut 4:24, an eloquent reminder that God's justice should motivate the Christian's faithfulness.

FINAL INSTRUCTIONS AND CONCLUSION

Heb 13:1-25

13:1-17 Various instructions. The sermon to the Hebrews seems to conclude at the end of chapter 12. If that is the case, chapter 13 is a kind of appendix which provides a variety of practical instructions and exhortations (vv. 1-17) and a number of features typical of the endings of letters (vv. 18-25). There is every reason to think the chapter was written by the author of the whole document: the style of writing is the same, and especially the use made of the Old Testament is similar. In addition there is no evidence that chapter 13 was added at some later time. We have already seen, for example in chapter 10 and elsewhere, how closely the preacher-author links practical matters of Christian living to his theological explanations, and in effect he continues the process in chapter 13. The point is an important one: as in the letters of St. Paul and other New Testament letters, practical Christian conduct is not a matter of indifference. It flows from one's understanding of the person and saving work of Christ.

The first six verses form a list of disparate instructions concerning brotherly love, hospitality, concern for prisoners and the suffering, fidelity in marriage, and avoiding love of money. The list may be rather conventional, but it is meant seriously. Christian conduct is not always distinctively different, but it is always distinctively motivated. In support of dependence on God and not on money, verses 5-6 quote Deut 31:6 and Ps 117:6 (in its Greek form).

Both verses 7 and 17 refer to "your leaders," using a term that is very general and not very common in the New Testament (see also v. 24). One cannot deduce from it what might have been the official leadership, if any, of the church in question. But the two verses refer to different leaders. The first are the former leaders who proclaimed God's word (message) to the community in the past. One is reminded of the people mentioned in 2:3.

They have passed away, but their lives remain as examples of faith, of insight into the invisible realm of God. In this context verse 8, perhaps the most memorable line in Hebrews, has an application. The statement that "Jesus Christ is the same yesterday, today, and forever" may well have an independent origin as a formula used in worship. Here it suggests that generations of church leaders may come and go, but the content of their proclamation, Jesus Christ, remains (a priest) forever. The leaders of verse 17 are contemporaries, whose function seems to be mainly to protect the community from harm. It is possible that verses 7 and 17 enclose the warning against "strange teaching" (vv. 9-16), with the implication that following the leaders would obviate the danger. But the passage is less than fully clear.

It is very difficult to be certain what situation is envisaged in verses 9-16, or even what the author is recommending. The "strange teaching" has to do with foods, but whether the context is Jewish food laws or some non-Jewish practice is unclear. Compare the somewhat similar warnings in Col 2:16, 20-23. The Old Testament background of the passage is Lev 16:27, which stipulates that some of the animals sacrificed on the Day of Atonement are killed outside the Israelites' encampment and burned there. Likewise, Jesus died outside the gate of Jerusalem as was traditionally believed (see John 19:17). The sanctuary and "outside the camp" are clearly understood in a symbolic way here, but there is little agreement on how, and interpreters offer even contradictory explanations. One possibility is that the author is warning against living the Christian life as though it were a sanctuary. One must go out into the everyday world to experience suffering where Jesus himself suffered. Since there is only one true sacrifice, the once-for-all sacrifice of Christ in the heavenly sanctuary, Christians can offer only analogous sacrifices of prayer, good deeds, and generosity (vv. 15-16).

13:18-25 Conclusion. The final verses remind us very much of the conclusion of a letter. They include a request for prayers for the author (18-19), a rather elaborate blessing or prayer (20-21), reference to what has been written (22), news of Timothy and mention of a planned visit (23), greetings (24), and a final blessing (25). Several of these features can be paralleled, for example, in 1 Thess 5:23-28, where we find a long blessing or prayer, a request for prayers for the author, greetings, and a final blessing. 1 Thessalonians is also a letter in which Timothy figures prominently (see 1:1; 3:2, 6). The author of Hebrews uses these letter features because he is sending his sermon in writing. Note that verse 22 refers to writing, not a letter, but a "message of encouragement" (or exhortation), that is, a sermon. In its only other New Testament usage, in Acts 13:15, this expression refers to a synagogue sermon of Paul.

The very beautiful blessing of verses 20-21 is often thought to have its origin in the worship of the Christian community. That may be so, but in its reference to "the blood of the eternal covenant"—a brief summary of the argument of chapters 8-10—and its use of Old Testament language, it may also have been composed by the preacher as a solemn conclusion to his sermon, which is mentioned in the next verse. It is not certain that the final phrase, in Greek "to whom be glory forever," points to Christ. That is possible in such passages (for example, 2 Pet 3:18), but it would be more usual for it to refer to God (for example, 1 Pet 5:10-11). The biblical background of the opening statement is Isa 63:11, which refers to God's having raised up from the sea the shepherd of the sheep, that is, he saved Moses and the Israelites from the Red Sea during the Exodus. There is no clear reference to the resurrection of Jesus here. The word "brought up" is not a resurrection word in the New Testament. Instead, the passage refers to bringing Christ from the dead up into heaven, which has been the basic picture throughout the sermon ever since 1:3. Though one must assume that the author knew about the resurrection of Jesus, it is not a central part of his theology.

What ought to be concrete hints about the origin of Hebrews in the final verses actually gives us little help. Timothy (v. 23) was a well-known figure in the early church, as is shown in the letters of Paul, the letters to Timothy, and the Acts of the Apostles. But how he relates to the author is not stated ("our brother" means merely our fellow-Christian). The second part of verse 24, which says literally, "Those from Italy greet you," does not help us locate the document since it could mean writing from Italy itself (probably Rome) or

REVELATION

Pheme Perkins

INTRODUCTION

A book for troubled times

The past ten years have seen an explosion of interest in the Book of Revelation at all levels, from that of the biblical scholar down to the casual Bible reader. From one end of the globe to the other, people are asking questions about Revelation. Why the attraction of this complex, often bizarre writing, which seems as far as one could get from our modern world of science and technology? Of course, most of the questions are based on a misunderstanding of Revelation, which assumes that it is a symbolic code predicting the exact persons and events that are leading to the end of the world. This type of understanding has existed in heretical Christian circles since the second century A.D. A group of Montanists even went off into the Phrygian wilderness to see the heavenly Jerusalem descend out of heaven. Like such prophets ever since, they were disappointed in their expectations. The church did not end Sacred Scripture with this book in order to provide glorified predictions of future events.

Anyone who expects predictions of that sort misses the spiritual message of Revelation. It is this spiritual truth that should compel present interest in the book. Despite scientific progress, despite communications media which give us greater and greater access to information and events, despite national and international efforts to relieve human suffering, the world seems more out of joint than ever. Senseless brutality, war, oppression, starvation—wherever we look civilized societies seem to be coming apart at the seams.

Perhaps the best index of our distress is in our movies. The popular movies *Star Wars* and *The Empire Strikes Back* picture a future in which most of the universe has been subjected to evil forces. The "high-tech" background of these movies also mirrors our society. The power of good, "the force," seems reduced to its last card in young, inexperienced, and spiritually undisciplined Luke Skywalker. These movies are not like the old Westerns to which they are often compared. There we always know that the "good guys" will win. They are bigger, better looking, smarter, have better horses, etc. The *Star Wars* movies, on the other hand, no longer provide the good with such an overwhelming advantage. *The Empire Strikes Back* ends with the hint that Luke's own father may have deserted the force to head the empire. Thus, these movies give a striking portrayal of the uncertainty of technological progress and of its futility in the face of evil and spiritual confusion. At the same time, they evoke hope for a time of spiritual renewal.

The Book of Revelation is like such a movie of its time. We find cosmic distances between earth and heaven; the good represented by a small, persecuted group of humans on earth; heavenly aid and inspiration to sustain them; strange, symbolic animals, and cosmic warfare between the forces of good and evil. So, we might ask ourselves what this Christian prophet from the end of the first

1265

century has to say to the end of the twentieth. What letters would he be writing to our churches? What would he say about the spiritual disorientation of Christians today? The growing interest in the Book of Revelation shows that people have an instinctual feeling for its message. They are looking for a vision of the struggle between good and evil which does not leave inspiration to modern filmmakers or, for that matter, to simplistic prophets of doom.

Revelation as an apocalypse

A person who has never seen the *Star Wars* movies will not understand the comparison in the previous section as well as one who has. Most twentieth-century readers are in a similar position with regard to Revelation. It is full of images that have a long history, stretching from ancient Near Eastern myth through the Old Testament prophets to Jewish apocalypses like the Book of Daniel. These images were also being used and reused in Jewish writings from New Testament times. Some images in Revelation might also evoke Greek mythology, which would be familiar to its readers from the consistent use of such themes in the decorative arts.

Apocalypse is the Greek word for "revelation." From Daniel at the end of the Old Testament to Revelation at the end of the New, and even beyond the time of Revelation, we have a wide variety of such visionary writings from Jewish and Christian circles. They were a form of expression that the audience was familiar with, just as people today are familiar with the *Star Wars* type of film, even if they have not seen the above examples. Read Dan 7–12. Much of the imagery in Revelation derives from Daniel and from the imagery of Old Testament prophets. These chapters of Daniel contain a series of visions of the course of world history. The cycles of visions overlap and provide alternate pictures of the same events. Revelation uses cycles of visions in the same way. Daniel and Revelation are both addressed to a community suffering persecution. When Daniel was written, the Syrian ruler of Palestine had been trying to force people to renounce Judaism. Many who refused were put to death. Reflection on the significance of their martyrdom led to a theology of martyrdom. The blood

of these martyrs was seen as expiation for the sins of those Jews who had not remained faithful to their religion.

That theology of martyrdom played an important part in early Christian understanding of the death of Jesus. His blood was seen as an expiation for the sins of the whole world. Revelation presents us with this picture of Jesus as the faithful martyr. He can use the Danielic picture of the faithful martyrs to encourage Christians who face persecution. Just as Antiochus failed to wipe out Judaism, so the new imperial beast, Rome, will fail to destroy the Christian faithful. Notice the image of "one like a Son of Man" ascending to God's throne in Dan 7. Originally, the "Son of Man" who receives dominion over the world referred to the martyrs of Israel. Once again, Revelation is able to apply that image to Christ. Jesus is revealed as the heavenly Son of Man in the opening verses of the book.

The Jewish apocalypses 4 Ezra and 2 Baruch, which were written about the same time as Revelation, address the suffering and spiritual disorientation felt by the Jews after the Romans had destroyed Jerusalem and burnt down the temple. Like Revelation, 2 Baruch includes letters to those who are to receive the revelation. All three apocalypses are concerned with the question of why God does not step in and send the messianic age by destroying evil—especially the Satanic embodiment of evil in the Roman Empire. All three answer with symbolic visions of world history unrolling according to a plan that God has measured out. They promise the faithful that they are much closer to the end of history than to its beginning. They reassure the suffering with the certainty of divine judgment on those who do evil and happiness for those who have endured. Those who have suffered and died out of faithfulness to God are not forgotten. They are enjoying happiness and peace. Though the images and themes of Revelation seem strange to us, these parallel examples show that they were well known at the time the book was written.

All of these apocalypses come from people oppressed by imperial powers. That situation is another reason that they use highly symbolic language, which only people familiar with the tradition of interpreting such images could understand. Criticism of political rulers could be dangerous business. Some ancient philosophers criticized tyrannical political power, but they would often wait until a particular emperor had been assassinated and was out of popular favor before making critical remarks. The Jewish writers use an additional device both to protect themselves and to lend authority to their visions. They present their writings as the secret, recently discovered revelation of a famous person from an earlier time of persecution. Daniel was a wise man at the court of the Babylonian king three centuries earlier. Baruch was a scribe at the time of the Babylonian Exile and an associate of the prophet Jeremiah. Ezra was a scribe who brought some people back to Palestine from the Exile when the Persians came to power almost a century later. These sages of Israel are claimed to have left symbolic revelations of the future sufferings that had now come upon Israel.

The reader of Revelation will immediately notice a difference. The author does use the tradition of symbolic language and has the evils of Babylon stand for the evils of the Roman Empire, but he does not hide behind a pseudonym. He tells us who he is and where he is: a Christian prophet named John, on the island of Patmos. On the artistic plane, there is an immediacy and sweep to his revelation that is different from his Jewish contemporaries. They engage the revealing angel in extensive dialogues about evil and divine justice. Their visions are said to take place over a lengthy period, often punctuated by periods of fasting and isolation. John's vision does not include such theological dialogue. It appears to happen all at once, so that the reader is swept through scene after scene. Like an epic movie, these scenes are linked together with a dramatic sound track—the chaos and disorder of battle, the thunder of horses, the sound of trumpets, and the beautiful pauses in heaven when the heavenly hosts sing praises to God and to Christ. The onrush does not stop until we find ourselves in the peace of the new Jerusalem.

In this study of Revelation, we will break up the book and trace the background of its symbolic visions. Such a process, however, ruins its dramatic sweep. Try reading the whole through without stopping. It is best to read it through aloud, since most people only came to know Revelation as they heard it read—probably during a liturgical assembly.

The details of this study should contribute to that vision of Revelation as a whole.

The author and his situation

People often assume that Revelation was written by the same person who wrote the Fourth Gospel. However, the author does not identify himself as the evangelist. In fact, he even refers to the apostles as a separate group from the past (18:20; 21:14). Even in ancient times people recognized that the two books could not have been written by the same person, since they do not have the same style. But the use of Revelation by heretical groups had led many Christians to be suspicious of it. By treating the John of Revelation as though he were John the evangelist, it was possible to win recognition for Revelation among Christians who might otherwise have rejected it. Today we do not require such a fiction about the author. We recognize that the church has included this writing in Scripture because it does contain an authentic and important vision of Christian faith.

Revelation opens with seven very stylized letters to churches in cities in Asia Minor. However, the author clearly expects that the whole book will be read. That means that all seven letters are intended to instruct all Christians, not just those in the particular churches. Doubtless, Christians living in Asia Minor at the end of the first century were able to understand the symbolic allusions to people and events better than we can today. However, some general problems emerge clearly enough. Some Christians are becoming lax. They seem to have lost interest in testifying to their faith. Others are being led astray by false Christian teachers and prophets, both men and women. It is harder to tell what the references to the "synagogue of Satan" and to "those who claim to be Jews but are not" mean. Some scholars think that the Jewish population of the cities mentioned was responsible for the persecution of Christians. Others suggest that Christians were trying to avoid suspicion and persecution by claiming to be Jewish.

The visions show us faithful Christians who are liable to persecution, and sometimes martyrdom, for failure to worship the emperor. There is no evidence for a formal decree enforcing such veneration throughout the empire. The persecution referred to in Revelation must have been a local phenomenon. Perhaps it was even instigated by local officials or other citizens who wanted to demonstrate their own loyalty to Roman imperial rule. Tradition associates Revelation with the period of the emperor Domitian (assassinated A.D. 96). He emphasized the monarchic side of imperial office and ruthlessly executed those in his own circles whom he suspected of disloyalty. Though he sometimes tried to gain favor in the provinces by removing a particularly unpopular local official and though his rule was a time of prosperity in Asia Minor, he was not universally loved. His assassination was greeted with outbursts of violence against his statues. Clearly, Christians were not the only Roman subjects who were discontented.

People often find it hard to understand "emperor worship." They think that it meant putting the emperor in the place that we reserve for God. Revelation agrees, but most people would have been puzzled by that attitude. Remember, the ancients had many gods. They also believed that some humans were exalted to dwell with the gods after death. Roman art depicts the soul of the emperor being carried up into such heavenly company from the time of Julius Caesar on. Veneration of living emperors began with his successor, Augustus. Often it simply meant using the same language about the emperor and the benefits he bestowed on humanity as was used about the gods in prayers and hymns. Private citizens or individual towns might honor the emperor by establishing holidays and offering sacrifices and holding festal games in his name. They might send an emissary to the emperor's court to inform him of those honors. They hoped, of course, that the emperor would respond by showering his divine favor on their city—perhaps granting relief from some form of taxation. Towns would also vie with their neighbors to see who could come up with the most lavish honors. These practices, then, involved a large measure of civic pride and even local political maneuvering. All this activity was in the hope of gaining some advantage from this distant figure whose statues and images were everywhere, who was felt to control the whole world, and yet whom most people would never see.

Such civic occasions were not the only ones on which a person who refused to venerate the emperor could be exposed to ridicule or suspicion. Elements of emperor worship formed part of everyday life. Slaves and people who had suffered losses in court suits might flee to a statue of the emperor in hopes of obtaining mercy from this distant person who represented "all-seeing" justice. Of course, such hopes were rarely fulfilled, but the mere fact that people had heard stories of people being so helped kept the hope alive. Most formal business and legal transactions were sealed with oaths sworn to the gods and the emperor. People might be asked to swear such an oath when receiving a loan or paying taxes. Local trade guilds might have banquets at which toasts were spoken in honor of the emperor. Perhaps the meal would begin with a libation being poured out in his honor. Even in private homes such libations might be offered at the beginning of the meal.

Jews avoided such situations by avoiding business and social contact with non-Jews. They were well known among non-Jews for their refusal to participate in the various manifestations of civic pride and solidarity. Consequently, they had the reputation of being "haters of humanity." Christians were in a different position. Most belonged to that larger non-Jewish community. Further, they could not carry out the task of witnessing to their faith if they withdrew from contact with the larger world. However, we can see as early as 1 Corinthians that Christians had problems in their social contact with non-Christians. 1 Cor 8 and 10 discuss the various sorts of banquets that a Christian might attend. St. Paul told Christians that they did not have to isolate themselves. They did not even have to avoid meat that had been used in sacrifice to a pagan god and then sold in the market, but they had to avoid compromising their faith in two ways. They could not accept an invitation to a banquet held in a temple honoring a pagan god (1 Cor 10:14-22). While they could accept invitations to the homes of pagan friends and eat whatever was served, they had to refuse to eat meat if someone made a point of telling them that it had been used in a sacrifice to an idol (10:27-32).

St. Paul also tried to deal with the question of Christian loyalty to the political order in Rom 13:1-7. Even though Christians know that all authority is based in God and that Jesus' return will soon bring human authorities to an end, they should still obey those in power, since their role is to see that good is promoted and evil punished. 1 Pet 2:12-17 echoes the same sentiments. Christians are even instructed to "honor the emperor." Since this benign view of poitical power was widely held in early Christianity, we can presume that it may have contributed to the confusion felt by Christians in Asia Minor. Should they avoid persecution, giving offense, by going along with local customs and demands? What was the difference between not asking questions about the meat and, perhaps, pouring a little libation in honor of the gods? If authorities are to be obeyed, then shouldn't one just swear the oaths required? Considering the social context of emperor worship, how easy it might be for Christians to come to such a conclusion. Perhaps some of the false teachers mentioned in the letters taught Christians that they could make such accommodations. John wants to make it clear that there is a big difference: Using language about the emperor as though he were a god or participating in rituals that honored him as such was equivalent to denying that one is a Christian. That is equivalent to joining forces with Satanic power.

The theology of Revelation

Revelation addressses serious questions about how Christians are to live in a larger, often hostile society. We may not know people today who are compelled to such veneration of political power, but we do not have to look far in the morning paper to read of the harassment or even murder of those who oppose governmental oppression in the name of Christian love and concern for the poor. The most perplexing cases are those in which governments of so-called Christian countries seem to promote policies of oppression that run directly counter to the ethical teaching of Christianity. Revelation speaks about such experiences. It warns us against the temptation to be silent or look the other way in the presence of evil and injustice.

There are also the smaller situations of daily life in which Christians prefer to remain silent and apathetic. Some would require us to act as a group, a church, or group of churches to oppose wrongs in the local community. Others, like the situation of the Christian at a friend's banquet, are more individual. Perhaps we allow people to slander or make fun of what we believe in rather than speak up. We would rather avoid controversy than question opinions, attitudes, and practices that we think are wrong. Of course, sometimes people remain silent because they do not know how to speak in defense of what they believe. People often want to defend their beliefs but lack the words with which to do so. We need to do everything we can to help one another become more articulate believers. After all, as Revelation so often insists, no Christian is immune from the obligation to bear witness.

Finally, the grand sweep of Revelation should lead us to resist the kind of pessimism that looks at the vastness of evil in the world and decides that any effort to change things would be a waste of time. Such judgments are false because Christians are not to measure what is true or right by statistics. Such judgments are arrogant because God is the only one who can determine "what's worth it." Such judgments are demonic because they only contribute to the hold that evil and pessimism have over human lives. Revelation is not a book aimed at scaring Christians into being good. It is a book to encourage them in the face of the most awful shape that evil can assume: when it takes on all the trappings of divine, imperial power; when it also has the force of local opinion behind it; when even some religious leaders are lined up against the few who would resist. Yet, it is the faithful few who share the victory that Christ's death has won over evil.

Structure of Revelation

Revelation has a complex structure. Many scholars think that the author put together vision accounts that were originally separate. While this subject of source analysis is beyond the scope of this commentary, please note that the author announces the next cycle of visions before he is finished with the cycle he is recounting. Such passages are similar to the flashes forward and backward in movies. The broad skeleton of the book seems to be built on the series of seven used to organize the vision cycles. In addition, the visions are presented as the contents of two scrolls: one, opened by the Lamb, dominates chapters 5–10; the other, eaten by the prophet, covers chapters 11–22. The second half of the book also has a dualistic axis embodied in the struggle between God and Satan, which is presented as the contrast between two cities—Babylon (= Rome) and Jerusalem.

OUTLINE OF THE BOOK OF REVELATION

COMMENTARY

PROLOGUE

Rev 1:1-18

The prologue has two parts. The first is a titular introduction to the Book of Revelation as a whole (vv. 1-3). The second is an introduction to the first section, the letters to the seven churches (vv. 4-8).

1:1-3 Heed this revelation. The opening words of the book are: "The revelation of Jesus Christ." The word "revelation" has a special meaning here, just as it does elsewhere in the New Testament. It does not refer to any sort of divine inspiration. Rather, it means knowledge of how the world will stand under God's judgment when history comes to an end. Such knowledge does not require detailed predictions about the events or timing of the end of the world, the sort of false interpretation often given of Revelation; what it requires is an understanding of the conditions for salvation, whenever that final judgment comes. We have already suggested in the Introduction that Revelation seeks to correct Christians who are confused about what is required for salvation.

The opening sentence is awkward, since everyone responsible for this revelation is included. The message in Revelation is both a messsage from Jesus to his churches and from God about the coming judgment. The seven letters are tied to a vision of Jesus as the heavenly Son of Man. The visions which follow the letters introduce angelic mediators, who interpret what John sees. Such angels are a common feature of Jewish apocalypses. As we have already seen, this apocalypse is un-

usual in being attributed to a living prophet rather than to a famous figure of the past.

Several expressions in this section are used to conclude the book. The promise to show "what must happen soon" (v. 1) reappears at 22:6. In 22:16, Jesus is the one who sends the angel. Similar promises to reveal "what will happen in the last days" appear in Dan 2:28f., 45. There "what is to happen" refers to the destruction of human empires and the establishment of the eternal rule of God. The same structure informs the visions that are to come in Revelation.

Some scholars think that "servants" in verse 1 only refers to a school of Christian prophets who were seeking such visions; however, we agree with those who feel that it refers to all Christians. The next verse pronounces a blessing on all who read, hear, and heed the message. It suggests that Revelation is to be read aloud in the liturgical assembly and is addressed to all. A similar beatitude appears in the conclusion (22:7). The solemn announcement of beatitude in a liturgical assembly carries a note of warning. Those who do not heed the revelation will not find themselves included in salvation. These beatitudes may reflect Luke 11:28, "blest are they who hear the word of God and keep it." Revelation contains the only beatitudes outside the Gospels. In keeping with the number symbolism of the book, there are seven (1:3; 14:13; 16:15; 19:9; 20:6; 22:7, 14). The others refer to the blessings of salvation.

Verse 2 introduces important words in the vocabulary of Revelation, "testimony/witness." The same Greek word underlies both English words. The parallel phrases "word of God" and "testimony of Jesus Christ" suggest that Revelation uses "witness" in a wider sense than that of a martyr who dies for the faith. In verse 9 (RSV) we learn that John was exiled to Patmos "on account of the word of God and the testimony of Jesus" (the New American Bible has interpreted this sentence by adding words that are not in the Greek). Here in verse 2, John places the whole revelation in the category of "word of God and testimony of Jesus." Since he can use the same expression in both contexts, we should presume that the content of this revelation is not a complete surprise. He already holds to the principles that are expressed in these visions. He has already opposed the "beast" in some way. Perhaps he was also worried by the laxity that he saw growing up among Christians. The revelation will bring together and clarify those experiences and concerns. The prophet can say for sure that Christians must not be taken in either by false teachers or the desire to avoid hardship and embarrassment. Instead, they must heed this vision of God as the sovereign ruler of the world.

1:4-8 A message to the churches. This section begins with the standard opening for a letter. Once again, multiple testimony is behind the message in the coming letters. John is the mouthpiece for God and Jesus. "Grace and peace" was a common early Christian greeting for the opening of a letter. The last verse will come back to this letter introduction with the concluding benediction: "The grace of the Lord Jesus be with all" (22:21). The greeting ends with verse 5a. It is followed by a doxology (vv. 5b-6) and two prophetic oracles.

Balancing lists of titles set off the names of the senders of the letter, God and Jesus. Instead of the standard expression for the divine "is, was, and always will be," God is described as the One "who is and who was and who is to come." The standard formula might be misunderstood. It might suggest that God will not do anything about manifesting his sovereignty over evil. The seven spirits before the throne use Jewish liturgical images. They can have a number of interpretations: seven archangels; the seven eyes of God (so Zech 4:10); seven lights (as in the Jewish apocalypse 2 Enoch 6, 11). The three parts to the name of Jesus parallel the name of God. "Faithful witness" may refer to all of Jesus' testimony and not simply his death, since Revelation often uses "witness" in a more general sense. "First-born of the dead" refers to Jesus' resurrection. It appears in a hymnic passage celebrating Jesus' cosmic rule in Col 1:18. Finally, "ruler of the kings of the earth" begins to introduce the political overtones of the message. Jesus already rules those who are using their power to harass his followers. The doxology which follows upon verse 5a calls Christians to give glory to Jesus for the salvation that they have received. Doxologies and hymns of praise are an important part of the prophetic insight of Revelation. They teach Christians that they already owe God thanks for his victory and salvation. They do not have to wait until the final destruction of evil for victory.

Two prophetic sayings conclude this section. The first is a combination of Dan 7:13 and Zech 12:10. Early Christians used this saying as a judgment oracle against those who reject Jesus (Matt 24:30; John 19:37). Oracles of judgment such as this one have a dual perspective, since they also point to the salvation promised the faithful. Revelation itself is to be read from this perspective. Judgment against evil and its forces represents the salvation of those who are faithful.

The final saying reminds the hearer that this revelation comes from the one who is truly God. Revelation uses "Alpha and the Omega," the first and last letters of the Greek alphabet, for both God and Christ (1:17; 2:8; 21:6; 22:13). "The almighty"(pantokratōr) is a divine title (4:8; 11:17; 15:3; 16:7, 14; 19:6, 15; 21:22). It sets God off as king against the power claimed by the empire in the later visions. The liturgical imagery of this section makes it clear from the beginning that this revelation comes with all the authority of God.

LETTERS TO THE CHURCHES

Rev 1:9–3:22

1:9-20 Prophetic call vision. The first vision of Jesus in Revelation commissions the prophet to write to the churches in Asia Minor. Though addressed to specific communities, these messages introduce a revelation addressed to the whole Christian community.

The problems in those churches were probably typical of those faced by Christians elsewhere. John's prophetic call is somewhat different from the Old Testament call stories. The Christian prophet is primarily a witness to the message from the risen Jesus. Jesus, not the prophet, is pictured as the one standing over against a wayward people with the words of judgment or consoling the faithful with those of promise.

The prophet makes it clear that he is a member of the community to which this revelation is addressed. "Distress," "the kingdom," and "endurance" present the conditions for Christian salvation. "Endurance" is a special term in the New Testament. It means more than just putting up with hardship. It is the virtue which enables people to remain faithful right through to the end, even though the final days of the world would be characterized by terrible distress and affliction for the righteous. Usually, people think of kingly rule as something that they will share with Jesus only in the future. However, John means more than that. He has already shown that Jesus is ruler of the kings of the earth. Therefore, he can speak of the Christian who endures the sufferings of the last days as already sharing in that rule.

Patmos was a small, poor island with no city on it. John makes it clear that his witness has led to his banishment there. He does not explain the situation further, since the Christians in Asia Minor were probably familiar with the circumstances. Early Christians substituted celebration of the "Lord's Day" for the Jewish sabbath, since it was the day on which Christ rose (see *Barnabas* 15,9; Ignatius, *Magnesians* 9). It was the day on which they met to celebrate the Eucharist (*Didache* 14). Thus, the author sets his visions at the most solemn liturgical time in the Christian week. The voice of God appears as a trumpet in the Old Testament (Ezek 3:12; Exod 19:16). A trumpet call was to signal the end of the world (1 Thess 4:16).

The number seven, which is the primary numerological symbol in Revelation, has many different associations. Some ancient authors would see the seven as the seven planets. The Roman emperor could be portrayed as holding seven stars (= the planets) as symbols of his universal dominion. Consequently, the image of Jesus holding seven stars provides a symbolic challenge to that claim of authority. He is the ruler of the cosmos. In the immediate context of the book, seven refers to the churches to which the letters are addressed (v. 20).

The description of Jesus is not intended as the representation of a visual image. Rather, the seer has brought together a number of images from the Old Testament to express the divine nature and authority of Jesus. The basic image combines the Son of Man who takes the throne in Dan 7:13-14 with the image of God, the Ancient of Days, who gives him that throne (Dan 7:9-10). Other elements in the description come from a vision Daniel has of a revealing angel in 10:5-6. Read those passages. A person familiar with Daniel would immediately recognize that Jesus is presented as an angelic, heavenly being who is both the source of revelation and the one who has dominion over the world. The sword in the mouth of the figure probably refers to the sword of the word of God (cf. Isa 49:2).

The initial reaction of fear at the appearance of the angelic or divine revealer is common in such visions (Isa 6:5; Ezek 1:28; Dan 8:18; 10:9-11). It is followed by reassurance (Dan 10:12). The description of Jesus had given him some divine attributes. Now he receives the titles of God: "first and last," "the one who lives." He merits these titles because of his death and resurrection.

One theme continuing throughout Revelation is the paradox of death and life. Jesus died and now lives. Those who are not faithful may live now, but they will die later when they are condemned at the judgment. If Christians can remain convinced that Jesus' death/resurrection has reversed the poles of life and death, that there is life far more important than anxious concern for our mortal bodies, then they will not be subject to fear and intimidation. Revelation tries to deal with that fear throughout its visions with vivid, almost grotesque portrayals of the reality of earthly life in contrast to the peace and glory of heaven. We make many decisions that are unconsciously motivated by our fear of dying—either actual death or symbolic death in the loss of something that we love or think we cannot live without. Thus, even if we are not faced with the threat of martyrdom, we still need to examine our own conviction about life/death. Is it really changed, reversed even, by our belief that Christ died and now lives? Or is it the same anxious concern with present self and security that motivates those who have no faith?

Some interpreters try to argue that the "angels of the churches" refers to the bishops of those communities. However, the letters never suggest that they are directed toward specific church leaders. Therefore, we would agree with those who assume that Revelation is thinking of the angelic guardians of those churches along the lines of Jewish speculation of the time which held that angels had been assigned to the different nations of the earth. This perspective also fits in with another feature of Revelation: The truth of external earthly events is found in the action in heaven which initiates them.

The letter pattern

The letter section provides prophetic evaluation, critique and encouragement to the churches mentioned. Each letter follows a pattern:

1. Command to write.
2. Prophetic messenger formula with a description of Jesus as the sender.
3. "I know" section.
   It includes some of the following elements: (a) "I know that" + description of the situation; (b) "But I have it against you" (censure); (c) command to repent; (d) "Look" + prophetic saying; (e) promise: the Lord is coming soon; (f) exhortation to hold fast.
4. Call to hear.
5. Promise of reward to those who are victorious.

These letters do not give us much information about the problems in the churches of Asia Minor. They speak in a cryptic way about situations that were familiar to the original audience. Their message is a prophetic warning that Christians must take care lest they lose the salvation that Christ has won for them. Ignatius, the bishop of Antioch, wrote letters to churches in the same area about two decades later (ca. A.D. 110). They show that some of the same problems mentioned in these letters continued to plague the churches in that area. Ignatius mentions heretical teachers. He says that they were denying that Christ was really human. They were also challenging the authority of the local church leaders. Other Christians are continuing to follow Jewish customs. They refuse to believe any teaching which is not contained in the Old Testament. The opposition in Ignatius' time seems to be more doctrinally oriented and better organized than that in the letters in Revelation. However, that strong opposition may have been the continuation of trends that are beginning as Revelation is written. If so, John's stern warnings against the false teachers is certainly justified. They would continue to plague the church.

2:1-7 To Ephesus. The city of Ephesus had undergone a great revival during the Roman period. That renewal would have given the populace reason to be enthusiastic about the empire. Consequently, we are hardly surprised to find this civic pride manifested in devotion to the emperor. At the same time, this city was also an important Christian center, since it had been part of the Pauline mission in Asia Minor.

The description of Jesus reminds the reader of 1:13, 16. The letter opens by praising this community for its endurance and its resistance to false teachers who claim to be apostles. Revelation usually limits the term "apostle" to the Twelve (so 18:20; 21:14). Presumably, people claiming to be apostles were using the term as it had been used during the time of Paul in reference to traveling missionaries (see Rom 16:7). Perhaps these traveling missionaries had been preaching the doctrines of the Nicolaitan sect mentioned in verse 6.

Though not in danger from false teachers, the Ephesian community has to be recalled to its former enthusiasm. The image of a fall from its former heights may have been based on the image of the fallen star in Isa 14:12a. The lampstand image recalls the single lampstand with seven lamps in Zech 4:2, which is in the divine presence. Revelation threatens Ephesus with removal of its lampstand.

The call to hear which forms a set part of the conclusion to the letters is a common prophetic warning. (It also appears in Rev 13:9; 21:7; 22:2.) The promise, eating from the tree of life, appears in first-century Jewish apocalypses as well. It shows that salvation reverses the curse of Adam. Revelation has already shown its audience that lost immortality is regained through Jesus.

2:8-11 To Smyrna. Smyrna was a fairly

new city north of Ephesus. It had a sizable Jewish population. When its bishop, Polycarp, was martyred in A.D. 155, conflicts between Christians and Jews were blamed. This letter leads off with the theme of life through death to encourage the suffering community. However, we cannot be sure whether Jews were the ones responsible for that suffering. It is possible that some Christians were trying to escape persecution by keeping to Jewish customs. (Compare the reference to those who will not admit to believing in Jesus because they prefer human glory in John 12:42-43.) Revelation must encourage this church to endure because more suffering awaits it. The "crown of life" image may be a combination of the crown of precious stones placed on the head of the righteous (Ps 21:4) and Yahweh as crown of hope (Isa 28:5). The audience might also have imagined it as similar to the crown given to victorious athletes.

Verse 11 explains the death that Christians really should fear: condemnation in the judgment or "the second death." They can avoid that death only by remaining faithful in their present suffering.

2:12-17 To Pergamum. Pergamum was an important city in Asia Minor. Its famous temple to Caesar was placed on a high, terraced hill. The city was known for its devotion to the cult of Augustus Caesar and the goddess Roma. This reputation for devotion to the emperor cult has earned the city the epithet "throne of Satan" in the eyes of the prophet. Perhaps refusal to participate in some form of that civic cult led to the death of the famous martyr Antipas.

The church is chided for following the teachings of the Nicolaitans. They are compared to the Israelites when they were misled by the false prophet Balaam (Num 25:1; 31:6). Some interpreters suggest that this sect might have taught that Christians could engage in ceremonial acknowledgements honoring the emperor. The condemnation of their eating "food sacrificed to idols" might indicate participation in ceremonial banquets, for instance. Ostensible paticipation would win such Christians freedom from persecution. They may have felt that such rites were not worship, since they did not believe that the emperor was divine. Revelation reverses their evaluation. Any form of participation in imperial cult is worship of Satan.

The promises of salvation pick up the two themes for which some are being condemned. Christians saw the "manna" as a prefiguration of the Eucharist, which in turn prefigures the final messianic banquet with Christ in heaven. The victors are also promised a new name. In Phil 2:6-11, Jesus receives the new name "Lord" when he is exalted in heaven. The new names received by the faithful are part of their share in the victory of Christ when they will eat the heavenly banquet. For the time being, both the manna and the new names remain hidden in heaven, but that should not cause Christians to abandon their glorious salvation.

2:18-29 To Thyatira. This city was less important than the previous three. Its citizens had lost their bid to have the emperor's temple built there instead of in Pergamum.

The church in this city appears to have been severely divided. The author encourages those members of the community who are remaining faithful. He castigates others who are following the teachings of a woman prophet. He calls her "Jezebel," after King Ahab's pagan wife, who caused her husband to worship the pagan god Baal (1 Kgs 16:31). He threatens her and her followers (= children; perhaps even disciples as prophets, just as in the Old Testament a disciple of a prophet might be a "son of a prophet"—see Amos 7:14). Jewish traditions frequently link sexual immorality with idolatry. Consequently, the combination does not provide us with any specific information about her group. We are told that they claim to know the "deep things" (RSV) of Satan, according to the author of Revelation. They must have claimed to know the deep things of God. Such an expression in a Jewish apocalypse of the period would most naturally express the claim to know the secrets surrounding the end of the world and the judgment. Perhaps their visions also legitimated participation in pagan cult. John's revelation will provide the true Christian knowledge of such deep things. The followers of this false prophecy are reminded that they must repent; nothing can be hidden from God who knows all (Jer 17:10). The violence of the punishments against the woman and her followers corresponds to the seriousness of their sin, perverting the true gift of prophecy. However, those in the community who do continue to resist Jezebel and her children will share not only the victory celebration but also the actual rule of Christ over the nations.

3:1-6 To Sardis. Rebuilt after it had been leveled by an earthquake in 17 B.C.E., this city was a famous port for the reshipment of woolens. The promise that the victors will go clothed in white (v. 5) may be an allusion to the city's wool trade. We cannot be sure what had given this city the reputation of "being alive" although it is really dead. Perhaps the Christians there were known for enthusiasm or spiritual gifts. The letter warns that they could lose everything if they do not pay attention to the commandments. Their deeds are not those of Christians. Since the author does not mention any specific faults or false teachers, the problem with this church may simply be a waning of their initial devotion. Each of the promises to the faithful contains a warning to those who are not faithful. They might find their names erased from the book of life. The author reminds them of two judgment sayings attributed to Jesus. He will deny those who deny him (Matt 10:32). They must watch out for the thief in the night (Matt 24:42-44; also as a warning of impending judgment in 1 Thess 5:2).

3:7-13 To Philadelphia. This small city lay in the earthquake zone to the southeast of Sardis. The church is not censured, but it is warned to hold out against those who claim to be Jews but are not. We cannot tell if this controversy was between Christians and Jews over who were the real people of God, the true Israel, or an internal conflict between those to whom Revelation is addressed and a group of Jewish Christians. Just as the author spoke of Pergamum as "Satan's throne" because of the emperor cult, so the Jewish problem here leads him to speak of their gathering as "Satan's assembly" or synagogue. Apocalypses of this type frequently designate opponents of God with Satan epithets. The use of Satan in both letters does not mean that the problem here is the same as in Smyrna.

Revelation alludes to several messianic prophecies to prove that Jesus is the true successor to David. Isa 22:22-25 seems to be the closest to this prophecy, since it refers to the key and the open door: "I will place the key of the House of David on his shoulder; when he opens, no one shall shut, when he shuts, no one shall open." Since the door is still open before this community, they still have the pos-

sibility of salvation if they continue to hold out. The letter even promises that the truth of their belief will be demonstrated when some of those who claim to be Jews are converted. Like the calls for repentance in other letters, this promise reminds us that the letters in Revelation are not proclaiming a fate that is already sealed. It is not too late for those being censured to repent. Those who are faithful must be encouraged to continue.

The concluding promises look forward to the coming of the new Jerusalem, which will conclude the visionary section of Revelation. Isa 22:23 makes the messianic steward a sure peg on which the whole weight of his father's house can hang. Again, the victors are promised a new name. Here we learn that the name is that of the victorious Jesus.

3:14-22 To Laodicea. Also in the earthquake belt, Laodicea lies east of Ephesus. We have completed our circle of cities. There had been a church in this area from the time of Paul (Col 4:13). This final letter is most often quoted for its imagery of "lukewarmness." Laodicea's water supply came from hot springs and arrived in the city lukewarm. The prosperity of the city and its trade form the basis for other images used by the prophet. It was known for its clothing industry, as a banking center, and for its medical school, which specialized in eye diseases. The problems of the church in this city are tied to the material prosperity in which Christians here live. They are neither poor nor suffering, but their prosperity is endangering their spiritual well-being.

The prophetic warnings draw on several images from the Old Testament. Only they can obtain gold who will pass the test of divine fire from Jesus. The Lord promises to separate the bad from the good among his people by refining them like precious metal in Zech 13:9. The promise of garments of salvation to cover the shameful nakedness of the people refers not only to the clothing industry of the city but also to the reversal of a prophetic curse: God will strip his enemies and expose their shameful nakedness. Isa 47:1-3 connects this curse with an image of the people as "bride." We will see that that imagery returns at the conclusion of the vision section. The new Jerusalem will be the true bride of the Lamb. Ezek 16:8-14 describes Israel as a young bride decked out for her wedding to the Lord. The bridal imagery appears in this passage because the first promise is a share in the divine wedding feast. The culmination of all promises of salvation in Revelation is a share in the victory which the lamb has won. Here the victors are promised a seat on the throne of Jesus and his Father at the festal celebration. Though the letters have been addressed to specific cities, both their warnings and their promises of salvation can apply to all Christians.

SEVEN SEALS

Rev 4:1–8:5

A new vision introduces the next section of the book. Some interpreters think that the letters and the visionary cycles were originally independent and were only combined when the book of visions we know as Revelation was put together. Even if they were originally independent, the imagery of the two sections fits together. The letters presuppose the visions of salvation that are coming in order to make their promises and warnings clear. We would not know that the concern with idolatry and with the throne of Satan refers to the emperor cult without the account of the beast in chapter 13, for example.

The various cycles of visions which make up the rest of Revelation overlap. The trumpets are introduced before the seals are concluded, and almost two chapters stand between the sixth and seventh trumpet. Apocalypses commonly included repetitious cycles of visions, which went over the same ground from a different perspective. The interlocking of the various cycles in Revelation suggests that its visions do the same.

Apocalypses also wish to show their audience that they are nearer to the end of the world than to its beginning. Symbolically, they make this point by having visions that encompass the past history of Israel. These past events may be from the salvation history of the Old Testament and/or from the recent experiences of the people under the Babylonian and Persian Empires such as we find in the visions of Daniel. In that way the audience can see the divine truth behind those past events and can be reassured that the future is no less subject to divine rule, however chaotic and confusing it may seem.

Revelation follows the same process. While reading through the visions carefully, notice that most of them have already been fulfilled from the standpoint of the author and his audience. One should never pay any attention to an interpretation of Revelation that applies to contemporary people and events the images which the author claims apply to the past. Revelation wants us to understand that the same divine judgment and guidance that were manifest in those past events are at work today, not that those past events have to be repeated in some way. When apocalypses come to describe the future events of judgment/salvation, they often move away from any connection to historical events and speak in the language of mythological symbols and metaphors. Revelation does the same. This shift in language reminds us that the seer is having a vision of the divine or symbolic truth that is to be worked out in the course of history. He is not trying to predict a sequence of historical events as they might be recorded in a history book or a newspaper.

It would also be a mistake to think that the imagery of wrath and punishment is the real foundation of Revelation. Both the letters and the visions make it clear that they seek to encourage Christians to remain faithful in a difficult and confusing time. Remember, John even has to contend with other Christian prophets who claim that they know the "deep things" of God. Revelation does not seek to teach Christians to glory in the expectation that others will suffer a terrible fate while they rest in the bliss of heaven. John sees that the victory that has been won in Christ is the beginning of a divine process of redemption that is to take in all of creation. Throughout the book hymns of rejoicing and celebration invite Christians to celebrate their salvation.

4:1-6a The divine throne. The Old Testament contains several visions of the heavenly throne and its surroundings. They introduce the mission of a prophet whose experience in the heavenly court gives him the authority to speak God's word to the people (1 Kgs 22:19; Isa 6:1-13; Ezek 1:4-26; Dan 7:9-10). Read the Ezekiel passage. It shows how familiar the scene in Revelation would be to a person who knew the earlier images. Not only is the vision of God's throne room a customary beginning for a prophetic revelation, but it also reminds the audience of this book of one of its major themes: God, not Caesar, is the ruler of the cosmos. The final letter promised that Jesus and his faithful ones would even share the divine throne at that final victory banquet. The next vision will show us the victorious enthronement of the lamb.

Visions of heaven often begin with the invitation to enter or to look through the open door into heaven (Ezek 1:1; Matt 3:16; Acts 7:56). Though the visions follow the letters, the author does not imply that everything in the letters has to happen before the events described in the visions will begin. The promise to show "what must take place in time to come" is the customary introduction to an apocalypse. As we have noted, such apocalypses may still contain visions that begin in the past, describe persons and events known at present to the audience, and then look to the future.

The seer has been commissioned in the visions which opened the book. After this first cycle of visions is over, he will be commissioned again. Now he provides a vision of the divine throne room. The scene combines images of the temple of Solomon in the Old Testament (see 2 Chr 3–5), throne of cherubim, brazen sea, incense, singing, and altar of sacrifice, with the scroll image of the synagogue, its elders and hymns, and the imagery of the heavenly court assembled in judgment (as in Dan 7:9-14). The crowns and white robes suggest that the twenty-four elders represent human rather than angelic figures. Some commentators think that they may represent the prophets of Israel.

The author has combined images of heavenly liturgy with those of the heavenly court assembled in judgment. When the lamb opens the scroll in the next scene, we see that judgment has begun to unroll. The piling up of images makes it clear where power and authority lie. Between the throne and the elders the image of the divine is manifest in a great storm. The seven torches are the seven spirits of God which ovesee the whole cosmos (Rev 5:6; see Zech 4:2). The bronze sea reflects that which stood before the temple of Solomon. It symbolizes the creative power of God, which is victorious over the sea of chaos. The cosmological mythology of the sea as the home of a great monster of chaos, which must be defeated by the divine storm god before the world can be created, becomes even more explicit later in Revelation. The empire is embodied in the beast which comes from the sea. God as creator imposes order by defeating the sea monster.

4:6b-8 The four heavenly creatures. In Ezek 1:4-20 the prophet first sees a great storm wind. Within it he finds the throne chariot of God being drawn by four creatures. Ezekiel supposes that each creature has four faces: man, lion, ox and eagle. Revelation has assigned one face to each of the four throne bearers. The images may have been taken from Babylonian signs of the zodiac. The ox, Taurus, is an earth sign; the lion, Leo, a fire sign; the third, with the face of a man, may be Scorpio, since the scorpion was often drawn with a human face, and is a water sign. The eagle provides a sign for the fourth element, air. It also provides another sign of divine sovereignty over the Roman Empire. Thus the four creatures not only serve to identify the divine throne chariot but also proclaim divine rule over the four elements of the cosmos and over the signs of the zodiac. The final verse brings in the vision of the throne room in Isa 6:1-2. The creatures merge with the cherubim and seraphim of that scene. Later Christians gave each of the four evangelists one of the creatures as a symbol.

4:8b-11 The heavenly praises. The transition to the Isaiah vision is continued with the singing of the threefold "holy." God is glorified by all in heaven as the sovereign creator. This praise makes the implications of the symbolism clear: God is the creator and Lord of all that exists. Several writings from Jewish groups in the New Testament period contain descriptions of the divine throne and of the praises of angels in heaven. The liturgical setting suggests that the acclamations offered by worshipers on earth are an image of the real worship of God which takes place in heaven.

5:1-7 The Lamb receives the scroll. We now turn from praising the divine creator to the plan of redemption. In Ezek 2:9-10, the seer is shown a scroll, which was "covered with writing front and back, and written on it was: Lamentation . . . and woe." That scroll was unrolled before the seer so that he could see what was written on it. Revelation has introduced a slightly different image. The scroll is sealed. That image reflects the revelation of Daniel. There the visionary is told to seal up his revelation: "As for you, Daniel, keep secret the message and seal the book until the end time; many shall fall away and evil shall increase" (12:4). John's question about who can unlock the scroll really is addressed to such apocalyptic visions. It rejects the possibility that any apocalypse, any revelation except the Christian one, could unlock the secrets of God's plan for the end of the world. Thus, he makes it clear that as the successor to the prophets Ezekiel and Daniel, he is also the last. The hidden book is now to be opened by the Lamb and the unfolding of the final stages in the history of salvation can begin. The angel issues the summons to the whole cosmos to witness the opening of the book, a feat that cannot be performed by any creature in the cosmos.

The messianic prophecy of the Lion of Judah answers the call. The messiah is now present and worthy to open the book. 4 Ezra 11:36-46 has the Lion emerge and speak the sentence of doom against the fourth imperial beast, the Roman eagle. Here the opening of the scroll by the victorious Lion will begin the visions that spell the end of imperial power. Revelation combines other images with that of the Lion of Judah, the sprout of David from Isa 11:1-10, and the more general messianic image of victory. The Christian audience knows that the victory won by Christ was in his death and resurrection. This fact is symbolized in the vision of the messianic lion as the slaughtered lamb. Several images have been combined. Early Christian traditions identified Jesus with the passover lamb and with the defenseless servant of Isa 53:7, 10-12. In another Jewish apocalypse, 1 Enoch, the seer sees the Lamb of David grow into a great horned sheep, which defeats the hostile beasts that attack the people of God (89, 45-46; 90, 9-16). The Lion of Judah/Lamb in this vision also appears with the horns of a victorious ram. He has the flaming eyes of the seven spirits before the throne (1:4; 3:1; 4:5).

5:8-14 Praises for the Lamb. Once again, we hear the heavenly chorus sing praises. "New song" often appears in the call to worship in the psalms. Here it has the added significance of offering praise to the victorious Lord, enthroned in heaven. He has created a new people of God from all those on earth. Thus, the universality of God's cosmic rule is echoed in the univesal redemption won by the atoning death of the lamb.

As we hear the praises, the author widens the angle of vision so that we see the myriads of heavenly beings and then all creatures at the various levels of the cosmos praising the Lamb. Their praise is confirmed with the answering AMEN of the four throne creatures and the worship of the elders. The vision of the praise offered by all creation forms a high point in the book. It is the heavenly basis for the confidence that Christians are to have in the truth of the visions of divine victory that are to follow. The Lamb has already been enthroned victorious in heaven because he has won a new kingdom of priests. The Christian is shown that the whole cosmos praises God and the Lamb for their saving power.

6:1-8 The four horsemen. Revelation uses images which flow into one another. We have seen this process at work in the earlier descriptions of the divine. When the author now turns to describe the inner reality of earthly events, he blends together the mythic symbols, the prophetic allusions, and the hints at the historical events to which they correspond. The four horsemen allude to a very concrete set of experiences of people living in a war-torn area, the disasters wrought by wars and invading armies. The white horse and the bow were favorite weapons of Rome's hated enemy along the eastern frontier, the Parthians. Later, the Parthians are summoned by the voice of God to come from beyond the Euphrates and initiate the downfall of Rome (9:13-21). The vision predicts that Parthian attacks would bring the downfall of Rome. That expectation was a reasonable one, since Rome had suffered defeat at the hands of Parthia in A.D. 62. Parthia would not be the nation to sack Rome, but Rome would eventually fall through war with an enemy on her borders.

The images of a company of horsemen also evoke the prophets. Zech 1:8-15; 6:1-8 pictures riders on different colored horses sent to range the earth and to punish those who oppress the people of God. The terrors of war in these first visions all fit the periods of conflict in the region. The eruption of Vesuvius (A.D. 79) was followed by a devastating fire and plague in the city of Rome and by famine in Asia Minor.

The prophets also picture the horrors of war, famine, plague, and wild beasts as chastisement from God. Ezek 5:12-17 has God utter a terrible curse, which is the basis for this section. In Ezekiel the destruction will kill a third of the people by plague and hunger; a third by war; and the remaining third will be scattered in exile. Perhaps because there are so many more plagues to come, Revelation has its version of the Ezekiel curse carry off a quarter of the earth. The third horseman images the disorienting economic effects of war that might lead some to starvation. The fourth horseman represents death by plague. All of the evils brought by the horsemen referred directly to common experiences in the life of the region through its combination of prophetic images.

6:9-11 The fifth seal. This scene forms an interlude between the plagues of war and the destructive earthquakes of the next scene. It also introduces the theme of the martyr. Those who have suffered call out for vengeance. This cry is not a manifestation of personal animus or spite as some people often think. It is also a common feature of the apocalypse genre: the righteous make a call for God to give some definitive manifestation of his justice and truth. This manifestation would counter the appearances of a world which seems able to ignore God's justice without any ill effects, a world which can persecute or simply ignore those who speak out for God. The plagues brought by the four horsemen serve to remind the audience that the world is not as peaceful or prosperous as it might be.

The position of those calling out for vengeance reflects that of the Old Testament "just ones" between the temple and the altar in Matt 23:35. The prayer to God to come and avenge the blood of the righteous alludes to Ps 79:5-6, 10. That psalm was a prayer to the Lord not to continue being angry with his people but to avenge them against the enemies that had laid waste the nation. The words are those of a nation laid waste by war and its devastation; it can only call out to God for help. Here the martyrs are asking God to pronounce sentence on the rightness of their cause and to execute judgment. The visions in Revelation that began with the opening of the scroll make it clear that God has pronounced his sentence against the wicked. But he does not promise immediate execution of judgment. More is yet to come. People often object to the tone of

this passage, which seems to make God something of a sadist, unwilling to act until enough righteous blood has been shed. The New American Bible translation contributes to that impression by rendering the Greek "they are fulfilled" as "until the number was filled." The passage is not really about a quota. Apocalypses are concerned with the problem of righteous people who seem to suffer and die needlessly in God's cause. They often reassure their audience that such suffering is not endless, not going to go on forever, by imagining that there is a fixed time period or a set sequence of events that must transpire. Neither the righteous nor the wicked can force the events of history out of that pattern. It is part of the mystery of the divine plan. Revelation does not relish suffering. The book is built around the image of the Messiah as the sacrificed Lamb. Those who suffer for the sake of righteousness are assured that God is attending to their cause; their sufferings and struggles are acknowledged in heaven.

6:12-17 The sixth seal. This vision of cosmic catastrophe piles up all the metaphors that the author can find for the horrors of the final day of judgment. Compare the vision of the judgment in Mark 13:4-19. Several Old Testament prophecies are behind this passage. It begins with the earthquake as the sign of divine theophany (see 1 Kgs 19:11; Isa 29:6). This sign would be familiar to many of the audience, since several of the cities addressed were in an earthquake zone. There are to be signs in the stars and the moon (Joel 3:4); darkness (Isa 50:3); falling stars (Isa 34:4). The terrible cry of people for the hills to fall and cover them also appears in the prophetic traditions (Hos 10:8 ties it to the earthquake; Isa 2:10, 19; Jer 4:29). The "great day" of verse 17 appears in Isa 2:10, 19 (also Zeph 1:14). The question posed by this terrible vision, "Who can withstand it?" (see Nah 1:6; Mal 3:2) will be answered by the sealing of the righteous in the next chapter. Thus, the author has piled together all the horrors of the judgment as they were known from the biblical tradition. Those horrors form a prelude to the sealing, which assures the righteous that they can withstand, just as they have withstood persecution in the world.

7:1-8 Seal the 144,000 from the tribes of Israel. Normally, the announcement of the terrible day of judgment would be followed by the vision of the divine theophany, God coming forth in judgment. Revelation breaks into that pattern to answer the question of who can withstand by describing the sealing of two groups. Interpreters are divided over the identity of the 144,000. Some think that they represent the righteous of Israel. Others argue that they represent Christians, who could also speak of themselves as the "twelve tribes" (as in Jas 1:1). Such a Jewish Christian tradition may underlie this passage in Revelation.

Several passages in the Old Testament use the imagery of sealing to indicate that a person belongs to the people of God. Exod 28:11, 21 associates that sign with deliverance from the disaster of the final plague. The Egyptian plagues will appear later in the visions. Isa 44:5 describes a sealing of the Lord's chosen ones as writing the names "I am the Lord's," "Jacob," and "the Lord's" on the hand. We have seen that in the letters Revelation promises the victorious that they will be given a new name which is that of God, of the new Jerusalem, and of Jesus' own "new name" (3:12). Ezek 9:4 instructs one of those who are to scourge the city of idolaters to pass through first and mark the foreheads of all those who lament the abominations being practiced there with an "X" so that they will not be touched in the coming disasters. In addition to all of these Old Testament examples of sealing and salvation, the Christian audience would also remember their own tradition, which spoke of baptism as "sealing."

God is holding back the four angels who are about to let loose the divine storm winds. They will come from the four corners of the earth as signs of divine wrath (see 1 Kgs 19:11; Jer 49:36; Ezek 37:9; Zech 6:5).

7:9-12 The elect praise the Lamb. On the basis of the Ezekiel parallel, we might expect the new vision of doom to follow immediately. Remember we are still waiting for the seventh seal to bring this first vision cycle to a conclusion. However, Revelation is not simply a prediction of disaster. It also shows the heavenly basis of salvation and Christian hope. Consequently, we are shown a new vision. Just as in the previous vision of cosmic praise, the angle of vision widens until we see multitudes from all the earth praising the Lamb. All of the elect are singing praises and waving palms, a sign of victory (1 Macc 13:37, 51; John 12:13). As in the earlier glimpse of the heavenly liturgy, the hymn is antiphonal. The praises of the elect are answered by heavenly beings who say "Amen" and then offer their own song to God and to the Lamb.

7:13-17 Interpretation of the vision. Interpretation of the seer's vision by an angel is common in apocalypses (compare Ezek 37:3). This passage combines allusions to Ezekiel and Daniel. The tribulation through which these people have passed may be that of the judgment (Dan 12:1), which has just been announced. Verses 15-17 are somewhat problematic, since they seem to narrow the focus of the vision from all the elect to just those who have died for their faith. However, the author may be thinking of all as having a share in martyrdom, since they have been redeemed by the blood of the Lamb.

Several images of salvation from the Old Testament describe what awaits the elect. The righteous will not hunger and thirst (Isa 49:10; Ps 121:6). The sheep will have their shepherd (Ezek 34:23; Ps 23). God will wipe away the tears of the elect (Isa 25:8). Now that we have seen the salvation won for all the elect by the death of Jesus, we are ready for the opening of the final seal.

8:1-5 The seventh seal. The account of the seventh seal includes a verse which introduces the next cycle, the trumpets (v. 2). This interlocking is typical of the style of Revelation. We expect a grand, perhaps terrifying, vision of the divine warrior to follow the announced judgment. Trumpets belong to the announcement of the beginning of judgment (as in 1 Thess 4:16). They announce the appearance of the Lord. Thunder and lightning are also signs of divine presence. However, we do not have the terrifying epiphany of the Lord; instead, there is a half-hour silence followed by further prayers. The silence may reflect the "small voice" of the appearance to Elijah (1 Kgs 19:11-12; 2 Chr 2:17; Hab 2:20). Amos 9:1 pictures the Lord standing beside the altar as he announces to the prophet the judgment he is to bring against his people. Here an angel is offering up the prayers of God's people. Since that offering is followed by his hurling the burning coals down on the earth, we assume that the prayers are the same as those of the martyrs in the earlier chapter. God's people have asked for salvation; the symbolic response shows that their prayer is to be answered.

THE SEVEN TRUMPETS

Rev 8:6–11:19

This cycle is structured like the previous one. Four trumpets herald plagues to come upon the earth. The movement toward the culmination in which Satan is cast out of heaven is interrupted. First we see two faithful witnesses and their fate. Then the prophet is again commissioned by an angel and so prepared for the revelations which form the second half of the book. As in the previous series, the first four trumpets are a short, unified group, while the last three are longer and more diverse. This series is modeled on the plagues of Egypt. It teaches a sobering lesson. The plagues and disasters do not lead to repentance. Instead, the humans who survive continue in their idolatrous ways. This cycle is more intense than the previous one; a third rather than a quarter of the earth is to be affected.

8:6-13 The first four trumpets. The humans who survive this succession of plagues do not realize that they are suffering divine punishment. This series, like the earlier one, presents disasters which are not those of the final judgment. The vision combines images from various Old Testament prophecies with the plagues of Egypt. Ps 18:13 ties the appearance of God to save his people with casting fire and coals on the earth. Blood recalls the plague in Exod 9:24. The second trumpet announces the destruction of the fish in the sea (see Exod 7:18). The image of disaster created by a burning mountain falling into the sea has both historical and prophetic overtones. For the audience at the time, it might evoke the eruption of Vesuvius in A.D. 79, with its rivers of molten lava flowing into the sea and destroying everything in their wake. A burning mountain also appears in Jer 51:25. The Lord will send a destroying mountain against the empire of Babylon.

Allusions to the overthrow of Babylon continue in the next trumpet. The falling star recalls the taunting of the king of Babylon in Isa 14:12. In Jeremiah (23:15; 8:14; 9:14), the Lord threatens to give poisoned water, wormwood, to his people because they have abandoned his ways and gone astray into idolatry. The darkness of the final trumpet in this group recalls the darkness over the land of Egypt (Exod 10:21-29). The prophets frequently refer to the darkness of the day of judgment (Amos 8:9; Isa 13:10; 50:3; Joel 2:3, 10; Ezek 32:7-8). However, this darkness does not represent that of the final day; only a third of the heavenly bodies lose their light.

The first cycle of disasters recalled the trials of international wars. This cycle, disasters in nature, might be called forth by divine command. Verse 13 brings it to a culmination with the ominous vision of the eagle flying across midheaven and crying out three "woes" against the inhabitants of earth (compare the "woe" introduction to prophetic oracles of doom as in Amos 5:7-27, a prophetic announcement of three woes). The vision of the eagle in midheaven may also recall the comparison of the coming of the Son of Man in judgment to eagles/vultures gathering above a corpse in Matt 24:28. The woes announce the next three trumpets. Two will be described immediately; the third will be delayed as in the previous cycle.

9:1-12 The fifth trumpet. With the fifth trumpet we move out of the realm of earthly disasters into that of the mythological. Mythological beasts come forth to attack the inhabitants of the earth. As though we were watching a horror movie, these creatures come out of the earth to torture humanity. Though the fifth trumpet recalls the plague of locusts (Exod 10:13-15), these locusts are not the ordinary sort of grasshopper that sweeps across fields destroying crops. A great star falling from heaven, possibly Satan, has the keys to let these creatures out of the underworld. They do not harm nature, the grass, at all. Instead, they are sent to torment humanity. They are really scorpion-like creatures. Scorpions were known as "fiery dragons" (Deut 8:15; Num 21:6; Isa 14:29). The prophetic pattern for this vision can be found in Joel 1:4, where the locusts and grasshoppers are sent against humanity. However, Revelation has moved out of the realm of that prophecy, which describes a possible natural disaster, into the realm of the mythological and demonic. Their sting torments but does not kill. The intensity of human suffering at this plague leads to a repetition of the cry of the sixth seal: people wish to die and cannot.

(Compare Jer 8:3; Job 3:21; the most horrible suffering leads people to seek death, which they cannot find.)

Some of the features in the description of the locusts come from Joel: teeth, flight, warrior's attire and comparison with war horses (1:6, 2:4-5). The human face was part of the traditional iconography of the scorpion. Perhaps the woman's hair was also derived from astral symbolism. The golden crown will appear later in the crown of the beast. The leader of these creatures is probably the same angel/demon whose fall brought their release from Hades. They torment humanity for five months. Another cry of woe and warning brings this vision to its close.

9:13-21 The sixth trumpet. A new contingent of demonic creatures appears. These terrible horsemen do not signal earthly disasters; they attack and kill a third of humanity. The angelic voice from the altar announces the time for the release of these destroying angels. Such an angelic cry is associated with the trumpet announcing the day of judgment in 1 Thess 4:16. The association between the voice and the altar also reminds the readers of the plagues as answer to the prayers of the righteous. But this woe is not the end of the world, either. Only a third of the inhabitants of the earth are killed. These terrible riders are deliberately more lethal than the previous group. They slay with the fiery breath of their mouths and with the venom of their serpent-like tails.

In these two visions Revelation has moved beyond the metaphors of the Old Testament prophets and beyond metaphorical description of the horrors that might accompany natural disasters or human wars. The author has now moved into the realm of the mythological, of the demonic and of the terrifying. That move makes the conclusion of this series even more sobering. Even attack by such mythic beasts does not change humanity. The conclusion remains much the same as it had been throughout the Old Testament: those who are hardened against the word of God do not repent, no matter what happens to them. Suffering does not convert them. Terror does not convert them. Those who live through such times continue in idolatry and sin. More signs must occur before a terrified humanity recognizes that God is at work (11:13).

10:1-7 The small scroll. Once again we must wait for the final woe, the seventh trumpet. The seer will be commissioned once again, and those who are to be witnesses to God's actions in the last days will be established. God will not commence those final events without further prophetic testimony. This vision brings us back to the prophet Ezekiel. The cloud and the rainbow are signs of divine presence (Ezek 1:28). The angel's face shines with the glory of God. All the demonic images that we have just seen are erased in this new vision of the divine. The scroll scene will rework the scene in which the prophet eats a scroll in Ezek 2:8-3:3. Cries of thunder and the lion's roar both appear as signs that the day of judgment is beginning in the prophets (Amos 1:2; 3:8; Joel 4:16). The seven thunders also remind us of the seven spirits of God.

But the end is not yet. The prophet is not allowed to reveal what is said by the thunders. Daniel seals up the mysteries of his revelation (12:4) because they are for the generation that will live in the last days, not for the people at the time in which the book is said to have been written, several hundred years before the events to which it alludes. John, however, was not such a fictional work. It begins as a revelation to a Christian prophet well known to the audience, not as the words of a wise man long dead. The sealing up of what John hears suggests that it is not yet the end time. Lest the audience become alarmed by that new sign of delay, the angel swears an oath by God that the time of the end, the time of the seventh trumpet, is not far off. When that time comes, everything that God has announced to the prophets will come to pass.

10:8–11:12 Commissioning the prophet. The section in which John is commissioned again for the visions ahead recalls two actions from Ezekiel: eating a scroll and measuring the temple. Like Ezekiel, John is instructed to eat a scroll which tastes like honey (Ezek 2:8-3:3). The bitterness [NAB: "sour"] in the stomach recalls the bitterness of having to announce the day of the Lord (Zeph 1:14). Verse 11 is awkward: "they" [NAB: "someone"] tell the prophet that he must prophesy again. He is set over against nations and kings (as in Jer 1:10). Yet, we have not yet seen the prophet fulfill the first commission. The verse may simply be an awkward transition between the two different allusions to the prophet's vocation as being like that of Ezekiel.

Measuring the temple of God appears in Ezek 40:3. The prophet measures the temple in view of the fact that it is to be restored. Here the prophet's measuring represents preservation of part of the temple in the period leading up to the end time. The three and a half years during which the outer court is under Gentile dominion is roughly the 1290 days during which the temple was profaned in Dan 12:11. Dan 7:25 has three and a half years as the time during which the fourth and final beast will dominate the saints of God. In Dan 12:7, the revealing angel swears an oath by the Most High (compare the oath of the angel at 10:5-6), that the period of domination by this final empire will be three and a half years. Thus, the audience of Revelation would know that the vision is invoking that earlier tradition. Preservation of part of the temple from domination symbolizes preservation of a remnant, the holy ones of God. The saying in verse 2 may reflect an older Jewish oracle about the destruction of the temple, just as we find an oracle about the "times of the Gentiles" in Luke 21:24. As they hear these prophecies, both author and audience know that the Roman imperial armies had completely leveled the temple in Jerusalem almost a quarter century earlier. They were not looking for precise predictions about the time of domination, or they would not have preserved the Danielic three and a half years. They could see this prophecy as one of those historical allusions to the past which show that the events described and the expectations for the future all belong to the times in which they live.

11:3-14 Sign of the two witnesses. The dominion of the Gentiles is matched by the sign of the two witnesses. Two probably refers to the number of witnesses required by law. It is difficult to determine who the two witnesses are. Ezekiel has to prophesy against two false advisors to the city in 11:1-4. The witnesses to God might be an antitype to such false advisors. Other interpreters suggest that the two represent the two eschatological prophets Moses and Elijah. The signs that they perform recall Moses' sending the plagues on Egypt and Elijah's closing the heavens (1 Kgs 17:1). Verse 4 identifies the witnesses with the lampstand and olive trees that the prophet Zechariah saw next to the Lord (Zech 4:3, 11, 14). No human enemy can attack these witnesses, but they meet their death at the hands of a mythical beast. He is the beast from the sea who fights against God's holy ones in Dan 7:3-7, 19, 21. Here we have another example of Revelation's fondness for interlocking cycles of visions. This beast will be back in chapters 13 and 17. He is embodied in Roman imperial power and its deadly conflict with the truth of God's sovereignty.

Further allusions to Ezekiel structure the rest of the section. In the midst of Ezekiel's prophecy against the two false teachers, they die (11:13). The image of the corpses of the two prophets lying in the street recalls Ezek 11:6. The symbolic naming of Jerusalem as "Sodom and Egypt" reflects oracles against Sodom and Egypt in Ezek 16:26, 48, 53, 56. We have seen that an early Christian prophecy against the temple may be behind Rev 11:2. This section may also draw on such a tradition. Matt 23:29-30 calls the graves of the prophets to witness against Jesus' contemporaries.

The nations that are trampling the holy city are also the ones that will witness the exaltation/resurrection of the two dead prophets. This section preserves a traditional Jewish story pattern: the wicked kill and mock the righteous; the righteous are exalted/resurrected; the wicked see the exaltation of those whom they had despised and cry out lamenting their own condemnation. As with many of the passages in which the author moves toward the mythical, Revelation intensifies the grotesque and terrifying in its presentation. Refusal to bury a corpse was the worst punishment antiquity could imagine. An unburied corpse would render the whole city polluted. Yet Revelation shows us people staring at and even celebrating around the two corpses in the street. All the world is involved. The corpses lie there unburied for the symbolic period of three and a half days.

After that period, God acts. The bodies arise as in the dry bones vision of Ezek 37:10 and are carried to heaven like Elijah (2 Kgs 2:11). The earthquake associated with the end of the world was transferred to the crucifixion and resurrection of Christ in Matthew (27:52). The terror of the people watching the sign recalls another Old Testament prophecy which early Christians used for the reaction of the nations when they say the crucified return in glory, Zech 12:10. It is important to remember that in this "exaltation of the righteous" pattern, the wicked acknowledge their sinfulness at the end when they see the righteous person exalted. But that acknowledgment is too late. They are not saved by it. Thus, the nations worship, but they do so out of fear. They are admitting their sinful neglect of the prophetic word. The resurrection/exaltation stands over against the wicked as a sign of their own condemnation.

Verse 14 ties this long section back to the second woe, from which it departed. However, the traditions in these two sections seem to have had an origin in prophecies that were not originally part of the trumpet cycle. We are warned that the final trumpet is about to sound.

11:15-19 The seventh trumpet. We shift back into the focus of the earlier cycles with a vision of the victorious ascent of the Lamb to his throne. Perhaps the early Christian prophecies of resurrection/exaltation and vindication that are related to the images of the previous section help tie that vision to this one. We are lifted out of the terrors of the previous vision to the heavenly splendor of a new king assuming the throne. The angelic herald announces the beginning of his rule. We are somewhat removed from the woe associated with the seventh trumpet, since the ascent of the Lamb to his throne does not immediately provide the occasion for further destruction on earth.

This vision resumes the earlier vision of the Lamb in chapter 5. That vision concluded with a hymn which proclaims the Lamb worthy to rule (5:9, 12). This one moves beyond that acclamation. The elders are singing a hymn of thanksgiving to the Lamb for having assumed his rule over the nations. That hymn envisages the Lord's rule over the raging nations (Ps 99:1). It proclaims the judgment of those who are hostile to God's people as having occurred. Their sentence has been passed with the enthronement of the Lamb, even though it is clear that the Lord has not yet destroyed such powers from the face of the earth. Jewish legend held that the ark, lost in the destruction of Solomon's temple, would be returned in the messianic age. Here we see it resting within the heavenly temple. The vio-

lent storm surrounding the ark is a sign of divine presence.

This vision proclaims the present sovereignty of the Lamb. It provides a heavenly prologue to the horrors of the beast that are to come, much as the visions in chapters 4 and 5 provided a prologue to the first two vision cycles. We are about to move into events which affect the author and his audience. The beast, like the fourth beast from the sea in Daniel, represents the empire under which they live and the imperial ideology against which they must struggle.

UNNUMBERED VISIONS

Rev 12:1–15:4

A new series of visions contrasts the followers of the beast with the followers of the Lamb. Many interpreters think that the dragon's attack on the woman and her offspring is the third woe. They point to the woe in 12:12: "Woe to you, earth and sea, for the Devil has come down to you in great fury!" The author may also have thought of this section as divided into seven visions. However, he does not provide a numbered cycle for them, and there is no agreement among commentators as to how the section should be divided. All of the literary devices introduced in the first half of the book continue. Horrors on earth alternate with visions of heaven. Symbols loaded with mythological allusions collapse into one another. Present realities and future predictions overlap. We cannot always tell where one begins and another leaves off. The author takes traditional imagery for evil and intensifies it in the direction of the grotesque. However strange these visions may be, we must always remember that they are interpretations of the world that Christians are experiencing. They seek to point out the real truth about the powers at work in that world.

12:1-6 "A woman clothed with the sun." The story of the woman and the dragon draws upon a wealth of symbolism from the myths of the ancient Near East, from Jewish and Greek sources. Many parallels can be brought to the events in this section. We will be content with sketching a few of the major images in order to indicate how deeply rooted the symbol is in the mythic consciousness of humanity. An important function of the woman in Revelation is to provide an antitype to the image of Babylon as whore.

The "woman clothed with the sun" would easily remind the audience of the Roman use of the story of the sun god, Apollo. Roma, the queen of heaven, was worshiped as mother. The emperor Augustus claimed that he had brought about the golden age of kingship associated with Apollo, the sun god. The emperor Nero, who will play a large role in the beast visions to come, went even further. He claimed that as an infant he had been rescued from a serpent's attack just as the infant Apollo had been. The Apollo myth said that Python was seeking to kill Leto, who was pregnant with Apollo, Zeus' son. Zeus has the north wind rescue Leto by carrying her off to an island. Poseidon, the sea god, then contributes to rescuing the woman by covering the island with waves.

The similarities with the story in Revelation are obvious. The woman clothed with the sun is being pursued by a dragon. She is carried off to safety by an eagle. Then the earth contributes to the rescue by swallowing the dragon's water. Other mythological traditions also tell stories of the goddess-mother who must ward off attack from a serpent being. None of the stories is exactly identical to any of the others, any more than the story in Revelation is the story of Apollo. They all reflect an archetypal symbol of the heavenly mother and her divine child, who are attacked by the evil monster from the waters of chaos. The mother and child must be rescued from the forces of evil.

For the audience of Revelation, which has just seen the enthronement of the Lamb, this scene is a flashback to the primordial story of the birth/rescue of the divine child. It will provide a mythic explanation for the hostility between the followers of the beast and those of the Lamb. It is easy to see why later Christians identified the woman with Mary. However, Revelation stays with the archetypal meaning of the symbol. It does not descend to the level of identification with a single person. All of the images of "the woman" in these chapters are to be read on that transpersonal level. The children of the persecuted woman will also be described as those who must struggle with the dragon on earth. Thus, the sign of the woman in heaven becomes the mythic prototype of the earthly realities that are faced by the audience.

We have already seen that John never takes his images from a single source. The woman also evokes traditions from the Old Testament. Being clothed with the sun recalls the glory with which God, the creator, is clothed in Ps 104:1-2. The twelve stars in her crown have astral symbolism, standing for the twelve signs of the zodiac, but they can also stand for the twelve tribes of Israel (compare the moon and the eleven stars of Joseph's dream in Gen 37:9). Isa 7:14 pointed to the child about to be born as a messianic sign. The woman's labor pains reflect those of the daughter of Zion (Mic 4:10; Isa 26:17). Her cry is reminiscent of the voice calling out from the temple just before Zion gives birth to the Messiah in Isa 66:6-8. The imagery makes it clear that the child born to the woman is the Messiah. He shepherds the nation with a rod of iron (Isa 66:8; 7:14).

However, we find another of those delays that permeate the images of Revelation. In Isa 66, the woman's birth pangs are followed by the messianic age of salvation. Here they bring on an attack of the dragon, which is still not yet the final showdown between good and evil. The dragon is a mythological representation of the opponent of God. In ancient Near Eastern creation myths, the warrior storm god must conquer the dragon of the watery chaos before the world can be created. In Jewish apocalypses conquest of the beast signals the final destruction of the world and the beginning of the new creation. This beast represents an intensified image of the beast from the sea in Daniel. His color and the destruction of the stars link him with the agents of destruction in the first half of the book. As in Daniel, the beast has many heads to symbolize the many kingdoms (7:7). Stars are swept from the heavens (8:10). As in the trumpet visions, the destruction of the stars is limited to a third.

The dragon is the last of the heavenly signs. The rest of the mythic creatures will emerge from the seas or will be associated with the earth. The symbolic protection of the woman for three and a half years returns at the end of the chapter after the dragon is cast out of heaven. Her flight into the desert recalls the Elijah story (1 Kgs 17:1-7). Presumably, angels care for her in the desert (1 Kgs 19:5-7).

12:7-12 Victory in heaven. We have seen that Revelation consistently shows victories that remain to be won on earth as completed in heaven. The story of Satan's fall from heaven now emerges as a preliminary battle between Michael and Satan. It will show that the persecution and hostility experienced by Christians have their source in this ancient conflict. The myth of the fallen angels has been combined with the imagery of the god's victory over the monster of chaos. The story in Revelation maintains the timeless quality of its mythic symbols. The story of the myth was repeated annually in the cults of the ancient world. It had the quality of being an eternally valid expression of the divine victory over the sources of evil and disorder. Something of those overtones must attach to the heavenly representations of victory in Revelation. Like the myths of old, they would reassure the persecuted of the fundamental victory of order over chaos. Michael is traditionally the guardian of the people of God and the opponent of Satan (see Dan 10:13, 21; 12:1). The heavenly victory symbolizes his permanent dominion over Satanic forces.

Verse 8 recalls Dan 2:35; verse 9, Isa 14:12. The tradition that Satan's fall from heaven is linked with the messianic age also appears in sayings of Jesus (Luke 10:18; John 12:31). Verse 9 reminds the reader that the dragon being defeated is Satan. The hymn of victory in verses 10-12 sounds an ominous note. On the one hand, it celebrates Michael's victory over Satan and shows that victory to be realized in the victory of God's faithful people. On the other hand, it sounds a note of warning to those on earth.

Casting out of Satan, the heavenly accuser, belongs to the image of the victorious ascent of the Messiah. Satan's attempts to accuse the saints before God have been defeated by their fidelity and by the sacrifice of the Lamb. The jubilation of the hymn reflects Ps 96:10-13 and the rejoicing of the cosmos in Isa 44:23; 49:13. The previous hymns might lead us to expect this hymn to end on that note. Instead, a warning is given. The defeated, angry dragon will be even more severe in his persecution of the woman and her children on earth. Michael's victory has shown that his rule is coming to an end. What follows is a description of the messianic suffering of the faithful.

12:13-18 The woman's flight. The story of the woman's flight, first exhibited in heaven, is now repeated on earth. Eagle's wings as a sign of divine protection appear in the Old Testament (Exod 19:4; Deut 32:11; Isa 40:31). She is cared for again for the symbolic three and a half years. Associated with the waters (see Isa 29:3; Job 40:23), the dragon tries to use his element, raging flood waters, against the woman, but she escapes (Ps 32:6; 69:16). Rescue from raging waters emphasizes the image of the woman as people of God, rescued from the sea and the raging hostility of Pharaoh (Num 16:32; Deut 11:6; Isa 29:3-5, 10; 30:12).

Verse 17 makes it clear that the woman stands for the people of God. The dragon goes off to find her offspring. The specification of the righteous as those who "give witness to Jesus" makes the hostility against the Christians the expression of the dragon's anger. However, the author's references to those experiences are indirect, since he continues the practice of imaginative intensification of mythological symbols in this section. Prophetic predictions of salvation, stories of Israel's formation as a people of God, and archaic mythological symbols all blend together in the visions of conflict and salvation that are about to unfold. We have already seen that the letters suggest that many in the audience would not have seen their experience of Roman imperial power as Satanic. Some have probably worked out compromises with the surrounding environment.

13:1-10 The beast from the sea. The dragon's authority comes to rest in two beasts, one from the sea and one from the earth. The beasts symbolize the antichrist and false prophet of the end time in Jewish apocalyptic visions at the same time as they are the final embodiment of imperial power opposed to the rule of God, the final beast of Daniel's visions. We have seen that 4 Ezra pictured Rome as a great eagle emerging from the sea (11, 1). The sea indicates that the beast in question embodies the watery chaos monster of ancient Near Eastern mythology, the primordial source of all evil. The author identifies the beast for his audience by reminding them of a piece of esoteric numerology that would apparently have been well known to Christians in such circumstances: the number of the beast is 666 (13:18). This number is not a prediction of the future. All interpretations of Revelation that claim to attach the number to a present-day figure should be dismissed. This code is one which the author and his audience share. The best solution to the identity of the beast remains "Nero Caesar," since the Hebrew letters for that title add up to 666.

Several other features of Revelation suit the Nero legend and add to our conviction that Nero is the person to whom the author is referring. A legend circulated among the subject peoples of the eastern part of the empire that Nero had not died. He would return leading a revolt against Rome. Remember the Parthians of the first horseman? The legend held that Nero had fled to live among the Parthians. The period between A.D. 69 and 88 is punctuated by a series of revolts led by those who claimed to be Nero redivivus. We have a collection of Jewish prophecies from this period known as the Jewish Sibylline Oracles. The earlier oracles, from the period after the destruction of the Jerusalem temple by the Romans, picture Nero as leading a great victory of Asian forces over Rome.

In other words, the legend functioned for the Jews at the time much as it did for other conquered peoples in the East: it was a symbol of anti-Roman feeling and hopes for a revolt that would bring freedom and wealth to Asia. Later oracles in the fifth book continue to suggest that Nero is alive somewhere in the East, but they switch their view of Nero to one more like that in Revelation. Nero is identified as the mythological opponent of God in the last days. They make fun of his claims to divine birth. They seem to conceive of Nero as still living and fighting a terrible war against the king sent by God. Other passages both in the Jewish Sibyllines and in a Christian edition of a Jewish apocalypse from the first century, the Ascension of Isaiah, clearly identify Nero with Satan. They speak of him as performing cosmic signs, as claiming to be God, as setting up his image in all the cities and demanding worship from the peoples of the earth. Since Revelation appears to be earlier than all but the oracles in the fourth book of the Jewish Sibyllines, its image of the Satanic Nero may well be the earliest example of the perception that Nero would not return as savior of the eastern peoples but would embody the final outbreak of evil against God and his people.

Remember, most people seem to have thought that Nero was still alive, even though he was said to have died. That was not difficult to believe, since he had only been about thirty-one at the time of his death. Verse 3 describes a mortal wound on the head of the beast, which nonetheless lives. The story of Nero's coming from the East with Parthian troops seems to be referred to in 17:8-10, when the author speaks of the amazement of the peoples who see the beast who once existed, now does not exist, and will exist again. We have already seen that the image of the woman with the sun in chapter 12 serves as an antithesis to the imperial propaganda which pictured Nero in terms of the Apollo legend. Finally, the emperor who appears to have been on the throne at the time Revelation was composed also tried to appropriate the positive side of the Nero image. He used "Nero Caesar" as one of his official titles.

Considering the positive expectations of Nero in the populace at large, it was necessary to speak in a symbolic and guarded way. Criticism of Roman rule was dangerous to begin with. Revelation adds to that critique the presentation of Nero, a symbol of reversal for many opposed to that rule, that makes him the epitome of Rome's demonic power. At the same time, symbolic words about and allusions to Nero and the political affairs of the region were a common way of speaking. Both Jews and Christians would understand the type of writing embodied in the prophecies of Revelation. The author has not tried to conceal his meaning from those who are accustomed to such a way of speaking.

The two beasts, sea and land, have their counterparts in Behemoth and Leviathan of Job 40:15-27. They also reflect the beast of the final empire in Dan 7:3. Daniel divides world history into four empires, each represented by a beast and each hostile to God. Revelation is following a tactic that it used before when it compresses the four beasts into one and intensifies the grotesque nature of the beast by adding heads. The audience would have no trouble recognizing that the beast represented the empire of their experience, the Roman Empire. They would see the challenge to the Roman Empire's claim to enjoy the favor of the gods and even be ruled by a "divine" emperor in the picture of the beast as the embodiment of Satan. In addition to Jewish and Christian apocalypses, there is some evidence for "apocalyptic" thought among the conquered peoples of Egypt and Babylonia. Though the mortal conflict between the sovereignty of a "Satan" and the true God is not necessarily part of pagan apocalypses, they show a longing for national liberation, return to tradition, and to former glory that is much like the desires of their Jewish counterparts. The general development of eschatological expectations among peoples of the East after the conquests of Alexander the Great has been understood by some political philosophers as evidence of the "underside" of imperial conquest. The self-glorifying and even self-divinizing inscriptions and proclamations of the imperial rulers presented the empire as beneficent. So does the literature written by those who benefited from the opportunities given by imperial expansion. We have seen that those local, civic authorities who sought favor with the empire joined the proclamation of the benefits of the empire through the various cultic activities in honor of the emperor. Clearly, the local citizenry did not have a universally agreed upon assessment of the empire.

Indeed, Revelation portrays most of the world as awed by the beast. None could imagine that its power would be overthrown. Just as the beast is a double parody of both the emperor and the false messiah, the antichrist, so following the beast is not just a sign of loyalty to the empire. It is also a parody of true Christian discipleship. The wound which heals not only refers to the legends about Nero. It also parodies the true healing of mortality in the resurrection, Christ, who died and now lives. The two witnesses lifted up into heaven in chapter 11 can also be seen as the antitype of another imperial symbol, the apotheosis of the emperor. Art works represent the deceased emperor being carried up to the heavens to be with the gods. Some people even claimed to have seen the souls of deceased emperors ascending into heaven from their funeral pyres. Such false claims of imperial divinity contribute to the veneration of the emperor. Revelation has already shown its audience that the true exaltation is Christ's ascent to the throne from which he now rules. The acclamation which the peoples give the beast are a parody of the true hymns of praise that are sung in heaven to the Lamb. Verse 4 even parodies the celebration of God's triumph over his enemies in Exod 15:11. The audience already knows from the previous battle in heaven that

Michael, the heavenly angels, and even God's faithful ones can triumph over this beast which the world holds in such awe. The audience knows the answer to that rhetorical question, "Who can compare with the beast or who can come forward to fight against it?"

Verses 5-8 intensify the conflict imagery. The symbolic forty-two-month period represents the time of authority given any hostile power. Some interpreters suggest that the blasphemy referred to in verse 6 belongs to the titles of Domitian, the ruling emperor. He was called "dominus et deus," lord and god. These verses make it clear that the world itself is divided in two between the followers of the beast and the followers of the Lamb. Only those who belong to the Lamb will hold out against the dominion of the beast.

The story of the first beast ends with a prophetic oracle. The familiar call to hear suggests that it is directed to the followers of the Lamb and is not a woe oracle against the followers of the beast. The first part reflects Jer 15:2. The oracle may also be related to Matt 26:5. The oracle clearly warns the faithful of a period of suffering. Perhaps it also intends to instruct them that no human revolt will stop its blasphemy. Some interpreters point to the Jewish rebellion under Trajan about twenty years later as evidence that such warnings were in order. Revelation may also have an earlier Christian oracle from the time of the Jewish revolt in A.D. 66–70 in mind.

13:11-18 The beast from the land. The authority of the first beast is passed to a second. However, both beasts clearly represent the empire. Verse 12 suggests that the second beast represents the power of the empire as it was exercised by local authorities. We have already seen that the spread of the emperor cult in the East was due to the initiatives of local governments and private citizens. They usually thought to gain some imperial favor or recognition for their city. Verse 12 describes such a process at the same time that it hints once again that the beast is Nero. We have seen that the signs and wonders could belong to the Nero legend. However, they are also typical of the false prophets of the end time (see Matt 24:24). Calling down fire from heaven was considered a particularly impressive sign of divine power (see 1 Kgs 18:21-23 and the disciples' request of Jesus in Luke 9:51-56). Cities and temples might also claim signs and miracles as a way of gaining support for local shrines. The cultic imagery continues in verse 14 when the people are instructed to erect a cult statue. Failure to worship will carry a death penalty (compare Dan 3:2-3). We have no evidence for any attempt to enforce such veneration throughout the empire. Pliny's correspondence with Trajan two decades later shows that the Romans had no specific crime with which to charge those denounced as Christians. Pliny and Trajan are willing to dismiss those accused of being Christians if they will acknowledge imperial power by offering incense before a statue of the emperor. They also refuse to accept anonymous accusations against people. Should the accused comply with the imperial directive, the person who brought the charge would have to pay a penalty. Should the accused resist, he or she would be executed as a potential danger to the state. We do not know how such cases were handled in Asia Minor at the time of Revelation. Perhaps such problems are only beginning and John is warning Christians that the beast will eventually expand its demands.

We have no direct evidence for a practice of marking people on the forehead such as we find mentioned in verse 16. John may have created that image as an antitype to the sealing of Christian baptism. The "sign" which a person wears identifies him or her as a member of either the followers of the beast or the followers of the Lamb. There is no grey area in between. Verse 17 rapidly brings us back to the sober reality of refusing to comply with demands to venerate the emperor. Christians seem to be excluded from or at a disadvantage in commerce, an important activity in cities like Laodicea. The letter to that city certainly hints that Christians were as much involved in its commercial prosperity as any of the other citizens. Some interpreters think that the disadvantage came from a refusal to use coins, which often carried images of the emperor as divine on one side. However, even if Christians did use such coins, they might still face problems. They might refuse to swear oaths that accompanied many transactions if they mentioned the emperor as divine. Thus it would appear difficult for Christians to engage in commercial transactions with non-Christians without being willing to go along with customs which appeared to acknowledge the divinity and authority of the beast.

14:1-5 The followers of the Lamb. The scene now shifts back to the 144,000, those who bear the mark of the Lamb. Condemnation of imperial power will resume in chapter 17. Mount Zion was often pictured as the place where the Messiah would appear prior to his final battle with the forces of evil. Here the Lamb appears with his faithful ones. This image consolidates the opposition between the two groups, the followers of the beast and the followers of the Lamb. This group is described as the "first fruit" of the people of God. Verse 16:14 will show the gathering together of the nations at the end time.

The opening of this scene recalls prophetic announcements of the day of Yahweh (see Joel 2:27; 3:3-5). However, this gathering is not the end. Instead, we are given the antitype to the worship paid to the beast. The 144,000 learn the "new hymn" to be sung before the Lamb. Revelation sees the prophetic promises that the remnant of Israel will be purified and will dwell without sin on God's holy mountain as fulfilled in this group (Zeph 3:8-13; Isa 53:9). Perfection and holiness are characteristics of the true people of God redeemed by the Lamb. Since Christians are being warned against the idolatry of worshiping the beast, we find the customary assertions of sexual purity in the assertion that the followers of the Lamb "were not defiled with women." This verse does not mean that Christians were expected to be ascetics. Jewish prophetic language often spoke of idolatry as sexual immorality. Revelation will come back to this combination in the pictures of the whore of Babylon in chapter 17. The angel is about to announce the destruction of Babylon (14:8).

14:6-13 Announcements of judgment. Remember the three cries of woe from the eagle in midheaven (8:13)? Now an angelic herald flies across midheaven calling out oracles of divine judgment. These oracles warn against following the beast. At the same time as the announcement of divine judgment means woe for those who follow the beast, it represents salvation for the faithful. It summons them to repentance and endurance. Consequently, the first angel is pictured as proclaiming the "gospel," the eternal good news, to all the people on earth. The gospel message given by the angel is that the time of salvation is at hand; the creator of heaven and earth has assumed his throne. Thus, the hymns in other parts of Revelation which celebrate the victory of the Lamb are also announcements of the gospel according to Revelation. The announcement recalls the celebration of the victory of the Lord on his holy mountain in Isa 25:9-10. The angel in Revelation is summoning the whole world to pay homage to its victorious creator.

The second angel brings an oracle of woe against Babylon which combines Isa 21:9 and Jer 59:7. Jewish apocalypses always identify the ruling empire with the Babylonian Empire, so that in Daniel, Babylon is the Syrian Empire of Alexander's successors. Revelation, of course, identifies Rome and Babylon. Once again, drinking the "wine of her lewdness" refers to homage and idolatry. These images will be expanded in the vision of Babylon, the great.

The third angel concludes with a stern warning against worshiping the beast. The punishments combine a number of prophetic themes. Sinners drink the cup of divine wrath (Isa 51:17, 22; Jer 25:15). They experience the sulphur sent on Sodom and find themselves in everlasting torment (Isa 66:24; 34:9f.). The godless have no rest (Ps 95:11). Their torment contrasts with the peace which awaits the faithful (Isa 57:2, 10).

Verses 12 and 13 apply these oracles to the followers of the Lamb. They are encouraged to persevere. They are promised that their fate will not be like the death of those who worship the beast. Remember, all these cries of woe are not invitations for Christians to gloat over the eventual fate of their enemies. They are reassurance for those who might be tempted to give up, who might think that the "gospel" of God's rule over the world just couldn't be true, who might be in awe of the greatness and power of the beast themselves. Revelation uses all the symbolic resources at its disposal to show that God's salvation is the truth about power and dominion for all the nations of the world, that it really does matter whether or not one resists the power of the beast.

14:14-20 The eschatological harvest. This image of the angelic harvest of the earth combines two Old Testament passages, Dan 7:13 and Joel 4:13-16. The harvest takes place in two stages: first wheat, then grapes. The image of the Son of Man on the clouds is taken from Dan 7:13. Although early Chris-

tians usually applied the Son of Man image to the second coming of Jesus, the Son of Man here is an angel. He is subject to the command of another angelic voice from the temple. We have seen that pattern frequently in the earlier scenes of angelic workers of destruction. The first harvest recalls the saying about the lord of the harvest in Mark 4:29 and the angelic reapers of Matt 13:39. Opinion on the significance of the first harvest is divided. Some scholars see it as the destruction of the pagan nations that come to attack the Messiah on his holy mountain in the last days. Others point to the positive images of the wheat harvest elsewhere in the New Testament. They suggest that the first act of harvesting gathers the righteous prior to the judgment of the wicked. We favor the first opinion. Joel 4:13-16 gives the basic elements of this vision. The call to harvest with sickle and winepress is negative. After the harvest oracle, the prophet proclaims the holiness and salvation of the Lord's people on Mount Zion. Revelation has presented us with the elements of this prophecy in reverse order. We have seen the vision of the holy ones on Mount Zion (14:1-5). They have been promised that the Lord is coming in judgment (14:7). Now that harvest begins.

There is no question about the negative imagery attached to the grape harvest in the second half of the passage. The angel at the incense altar ties this vision back to the earlier visions of the trumpets. Before the trumpets began, he brought the prayers of the holy ones to God and then cast the coals from the censer down on the earth (8:3-4). Then he commanded the angel of the sixth trumpet to release the deadly horsemen from the banks of the Euphrates to kill a third of humanity (9:13). Now we find a third grim reminder of the deadly consequences of that angel's voice as he unleashes the trampling of the grapes of wrath. Verse 18 recalls Jer 25:30. Trampling the enemies of God in a great winepress was traditional (see Isa 63:1-6). The enemies of God are turned into a great sea of blood.

15:1-4 The song of Moses. Once again, just as we feel the narrative coming close to the great day of divine wrath and judgment, Revelation turns away. Verse 1 announces the final plagues, but they are interrupted by the song of the victors. Many interpreters think that the final woe, announced by the trumpets and then delayed, is represented in the vision of destruction that comes with the last cycle of seven—the seven bowls. In the interlude, we return once again to the heavenly temple. The images of the sea of the beast and the sea of blood are reversed in this image of a sea of glass and fire on which the victors over the beast stand to sing their hymn. The "song of Moses" and "of the Lamb" praises God and promises that all the nations of the earth will come to worship the Lord when they see his mighty deeds. It appears to be a collage of Old Testament passages (see Pss 111:2; 139:14; Amos 4:13; Jer 10:7; Pss 145:17; 86:9; Hos 6:5). This song looks forward to the universal recognition of God's rule which has been the theme emphasized again and again by the scenes of heavenly praise.

THE SEVEN BOWLS

Rev 15:5–16:21

This cycle brings to a conclusion the series of plagues on earth. Each of the cycles has repeated the theme of the coming judgment from a different perspective. Each has been more intense than the previous one. Each opens with a series of short plagues and concludes with more elaborate and mythological ones at the end. Like the trumpet cycle, the bowl plagues include allusions to the Exodus plagues. The image of the bowl combines two elements from the Old Testament traditions that have already been presented in the course of Revelation. Exod 27:3 describes the bronze basins used by the priest to carry out the ashes and fat from the sacrifices. Rev 8:3-5 has the angel at the altar of incense empty the censer of coals on the earth. Here, angels come out of the temple carrying bowls filled with the plagues. The second image, introduced in the vision of the winepress, is that of the cup of wine, which represents the wrath of God (Ps 75:8; Isa 51:17, 22). Also, like the previous plagues, these plagues do not bring people to worship God or to repent. They only continue to blaspheme the Lord, thus sealing their own doom.

15:5-8 The angels carry out bowls of wrath. Chapters 9 and 10 of Ezekiel provide the model for this section. In that section of Ezekiel, the scribe and six angels make up the needed seven. They are summoned to execute the guilty ones in the city of God. The scribe goes before the angels and marks the righteous to spare them from destruction. Revelation does not need such a process, since the righteous and the wicked already bear the seal of the one whom they follow. The description of the angels combines Dan 10:5-6 and Ezek 28:5. Ezek 10:4 describes the cloud of divine glory which fills the temple when the Lord is present. Here the smoke symbolic of his presence prohibits anyone from entering the temple until the plagues are carried out. In Ezek 10:6-8 the angels cast fire on the earth from the divine throne chariot. Here one of the chariot creatures gives the bowls to the angels.

16:1-11 The first five plagues. The first five plagues strike humans and water creatures with sores, blood, fire, and darkness. The voice which calls out from the temple may be that of God (see Isa 66:6), since no one can enter there, or that of the revealing angel (see Ezek 9:1). The intensification of these plagues is indicated by the affliction which hits the whole earth, not just a part of it. The third plague, which destroys all fresh drinking water, is accompanied by an antiphonal proclamation of the justice of God's judgment against those who have shed the blood of the righteous (see Pss 119:137; 145:17; 79:3; Isa 49:26). The fourth plague combines the apocalyptic sign in the sun with the casting of fire on the earth. Instead of darkening, as in other apocalyptic visions like the third trumpet, the sun flares up and burns people with its fire. The darkness of the final plague resembles the darkness over Egypt. It also recalls the destruction of the light of the heavenly bodies in the earlier plagues. Human suffering comes from the affliction with boils, as in the first plague of this series.

The fourth and fifth plagues are also linked to the earlier trumpet series in their emphasis on humanity's failure to repent. Instead of turning from wickedness, humans blaspheme God all the more as the cause of their suffering. This intensification of their hostility to God prepares the way for the summoning of destruction from the East. In Isa 46:11-13, Yahweh answers the hard of heart by summoning his man from the East. That summons is the prelude to salvation: the beautiful daughter of Babylon is reduced from luxury to slavery in Isa 47. Revelation will follow a similar pattern. We are about to see the luxurious daughter of Babylon and then to witness her fall. However, two more plagues intervene before we come to that vision.

16:12-16 Armies assemble in the East. We have already seen that people expected destruction from the Parthians in the East. We have also seen that Revelation turns to more grotesque and mythological images for the concluding plagues of a series. The sixth plague presents us with a ghastly image of the armies drawing up for battle. In a mockery of "preparing the way of the Lord," the river Euphrates is dried up to provide a way for the demonic armies. Like the Egyptian frogs (Exod 7:6-11; Pss 7:45; 105:30), they come forth. They work signs and assemble all the kings of the earth for battle. This assembling provides a demonic antitype for the assembling of the righteous with the Lamb in chapter 14. It translates into the macabre imagery of Revelation—the prophetic vision of the armies coming against Jeruslem in Zech 14:2-5. Zechariah shows us the Lord going forth against his enemies from Zion. When he stands on the Mount of Olives, it splits in two; the valley fills and a great earthquake ensues. Later in the same vision, the Lord strikes his enemies with a plague that causes their flesh to rot (Zech 14:12).

Verse 15 interrupts these predictions of disaster with warnings to the righteous to be on their guard. Related sayings about the second coming are common in the New Testament (see Matt 24:43; Luke 12:39; 1 Thess 5:2, 4; 2 Pet 3:10).

16:17-21 The seventh bowl. We have seen that the violent earthquake, lightning flashes, and announcement of judgment with "it is done" all belong to the scenario for the appearance of God at the end of the world. That theophany should, as in Zech 14, bring the final destruction of the wicked. Once again we will be put off. The description of Babylon and her destruction is being held off until the next section.

The final plague is ordered from the throne in the sanctuary and is accompanied by all the signs of a theophany. The division of the great city and its fall may have been derived from the image of the quake on the Mount of Olives. Revelation is recapitulating the woe of 14:3-16 and looking forward to the vision of the fall of the "great city" Babylon which

is to come in the next section of the work. Flight of the islands and mountains is a sign of the divine appearance (see Isa 41:5). Even the destruction of a multitude of cities and great hailstones do nothing to change the ways of humanity. As they have done in response to the earlier plagues, they continue to blaspheme. The evil of the last days is intensified by the punishments which God has sent against humanity.

BABYLON THE GREAT

Rev 17:1–19:10

All the delay and expectation, all the hints of the fall of Babylon will come to a head in this section. Her fall was announced in 14:8. Chapter 18 will finally show us her demise. First, a description of her appearance reminds the reader that Babylon represents the Satanic power of imperial Rome.

17:1-6 The great whore of Babylon. One of the bowl angels takes the seer to witness the destruction of Babylon. The seventh bowl identified Jerusalem as city of destruction with Babylon. The epithet "harlot" recalls the prophetic oracles against a faithless Jerusalem as well as against other cities (see Isa 1:21; 23:15-18; Ezek 16:15-35; 23:3-49). The drunkenness of the kings of the earth appears in Jer 25:15-29. There it is the cup of wrath from the hand of the Lord which is given to the nations.

There is no direct Old Testament image for the harlot riding on the beast. However, John may have created the image out of chapter 13 and pagan cultic imagery. The color of the beast reminds us of all the plagues of blood and fire that have been shed on the earth throughout the book. The interpretation in the second half of the chapter makes it clear that this vision is a variant of the earlier vision of the beast. The description of the woman combines several Old Testament images from Isa 3:16-24 against the finery of the daughters of Zion; Ezek 28:11-16 against the wealth and ostentation of Tyre; and Jer 51:7 against Babylon. In Jer 51:7, Babylon is the golden cup in the hand of the Lord which makes the nations drunk. Here they are drunk with the lewdness of the harlot (=idolatry) just as the beast was leading the world into idolatry in chapter 13.

The symbolic name on the forehead of the harlot recalls the other names which the faithful, whose blood she drinks, have received; the mark of the beast on the forehead of its followers, points to the seal on the foreheads of those who follow the Lamb (9:2). She is drunk with the blood of those faithful ones (16:16; 18:24; cf. the image of the land drunk with blood in Isa 34:7). The faithful martyrs reappear at the end of this section.

17:7-18 Interpretation of the vision of the whore. Like the earlier picture of the beast, this one is a symbolic expansion of traditional imagery. Like most symbolic accounts of history, the number of heads does not match a strictly historical account of the Roman emperors. It seems to best represent a rough sketch of the emperors up to the time of Domitian. Clearly, the beast that returns as the eighth, but is one of the seven, refers to Nero. The eagle vision of the Roman Empire in 4 Ezra has wings which may intend to represent all the emperors, but it only selects three to represent the heads: Vespasian, Titus, Domitian (11:29-32; 12:22-28). The best suggestion is that the emperors indicated represent those particularly hated. Since Revelation is close to contemporary Jewish apocalypses in its anti-Roman sentiment, we may use those sources to suggest a possible identification.

Caligula was the first emperor to cause opposition among the Jews when he demanded that his statue be set up in the temple. (Remember, the beast is accused of doing that in Rev 13:15.) Beginning with Caligula, the heads would represent Caligula, Claudius, Nero, Vespasian, and Titus. Domitian, "the one who is," is sixth. One further emperor is needed to fill out the number seven. As in many apocalypses, the author feels that he is almost but not quite in the last days. The rule of the seventh emperor is to be very short.

No one can miss the parallel between the beast and Rome, since the woman is enthroned on the seven hills of that city. Verse 11 associates the coming of the eschatological age with Nero's return from the East. The ten horns are taken from the vision in Dan 7:7, 27. They appear to represent allies of Rome, who suddenly bring the destruction of the harlot by turning viciously against her. Although Revelation uses more archaic and bizarre imagery than the Old Testament prophets, the author shares their conviction that the nations of the world finally do the Lord's bidding. He can turn the nations from friendship to hatred when that is necessary to the plan of salvation. Though the horns hint at the destruction of the harlot by the victorious Lamb and the revolt of her own allies, the full description of her fall awaits the next scene. Verse 16 alludes to a number of prophetic texts (Hos 2:4; Ezek 23:29; Jer 41:42; Mic 3:3).

This interpretation of the harlot vision repeats much of what the audience has already heard. The whole world is taken in by the beast except the followers of the Lamb. They have the insight and wisdom to know the truth about the times in which they live. They can identify the harlot as Rome and know the fate which awaits her. They are not taken in by her pretensions to divinity. The title of the beast, "existed once but exists no longer, and yet it will come again" (v. 8), may even be a parody of the title of God, "who is and who was and who is to come," from the opening of Revelation (1:4). They are certain of their salvation, since their names are recorded in the book of life (see Dan 12:1).

18:1-8 Fallen, fallen is Babylon. Rev 14:8 announced the fall of Babylon. Now a great angel from heaven announces that the condemnation passed by the heavenly court is upon her. This angel is more glorious than all the others we have seen (compare Ezek 43:2). Dan 4:27 provides the epithet "Babylon the great." Several Old Testament prophetic oracles against great cities are recalled in this passage (see Isa 13:21; 34:11, 14; Jer 50:39; 51:8). This passage comes closest to the condemnation of Tyre in Ezek 27:12-18. Nah 3:3-4 describes Babylon as a city of prostitution and drunkenness. Isa 23:17 refers to the drunkenness of the pagan nations. However, the oracles against Tyre bring out the theme of a city whose luxuries are due to trade and whose fall is not prevented by that great wealth.

The two angelic voices present the grounds for the condemnation of Babylon. When she is sentenced for her crimes, God will repay her double for all the evil she has done. The righteous are warned to flee Babylon, lest they become entangled in her sins. Similar warnings occur in the oracles against Babylon in Jer 50 and 51. Other passages from Jeremiah and Isaiah provide the pattern for the rest of the second announcement. Verse 5 is modeled on

Jer 51:9; verse 6, on Jer 51:15, 29 (also Isa 40:2). Verses 7-8 reflect Isa 47:1-9. But while Isaiah tells the boastful daughter of Babylon that she will suffer both loss of husband and loss of children in a single day, Revelation tells her that she will suffer all the plagues, death, mourning, famine, being consumed by fire, at once. The punishment of this Babylon will epitomize all the plagues described in the book at one time.

18:9-10 The kings of the earth lament. Those who had profited by the prosperity and sinfulness of the city now lament her fate. The inspiration for this whole sequence of laments is found in Ezek 26 and 27. The kings' lament alludes to Ezek 26:16. They see the city being destroyed by fire.

18:11-17a The merchants' lament. Like the kings of the earth, the merchants lament the overthrow of the great city. The description of her markets would suit any of the great trading ports of the Mediterranean. Her conquests in the East had made Rome famous as a center into which all the wealth and luxuries from those provinces flowed, even spices from faraway India. This great catalog of wares recalls that in Ezek 27. According to Ezek 27:13, Hellas demanded slaves.

Although no change of speaker is indicated, verse 14 appears out of place in the lament of the merchants. It probably represents an angelic condemnation like the longer one in verses 21-23.

Like the kings, the merchants draw back. They do not wish to share the fate of the city. They weep for all the great wealth that has been destroyed along with her.

18:17b-19 The seamen's lament. The final group to bewail the fate of the city are those whose ships bring her the wealth of the world. Each lament has followed the same pattern:

1. Introduction: "Alas, alas, great city . . ."
2. Statement of the relevant loss: kings—power; merchants—goods; shipowners—profit from trade.
3. Formal conclusion: "In one hour," destruction. The seamen's lament has a parallel in Ezek 27:29.

These laments paint a striking picture of the fall of a great trading center. Those who had benefited from her glory stand at a distance and watch her burn to the ground. Situated between two angelic proclamations of her judgment, they provide a strikingly human touch in the midst of an intense drama of divine and mythic symbols.

18:20-24 Rejoice! Babylon perishes! The call to rejoice contrasts with the laments of the previous section. It is the antitype of the rejoicing of the people in the city (=Jerusalem) over the death of the two witnesses in 11:8, and it contrasts with the call to rejoicing in 12:12. There the heavens could rejoice at the destruction of the beast, but those on earth had to expect woe. This call is the answer to the prayers of the saints. All who have suffered at the hands of the city are called to rejoice. The model for this summons appears in Deut 32:42; the nations are called to praise God for avenging the blood of her servants. Jer 51:48-49 summons the heavens and the earth to sing for joy over the destruction of Babylon. The legal grounds for the divine sentence, the "slain of Israel . . . the slain of all the earth" (Jer 51:49), is the same one that is found at the end of this passage. The city falls because of the blood of the prophets and saints.

The summons to rejoice and the legal sentence frame a final angelic cry as the destroying angel hurls a great millstone into the sea. The angel is enacting the conclusion to the great prophecy against Babylon in Jer 51:63-64. The prophet was told to bind the words of his prophecy against Babylon to a stone. As he cast the stone into the Euphrates, he was to say, "Thus shall Babylon sink. Never shall she rise, because of the evil I am bringing upon her." Rev 18:21 echoes those words, "With such force will Babylon the great city be thrown down, and will never be found again." The angel goes on to catalog the signs that she will never again rise as a city. That catalog continues to echo Ezek 27 with echoes from similar prophecies (see Isa 23:8, 27; Jer 25:15-17; 49:38). This city will never rise from the ashes of its destruction.

Even the announced destruction of the great city does not bring the story to its conclusion. The story of Revelation is about more than the fall of Roman power. It is about the conflict between God and those faithful to him and the forces of evil. The city embodies the beast, but the beast itself must be destroyed. It is the activities of the beast which underlie all the empires that are opposed to God. Before that story is told, we have another interlude in heaven to give thanks for the divine act of salvation that has just been described.

19:1-10 Hymn of divine victory. The heavenly assembly sings another victory song. God's judgment and justice are praised. It is important to recognize the theological perspective of such a hymn. The avenging of the martyrs represents more than the personal desire to see a wrong punished. It represents proof that God and his justice do rule the world. His judgments of the glory and power of Rome are the right ones. Thus, such victory hymns celebrate a world in which divine justice will win out in the affairs of humanity and nations, however much the evidence appears to go against that truth.

Verse 4 returns us to the divine throne room. One of the creatures of the throne calls to all the servants of God, all in the cosmos, to praise him (see Ps 135:1). That call is answered with a psalm of rejoicing by the great assembly (see Ps 118:24). Just as the earlier hymns had given us a glimpse of the future victory of God, so this hymn gives us a glimpse of the salvation which is about to come, at the wedding feast of the Lamb. The bride is the antitype to the prostitute Babylon. That contrast will be made more explicit when the heavenly Jerusalem is revealed. Here the bride's dress is interpreted as the virtuous deeds of the righteous. They are to share in the salvation of the Lamb at that great wedding banquet. This scene also evokes another part of the ancient myth of the defeat of the monster of chaos, which is about to be played out. The victorious young god would celebrate a banquet on the divine mountain. Since fertility and new creation followed from the divine victory over the forces of chaos, some forms of the myth celebrate a sacred marriage as part of the manifestation of the new divine rule.

Verse 10 is somewhat awkward. Verse 9 would provide a suitable conclusion to the section with its beatitude on those who will partake of that feast. Suddenly the seer worships the angel. While such a response might occur at the first appearance of an angel to make a revelation, it hardly makes sense here. Certainly the seer knows that God and the Lamb are the objects of heavenly worship. Perhaps this verse represents an independent piece about the truth of Christian prophecy—every true spirit testifies to Jesus—that the author has included to authenticate his Christian vision of the victory of God over his enemies.

UNNUMBERED VISIONS

Rev 19:11-21:8

It indeed seems that "delay is the stuff of which Revelation is made." We find another series of visions before we see the bride at the wedding feast. These visions also reflect the mythic patterns of divine victory. God has yet to overthrow the monster and establish his divine presence on earth. The wedding feast can only take place as part of this final cycle, which brings the mythic allusions in the book to their completion. The mythic pattern of new creation also includes the building of a new temple to the god. Here the theme will be somewhat altered, since the new Jerusalem will be the dwelling place of the Lord. The basic elements of the pattern of divine combat and victory celebration can be found in the concluding sections of Revelation. They have been expanded by the addition of other materials, as is common in all the visions of Revelation. We actually have a double victory over the beast. Such a victory appears in some versions of the myth when the god must conquer chaos and death in separate battles. The basic elements in the pattern are:

1. Divine warrior appears (19:11-16)
2. Threat to divine sovereignty (19:19; 20:8-9a)
3. Combat and victory (19:20–20:3; 20:9b-10)
4. Victory shout (19:17-18)
5. Manifestation of divine kingship (20:4)
6. Salvation (20:5-6; 21:4; 22:1-5)
7. Renewal of creation/ sacred marriage/ building of temple (21:1-3, 9-27)

The victory shout actually comes before the divine victory rather than afterwards, as it would in the mythic stories. We have seen many examples of the "anticipation" of salvation, even the enthronement and kingship of the Lamb, in Revelation. Such anticipation forms part of the author's concern with assuring the audience of the present certainty of salvation.

When the author structures his story in accord with an archaic, mythic pattern as he has done here, we see that much more is involved than a simple prediction of historical events. The eternal realities imaged in that myth are shown to be fulfilled in the Christian story. The psychological power of those symbols to assure people of the order of the cosmos is evoked through the narrative. We no longer view the world in the dimensions of profane time or ordinary history. We view it from the perspective of divine time.

If the author is imaging Christian salvation as the fulillment of the most archaic, mythic hopes for salvation, then he has moved quite beyond the level of historical predictions. He has even moved beyond the level of social critique. The condemnation of Rome ended in chapter 18. Now, even the struggle with Rome is but an episode in the greater struggle with the primordial forces of evil and chaos for control of the world. Revelation was right about the Roman Empire, which had seemed both divine and immortal to many of its contemporaries. That empire, like all such empires, did collapse. Revelation is right: even the worst disasters will not turn those who do not have prophetic insight into God's view of truth and justice to the Lord. Humanity can continue to ignore, or worse, to blaspheme God, even in the face of unspeakable horrors. When Revelation keeps asserting that the rule of God is victorious over evil, it does not do so out of a naïve optimism about humans and their behavior; rather, it claims that the only source of confidence in salvation can be the victory of God.

Now we come to the final movement in our journey, the final intensification of the images of salvation. Revelation shows us that all human hopes for salvation must be realized in the rule of God and the Lamb. The mythic patterns are taken up because, like the Old Testament prophecies, they are fulfilled in the Christian story of divine victory.

19:11-16 The messianic warrior. Christ wins the real victory in his death. Consequently, Revelation places much less emphasis on description of the messiah-warrior and his battle with the foes of the Lord than we might expect. Unlike other apocalypses of the period, the righteous do not participate in an earthly war paralleling the conflict of the divine warrior and Satan. All elements of conquest in this book are on the divine level. Human armies are not involved. This ap-

proach is quite different from the War Scroll that was found among the writings of the Essenes at the Dead Sea. That Jewish sect had a scroll which claimed to give instructions as to how the army of the righteous was to draw up for the wars that would be part of the messianic victory. It gave instructions about what was to be written on the trumpets and standards of the assembled hosts, and it included the hymns of victory that the army of the Lord would sing after defeating its enemies.

The Messiah finally appears for battle. Like the armies in the War Scroll, names are inscribed on his person and his equipment. But he comes only at the head of divine armies, not human ones. The names designate this rider as the source of divine salvation; he is not the earlier horseman of destruction (6:1-2). The description of the rider contains a string of his divine names: Faithful and True, Justice, unknown name, Word of God, and, finally, the divine acclamation, King of Kings, Lord of Lords. The unknown name may refer to the "new name" God gives Jerusalem when he bestows salvation on her in Isa 62:2. All these names signify divine sovereignty and salvation.

The flaming eyes of Dan 10:6 are familiar from Rev 1:14 and 2:18. The messianic crown evokes the Psalms (Pss 21:4; 132:18), the title "King of Kings," and, of course, the many crowns worn by the beast. The rider goes forth to battle in blood-stained garments much as God does in Isa 63:1-3. The sword in the mouth recalls Isa 11:4 and 49:2; the rod, Ps 2:9. We are already familiar with the divine winepress from Rev 14:10 and 17:6 (see Isa 63:2; Joel 4:13). The combination of names, images and symbols attached to the divine warrior makes it clear that no one will escape this judgment. God is taking the field against the embodiment of evil.

19:17-21 The vultures' feast. As in the other mythic sections, this battle between the divine warrior and the beast is hardly described. Instead, ominous birds once more appear in midheaven. They are gathering to feast on the enemies of God (see Num 16:30; Isa 63:1-6). The curse against Gog in Ezek 39:4 warns that he will fall on the mountains of Israel and be given to the birds as food. So many will be killed that God will summon the birds and the wild beasts to come to a great sacrificial feast, to dine on the bodies of the fallen warriors and their horses (Ezek 39:17-20). So here the birds are summoned to feast on all who had followed the beast. Some interpreters suggest that this feast is a gruesome parody of the heavenly victory feast that follows the defeat of the beast in the mythic cycle. Once again, a delay; the inhuman enemies of the divine warrior, the beast, and the false prophet are not slain but imprisoned in Hades.

20:1-6 A thousand-year reign. This section has combined several apocalyptic themes. Speculation about a thousand-year reign of the Messiah is uncommon. However, the section of Ezekiel on which the author has been drawing does contain a doubling of the end-time images of salvation: the Messiah rules; Gog and Magog are defeated; the new Jerusalem is described (Ezek 37-43). This passage in Revelation pictures a rule by the Messiah prior to the defeat of Gog and Magog. Before that reign can occur, an angel imprisons the dragon in the abyss. He resembles the star-like angel with the keys to the abyss in Rev 9:1. The descent into Hades continues the imagery of Satan's fall from 12:9.

The significance of the throne imagery in this passage is not clear. At the end of the last letter, the victors are promised that they will share the throne of God/Jesus (3:21). Traditionally, the righteous or some group of them ascended thrones to judge the wicked (see Dan 7:9, the beast; Matt 19:28-30, the nations; also 1 Cor 6:2). Though Revelation has those sitting on thrones empowered to pass judgment, it is not clear whom they would be judging, since the messianic kingdom is established on earth, and the final judgment is yet to be described.

This section also seems to have mixed traditions about the resurrection. Images of resurrection in the first century vary between a general resurrection for a judgment, which separates righteous from wicked people, and resurrection as the reward for the righteous. The awkward distinctions in verses 4 and 5 may represent a combination of both traditions. The faithful witnesses are rewarded with an early resurrection and share the thousand-year reign. Verse 6 makes it clear that that resurrection is a definitive sign of salvation. Others will be resurrected at the judgment.

20:7-10 Against Gog and Magog. As in the previous battle scene, there is little description of the actual battle. In the tradition upon which Revelation draws (Ezek 38:22, 39), the armies are made up of people from among the nations. Either Revelation assumes that some have survived the previous destruction, since the dragon is said to be prevented from leading the nations astray, or one must assume that this army is made up of the dead/resurrected. The traditional image has the nations draw up against the people of God who are with the Messiah in Jerusalem (= the beloved city). That seems to be the tradition behind this battle. Revelation does not specify the nature of the opposition any further. What is significant is the final and eternal imprisonment of the devil, the beast, and the false prophet.

20:11-15 Judgment of the dead. God appears on his throne to execute judgment (compare Dan 7:9). This image of judgment presupposes a universal judgment of all those who are dead, wherever they may be. All that is hostile to God is cast into the fire of judgment, the second—and real—death. This punishment includes the destruction of both death as enemy and the underworld (see Isa 25:8; 1 Cor 15:26).

21:1-5a New heaven and earth. This section closes with the vision of a new heaven and earth that replaces the old creation, which has finally passed away (see Isa 65:17). The author is not interested in the implications of the image of a new creation which he has taken from Isaiah. Consequently, we cannot push this verse for information about the renewal of the natural world, as some interpreters concerned with ecology have tried to do. The real centerpiece of the new creation is the new Jerusalem (see Isa 52:1-3). The holy city will be the true dwelling place of God and also of the bride in the final section of the work. The throne voice announces that the promises of divine presence are fulfilled in this city (see Ezek 37:27; Zech 2:14; Jer 38:33). This city of divine presence and peace forms a striking contrast to the fallen Babylon (see Isa 25:8; 35:10; 65:19). In Isa 43:18-19 the Lord tells Israel not to remember the old things, since he is doing "a new thing." Revelation proclaims that that promise is finally fulfilled. God is making all things new.

21:5b-8 Second conclusion. These last chapters anticipate the conclusion of the whole with injunctions to the seer to record the trustworthy vision which he has received (see 19:9). The following section resumes the vision of the bride of the Lamb with an introduction that is parallel to the vision of the whore of Babylon (compare 21:9 and 17:1). This interruption also provides Revelation the opportunity to anticipate the bridal scene and the marriage feast (already anticipated once in the hymn of 19:7-8). The command to write and the divine name Alpha and Omega also bring us back to the beginning of the book (1:11, 19). The exhortations in this section are reminders of the exhortations in the opening letters, as are the promises to the victors (largely derived from the prophetic sayings in Isa 55:1-6). The passage seems to recapitulate the warnings of those letters. Verse 8 warns against various vices and idolatry. Thus, the section reminds the audience that the lessons of the book are to be applied to their own situation. They must heed the revelation and repent, lest they find themselves excluded from the final salvation. Now we find one final image of that final salvation, the new Jerusalem.

THE NEW JERUSALEM

Rev 21:9–22:5

We finally see the new Jerusalem in all her glory. This vision of the city in which God truly dwells rounds out the condemnation of all the false claims of the beast and Babylon in the previous chapters. It also represents the final gathering of the community which belongs to the Lamb.

21:9-21 The bride of the Lamb. The introduction to the vision of the bride deliberately recalls the introduction to the vision of the whore of Babylon. The two cities are antitypes of one another. Much of the imagery of the city also derives from Ezekiel: the city on the mount from 40:2; the city full of the glory of God from 43:2-4. The description of the walls primarily draws upon Ezek 40:5; 48:31-35, though other prophetic descriptions of the walls of Jerusalem might also lie behind this passage (see Jer 30:18; Isa 26:1; 60:10, 18; 62:6). Angelic watchers appear in Ezek 49:12 (also Isa 62:6, 10). Ezekiel's gates represent the twelve tribes (43:31-34). For Revelation, the Twelve are the apostles. The use of Ezekiel imagery has switched from description of the

woman as bride to the architectural features that define the city.

The next actions continue that image. Like Ezekiel (ch. 40), the seer measures the city. The measurements emphasize the perfection and size of the city. The stones in the walls seem to be based on Exod 28:17-20 (also 39:10-13; 36:17-20). Some interpreters try to give astrological interpretations of the various stones. If the author was acquainted with such traditions, he does not give any indication that he is exploiting that symbolism in the description about the city.

21:22-27 Divine presence in the city. This city is introduced as quite different from its prototype in Ezekiel when we learn that there is no temple there. The presence of God and of the Lamb makes the whole city a temple. Metaphors derived from Isaiah are used to describe the divine presence in the city; the basic passage is 60:1-20. Most of the elements of this passage can be found there. The glory of the Lord fills Jerusalem, so that she has no need of heavenly bodies to provide light (60:19-20; also Isa 24:33). The kings of the earth come bringing their wealth (60:3, 11). The city gates are always open (60:11a). The city is one of holiness. Nothing profane enters. Only the righteous live in this city (60:21; also Isa 35:8; 52:1; Ezek 44:9). Revelation has taken the vision of Isaiah and made appropriate additions to suit the images of the Lamb and the book of life. In so doing, it has proclaimed that vision fulfilled. The glory of divine presence is shared between God and the Lamb. The righteous who dwell in the city are faithful Christians.

22:1-5 The water and the trees of life. The vision of the new Jerusalem concludes with an image of the blessedness and immortality of those who inhabit it. The life-giving water flowing from the thrones of God and the Lamb recall the image of the streams of water flowing from the temple mount in Joel 4:18 and Ezek 47 (also Jer 2:13; Pss 46:5; 36:10). The tree of life from Gen 2:9 has been combined with the trees by the stream from Ezek 47:12 to provide twelve fruit-bearing trees. They provide the healing predicted for the pagan nations in Joel 1:14; 2:15. Just as nothing profane can enter the city, so nothing cursed can dwell in the grove near the stream (see Zech 14:11). These final verses bring Revelation to a fitting close by summarizing the promises that have been made to the elect throughout the work. Those promises are all fulfilled in the heavenly city.

EPILOGUE

Rev 22:6-21

Revelation concludes with a collection of separate prophetic oracles. They testify to the authenticity of the revelation contained in the book. The speaker shifts from oracle to oracle. We hear words of the revealing angel, of Jesus, of the Spirit, and of the prophet. Three themes are reiterated throughout: heed the revelation; the end is near; the righteous are rewarded. The "I am coming soon" of the opening exhortations ties this conclusion back to the initial revelation (1:1; 2:16; 3:11; 22:6b, 7, 12, 20).

The nearness of the Lord's coming is often tied to exhortations to remain faithful. That combination suggests that the phrase was part of the regular ethical exhortation of the churches addressed. It was not primarily directed at calculating exactly when the end would be; rather, the phrase assures the audience of the Lord's coming so that they will continue to be faithful. In Rev 2:16 it belongs to the exhortation against the Nicolaitan heresy. In Rev 3:11 it encourages perseverance.

As in the conclusion to Daniel (12:5), the author signs his name to the revelation to attest to its authenticity. Unlike Daniel (12:10), the words of the revelation are not sealed. For the second time the seer is rebuked for worshiping the revealing angel (also 19:10). Both the angels and the faithful stand together in praising God, as we have seen throughout the book in the scenes of the heavenly liturgy.

The oracle confirming the division between righteous and wicked in the last days also confirms a phenomenon to which the visions have given us dramatic testimony. The various plagues did not bring humanity to repentance. The prophecy does not convert the wicked from their ways (compare Ezek 3:27; Dan 12:10).

Jesus speaks with his divine authority, Alpha and Omega, to affirm the reward that is to be given to each. The beatitude (v. 14) is a variant of 7:14, which now includes the new visions of the holy city, in which nothing profane dwells with the tree of life. Verse 15 cites a catalog of vices to indicate the evils that cannot be allowed to enter the new city (see Joel 3:22–4:17; Rev 21:7-8).

Verse 16 has Jesus authenticate the angel of 1:1 as his messenger. The messianic titles given Jesus come from the Old Testament: root of Jesse (Isa 11:10); star of Jacob (Num 24:17); morning star (Isa 9:1; 60:1).

The summons to "come" in verse 17 allude to the liturgical practice of summoning the righteous to the Eucharist. Here we find an antiphonal summons to come and receive the promised reward. Another part of the same liturgy was the prayer to the Lord to come. Paul indicates that it was spoken in Aramaic, *Marana tha,* "Lord, come!" (1 Cor 16:22). It was also connected with the pronouncement of a formula excluding all nonbelievers and all who are not holy. The catalog of vices in verse 15 could function as such a formula for Revelation. Thus, the audience is reminded that the summons into the liturgical assembly is an image of that final summons to the gathering of the holy ones of God. We are also reminded that Revelation was read in such a community gathering.

The final verses provide further testimony to the truth of the prophecy. The curse against those who tamper with the words of such a revelation derives from Deut 4:2. Such curses also appear in Jewish apocryphal writings from New Testament times. Jesus' own testimony to the truth of the revelation is answered by the liturgical prayer for his coming. A common conclusion in Pauline letters ends Revelation. It reminds us, as much of the epilogue has, that the revelation is given to the audience which has also heard the warnings and promises in the letters. They must apply these visions to their situation. Those who are praised should continue, confident in the salvation that they have been promised. Those who are called to repent should heed the warning, lest they be found among the hardened and blasphemous who will not listen to any of the words of the Lord.

The message of Revelation does not depend upon calculations about the time of the second coming of the Lord. People must be convinced about the "nearness of the Lord" and the certainty of the Christian vision of salvation if they are to heed the warnings in the book. Many of the questions raised by Revelation continue to create problems for Christians. They must question false claims of political and economic systems when they destroy values that Christians are committed to. They must question the nature of human compliance with evil and injustice. Christians must also face the dangers of sectarian groups which pervert the gospel by claiming to have esoteric wisdom not available to others, "to know the depths of God." They must also ask whether they really believe in God's rule over the cosmos, which Revelation presents as real and active. Or, perhaps, Christians really feel that God is "far off' and not really concerned with the problems of our day beyond some record-keeping of individual transgressions. Perhaps the justice demanded in the prophets to whom Revelation is constantly alluding does not seem to count for much in the complexities of the modern world. Revelation would never tolerate such an attitude among Christians. It has used all the mythic and symbolic resources at its disposal to show Christians the dangers of a false estimate of the powers of this world. Christians live on the edge of times. They take their values from the gospel and from the way God sees things. They should always expect that "the Lord is coming soon!"

A first-rate, well-informed, and powerfully relevant commentary
to open windows of insight into sacred Scripture

SACRA PAGINA

Daniel Harrington, S.J., Editor

Sacra Pagina is a multi-volume commentary on the books of the New Testament. The goal of this exciting series is to provide sound, critical analysis without any loss of sensitivity to religious meaning. This series is therefore catholic in two senses of the word: inclusive in its methods and perspectives, and shaped by the context of the Catholic tradition.

The expression "Sacra Pagina" ("Sacred Page") originally referred to the text of Scripture. In the Middle Ages it also described the study of Scripture to which the interpreter brought the tools of grammar, rhetoric, dialectic, and philosophy. Thus *Sacra Pagina* encompasses both the text to be studied and the activity of interpretation.

The volumes in this series present fresh translations and modern expositions of all the books of the New Testament.

"I rejoice in recommending one of the most gracefully erudite, historically astute, and theologically rewarding commentaries available in a frugal market."

Theological Studies

Written by an international team of Catholic biblical scholars, *Sacra Pagina* is intended for biblical professionals, graduate students, theologians, clergy, and religious educators. The volumes offer basic introductory information and close exposition, with each author adopting a specific methodology while maintaining a focus on the issues raised by the New Testament compositions themselves.

The Second Vatican Council described the study of "the sacred page" as the "very soul of sacred theology" (*Dei Verbum* 24). This series illustrates how Catholic scholars contribute to the council's call to provide access to Sacred Scripture for all the Christian faithful. These volumes open up the riches of the New Testament to invite all Christians to study seriously the "sacred page."

Rights: World

Place a Standing Order & Save $5 Per Volume!

To place a standing order for the *Sacra Pagina* series (5034-1), simply call our toll-free number: 1-800-858-5450.
Volumes will be billed at a savings of $5.00 off the cover price and shipped to you as they are published.
(If you have already received certain volumes in the series, simply inform the customer service representative with whom you speak.)

Upcoming Volumes in the Series

The Gospel of Mark (5804-0)
The Gospel of John (5806-7)
1 Corinthians (5809-1)
2 Corinthians (5810-5)
Letters of John (5812-1)
Pastoral Epistles (5814-8)

Hebrews (5815-6)
James (5816-4)
1 and 2 Peter/Jude (5817-2)
Colossians and Ephesians (5819-9)
Philippians and Philemon (5820-2)

THE LITURGICAL PRESS
St. John's Abbey Collegeville, MN 56321
Phone 1-800-858-5450 • Fax 1-800-445-5899

First and Second Thessalonians

Earl J. Richard
The letters First and Second Thessalonians are traditionally associated with the Pauline foundation of the Macedonian Church at Thessalonica. The first is seen as representing Paul's earliest epistolary efforts and as providing two successive moments in his long relationship as advisor to that community. Soon after leaving the area for the southern province of Achaia, Paul addresses the concerns of the new Gentile converts and at a later period responds more directly to queries received from the thriving and successful community. The second document, written in Paul's name and at a later date, attempts to calm the apocalyptic fervor of the community by reiterating its traditional eschatological and Christological teaching.

After treating these introductory matters, this study provides a new translation of each section of the canonical text, explains in notes the pertinent textual and linguistic features of the text, and then offers in a series of interpretive messages a literary, rhetorical, and thematic analysis of the biblical documents.
5813-X Hardcover, 456 pp., 6 x 9, $29.95

The Acts of the Apostles

Luke Timothy Johnson
This commentary treats Luke-Acts as an apologetic history. It takes with equal seriousness both Luke's literary artistry and his historical interests, fitting his methods comfortably within the ancient standards of historiography. This perspective illustrates in particular that Luke's historical narrative serves a definite religious intent. Tracing that intent through the specific contours of Luke's story is the special contribution of this commentary.
5807-5 Hardcover, 592 pp., 6 x 9, $29.95

> *"This is an excellent commentary and a very important contribution in the series."*
> **Louvain Studies**

Coming Soon!
Romans (5808-3)

The Gospel of Matthew

Daniel Harrington, S.J.
Matthew wrote his gospel from his perspective as a Jew. It is with sensitivity to this perspective that Father Harrington undertakes this commentary on the Gospel of Matthew.

After an introduction, he provides a literal translation of each section in Matthew's Gospel and explains the textual problems, philological difficulties, and other matters in the notes. He then presents a literary analysis of each text (content, form, use of sources, structure). Bibliographies direct the reader to other important modern studies.
5803-2 Hardcover, 448 pp., 6 x 9, $29.95

> *"This is a balanced, well-informed, centrist commentary, with which the reviewer usually agrees and which he can heartily recommend."*
> **Revue Biblique**

The Gospel of Luke

Luke Timothy Johnson
What makes this commentary on Luke stand apart from others is that, from beginning to end, this is a literary analysis. Because it focuses solely on the Gospel as it appears and not on its source or origin, this commentary richly and thoroughly explores just what Luke is saying and how he says it.
5805-9 Hardcover, 480 pp., 6 x 9, $29.95

> *"The name of the editor is a guarantee of their high quality."*
> **Liguorian**

> *"If [Matthew and Luke] are any indication, this series will become a classic. Both books are landmark commentaries."*
> **Catholic Library World**

Revelation

Wilfrid J. Harrington, O.P.
More than any other New Testament writing the Book of Revelation demands commentary. Its often bewildering text is easily open to less than scholarly interpretation.

Father Harrington brings his scholarship to the Book of Revelation and conveys its Christian message. He puts the work in its historical and social setting—a first-century C.E. province of the Roman Empire—and explores its social and religious background and its literary character. Through Father Harrington we hear clearly the challenge of John, the prophet, to the Churches of his time—and to ours—not to compromise the Gospel message.
5818-0 Hardcover, 296 pp., 6 x 9, $29.95

> *"This book of scripture is endlessly fascinating and open to ceaseless speculation. Harrington provides scholarly and thoughtful insight."*
> **National Catholic Reporter**

Galatians

Frank J. Matera
Paul's Letter to the Galatians has played a major role in the history of theology, especially in the Church's teaching on grace, faith, and justification. This commentary argues that Paul's doctrine of justification by faith is essentially social in nature and has important ecumenical implications for the Church today. In its original setting, Galatians established a foundation for the unity of Jewish and Gentile Christians: all are justified by the faith of Jesus Christ.
5811-3 Hardcover, 272 pp., 6 x 9, $24.95

> *"Uniquely explained and scholarly presented, this presentation of the meaning of the Letter to Galatians, as one of the most influential of the New Testament, should be powerfully relevant to contemporary peoples."*
> **Emmanuel**

THE LITURGICAL PRESS
St. John's Abbey Collegeville, MN 56321
Phone 1-800-858-5450 • Fax 1-800-445-5899

COLLEGEVILLE

𝓛ooking for a Bible commentary that is comprehensive yet succinct? One that avoids intricate arguments, hypotheses and debates, yet contains the latest in biblical scholarship? Fortunately there is *The Collegeville Bible Commentary*—a simpler and easier way to read and understand the Bible. Directed to the non-specialist reader, teacher, and lover of the Bible, *The Collegeville Commentary* series fulfills an essential pastoral need. Its scholarship has stood the test of time and continues to provide a fresh approach for adults beginning Bible study and those looking for help in understanding and appreciating the Good News. Individuals and groups, including an established and respected Scripture study program, trust *The Collegeville Bible Commentary* and its family of resources for its comprehensive, educational, and straightforward presentation. The revised New American Bible translation is used, maps and photos throughout the series illustrate lands of biblical importance.

The Collegeville Bible Commentary's content and merit remain as solid as its longstanding purpose: to give catechists, clergy, readers, and preachers a valuable resource for reflection and prayer with God's Word.

A contemporary classic!
The Collegeville Bible Commentary
One-Volume Hardcover Edition
The one-volume, hardcover edition of *The Collegeville Bible Commentary* was prepared to meet the needs of those students of the Bible who need reference to more than one book of the Bible or who prefer to use their own Bible. The full Scripture texts are not included in this commentary-only edition.

Thirty-two pages of full-color maps illustrate places of biblical importance.
1484-1   Hardcover, 1,344 pp., 7 x 10, $54.95
Rights: World

The Collegeville Bible Commentary
Two-Volume Paperback Edition
Now *The Collegeville Bible Commentary* is available in an affordable two-volume paperback edition. Special "ease" binding allows the volumes to lay open without assistance. Perfect for classroom use or personal study.
Rights: World

Old Testament
2210-0   Paper, 880 pp., 7 x 10, $21.95

New Testament
2211-9   Paper, 464 pp., 7 x 10, $16.95

Old and New Testament Set
2212-7 $35.95

". . . the most accessible single-volume guide to the Bible issued under any auspices."
The Christian Century

"The straightforward and nontechnical presentations transmit the best of modern biblical scholarship to a wide audience."
America

". . . a magnificent one-volume commentary . . . a fine reference volume for the parish library and the CCD faculty shelves."
Msgr. Charles Dollen
The Priest

THE LITURGICAL PRESS
St. John's Abbey Collegeville, MN 56321
Phone 1-800-858-5450 • Fax 1-800-445-5899

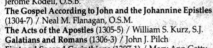

The Bible Today

God's Word in the World

Gain a deeper, richer, knowledge of God's Word with this award-winning magazine. *The Bible Today* offers a comprehensive look at the very latest information on Scripture from the most recent and best biblical scholarship. It explores Scripture through illustrated articles and commentary that focus on a particular theme or book of the Bible.

As you journey through the pages of *The Bible Today*, it's easy to picture yourself experiencing the events of the period, visiting significant places, and meeting the people whose stories still live on in the present.

Published six times a year in understandable and instructive language, *The Bible Today* is ideal for individual or group study of the Bible. *The Bible Today* features:

The Bible On . . . —biblical scholars explore how the biblical tradition can shed light on contemporary concerns or offer an introduction to a particular book of the Bible.

Puzzling Passages—each issue examines a notoriously difficult passage from the Bible. You are provided with a brief description of the problems related to the text and suggestions from the author on how to solve the puzzle.

Seers' Corner—beautifully illustrated text helps you experience for yourself important events, people and places of the ancient and modern biblical world.

The Bible in Ministry—helps you discover ways of using the Bible responsibly and effectively in your ministry.

Book Reviews—offer you a wealth of information on recent books.

Announcements—alert you to workshops, tours, or other Scripture-study related events.

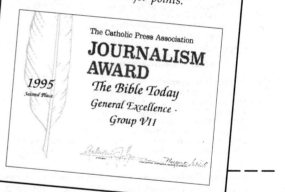

During its 1995 annual convention, the Catholic Press Association honored The Bible Today with a second-place award for general excellence. Judges commented that "innovative themes (The Bible on the Economy, for instance) and substantive, brief articles make this journal easy to read for lay readers and no waste of time for scholars. Photography accompanying articles often highlights their major points."

The Catholic Press Association

JOURNALISM AWARD

The Bible Today

General Excellence - Group VII

1995
Second Place

THE LITURGICAL PRESS
St. John's Abbey, P.O. Box 7500
Collegeville, MN 56321-7500
1-800-858-5450, ext. 2223
Fax: 1-800-445-5899

Please enter my subscription for
❏ One year (six issues), $22.00 ❏ Two years, $43.00
❏ One year, foreign, $26.00 ❏ Two years, foreign, $51.00
❏ One year, libraries, $30.00
❏ Please bill me. ❏ I enclose payment.

NAME_____

ADDRESS_____

CITY_____

STATE/ZIP_____

Send a gift subscription
❏ One year (six issues), $22.00 ❏ Two years, $43.00
❏ One year, foreign, $26.00 ❏ Two years, foreign, $51.00
❏ Please bill me. ❏ I enclose payment.
Please allow 6 to 8 weeks for delivery of your first issue.

NAME_____

ADDRESS_____

CITY_____

STATE/ZIP_____

DONOR'S NAME_____

ADDRESS_____

CITY/STATE/ZIP_____

Prices subject to change without notice